A THEOLOGICAL WORD BOOK OF THE BIBLE

Edited by

ALAN RICHARDSON D.D.

SCM PRESS LTD
BLOOMSBURY STREET LONDON

334 01620 7

First published 1950
Second impression 1950
Third impression 1951
Fourth impression 1954
Fifth impression 1956
Sixth impression 1957
Seventh impression 1962
Eighth impression 1965
Ninth impression 1967
Tenth impression 1969
Eleventh impression 1972

Printed in Great Britain by offset by
Fletcher & Son Ltd, Norwich

THE CONTRIBUTORS

Matthew Black, *Professor of Biblical Criticism, University of St Andrews*

E. C. Blackman, *Professor of New Testament Literature and Exegesis, Emmanuel College, Victoria University, Toronto*

L. H. Brockington, *Lecturer in Aramaic and Syriac, University of Oxford*

J. Y. Campbell, *Professor Emeritus, Westminster College, Cambridge*

H. J. Carpenter, *Bishop of Oxford*

J. O. Cobham, *Archdeacon of Durham and Canon Residentiary of Durham Cathedral*

C. E. B. Cranfield, *Reader in Theology, University of Durham*

G. Henton Davies, *Principal, Regent's Park College, Oxford*

C. F. Evans, *Professor of New Testament Studies, King's College, London*

Reginald H. Fuller, *Professor of New Testament, Union Theological Seminary, New York*

Kenneth Grayston, *Professor of Theology, University of Bristol*

R. J. Hammer, *Lecturer in Christian Doctrine, The Queen's College, Birmingham*

A. G. Hebert, *late Society of the Sacred Mission*

George S. Hendry, *Professor of Systematic Theology, Princeton Theological Seminary, Princeton, New Jersey, U.S.A.*

George Johnston, *Professor of Divinity, McGill University, Montreal*

James S. McEwen, *Regius Professor of Church History, University of Aberdeen*

John Marsh, *Principal of Mansfield College, Oxford*

C. R. North, *Emeritus Professor of Hebrew, University College of North Wales, Bangor*

Ronald H. Preston, *Canon of Manchester; Lecturer in Christian Ethics, University of Manchester*

A. M. Ramsey, *Archbishop of Canterbury*

THE CONTRIBUTORS

O. S. Rankin, late *Professor of Old Testament Language, Literature and Theology, New College, University of Edinburgh*

J. K. S. Reid, *Professor of Christian Dogmatics, University of Aberdeen*

Alan Richardson, *Dean of York*

J. N. Schofield, *Lecturer in Hebrew and Old Testament Subjects, University of Cambridge*

R. Gregor Smith, *Primarius Professor of Divinity, University of Glasgow*

Norman H. Snaith, *formerly Principal of Wesley College, Headingley, Leeds*

F. J. Taylor, *Bishop of Sheffield*

J. P. Thornton-Duesbery, *Master of St Peter's College, Oxford*

R. C. Walls, *Lecturer in Divinity, University of Edinburgh*

W. A. Whitehouse, *Professor of Theology, University of Kent*

R. R. Williams, *Bishop of Leicester*

PREFACE

By entitling this volume *A Theological Word Book of the Bible* it is hoped that a clear and concise indication might be given of its content and purpose. The adjective 'theological' is intended to indicate a limited aim—namely, to elucidate the distinctive meanings of the key-words of the Bible. Historical, geographical, archaeological and philological details are not elaborated, except—and this is very important—in so far as they are necessary for theological understanding. This must not be taken to imply that such considerations are of little moment: the Christian faith is founded upon actual events of history, and hence theological interpretation and historical investigation can never be separated from each other. The contributors were asked, however, to focus attention upon the theological meanings of the words with which they deal, because it would appear that it is precisely at this point that the ordinary reader of the Bible, as well as the preacher and the teacher, requires clear and positive help. There are many excellent works available to-day from which a knowledge of biblical history and literature may be derived, whereas we know of nothing that is comparable to this attempt at the theological elucidation of the whole Bible. Thus, while every writer has based his contribution upon a scholarly study of the Bible, with the aid of every resource which modern historical and literary criticism can provide, he has presented the results of this study in such a way as to help the reader to understand the real import of the biblical words without confusing him with all the complicated technical apparatus of biblical science. The text of the English Revised Version of Holy Scripture has been used, and all Hebrew and Greek words have been transliterated into English characters.

When the aim of this *Word Book* has been thus understood, the principles governing the choice of words to be treated and words to be omitted will become apparent. Words of prime theological importance have been dealt with at length, others more briefly. Many words to be found in the Bible have not been treated at all, but this does not necessarily mean that they have no theological interest. Considerations of space and time have imposed restrictions upon our enterprise, and a certain degree of selection was, of course, inevitable. All selection is in a measure subjective, and no two students of the Bible would have made precisely the same list of words to be treated. The Editor, while acknowledging his indebtedness to a great number of friends and advisers whom he has consulted, accepts responsibility for the words finally selected or omitted. The principle of selection is simply that of theological interest: such words as have acquired specific biblical-theological meaning—including proper names—have been treated as fully as space permitted. Thus, for reasons which should now be sufficiently obvious, articles will be found upon, for example, Abraham, Isaac, David, Elijah or St. John the Baptist, but not upon Amos, Daniel, the Herods or St. John the Divine.

PREFACE

All the words of the Bible are intricately related to one another in meaning, and cross-references have been plentifully supplied both in order to assist understanding and to avoid repetition; the system of cross-reference is so simple that it requires no explanation here. No attempt has been made to ensure uniformity of outlook or presentation amongst the contributions of the various writers in this book; nor even to standardize the spellings of transliterated words (e.g. Jehovah, Jahweh, Yahweh), since it was felt that the authors' preferences in such matters should be respected and that the divergences are hardly likely to mislead the reader. It will not, however, escape the careful reader that the unanimity of the contributors upon essential matters is indeed remarkable and affords striking proof that in the renewed emphasis upon biblical theology, which is such a notable feature of Christian thinking in our time, a sound foundation for Christian unity is being laid. The volume as a whole doubtless possesses considerable significance as presenting a cross-section of the mind of representative English-speaking biblical scholars at the middle of the twentieth century. Broadly, it may be said that, while accepting *ex animo* the methods of scientific criticism, the common point of view is that the key to the biblical revelation is Christ, who is the proper subject both of the Old and of the New Testaments. It is because of the continuity of the Old Israel with the New, and because of the fulfilment of the Old Covenant in the New Covenant of our Lord and Saviour Jesus Christ, that it was understood from the outset by those who planned this volume that it must be a word book of the whole Bible, and not merely of the New Testament. The character of the biblical revelation as culminating in the incarnate Word of God gives to a study of the words of the Bible a seriousness and urgency which no merely secular study of words can have. It is because the living Word of God is to be encountered in the Bible, wrapped in the 'swaddling-clothes' of poor, inadequate and fluctuating human words, that the strictest historical, literary and philological scrutiny is an indispensable discipline of all biblical theology. Such a discipline lies unobtrusively behind all the articles in this book, which owes its conception to the conviction that the words of the Bible are not merely interesting objects of academic research, but are indeed the words of eternal life.

It is scarcely possible to render due acknowledgment to all those through whose suggestion, encouragement and advice this work has been brought to completion. The debt that is owed to the several contributors, who have so freely given of their time and learning, is sufficiently obvious. The active co-operation and support of the Board of the S.C.M. Press, and of its former Editor, Dr. Hugh Martin, in particular, have rendered feasible the seemingly impractical venture of carrying out such a project during the unfavourable conditions of the nineteen-forties; in the earlier stages of the work assistance and encouragement of especial value was received from individual members of the Board, notably the Bishops of Bristol and Manchester, Dr. John Marsh of Nottingham University and Mr. Eric Fenn of the British and Foreign Bible Society. Miss Kathleen Downham, the Assistant Editor of the Press, has rendered invaluable service at every stage of production. The Rev. Edmund Leigh, M.A. (Cantab.), Vicar of Kirk Merrington in County Durham, has read through much of the work in the proofs. The Camelot Press, the printers of this work, are to be congratulated upon their skill and care in setting the type, and upon the acumen of their reader's comments in proof. For such errors and imperfections as remain the Editor must accept entire responsibility.

ALAN RICHARDSON

The College
Durham

ABBREVIATIONS

IN addition to the usual abbreviations employed in most works of reference, the following have been used in this book:

AV: Authorized Version (the translation of Holy Scripture authorized by King James I in 1611).
RV: Revised Version (of the above, 1884).
EVV: English Versions (both the above).
ARSV: American Revised Standard Version of the New Testament (1946).
OT: Old Testament.
NT: New Testament.
LXX: Septuagint Version (the Greek Old Testament).
BCP: Book of Common Prayer (1662).
HDB: Hastings' *Dictionary of the Bible.*
HDCG: Hastings' *Dictionary of Christ and the Gospels.*
HERE: Hastings' *Encyclopaedia of Religion and Ethics.*
ICC: International Critical Commentary.
JTS: Journal of Theological Studies.
RGG: Die Religion in Geschichte und Gegenwart.
TWNT: Theologisches Wörterbuch zum Neuen Testament (ed. by G. Kittel).

A THEOLOGICAL WORD BOOK OF THE BIBLE

AARON, SONS OF *v.* SACRIFICE III(*a*)

AARONITES *v.* SACRIFICE III(*a*)

ABBA *v.* FAMILY

ABOMINATION

Translates 4 Heb. words: *to'ebah* (most frequent), *sheqez* (techn. of flesh of prohibited animals), *shiqquz* (almost always of idolatry), and *piggul* (techn. of stale sacrificial flesh). Apart from *piggul*, LXX mainly trans. by *bdelugma*, which also represents all NT occurrences except one.

A primitive offshoot of the numinous is an irrational sense of repugnance for people and things. Thus the Egyptians loathed shepherds (Gen. 46.34) and could not bear to eat with Hebrews (Gen. 43.32). The Israelites themselves loathed certain groups of people and excluded them from the community; but not Edomites because they were kinsmen, or Egyptians because Israel had dwelt in their land (Deut. 23.7). An individual might be loathed because of sickness (Ps. 88.8) or affliction (Job 19.19), and the honour formerly due to him would be completely reversed. Or, again, the Hebrews could not make their proper sacrifices in the presence of Egyptians, since they would use animals regarded by Egyptians as unlawful and repugnant (Exod. 8.26). The Hebrew lists of prohibited foods (Deut. 14.3–20, Lev. 11.2–23) closely connect a. with uncleanness (*q.v.*), and were based, not on natural loathing, but on reverential dread, since unclean animals were the divine animals of the heathen. The fact that creeping things and abominable beasts could be objects of veneration (Ezek. 8.10) must lie behind the action of apostates who ate 'swine's flesh, and the a. and the mouse' (Isa. 66.17). During the exile the distinction of Jews from other people was maintained by observing the food and purity laws, and their original meaning was forgotten; but although the compiler of the Priestly Code no longer knew why certain animals were forbidden, a. still kept its original sense of numinous repugnance.

This primitive, unreflective repugnance is already, therefore, closely related to idolatry, explicitly so in Deut. 32.16f.: 'with a. provoked they him to anger, they sacrificed . . . to new gods that came up of late, whom your fathers *dreaded* not.' Deut. 13.13ff. condemns those who draw off the people to worship other gods, and a city infected by them is to be totally destroyed and put to the BAN (devoted to the Lord, 5.17; cf. Deut. 20.18). This application of the ban provides the transition to the phase: 'A. to the Lord' (so Deut. 7.25–6 of the precious metal covering a captured image) which is frequent in Deut. as the ultimate ground of a prohibition, e.g. 'Thou shalt not sacrifice unto the Lord thy God an ox, or a sheep, wherein is a blemish . . . for that is an a. unto the Lord thy God' (Deut. 17.1; in a context dealing with idolatry this must refer to some special feature in the rites of the surrounding heathen). Thus a. is whatever is repugnant to the life of the people centred on its God.

IDOLATRY (*q.v.*) reverses the proper order of life and overturns the worship due to the Lord. Deut. 17.4, 5 prescribes stoning for the person who does the abominable thing of worshipping other gods (sun, moon, host of heaven) because this *transgresses the covenant*; therefore Israel must not ask: 'How do these nations serve their gods?' (Deut. 12.30). Jeremiah complained that the people were not ashamed of committing a., for 'the stork . . . knoweth her appointed time . . . but my people know not the ordinance (*mishpat*) of the Lord' (8.7, 12). (For an image as a. to the Lord, e.g. Deut. 27.15; cf. Exod. 20.4.) In post-exilic times the a. of idolatry is closely linked with the separatist preservation of the Jewish manner of life (Ezra 9.1,11,14, Mal. 2.11, Ezek. 44.6f.).

Thus a. became the conventional term for idolatrous practices, e.g. II Kings 23.13, 'Ashtoreth the a. of the Zidonians, etc.'; and several passages give detailed accounts (II Kings 21.2ff., Ezek. 8.6ff.). In Dan. 9.27, 11.31, 12.11 are found variant forms of *shiqquẓ shomem* (the appalling a.), a contemptuous form of *Ba'al shamayim* (the Lord of Heaven), which refer to the rites (altar and idols) of Olympian Zeus installed in the Temple sanctuary by Antiochus Epiphanes (I Mac. 1.54ff.). The phrase occurs again in Mark 13.14, 'the a. of desolation' (which causes desolation), and is explicitly referred by Matt. 24.15 to Daniel. The cryptic 'let him that readeth understand' almost compels a political reference (and not a purely spiritual one), and it is usually taken to be Caligula's order for his statue to be set up in the Temple (AD 40). If so, it is necessary to believe that the words were not spoken by Jesus, but by the author of the Gospel who believed that the order would be carried out and would precipitate a fatal outbreak. In fact, it was not carried out because the emperor died; and Luke's alteration of the words (21.20) looks as if he understood the reference and knew it to be unfulfilled. Closely connected with these passages is 'the man of sin (lawlessness, RV margin)' of II Thess. 2.3, usually interpreted of the Roman emperor, through the LXX trans. of a. by 'lawlessness' (26 times, all but one in Ezek.; cf. Ezek. 6.6ff. and frequently for desolation following upon idolatrous a.).

Many passages connect idolatry with ethical irresponsibility. Jeremiah's Temple address (7.1–15) shows the intimate relation of the ethical and the ritual, based on Deut. itself; cf. Jer. 6.13–15. By the time of Ezekiel's public address to the exiles in 585–575 BC, the scope of a. is as wide as the law itself. The refs. in Rev. fall into place here, as well as the inclusion of 'abominable idolatries' in the list of Gentile profligacies in I Pet. 4.3. (The word trans. a.= lawless, godless, usually with ref. to some religious law or tradition, and so may well have borne the primitive sense of 'repugnant'.) A. is closely related to sexual offences (Deut. 23.18, ref. to cultic prostitution), and idolatry is frequently described by sexual metaphors: Jer. 13.27, 'their a. are adulteries, neighings (=lust), lewdness of whoredom'; cf. Ezek. 16 *passim*. Ezek. clearly expresses the nemesis of idolatry, by which the abominable things which people perform recoil upon them and rot away the national life (7.3ff., 20.4ff.). Cf. Hos. 9.10, 'they became a. like that which they loved'.

The way is now clear for regarding all ethical faults as a. Thus the list of sexual offences in Lev. 18.6–23 is summed up as 'these a.' which were done by surrounding nations. Homosexuality, as an outstanding reversal of what is natural, is especially singled out. Prov. 6.16–19 lists pride, lying, shedding innocent blood, wicked scheming, mischief, false witness, and sowing discord as a. to God; but the germ of this development is seen in Deut. 25.16 (thrice repeated in Prov.), which similarly condemns false weights. Luke 16.15, 'What is exalted among men is an a. in the sight of God', derives from the refs. in Prov. to pride (e.g. 16.5). The final meaning of a. develops the sense of reversing what is natural (cf. interchange of garments in Deut. 22.5, and numbering the people in I Chron. 21.6), and becomes in Prov. *anything repugnant to the true nature of person or thing*, e.g. 'a. to kings to commit wickedness', because it is the king's nature to do what is right (Prov. 16.12); 'he that justifies the wicked and condemns the righteous is a. to the Lord' because he perverts the nature of justice (Prov. 17.15). Cf. also Prov. 29.27, 13.19, 24.9, 3.32, 8.7, 15.8f.; and so interpret Tit. 1.16: men whose natures are wholly perverted. (*V.* also ANTICHRIST.)

KENNETH GRAYSTON

ABRAHAM

Whether or not anything can be established concerning an historical Abraham from the traditions about him collected in Gen. 11–25, he certainly became an important symbol in Jewish national life and thought and in the biblical theology. The Jews regarded him as the father of their race (cf. Matt. 3.9), which was 'the seed of Abraham' (e.g. Ps. 105.6, Luke 1.55, John 8.33,37, Rom. 4.13, 9.7, etc.); all faithful Jews participated in the righteousness of A. and would enjoy his reward (the 'Merits of the Fathers'); the rabbis held that A. would welcome the faithful into Paradise, and indeed the expression 'A.'s bosom' was merely a synonym for Paradise (cf. Luke 16.23). A. was thus the symbol of the beginning and ending of Jewish existence. It is significant that St. Matthew thinks it unnecessary to trace back the genealogy of Christ beyond A. (Matt. 1.1f.). In the traditions of Gen. 11–25 A. is represented as a righteous man who enjoyed close and constant communion with God; the later tradition stresses his *obedience* to the 'commandments, statutes and laws' of God (Gen. 26.5, a redactor's passage; cf. 22.18, Heb. 11.8), and hence, it came to be believed, God elected him to be the instrument of his purpose and the father of his chosen nation. St. Paul is particularly anxious to controvert the view that God's choice of A. was due to any righteous works on his part: it was a free exercise of the divine mercy, and A.'s faith was not merely one of 'the works of the law', as the rabbis supposed. Paul's arguments may seem to us to be sometimes tortuous and far-fetched, but the truth he was seeking to establish was important and simple: God did not choose the Jews because they were virtuous above all other nations (or had 'a genius for religion'), but simply because he was God. If the rabbis claimed that God chose A. because of his obedience (typified in his willingness even to sacrifice Isaac; Gen. 22.12,18, 26.5), Paul replied that A.'s faith preceded his works, since he would not have obeyed had he not first believed God's promise; and he quotes Gen. 15.6, 'A. believed God, and it was reckoned unto him for righteousness' (Rom. 4.3, Gal. 3.6 and contexts: contrast the opposite use made of Gen. 15.6 in Jas. 2.23, where the rabbinic conception of faith as merely one of the works of the law is maintained; cf. Tit. 3.8). God's covenant with A. (*v.* COVENANT) preceded the giving of the law by 430 years (Gal. 3.17), and A.'s righteousness was not of law but of faith (Rom. 4.13). A. was thus 'justified' (*q.v.*) or reckoned righteous while still uncircumcised, and circumcision was 'the seal (*q.v.*) of the righteousness of the faith which he had while he was in uncircumcision' (Rom. 4.11). Circumcision itself (the supposed badge of A.'s covenant: Gen. 17.11,14), which had become the proud and exclusive token of Jewish nationalism, is viewed by Paul as nothing less than a pledge of the admission of the Gentiles to the status and privileges of A.'s seed (Rom. 4.11). Paul is, in fact, bringing out something which is implicit in the OT accounts of God's covenant with A. and which is inherent in the biblical conception of God's choice of the Jews as an elect nation, viz. that the Jews were not chosen for special privileges as over against other nations, but in order that God's will for the salvation of all mankind might be realized: 'in thy seed shall *all* the nations of the earth be blessed' (Gen. 22.18). It should be noted that in the story of the making of the covenant at Sinai this universalism is again explicit: all the earth is Jehovah's, and Israel is to be 'a kingdom of priests' to the other nations (Exod. 19.5f.). Paul has seen how in Jesus Christ this promise has come true—he has witnessed it with his own eyes: in Christ there is neither Jew nor Greek (Gal. 3.28). The true seed of A. now includes both circumcised Jews and uncircumcised Gentiles who believe in Christ; circumcised Jews who reject Christ are no longer the seed of A. (Rom. 9.7 and context). God's promise to A. is fulfilled in Christ: 'the Scripture, foreseeing that God would justify the Gentiles by faith, preached the gospel beforehand unto A., saying, In thee shall all the nations be blessed. So then they which be of faith are blessed with faithful A.' (Gal. 3.8f.; cf. Rom. 4.18–25). Upon the Gentiles has come the blessing of Abraham in Christ Jesus (Gal. 3.14). *V.* also COVENANT.

ALAN RICHARDSON

ACCESS

In the Oriental world the court of a king usually had amongst its officers a functionary whose business it was to bring visitors or suppliants into the royal presence. Anyone seeking access to the king or desiring his interest in some project would first have to gain the goodwill of this official, who would in some measure act as a guarantor of the genuineness and good intentions of all those persons whom he introduced into the royal presence. (Cf. the introduction of Saul into the Jerusalem church by Barnabas, who stood surety for him; Acts 9.27–8. Note the two stages, a first introduction for Saul, and, as a result, liberty of access.) More generally, the same Gk. word might signify one who introduced another as an intermediary (*v.* MEDIATOR). The word 'access' as used in the NT (Rom. 5.2, Eph. 2.18, 3.12, I Pet. 3.18, where the verb is used actively) signifies the actual entry into the royal presence and favour. The biblical understanding of God as the king of all the earth (Ps. 29.10, 47.7, 96.10, 99.1 and many other places) made it possible to use this language in describing access into his presence, which man does not possess as an independent right, but which is secured to him by the work of Christ (Heb. 10.19–22). The word thus throws light on the mediatorial work of Christ and symbolizes the first decisive introduction or admission of the sinner into the very presence of God and the subsequent liberty of approach which such an introduction brings with it. In Rom. 5.2, Eph. 2.12–18, the thought assumes (1) a separation from God with the necessary exclusion from covenant-privileges which is the inevitable position of every man (Rom. 3.23) as a sinner; (2) the desperate human need to gain entry into the presence of God by finding someone able to make the required introduction; (3) the decisive ending of this state of separation by the removal of barriers (Eph. 2.15–18) and the securing of the right of access by the death of Christ (cf. I Pet. 3.18, where Christ in his suffering is said to have had this end in view), which is the justification (*q.v.*) of the sinner (Rom. 5.1). This right of access is to God himself, through Christ who by his self-sacrifice can take the sinner by the hand and lead him into the presence of God (cf. Heb. 4.16, 10.22, urging believers to draw near and claim the right won for them by Christ) through the power of the

Spirit (Eph. 2.18). Thus a change in the relations of God and man (and of men with each other) is the result of the death of Christ. The passage in Eph. 3.12 emphasizes the continuing liberty of approach which is the right of those who have faith in the prevailing efficacy of Christ's work (Rom. 5.1; cf. Rom. 3.25, Heb. 11.6). (*V.* also MEDIATOR, RECONCILE.)

F. J. TAYLOR

ACCOMPLISH *v.* FULFIL

ACCURSED *v.* DEVOTE

ADAM, MAN

The Biblical View of Human Nature. The Bible consistently teaches the paradoxical character of human nature. On the one hand, man is 'but a little lower than God'; he is crowned with glory and honour and (under God) holds the *dominium* over the beasts and the whole world of nature (Ps. 8.4–8). On the other hand, man is 'like unto the beasts that perish' (Ps. 49.12,20; cf. Ps. 144.3f.); his mortality is the outward and visible sign of the inner corruption of his nature (*v.* DEATH). The great philosophers and poets of all ages have generally agreed with this fundamental biblical perception of man's paradoxical character: man is at once 'the glory and scum of the universe' (Pascal); he is 'the quintessence of dust' (Hamlet). The realism of the biblical view stands in sharp contrast to the naïve optimism of naturalistic humanism and the cynical pessimism of Marxist notions about 'economic man'. The Bible knows alike of man's wretchedness and of his high destiny. All men die: all men are sinful; death is the corollary of sin and its symbol in the natural order (cf. I Cor. 15.56); but the Bible speaks of man's redemption from sin and conquest of death, of a salvation which is available for him when once he has abandoned his trust in human resources alone (cf. Jer. 17.5).

The Myths of the Creation and Fall. This paradoxical view of human nature which pervades the whole Bible receives striking expression in the myths of the Creation and Fall of Man in Gen. 1–3. According to the former, man is made in the IMAGE OF GOD: this means that man shares with God the power of understanding truth, of creating what is beautiful and of doing what is right; in this man differs from every other living creature upon earth. But according to the latter myth, man's desire to be on an equality with God has led to that rebellion against God's will which is the essence of sin (pride)—the attempt to claim for himself the glory and honour which properly belong to God alone (cf. Rom. 1.21–3). Man's capacity for truth, beauty and goodness is thus seriously impaired, and God's image in man is defaced. But it is not destroyed. The only sense in which the Bible may be said to teach the total depravity of man is in its recognition that every part of man's nature is corrupted by his rebelliousness (pride); there is no part of him (e.g. his reason) which remains unaffected by the 'Fall'. There still remain in man, though fallen, vestiges of the divine image and likeness, e.g. his capacity, however fragmentary and distorted it may now be, to exercise reason, conscience or creative workmanship. Man is a sinner, but he *knows* that he is a sinner: he knows that there is truth, beauty and righteousness, even though he does not attain to them. If he were utterly depraved, man would not know that he was a sinner, and would therefore not be capable of sinning: his nearest approach to complete depravity occurs when he thinks that he is a truth-loving and right-acting person, when his pride obscures from his eyes the real truth about himself.

Later Christian theology has expressed these truths in the doctrines of *Original Righteousness* and *Original Sin.* (These terms are not found in the Bible.) The doctrine of Original Sin is not so much an *a priori* theory as an empirical description of human nature: we all of us tend at every moment to put ourselves in the place of God by setting ourselves in the centre of the universe. The new-born infant comes into the world as the centre of his own universe, and all his education will consist in learning that he is not the centre of things. Yet every time we mention Original Sin we ought also to mention Original Righteousness: this is the other side of the paradox. The vestiges of the divine image remain in us; we know that we are self-centred and we know that self-centredness is wrong. No man-made technique of psychology or pedagogy can completely adjust us to society; our deepest need is for community, for reconciliation, for right relationships with our fellow men and with God. We need a salvation which no human technique can bring.

The time-element in the myths of Creation and Fall (as in all the biblical myths) must be discounted: it is not that *once* (in 4004 BC—or a hundred thousand years ago) God created man perfect and then he fell from grace. God is eternally Creator; he is eternally making man and holding him in being and seeing that his handiwork is good (Gen. 1.31). And just as creation is an eternal activity, so the 'Fall' is an ingredient of every moment of human life; man is at every moment 'falling', putting himself in the centre, rebelling against the will of God. Adam is Everyman.

Adam. The word means originally a human being (cf. Gen. 2.5) or mankind collectively (Gen. 1.26). Only for the purposes of the myth does it become a proper name. (The precise etymology of the word is doubtful.) Thus we may claim biblical sanction for the statement that Adam is Everyman. The myth was, of course, taken literally for centuries; it was traditionally held that Adam was the first human being, for whom a 'help-meet', Eve, was created, and that this pair lived for an indefinite while in the perfection of unfallen humanity (cf. R. South, 1634–1716: 'An Aristotle was but the rubbish of an Adam, and Athens but the rudiments of paradise', *Sermons*, I, ii). The sin of the first parents of our race, it was held, was transmitted like a physical defect to their posterity, and this was what was often meant by Original Sin. To-day we do not interpret the Genesis myths thus literally. But nevertheless we assert their amazing insight into the truth about human nature. Man desires to be as God, to put himself into the place of God; he is only too ready to believe the Serpent's lie (Gen. 3.4), to forget his mortality and his creatureliness; he is unfit to live in paradise and must toil in the ground that is cursed for his sake (*v.* WORK); his sense of shame is aroused by the knowledge of his guilt. Nevertheless, he is God's son (cf. Luke 3.38), though, like the prodigal in Luke 15, he has forfeited his inheritance as a son. How is he to receive it again? The NT supplies the answer and deepens and completes the biblical doctrine of human nature.

Christ, the Last Adam. It is St. Paul who develops the Christ-Adam parallel, or rather contrast. He speaks of Christ as 'the Second Man' and 'the Last Adam' (I Cor. 15.45,47); he does not actually use the phrase, 'Second Adam' (cf. Newman's 'A Second Adam to the fight and to the rescue came'). Adam is 'a figure (*tupos*) of him that was to come' (Rom. 5.14). Paul stresses the solidarity of the whole human race with Adam in his sin and its consequence, death (Rom. 5.12); he doubtless thought of Adam's sin as being transmitted by heredity, or perhaps he thought of all men as being 'in Adam', i.e. in Adam's loins, part of the corporate personality of Adam as the ancestor of the whole race. To-day we would put it differently but still mean what St. Paul meant: in virtue of our common, fallen humanity—the 'old man' in us (Rom. 6.6, Eph. 4.22, Col. 3.9)—the terrible truth is not merely that we shall die but that we deserve to die (*v.* DEATH); but our salvation is achieved through our solidarity with Christ in his righteousness and its consequence, the conquest of death, through our baptism and incorporation into the new humanity of Jesus Christ, which is the Church, his Body. 'As in Adam all die, so also in the Christ shall all be made alive' (I Cor. 15.22). In this sense, *extra ecclesiam nulla salus*. By 'one man' (Adam), St. Paul is saying, sin and death entered into the world; so also by one Man (Christ) righteousness and life have now entered in. The original intention of God in the creation, frustrated by Adam's Fall—Paul does not quite use the expression 'Fall', but he comes near to it in the *paraptōma* of Rom. 5.15 (*v.* FALL)—is now capable of fulfilment through the restoration achieved by Christ: 'if any man be in Christ, there is a new creation' (II Cor. 5.17, RV marg.; cf. Gal. 6.15). The Church, the body of redeemed humanity, is the new creation, the second creation, wrought by God (like the first one) through his Word—but this time his Incarnate Word. St. Paul explicitly teaches that the defaced image of the Creator is being renewed: the old humanity is being put off and the new humanity is being made, in which the former distinctions of race, religion, culture and class are being done away (Col. 3.9–11). The whole passages Rom. 5.12–21 and I Cor. 15.22,45–9 should be carefully studied in this connexion; also Phil. 2.5–11, where Paul is clearly contrasting Christ's action in emptying himself of his divinity with Adam's act of grasping at equality with God (so McNeile in *HDB*, one-vol., p. 12), though Adam is not mentioned by name in this passage. (*V.* also WORK.)

BIBLIOGRAPHY

E. Brunner: *Revelation and Reason*, London (1947). J. S. Whale: *Christian Doctrine*, Cambridge (1941), Chap. II. J. Baillie: *Our Knowledge of God*, Oxford (1939), pp. 17–34.

ALAN RICHARDSON

ADOPTION

OT: In primitive Semitic society fatherhood was presumptive rather than actual. Heb. *AB* (Father) does not imply paternity but means 'protector', 'nourisher'. Hence adoption as such was unknown in Semitic society, for it is relevant only where 'being a father' means primarily paternity. (See Guillaume, *Prophecy and Divination*, p. 75, and cf. Pedersen, *Israel*, p. 14.) Instead, we have the idea of 'becoming a son', i.e. entering an already existing family and sharing the protection and nurture of a father with its reciprocal obligations, rather than the assumption of a fictitious paternity. Four instances occur of something more akin to adoption, all outside Palestine: Exod. 2.10 (Moses); I Kings 11.20 (Genubath); Esth. 2.7 (Esther); and possibly also Gen. 48.5 (Jacob gives Joseph's sons, Ephraim and Manasseh, the status of his own sons).

According to Levirate laws (*v.* MARRIAGE and *HDB* III, p. 269), the brother of a man dying without issue entered into a union with the widow to provide the deceased with an heir, the firstborn of this union receiving the name of the deceased. Some Fathers, notably Augustine, call this a., but it is essentially different from a., where the adopting parent exercises a free choice.

The idea of 'becoming a son' is used of the relationship established by God with Israel through the Exodus (cf. Exod. 4.22–3, Hos. 11.1), thus ruling out any idea of crude physical paternity as in pagan mythologies. It is also used of the relation between Yahweh and the King of Israel (II Sam. 7.14, I Chron. 28.6), and also used of the ideal Davidic King (Ps. 2.7, 89.26,27) and therefore applicable to Messiah (*v.* FAMILY).

NT: The word a. occurs only in the Pauline Epistles, and always as a theological metaphor (Rom. 8.15,23, 9.4, Gal. 4.5, Eph. 1.5). Paul was able to use the Gk. word for a. (*huiothesia*) because both word and practice were familiar in the Graeco-Roman world. (For Gk. customs of a. see *ERE* (1908), I, pp. 107–10, and Roman, *ibid.*, pp. 111–15.)

In Rom. 9.4, a. is used of the OT covenant relationship between God and Israel. It denotes: (*a*) The *origin* of the sonship, i.e. not the common property of all men by creation, an unbiblical idea (Dodd, *Johannine Epistles*, p. 67f.), but conferred by God's free choice through an historical event. This choice is not determined by any quality or achievement of Israel, but is a sheer act of grace (Rom. 9.11). (*b*) The *status* thereby conferred, a relationship of fatherly favour and filial obedience (see Manson, *Teaching of Jesus*, p. 91). (*c*) The *heritage* thereby secured to the adopted, the peculiar privileges of Rom. 9.4—a. comes first and controls the rest.

It is apparent from Gal. 4.1–3 that this OT a. was potential and awaited fulfilment: the adopted sons were under 'guardians and stewards' until the time appointed of the Father. Paul proclaims that with the sending of the Son this time has now come (Gal. 4.4), and with it a new and perfect a. (Gal. 4.5). (*a*) *Origin* of the new a.: three moments: (i) it is determined by God before creation: our a. is not occasioned by any quality or merit we already possess (Rom. 8.29, Eph. 1.4,5); (ii) he sent his Son, who accomplished the deliverance which secured our a. (Gal. 4.5); (iii) we received the title deeds of a. when we put on Christ (Gal. 3.26,27), and were sealed with the Holy Spirit of promise (Eph. 1.13). See BAPTISM and LAYING ON OF HANDS. (*b*) The *status* thereby conferred is a participation in the Sonship of Christ (Gal. 4.6) which is his by right (Rom. 1.3,4). (*c*) the *heritage* thereby secured: 'the unsearchable riches of Christ' (Eph. 3.8), the possession of the Spirit and the right to call God, Father (Gal. 4.6, Rom. 8.15). A. is a singularly appropriate word to denote a status to which Gentiles as well as Jews are admitted.

But this a., though a reality, is at present *hidden* (Rom. 8.18–19), obscured by the sufferings of the Christians and their subjection to the bondage of corruption (Rom. 8.18,21,23). Hence we wait for our 'adoption, the redemption of our body' (Rom. 8.23) at the Parousia and Resurrection. This ultimate adoption is not qualitatively or quantitatively different from our present adoption. It is the same adoption made manifest (cf. the verb 'see' in vss. 24 and 25), and is parallel to the hidden Sonship of the Messiah in the humiliation of his earthly life and his manifest Sonship after his exaltation. (Cf. I John 3.1–3 and 4.17*b*.)

The theology of a., though specifically Pauline, is paralleled in the Johannine writings (John 1.12, the OT expression of 'becoming a son'; and I John 3.1ff.), and is grounded in the synoptic saying that those who do the will of God (i.e. those called by Jesus and who respond to the call) are his brothers and sisters (Mark 3.35), which means also that they share his filial relationship to the Father (Matt. 6.9, Luke 11.2, Mark 14.36).

Also *v.* INHERIT NT(*a*).)

R. H. FULLER

ADULTERY, FORNICATION, HARLOT, WHORE, etc.

'Adultery' (*n'p, moicheia*) is sexual intercourse of a man with another man's wife (Exod. 20.14, Deut. 5.18, Lev. 20.10), and the law is that both man and woman are to be put to death; or of a married woman with any man (Num. 5.11–31, ordeal of jealousy). A married man who has intercourse with an unmarried woman is not regarded by the OT as an adulterer. The pronouncements of Jesus on divorce, closely related to Rabbinic discussions especially in Matt., change and define the position (Matt. 5.32, 19.9, Mark 10.11f., Luke 16.18). Four statements are made: a man who divorces his wife [except for fornication, Matt.] commits adultery if he marries another (Matt., Mark, Luke); a man who marries a divorced woman commits adultery (Matt., Luke); a man who divorces his wife except for fornication makes her an adulteress (Matt.); a woman who divorces her husband [which contradicts Jewish law] commits adultery if she marries another (Mark).

FORNICATION (*znh, porneia*) is sexual intercourse outside marriage or even sensuality in general. In the OT there is no condemnation of sexual relations that do not violate the marriage bond; at the most Prov. advises against it as unwise and destructive (7.5–27). Opposition to fornication arises entirely from its connexion with religious prostitution (cf. Lev. 21.7,9).

In this connexion both words are used for idolatry, especially when other nations are involved (e.g. Hos. 1.2, 2.2ff., 9.1, Jer. 3, Ezek. 16, 23). In Egypt and Babylonia the marriage of the god, accomplished in the person of the king, was part of the fertility rites. The holy marriage acquired independent character, with bands of priestesses (or even men and boys) at the temple for men to visit, and so produce a blessing for the participant and the community. Via Canaan, this practice penetrated Israelite life (e.g. Amos 2.7f., Mic. 1.7—a special word *qdšh*, 'holy women', is sometimes used) and dominated the cultus throughout the monarchical period (in the royal temple at Jerusalem, I Kings 14.24), though attempts were made to destroy it. It is this cult that was condemned by the prophets, and their attitude is reflected in the Law of Holiness and Deut. (Lev. 19.29, Deut. 23.17f.).

In the NT the metaphorical sense appears (e.g. fornication, Rev. 17 and freqt.; Matt. 12.39, Mark 8.38, adulterous generation = unfaithful to God). *Porneia* may have the general sense of 'adultery' (Matt. 5.22, 19.9), though it may mean 'marriage within the forbidden degrees, incest' as it does in I Cor. 5.1 and possibly in Acts 15.20f. (Lake, *Beginnings*, V, 207). In Jude 7 it means 'sodomy'. In I Cor. 6.9 it is said that fornicators, idolaters, adulterers, etc., shall not inherit the Kingdom of God (cf. Mark 7.21f.), and in Heb. 13.4 that God shall judge such perverters of marriage. Yet Jesus said that publicans and harlots precede the elders of the people into the Kingdom (Matt. 21.31f.). Even though he said that a man that looks on a woman to lust after her is an adulterer (Matt. 5.27f.), he treated the woman taken in adultery with great compassion (John 8.3ff.). Thus the NT condemnation proceeds from the sovereignty of God working to restore mankind to himself: so in I Cor. 6.13ff. the body is meant to glorify God as a temple of the Holy Spirit, a member of Christ whose inner being is destroyed if it is prostituted.

KENNETH GRAYSTON

ADVERSARY (SATAN, ENEMY, FOE, DEVIL, DEMON, BEELZEBUB)

In the OT 'adversary' translates two Heb. words meaning: one who distresses someone, and one who strives (often in law) against another. In the NT there is a Gk. word with the second meaning, and also one meaning 'to lie in wait against'. In I Sam. 1.6 and Lev. 18.18 the word has the technical meaning of 'a fellow wife', but with a Heb. nuance of 'one who causes distress'. In the OT Israel's FOES are often thought of as ENEMIES of Yahweh and of righteousness, and the belief in Yahweh's ruthless zeal against evil is expressed in the demand for ruthlessness to enemies (the ruthless God is seen too in the NT; cf. Matt. 13). In the Psalms many expressions of personal enmity probably arise from the fact that some Psalms were part of the ritual of trial by ordeal; the adversary is the accuser at whose instigation the trial is held. The accused, when found innocent, demands the fulfilment of the legal requirement that the punishment which would have been his falls on the head of the false accuser.

The SATAN is another name for an adversary or accuser; his function, like that of the royal official, 'the king's eye', is to bring a misdemeanour to the notice of God. It has the ordinary meaning of adversary (Num. 22.22, I Sam. 29.4); later, still with a definite article, it is used for the supernatural adversary *par excellence* (Job 1f., Zech. 3); later still as a proper name (I Chron. 21.1; cf. II Sam. 24.1), and so in the NT (Matt. 4.10 + 35 times); always he is thought of as subordinate to the God who does evil as well as good (Isa. 45.7), but he can allure man to an action which brings God's wrath (I Chron. 21.1). The opposition between God and Satan becomes clear in the NT: he tests Jesus in the wilderness (Matt. 4.10); is leader of the kingdom of evil (12.26); is responsible for the sin of Peter (16.23), Judas (Luke 22.3), and Ananias (Acts 5.3); he causes disease (Luke 13.16). He has been defeated (Luke 10.18), but still tries to get advantage over us (II Cor. 2.11). Another name for this prince of devils is BEELZEBUB (Matt. 10.25), used mostly of demon possession (12.24); the Eng. word comes from the Heb. name for the God of Ekron, Baalzebub (II Kings 1) used by the Jews as a derisive name for Baalzebul, the Lord of the High Place, and it is the form with a final 'l' which is used in the Gk. NT.

In the NT the DEVIL is identified with Satan (Matt. 4.1), but the word (DAEMONS) is also used for the many evil spirits under his control who possess men (Matt. 7.22) and animals (8.31). In the OT the word is used for the goat-like satyrs (Lev. 17.7), and for heathen gods (Deut. 32.17).

The whole realm of these ideas is easier to understand in the context of the Heb. belief that human personality is open to invasion from the Spirit of God (Judg. 6.34), and of the vivid concrete form of Heb. thinking. The theological question which arises in our day is how far the biblical language about the Devil, demons, etc., is to be taken literally or how far it is to be regarded as 'picture-thinking', i.e. as a mythological attempt to express the reality and extent of evil in the universe, existing outside and apart from (though not without influence upon) the human sphere. (*V*. also TEMPT; SPIRIT, I(d); ANTICHRIST.)

J. N. SCHOFIELD

ADVOCATE *v.* SPIRIT IX(*d*)

AFFLICTION *v.* SUFFER

AGE, AGES *v.* TIME

ALMIGHTY *v.* GOD, GODS III

ALMS-GIVING *v.* POOR

ALTAR *v.* SACRIFICE II(*c*) and (*e*)

AMAZE *v.* ASTONISH

AMBASSADOR, AMBASSAGE

Ambassador (II Chron. 35.21, Isa. 30.4, 33.7) and Ambassage (Luke 14.32, 19.14) are both used in their literal sense. In II Cor. 5.20, Eph. 6.20, and perhaps Philem. 9 (RV marg.), St. Paul describes himself as an 'ambassador for Christ', 'an ambassador in bonds'. The term employed (noun and verb alike) was used technically of the Roman Emperor's personal representative in the East (Deissmann, *Light from the Ancient East*, 379). Thus the Apostle, and by inference any evangelist (II Cor. 5.20), not merely speaks on behalf of Christ, but actually represents him and acts for him among men.

J. P. T.-D.

AMEN

Transliterated into Gk. and modern languages, this Heb. word has continued a liturgical usage which originated in OT times, at least as early as the Exile in Babylon (cf. Deut. 27.15ff., Ps. 106.48). In the Gospels we find a different though related meaning, viz. 'truly' (AV and RV 'verily'), giving a solemn emphasis. This is common, and confined to utterances of Jesus. In St. John's Gospel the *amen* is always doubled.

Elsewhere in the NT the original liturgical sense predominates, and it expresses assent to a prayer or wish. Paul uses it five times at the end of an Epistle, and this is copied in other Epistles. Almost without exception in the NT *amen* expresses the feeling of an individual, but we find the corporate usage in Rev. 5.14, 19.4 (cf. I Cor. 14.16, II Cor. 1.20), and there is no doubt that the practice of the primitive Church followed that of the synagogue. Rev. 3.14 calls for special notice. Here the phrase 'the Amen' is used with ref. to the heavenly Christ, and the meaning is clearly 'the true and reliable one'. The author probably had in mind Isa. 65.16, where the Heb. actually has 'God of Amen'. (Also *v.* TRUTH.)

E. C. BLACKMAN

ANATHEMA *v.* DEVOTE, CURSE II

ANGEL

This word is used in the Bible to translate Heb. and Gk. words meaning 'messenger'; but usually in Eng. it denotes a superhuman being. In the early popular writings in the OT the word is used in the sing. in the phrase 'the angel of the Lord' or 'of God' (the trans. 'an angel of the Lord' is grammatically inadmissible) to denote an appearance of God himself in human form (Gen. 16.7–14, 22.11–15, Exod. 3.2, Judg. 2.1ff., 5.23, 6.11–24, 13.3ff.); the heavenly visitor always betrays his identity by word or act, and in each story is at some point treated as God (cf. Gen. 16.13, 31.13, Exod. 3.4, Judg. 6.14, 13.22). Clearly the phrase is used thinly to veil a theophany, for in the popular belief God could appear in human form. Our clear-cut distinction between natural and supernatural did not exist: man is a body animated by the breath (Gen. 2.7) or spirit (Eccles. 12.7); he is open to the invasion of the spirit of God which can clothe itself in Gideon (Judg. 6.34) or rush upon Samson (Judg. 14.6).

In popular Heb. thought there was also a belief that there existed a rich background of supernatural beings attendant on God; they ascend and descend the heavenly ladder (Gen. 28.12) and are distinct from God (cf. Gen. 32.1); Jacob meets two companies of them (Gen. 32.1). These supernatural beings are called sons of God (Job 1.6, Ps. 89.6; cf. Dan. 3.25), Gods (Ps. 8.5), hosts of heaven (I Kings 22.19), God's ministers (Ps. 103.21). As man was not thought of as an individual but as part of the corporate personality of a group, so God was not conceived as a lonely individual.

Later Jewish thought regarded angels as intermediaries between man and God (Ezek. 40.3, Zech. 2); they bring God's help (Dan. 3.28, Ps. 91.11, Acts 8.26, Heb. 1.14); God's revelation (Matt. 1.20, Acts 10.3); man's intercession (Zech. 1.12, Job 5.1). But the priestly writings of the OT avoid the phrase 'the angel of the Lord', and the Sadducees in the NT (Acts 23.8) did not believe in angels. In Dan. and the Apocrypha, names are given to individual angels and they are arranged in an hierarchy: Gabriel (Dan. 8.16), Michael (Dan. 10.13), Raphael (Tob. 3.17).

Popular beliefs are seen in the NT. There

are countless hosts of angels (Matt. 26.53); Gabriel reveals God's will (Luke 1.19); angels share God's joy (Luke 15.7); accompany the Son of man (Matt. 16.27); and stand in the presence of God (Matt. 18.10). The doctrine of 'guardian angels' is found in Matt. 18.10 and Acts 12.15. The Christian Church adopted largely the belief in angels and used it to express the experience of the unseen spirit world of guardian beings sent to minister (Heb. 1.14).

J. N. SCHOFIELD

ANGER *v.* WRATH

ANOINTED *v.* CHRIST

ANOINTING *v.* SACRIFICE III(*d*)2

ANTICHRIST, MAN OF SIN

The word 'Antichrist' occurs only in St. John's Epistles (I John 2.18,22, 4.3, II John 7), and 'the Man of Sin' only in II Thess. 2.3. But the idea occurs in various places in the OT and the NT. It is that, as the darkest hour is that which precedes the dawn, so before the final victory of God and the establishment of his Kingdom, all the forces of evil must be unleashed and do their worst. The final blasphemy will be seen when 'the Man is revealed, the son of perdition, he that opposeth and exalteth himself against all that is called God or that is worshipped; so that he sitteth in the temple of God, setting himself forth as God' (II Thess. 2.3–4). In St. John's Epistles the Antichrist is identified with those who 'deny that Jesus is the Christ', 'deny the Father and the Son', and do not confess 'Jesus come in the flesh' (I John 2.22, 4.2–3); and 'even now there have been many Antichrists'. Here, in contrast with St. Paul, is a conception of a plurality of Antichrists. Christians in many generations have believed that Antichrist was to be discerned in their day. We in our day can nevertheless be right, perhaps, in thinking that in our own day more complete embodiments of Antichrist have appeared than ever before. But everywhere in Scripture where this fearful uprising of evil is described, it is against the background of the advent of the Lord to overthrow evil and set up his Kingdom.

The idea first appears in Ezek. 38 and 39, the prophecy of Gog and Magog; it comes again in Zech. 14.2ff. where Jerusalem is to be taken and sacked, before the Lord comes to fight his battle and save his people. The men of the Maccabean persecution evidently believed that they were living in the last days; the Fourth Beast in the Son of Man vision, Dan. 7.21–7, is seen as a final uprising of evil, and the same thought is pursued in 9.24–7 and 11. From the evidence of Jewish apocalyptic writings (*Sib. Or.*, Book iii, IV Esdras 5.4,6, *Apoc. Bar.*, ch. xl, *Asc. Isa.*, ch. iv—summarized briefly in *HDB*, vol. III, p. 227), it may be concluded that 'there was among the Jews a fully-developed legend of Anti-Christ, which was accepted and amplified by Christians'.

In II Thess. 2, St. Paul's teaching is that 'the day of the Lord is *not* imminent'—the warning-bell for it has not yet rung—because the Man of Sin has not yet appeared (2.1–4). There are forces at work—the Thessalonians know what he means—which are holding him in check (5,6), though indeed 'the mystery of lawlessness' is plainly at work (7). But the time will come when the Lawless One will be revealed, and the Lord Jesus will slay him with the breath of his mouth (8ff.).

The teaching of Mark 13 is commonly held to be the same: Antichrist has not yet appeared. Antichrist seems to be alluded to in 13.14, where in defiance of grammar 'the abomination of desolation' (allusion to Dan. 9.27, 11.31, 12.11) takes a masculine participle. Matt. 24.13 adds the reference to Daniel, and the words 'standing in the holy place'; Luke 21.20 interprets of the Roman armies: 'when ye see Jerusalem compassed with armies.'

The texts in the Johannine Epistles have been summarized already.

In Revelation there is a fuller treatment of the uprising of evil. In 12 the Dragon, who is identified with the 'original Serpent' (i.e. the Serpent of Gen. 3) in verse 9, seeks in vain to destroy the Man-child who is the Messiah (5), and then the Woman who brought him forth (15). Then in 13.2–9 we read of the Beast, who makes war with the saints as in Dan. 7; and in 13.11–18 of the second Beast, who has 'two horns like a lamb', and persuades men to worship the Beast, enforcing his persuasion by the exclusion from commercial rights of all who do not accept the mark of the Beast. Immediately after this we are shown the true Lamb standing on Mount Zion with the 144,000 who have his Name and the Name of his Father on their foreheads (14.1). The trio of the Dragon, the Beast and the Beast who is the false Lamb reappears as the trio of the Dragon, the Beast and the False Prophet in 19.20 and 20.10.

In 19.11–16 is the Parousia, the appearance of the divine Warrior on the white horse, to fight the great battle with the trio of evil powers and all the kings of the earth (19.19–21). After this the Devil is bound for a thousand years; at the end of the millennium he is to be loosed for a little while (20.4,7) to deceive 'the nations which are in the four corners of the earth, Gog and Magog, to gather them together to the war' (8); they 'compass the camp of the saints about, and the beloved City'; then fire comes down from heaven to devour them, and there is an end of the Devil (9–10); then the last judgment, and the coming of the New Jerusalem. (*V.* also ABOMINATION.)

A. G. HEBERT

ANXIOUS *v.* CARE

APOCALYPSE *v.* REVEAL

APOSTLE

An apostle (Gk. *apostolos*) is one sent forth (from *apo-stellein*, to send forth), a messenger, especially one authorized to act in a particular matter for the one who sends him. In the earliest instance of the word in Gk. literature, a herald sent to arrange a truce is called 'the apostle' (Herodotus i. 21); cf. for the combination of the two words II Tim. 1.11, 'a herald (EVV, preacher) and apostle and teacher'. This general sense of the word, rare in ordinary Gk., is found in the NT in John 13.16 (EVV, 'he that is sent'), II Cor. 8.23, Phil. 2.25 and (probably) Luke 11.49.

In the Gospels of Mark, Matt., and Luke (the only instance of the word in John is in 13.16) it is used of the twelve disciples whom Jesus chose 'that they might be with him and that he might send them forth to preach' (lit., 'to be heralds'), Mark 3.14. Mark and Matt. each use the word only once, Mark 6.30, Matt. 10.2. Luke alone says that Jesus himself called them apostles when he chose them and sent them forth on their mission, Luke 6.13. (The words, 'whom also he named apostles', found in many MSS at Mark 3.14, are a gloss from Luke—*v.* RV margin.) In four other passages in Luke 'the apostles' means the Twelve. In 24 out of the 26 occurrences of the word in Acts 'the apostles' means either the eleven original apostles, or the Twelve after Judas' place had been taken by Matthias. But in 14.4,14 Paul and Barnabas are called apostles, although in 9.27 they are by implication distinguished from 'the apostles'.

In the letters of Paul, except for the two instances of the general sense mentioned above, 'apostle' always means 'apostle of Jesus Christ'. The full phrase is used chiefly in the opening salutations, of Paul himself, but also in II Cor. 11.13 and I Thess. 2.6 ('apostles of Christ'). Plainly the title is not confined now to the Twelve, cf. especially I Cor. 15.5,7, 'to the twelve . . . then to all the apostles'. Since Paul is here referring to a tradition which he had himself 'received' (vs. 3), it would seem that this wider application of the title did not originate with him, but was current in the early Church. It is not possible, however, to determine either who were called apostles or what the qualifications of an apostle were. On the most natural interpretation of Rom. 16.7 ('of note among the apostles'), Andronicus and Junias, of whom we know nothing more, were apostles, and Gal. 1.10 may imply that James, the brother of the Lord, was an apostle. The reference in II Cor 11.13 to 'false apostles', who 'fashion themselves into apostles of Christ', shows that the claim to be an apostle could be made falsely, and so, that there was no easy way of knowing whether it was justified or not. Paul's own claim to be an apostle was challenged by his opponents, and so he insists that he is 'an apostle, not from men nor through man, but through Jesus Christ and God the Father' (Gal. 1.1). In II Cor. 12.12 Paul speaks of 'the signs of an apostle' which he had 'wrought' among the Corinthians, but it is not clear that such 'signs and wonders and mighty works' could be wrought only by an apostle; in I Cor. 12.28f., (workers of) miracles are mentioned as a distinct group of Church workers, after apostles, prophets and teachers. From this passage it is clear that apostleship was the highest office in the Church: cf. also Eph. 4.11. Within the apostleship Paul was not prepared to recognize distinctions of rank; if he speaks of 'the very chiefest apostles' (better, 'those pre-eminent apostles', RV margin), II Cor. 11.5, 12.11, it is ironically, and if from one point of view he holds himself 'the least of the apostles', I Cor. 15.9, from another he claims to be 'not a whit behind the very chiefest apostles', II Cor. 11.5. It is precarious to infer from I Cor. 9.1, 'Am I not an apostle? Have I not seen Jesus our Lord?', that one necessary qualification for true apostleship was to have seen the risen Christ. It is even more precarious to infer from Paul's insistence that he did not receive his own commission as an apostle 'from men or through man' that there were other apostles whose commission came to them, not directly from God and Christ, but through the Church. The account of the appointment of Matthias as an apostle, Acts 1.23ff., suggests that 'the brethren' did no more than recognize God's choice of him to be an apostle in place of Judas. According to Acts 13.2f. Barnabas and Paul were 'separated' for the work to which the Holy Spirit had called them in the Church at Antioch with fasting, prayer, and the laying on of hands. This certainly looks like ordination to office, but Paul himself would not have admitted that it was his ordination as an apostle—God had separated him, even from his birth, and then had called him, at his conversion, that he might preach Christ among the Gentiles (Gal. 1.15f.). And Peter and the other leaders in the church at Jerusalem recognized that he had a divine commission as authentic and full as their own (Gal. 2.7f.).

From what Paul says of himself it is plain

that the chief work of an apostle was simply to preach Christ (Gal. 1.16) or to preach the gospel (I Cor. 1.17), and to preach it, in the first place, to those who had not yet heard it. His authority over the churches he founded was such as resulted naturally from the fact that he was their founder; Paul carefully refrains from claiming authority in the church in Rome, which he had not founded (cf. Rom. 1.11f.). But what exactly distinguished apostles from other preachers of the gospel is not clear; Silvanus and Timothy were associated with Paul in preaching Christ at Corinth when the church there was founded (II Cor. 1.19), but neither is ever called an apostle (*v.* especially II Cor. 1.1, Phil. 1.1, Rom. 16.21). All that can be said is that, after Paul, the Church soon came to restrict the use of the title to the Twelve and Paul himself. Paul's apostleship, however, seems to have been regarded as exceptional, for in Rev., although the wider use of the title appears to be implied in 2.2, 'the twelve apostles of the Lamb' are mentioned as if they were the only apostles, 21.14.

The author of the epistle to the Hebrews seems to avoid using the word in its usual Christian sense (cf. 2.37), but does use it once of Christ himself, who is called 'the apostle and high priest of our confession', 3.1; here the word has its original sense of one authorized to speak and act for the person who sends him. (Also *v.* MINISTER.)

J. Y. CAMPBELL

APPOINT

This English verb is used to translate a number of Heb. and Gk. verbs, and the precise meaning has often to be determined from the context. The RV often uses some other word where the AV has 'appoint' and uses 'appoint' where the AV has some other word; yet the meaning is usually sufficiently clear whatever rendering is used. But in Acts 1.7, e.g., RV margin: 'times or seasons which the Father hath *appointed* by his own authority' is probably preferable to the text, 'hath set within his own authority'. It was a widely held belief that God himself had determined beforehand the exact time of important happenings; hence the frequent occurrence of the phrase, 'the time(s) appointed'. (Also *v.* FULFIL.)

J. Y. C.

ARK *v.* PRESENCE, SACRIFICE, NOAH

ARMAGEDDON or HAR-MAGEDON

This is the name of the last great battlefield (Rev. 16.16), and probably contains a reference to the Hill (Heb. *Har*) of Megiddo in northern Palestine overlooking the plain of Esdraelon, in which many of the decisive battles of Palestine were fought (Judg. 5, I Sam. 31, II Kings 23). The word is also probably influenced by Ezek. 38f., which speaks of the last great battle taking place on the mountains of Israel. In post-biblical Christian tradition the word becomes the name for the final battle between good and evil at the end of the age.

J. N. S.

ARMOUR

As offensive weapons, it is probable that the early club or staff and sling were never entirely replaced by the later bow, javelin, spear, sword and dagger. In the stories of Joshua's conquest of Palestine he is said to use his javelin as a signal (Josh. 8.18), and this same short spear is mentioned by Jer. 6.23, 50.42, and in the interesting list of weapons useless against 'leviathan' (Job 41.1). The SLING could be an accurate weapon: there were 700 chosen Benjamin left-handed men who could sling at a human hair and not miss (Judg. 20.16), and David with a carefully chosen stone defeated Goliath (I Sam. 17.40). The metaphor of the sling was used of God's destruction of the inhabitants of a land (Jer. 10.18) and of the fate of the wicked as slung out of God's sling (I Sam. 25.29).

Spears are first mentioned in the OT in Israel's fight with the Philistines (I Sam. 13.19ff.); like swords, they needed to be made and sharpened by a smith, and the Philistines allowed no smiths among the Israelites. In the ideal peaceful world spears will be pruning-hooks (Micah 4.3).

SWORDS are more commonly mentioned from the whirling flame of the sword guarding the way to Eden (Gen. 3.24) to the sword—the sharp Word of God—which slew the remnant of the followers of the beast (Rev. 19.13ff.). Petrie discovered an iron-smelting furnace and sword factory at Gerar dating from *c.* 1300 BC (Duncan, *Digging up Bible History*, I, p. 144); and copper-smelting furnaces have been found in Transjordan (N. Glueck, *The Other Side of Jordan*). Greeks and Philistines are claimed to have used straight, pointed, two-edged swords for both cut and thrust, but from Egyptian monuments it seems probable that a more sickle-shaped one was used for cutting. The sword is used symbolically for God's judgement (Deut. 22, Ps. 149), his Word (Eph. 6.17, Heb. 4.12); the tongue of the wicked (Isa. 49.2); the harlot (Prov. 5.4); strife (Matt. 10.34).

Just as 'sword' does not always refer to the same weapon—it may be wood, bronze or iron—so bows and ARROWS, the commonest weapon in early warfare, could be of various kinds. Heb. uses the phrase 'tread the bow' as though referring to a large, powerful one. The arrows had flint or metal heads. Arrows were used for divination—the quiver was shaken (Ezek. 21.19ff.). Like the word 'sword', arrow is used metaphorically. The rainbow is God's bow in the sky (Gen. 9).

There is also defensive armour. The Philistine Goliath had a bronze helmet, a scale coat-of-male, weighing about 2 cwt., bronze leg-shields, and a shield borne by another man (I Sam. 17.5); Saul had similar garments. Isa. 59.17 speaks of God as putting on righteousness as a coat-of-mail, and victory or deliverance as a HELMET. Paul pictures the Christian as clad in the same armour (Eph. 6.13ff.); in I Thess. 5.8 the helmet is 'the hope of deliverance'. SHIELDS were of two kinds: the large one carried by Goliath's armour-bearer, and used by heavy infantry; this shield is used figuratively of God's goodwill (Ps. 5.12), truth (Ps. 91.4), or faith (Eph. 6.16); and the smaller round shield, carried by the warrior himself, often used figuratively of God himself (Gen. 15.1 and Pss.) or his deliverance (Ps. 18.35). The BREASTPLATE worn by the priest appears to have been a square object adorned with precious stones and containing pockets for the sacred lot (Exod. 28, Lev. 8.8).

J. N. SCHOFIELD

ARROW *v.* ARMOUR

ASCEND

The only instances of the word 'ascend' that call for any comment are those which refer to ascending to heaven. In the Bible, heaven, the dwelling-place of God and his angels, is thought of as spatially located above the earth and the sky, just as Sheol or Hades, the abode of the spirits of the dead, is thought of as located below the earth. Thus, in Judg. 13.20, the angel of the Lord who had appeared to Manoah and his wife '*ascended* in the flame of the altar' when it '*went up* toward heaven from off the altar'. Even when it was realized that God's presence was not confined to heaven (cf. Ps. 139.8, 'If I ascend up into heaven, thou art there: if I make my bed in Sheol, behold, thou art there'), it was still natural to speak of going to where God 'dwelt' as ascending. So the return of our Lord, after his resurrection, to God from whom he had come, is commonly called his Ascension. It is doubtless accidental that, neither in Gk. nor in Eng., are the words 'ascend', 'ascension', or their equivalents, used in the account of this in Acts 1.9ff. From the beginning it was the Christian conviction that Jesus had not only gone to be with God, but had been exalted to a position of authority 'at his right hand' (cf. Acts 2.33). In this regard *his* Ascension was unique. Whether it was also regarded as unique simply as an Ascension to God, it is not possible to determine, for both among Jews and Christians there seem to have been different opinions about the possibility of men ascending to heaven. In the OT there is the story of Elijah's ascent into heaven 'by a whirlwind' (II Kings 2.11), and in non-canonical Jewish writings similar stories are told of other OT characters. In Rabbinic writings the souls of the righteous dead are sometimes said to dwell in the highest of the seven heavens. In a particularly difficult passage in Rev. 11.1–13, we have the strange story of two unidentifiable 'witnesses' who are put to death in Jerusalem by their enemies, raised to life after three and a half days, and who then 'ascend into heaven in the cloud' before the eyes of their enemies. In the letter to the Philippians, too, Paul speaks of his own death as meaning that he will be 'with Christ', which surely must mean being with him in heaven (1.23). On the other hand, it was a widely accepted Jewish doctrine that no man could ascend into heaven (however this was harmonized with the stories just mentioned), and this doctrine was accepted by Christians also —cf. John 3.13, 'No one has ascended into heaven except he who came down from heaven, the Son of Man'. (*V.* also ASCENSION.)

J. Y. CAMPBELL

ASCENSION

The 'ascension' or 'exaltation' of Jesus Christ was a regular theme of the preaching of the primitive Church. A variety of words and phrases was used to describe this climax of the gospel history: to take up (Acts 1.2, 1.11, I Tim. 3.16), to exalt (Acts 2.33, 5.31), to sit down at the right hand of God (Eph. 1.20, Heb. 1.3, 10.12), to go up or ascend (Acts 2.34, John 3.13, 6.62, 20.17, Eph. 4.8–10). The Apostles accepted the Ptolemaic astronomy of the time, and they thought of Jesus as having gone to a place beyond the sky called heaven from whence he would return (Acts 1.11, Phil. 3.20, I Thess. 1.10). But their belief involved more than this, for the phrase 'at the right hand of God' meant not a place, but a participation in the sovereignty of God over all things. The exalted Jesus had entered a state and an activity which transcended the limitations of place altogether (cf. John 14.3, Eph. 4.10, Col. 3.1).

In a number of passages the Resurrection and the Ascension are not apparently distinguished as two events (cf. Acts 2.32f., Rom. 8.34, Col. 3.1, Phil. 2.9, I Tim. 3.16, Eph. 1.20, I Pet. 3.22). But there is a clear distinction between them in theological meaning. It was one thing to assert that Jesus had been raised from death: it was another thing (however closely connected) to assert that he now shared in the sovereignty of God over heaven and earth.

The account of the Ascension as a distinct event is found only in one of the NT writers. At the end of St. Luke's Gospel it is recorded that Jesus led the Apostles over against Bethany, blessed them and was parted from them; and they returned to Jerusalem rejoicing. It is the record of an impressive final parting; but it cannot with confidence be called a record of the Ascension, for the words 'and was carried up into heaven' are omitted in Western MSS. and are doubtful. But there is a second account in Acts 1.9–11, where Jesus in the presence of the Apostles 'was taken up, a cloud receiving him from out of their sight'. The story has some resemblances to the story of the assumption of Elijah in II Kings 2. Like all miracle stories, it has its special difficulties; and it has been asked: What happened to the body of Jesus? Could it have travelled to a local heaven? Or could it have been withdrawn from space altogether? The real point is that these questions have already arisen in connexion with the Resurrection. *Then*, in the belief of the primitive Church, the body of Jesus had been raised and glorified, passing to a mode of existence akin to the 'spiritual body' mentioned in I Cor. 15.44 (*v.* RESURRECTION). Subsequently there was the series of manifestations of Jesus to the Apostles, each of the series ending with his withdrawal from their sight; and 'the only difference between the Ascension and the previous withdrawals was that the Ascension was the last of them' (J. H. Bernard). The episode in Acts 1.9–11 need not be identified with the 'glorifying' of Jesus; and perhaps it may best be understood as an enacted symbol to reveal to the Apostles that the series of appearances to them was ending, that Jesus was entering upon a new mode of existence and activity, and that he was not only raised from death, but exalted into the glory of God—the cloud being a recognized symbol of the divine presence (*v.* PRESENCE). The belief in the exaltation of Jesus is attested widely in the NT, and it may not have depended upon the episode recorded in Acts 1. But the episode conveys by its imagery a truth about the consummation of the earthly life of the Lord which can never be conveyed without recourse to the imagery of movement upwards.

The importance of the Ascension is drawn out specially in the discourse in John 14–16, in Eph. and in Heb. The bringing to an end of the visible intercourse between Jesus and the disciples is the prelude to a new manner of relation between him and them, and to a new stage in his activity on behalf of the human race. The ascended Christ is *King*, all things being ultimately beneath his sovereignty (cf. Eph. 1.20, Phil. 2.9–11, Heb. 1.3, I Pet. 3.22, Rev. 5.11–13). The ascended Christ is *Forerunner*; in him our human nature has reached its final goal, and the Father's acceptance of him is the ground of the acceptance of mankind in him (cf. John 14.3, Heb. 6.20, 10.19–22, Eph. 2.6). The ascended Christ is *Priest*: he for ever intercedes for the human race as one who has known temptation, suffering and death (cf. Rom. 8.34, Heb. 4.14–16, 7.25f.); and his sacrifice, which was once for all wrought in history upon the Cross, remains for ever in virtue of his presence with the Father (cf. Heb. 7.23–5, 9.24, I John 2.1–2, Rev. 5.6). Upon the ascended Christ, no less than upon the events which preceded his exaltation, the Church depends for its existence and its characteristics. Its worship is a participation in his priesthood; its work in the sanctification of human lives rests upon his glorified manhood as the forerunner; and its preaching is the setting forward of his kingly rule.

A. M. RAMSEY

ASHAMED *v.* SHAME

ASHERAH *v.* GOD, GODS IV

ASHTAROTH *v.* GOD, GODS IV

ASSEMBLY *v.* CHURCH

ASSYRIA and BABYLONIA

These are the names for the district between the Tigris and Euphrates. It is difficult to separate the two kingdoms geographically, historically or ethnologically. Usually Assyria is the name given to the northern section with Assur as its capital, and Babylonia is the name for the southern part whose earliest capital was Ur. Assyria is a rich alluvial plain formed by river deposits. Babylonia runs south to the sea marshes, which are extending about 115 ft. a year through silting. Eridu, an early sea-port for Ur, is now 130 miles from the sea.

The early inhabitants, the Sumerians, gave way about 2500 BC to Semitic conquerors—the kingdom of Sargon of Agade known as Accadian—who gradually encroached on the western nomads until a raid from Hittites of Asia Minor overthrew the short-lived first Babylonian dynasty (of which Hammurabi is the best-known ruler) about 1750 BC. Power was then seized by Kassite tribesmen from the hills in the north-east, and for 600 years Assyria was independent of Babylonia and closely linked with the Mitanni kingdom on the west. During this period the Assyrians—

a mixed Semitic race whose language was kin to Accadian—rose to power and were dominant until Nebuchadrezzar I asserted Babylonian supremacy about 1150 BC. Fifty years later Tiglath-pileser I revived the Assyrian Empire, and, though weakened by Aramaean and Chaldean incursions between 1050 and 950 BC, the Assyrians dominated Mesopotamia and Palestine until the foundation of the New Babylonian empire under Nabopolassar in 625 BC. In 539 BC the country was again invaded from the east, by Medes and Persians under Cyrus. The Persian Empire in its turn fell before Greek invaders, but the western domination of Mesopotamia by Greek and Roman was continually and successfully challenged by eastern tribesmen, the Parthians.

Excavations in progress in Mesopotamia since 1841 have yielded a rich harvest of exact historical information and have shown how profound was the influence of the country on the language, literature and religion of Palestine. The Sumerians were the founders of civilization in the Near East, and their influence spread to India on the east and, through Palestine, to Egypt on the west (cf. *The Sumerians*, C. L. Woolley). Their legends, myths, legal codes, and cultus, taken over by their Semitic conquerors and adapted by the early Babylonians and the Assyrians, have much in common with parts of the Pentateuch: the stories of creation and the flood, and the Mosaic law-codes cannot be treated in isolation from the Mesopotamian parallels. It has also become increasingly clear that the study of the Psalms can gain much from a knowledge of the long liturgies sung in the old Sumerian temples in accordance with a careful calendar; the form of many of the Psalms has much in common with Mesopotamian hymns of the king-cult, hymns of praise, and private and public penitential psalms. Methods of atonement for ethical and ceremonial sins by means of magic and ritual, and methods of divination by priests and cult-prophets, show that, at least, there was a large religious heritage common to the whole Near East.

The Assyrians were a warlike people, and their empire was built on military organization. In religion they were intolerant, and they prided themselves on their ruthless cruelty in warfare. Their wickedness and cruelty, like that of the Babylonians, became proverbial in Palestine; years after Nineveh had fallen her name was used by the editor of the book of Jonah as a symbol of the worst of sinners whom the merciful God was willing to pardon; and in Revelation, Babylon is used as a code-word to denote Rome, the persecuting oppressor. (*V.* also CITY.)

J. N. SCHOFIELD

ASTONISH, AMAZE, MARVEL

These and their related words record the experiences of individuals confronted with the unexpected, and describe these experiences, whether of bane or blessing, in ejaculations or in questions, in acts of grieved astonishment (e.g. Ezek. 3.15, Ezra 9.3f.), in affirmations or in confessions of fear (Jer. 4.9). It should be noted that expressions of astonishment are not, of course, confined to the terminology, and, further, that in Hebrew thinking there is a close connexion between surprise, fear and desolation.

Most important are those references which describe the astonishment caused by some divine manifestation or activity (Job 17.8, Dan. 8.27). Noteworthy is Jacob's experience at Bethel (Gen. 28), and especially his affirmation (vs. 16ff.). Especially will the actions of God in the future cause astonishment, for Israelites and Jews (I Kings 9.8, Jer. 18.16) and the peoples (Jer. 49.17, Lev. 26.32, Ezek. 27.35, 32.10) will be astonished. Conditions in the Messianic Age will be astonishing. Reversal of natural conditions (e.g. Isa. 11.6–9,35), the qualities and titles of the Messiah (Isa. 9.6f.), and the character and destiny of God's servant (Isa. 52.13–53.12), of whom it is said: 'As many were astonished at thee, so shall he startle (rather than sprinkle) many nations,' (52.14f.), evoke astonishment.

It should also be noted, in view of what follows below, that Isa. 59.16, 63.5 suggest the astonishment of God, while in Jer. 2.12, we read that Israel's idolatry calls forth this oracle: 'Be astonished, O ye heavens at this, and be horribly afraid, be ye very desolate, saith the Lord.'

Of most importance is that twofold astonishment which is described in the Gospels. There is first those expressions of astonishment caused by Jesus himself. His hearers were astonished at his authority (Mark 1.22), at his doctrine (Matt. 7.28), at his words (Mark 10.24), at his proposed journey to Jerusalem (Mark 10.32), at his wisdom and marvellous deeds (Matt. 13.54). The people are compelled to ask, 'Is not this the carpenter, the son of Mary? . . .' Their astonishment is the fruit of the contrast between what they know of him as one of themselves, and what they now discover about him. So painful does this contrast become, that 'they were offended in him' (Mark 6.3).

The Gospels also witness to the astonishment of Jesus Christ himself, and it is in his astonishment that the real importance of this study is to be found. This astonishment is recorded in several places in the Gospels, as for example in his questions. Thus he asks the disciples, after stilling the storm, 'Why are ye so fearful? how is it that ye have no faith?' (Mark 4.40). The implied astonishment of his questions witnesses to the contrast between their dread and his calm serenity. Similarly, the experiences of teaching and healing in his own country issue in the following statement: 'And he marvelled because of their unbelief' (Mark 6.6). There is an unmistakable element of astonishment in this marvelling of Jesus. It is not merely due to the contrast between what he expected to find in the way of unbelief in the people, and what he actually did find of unbelief among them; it is due also to the contrast between their unbelief and his belief.

Mark 14.33 records that Jesus 'began to be sore amazed (cf., e.g. 9.15, 16.5f.), and to be very heavy'. This passage clearly shows that Jesus is now amazed by something within himself, that is, by the depth of suffering and of doubt of which a human mind could be capable. This experience is only partially interpreted, when it is regarded as a testimony to the reality of our Lord's humanity, for it also witnesses to a divine astonishment at the depths of human suffering.

The study of 'astonishment' in scripture is thus important because it leads to the astonishment of our Lord himself. The external facts and internal experiences which created his astonishment witness to a certain 'divine innocence', which in turn is a clue to and a confirmation of his divinity.

G. HENTON DAVIES

ATONE, ATONEMENT

OT: The words used in the Bible to describe the taking away of sin need to be studied in their biblical context (*v.* art. SACRIFICE, in which they all occur) and also as permanently belonging to the vocabulary and thought of the Israel of God which is the Church. The Heb. word for 'atone' is *kaphar,* with its derivatives (Gk. *hilaskesthai* and derivatives). It is disputed whether *kaphar* denotes primarily an atoning action directed towards God ('propitiation') or towards the offence ('expiation'). But both meanings are biblical and are expressed also in other words. Great caution is, however, necessary in using the words 'propitiation' and 'expiation', because these are all too readily interpreted in the light of the meanings which they bear in the Greek and Latin classics; much harm has come from this source to traditional expositions of the doctrine of the Atonement.

(*a*) *Propitiation.* Buchanan Gray (*Sacrifice in OT,* pp. 67–81) and others regard this as the primary meaning of *kaphar* and 'atonement'; by sacrifice or other means the wrath of God is turned away and he is reconciled to man. In Gen. 32.20 *kaphar* is used of Jacob 'appeasing' Esau with a present; and an action directed God-wards is taken to be the meaning of 'atonement' in Lev. 16.10, 17.11, and many other places where the word occurs. For the idea, compare David's 'Let him smell an offering', I Sam. 26.19: the sacrifice offered to Chemosh by King Mesha of Moab in II Kings 3.26, whereby 'wrath' is turned away from Moab and diverted against Israel; and the phrase 'a sweet savour' regularly used of burnt-offerings, Gen. 8.21, Exod. 29.25, etc. (cf. Eph. 5.2), commonly interpreted as a 'soothing odour'. The prophets, however, whose criticism of the offering of sacrifice and of the sacrifices themselves constitutes a very important part of the OT doctrine of sacrifice, deny that sacrifice *of itself* can thus have an effect on God; man cannot thus buy God's favour, since man's relation to him is personal, and he wants men's own love and obedience. In one place, however, such an offering is called a sacrifice, an *'asham,* a guilt-offering; this is the redemptive self-oblation of the Servant of Jehovah (Isa. 53.10). Here the redemptive action of the Servant is said to originate with Jehovah himself. Elsewhere, God himself appears similarly as the subject of the verb *kaphar*: Ezek. 16.63, Ps. 78.38 ('forgive'), II Chron. 30.18 ('pardon'), Deut. 21.8, 32.43; cf. Luke 18.13 ('be merciful'), Ps. 79.9, Dan. 9.24. Cf. also the *kapporeth,* the covering of the sacred Ark, translated 'mercy-seat', Lev. 16.2, etc.

(*b*) *Expiation.* It has been held by others that the 'atoning' action is primarily regarded as having a direct effect on the sins, 'covering' them or 'blotting them out', i.e. 'to make or treat as harmless, non-existent, or inoperative, to annul (so far as God's notice or regard is concerned), to withdraw from God's sight, with the attached ideas of reinstating in his favour, freeing from sin, and restoring to holiness' (Driver in *HDB,* IV.131). Even if this be not the proper meaning of *kaphar,* the idea certainly occurs in the words 'cover' and 'blot out'; and in Isa. 6.7, 22.14, 27.9, Ps. 65.3, 79.9, *kaphar* is translated 'purge'. *Kasar,* 'cover', is used of sins in Ps. 32.1, 'Blessed is he . . . whose sin is covered'; Ps. 85.2, Neh. 4.5, Job 31.33, Prov. 17.9; cf. I Pet. 4.8. In Lev. 16.13 it is used of the cloud of incense covering the mercy-seat as the high priest enters the Holy of Holies, 'that he die not'; seemingly a smoke-screen is interposed between sinful man and the divine Presence. Perhaps the incense in Num. 16.46–8 is thought of as making a similar barrier: atonement is made (*kaphar*) and the plague stayed. In I Sam. 12.3 and Amos 5.12, *kopher* is used of a bribe to screen a murderer; in Exod. 30.12 it is used of the half-shekel paid by all Jews 'as an atonement for their souls', perhaps to avert a plague such as might be apprehended in view of II Sam. 24. Others have held that *kaphar* means in the first place 'to wipe away'; this is the proper meaning of *machah* ('blot out'), used of sins in Ps. 51.1,9, Isa. 43.25, 44.22, Jer. 18.23, where note the parallelism: 'forgive not (*kaphar*) their iniquity, neither blot out (*machah*) their sin from thy sight.' (See Driver, *HDB*, vol. IV, art. 'Propitiation', and Buchanan Gray, *Sacrifice in OT*, pp. 68ff.).

NT: What happens to these conceptions when they pass over into the NT? (*a*) It cannot be right to think of God's wrath being 'appeased' by the sacrifice of Christ, as some 'transactional' theories of the Atonement have done; for as in OT God is sometimes the subject of the verb *kaphar*, and as he is behind the redemptive action of the Servant in Isa. 53.10, so in NT it is God who in Christ reconciles the world to himself (II Cor. 5.19), who so loved the world that he gave his only-begotten Son (John 3.16), to be the propitiation for our sins (I John 4.10). Cf. Rom. 3.25: 'whom God set forth to be a propitiation' (*hilastērion*), a word which T. W. Manson would translate 'the mercy-seat': as the *kapporeth*, the covering of the Ark in the Tabernacle, was the place of propitiation as being the place where God's forgiving mercy was shown, so now the cross of Christ is the place where his saving mercy has been manifested (in *Journal of Theological Studies*, Jan., 1945, Vol. XLVI, No. 181–2, pp. 1–10). It cannot be right to make any opposition between the wrath of the Father and the love of the Son. By the sacrifice which God has provided (cf. Gen. 22.8 and John 1.29), reconciliation is made. 'He is our Peace', Eph. 2.14–16. (*b*) It can, again, be right and truthful to think of the Atonement as a 'covering' of sins, whereby they are treated as non-existent and the sinner as if he had not committed them. It is not, indeed, that our sins are condoned and conveniently forgotten; we must confess them, and find absolution and forgiveness (I John 1.8,9). But we have been baptized (washed, John 13.10), reconciled, united with Christ as members of his Body; thereby the root of sin, which is the pride and self-love of the ego, has been extracted, and the process of healing from the bottom initiated. Thus we share in the righteousness of Christ; and here we must banish any notion of a legal or forensic imputation of merit, for we are justified and made righteous, not in the sense of possessing a righteousness all our own (Phil. 3.9), but because we belong to Christ. And this is true, however much yet remains to be done in mortifying the old Adam and attaining to the fulfilment of our vocation (Phil. 3.12–14). Thus our sin is 'covered' in the sense of William Bright's eucharistic hymn, 'Look, Father, look on his anointed Face, And only look on us as found in him'. For if we run away from him, and separate ourselves from him, we become immediately subject to the 'wrath of God' (John 3.36). (*V.* also SACRIFICE.)

A. G. HEBERT

AUTHORITY

In the NT 'authority' is usually the trans. of the Gk. word *exousia*, which strictly means derived or conferred authority, and so is often said to be 'given', as, e.g. in Matt. 9.8, 10.1, 21.23, 28.18. For both Jewish and Christian thought the ultimate, though not necessarily the immediate, source of all authority whatever is God himself; cf., e.g. Dan. 2.37f., John 19.11, and esp. Rom. 13.1: 'There is no authority except from God.' It is therefore not strictly accurate to speak of God himself as having 'authority', and there are in fact only three instances of this in the NT, Luke 12.5, Acts 1.7, and Jude 25; yet this slight extension of the meaning of the word is so natural that it is surprising that there should be but three instances of it. Since authority is valueless without the POWER to make it effective, the distinction between authority and power is a fine one, and it is often ignored in the EVV. Thus in Matt. *exousia* is trans. 'power' four times in the AV (9.6,8, 10.1, 28.18); the English Revisers changed this to 'authority' in 10.1 and 28.18, the American in all four places. On the other hand, 'authority' is sometimes an over-translation, e.g. Heb. 13.10, 'an altar, whereof they have no right (*exousia*) to eat which serve the tabernacle', I Cor. 9.4,5,6, 12,18, where the RV correctly substitutes 'right' for AV 'power'. In John 1.12 translators and interpreters differ as to whether 'right' or 'power' is the better rendering of *exousia*.

By a natural extension of the meaning of the word *exousia* sometimes denotes the sphere in which authority is exercised, e.g. Luke 23.7, 'Herod's jurisdiction'. Much oftener in the NT it denotes the holders of authority. In Rom. 13.1ff. and Tit. 3.1 the authorities to whom Christians are to be obedient are clearly the civil magistrates of the Roman Empire. But elsewhere the word denotes spiritual or angelic beings to whom God delegated authority in his universe. Originally these were good: they were created in Christ, Col. 1.16, and so he is 'the head of every ruler and authority', Col. 2.10. (Here the concrete, personal, sense is easier than the abstract, 'of all rule and authority'.) But they have become evil, and now abuse their authority over men—collectively they are 'the dominion (*exousia*) of darkness' from which Christ has delivered Christians, Col. 1.13. Already Christ is set, at

God's right hand, 'far above every ruler and authority and power and lordship', Eph. 1.21; cf. I Pet. 3.22. In the end he will utterly destroy them all, and hand over the Kingdom to God the Father, I Cor. 15.24. Meanwhile, though they cannot separate us from the love of God which is in Christ Jesus our Lord, Rom. 8.39, they retain some of their power, and so Christians have to contend, 'not against flesh and blood, but against the rulers, against the authorities, against the world-potentates of this darkness, against the spirit-forces of evil in the heavenly sphere', Eph. 6.12.

(The use of the word *exousia* in I Cor. 11.10, where it evidently means the head-covering which Paul says women ought to wear in church, is still an unexplained puzzle.) (*V.* also MIGHT, MIRACLE.)

J. Y. CAMPBELL

AVENGE *v.* REWARD

AWE *v.* FEAR

* * *

BAAL, BAALIM *v.* GOD, GODS III

BAAL-BERITH *v.* GOD, GODS IV

BAALZEBUB *v.* ADVERSARY, GOD, GODS IV

BABEL *v.* CITY

BABYLON *v.* CITY

BABYLONIA *v.* ASSYRIA

BAN *v.* DEVOTE

BAPTIZE, BAPTISM

Both words go back to Gk. *bapto*=to dip (e.g. Homer, *Odyssey*, ix.392, of a brazier dipping hot steel in water to temper it). From this comes the intensive form, *baptizein*, to dip, plunge under water, sink or swamp (often used metaphorically, e.g. Josephus, *Jewish War*, 4.3.3., says of the refugees who fled to Jerusalem that they 'swamped' the city). The nouns *baptisma, baptismos*, do not occur in classical literature.

In the LXX *bapto* is used frequently for dip (e.g. Ps. 67.23, of dipping the foot in the blood of enemies). *Baptizein*, used rarely, is of more importance, esp. II Kings 5.14 of Naaman, who 'dipped himself (middle, *ebaptisato*) in Jordan seven times'. Cf. also Jdth. 12.7, 'She washed herself at the fountain of water in the camp'; Ecclus. 34.25, of being cleansed from, i.e. from the defilement of, a dead body. In II Kings 5.14 *baptizein* translates Heb. *tābhal*, which is often translated simply 'dip'. But *baptizein* has a more intransitive flavour than *bapto*: it almost means 'wash', in our sense of 'to wash oneself'. The nouns *baptisma, baptismos* do not occur in Gk. OT.

In the NT refs. are many:

I. JOHN THE BAPTIST

About half the total number of refs. to the various cognate words concern John the Baptist and his work. Most of these refs. are in the Gospels, and in their present form are later in date than, e.g. St. Paul's Epistles. But the belief that John the Baptist's movement ushered in Christ's Messianic work is embedded in all four Gospels, so it will be convenient to deal with John's b. at this point. The story of John the Baptist occurs in Mark and Q, and therefore formed part of the earliest Christian tradition. Josephus (non-Christian Jewish historian, *c.* AD 90) relates the story of John the Baptist (*Antiquities*, xviii.5.2). He says John the Baptist commanded the Jews to come to b., and to use the washing for the purification of the flesh, the candidates having already put away their sins.

In NT, John is called 'the Baptizer' (Mark 1.4, 6.14,24) and 'the Baptist' (Mark 6.25, 8.28, Matt. 3.1, 11.11,12, 14.2,8, 16.14, 17.13, Luke 7.20,33, 9.19). Crowds 'were baptized of him in the river Jordan, confessing their sins' (Mark 1.5). He preached 'the baptism of repentance' (Mark 1.4). 'The baptism of John' (Mark 11.30) was well known enough to be discussed between Jesus and the Pharisees. John's b. therefore is presented as a washing in Jordan, symbolic of, and accompanied by, repentance. John was the agent. It had a strong eschatological colouring. Those who came to it were said to be fleeing from the coming wrath (Luke 3.7). It was a prophetic, symbolic act, perhaps meant to appear similar to the b. necessary when a Gentile became a proselyte Jew. To be a real Jew, John's b. proclaimed, it was necessary to undergo cleansing, moral and ritual. (Contemporary evidence for the b. of proselytes in NT times is scanty, but it receives ample testimony in the *Mishna*, and is not likely to have been introduced into Judaism after the arrival of Christian b.) According to Acts, there were places (Alexandria and Ephesus) where John's b. was known and practised (without any Christian completion) as much as 30 years afterwards (Acts 18.25, 19.1–7). This suggests that a Messianic movement of cleansing and repentance was widely spread, that it was connected with b., which had been the principal work of its founder. It can hardly have failed to suggest the custom to Jesus and his followers, and to influence the meaning which they in turn attached to their b. The fact that Jesus himself submitted to John's b. shows that there was a link, if not a recognizable continuity, between his movement and John's.

II. ST. PAUL

The earliest strata of the NT writings (as writings) are the Epistles of St. Paul (say AD 48–62). He refers to baptism (or to closely associated conceptions) some 17 times. The following are some of the most important passages: Gal. 3.27: 'As many of you as were baptized into Christ did put on Christ'; I Cor. 1.13: 'Were ye baptized into the name of Paul?'; I Cor. 10.2: '(Our fathers) were all baptized unto Moses in the cloud and in the sea'; I Cor. 12.13: 'In one spirit were we all baptized into one body'; Rom. 6.4: 'buried with him through b. unto death' (cf. Col. 2.12); Eph. 4.5: 'One b.'; Eph. 5.26: 'having cleansed it (i.e. the Church) by the washing of water with the word'; I Cor. 6.11 (of the Corinthian Christians): 'Ye were washed, ye were sanctified, ye were justified, in the name of our Lord Jesus Christ, and in the Spirit of our God'.

What general meaning must be given to b. in the light of these quotations? St. Paul does not find it necessary to *define* b. He refers to it, assuming that his readers know what it means. This was natural, for they, like him, had been baptized. He does not refer specifically to *the water* of b. except in Eph. 5.26 and, by implication, in I Cor. 10.2, but in view of the general use of the word in OT and NT there can be no doubt that it was to b. in water that he referred. B. seems to have been universal in the Christian Church. It was b. 'into Christ', i.e. into union with him, into possession by him, into all the benefits, e.g. justification and sanctification, which flowed from being linked to him. He does not say that b. involves the gift of the Spirit, but he links the Spirit with the whole experience of conversion and b. (Gal. 3.1,2, I Cor. 6.11, 12.13). Union with Christ involved sharing in his death and resurrection, of which b. was an obvious sign and symbol. There is no need to go to the Mystery religions for an explanation of the meaning of the Pauline b. The Messianic age had dawned, and both Jew and Gentile could enter it by faith, the proof and expression of which was the acceptance of b. In this sense, b. was eschatological. To accept it meant to enter the new creation, which existed for all those who were 'in Christ'. At the same time, the convert became himself part of the new creation. There was a new creature in a new creation. B. initiated converts into an organism (I Cor. 12.13). Thoughts like this, and those connected with death and resurrection, suggest that b. moved in the same circle of ideas as the Eucharist. Both were sacraments of union with Christ, leading to union with and in Christ's body. One was the sacrament of initiation; the other of continuing fellowship.

III. THE ACTS OF THE APOSTLES

In the light of the known Pauline usage, we can examine the picture presented in the Acts. There are 27 refs. to b. in Acts (almost exactly 1 ref. per chapter). It is very clear that b. is the normal, indeed the invariable, gateway to membership in the Church. At Pentecost Peter calls on all to 'repent and be baptized', in order to receive the promised gift of the Spirit (2.38). 'They that received his word were baptized' (2.41). Men and women converts in Samaria were baptized (8.12). Other converts baptized include the Ethiopian Eunuch (8.36–8), Paul himself (9.18), Cornelius and those with him (10.47–8), Lydia at Philippi (16.15), the jailor and his household (16.35), many Corinthians (18.8), a group of 12 men at Ephesus (19.3–5).

A careful examination of these and other passages reveals a picture in no way incompatible with that derived from St. Paul's Epistles, though a few new points emerge. Union with Christ is not stressed as the supreme result of b., but b. is in, or into, 'the name of Jesus Christ', which means much the same thing. B. is closely connected with acceptance of the gospel message (Acts 2.41, 8.12,36, especially when followed by 8.37, a verse of ancient but unconvincing authority; 16.15). Like the Fourth Gospel, Acts speaks of 'believing' rather than of 'faith' in the abstract. The eschatological side is shown in the whole setting of Peter's speech at Pentecost (see esp. Acts 2.16–21) and in the description of Philip's preaching in Samaria ('they believed Philip preaching good tidings concerning the Kingdom of God and the name of Jesus Christ', Acts 8.12). B. meant, for Jews, qualifying to receive the benefits of the Messianic age now dawning; for Gentiles, it meant the same, but the meaning of Messiahship had to be explained first (see Acts 18.31). The connexion with forgiveness of sin is rather clearer than in St. Paul: see, e.g. Acts 2.38, 22.16. In the latter passage b. is explained as 'washing away sins'. This is not really different from what is implied in I Cor. 6.11, but the point is made here with greater clarity. Finally, the connexion between b. and the gift of the Spirit is raised more pointedly than elsewhere. In Acts 2 it is implied that b. itself opens the way for converts to receive the promised gift. In the story of Philip's work at Samaria b. is not enough to bring the gift. It is necessary for the Apostles to come and lay their hands on the baptized (*v.* LAYING ON OF HANDS). In the story of Cornelius, the gift of the Spirit precedes b.

itself. Thus there is no clear pattern, but it is plain that b. was closely connected with the gift of the Spirit. Alone or with 'confirmation', it brought the gift: the gift, if present, justified the rite of b., even in the case of a Roman officer. There are three references (Acts 1.5, 11.16, 19.4–6) to the contrast between John's b. and that which Christ performs—b. with the Holy Spirit, but there is no suggestion that b. with the Holy Spirit makes water-b. unnecessary or irrelevant.

The major part of the NT evidence has now been considered, but a number of special passages calls for brief mention.

IV. I PETER

The crux in I Pet. 3.21. 'Water: which also after a true likeness (or "by way of an antitype") doth now save you, even b., not the putting away of the filth of the flesh, but the interrogation of a good conscience toward God.' The Gk. of this passage presents many problems, but the main facts stand out. A passing reference to water suggests the thought of b. which is said to 'save' the readers—though only when it carries with it a moral and spiritual cleansing, a renewed fellowship with God, based on the supreme saving act of the resurrection of Christ.

V. LATER USAGE

(*a*) The command to b. in Matt. 28.19 is thought to show the influence of a developed doctrine of God verging on Trinitarianism. Early b. was in the name of Christ. The association of this Trinitarian conception with b. suggests that b. itself was felt to be an experience with a Trinitarian ref. It expressed and epitomized repentance towards God, faith towards our Lord Jesus Christ, and the renewing gift of the Holy Spirit. Mark 16.16 comes in the late appendix to Mark, but testifies to the belief that b. had always been part of the Christian programme.

(*b*) *The Fourth Gospel* has 13 refs. to b., but 10 of them relate to contrasts and comparisons between John's b. and a supposed contemporary b. by Jesus and/or his disciples. The sentence, 'I baptize with water', leads in St. John (1.26) not to the direct assertion, 'But he will baptize you with fire and Holy Spirit', but to the statement, 'There standeth one among you whom ye know not'. The picture of the unrecognized Messiah is built up, and only in 1.33 do we reach the point that he it is that baptizes with the Holy Ghost. There seems some doubt in the writer's mind as to whether Jesus did, or did not, personally baptize (3.22; cf. 4.1–2). Much of the material would be compatible with the view that the writer is telling the story with his eye on some who still clung to John's b. (this is quite possible if the Gospel emanates from Ephesus, the scene of the *enclave* which was clinging to John's b. of which we read in Acts 19.3–5).

More important is the passage in John 3.5, 'Except a man be born of water and the Spirit, he cannot enter the Kingdom of God'. It is impossible to state definitely whether the writer wishes to stress either of the two media, to the implied detriment (though not necessarily the exclusion) of the other, or whether he wishes to stress the necessity of both media, and their mutual relationship. A *prima facie* view suggests that 'water and the Spirit' is one complete phrase, which, taken as a whole, means b. as understood in the early Church. Here then, if that is the true view, b. is thought of primarily as the gateway to the new birth. This is not incompatible with St. Paul's words in Rom. 6.4 (see above), but the centre of gravity is now on rebirth to a spiritual life rather than on identification with Christ in his death and resurrection.

(*c*) *Titus 3.5.* 'According to his mercy he saved us, through the washing (=bath) of regeneration and renewing of the Holy Ghost, which he poured out upon us richly, through Jesus Christ our Saviour.' The word 'bath' (Gk. *loutron*) is used very little in NT and the Fathers (once in NT, once in Justin Martyr, once in Clement of Alexandria), perhaps because of the pagan associations of 'the baths' (unwelcome to Jews and Christians), perhaps because the idea of cleansing was not at any rate the only idea involved in the baptismal washing. Here we find b. connected with the new birth (cf. John 3.5) and with 'the renewing of the Holy Ghost' (cf. I Cor. 6.11, as well as John 3). A. Oepke (*TWNT*, article on Baptism) says, in ref. to this passage and that from John 3, 'Deutero-paulinism (Titus 3.5) and Johannine theology (John 3.5) approach more closely the Hellenistic thought of regeneration, whilst St. Paul remains essentially critical in his attitude to Hellenism, but the former do not leave the line of a theology based on soteriological history'.

VI. *BAPTISMA* AND *BAPTISMOS*

In most cases in the NT 'baptism' corresponds to Gk. *baptisma. Baptismos* occurs three times in NT (Mark 7.4: 'washings of cups and pots and brazen vessels'; Heb. 6.2: 'teaching of baptisms'; Heb. 9.10: 'meats and drinks and divers washings'). All these instances, with the probable exception of Heb. 6.2, refer to ceremonial washings—dippings of things, including perhaps dipping of hands—and the evidence clearly suggests that *baptisma* was the only fully accepted word for Christian b. In Heb. 6.2 *baptismos* may mean Christian b. when contrasted with its possible rival, John's b.

VII. METAPHORICAL USE

We have seen that Josephus could use *baptizein* metaphorically for 'swamp'. We find two examples of this use in NT (Mark 10.38f., Luke 12.50). Jesus uses the word in connexion with his coming suffering, possibly with an oblique ref. to passages like Ps. 42.7*b*, 'All thy waves and billows are gone over me'. The passages have some bearing on the doctrine of Christian b. Perhaps they may have strengthened the idea that b. was a real identification with the sufferings of Christ. If, as is commonly thought, I Pet. is a homily intended for newly-baptized converts, the stress on the sufferings of Christ and his followers in that Epistle would come in very appropriately, quite apart from the historical circumstances of an outbreak of persecution.

VIII. CONCLUSION

The total NT evidence suggests the following picture. Christian b. followed on John's b. incorporating its ideas of repentance and deliverance from wrath and adding those of union with Christ and admission to the Christian Church. It was universal as the means of entry to the Church in the Apostolic Age (and later). Households were baptized, but there is no indication whether these included infants. They probably were included, on the strength of the idea in I Cor. 7.14. B. was the means whereby the convert was united to Christ, with all the attendant benefits and responsibilities of such union, including esp. the reception of the gift of the Spirit. But this could be delayed until a stage later than b. itself, as we see from Acts 8.17 (*v.* LAYING ON OF HANDS). For the ideas underlying the practice of Christian b., e.g. re-birth (regeneration), etc., *v.* BIRTH. (See W. F. Flemington, *The NT Doctrine of Baptism*, London, 1948.)

R. R. WILLIAMS

BARBARIAN

From a Gk. word used by Homer to describe the language of the Carians; throughout Gk. literature it means one who does not speak Gk., and originally it was not used offensively. Paul includes Jews among barbarians; he used the common phrase to denote the whole world, 'Greeks and Barbarians' (Rom. 1.14). In Col. 3.11 'Barbarian and Scythian' is added to the pairs mentioned in the par. passage in Gal. 3.28 to emphasize the fact that neither those who lacked culture nor even the proverbially cruel, unjust, uncultured Scythians (cf. II Macc. 4.47, III Macc. 7.5) are shut out from the unity in Christ (Lightfoot, *Epistles of Paul, Colossians and Philemon*, p. 215). The word is used for those who speak an unintelligible language (Acts 28.2, I Cor. 14.11).

J. N. S.

BEAR *v.* BIRTH

BEAST *v.* ANTICHRIST

BEATITUDE *v.* BLESS

BEELZEBUB, BEELZEBUL *v.* ADVERSARY, GOD, GODS IV

BEGET *v.* BIRTH

BELIEVE *v.* FAITH

BELOVED *v.* LOVE

BETROTHAL *v.* MARRIAGE

BIRTH, BEGET, BEAR, REGENERATION, etc.

OT: These words usually represent the Heb. root *yalad* (in Qal both 'beget' and 'bear', in pass. forms 'be born'). Literal in vast majority of instances. Used metaphorically of origin of Jerusalem-Israel (Ezek. 16.3f.); of rebirth of Israel after Exile (Isa. 66.8f.; cf. metaphor of resurrection, Ezek. 37.1–14); of Zion's children (Isa. 49.21, 54.1ff.; cf. Gal. 4.26); of planning evil (Isa. 59.4; cf. II Tim. 2.23). An important ref. is Ps. 2.7 (also 110.3 in LXX text), with which cf. II Sam. 7.14, Ps. 89.26f.; and *v.* MESSIAH. In Prov. 8.25, LXX makes it clear that it is God who begets Wisdom, where Heb. less definite.

NT: Often literally. For b. of Jesus *v.* VIRGIN BIRTH. Our concern here is NT use of metaphor of b. in connexion with the Christian life. It will make for clarity, if we distinguish (*a*) its use to denote an *event*, the actual entry on the Christian life, and (*b*) its use to denote the ensuing *state*, the relationship (begotten of God, i.e. child of God).

(*a*) The NT indicates the absolute contrast between two kinds of life and the momentousness of the passing from the one to the other by metaphors of creation (II Cor. 5.17, Gal. 6.15, Eph. 4.24, and perhaps also John 20.22 in the light of Gen. 2.7), resurrection (Eph. 2.1,5f., Col. 2.12f.) and birth (John 1.13, 3.1–8, I Pet. 1.3,23, 2.2, Jas. 1.18, Tit. 3.5, and also numerous refs. in I John, which concern us more under (b). The need for radical renewal, already recognized in OT (e.g. Jer. 31.31–4, Ezek. 11.19, 36.26f., Ps. 51.10) is most clearly expressed in John 3.3,5. The new life is spiritual, and can be originated only by God. (In John 3.3,7—RV margin 'from above' is correct trans.) The change can be effected only by God, and is sheer miracle. Just as a man's natural b. cannot be of his own doing, so his spiritual b. is something he neither effects nor co-operates in, but simply receives. (All three metaphors—creation, resurrection, birth—alike stress this.)

This rebirth is associated with baptism: Tit. 3.5, John 3.5 (or does this refer to John's baptism, the meaning being that Nicodemus has to confess to being a sinner?), and Rom. 6.3f., though here the b. metaphor is not used. But baptism is rather the outward sign and seal of the inward change than itself the effective cause of the change, as is shewn by Acts 10.44–8, by the part of the Word of God in the new b. (I Pet. 1.23–5, Jas. 1.18), and by the emphasis on faith in connexion with baptism (e.g. Mark 16.16, Col. 2.12). The entry on the new life is intimately associated with the Holy Spirit in John 3 (cf. I Cor. 12.3). The new b. is a miracle and occurs when the Holy Spirit enables a man to believe in Jesus Christ.

What is the source of the b. metaphor? It has been suggested that this whole set of ideas has been taken over from the pagan mystery religions; but there are several facts that make this unlikely (though C. H. Dodd, *Johannine Epistles*, p. 68, still maintains it). First, there are big differences between the ideas of renewal in the Mystery religions and in the NT, which become plainer on closer examination. The NT has no idea of a rebirth worked by a magical cult-act, but the rebirth is a matter of faith in Christ. As a matter of fact, there is no certain ref. in pre-Christian Mystery religion to a being begotten of God, only to some ritual adoption (cf. Büchsel, *TWNT*, I, p. 668). It is also to be remembered that those passages in Mystery religion literature, which are the nearest parallels are actually later than NT. So Hermetica 13 (cf. John 3) is dated by W. Scott 3rd cent. AD, and was most likely influenced by Christian ideas. A much more probable source of the metaphor is to be found in Judaism. The metaphor was current later—and probably also in NT times—for the conversion of a Gentile, e.g. 'A proselyte who has newly come over is like a new-born child' (*Jebamoth* 22*a*, Babylonian Talmud). The Rabbis also regarded the winning of a proselyte as a fulfilment of the OT command to be fruitful (Gen. 1.28, 9.7), i.e. as an act of begetting. It is worth mentioning that in Judaism the metaphor of creation is also used in connexion with the conversion of Gentiles. Büchsel suggests that the words *palingenesia* (regeneration) and *anagennao* (beget again, I Pet.) had become common Gk. words as a result of Stoicism. Some have suggested that the idea of rebirth is implicit in Jesus' saying (Matt. 18.3, Mark 10.15, Luke 18.17), and that this lies behind John 3.3.

It is sometimes said that the b. metaphor is not found in Paul (Tit. 3.5 not generally being regarded as Pauline), and that he uses creation and resurrection instead. But this is hardly true in view of I Cor. 4.15, Gal. 4.19, Philem. 10, where the idea is present. (Cf. Rabbinic use mentioned above. It is more likely that Paul has the same general idea in mind than that this is merely a stronger form of the common Jewish use of father-son relation to denote teacher-disciple relation as in II Kings 2.12, Matt. 23.8–10.) There is a parallelism between the Pauline idea of adoption and the Johannine of being born from above, both as far as the actual event and the succeeding state are concerned. Paul thinks rather in terms of Roman law and of legal status, John in terms of the origin of the new life. Cf. being born of the Spirit (John) with the Spirit of adoption crying in us, 'Abba, Father' (Paul). For both, the renewal means the beginning of faith in Jesus Christ and is inseparably bound up with him. For both it is an act of the sovereign grace of God.

(*b*) We must now glance briefly at the use of this metaphor, where the stress is not so much on the actual event of spiritual b. as on the ensuing state or relationship to God. Here our main concern is I John, but we must try to see how far the ideas there expressed are paralleled elsewhere in NT. The refs. in I John are 2.29, 3.9, 4.7, 5.1,4,18. Here we have repeatedly the perfect tense; the stress is not so much on the event now in the past as on the relationship implied by it. In fact, the expression 'whosoever is begotten of God' (in Gk. perfect tense) is the equivalent of the other expression 'child of God' (3.1,2,10, John 1.12f.). Cf. opposite idea of children of the devil (3.10).

Great stress is laid on the ethical implications of this b. from God, just as it is in the other NT writings. But the uncompromising way that 3.9 (cf. 3.6) and 5.18 are put raises a problem. What does 'Whosoever is begotten of God doeth no sin . . . cannot sin . . .' mean? Superficially at any rate it seems to contradict 1.8–10, 2.1. C. H. Dodd mentions (*op. cit.*, pp. 78ff.), but is not content with, the grammatical explanation that in 2.1 the verbs are aorist and indicate single or occasional acts of sin, while in 3.4–10 and 5.18 the relevant verbs are in the present and indicate habitual action. Instead, he suggests that the writer shared the idea, which he thinks was popular among Christians of the time (taken from Jewish eschatology), that in the last days the people of God would be free from sin; and that anyway he writes with different purposes in view —in 1.8–10 against the self-complacent, in 3.9 and 5.18 against those who think ethics unimportant so long as one is 'enlightened'. But, before we accept this as the final explanation, we should ask whether the following Pauline ideas can give any light on the matter: the *old* and the *new man* (Rom. 6.6, Eph. 4.22,24, Col. 3.9f.); the *outward* and the *inward man*

(Rom. 7.22, II Cor. 4.16, Eph. 3.16); our real life hid with Christ in God and 'Christ *who is* our life' (Col. 3.3f.); the strange distinction between 'I' in Rom. 7.17 and 'me'='my flesh' in vs. 18; and the whole teaching on justification. It is noticeable that Paul speaks of 'putting on' Christ (Gal. 3.27, Rom. 13.14), the new man (Eph. 4.24) and the breastplate of righteousness, i.e. justification (Eph. 6.14). Paul envisages a conflict that is not yet resolved. May it not be that John also envisages a conflict, and that 'he that has been begotten from God' and that 'cannot sin' is meant to be a description not of the entire psychological and moral state of the empirical Christian, but of that 'new man' that is in conflict with the old so long as the Christian is in this world?

See further: W. F. Howard, *Christianity according to St. John*, pp. 197–201; F. Büchsel, K. H. Rengstorf, in *TWNT*, I, pp. 663–74, 685–8; J. Orr, in *HDB*, pp. 787–9; and on I John 3.9, 5.18, K. Barth, *Kirchliche Dogmatik*, 1/2, pp. 439–41; W. Grundmann in *TWNT*, I, pp. 310f. See also commentaries on John and I John.

C. E. B. CRANFIELD

BIRTH (OF JESUS) *v.* VIRGIN (BIRTH)

BIRTHRIGHT *v.* FIRSTBORN

BISHOP *v.* MINISTER

BLAMELESS *v.* INNOCENT

BLASPHEME, BLASPHEMY

These words occur a dozen times or so in OT. Properly, the verb 'to blaspheme' has for its object the Sacred Name, and is thus opposed to confessing the Name, hallowing it, honouring it. In Lev. 24.10–23 a half-caste Israelite blasphemes the Name and curses, and is put to death. (In I Kings 21.10,13, where, according to AV, Naboth is accused of 'blaspheming God and the king', the word should be rendered 'curse', as in RV.) In II Kings 19.6,22=Isa. 37.6,23, the envoy of the king of Assyria 'blasphemes the living God'; cf. Ps. 44.16, Isa. 52.5 and Ps. 74.10,18, blasphemy of Gentiles; and Ezek. 20.27, Isa. 65.7, of idolatrous Israelites.

In the NT the Greek word *blasphemia* is used of reviling, or abusive language towards men, in Mark 7.22, I Cor. 4.12, 10.30, Eph. 4.31, Col. 3.8, I Tim. 6.4; or of slanderous reports about St. Paul, Rom. 3.8. But its proper meaning is blasphemy against the holy Name of God or of Jesus, as when men who revile the Christians 'blaspheme the holy Name which has been invoked upon them' in their baptism (James 2.7).

Three passages call for special explanation:

(*a*) *The Blasphemy against the Holy Ghost*, Mark 3.29, Matt. 12.32. The scribes who have accused Jesus of casting out devils by Beelzebul are warned by him that whereas there is forgiveness for all sins and blasphemies, 'he who blasphemes against the Holy Ghost hath never forgiveness, but is guilty of [under the power of] eternal sin' (Mark 3.28–9). There is forgiveness for all sins where there is repentance. But just as the time will come when God's faithful servants, having endured all their temptations and won their victory, will be beyond the reach of temptation, having entered into the Sabbath-rest which remaineth for the people of God (Heb. 4.9); so those who persistently refuse to listen to God's voice, and harden their hearts, will lose the power to listen, having become insensitive. The one will attain to 'eternal life'; the other to the death of the soul, which is the 'eternal sin', spoken of here. People who are distressed in their souls for fear that they have committed the sin against the Holy Ghost should in most cases be told that their distress is proof that they have not committed that sin.

(*b*) *Speaking a Word against the Son of Man*, Matt. 12.32; cf. Luke 12.10 where the word 'blasphemy' is not used, but in the context of the blasphemy against the Spirit, it is said that a word spoken against the Son can be forgiven. This is difficult, for elsewhere he says, 'he that rejecteth me rejecteth him that sent me', Luke 10.16; and cf. Mark 3.30, where Mark explains the occasion of the warning about the blasphemy of the Spirit: 'because they said, He hath an unclean spirit'. Hence some have held (e.g. Driver in *HDB*, IV, p. 588) that 'Son of Man' in Matt. 12.32 is a mis-reading of 'sons of men' in Mark 3.28; but this does not explain Luke 12.10. We must therefore interpret our Lord as saying: Though he who rejects me rejects him that sent me, yet not all who seem to reject have really rejected. They may have been misinformed; or some disciple of mine may have given a wrong impression.

(*c*) *The Cry of 'Blasphemy' against Jesus at His Trial*. See Mark 14.61–6. The high priest has asked him, 'Art thou the Messiah the Son of God [the Blessed]?' He replies 'I am: and ye shall see the Son of Man sitting on the right hand of God [power] and coming with the clouds of heaven', thus quoting Ps. 110 and Dan. 7. They cry 'Blasphemy!'—but why? It is not the assertion that he is Messiah, for that would be to make any claim to Messiahship blasphemous—even that of God's chosen, when he came. It can hardly be the attribution to himself of the Son of man prophecy. But it could be the coupling of that with the assertion that he will be seen seated at God's right hand. We gather from Mark 12.35–7 that the scribes did not know how to interpret Ps. 110.1. And the claim that he is Messiah *in this sense* could and would be taken as blasphemous; as indeed the Jews say according to John 10.33, 'For a good work we stone thee not, but for blasphemy, and because that thou, being a man, makest thyself God'. And this has been the Jewish accusation ever since, that we have deified a man; for to them 'Messiah' means a human prince and deliverer. Compare the martyrdom of St. Stephen, Acts 7.55–8, where the word 'blasphemy' does not happen to be used; but he sees the Son of man at the right hand of God, and he suffers the penalty of blasphemy, death by stoning. (*V.* also CURSE, NAME.) A. G. HEBERT

BLESS, BLESSED, BLESSING

In the Bible blessing means primarily the active outgoing of the divine goodwill or grace which results in prosperity and happiness amongst men. In the OT this prosperity or blessedness is usually measured in material things—long life, increase of family, crops and herds, peace, wealth (Gen. 1.22, Deut. 33.11, II Sam. 6.11, etc.); but in the Wisdom writers wisdom itself is the chief result of the divine blessing; righteousness and peace are held to be the marks of the coming Messianic blessedness on the part of the later apocalyptic writers. Jesus gives a much more profound and spiritual connotation to the idea of blessedness in the Beatitudes (Matt. 5.2–12) and elsewhere. Even when the blessing is pronounced by men it is to be understood that it is a divine blessing that is imparted, because such men stand near to God, as in the case of the priestly orders (Lev. 9.22, Aaron) or in that of saintly individuals (Gen. 48.14ff., Jacob). Two outstanding instances of this latter type are to be seen in Gen. 27 (Isaac's blessing of Jacob) and Num. 23 (Balaam's blessing of Israel); here the word spoken is prophetic in character and has a self-fulfilling efficacy (*v.* SPEAK) and cannot be recalled. The action symbolic of blessing was often that of LAYING ON OF HANDS (*q.v.*), an action used by Jesus himself (Matt. 19.15); sometimes it was that of uplifting the hands (Lev. 9.22). Finally the circle of blessing is completed when man blesses God; God's blessing does not return to him void; it is reciprocated by the Church's response: 'Blessed be the God and Father of our Lord Jesus Christ' (II Cor. 1.3; cf. Rev. 7.12, etc.)—a response which christianizes ancient Jewish usage found frequently in the Psalms and elsewhere (cf. esp. also 'the Benedictus', Luke 1.68). For the 'Blessing' spoken before a meal in a Jewish household and its connexion with the Eucharist, *v.* THANK OT(*b*) and NT(*c*). *V.* also CURSE. A. R.

BLOOD

The Heb. word for blood as the name for the fluid which circulates in the human body had a further significance beyond the literal meaning which is usually apparent from the context. The brethren of Joseph after selling him to the merchant-men going to Egypt, took his coat and dipped it in the blood of an animal and presented it thus stained to their father. It had the desired effect (Gen. 37.31,33) since Jacob at once concluded that his favourite son had been killed by a wild beast. Blood could thus be used as a symbol for death (Ps. 30.9) and particularly violent death, since the loss of a considerable amount of blood through injury or wound brought to an end life in its fullness. In three passages (Gen. 9.4, Lev. 17.11, Deut. 12.23) it is emphatically asserted that 'the blood is the life', but an examination of the contexts of the sayings shows that blood means not life which can be released from the flesh for further activity by letting the blood flow, but the very life of the body which is ended when the blood is shed. It is hardly likely that blood could signify life released (Westcott, *Epistles of St. John*, additional note on I John 1.7; Vincent Taylor, *The Atonement in NT Teaching* in several places), for early Hebrew thought had no adequate conception of a spiritual survival after death. The concrete reality of human flesh-and-blood existence was the foundation (Matt. 16.17, I Cor. 15.50, Gal. 1.16, Eph. 6.12, Heb. 2.14) of Hebrew thinking about human personality; so that blood was frequently used as a word-symbol for death as the end of life. Thus a murderer was said to have blood upon his hands or head (II Sam. 1.16, I Kings 2.37, Josh. 2.19, Prov. 28.17, Jer. 26.15), where the phrase was equivalent to bearing the guilt of another man's death. To conceal a man's blood (Gen. 37.26) was to conceal his death, to murder a man was to sin against innocent blood (I Sam. 19.5, Matt. 27.4; cf. I Kings 2.5), to drink a man's blood was to gain some advantage through taking his life (I Chron. 11.17–19, John 6.53–6; cf. 'eating flesh' in Ps. 27.2 and John 6.53,56).

In the NT the word carries the same meaning of bodily existence terminated by death, frequently violent death. To resist unto blood (Heb. 12.4) means to die rather than to yield. Judas confessed that he had betrayed innocent blood (Matt. 27.4); Pilate repudiated responsibility for the death of Jesus by declaring that he was innocent of his blood, while the mob accepted the responsibility with the shout, 'his blood be on us and on our children' (Matt. 27.24–5; cf. Acts 5.28, Rev. 6.9–10, 17.6, 18.24). Blood which was thus shed violently, i.e. the death of the innocent, might be required of the murderers either by human administrators of justice or by God, so that it could be described as coming upon them in judgment (Matt. 23.29–30,34–6).

The Bible presents physical life as the creation of God; who alone has the source of life, and man has no independent right to shed blood and take life. If he does so, he will be accountable to God for what he has done and his own life will be forfeit (Gen. 9.5–6; cf. Exod. 20.13). Thus the blood of a man after his death may have profound effects, not through the persistent activity of a life released, but because of the significance of the life taken (Gen. 4.10, Job 16.18, Ezek. 24.7–8, Heb. 12.24; cf. Denney, *The Death of Christ*). The idea of blood speaking is a particularly vivid way of describing the meaning of a violent death and is typical of the realistic imagery of Heb. speech. Animal life as well as human life was considered to belong to God and could only be taken by divine permission. The strict prohibition of the drinking of blood (Gen. 9.4–5, Lev. 17.3–7,10–14, Deut. 12.15–16,20–8, I Sam. 14.32–5) which was to be poured out before God on the altar or on the ground was the appointed way of recognizing that the mystery of the source of life was with God, and man might not presume to appropriate it. The subsequent meal was not a feeding upon the life of the animal but upon its flesh, and the eating was made possible only at the cost of the animal's death. The shed blood of animals which men were forbidden to drink was given by divine appointment to make atonement (*q.v.*) for sin (*q.v.*) and to effect cleansing (*q.v.*) (Lev. 17.11–12). The description of the first Passover ritual (Exod. 12.1–20, P) shows that the blood was the visible sign of life taken, and the participants in the feast within the house enjoyed the benefits (being sheltered from the visitation of death) of the sacrificial death of the victim.

These categories of thought—blood as the token of life violently ended: the greatest offering being the giving of life or blood (John 15.13), the greatest crime to take blood or life, the greatest penalty to have one's life or blood taken and blood or life being the only adequate atonement for blood or life which man cannot give as his own life is already forfeit (Ps. 49.7–8) and he has nothing which is not God's (Ps. 50.9–10) to give—supplied by the language and cultus of the OT, are used to set forth in the NT the significance of the death of Christ. In him all these meanings are summed up and fulfilled. The phrase 'the blood of Christ' is used much more frequently in the NT than either the death of Christ or the Cross of Christ (cf. V. Taylor, *The Atonement in NT Teaching*, 2nd ed., p. 177), especially in Pauline Epp., Heb. and I John. It is a pictorial way of referring to the violent death upon a cross of shame voluntarily endured for men by Christ (Rom. 3.25, 5.9). The shedding of his blood upon the Cross (John 19.34) brought to an end his earthly life so that 'the blood of Christ' indicates the significance which that death bore and still bears for men (Rom. 5.9). It has a decisive once-for-all quality about it so that those who are said to be sprinkled by his blood (Heb. 10.19–23, 12.24, I Pet. 1.2, I John 1.7; cf. Heb. 9.14, 13.20—imagery drawn from the sealing of a covenant, *q.v.*), or who drink it, are receiving the benefits of his death and find shelter from threatening dangers (John 6.53–6, note the parallel with eating the flesh of the Son of Man in the same chapter). The life of the sinner was forfeit and lay under sentence of death until Christ by the shedding of his blood in the suffering of death gave release and cleansing to the sinner (Eph. 1.7, I Pet. 1.18–19, Rev. 1.5, 5.9). It is the death of Christ and not his life released which has effected a universal reconciliation through the act of suffering accomplished in history (Col. 1.20). The blood of his cross can only mean the pouring out in death of his earthly human life, a deed which availed and still avails to put men right with God. (*V.* also SACRIFICE.)

F. J. TAYLOR

BOAST *v.* PRIDE

BODY

(1) In the first place the word signifies the natural body of man (Prov. 5.11, Dan. 4.33, I Cor. 15.44) constituted by the creative act of God (Gen. 1 and 2), adapted to the conditions of earthly life (I Cor. 12.12, 15.38), and therefore as bearing the sign-manual of divine handiwork, not to be despised as in some way inferior to the soul or a hindrance to the higher life of man. On the contrary, for Heb. thought (unlike Gk.—Gnosticism was a Gk. not a Heb. heresy), the body was to be reverenced (I Cor. 6.15–19; cf. John 2.21). For this reason it was possible to use the word body with the meaning of self, person, personality or whole man; and indeed neither Heb. nor Gk. had words to express these concepts. 'The body is a perfectly valid manifestation of the soul and therefore body and man may be interchangeable terms' (L. S. Thornton, *Common Life in the Body of Christ*, p. 298). Thus in Rom. 12.1 'present your bodies' means present yourselves in the fullness of human life and activity. In I Cor. 6.15–18 the argument is based upon the significance of the body not as a thing apart from the real self, but essentially one with it. Sexual activity involves the whole man, and sexual union is a union not merely of two physical organisms but of two persons. It is on the basis of this profound

understanding of human personality and sex that the apostle condemns sexual irregularities for the damage they cause to the integrity of the persons involved in them.

(2) The NT also speaks of a spiritual body (cf. IMMORTAL, HELL) which men will receive at the resurrection (I Cor. 15.44; cf. II Cor. 5.1–6: 'a house not made with hands, eternal in the heavens') in contrast to the body of flesh and blood which cannot inherit the Kingdom of God (I Cor. 15.50). What Paul means is not that there is to be a restoration of the fleshy particles of the deceased, but that each individual will have bestowed upon him, as God sees fit (I Cor. 15.44), a spiritual body—that is, a body of another order than flesh and blood. The Gk. view of immortality as absorption into the Infinite is repudiated and the Christian doctrine of resurrection (*q.v.*) asserted, which, taking seriously the body, postulates an organ of personality, expressing and defining it and adapted to the conditions of life in the eternal order, even as the body of flesh and blood serves the same ends in the present order. The relation between the mortal body and the risen body can be expressed as 'identity of essence, distinction of form' (Thornton, *op. cit.*, p. 299), or more shortly, identity with a distinction. There is to be understood in this teaching some continuity with the earthly body as well as the idea of a new spiritual organism.

(3) In the third place the word is used to describe the whole community of Christians as the body of Christ (I Cor. 12.12ff., Rom. 12.5ff.). There can only be one body of Christ, as Christ is one and not divided (I Cor. 1.13); and it is into that one body (I Cor. 12.13, Col. 1.24) that Christians are baptized and in that body they are set by God in their appropriate places, even as limbs are by the creative act of God set in the physical body to fulfil the several functions required to enable the whole life of the body to be articulated according to the divine intention. Bishop Rawlinson (*Mysterium Christi*, ed. Bell and Deissmann, p. 225) and Dr. Thornton (*op. cit.*, p. 330), noting the emphasis on unity in the chief contexts in which the concept 'body of Christ' is used, have suggested that the source of the idea is to be traced to participation in the one eucharistic loaf, the symbol of the broken body of Christ (I Cor. 10.16–17). Others, e.g. W. L. Knox (*St. Paul and the Church of the Gentiles*, p. 160ff.; also in *JTS*, xxxix, 1938) and T. W. Manson (*JTS*, xxxvii, 1936), think that the expression is derived from Stoic thought, in which the whole world is sometimes depicted as a great body with the supreme earthly ruler as its head. Whatever the origin of the concept, Paul uses it in Rom. 12.5ff. and I Cor. 12.12ff. to express the close identification of Christ with his people (cf. Acts 9.4–5, where persecution of Christians is represented as persecution of Jesus) and the spiritual solidarity of the members of the body without distinction of race, sex, learning or social status. The people of God cannot therefore be other than one as the body of Christ and this essential unity of all Christians leads the apostle on to a discussion of the mutual helpfulness of each limb in the body (I Cor. 12.14–25, Rom. 12.6–8). Every member has his own appointed place and an indispensable function, so that all depend on each and each depends on all. The full life of the body is impossible (Eph. 1.23, Col. 1.19, 2.9) unless each limb makes its own distinctive contribution to the whole body, without presuming to attempt a function which is not its own. In the later Epistles, Eph. and Col., the word body has become a designation not merely for the local church but for the universal Church. Thus, in Col. 1.22,24 Christ died in the body of his flesh but has gained a new body in the Spirit—the men and women who have been raised with him: in Eph. 1.22–3 the Church is the body of Christ in the sense that it is to present Christ to the world in all his fullness (*q.v.*). The life of this body is developed with ever greater significance as time goes on, so that it can be described as the fullness of Christ in the world, even as Christ manifested to the world the fullness of God (Col. 1.19, 2.9, Eph. 1.23). Only as the body comes to full growth and perfect stature (Eph. 4.16) can it be the instrument for the accomplishment of the divine purposes and so complete the work of Christ which the NT describes paradoxically as finished and yet incomplete. In the earlier Epistles, and in Rom. and I Cor., Christ is conceived as the whole body of which Christians are members in particular; in Eph. and Col. the Church is the body and Christ is the head (Eph. 1.22, 5.23ff., Col. 2.19), thus suggesting the absolute dependence of the Church upon Christ for its very existence, its growth and strength. The fullness which is in the head flows into the body and maintains the order of the body. But the figure not only signifies the dependence of the Church on Christ for life and strength, but asserts his sovereignty over it, since the directing force is in the head, and the body must be guided and controlled by its head (Col. 2.10). The way had been prepared for such a usage by the Heb. idiom of using the head (like the body) as representative of the whole personality: 'Your blood be upon your own heads' (Josh. 2.19, I Sam. 1.16, Acts 18.6); cf. the proverb that kindness to an enemy heaps coals of fire on his head (Prov. 25.22, Rom. 12.20). When the Apostle speaks of the headship of Christ he is

using Heb. psychology and proclaiming the unity of purpose which must be a feature of the life of the Church. As a centre of life the head dominates the body, the separate organs of which in subordination to the head contribute to the fullness of the whole personality 'according to the working in due measure of each several part' (Eph. 4.16). Christ as head is described 'as the saviour of the body' (Eph. 5.23), as it is the head on which the safety of the whole body depends because of the sense organs which are located in it, yet the body is necessary (Eph. 1.22) to the completion of the life of the head.

(4) The concrete realism of Heb. thought is manifested in the accounts of the Last Supper (Mark 14.22, Matt. 26.26, Luke 22.19, I Cor. 11.24), where the broken bread is identified with the body (the earthly body about to be broken) of the Lord (cf. prophetic symbolism). An unworthy participant in the supper is said by the Apostle to be guilty of the body of the Lord, to carry a serious measure of responsibility for the rejection of Christ at the hands of wicked men. (*V.* also CHURCH, THANK.)

F. J. TAYLOR

BOND, BONDAGE

The institution of slavery was a familiar feature of life in the ancient world, and the Book of the Covenant (Exod. 21) laid down directions for the treatment of Hebrew slaves (cf. Gen. 16.1–2, 30.3–4). In the Roman world into which the Gospel spread in the first century, slavery was accounted an essential foundation both of domestic and of State economy. St. Paul was at pains to emphasize that such secular divisions of humanity into bond and free had no significance in the Church of God, for in Christ all were at one with one another, whatever the economic or social status of the members (Gal. 3.28, Col. 3.11), and no one was debarred from receiving the highest spiritual gifts by reason of his status as one of the despised class of slaves (I Cor. 12.13). In this assertion of the essential spiritual equality of the slave with the free man and his sharing in the redeemed humanity of the new creation was contained the germ of the much later Christian witness against slavery and the slave trade. The apostolic writers in recognizing the fact of spiritual freedom for all believers (Philem. 16–18) could yet urge Christian slaves to give loyal and ungrudging service to their masters (Eph. 6.5–9, Col. 3.17,22–5, Tit. 2.9).

In a figurative sense the word bond is used in several passages with the meaning of ligament or uniting force. In Eph. 4.3 peace is the bond which holds together Christians in unity. In Col. 2.19 there is reference to the bands which hold together the body of Christ, and in Col. 3.14 love is defined as that force which unites perfectly all Christian graces. The fetters which sin binds upon a man, making him the prisoner of evil, are mentioned in Acts 8.23, where the sorcerer Simon Magus is judged to be in the bond of iniquity—that is, held in the grip of sin.

St. Paul in expounding the superiority of the Gospel of Christ over the Law makes use (in Rabbinic fashion) of an allegory based upon the concept of slavery and freedom. The story of Hagar and Sarah and the status of their sons is allegorized to represent the inferiority of the Law to the Gospel. The Law in requiring painful obedience reminds the Apostle of the servitude of slaves, while the Gospel bestows upon men the freedom of Christ, so that they are like sons in a father's household. For those who have received the word of the Gospel, the yoke of bondage has been broken (Gal. 5.1). In another passage a similar idea is expounded from the marriage tie. The bond which holds a wife to her husband is of force until his death, but after that she is free once more to marry, if she so wishes. So Christians have in Christ died to the Law, who met its requirements fully, and are now free from the necessity of obedience to it as a principle of life (Rom. 7.1–6,25). In Rom. 6.15–23 man is pictured as the bondslave of sin (cf. Heb. 2.15, fear of death) and as having surrendered himself to do wrong; he is now under obligation to engage in sinful activity, so that his whole self (cf. body and members) has become an agent of wrongdoing. But those who have been accepted of God have had the old slavery broken and have become 'slaves' to righteousness and in bondage ('glad and free', Gal. 5.1; cf. John 8.31–2, Rom. 8.2, II Cor. 3.17, Jas. 1.25) to the will of God 'whom to serve is perfect freedom'.

The paradox of Christian obedience (cf. DEBT, DEBTOR) as the meaning of freedom is well expressed in Paul's frequent description of himself (Rom. 1.1, Phil. 1.1) as the slave of Jesus Christ, branded (Gal. 6.17) with the marks of his master's ownership. This language is a continuation of the OT tradition of speaking of oneself as 'Thy slave' or 'Thine handmaid' in addressing an equal or a superior and (most commonly) by worshippers in their approach to God. In the prophetic writings God is represented as addressing his people as 'my servant (slave) Jacob' (Isa. 45.4, Jer. 30.10, 46.27, Ezek. 28.25, 37.25). The final inadequacy of the concept slave to express the truth about Christian obedience-in-service is presented in the last discourse of the Lord in the Fourth Gospel (John 15.11ff.), where the title slave is exchanged for friend (cf. the title of Abraham, Isa. 41.8, II Chron. 20.7, Jas. 2.23), since the friend, unlike the slave, is made privy to the thoughts and intentions of the Lord and given a share in the realization of his purposes. (*V.* also FREE, SERVANT.)

F. J. TAYLOR

BOOTH *v.* SACRIFICE IV(*d*)

BOW, RAINBOW

In the OT the metaphor of Jehovah's war-bow is used to denote his avenging power (e.g. Ps. 7.12); perhaps in the Noah-myth, when he sets his bow in the cloud, the meaning is that God has laid aside his vengeance and will show mercy (Gen. 9.12–17). In the myth the rainbow (in Heb. the same word as war-bow) becomes the mercy-sign of God's everlasting covenant with Noah, i.e. with all mankind (*v.* NOAH). The rainbow, which against the darkest cloud betokens the shining of the beneficent sun, is a fitting symbol of God's mercy; and the Noah-myth gives biblical sanction for holding that man's 'natural piety' in the presence of this beautiful phenomenon of nature is not misconceived (cf. Wordsworth's 'My heart leaps up', or O. Wendell Holmes's 'Lord of all being', *Songs of Praise*, 564). In Ezekiel's vision of the Almighty on his throne, girt about with fire (of judgment), a rainbow surrounds the scene (Ezek. 1.28); this is probably intended as a token of mercy, and it is identified with the glory of the Lord. Rev. 4.3 and 10.1 speak of a rainbow (Gk. *iris*) after the manner of Ezek.; in Rev. 6.2 a different Gk. word (*toxon*, a war-bow) is used.

A. R.

BREAD

Heb. *lechem* occurs 298 times in OT; Gk. *artos* 98 times in NT. The false spirituality that tries to ignore bread, economics, etc., as mundane, or to limit God's concern to things spiritual, meets no encouragement in Bible. The physical need for b., serious in itself, points to a still more serious need.

OT: *Lechem* can mean either b. specifically or food in general. In great majority of cases both AV and RV render 'bread', but sometimes other words, especially 'food', 'meat' (where AV has meat, RV often has bread). Ps. 44.11 and Lev. 3.11 contain examples of *lechem* referring to flesh-food.

Adam, driven out from Eden, is told that in future he is to get b. by hard toil, Gen. 3.19. B. and wine often together as main food and drink, e.g. Gen. 14.18, Judg. 19.19. Similarly b. and water, e.g. Gen. 21.14, Exod. 23.25, 34.28. B. and raiment—necessities of life, Gen. 28.20, Deut. 10.18 (EVV food). Ravens bring Elijah b. and flesh, I Kings 17.6. Men go without b. when fasting, Exod. 34.28, II Sam. 12.17; or in sorrow, I Kings 21.4f., Ezra 10.6. To eat b. with someone established a mutual obligation, Ps. 41.9. The Egyptians regarded it as an abomination to eat b. with a Hebrew, Gen. 43.32 (cf. Gal. 2.12, etc.). B. is a gift of God, e.g. Ruth 1.6, Ps. 104.15. Used of manna, Exod. 16.4; cf. Neh. 9.15, Ps. 105.40. The lesson drawn in Deut. 8.3 from the gift of manna is that God is not limited to any particular means for sustaining human life; but when this is quoted in the NT it is given a different meaning. We may also notice the use of b. in such phrases as *b. of affliction* (I Kings 22.27); *b. of toil* (Ps. 127.2); *b. of tears* (Ps. 80.5), i.e. b. accompanied by, or earned by, these. Sometimes metaphorically, as in Ps. 42.3 (meat); of the benefits given to those who obey God (Isa. 55.2); b. and wine stand for the benefits offered by divine Wisdom (Prov. 9.5).

B. played an important part in Heb. worship. Various kinds of b. were offered with the sacrifices, e.g. it is among the offerings used at consecration of priests, Exod. 29. Generally b. offered on the altar had to be unleavened, Exod. 23.18, 34.25, Lev. 2.11, 7.12. But there were exceptions, Lev. 7.13, 23.17: in both these cases the priest was to eat it, 7.14, 23.20. The latter was 'the b. of the firstfruits'. The avoidance of *leaven* in b. offered in worship was due to the fact that leaven was regarded as a form of corruption. This reflected in the fact that, where leaven is used metaphorically in Bible, it always has a sinister sense, except in Matt. 13.33=Luke 13.21.

The FEAST OF UNLEAVENED BREAD (Exod. 12.15–20) was the continuation of one of the three great agricultural festivals which the Israelites found in Canaan, and to which was joined the nomadic festival of Passover. It was kept at the beginning of barley harvest. During the 7 days of the feast it was strictly forbidden to eat anything leavened or even to have leaven in the house. The aetiological suggestion in Exod. 12.34,39 and Deut. 16.3 represents the tendency to attach an historical meaning to the agricultural festivals; but most likely the original motive of the prohibition was to save the new year's produce from contamination by the old. Usually some dough was saved from each baking and allowed to ferment and then used to leaven the next baking. The Feast of Unleavened B. broke this continuity and marked the new start of the new year (Exod. 12.2). Later there developed a tendency to give a spiritual or ethical interpretation to ritual. Cf. I Cor. 5.6–8, which gives a clue to its message for us: forgiveness marks the break with the old life and provides the new start; but the forgiven man must strive to become by obedience what he is by justification. Linked, as it was, with the Passover, it was both a reminder of the new beginning given to runaway slaves by God's act of deliverance and a promise of a yet more significant new beginning to be given in Christ.

The earliest mention of SHEWBREAD is I Sam. 21. We hear of it later in Solomon's Temple and in the Priestly description of the Tabernacle. It is usually called *lechem panim* (bread of the presence), but the Chronicler prefers *lechem ma'areketh* (bread of arrangement—so called because arranged in 2 piles of 6 loaves each): both names are represented by 'shewbread' in AV and RV. It is also called 'continual b.' (Num. 4.7; cf. II Chron. 2.4). For the table of shewbread see I Kings 6.20 (RV margin), 7.48, and in P, Exod. 25.23–30, Num. 4.7. It was in the Holy Place in front of the Most Holy Place or Holy of Holies (cf. Heb. 9.2f.). A section of the Levites was allotted the job of preparing the shewbread (I Chron. 9.32). For detailed instructions, see Lev. 24.5–9, and for the accompanying wine see Exod. 25.29 (RV), Num. 4.7. The shewbread was not a sacrifice in strict sense, but an offering originally thought of as a meal for the god. At one time perhaps connected with the zodiac, as the number 12 (Lev. 24.6) suggests, though the number would later suggest the 12 tribes, and the offering would be interpreted as a rendering of thanks to God. There are parallels outside the Bible, e.g. the Roman *lectisternium*.

The phrase 'the b. of their (thy, his) God' (Lev. 21.6,8,17,22, 22.25) does not refer specifically to b., but rather food in general. Cf. Lev. 3.11, where *lechem* is translated 'food', and the context shows it to be flesh.

NT: The following groups of occurrences of word b. may be noted. (*1*) Christian obligation to earn one's own b. (II Thess. 3.8,12). (*2*) In the Lord's Prayer, Matt. 6.11—God interested in our material needs; b. his gift. (*3*) But b. not everything. Jesus, tempted to work a miracle for satisfaction of his own hunger, replies to the tempter by quoting Deut. 8.3. Physical hunger points beyond itself to a deeper need. (*4*) In accounts of miracles of feeding (Mark 6.35ff. and parallels; Mark 8.1ff. and parallels; John 6. 1–13). (*5*) In the discourse in John 6.25ff. Jesus is himself 'the true bread out of heaven' (ref. back to manna of Exod. 16), 'the bread of God . . . which cometh down out of heaven and giveth life to the world', 'the b. of life', 'the living b.', and he says: 'The b. which I will give is my flesh, for the life of the world'. Judaism expected a second manna-miracle, e.g.: 'As the first Redeemer caused manna to descend, so shall also the last Redeemer cause manna to descend' (*Qoheleth Rabba*). Philo saw in the manna a type of the Word (*Logos*) (*v.* J. Behm in *TWNT*, I, p. 476). The background of the Johannine discourse is threefold—the miracle just performed, the OT gift of manna, the Christian Eucharist. (*6*) In a number of passages including those mentioned under (*4*), also Luke 24.30, John 21.13, Acts 27.35, and the accounts of institution of Eucharist, the words take, give thanks (or bless), break, give (or distribute) occur in connexion with b. (*7*) For b. in Eucharist *v.* THANK. But we may here note one idea connected with it. In I Cor. 10.17 the one b. or loaf of which all partake is a symbol of the unity of the Church. Cf. Didache 9.4: 'As this broken bread was scattered upon the tops of the mountains and being gathered became one, so gather thy Church from the ends of the earth into thy kingdom.' Also Cyprian, *Ep.* lxii.14 quoted by C. A. Anderson Scott, *Christianity according to St. Paul*, p. 195. (*8*) John 13.18 looks back to Ps. 41.9. (*9*) 'To eat b. in the kingdom of God', Luke 14.15; cf. 'to sit down (i.e. recline at meal-table) in the kingdom of God', Luke 13.29, also 22.16,30, Rev. 19.9; and the parable of Great Supper/Marriage Feast, Luke 14.16ff., Matt. 22.1ff. The meaning is to partake of final blessedness. (*10*) Of the Baptist 'eating no b. nor drinking wine', Luke 7.33. (Also *v.* THANK NT(*c*) and (*d*).)

C. E. B. CRANFIELD

BREAKING OF BREAD *v.* THANK NT(*c*) and esp. (*d*) and BREAD NT(7)

BREAST

Frequently of women, especially with reference to the suckling of children; more rarely of men. To smite the b. was a sign of grief (Luke 18.13, 23.48). Also of animals. In the sacrifices the b. of the victim was part of the priests' share (Lev. 7.31). It was presented by being solemnly waved to and fro before the altar. Hence the name *wave breast* (Lev. 7.34, etc.). Cf. 'heave thigh' (AV heave shoulder).

Metaphorical. To suck the milk of the nations and the b. of kings, Isa. 60.16, i.e. to enjoy the wealth of the nations and their kings (cf. 49.23, 66.12). In Isa. 66.11 of Jerusalem: the restored people are to 'suck and be satisfied with the breasts of her consolations'. Jerusalem is here thought of as the mother of her citizens. Cf. Gal. 4.26; also Calvin, *Institutio* IV.i.4 on the Church.

C. E. B. C.

BREASTPLATE *v.* ARMOUR

BREATH *v.* SPIRIT I(*b*) and MIND

BRIDE *v.* MARRIAGE

BRIDEGROOM *v.* MARRIAGE

BROTHER *v.* FAMILY

BURN, FIRE

There is one point here of special interest—namely, the distinction in Heb. between *qatar*, to burn incense and sacrificial offerings which ascend as a sweet savour (as in Exod. 30.7, I Kings 3.3), and *saraph*, used of destructive burning, as, e.g., of the city of Ai (Josh. 8.28) or of dead men's bones on an altar to desecrate it (II Kings 23.16). For the two meanings, see Lev. 4.10,12, or 16.25,27. *Saraph* is however also used contemptuously of human sacrifices offered by the Sepharvites, II Kings 17.31, and by Israelites, Jer. 7.31, 19.5, where it might be rendered 'to murder their sons in the fire for burnt offerings unto Baal'. Another word *ba'ar* is used of burning wood to keep the altar fire alight (Neh. 10.34) but not of the burning of the victims. The metaphorical use of FIRE in NT is usually in the destructive sense, and so of the fire of judgment. Thus Matt. 3.11, 'He shall baptize you with the Holy Ghost and with fire', is best explained by vs. 12, which speaks of the burning of the chaff in language taken from Mal. 4.1, as if to say: 'for the saved, a baptism with Holy Spirit, but for the damned a very different sort of baptism'. But the tongues of fire on the apostles' heads at Pentecost, Acts 2.3, may be the sacrificial fire; and similarly Mark 9.49, where, following on a series of refs. to the penal fire of Gehenna in vss. 43, 45, 48, come the words 'for every one shall be salted with fire', which seem to require for their explanation the addition in D, 'and every sacrifice shall be salted with salt': as if to say, 'Salt and fire are sacrificial things (cf. Lev. 2.13); the disciples' lives are to be offered in sacrifice; let them have salt also in themselves, and be at peace with one another'. The distinction has been preserved in the devotional language of the Church, which speaks both of the fire of judgment, and of the sacrificial fire of the Holy Ghost, as in 'Come, Holy Ghost, fill the hearts of thy faithful people, and kindle in them the fire of thy love'.

A. G. HEBERT

BURNT-OFFERING *v.* SACRIFICE I(*c*)

* * *

CALL, CALLED, CALLING

[VOCATION occurs once in AV, Eph. 4.1, where it renders the word elsewhere (10 times) always translated 'calling'. RV rightly renders it by 'calling' here also.]

I. We may first notice two literal uses of the word, both of which form a basis for its technical employment in biblical theology. (A) *To give a name to* a person or thing. Freq. from Gen. 1.5 onwards: 'God called the light Day, and the darkness he called Night.' So in NT, Matt. 1.21, 'Thou shalt call his name JESUS'. (B) *To summon*; e.g. Gen. 12.18, 'Pharaoh called Abram'; Matt. 2.7, 'Herod privily called the wise men'. Under this head belongs the common use of the word for *calling for help* and so *calling upon God*; e.g. Gen. 4.26, 'Then began men to call upon the name of the Lord'; II Cor. 1.23, 'I call God for a witness'. But this use does not lead to any theological development.

II. *Theological Developments.* (A) To give a name to someone or something readily leads to the idea of *claiming him or it for your own possession and appointing him for a particular destiny*, which in some cases may be expressed by the name that is given, since for the Hebrew the name often symbolized the nature (*v.* NAME). Thus Abram becomes Abraham and Jacob becomes Israel (Gen. 17.5, 32.28). (The etymological difficulties, for which *v.* the commentaries *ad loc.*, do not affect the principle.) So Simon is surnamed Peter (John 1.42). Specially noticeable is Isa. 43.1, when the Lord addresses Israel: 'I have called thee by thy name, thou art mine'; cf. 45.3f. (of Cyrus), 62.2, Rev. 2.17, 3.12. See also Hos. 1.4,6,9, 2.1,16–17,22–3. The same idea occurs in the case of those 'upon whom the name of the Lord is called' (? in baptism), Acts 15.17, Jas. 2.7. The climax is seen in I John 3.1: 'Behold what manner of love the Father hath bestowed upon us, that we should be called the children of God.'

This leads to (B) *the technical sense of 'calling' in biblical theology*. The Bible tells the story of a People foreknown and foreordained, and in due time *called* (Rom. 8.29f.) to their divine destiny. Throughout God takes the initiative in summoning them. Their part is to respond to his calling—though too often, nationally and individually, they fail to do so. It is not always easy to draw a sharp line between the literal and the biblical-theological uses of the words, but the theological import becomes steadily clearer; and what is related as plain fact in the historical books receives its significant illumination in the prophets, and becomes fully and consciously technical in the apostolic writings of the NT. It is, of course, obvious that many diverse actions are part of this 'calling', even though the word itself is not always used.

This calling, with its attendant idea of separation, calling *out* (cf. CHURCH), may be said to begin with the order to Abram to move from Haran (Gen. 12 does not use the actual term, but Heb. 11.8, referring to it, does; cf. Isa. 51.2). See also Gen. 21.12, cited in Rom. 9.7, Heb. 11.18: 'In Isaac shall thy seed be called.' Moses is 'called' to the Burning Bush (Exod.

3.4) and charged with the deliverance of the captives in Egypt. Later (19.20, 24.16) he is 'called' to the top of Sinai to receive the Book of the Covenant. Hosea (11.1) speaks definitely of the whole process as a vocation: 'I called my son (Israel) out of Egypt', and the *thought*, if not the word, is present in his picture of Israel as the Bride, wooed and won by God in the wilderness (chs. 1–3). Above all, Deutero-Isaiah constantly sees the history not only of Israel but of all nations, as dependent upon the calling of God (e.g. 41.2,4,9, 42.6, 44.7, 46.11, 48.13,15, 49.1, 51.2, 54.6).

In the NT Jesus *calls* men and they follow him, e.g. Mark 1.20, 3.13. Here the idea of 'vocation' is clear ('*Christus ruft und damit beruft*', K. L. Schmidt). Similarly he 'came not to call the righteous, but sinners', Mark 2.17 and parallels; Luke 5.32 explicitly adds 'to repentance'. This gracious calling is part of the Church's preaching from the first; cf. Acts 2.39.

In the apostolic writings (chiefly, but not exclusively, in St. Paul, for cf. Heb. 3.1, 9.15, I Pet. 1.15, 2.9,21, 3.9, 5.10, II Pet. 1.3,10, Jude 1, Rev. 17.14, 19.9) 'call', 'calling' and 'called' are technical terms of theology, and even where this is not obvious on the surface it must still be allowed for.

(*a*) The verb 'to call'. The 'caller' is God (Rom. 9.11, Gal. 5.8, etc.), and the divine purpose in which 'calling' is one stage is set out in Rom. 8.28–30. The calling is into God's kingdom and glory (I Thess. 2.12); to salvation (II Thess. 2.13–14); to eternal life (I Tim. 6.12); to God's marvellous light (I Pet. 2.9). It has a moral content and purpose; 'not for uncleanness, but in sanctification' (I Thess. 4.7); for patience in suffering (I Pet. 2.21); for freedom (Gal. 5.13); for peace (I Cor. 7.15, Col. 3.15). The basis of the calling is the free grace of God and of his Christ (Gal. 1.6,15). It reaches men through the Gospel (II Thess. 2.14). It sets before them a glorious hope (Eph. 4.4).

(*b*) The noun 'calling' is similarly used. It is of God, who will not go back upon it (Rom. 11.29); 'a high (lit. upward) and heavenly calling' (Phil. 3.14, Heb. 3.1). It is filled with hope (Eph. 1.18, 4.4). It must be held sure (Eph. 4.1, II Pet. 1.10; and cf. the whole passage Heb. 3.1–4.13, where the fact of the believer's calling is made the basis of exhortation to steadfastness).

(*c*) The verbal adjective 'called' is sometimes used absolutely of the call to salvation (Rom. 1.6,7, I Cor. 1.2,24, Jude 1, Rev. 17.14), but also of calling to a particular office (Rom. 1.1, I Cor. 1.1; cf. Heb. 5.4, and see also Acts 13.2 and 16.10).

Throughout these passages it is implied that the call has been not only uttered, but obeyed. The called (*klētoi*) are identified with the chosen or elect (*eklektoi*); cf. Rom. 8.33, 16.13, Col. 3.12, and esp. Rev. 17.14. But in the Gospels (Matt. 22.14; cf. 20.16 in certain MSS.) the 'called' are distinguished from the 'chosen'. This difference in usage should be frankly admitted (cf. Lightfoot on Col. 3.12), but too much should not be made of it, esp. as we do not know what Aramaic words our Lord originally used. (*V.* also CHOOSE, DETERMINATE, SAINT, WORK.)

J. P. THORNTON-DUESBERY

CANAAN (twice in AV (*NT*) CHANAAN)

The meaning of the word is not clear; it may be from a Hurrian word for 'land of purple', or from a Heb. word 'to be humble' and so 'lowland' (G. A. Smith, *The Historical Geography of the Holy Land*, London, 1896). In the present form of the tradition in Gen. 9f. the name goes back to a son of Ham and grandson of Noah and recognizes the fact of Egyptian domination in Palestine. The Egyptian letters of the 14th cent. BC found at Tell El-Amarna use the name for all the coastal plain of Palestine and Phoenicia; later, as the Canaanites spread, it became the name for all western Syria. Josh. 11.3 and Judg. 1.9 use it for all pre-Hebrew inhabitants of the land of Palestine in east and west, and Isa. 19.18 describes the languages spoken in Palestine—Hebrew, Phoenician, Moabite—as the Canaanite tongue. It is possible that in some places the word Canaanite=merchant (Zech. 14.21). In the NT (Matt. 10.4, Mark 3.18, Luke 6.15, Acts 1.13) Simon the apostle is distinguished from Simon Peter by the title 'the Cananaean' (AV, Canaanite) from the Gk. *Kananaos*; the Aramaic original may denote that he was a native of Cana in Galilee or that he was a Zealot, a member of a Jewish patriotic underground movement active against the Roman occupying forces.

Archaeology has provided excellent knowledge of the land before the Israelite invasion: the story of Sinuhe, an Egyptian nobleman who fled to the land in the 12th cent., describes the nomadic character of many of its inhabitants; the Tell El-Amarna tablets reveal the political condition of the country, with its independent, disunited city-states; the Ras Shamra tablets show the religion of the land and reveal more clearly how much later Heb. religion incorporated from these earlier inhabitants. The height of Canaanite influence is seen in the OT description of Solomon's Temple, and Canaanite literature had a profound influence on the OT. Bible history represents the Canaanites as finally conquered by Israel in the time of Solomon (I Kings 9.20f.)

The extermination of these original inhabitants was ordered by God according to the accounts in Josh., but in Judg. 1 there is another story of the invasion and it is suggested that Canaanites were retained in the land to test Israel (Judg. 2.22) and to teach them how to fight (3.1). It seems probable that the writers of Josh., realizing the bad influence of Canaanite customs and beliefs and believing that God was always ruthlessly fighting against evil, regarded the complete extermination of these previous inhabitants of the land as part of the purpose of God, and represented Joshua, the ideal leader, as carrying out that purpose. The religious and literary circle from which the Book of Josh. came was strongly nationalistic, regarded Israel as in a peculiar sense God's own people and Israel's enemies as the enemies of God and, just as Jesus (Mark 9.43ff.) vividly demanded a clean cut between the Christian and everything that enticed him to evil whatever the cost, so these OT writers illustrated the same requirement of God by rewriting the story of Israel's conquest of the Holy Land. (*V.* also INHERIT.)

J. N. SCHOFIELD

CARE

'Care' (verb and noun) and deriv. (careful, -ly, -ness, careless, -ly) represent several distinct Heb. and Gk. words. This is further complicated by considerable divergence between EVV and also by the fact that the various Heb. and Gk. words, which are sometimes trans. by 'care' and deriv., are also elsewhere in the Bible trans. by quite different words, e.g. Heb. *daag* in AV be careful (once), be afraid (3 times), be sorry, sorrow (2), take thought (1). Its deriv. *deagah* care, carefulness (3), fear (1), sorrow (1), heaviness (1). *Betach* or *labetach* careless, -ly, without care (9), safely, in safety (26). Gk. *merimna* in AV care (6); in RV care (4), anxiety (2). *Merimnao* in AV care, have c., be careful (8); also take thought (11), where RV be ANXIOUS.

OT: Of anxious foreboding (root, *daag*), Ezek. 4.16, 12.18f., Jer. 17.8; of solicitude for another's welfare and attention to his wants (*charad*), II Kings 4.13; careless (*betach*) in good sense, e.g. Judg. 18.7 (RV, in security); in bad sense, of false sense of security, e.g. Isa. 32.9ff.

NT: The chief Gk. words that are sometimes trans. by 'care' and deriv. are *melei* (impersonal verb), *epimeloumai*, *merimna*, *merimnao*.

(*a*) *Melei*—of concern with or that, interest in, Mark 4.38, 12.14 (where the following words give the meaning), Acts 18.17; of c. for, I Pet. 5.7, I Cor. 9.9.

(*b*) *Epimeloumai*—to take c. of, Luke 10.34f., I Tim. 3.5.

(*c*) *Merimna* (noun), *merimnao* (verb) denote anxious concern for (oneself, one's life, others); anxious concern about or with (e.g. 'many things' in Luke 10.41; 'the things of the Lord', 'of the world', in I Cor. 7.32ff.); anxious striving after (e.g. pleasing one's wife, *ibid.*): absolute *anxiety*. The reference to the future is never far away.

The warnings in Matt. 6.25–34, Phil. 4.6, I Pet. 5.7 are not a prohibition of all human concern. (The NT presupposes that it is natural to men to be concerned for themselves, and so to be always striving after something). Rather they are directed against (*1*) the false orientation of men's concern, and (*2*) the element of anxiety in it.

(*1*) A man's whole understanding of himself, his real existence, is determined by the orientation of his concern. The word 'first' in Matt. 6.33 provides a clue to the meaning of NT warnings. When NT contrasts the c. or concern for 'the things of the Lord' with that for 'the things of the world' (I Cor. 7.32ff.) or 'the cares of the world' (Mark 4.19) or 'the cares of this life' (Luke 21.34), the intention is not that the Christian is to be withdrawn altogether from the world or forbidden to share the concerns of ordinary life, but that he is not to allow these to draw his heart away from the c. of the things of the Lord. Riches, for instance, are deceitful (Mark 4.19), because men tend to be so taken up with them that they forget the kingdom of God.

(*2*) Our concern is freed from the element of anxiety when on the one hand we are disillusioned of the notion that *we* by our concern can control the future and make ourselves secure, and on the other hand we learn to commit our concern to God with thanksgiving (Phil. 4.6, I Pet. 5.7). In so far as we submit our desires and cares to God (who is not the guarantor of our wishes, but the one who knows better than we do what our real need is), we are in that very act loosening our own hold upon them, and thereby we are released from anxiety. Moreover, the eschatological nature of the Christian life (the fact that we already belong to the age to come) should set us beyond the reach of the crippling power of anxiety, and produce a certain detachment of spirit (cf. I Cor. 7.29–31). How *can* those who really seek first the kingdom of God, who really are ready for its breaking in, be held captive by the anxiety of this world?

It follows that, when our concern (and therefore our whole being) has been reorientated by the Gospel, and also freed from the element of anxiety, we shall also be set free from our natural preoccupation with ourselves, and so have opportunity to be concerned for others. Such caring for others is laid upon us (I Cor.

12.25, II Cor. 11.28, Phil. 2.20). (For the above on *merimna*, *merimnao* the writer is largely indebted to R. Bultmann's article in *TWNT*, IV, pp. 594ff.)

(*d*) Three other Gk. words are occasionally trans. 'care', etc.: *phroneo*: Phil. 4.10 (AV; but RV, thought, take thought), Mark 8.33 (AV, savour; RV, mind), Col. 3.2 (AV, set one's affections on; RV, set one's mind on); *phrontizo*: Tit. 3.8 (be careful to); *spoude*: II Cor. 7.12, 8.16 (earnest care).

C. E. B. CRANFIELD

CAREFUL *v.* CARE

CARELESS *v.* CARE

CARNAL *v.* FLESH

CARPENTER *v.* WORK

CHARITY *v.* LOVE

CHASTEN, CHASTISE

The three OT words which, with their derivatives, are used for describing disciplinary punishment are chastise, chasten, CORRECT. All three represent, more or less indiscriminately, the two Heb. roots *yasar* and *yakhach*. The noun which is formed from the former root is common in Prov., where the regular equivalent in EVV is INSTRUCTION. The Gk. equivalent is therefore *paideia*, the regular word in classical Gk. for the instruction of the young, though at II Tim. 3.16 the Gk. word used definitely means 'putting right'. The atmosphere of the whole group of words is shown clearly in the many passages in Prov. (24 times) where the word 'instruction' is found, and also in two particular passages: Deut. 8.5, 'as a man chasteneth his son, so the Lord thy God chasteneth thee'; and Eph. 6.4, where fathers are urged to 'nurture their children in the chastening (so RV, but AV has 'bring up . . . nurture') and admonition of the Lord'.

In the NT the word 'chasten' is found more frequently than the word 'chastise' (9 AV and 10 RV against 3), whilst the word 'correct' is found twice. There is a distinction everywhere between chastisement and PUNISHMENT (*q.v.*), the former being disciplinary and confined to the people of God, and the latter being retributive and applicable to all who transgress. God does indeed chasten his people with calamity, but he does not abandon them (II Macc. 6.16), and we, as Christians, 'are chastened of the Lord that we may not be condemned with the world', I Cor. 11.32. On the other hand, there is punishment for sin, more clearly expressed in the OT than in the NT, though there are enough passages in the teaching of Christ, apart from those elsewhere in the NT, to make it clear that retributive punishment has a place in his teaching.

The whole conception of the chastening of the Lord belongs to a view of the world and God's part in it very different from that of the modern world. Our modern attitude is to ascribe the varied fortunes of man to natural causes or to human causes. We may adopt the full Marxian attitude of finding economic reasons for everything that happens, or we may take a general rationalist, humanist view whereby we explain everything in scientific and human terms. In any case, we are involved in interpreting the conception of the chastening of the Lord as a figurative phrase. We do not think of God as being always directly active in this world. We tend to say that suffering is the direct result of sin, ours or someone else's, and where we cannot say this we ascribe it to 'natural causes' and we say it is the sort of thing that is inevitable in a world like this. We agree with Heb. 12.11 that 'all chastening seemeth at present to be not joyous, but grievous', and we would further agree that we can be thankful for it afterwards when it has yielded 'peaceable fruit'; but we do not think of God as directly concerned in the matter, and we regard our own attitude as being decisive. We hesitate to say of any suffering that God has definitely brought it upon us, but tend to say that, when once the suffering is present, it can be so met as to produce 'works of righteousness'. This is not the Bible attitude, which regards God as being active in his world and directly responsible for what happens in it. This attitude of responsibility is maintained even when the suffering seems to be so severe that Satan is said to be immediately responsible, I Cor. 5.5, II Cor. 12.7, I Tim. 1.20. Such passages show that the NT writers were already having difficulty over the direct action involved in the conception. (*V.* also CORRECT, PUNISH.)

N. H. SNAITH

CHASTISE *v.* CHASTEN

CHEMOSH *v.* GOD, GODS IV

CHERUB, SERAPH

The Heb. name for the winged sphinx with human head. The idea is not distinctively Heb., but moved westward from the north-east; it was known in the mythological records of Mesopotamia from a very early period, and the name was used of the winged, human-headed and animal-bodied colossi which were regarded as divine intercessors placed at the entrances to sanctuaries and as guardians placed at the entrances to royal palaces. The idea appears to have entered Heb. thought through Canaanite influence: representations of them were found on the incense altar at

Taanach, the model shrine at Megiddo, and on the inlaid ivories at Samaria. In Solomon's temple they were part of the decorative motif on the walls and hangings, and there were two 15 ft. high in the inner shrine (I Kings 6.23); in I Chron. 28.18 they are connected with the chariot of the sun-god, just as at Megiddo a male cherub wears a sun disc on its forehead. Gen. 3.24 speaks of a cherub as guardian of the road to Eden (Ezek. 28.14); Ps. 18.11 represents God as riding through the sky on a cherub which is equated with the wings of the wind; God rides on cherubim (II Sam. 22.11) and is enthroned on them (II Kings 19.4). Their wings are emphasized in Exod. 25.20 and Isa. 6. Perhaps originally they symbolized God as superhuman, possessing the intelligence of man and the power of animals, and became the visible symbols of the invisible gods they guarded or served. Ezekiel's picture (1.4ff.) of the throne of God borne by cherubim is used to enhance the majesty of God, and there, as in the book of the Revelation, there is a difference from the earlier representation: there is a human body, four-headed to show the human, lion, ox, and eagle.

The seraphim may be different, although in Isa. 6 seraphim are used apparently for the two cherubim in the holy place of the temple. The word appears to mean 'the burning ones', and elsewhere in the OT it is used of the fiery flying serpent inhabiting the desert (Isa. 14.29, 30.6) and of the brazen image of a serpent made by Moses (Numb. 21.8) to heal the people dying of serpent bites (cf. John 3); II Kings 18.4 refers to this figure as a serpent and states that Hezekiah destroyed it because the people were worshipping it.

In later Christian thought the four-headed cherub was regarded as the symbol of the fourfold Gospel: Matthew the human, Mark the lion, Luke the ox, and John the eagle.

J. N. SCHOFIELD

CHILD *v.* FAMILY

CHOOSE, CHOSEN, ELECT, ELECTION

It is the firm conviction of the OT writers that God chose Israel rather than that Israel chose God. The whole of the story of the patriarchs has this *motif.* It begins in the choice between Abel and Cain; it is continued in the choice between Isaac and Ishmael, Jacob and Esau, Joseph and his brethren. The idea of the covenant, which is the form of the expression of God's choice, is traced back from Sinai to the 'covenant with Abraham, with Isaac, and with Jacob', Exod. 2.24. The idea is expressly set forth in Amos 3.2: 'You only have I known of all the families of the earth.' God had a personal and intimate relationship with Israel such as was not given to other peoples. Knowledge, amongst the Hebrews, tended to be personal rather than intellectual, and practical rather than academic. When the psalmist says (Ps. 1.6) that 'the Lord knoweth the way of the righteous', he means that God is himself personally acquainted with every step which the righteous man takes, not that he is aware of the road and can trace it out, so to speak, on a map. God's concern is not so much with the road as a road, but with the man who is walking along it. This particular concern with the wayfarer is what is involved in the idea of God's choice of Israel.

The OT writers could never understand the reason for this choice. Amos does not attempt to provide a reason; he contents himself with the statement of the fact of the choice. The Deuteronomic writers attempt to find reasons for it, but the reasons they give do but show their inability to solve the mystery. They say that it was because 'the Lord had a delight in their fathers to love them' (Deut. 10.15). They knew it was not because Israel was good, nor was it because Israel was great in numbers (7.7). In Deut. 9.4f. the people are definitely warned against thinking that they were chosen because of their righteousness. It was because God loved them (Deut. 23.5) that he turned Balaam's curse into a blessing. The reason for God's choice of Israel is to be found in God alone, and not in Israel, in anything they were, or in anything they had done. It was his good pleasure, and he chose them 'for his Name's sake'. The whole OT emphasis is that God's love for Israel was wholly unmerited by Israel. His choice of Israel was irrational in the sense that there is no reason for it which men can find amongst men. His choice is arbitrary in the sense that it depends solely upon his sovereign will. But it is not irrational in the sense that there is no reason at all for it; neither is it arbitrary in the sense that it is capricious. It is God's will, his own choice, and the reason for it is to be found in his nature (cf. Job 42.3, Isa. 55.8f., Rom. 11.33).

The Bible is emphatic that the choice is with God rather than with man. This is the basis of the Biblical doctrine of election. 'Ye have not chosen me, but I have chosen you' (John 15.16). There is something of the nature of exclusiveness about God's choice. This must of necessity be the case if some are chosen and others are not chosen. This does not mean, however, that God chooses ('elects') some to eternal life and elects others to damnation. God does indeed reject some, but this is not an arbitrary rejection even in the limited sense of arbitrariness which we would allow in his choice. His rejection is on the ground of a persistent stubbornness in unrepentant wickedness. Ephraim is rejected (Ps. 78.67) and Judah is chosen, in spite of what Amos said. Indeed Amos himself speaks of the rejection of Israel-Ephraim, when he says in the end that God's bringing of Israel out of Egypt comes to mean no more than his bringing the Philistines from Caphtor and the Syrians from Kir (Amos 9.7). He calls many, but he chooses few (Matt. 22.14). It is tempting to say that he calls all men, but few respond to his call. But this is not sound NT teaching, which insists that the choice is with God and not with man. In the Gospels there is a distinction between the 'called' and the 'chosen'. The former are those who are 'summoned to the privileges of the Gospel, and the elect those appointed to final salvation'; so Lightfoot, *Epistle to the Colossians*, in his note on Col. 3.12 (*q.v.*). In the Pauline Epistles there is no such distinction between the two words. Men are 'chosen out' from the world and are 'called' to Christ.

The whole problem is one of freedom, and our difficulty arises from the fact that we persist in thinking of freedom as an absolute. Actually there is no such thing as absolute freedom in this world; it is always relative. If we begin by assuming an absolute freedom for God, we find it difficult to ascribe any freedom to man. Conversely, if we begin by assuming freedom for man, we find it difficult to secure a proper freedom for God. The solution is to be found in Christian experience rather than in intellectual and logical terms. The idea that man chooses belongs to 'first principles of Christ'; the extent to which a man knows that God chooses is the measure of his progress towards perfection (cf. Heb. 6.1). At conversion a man is very sensible of the fact that he has a choice between Christ and not-Christ, between life and death (cf. Deut. 30.15–20). He is certain of nothing more than this. He is right, for it is a real and true choice. But afterwards that same man grows more and more conscious that even those very first stirrings in his own heart which led him to choose Christ were the work of the Holy Spirit. He becomes growingly sure that he was chosen rather than that he chose. He becomes more and more sure also that this choice of God's depended upon God's love and not upon his own deserving of it. It was because 'he had a favour unto me'. Further, this same man is not prepared to follow the logic of this statement along normal human lines to its conclusion, for then he will find himself saying that God has not chosen certain others, from which it is but a small step to say that he has elected some to damnation. He therefore stops short in his logic when he comes to the end of his own experience, because, since he is dealing with an action of God rather than with an action of man, he knows that he is in a realm too deep for human thought. We say, therefore, that the idea of a human choice is the language of the newly converted, but that the certainty of the divine choice is the language of the sanctified. (Also *v.* DETERMINATE.)

BIBLIOGRAPHY

N. H. Snaith: *Distinctive Ideas of the Old Testament*, London (1944). C. H. Dodd: *Epistle to the Romans* (Moffatt Commentaries), London (1932).

N. H. SNAITH

CHOSEN *v.* CHOOSE

CHRIST

'Christ' is the Eng. form of the Gk. verbal adj. *Christos*, ANOINTED, which is used about 40 times in the Gk. version of the OT to trans. the Heb. participle *mashiach*, which has the same meaning. Later the Heb. word was taken into Gk. in the form *messias* (John 14.1, 4.25); from this are derived the Eng. forms, *Messias* and *Messiah*.

In Israel in early times high priests (Exod. 29.7) and kings were anointed with oil; this was a sign that God had chosen them for their offices, and it is recorded of both Saul and David that, when they had been anointed, the Spirit of Yahweh came upon them mightily (I Sam. 10.6ff.–16.13). So 'Yahweh's (or "my", "thine", "his") anointed' came to mean 'the King of Israel'. This use of the phrase is found chiefly in I and II Samuel, and usually the ref. is to Saul, e.g. I Sam. 24.6,10. In Ps. 2.2, 18.50, 20.6, 132.10,17 the ref. is to some later king. In Ps. 28.8, 84.9, 89.38,51, the phrase seems to be used of the people collectively rather than of their king; cf. also Hab. 3.12 (this chapter is a psalm), where the parallelism of the phrases 'the salvation of thy people' and 'the salvation of thine anointed' suggests that this is the meaning. In Ps. 105.15 (=I Chron. 16.22), the only passage in which the word is used in the plural, the context shows that it refers to the patriarchs, who, though not literally 'anointed', were consecrated to God's service (cf., for the figurative use of the verb, Isa. 61.1). It is very remarkable that in Isa. the term is used only once, and then of the Persian king, Cyrus, Isa. 45.1. In a very obscure passage in Dan. (9.25f.), it is quite uncertain who is meant by 'an anointed one, a prince' (AV, the Messiah the Prince) and 'an anointed one' (AV, Messiah), but the latter phrase probably refers to the high priest Onias III, deposed in 175 BC, and so the former may refer to Jeshua, the first high priest after the restoration (cf. Ezra 3.2). In Zech. 4.14, where the AV has 'the two anointed ones', the literal rendering, given by the RV, is 'the two sons of oil'.

In the OT, therefore, the term, 'the anointed', whether alone or with the usual addition of 'Yahweh' (or the equivalent of this), is never used with a future ref. to the king whom God would one day raise up to rule over the restored Kingdom of David. Later, some of the passages in the Pss. which originally referred to an actual king of Judah were interpreted 'messianically'. But the earliest evidence for this interpretation is in the NT; it is not found in extant Jewish writings earlier than the 3rd cent. AD.

In Jewish writings of the period between the OT and the NT, refs. to the Messiah are remarkably few. By far the most important of them is in the 17th of the Psalms of Solomon, a long psalm which can be dated about 50 BC, and which is entirely concerned with the character and achievements of the king whom God will raise up, in his own good time, to deliver his people from their godless enemies, and to reign over them in faithfulness and righteousness. This king will be strong only 'in fear of God' and 'in holy spirit'; he will overcome the enemies of his people, not by military force, but by 'the word of his mouth'. He will gather a righteous people, who will all be sons of their God, and among whom there will be no unrighteousness any more. Being himself free from sin, and endowed by God with wisdom and understanding, strength and righteousness, he will bless the people of the Lord in wisdom with gladness. But the blessings of his reign are for Israelites only; other peoples, if they are not destroyed or reduced to servitude, are at best permitted to come from the end of the earth to see his glory. The psalm ends with the prayer, 'May the Lord hasten upon Israel his mercy; may he rescue us from the uncleanness of profane enemies. The Lord himself is our king for ever and ever.' The king who is here described is quite clearly 'the Messiah', but in this psalm he is not actually called by that title. He will be 'anointed-of-(the)-Lord', but this is a predicate rather than a title. In the next psalm (the 18th), however, 'his (=the Lord's) anointed' does seem to be used as a title.

Probably the chief reason for the remarkable infrequency of the term 'the Messiah' in the extant Jewish literature of this period is that the expectations of the way in which God would 'visit and redeem his people' (Luke 1.68) varied greatly; sometimes God himself was expected to intervene directly on their behalf, and sometimes the agent of their redemption was an angelic being from heaven. But the title 'the Messiah' was used only of the human 'son of David' whom God would raise up to be the king of a restored Davidic Kingdom.

In the Gospels of Mark, Matthew, and Luke the title *Christ* occurs much less often than might be expected. Jesus never openly claims to be the Messiah. When he asked his disciples, at Caesarea Philippi, whom the people generally supposed him to be, the answer was, 'John the Baptist, or Elijah, or one of the prophets' (Mark 8.27f.). And when Peter declared him to be the Christ, Jesus' response was to charge his disciples to tell no one about him (Mark 8.29f.; cf. Luke 9.20f.). Matthew records that he first called Peter blessed, because this knowledge could have come to him only by revelation from God himself (Matt. 16.13–20). It is difficult to understand how Mark and Luke could omit this part of the story if they knew it, or how they could have failed to know of it if Jesus really did reply in this way. But as they stand, Jesus' words to Peter indicate that he himself had not yet given any indication even to his most intimate disciples that he was in fact the Christ. Mark tells us that at his 'trial' before the Sanhedrin Jesus frankly admitted that he was the Christ (Mark 14.61f.), but according to both Matthew and Luke he refused to give a direct answer to the high priest's question (Matt. 26.63f., Luke 22.67f.). In any case, his reply was taken as an admission that he was the Christ, and it was as a pretended Messiah, 'King of the Jews', that he was sent to the cross (cf. Mark 15.26,32). Yet it is clear that his enemies could produce no other evidence that he had ever made this claim for himself.

In the Gospel of John, on the other hand, Jesus is acknowledged to be the Christ from the very beginning of his public ministry (John 1.41,49). Only once does Jesus quite explicitly claim to be the Messiah (John 4.25f.), but it is made perfectly plain that he never attempted to conceal the fact that he was the Messiah (cf. John 10.24f.). Here there is a clear contradiction between John and the other Gospels, and there can be no doubt that the evidence of the earlier gospels is the more trustworthy.

Unfortunately, this means that there is no sufficient evidence to show whether or not Jesus in fact believed himself to be the Messiah. It is often said that he knew himself to be the Messiah, but not the Messiah whom the Jews expected. But why should he have used the term at all, if he had to give it a new and different meaning? To do this, without explanation, would only have misled his hearers. There is some evidence that even after the resurrection the disciples expected Jesus to do just what the Messiah of the Jews had been expected to do—'restore the kingdom to Israel' (Acts 1.6f.); cf. also the request of the sons of Zebedee that they might have the chief places in Jesus' kingdom (Matt. 20.20ff., Mark 10.35ff.) (though Mark has 'glory' instead of 'kingdom'). It is also to be noted that Peter, in his address to the crowd on the day of Pentecost, speaks of God having made the Jesus whom they had crucified 'both Lord and Christ'; in the context, this seems to mean that it was by raising Jesus from the dead that God had made him 'Christ'. But here there is no clear indication of the meaning which Peter gave to the title 'Christ', except that since he was speaking to Jews he would naturally be understood to use it in its Jewish sense.

It is, however, clear that in Christian usage the word first acquired a new and different meaning, and then lost all real meaning, and became simply a proper name like 'Jesus' itself. The latter development was all but inevitable among Gk.-speaking Gentile Christians, who were not interested in a 'Christ' who should restore the kingdom to Israel, and who did not understand the literal meaning of the word—they probably often took it to be an adj. meaning 'good', 'kind' (*chrēstos*), which was pronounced in the same way though spelled differently (*v.* also art. CHRISTIAN). What is much more surprising is that Paul, Jew though he was, hardly ever uses the word except as a proper name, which can be combined with, or substituted for, the name Jesus, without any thought of its special meaning. (The fact that the order may be either 'Jesus Christ' or 'Christ Jesus' may perhaps be an indication that some sense of the original meaning of *Christ* survived, since when both parts in such a combination are strictly proper names the order is not variable, e.g. 'Simon Peter'.) (Also *v.* PROPHECY, I, FAMILY, II; and for Christ as High Priest, SACRIFICE V(*c*).)

J. Y. CAMPBELL

CHRISTIAN

This name for the followers of Christ occurs only 3 times in the NT (Acts 11.26, 26.28, I Pet. 4.16), and the only definite information we have about its origin is the statement in the first of these passages, that 'the disciples were called Christians for the first time in Antioch'. The name does not seem to have been generally used by Christians themselves until the middle of the 2nd cent. AD, and even then it is used chiefly by apologists writing for pagan readers. But the Roman historian Tacitus says that it was used by the populace in Rome in the time of Nero (Annals, XV.44.3). In the important MS of the NT, the Codex Vaticanus, the spelling *Chrēstian(os)* is found in all three passages, and the same spelling is common in early inscriptions. This points to a derivation, not from *Christos*, but from *Chrēstos*, which is presumably the common Gk. adj. *chrēstos*, 'good', 'kindly', regarded as a proper name. (The ending *-ianos*, which is Lat. rather than Gk. in origin, does not seem to have been used except in formations from proper names; cf. in the NT itself *Herōdianoi*, Mark 3.6, etc.) The two names were at this time pronounced in almost the same way. Christians sometimes accepted this implied derivation without remark, but they can scarcely have invented it for themselves. It is therefore probable that the name was originally invented and used by non-Christians.

J. Y. C.

CHURCH, ASSEMBLY

Eng. 'church' (cf. Scottish *kirk*, Dutch *kerk*, German *Kirche*) is generally derived from Gk. *kuriakon* 'the Lord's house', a building for Christian worship. *Kuriakon* does not occur in this sense in the Bible. Until long after the 1st cent. Christians had no Church buildings. 'Church' in NT translates Gk. *ecclesia*, which always means an assembly of people, and cannot mean a building.

OT: 'ASSEMBLY'

'Church' does not occur in AV or RV of OT. *Ecclesia* is, however, used by LXX to translate two Heb. words, *'edhah* and *qahal*. Whereas AV translates both these indiscriminately by 'congregation' and 'assembly', RV consistently renders *'edhah* by 'congregation' and *qahal* by 'assembly'. In AV 'assembly' is also used for 6 other Heb. words; none of them is frequent. Some have a religious, none a theological connotation like *'edhah* and *qahal*.

'Edhah, the older word, comes from a root meaning 'to appoint', hence, 'a company assembled together by appointment'. In P with the qualification 'of Yahweh' (denoting *who* assembles) and with 'of Israel' (denoting who is assembled), it signifies the company of Israel of the Exodus.

Qahal comes from a root meaning 'to call', and originally meant the assembling of the community for counsel, or the mustering of men of military age for war. Deut. uses it of the people assembled to hear the Law at Horeb. Qualified like *'edhah* by 'of Yahweh' or 'of Israel', it acquires the same meaning of 'the people of God', and in post-exilic writings almost replaces *'edhah*. Its use on certain solemn occasions, as in Deut. at the giving of the Law, in I Kings 8.14ff. at the dedication of the Temple, and at the republishing of the Law by Ezra, emphasizes the truth that the people of Israel are constituted by the word of Yahweh as the bearers of the divine covenant and promise.

See Brown, Driver and Briggs, *Hebrew Lexicon* on *'edhah* and *qahal* and *TWNT*, *ecclesia*. Cf. Hort, *Christian Ecclesia*, ch. I, and

Hoskyns and Davey, *Riddle of the New Testament*, p. 25ff.

ECCLESIA IN LXX

The translators of the Pentateuch translated both *'edhah* and *qahal* by *ecclesia*, but later reserved *synagoge* (SYNAGOGUE) for *'edhah*, and *ecclesia* for *qahal*. Like *qahal* it is rarely used absolutely in a technical sense but normally with the qualifying genitive 'of the Lord' or 'of Israel', expressed or understood. The phrase '*ecclesia* of the Lord' acquires the same theological content as Heb. '*qahal* of Yahweh'. In popular Hellenistic Jewish usage '*synagoge*' acquired the more restricted meaning of the local Jewish community assembled for worship and thence the building used for such assembly. *Ecclesia* seems never to have undergone this development, but to have retained its theological connotation. This is probably the consideration which led the early Gk.-speaking Christians to adopt the term *ecclesia* to designate the reconstituted, Messianic, people of God.

THE GOSPELS

Ecclesia occurs three times, once in Matt. 16.18 and twice in Matt. 18.17. The latter, if an authentic saying of Jesus, must refer to a local Jewish community, and is therefore irrelevant for the origin of the specifically Christian use of *ecclesia*. If a Church rule put into the mouth of Jesus (so Streeter, *Four Gospels*, p. 258), it is irrelevant for the teaching of Jesus himself on the *ecclesia* in its Christian sense.

In Matt. 16.18 *ecclesia* clearly refers to the future Christian community. The authenticity of this saying has been widely questioned, but the tendency of most recent critical scholarship is to vindicate it. See K. L. Schmidt in *TWNT*, III, pp. 522ff., and *Die Kirche des Urchristentums*, also Linton, *Das Problem der Urkirche*, and Liechtenhan, *Die Urchristliche Mission*. The arguments of these critics are conveniently summarized for English readers by Lowther Clarke, *Divine Humanity*, pp. 158–63, and Flew, *Jesus and His Church*, Ch. IV. If this saying is authentic, it is unlikely that Jesus used the Gk. *ecclesia*. Schmidt suggests Aramaic *kenushta*, which, though it meant primarily a local Jewish community, might connote the 'Messianic remnant' which Jesus came to call out of the Israel of the Old Covenant, thereby reconstituting it as the eschatological community which will enter the Kingdom of God or the Age to come.

Although *ecclesia* does not occur elsewhere in the Gospels, the Messianic community appears under other designations. It is the 'flock' of Matt. 26.31, the 'little flock' of Luke 12.32 (see Flew, *op. cit.*, pp. 53f.); the 'twelve' who are the nucleus of the community. Jesus calls himself the 'Son of Man', and 'if Jesus called himself the Messiah in the sense of Dan. 7, it throws new light on his foundation of his Church. The Danielic Son of Man is more than an individual figure, he is the representative of the "people", the "saints of the Most High", whose self-appointed task is to represent and embody this people of God, the ecclesia.' (Schmidt, *TWNT*, III, p. 525.) The case has been argued even more strongly by Manson (*Teaching of Jesus*, pp. 227–36; but in view of the Book of Enoch his arguments are by no means certain; see Flew, *op. cit.*, p. 75). The arguments of Schweitzer and others that he cannot have intended to found a Church because he anticipated an immediate End are irrelevant because *ecclesia* in NT usage is itself an eschatological term—the community which is promised the Kingdom of God (see Flew, *op. cit.*, Ch. I).

ACTS

Ecclesia is first used of the Christian community which had been gathered at Jerusalem by the preaching of the apostles (Acts 5.11, 8.1,3). This community consisted of those who, with the Apostles, had accepted the belief that Jesus was the Messiah, had been baptized and had received the forgiveness of sins and the gift of the Holy Ghost (Acts 2.37–41). They continue at first as a sect within Judaism, attending the Temple, but, unlike the unbelieving Jews, they are the true, eschatological community, which as such has already received the Spirit of the Messiah. This is why *ecclesia* rather than *synagoge* is the designation of this community. The prime fact about it is not that it is a local assembly, but that it is the people of God who are heirs of the promises. This *ecclesia* is continuous with the people of the OT, who are also, as in LXX, called *ecclesia* (Acts 7.38).

As Christianity spreads from Jerusalem outwards, *ecclesia* acquires two distinguishable, but closely connected meanings. It is used in the sing. in the sense of a local Christian community, as it had in the earlier chapters been applied to the original church at Jerusalem, 11.26, 13.1, 14.27, 15.3 (Antioch in Syria), 18.22 (Caesarea), and 20.17 (Ephesus). It can also be used in the pl. of a number of such local Christian communities, as in 15.41, 16.5. But the word can also be used in a wider sense in the sing. of the 'whole church' as far as it then existed in Judaea, Galilee and Samaria (9.31). And see esp. 20.28, where, though reference is primarily to the Church in Ephesus which the bishop-presbyters are to tend, the qualifying clause 'which he hath purchased with his own blood' clearly points beyond the Church at Ephesus, so that the whole passage might be paraphrased 'feed that local embodiment of the universal church which Christ purchased'. 'It is not that the *ecclesia* is divided into *ecclesiai*. It is not that the *ecclesiai* are added up to make the *ecclesia*. Rather, the *ecclesia* is to be found in the places named' (K. L. Schmidt, *op. cit.*, p. 506).

PAULINE EPISTLES

First, Paul uses as Acts of separate local Christian communities both in sing. and pl.

Singular, of the church in a particular city (Cenchreae, Rom. 16.1; Corinth, I Cor. 1.2 and II Cor. 1.1; Thessalonica, I Thess. 1.1 and II Thess. 1.1; Laodicea, Col. 4.16). Of house-churches, I Cor. 16.19 (Aquila's and Priscilla's), Col. 4.15 (Nympha's) and Philem. 2 (Philemon's). Other phrases implying a local sense are: I Cor. 4.17 (every church), and Phil. 4.15 (no church). Cf. also I Tim. 3.5 and 5.16.

Plural. The churches of Judea (I Thess. 2.14, Gal. 1.22); Galatia (I Cor. 16.1); Asia (I Cor. 16.19); Macedonia (II Cor. 8.1); more generally 'all the churches of Christ' (Rom. 16.16); I Cor. 7.17 ('all the churches'); I Cor. 11.16 ('all the churches of God'); I Cor. 14.33 ('all the churches of the saints'); II Cor. 8.18,19,23 ('the churches').

A more restricted use appears in I Cor. 11.18, 14.19,23,28,34 (pl.), 35 of the local Christian community assembled together specifically for worship. Dix (*Shape of Liturgy*, p. 19) regards this use as primary. 'Until the third century the word "church" means invariably . . . the solemn assembly for the liturgy, and by extension those who take part in this.' This is true so long as we remember that the liturgical assembly is the local embodiment of the whole people of God. This is clear from I Cor. 1.2 and II Cor. 1.1, 'the church which is in Corinth', not 'the Corinthian church'. In I Cor. 15.9, Gal. 1.13, Phil. 3.6, Paul says he persecuted 'the church of God' which included other local manifestations of the one Church besides that at Jerusalem. In I Cor. 12.28, he speaks of the universal Church, susceptible of local embodiment, just after he has for the first time expounded the theme of the Christian community as the Body of Christ (I Cor. 12.12–27). In Eph. and Col. this theme is further developed. Christ is the Head of the Church which is his body (Eph. 1.22, 5.23, Col. 1.18,24), while the cognate metaphor of the Church as the spouse of Christ is elaborated in Eph. 5.23–32; cf. II Cor. 11.2 for the germ of this idea (cf. Rev. 21.2, 9, 22.17). See articles BODY and MARRIAGE, and cf. Chavasse, *The Bride of Christ*.

The roots of this developed doctrine of the Church lie in the quite casual and unselfconscious designation of the Christian community in its local embodiments as the 'Church *of God*' (see esp. I Cor. 1.2 and II Cor. 1.1, and cf. Acts 20.28—a genuine Pauline reminiscence?), and in the further specification that the Church of God is the 'church of God *in Christ*', I Thess. 2.14; cf. Gal. 1.22 (in Christ) and Rom. 16.16 ('of Christ'). Paul does not speak of a Christian church or congregation side by side of other churches, Jewish or pagan, but of the assembly *of God in Christ*. The Church is the Messianic community. It is not an assembly of men initiated by their own volition, it originates in the redemptive act of God in Christ and lives through its unity with the Messiah in his death and resurrection and through the indwelling of his Spirit. The doctrines of the Body and Spouse bring out the implications of this earlier conception.

The Pastoral Epistles add nothing except that I Tim. 3.15 calls the *ecclesia* 'the house of God'. The metaphor is already implicit in the genuine Pauline Epistles, which speak of the 'edifying' or 'building up' of the Church.

REST OF NT

Hebrews uses *ecclesia* twice, Heb. 2.12 (RV margin, 'church'; text 'congregation'). This is a quotation from LXX, Ps. 21.23=Heb. Ps. 22.22. The original referred to the old Israel. Heb. reapplies it to the new. Heb. 12.23 speaks of 'heavenly Zion' as the 'general assembly' (*paneguris*) and 'church' (*ecclesia*) of the firstborn. If *ecclesia* is here used in its technical sense=the Messianic community, it is the only example in NT of 'Church' used for the Church triumphant in heaven. Other critics hold that *ecclesia* here is non-technical, and=a festive assembly, almost a synonym for *paneguris* (so Schmidt, *TWNT*, III, p. 516). Rev. uses *ecclesia* 20 times, sing. and pl. of a local Christian community.

PARALLEL EXPRESSIONS

The Messianic community is designated by other terms than *ecclesia*. There is a whole group of passages where OT expressions applied to Israel are transferred to the *ecclesia*:

Gal. 6.16, Israel of God; cf. Rom. 9.6, and see JACOB.

Gal. 3.29, seed of Abraham.

Jas. 1.1, twelve tribes of the dispersion; cf. I Pet. 1.1.

I Pet. 2.5, spiritual house; cf. I Tim. 3.15 and see above.

I Pet. 2.5,9–10, elect race, royal priesthood, holy nation, people of possession, people of God.

Especially important are those passages which speak of the Church as the Temple (I Cor. 3.16,17, II Cor. 6.16, Eph. 2.21); as the olive (Rom. 11.17*b*–24); and of Messiah and his people as vine and branches (John 15.1–8). All these parallel terms bring out the continuity and also the eschatological renewal of the Old Israel in the Christian *ecclesia*. There are only three instances of *ecclesia* in the classical Gk. profane sense of the *assembly* of citizens in a Gk. city state, Acts 19.32,39,41.

SUMMARY

'The Church in NT is never triumphant, always militant. The Church triumphant would be identical with the Kingdom of God, and therefore no longer *ecclesia*. The NT knows no distinction between a visible and an invisible church. The Christian community is as visible and as bodily as the individual Christian. The fact that a number of separate local communities grew together gradually as an organization creates the impression of a development from separate local churches to one universal Church. But this impression is not decisive. The important fact is that the local congregation was conscious of itself as the representative of the universal church' (K. L. Schmidt, *TWNT, op. cit.*, p. 537).

R. H. FULLER

CIRCUMCISION *v.* ABRAHAM, COVENANT, SEAL

CITY

The equivocal attitude of the Bible towards that culminating point of human social organization, the city, constitutes a good example of the biblical dialectical point of view. On the one hand, a city may be a lovely and noble place: the earthly Jerusalem is to be God's dwelling-place and the joy of the devout Israelite (e.g. Pss. 122, 137); it has often been noted that the Bible-story begins in a garden and ends in a city—the New Jerusalem coming down from heaven (Rev. 21). On the other hand, cities may become the habitation of all that is vile, oppressive and horrible in human life: various cities in the Bible become symbols of different aspects of human depravity—Sodom and Gomorrah and the 'Cities of the Plain' (Gen. 18, 19), Nineveh, Babylon (used as a symbol for Rome in I Pet. 5.13, Rev. 16.19, 17.5, 18.10,21). But the chief interest is centred in Jerusalem itself, the city which never realized its high possibility and promise, yet remained the 'type' or symbol of heaven itself —'Jerusalem which is above' (Gal. 4.26). It is significant that the writer to the Hebrews thinks of the 'social joys' of heaven in terms of a city 'whose architect and maker is God' (Heb. 11.10,16). The earthly Jerusalem symbolizes the redemption that is to come, yet she herself always stands under judgment—whether it be that of Jeremiah and the prophets, or that of the Messiah himself (cf. the Barren Fig-tree, Mark 11.12ff., 13.2). The attitude of Jesus, loving Jerusalem but weeping over its sins and fate (Luke 19.41–4), is the supreme expression of the equivocal biblical attitude towards the achievement and failure of human civilization; this attitude had already been foreshadowed in the myth of the Tower of Babel in Gen. 11.1–9, in which man's inability to build for himself a stable and intrinsically valuable secular civilization is clearly depicted. The myth also explains the varieties of human languages as being in some sense the result of human sinfulness; and the Pentecost-story of Acts 2 shows how in the new divine society, the Church of Christ, a new and universal language of the Spirit is able to undo the effects of man's Babel contumacy, as he listens, not to the boasting of his own secular achievements, but to the preaching of the wonderful works of God.

A. R.

CLEAN *v.* UNCLEAN

CLOUD *v.* PRESENCE

COLLECTION *v.* FELLOWSHIP

COMFORTER *v.* SPIRIT, esp. IX(*d*)

COMMAND

This word, its derivatives, and its associates (*v.* LAW, COMMANDMENT, STATUTE, ORDINANCE) must be understood in reference to the personal activity by which God exercises authority over all things. The universe and its inhabitants exist by the command of God (Ps. 33.9); history is providentially controlled, for God by his command is able to give or withhold in his good pleasure (Lev. 25.21); and the ultimate purpose for which this effective control is exercised is to create a community which, in all the detail of its life, will show the characteristics of the people of God, and thus bring credit to him. The Bible discriminates between the many forms in which the command of God reaches men, making them subject to his claim as responsible personal beings. It exhibits the complete significance of this event. But what is implied by this range of words can only be properly grasped by those who hold firmly to the thought of God's concrete act of commanding.

The command of God is taken to be the underlying principle of all creaturely being. It is an ever-present element in the Word of God, and the biblical testimony to it is co-extensive with its testimony to the Word. The

Bible's chief concern is with the communication of the Word of God to men, an activity which it exhibits by reference to the covenant (*q.v.*) God makes with mankind. The covenant exists on the twofold basis of gospel and command: a declaration of the act of God by which it has been initiated, and a declaration of the obligations for which man is now responsible before God. In the OT the covenant is offered to Israel in circumstances where, for its fruition, immediate and perfect obedience to the command is necessary on the part of every member of the community (Deut. 5.27–30). To this end, Israel was made peculiarly aware of the command as the Law given through Moses (*q.v.*). In the NT the fruition of the covenant is assured by the perfect, representative, and sacrificial obedience of Jesus Christ, in virtue of which God exercises commanding grace (*q.v.*) over man's actions and decisions. That for which man is now responsible before God is 'that ye believe on him whom he hath sent' (John 6.28,29). The Law, the Commandments, etc., regarded as historical manifestations or products of the fundamental activity under discussion here, must still be respected as valid pointers to the command (Matt. 5.17–20) until the day when the new creation is revealed in glory. But Christians must not fall into the error of Judaism and identify the command of God with any of these manifestations or products.

The complementary term for command is promise; and this pair of terms should not be confused with the other complementary pair 'law-gospel', whose significance arises in a slightly different context. The element of promise is present in law, just as the element of command is present in gospel. In the Bible, however, and in theology, the term law is sometimes used to denote the more fundamental reality of command (*v.* LAW).

The command of God is always the action of the one gracious God upon man's life, determining that life in accordance with the divine purpose. The action of the commanding God has a constant character and direction, and the various manifestations of his command, though they are not to be understood as literal prescriptions to be followed slavishly (Matt. 23.23, 25.31ff., Gal. 5.13–14), indicate the reality of God's present rule. The command itself applies more concretely and definitely to the actual decisions of every man's life than would be possible were it to be identified with any general rules or prescriptions. From the words of Jesus (Mark 12.29–31), echoed by Paul (Gal. 5.13,14), it is clear that the effect of the command is to bind man with God and with his neighbour in a relation of love, and to determine his life through the duties which flow from love. The significance of the various codes which express the command, for the fulfilment of man's responsibility in face of the command, is discussed elsewhere (*v.* LAW-CODES).

W. A. WHITEHOUSE

COMMANDMENT

This term, the first in the familiar formula describing the legal code in Deuteronomy, 'the commandments, the statutes, and the judgments', has a fairly clear significance in comparison with other legal terms. It means an edict or decree from a person possessing authority. The Heb. word which it translates has one natural equivalent in Gk., *entolē*, so there is genuine continuity of meaning throughout the Bible. It is often used in a general sense to denote a charge given by a divine or by a human authority. Sometimes it refers to any particular instance of God's command, or any precept having divine authority. In such cases, a deliberate reference is intended to the source, in the personal authority of God, from which the charge in question arises.

In the NT (Matt. 5.17ff., Mark 10.19), and in Christian theology, the term is used with special reference to the Decalogue, or Ten Commandments (Exod. 20.1–17, Deut. 5.6–21). This can almost certainly be traced in the Deuteronomic formula, and perhaps in the Code of Holiness, for the grouping of phrases in Lev. 26.14,15 may indicate that obedience to statutes and judgments is the concrete form of fulfilling the more fundamental commandments which are the *sine qua non* of the covenant relation. Paul's phrase 'the law of commandments in ordinances' (Eph. 2.15) can be taken to mean that the ordinances developed in Judaism represent one way of interpreting the more fundamental demand. The term 'commandments' carries with it in its specialized use the suggestion of an explicit formulation of God's command which is inalienable and binding on all men. And that formulation has come to be identified with the Decalogue. Is there a basis for this use of the term within the Bible itself?

The OT places the history of Israel within a setting which is universal. The patriarchal and Mosaic covenants were made for a limited purpose, with one race, in order that the purpose of God, begun with Adam and expressed in the covenant with Noah, might be fulfilled. At some stage of Israel's history, it would seem to have been a matter of importance that the command of God to man as such be discriminated from the special command to Israel. The relation between the Commandments and all other codes is discussed in this context in Deut. 5 and 6. The

Commandments are delivered by the voice of the Lord direct to the people. Provision is made for other charges to be given indirectly, but these lack the marks of permanence and universality which are seen in the Ten Words. In Deut. 13.1–5 and 18.9–22, it is made clear that legitimate modifications of Israel's religious and social life may take place, but only within the covenant whose framework is safeguarded precisely by the fundamental Commandments.

The Christian Church, faced with the question of how relevant for its own life is the witness given by the OT to the command of God, pointed eventually to the Decalogue as the *sine qua non* of life within the new covenant. In I Tim. 1.8–11, the particular evils which it is the office of 'the law' to restrain are specified in an order corresponding to the Ten Commandments, 'according to the gospel of the glory of the blessed God' (cf. also Rom. 13.8–10). Influenced probably by a right interpretation of Deuteronomy, the Church conceived God's action with all mankind as a personal action with men who are already in covenant with him. Human status is inconceivable apart from this primeval covenant. The fullness of God's action has been made explicit within the special tradition of Israel and the Church, and that includes explicit publication of the terms of this primeval covenant in the Decalogue.

This leads to the further point that the Decalogue may be interpreted as a promulgation by divine positive law of obligations of which man as such is aware, naturally though obscurely (*v.* LAW; also, generally, LAW-CODES; COMMAND, STATUTE).

W. A. WHITEHOUSE

COMMON *v.* FELLOWSHIP

COMMUNION *v.* FELLOWSHIP

COMPANION *v.* FELLOWSHIP

COMPANY *v.* FELLOWSHIP

CONCUBINE *v.* MARRIAGE

CONCUPISCENCE *v.* DESIRE

CONDEMN, CONDEMNATION

There are two uses of the verb. The first is of final condemnation and judgment (*q.v.*), and this is the regular significance of the noun. The second is the milder sense of a verdict given against a man, either in the courts by the judges or in the common judgment of men. In Deut. 25.1 the reference is definitely juridical. Two men come to the judges in order that a dispute may be settled. The judges 'shall justify the righteous, and condemn the wicked', that is, they shall give the verdict in favour of the man who is in the right and against the man who is in the wrong. In Isa. 50.8f. the scene of judgment is the world of affairs. The Servant of the Lord maintains that God will vindicate him in the future and that no adversary will be able to humiliate him as in the past. In Matt. 12.7 the reference is to adverse judgments which men wrongly make concerning each other.

N. H. S.

CONFESS, CONFESSION

In the OT both the verb and the noun usually refer to the open acknowledgment of sin, whether by the individual or by the community. Such confession brought God's forgiveness: 'I acknowledged my sin unto thee, and mine iniquity have I not hid: I said, I will confess my transgressions unto the Lord; and thou forgavest the iniquity of my sin' (Ps. 32.5; cf. also Prov. 23.13). Confession of sin to God necessarily involved acknowledgment of him as the God to be worshipped and served: 'When thy people Israel be smitten down before the enemy, because they have sinned against thee; if they turn again to thee, and confess thy name, and pray and make supplication unto thee in this house: then hear thou in heaven, and forgive the sin of thy people Israel' (I Kings 8.33f.). This acknowledgment of God naturally passed into praise and thanksgiving, and the same Heb. word which is translated 'confession' in Josh. 7.19 and Ezra 10.11 is elsewhere translated 'praise' (e.g. Ps. 42.4) or 'thanksgiving' (e.g. Ps. 100.4); very often it has the concrete meaning of a thank-offering (e.g. II Chron. 29.31) or sacrifice of thanksgiving (e.g. Lev. 7.12f.).

In the NT also the verb is used of confession of sins, but only some 5 times, Matt. 3.6, Mark 1.5, Acts 19.18, Jas. 5.16, and I John 1.9. As in the OT, such confession is assured of God's forgiveness (I John 1.9). But oftener it means to acknowledge, admit, declare, that something is so (John 1.20, Acts 24.14, Heb. 11.13, I John 4.2f.). In Matt. 7.23, I Tim. 6.12, Tit. 1.16, the AV uses 'profess' instead of 'confess' to render the same Gk. verb. A special development of this meaning is, to make a profession of faith, as in Phil. 2.11, 'that every tongue should confess that Jesus Christ is Lord'. Rom. 10.9 ought to be trans. similarly 'if thou shalt confess with thy mouth, "Jesus, is Lord"'; this was probably the earliest baptismal creed of the Church. This is referred to in I Tim. 6.12, 'and didst confess the good confession in the sight of many witnesses' (RV). In the same passage, vs. 13, Jesus himself is said to have 'witnessed the good confession' before Pontius Pilate. Other forms of the Christian confession of faith are that Jesus is the Son of God (I John 4.15) and the Christ (John 9.22). In John 12.42 the meaning is probably 'they did not confess *it*', i.e. that they believed on Jesus, as in RV text, rather than 'confess him', as in AV, RV margin; cf. Acts 23.8, 'the Pharisees confess both', i.e. acknowledge both doctrines. It is only in one saying of Jesus himself that 'confess' is used with a personal object, 'Everyone therefore who shall confess me before men, him will I also confess before my Father in heaven' (Matt. 10.32; cf. Luke 12.28); the Gk. here is unidiomatic (lit. confess in me, in him), but the meaning is made sufficiently clear by the contrast with 'deny me' (him) in the next verse. The same meaning is expressed slightly differently in Rev. 3.5, 'I will confess his name before my Father'.

In Heb. 3.1, 4.14, 10.23 'confession' (RV; AV, profession) comes very near to meaning simply 'our religion'. The precise meaning of a rather cumbrous phrase in II Cor. 9.13, 'the obedience of your confession unto the gospel of Christ' (RV), is uncertain, but the noun confession (used only here by Paul) seems to have the active sense of the making of a profession of faith, or, more generally, the acceptance of the Christian religion.

The AV rendering of the quotation from Ps. 18.49 in Rom. 15.9, 'I will confess to thee', is certainly misleading if not actually wrong; the RV rightly changes this to 'I will give praise to thee'—the wording might well have been made to agree with that in the psalm, 'I will give thanks to thee'. (Also *v.* THANK.)

J. Y. CAMPBELL

CONFIRM

This word is used only in a general sense (=strengthen, establish) in the NT, e.g. Acts 14.22, 'confirming the souls of the disciples'. It is not used in connexion with the laying on of hands (*q.v.*).

R. R. W.

CONQUER *v.* VICTORY

CONSCIENCE

The Gk. word rendered 'conscience' (and etymologically similar to the Latin *conscientia*) signifies properly 'co-knowledge', a second reflective consciousness which a man has alongside his original consciousness of an act. This second consciousness is readily personified, as in Rom. 2.15, 9.1.

The developed idea of conscience is absent alike from cl. Gk. philosophy and from the OT. For both, actions could be judged by reference to an external authority, that of the City State or that of the Mosaic Law. This is not to deny the practical activity, in individuals, of what we call 'conscience' today. The Hebrews regarded it as the work of the 'heart', e.g. I Sam. 24.5, II Sam. 24.10, Job. 27.6: 'David's heart smote him'; 'my heart doth not reproach me for any of my days' (RV marg.). But the presence of an external authority made the developed idea of a second consciousness unnecessary.

In the Hellenistic world, however, where Jew and Greek met and exchanged ideas in the last three centuries B.C., a growing individualism changed the position. 'Conscience' appears in Menander, in Cicero and in the Stoics. The Gk. version uses the word in rendering *madda'* (thought) in Eccles. 10.20, and one reading of Ecclus. 42.18 gives 'The Most High knoweth every conscience (inner thought)'. Wisd. 17.11 is explicit: 'Wickedness . . . being pressed hard by conscience, always forecasteth the worst.' This brings us to the threshold of the NT and the distinctively Christian use of the word.

It is absent from the Gospels (John 8.9, AV, 'convicted by their conscience', is rejected by RV as a gloss), though the *idea* appears in such a passage as Matt. 6.22–3: 'the light that is in thee'. But it is frequent in the Pauline Epp., Heb. and I Pet.; and also occurs in two Pauline speeches in Acts. (I Cor. 8.7, AV, 'with conscience of the idol' is rightly replaced in RV by a quite different, though rather similar, Gk. word, thus giving 'being used until now to the idol'.)

'Conscience' in these writings belongs to all men alike (cf. Rom. 2.15). For the most part it bears witness to, or pronounces judgment upon, actions already performed; e.g. Acts 24.16, Rom. 9.1, Heb. 9.14, I Pet. 3.16,21. But it is too much to say (Lake and Cadbury on Acts 23.1, *Beginnings of Christianity*, IV, p. 286) that the idea of 'a guide for conduct is not included in the term'; cf. Rom. 13.5 and still more I Cor. 8.10, where the reference is surely future. Conscience covers the whole of life, not merely the specifically 'religious' duties, but civil obligations (Rom. 13.5) and matters of purely 'private' choice (I Cor. 10.25–9). A man who accepts its arbitrament and returns in penitence when he has fallen away from its standards may claim a 'good' conscience (Acts 23.1, I Tim. 1.5,19, Heb. 13.18, I Pet. 3.16,21); 'pure' (I Tim. 3.9, II Tim. 1.3); 'void of offence toward God and men' (Acts 24.16). On the other hand, the conscience may be imperfectly informed (I Cor. 8.7–12), or even, through persistent rebellion, defiled and seared (I Tim. 4.2, Tit. 1.15). Finally, I Pet. 2.19 (in its Greek form a unique phrase) establishes the point that the final authority of conscience rests upon God's Will. 'It is at this point that the concept becomes specifically religious. . . . The point is one of importance in an age when conscience is often invoked as though it meant no more than a personal prejudice obstinately held, e.g. by anti-vaccinationists. St. Peter's phrase guards the word from becoming thus emptied of its true content' (E. G. Selwyn, *First Ep. of St. Peter, ad loc.*).

J. P. THORNTON-DUESBERY

CONSECRATION (OF PRIESTS) *v.* SACRIFICE III(*d*)

CONSENT

As a verb this renders various verbs with the meaning 'be willing'. Once it stands for *shama*', listen. In Acts 8.1 it signifies 'approve'. The substantival use needs no explanation. The phrase 'with one consent', Ps. 83.5, is lit. 'with one heart', and in Zeph. 3.9, it is 'with one shoulder'. In Hos. 6.9, however, read with RV, 'toward Shechem' (not AV, 'by consent', as in Zeph. 3.9).

E. C. B.

CONTRIBUTION *v.* FELLOWSHIP

CONTRITE

Occurs in EVV only at Ps. 34.18, 51.17, Isa. 57.15 and 66.2. See REPENT.

CONVERSATION (AV only)

This word is found only in AV, where it always bears the archaic sense of 'behaviour', 'conduct'. In the OT it occurs twice in Pss. (37.14, 50.23) for Heb. *derek* (way). In the NT Epistles it represents *anastrophe* (behaviour, manner of life), Gal. 1.13, Eph. 4.22, etc.; *politeuma* (citizenship, commonwealth), Phil. 1.27; and *tropos* (manner), Heb. 13.5. In every case RV substitutes a more up-to-date rendering.

CONVERSION, CONVERT *v.* REPENT

CORNER-STONE

This phrase occurs only twice in the OT, Job 38.6 and Isa. 28.16; in both passages it is used figuratively, and so its literal meaning cannot be determined with certainty and precision. But a corner-stone would appear to be a stone in the foundation of a building. This meaning fits the use of the Isaiah passage in I Pet. 2.6; here Christ is the corner-stone of that spiritual house which is the Christian Church, just as in I Cor. 3.11 he is said to be the foundation of it. In the next verse, I Pet. 2.7, a quotation from Ps. 118.22, 'The stone which the builders rejected is become the head of the corner', is combined with a phrase from Isa. 8.14, 'a stone of stumbling and a rock of offence'. It is doubtful whether the NT writer was concerned whether his OT quotations were altogether congruous with one another or not, yet it seems possible that a stone at the corner of the foundation of a building might on occasion be a stumbling-stone. So he may have taken 'the head of the corner' to be the same thing as a 'corner-stone'. It is, however, almost certain that its proper meaning, and the meaning which it has in the psalm, was different; it was the top-stone, or coping stone, which completed the whole building, 'the head stone' of Zech. 4.7. Such a stone was both conspicuous and important, and would be carefully selected and finely wrought. In Ps. 118 'the head of the corner' is Israel, which, despised by other peoples, has nevertheless been chosen by God for the chief place in his building. Our Lord is reported to have applied this passage to himself (Mark 12.10=Matt. 21.42=Luke 20.17), and later Peter says of him, 'This is the stone which was rejected by you, the builders, which became the head of the corner' (Acts 4.11). He had been rejected by the religious leaders in Israel, but God had chosen him to be the head of a new Israel.

The Gk. word which is used to translate 'corner-stone' in Isa. 28.16 (but not in Job 38.6) was long supposed to be a purely biblical word, coined specially for this passage, so that this determined its meaning. If so, it ought to be translated, in I Pet. 2.6, 'corner-stone', not 'chief corner-stone' (as in the EVV, which in this follow the Vulgate); it is, moreover, exceedingly doubtful whether this is really a possible meaning of the word taken by itself. Recently it has been pointed out that the word is used in at least one other passage, not dependent on Isa. 28.16, in which it plainly means, not a foundation-stone, but a top-stone, i.e. very much what 'head of the corner' means. It is therefore possible that the Gk. translators, rightly or wrongly, took this to be the meaning in Isa. 28.16, as did the Syriac translators, who render the phrase 'head of the wall'. If the refs. to the foundation make it difficult to accept this as the true meaning in the Isaiah passage, it may still be the meaning intended in Eph. 2.20, the only other passage in the NT in which the word occurs. There the foundation of the 'holy temple' which is the Christian Church is said to be 'the apostles and prophets', and Christ Jesus himself is the 'corner-stone' by which the whole building is held together. If in such a figure Christ is not to be, as in I Cor. 3.11, the foundation, it would seem that the only other part of the building which he might fitly be said to be is the coping-stone, which completes the whole. And such a coping-stone may be said to hold together the whole building as no other stone, whether at a corner or elsewhere, can be said to do. But it must be remembered that no such figure is ever perfectly exact in its application or fully adequate to express what Christ is in and to the Church.

J. Y. CAMPBELL

CORRECT, CORRECTION, REPROVE, REPROOF, REBUKE

These words are all used of God's attitude to sinners, and they are progressively stronger and more ruthless. The word 'correct' is almost an exact synonym of 'chasten', 'chastise' (*q.v.*), for though chastening can be severe (Jer. 30.14, Ps. 118.18), yet correction can be 'in measure' (Jer. 30.11, 46.28). The word 'reproof' is used frequently in Prov. in company with the word 'instruction', so that it is largely used of that reproof which is designed to discipline and correct. On the other hand, it is used of bringing disaster where there is no intention of producing repentance. For example, 'Yea, he reproved kings for their sakes' (I Chron. 16.21) where the reference is to the complete destruction of the two kings of the Amorites. The idea of condemnation is more prominent in the word 'rebuke', and is used of God rebuking the heathen (Ps. 9.5), the Red Sea (Ps. 106.9) and Satan (Zech. 3.2).

In the NT the word 'correction' is rare, being used once (Heb. 12.9) for parental discipline and once for 'being set right' by the admonitions and warnings of Scripture (II Tim. 3.16). Similarly, the words 'reprove' and 'reproof' are rare in the NT, being used either as a synonym for 'correction' (II Tim. 3.16) or for being told quite clearly that one is in the wrong (Luke 3.19 and 5 times elsewhere). The NT use of 'rebuke' is mixed, either in the mild sense of contradict (cf. Peter contradicting Jesus, Mark 8.32), or in the stronger sense of reprove, condemn (Tit. 1.13, 2.15). (Also *v.* CHASTEN, PUNISH.)

N. H. SNAITH

COUNSEL

OT: The word in its biblical usage carries the meaning 'advice' as in common parlance. There is, however, a distinctively Hebraic mark upon it which is worth noting. When Hebrews gave or received advice, there was no mutual recognition of a 'take it or leave it' principle. Counsel was thought expressed in words, and awaiting its further translation into action; it could not be left, as it were, 'in the air'. There was a certain objectivity in it. Some account needs here to be taken of the whole primitive conception of the objectivity of the spoken word (cf. Isa. 55.11 and see, further, WORD). For the close connexion between counsel and thought, cf. Ps. 33.10, noting the parallelism between 'counsel of the nations' and 'thoughts of the peoples'; cf. also vs. 11. When counsel has been acted on, it may be said to 'stand' (Ps. 33.11); or to be 'filled' (Ps. 20.4); or 'completed', made whole (Isa. 44.26). Alternatively, it may be 'defeated' (lit., broken; cf. II Sam. 15.34, Ps. 33.10, where the verb *parar* means this, rather than 'bring to nought' as AV and RV read; it is also used of breaking a covenant); or 'swallowed up' (Isa. 19.3, where read RV margin). Yahweh can always do this (Isa. 8.10, Ps. 33.10, Jer. 19.7, where we have the verb 'make void', AV and RV, lit. 'empty').

To reject counsel is to 'shame' it (Ps. 14.6) or 'despise' it (Ps. 107.11), i.e. the one who gave it. The ideal ruler of Isaiah's vision is to be equipped by the spirit of God with counsel (Isa. 11.2, where the context clearly means good counsel, synonymous with wisdom, etc.); in fact, is to be a 'marvel of a counsellor' (Isa. 9.6). A messianic passage of Zechariah (6.13) speaks of a 'counsel of peace' between the 'Branch', i.e. Messiah, and the High Priest. (The ref. is probably to Zerubbabel and Joshua.) A prophet stands in the counsel of Yahweh (Jer. 23.18, using a rare word, *sod*, which means council chamber or group of advisers). For the same idea, cf. I Kings 22.19ff.

NT: The word counsel occurs less frequently in NT, and then mostly in the sense of advice. God's counsel is immutable (Heb. 6.17) and man's by implication is not (for this contrast, cf. TRUTH). Man's counsels, good and bad, are patent to God, who, as perfect Judge, 'makes them manifest' (I Cor. 4.4f.), i.e. God will ultimately reveal how much or how little praiseworthy are not only the actions of men, but even their inner life, 'the counsels (lit., wishes) of the hearts'. (The context of I Cor. 4 is dealing with the Christian minister, but the wider applicability is obvious.) St. Paul does not speak of God 'breaking' the counsels of men, as do the OT passages above considered, but of showing them up at their true value. But though no human counsel, however dark, is hidden from God, the divine counsels transcend human wisdom and remain inscrutable. See Rom. 11.33f. and cf. Isa. 40.14.

E. C. BLACKMAN

COUNTENANCE *v.* PRESENCE

COVENANT

The idea of c. is fundamental both to OT and NT. The religion of Israel has its origin in the c. under Moses, while Jesus came to initiate a New C. sealed by the c. sacrifice of his death. The Church named the two components of her Scriptures from the covenants they record, at least 'from the end of the second century' (B F. Westcott, *The Bible in the*

Church, p. 5); but the germ of later usage is found in II Cor. 3.14, and is indeed implicit in Exod. 24.7. The Hebrew word *berith* is translated *diathēkē* in LXX and NT, and *testamentum* in the Vulgate, particularly in Pss. and NT (though in other books *foedus*, *pactum* and *amicitia*); hence *testament* normally in Tyndale's NT translation. AV normally uses c. in OT and in all but 13 instances in NT; while RV almost invariably translates c. But *Testament* remains as the title of the components.

OT

(*i*) *Etymology of Berith.* Quell in *TWNT*, II, pp. 107–8, states that the attempt to expound the nature of *berith* from the etymology of the word has led neither to an unanimous nor a convincing issue. Of explanations offered he prefers that *berith* is the Heb. equivalent of the Assyrian *beritu*, 'bond' or 'fetter'. *N.B.* unique use of *masoreth* (tradition) with *berith* in Ezek. 20.37, with the meaning of 'bond'. (For discussions, see *TWNT*, *HDB*, I, p. 509, V, pp. 630–2, Cheyne, *Encyc. Bib.* I, cols. 928–9, A. Lods, *Israel*, p. 202.)

(*ii*) *Berith between Men or Tribes.* 'A covenant means artificial brotherhood, and has no place where the natural brotherhood of which it is an imitation already subsists' (W. R. Smith, *Religion of Semites*, p. 318; cf. J. Pedersen, *Israel*, I–II, p. 285). A c. may be between individuals (Gen. 21.27, 26.28, I Sam. 18.3); between husband and wife (Mal. 2.14); between tribes (I Sam. 11.1, Judg. 2.2, Exod. 23.32); between monarchs (I Kings 20.34); between a king and his people (II Kings 11.4, II Chron. 23). It creates rights and duties (II Sam. 9), but does not necessarily place the parties on an equal footing. It may be forced on the vanquished by a conqueror (I Kings 20.34). It may be sealed by gifts (Gen. 21.27, 24.42–8, I Sam. 25.5–35); by a handshake (Ezek. 17.18, Ezra 10.19, II Kings 10.15); by a kiss (I Sam. 10.1); by a common meal (Gen. 26.27–31, II Sam. 3.17–21, Ps. 41.9); by eating salt (Ezra 4.14, Num. 18.19, II Chron. 13.5); by a sacrificial meal (Gen. 31.44–6 [JE] 51–4 [E]); in a sacred place (I Sam. 23.18, II Sam. 5.3, II Kings 11.4, 23.3, Jer. 34.15,18; cf. J. Pedersen, *Israel*, I–II, pp. 263–310).

(*iii*) *Yahweh's Berith with Israel.* The history and religion of Israel presumes an historic covenant between Yahweh and Israel. Yet the origin of the idea of a c. between Yahweh and Israel is obscure. E. Meyer, *Die Israeliten und ihre Nachbarstämme*, found the origin in the cult of the Shechemite deity, Baal-berith, whose sanctuary in Shechem became a Yahwist sanctuary (Judg. 8.33, 9.4,46). This is the origin of the later Shechem covenant (Josh. 24.1–27) which is not easy to explain if the Horeb-Sinai covenant was in fact earlier. This theory has recently been argued afresh by C. A. Simpson in *The Early Traditions of Israel*, pp. 456, 647–9.

The dominant tradition, however, seems to imply that the Horeb-Sinai covenant is the original c. between Yahweh and Israel. It is to this c. that the prophets (Amos 3.1,2, Hosea 2.15, Jer. 7.22–6, 31.32, Ezek. 16.3–8,60, 23.1–8) look back. The character of this c. is succinctly stated by Jeremiah, 'I will be your God and ye shall be my people' (Jer. 7.23, 31.33). In the Exodus narratives Yahweh calls Moses, reveals his name to him (according to E), sends him to deliver Israel from Egypt (Exod. 3.1–14), and then, the deliverance accomplished, makes a c. with the Israelite confederation (Exod. 19.4–5) at the mount of God (Horeb in E followed by D; Sinai in J followed by P), which is the foundation of the religion of Israel (R. Kittel, *Religion of the People of Israel*, pp. 49–57, Lofthouse in Peake, *The People and the Book*, pp. 231–8, Lods, *Israel*, p. 314). A c. is sealed with sacrifice (Ps. 50.5). Yahweh's c. with Israel is sealed (Guillaume, *Prophecy and Divination*, p. 88, Kennett, *Church of Israel*, p. 104, R. Kittel, *op. cit.*, p. 48, Lods, *op. cit.*, p. 280) in E by blood on the altar and the people (Exod. 24.3–8), and in J by a sacrificial meal (Exod. 24.1,2,9–11).

J, who carries the knowledge of the name of Yahweh back to Seth (Gen. 4.26), tells of the c. between Yahweh and Abram being sealed by passing between divided animals (Gen. 15.17–18; cf. Jer. 34.18).

In P the c. is carried back to Noah (Gen. 9.8–17): 'the story stands as witness that God's covenant, though historically it was made with Israel, is applicable to the whole human race' (C. H. Dodd, *The Bible To-day*, p. 114). As a further extension of the same principle, we find the c. carried back to Adam in Ecclus. 17.12.

It is difficult to avoid the conclusion that the Horeb-Sinai c. was the original as it was certainly in the minds of the prophets the fundamental c. Here too was the nucleus that, expanded, became the Torah or Law. The covenant involved obedience to Yahweh's oracles (Exod. 15.25, 18.16,20, 24.7 [E], 34.10*a*, 14*b*,17–27 [J]). The primitive Decalogue, expanded into the Book of the Covenant (Exod. 20.22–23.33), was developed and revised in the Deuteronomic Code and the Holiness Code (Lev. 17–26), but all were ascribed to Moses. In D. the Horeb c. is emphasized (Deut. 4.13, 5.2ff.), but the promise to Abraham, and now also to Isaac and Jacob, is mentioned. The ten words, written on tables of stone (Exod. 31.18, 32.15,16 [E], 34.1,4 [J]) were placed in the ark, which in D. is called the ark of the covenant (Deut. 10.1–8). Thus c. begins to be almost a synonym for Torah or Law (Deut. 29.9–21; cf. Ps. 25.10, 50.16).

Yahweh is a God who initiates covenants (W. Eichrodt, *Theologie des Alten Testaments*) and they are his ordinances (*HDB*, V, p. 630*b*). Indeed, 'covenant making' is an attribute of Yahweh expressed as *hesed*, 'mercy' (N. H. Snaith, *Distinctive Ideas of OT*, pp. 94–130). So within the c. with Israel we find further covenants. The promise to David (II Sam. 7.11–13,16) is reinterpreted as a c. (II Sam. 23.5). The later covenants were reaffirmations in new situations of the original covenant (II Kings 11.17, 23.3, Neh. 10.28ff.).

The prophets sought to recall unfaithful Israel to faithfulness to the c. (Amos 3, Hosea 2, Jer. 7). Yahweh is a forgiving God (Jer. 31.34) who will restore the c. relationship (Zech. 8.8). The c. was interpreted as a marriage c. (Ezek. 16.8,60): Israel is the wife (Hos. 2.16, Jer. 3.4,8, Isa. 54.5); in the days of her virginity there was no sacrifice (Amos 5.25, Jer. 2.1–3, 7.22), for sacrifice is consummation (Hos. 2.15, 3.3–4), and sacrifice to other gods is adultery (Hos. 1–3, Exod. 34.14–16, Deut. 31.16, Jer. 3, Ezek. 16,23). Yahweh remains faithful to the marriage c. and restores Israel to the original relationship (Hos. 2.14–23, Jer. 3.1,14, Ezek. 16.60–3, Isa. 54.1–8, 61; cf. C. Chavasse, *Bride of Christ*, L. S. Thornton, *Common Life in Body of Christ*, pp. 223–4). But the prophets saw the danger of legalism implicit in the c. conception (Gen. 17.1–21 [P], Exod. 31.18, Deut. 4.13), and looked for a New C. with the law written in the heart (Hos. 2.19,20, Jer. 31.31–4, Ezek. 16.60–3, Isa. 61.8). It was to initiate this New C. foretold by Jeremiah that Jesus came, as his word over the cup at the Last Supper shows.

NT

While the c. conception seems to be present in the mind of Jesus in Luke 22.29f. (R. Otto, *Kingdom of God and Son of Man*, pp. 268, 289–95; against N. Flew, *Jesus and His Church*, p. 106), only at the Last Supper does Jesus explicitly speak of the New C.: 'This cup is the new covenant in my blood' (I Cor. 11.25; cf. Mark 14.24 [Luke 22.20]). J. Behm in *TWNT*, I, p. 136, contends that the Pauline form is the original one. Mark has changed the word over the cup to conform to the word over the bread (Exod. 24.8). 'The word in the Pauline form declares that the blood, i.e. the death, of Jesus seals the new *diathēkē*.' G. Dix, in *Shape of Liturgy*, p. 68, follows Behm. (For priority of Markan word, V. Taylor, *Jesus and His Sacrifice*, pp. 125–39, 203–6; of Lukan in sense of 22.29, R. Otto, *op. cit.*, p. 274.) The circumstances in which this unique word was spoken make it the key to Jesus' understanding of his mission (Behm, *op. cit.*, p. 137; against E. W. Barnes, *Rise of Christianity*, p. 288). The New C. is a correlative conception of the 'Kingdom of God' (*q.v.*). From this word over the cup arises the NT interpretation of the cross as sacrifice (G. Dix, *op. cit.*, pp. 74–7; against J. Klausner, *Jesus of Nazareth*, p. 329). Jesus' purpose to initiate the New C. through his sacrificial death finds its fulfilment in the pouring forth of the Spirit (Acts 1.4,5 2.14–18,38,39, 4.31, 19.1–6, Gal. 3.3,5, 4.6, 5.16–18,25). I Cor. 12–14 is a discussion of problems arising from the reality of spiritual gifts.

In Paul and Heb., the New C. is an ordinance of salvation from God. Covenants figure among the privileges of the old Israel (Rom. 9.4). The New C. brings forgiveness (Rom. 11.27, citing Isa. 59.21). It is as a minister of the New C. that Paul has confidence, and the New C. is spirit, not letter (II Cor. 3.6; cf. Jer. 31). The old c. signifies the content of the Law of Moses, which had a glory of its own such that it must be veiled to Jewish eyes, but that veil is done away in Christ (II Cor. 3.7–14). For Paul, there are two covenants, but one will of God, who is the end of the Law, the fulfilment of all promise (note one plural use: 'covenants of promise', Eph. 2.12—various reaffirmations to Israel of the promise to Abraham). Gal. 3.15ff. is typically Rabbinic exegesis, stressing c. with Abraham before the giving of the Law.

In Heb. Jesus is the mediator of the New C. (8.6, 9.15, 12.24) through his blood (9.12,14, 10.19,29, 12.24, 13.12,20) once offered (9.26,28), whereby the first c. and its ordinances (9.1–10), dedicated with blood by Moses (9.18–22) and annually renewed (9.25, 10.3) yet ineffective to take away sins (10.4), have been abolished (8.7,13). The New C. fulfils Jer. 31 (8.8–12, 10.16) and puts away sins (9.14,15,26, 10.17–18). Where in 9.16 the author uses the illustration of a testator, it is *ad hominem* and moves away from his real thought (Behm in *TWNT*, II, p. 134).

J. O. COBHAM

COVER

Apart from the ordinary literal meaning conveyed by the English word, discussion of this term is really a part of the meaning of sacrifice (*q.v.*). In the OT there are many examples of the use of a word in relation to sacrifice which has its root meaning, to cover or to appease. The sin offering and the guilt offering, which are post-exilic sacrifices, are offerings designed to 'cover' unwitting transgressions (cf. Job 1.5) and acts of ritual defilement (Lev. 16.33, Ezek. 43.26, II Chron. 29.24) or offerings where restitution is not possible. Through these appointed means (cf. Gen. 22.8) sin is covered so that it no longer stands as an obstacle between God and worshippers. In the passages quoted and in Lev. 1.4, Num. 15.25, the word has acquired the general meaning of 'make atonement', through the worshippers being covered by that offering which God regards as sufficient and satisfactory. In other contexts, where God is the subject, it is translated 'forgive' (Deut. 21.8, Ezek. 16.63), 'make expiation' (Deut. 32.43), 'pardon' (II Chron. 30.18, Ps. 78.38) or 'purge away' (Ps. 69.18, 79.9). In Lev. 16.30 the sacrifice of the day of atonement is 'to cleanse you', so that when God looks upon men he no longer sees their sin, which has been 'covered' by the appointed sacrifice, and accepts them to his favour. For a fuller treatment of this whole theme, *v.* under ATONE.

F. J. TAYLOR

COVET *v.* DESIRE

CREATE, CREATION, CREATOR *v.* GOD, GODS I, II, ADAM, WORK

CROSS

The English word has come to have a more restricted meaning than the Gk. which signifies an upright stake to which a victim could be bound or upon which he could be impaled, as well as the cross made of various shapes. In the NT, however, cross has the usual English meaning and does not indicate a stake. Most references are to the crucifixion of Jesus Christ. It was a punishment practised by the Phoenicians and the Persians and adopted by the Romans, but by them reserved for slaves and foreigners. Great indignation was excited when Roman citizens were crucified by Galla in Spain and Verres in Sicily. The normal Jewish mode of execution was by stoning (Lev. 20.2, Deut. 13.10, 17.5), though dead bodies were hanged to the accursed tree (Deut. 21.23). In Palestine crucifixion was frequently used by the Romans for the punishment of highway robbery, sedition or tumult, and the cross was a familiar sight in many places. Thus our Lord could use the familiar procedure of the closing stages of the career of a condemned criminal to describe one aspect of discipleship to himself (Mark 8.34, Matt. 16.24, Luke 9.23). In the NT two elements are particularly emphasized, the suffering involved (Heb. 2.9, I Pet. 4.13) and the shame (Heb. 12.4, 13.13). The shame was emphasized by the custom of compelling the victim to carry the cross or at least the transverse part of it to the place of execution (Mark 15.21, Matt. 27.32, Luke 23.26, John 19.17) and by his being stripped of his clothes. Further, to the Jew it was the public demonstration of servitude to the Roman overlord. Thus the crucifixion of Jesus, accomplished by the Jewish leaders through surrendering him to the Roman governor, publicly discredited him and brought him under the ancient curse on those who were hanged upon a tree (Gal. 3.13). In some passages the cross is referred to as the tree (Acts 5.30, 10.39, 13.29). Many of the early preachers, to whom the cross was the scene of a divine victory over the powers of evil (Col. 2.15), found that it was an offence (Gal. 5.11) alike to the Jew with his messianic hopes and to the Greek with his humanist culture (I Cor. 1.23–4). To the believer, the recollection of the ignominy and pain of the cross only served to intensify the realization of the depth of Christ's love for men (Eph. 3.18–19) and the profound meaning of his death as a voluntary submission to the demands of the moral law on behalf of sinners (Phil. 2.8). It was not merely that Christ had died but that he had died on the cross which caught the imagination and moved the will. So the cross became a brief designation of the saving work of Christ in reconciling (*q.v.*) God and man (Col. 1.20; cf. II Cor. 5.19) and men who hitherto had been kept at enmity by racial antagonisms (Eph. 2.16–18). The Gospel could be described as the word of the cross (I Cor. 1.18), the word which the cross itself preaches and which Paul resolved should be the touchstone of all his teaching (I Cor. 2.2). The apparent weakness of the cross was really a demonstration of the restrained power of divine love (II Cor. 13.4, I Cor. 1.24–5). The curse of the law which rested upon all who had not kept it in its entirety or had ignored it altogether (Gal. 3.13, Col. 2.14) was borne by Christ as the willing victim and in being nailed to the tree he took this curse right away. (*V.* also CURSE (ii).)

F. J. TAYLOR

CRUCIFY *v.* CROSS

CURSE

This art. is divided into three parts: (i) the general meaning of 'curse'; (ii) the curse attached to crucifixion (Gal. 3.13f.); and (iii) the curses pronounced upon enemies in the Psalms. For ACCURSED *v.* under DEVOTE.

(i) *The General Meaning of 'Curse'*. 'Curse' is the contrary of 'blessing'. As a word of blessing spoken in Jehovah's Name expresses (and also conveys) that which proceeds from his gracious favour—health, strength, wisdom, prosperity, success, and all that is comprehended under the word *shalom* (peace, *q.v.*), so a curse expresses (and also conveys) that which proceeds from his wrath—disease, ill-success, ruin, desolation, death. Because the two are felt to be parallel, the word *barakh*, bless, is sometimes used with the meaning of 'curse' (presumably a euphemism, to avoid the dreadful word): I Kings 21.10,13 (Naboth), Job 1.5,11, 2.5,9. The parallel reappears in Matt. 25.34,41. The primary word for 'curse' is *'arar*. It is used of the blessings and cursings to be pronounced respectively from Gerizim and Ebal upon obedience and disobedience to God's commands in Deut. 27. It is, however, Deut. 28 that deserves to be called the *locus classicus* for the ideas of the blessing and the curse, every variety of either being specified in vss. 1–14 and 15–68—the latter in the light of the judgment of God upon Israel in the exile. In II Kings 9.34 Jezebel is called 'this cursed woman' in virtue of the word of Jehovah pronounced by Elijah, of doom on king Ahab and his house, and on her, after the affair of Naboth (I Kings 21.21–4); the word 'curse' is not used in that passage, but a curse it was. Curse on disobedience to the Covenant, Jer. 11.3 and on disloyalty to God in general 17.5; cf. vs. 7. Among the other words, *qalal* is used of Shimei reviling David (II Sam. 16.5–13); of a man cursing his father or mother (Exod. 21.17), quoted Mark 7.10; and it is the word used of the curse attaching to every man hanged on a tree (Deut. 21.22f.). The word *cherem* ('devoted thing'), often rendered 'accursed' in AV, is treated under DEVOTE.

(ii) *The Curse attached to Crucifixion* (Gal. 3.8–14). When Caiaphas decided that Jesus must be crucified, there can be no doubt that his intention was to attach to him the curse of Deut. 21.22–3: 'he that is hanged (on a tree) is accursed of God', so that every Jew would regard it as demonstrated that this was not God's Blessed One but a blasphemous impostor on whom God had broken out, and would say 'Jesus is anathema' (cf. I Cor. 12.3). This decision involved much risk; Jesus must be condemned by the Sanhedrin first, and then by Pilate, and at both points the plan came near to failure. This shows that Caiaphas regarded the risk as worth taking; for if it had been a matter merely of getting rid of him, it would have been easy to have him murdered in the garden of Gethsemane. But the plan succeeded. Saul the Pharisee, with the rest, regarded the curse of crucifixion as resting on Jesus. He deals, therefore, with this point in Gal. 3.8–14. There had been God's promise to Abraham, that in him all nations should be blessed: this was the final term of God's purpose in history, that the Gentiles should be justified through faith (vs. 8). But then there was the Curse: God's wrath rested on the sinners who broke his commandments; here he quotes Deut. 27.26, and shows how this curse rests on all who are under 'the works of the Law' (vss. 10–12). Christ, who came to bear his people's sin, accepted this curse on himself; and it was worked out in the suffering and death which he bore. Thus there was indeed a Curse resting on the Crucified; he 'became a curse for us' in being hanged on a tree, according to Deut. 21.22–3 (vs. 13). But it was impossible that the Son of God, on whom the fullness of the divine Blessing rested, should be overwhelmed by the curse. Its effect exhausted itself in his death on the cross; and in dying he 'redeemed us from the curse of the Law', so that through his resurrection the Blessing of Abraham might be saved for the Gentiles, and the messianic gift of the Spirit be poured out upon them (vs. 14). (*V.* also CROSS.)

(iii) *The Curses pronounced upon Enemies in the Psalms*. In several psalms (notably 69, 109, but also many others, including such a psalm as 54) vengeance is invoked upon enemies, and prayer is made for all manner of evil things to happen to them. This appears to be, and in a real sense is, contrary to the teaching of our Lord that we should love our enemies and pray for those who would do us harm, to his example in praying for those who nailed him to the cross 'Father, forgive them', and to his act in giving his life as 'a ransom for many'. Hence these psalms are regularly held up as marking the contrast between the OT and the NT; and the traditional practice of the Church in using them in divine worship is widely condemned. The difficulty must not be evaded. There is an advance in NT on the teaching of OT: 'Ye have heard that it was said to them of old time . . . but I say unto you . . .' The question, however, is not a simple one. The following considerations need to be borne in mind:

(1) Jeremiah is without doubt one of the greatest of OT saints; and in the midst of his cruel sufferings for the cause of the Lord he breaks out into prayer for vengeance: 'Remember how I stood before thee to speak good for them. . . . Therefore deliver up their children to the famine, and give them over to the power of the sword' (Jer. 18.20f.; cf. 17.18). He appeals to the Lord's judgment (11.20), and his imprecations are upon the Lord's enemies, not personal enemies. Here it is necessary to be aware of the great danger which besets the servants of the Lord in all ages of simply identifying their cause with God's cause and their enemies with his enemies. If Jeremiah escaped this danger, it does not follow that all the psalmists escaped it; we, however, are not called to sit in judgment on them.

(2) But then who are the Lord's enemies? In early times it is assumed that Israel's enemies, such as Amalek and Moab, are the enemies of the Lord: in later times, the 'ungodly' who persecute the 'poor'. Yet the matter is not so simple; the prophets accuse Israel as a whole

of sin, and they also accuse themselves (Isa. 6.5). One of the words for 'sin' is *pasha*', to rebel; and in rebelling against the Lord Israel took sides against him, and the Lord 'their saviour' (Isa. 63.8) 'was turned to be their enemy, and himself fought against them' (vs. 10). The sin of man, and above all Israel's sin, must provoke his wrath.

(3) F. D. Maurice once spoke of the Bible as 'the book of the wars of the Lord'; and when we take a view of the OT as a whole, we see it as the story of the mighty conflict of the Lord God against all that in his world which opposes his will. In this whole conflict, the wars of Israel against Amalek and Moab, and the struggles of Jeremiah and the psalmists against overpowering enemies, appear as but episodes in the Lord's conflict, of which the climax is pictured in Isa. 59, where after a pathetic lament over the helplessness of his people, we read in vss. 15–18 how the Lord himself girds on his armour to fight his own battles to win victory over his enemies. Who then are Christ's enemies? He hates no one, for he has come to reconcile men to God. But his wrath blazes out against the scribes with their hardened hearts (Mark 3.5), against their manifold hypocrisies (Matt. 23), against him who leads one of the little ones into sin (Mark 9.42), and he pronounces judgment on sinful Jerusalem (Luke 13.34f.). Could Christ then accept and use the 'cursing psalms'? The answer to this question is not 'God forbid'; for there are elements in them which belong to his mind. He has come to save sinners, not in the first place to judge them (John 3.17); yet salvation involves judgment, because it is the coming of the Light of the World into the world, and men, loving the darkness rather than the Light, are thereby judged (vss. 18f.). There is such a thing as the Wrath of the Lamb. If Christ be thought of as using these psalms, all personal vindictiveness (if there is any there) will drop away, and the words will express the Lord's wrath against sin, which takes form in the mischief and ruin which the sinner by his sin draws down on himself.

(4) Can these psalms then be rightly used in Christian worship? In justice to the traditional practice of reciting the whole psalter as it stands, it needs to be pointed out that the regular interpretation given by St. Augustine and all the standard writers is that the psalms are recited as the prayer of Christ and of the members of his body: in them is heard the voice of Christ and of his people, praising God and praying to him in Christ's name. Therefore when the 'cursing psalms' are recited, judgment is there being pronounced on all man's rebellion against God, including (for each worshipper) *his* rebellion and disobedience; each worshipper must see in them the judgment which his own sins have deserved. It is not indeed to be expected that all who attend church in these days will understand this; but that means that Church people need more help than they usually get about the use of the psalms in worship, as indeed about the Scriptures in general. Yet even so it may be that psalms such as 101 or 131, in which the psalmist professes his own virtue and faithfulness to God—psalms which are fully true only when used of Christ, as expressing his Righteousness—are more dangerous to the ordinary Christian, whose chief peril is self-righteousness, than the psalms which invoke vengeance upon enemies; for all Christians know that it is wrong to hate their enemies.

A. G. HEBERT

* * *

DAGON *v.* GOD, GODS IV

DAMNATION

An infrequent NT rendering of words which elsewhere are translated by 'condemnation' and 'judgment' (*q.v.*).

DARKNESS *v.* LIGHT

DAVID

The Jews rarely enjoyed the privilege of wielding the rod of empire, and it was natural that they should think of David, who had established his throne in Jerusalem and exercised wide and weighty rule, as the ideal king—a picture which became ever more attractive as the historical D. was left further behind in history and as mounting oppression by pagan empires tyrannized their lives. From the point of view of theological interest, the most important chapter from the history of D. is II Sam. 7, in which God refuses D.'s request to build him a temple but promises him an everlasting dynasty: 'thy throne shall be established for ever' (vs. 16). In times of adversity the Jews comforted themselves with this promise and besought God to redeem it (*v.* esp. Ps. 89.20–52; vss. 28, 34, 39 refer to God's covenant with D.). The prophets proclaim God's fidelity to his promise (cf. Amos 9.11, Hos. 3.5, Isa. 9.7, 16.5, 37.35, Jer. 23.5f., 33.15ff., Ezek. 34.23f., 37.24f., Zech. 12.7ff.); and the expectation of a ruler of D.'s line who shall excel D.'s triumphs continues beyond the end of the OT period (cf. Ecclus. 47.11, I Macc. 2.57, and esp. Ps. Sol. 17—a remarkable prophecy of a Messianic King who shall be D.'s son). By NT times it was common rabbinic teaching that the Messiah would spring from the royal line of D. (Mark 12.35), and indeed the expression 'Son of David' was a mere synonym for 'Messiah' (Mark 10.47f., Matt. 21.9: hence the indignation of the Sadducees in 21.15). Jesus himself would appear to have attempted to correct any false notions about his Messiahship which might have arisen through the suggestion that the Messiah should be a conqueror like D., for he emphasizes that 'David' (i.e. Ps. 110) himself had called the Christ 'Lord'—implying that the Messiah is incomparably greater than King D. and that the Messianic Kingdom is not to be reduced to the dimensions of a merely Davidic empire (cf. John 6.15, 18.36). Nevertheless, Jesus does not rebuke Bartimaeus for hailing him as D.'s son: D.'s Son, who is also D.'s Lord, has come to claim his inheritance in D.'s city (Jerusalem); but the throne which he receives is a cross outside the city wall—so far removed is his royalty and empire from D.'s. Jesus claims Kingship (Mark 15.2, John 18.37), but the NT writers do not lay any stress on the Davidic kingship as a type of Christ's; they are entirely concerned to assert the Davidic ancestry of the Lord (Matt. 1.1,20, Mark 10.47, Luke 2.4, John 7.42—note the significance of the birth at Bethlehem—Rom. 1.3, II Tim. 2.8, Rev. 5.5, 22.16). In Christ the promise made by God through Nathan (II Sam. 7) is fulfilled.

ALAN RICHARDSON

DAY, DAY OF THE LORD *v.* JUDGE, TIME

DAY OF ATONEMENT, FEAST OF *v.* SACRIFICE IV(*e*)

DAYSMAN *v.* MEDIATOR

DEACON *v.* MINISTER

DEACONESS *v.* MINISTER

DEATH, DIE, MORTAL, MORTALITY

The Heb. term (*maweth*) and the Gk. term (*thanatos*) commonly denote physical death in the sense of the observable dissolution of all living things. But, like other biblical words, they acquire a peculiarly biblical overtone. The Bible never for one moment allows men to forget their mortality: man is akin to God, he is 'visited' by God, yet he differs from God in that he shares their mortality with the beasts that perish (Pss. 144.3f., 49 *passim*). The illusion of natural or inherent immortality is the Serpent's lie (Gen. 3.4). The Hebrews, like other primitive peoples, did not regard death as utter non-existence; death—'being gathered to one's fathers'—meant joining the departed souls in the underworld (*Sheol*), a dreary, meaningless existence where one was cut off from 'the land of the living' and from the presence of Jehovah (cf. Ps. 88.10–12 and many other passages). It is clear from a perusal of the Psalter that the distress which the approach of death caused to the genuinely religious consciousness of the men of the OT resulted not from the fear of extinction, but from the expectation that all intercourse with God would be at an end (*v.* HELL).

As soon as the religious awareness developed that sin was also a barrier to man's intercourse with God, it became clear to the men of the Bible that there was a connexion between death and sin. In the OT this insight is most clearly expressed in Gen. 3 (the myth of the Fall: 'dust thou art, and unto dust shalt thou return', vs. 19). The notion of some kind of penal connexion between sin and death is focused in such prophetic teaching as Ezek. 18 ('the soul that sinneth, it shall die'), but it is also clearly taught that Jehovah takes no pleasure in the death even of the wicked. Nor does the OT encourage the sentimental notion that death is 'natural', a necessary and beneficial aspect of the ordering of nature; on the contrary, death is evil (Deut. 30.15,19), bitter (I Sam. 15.32), horrific (Ps. 55.4f.): in short, it is unnatural, though the Bible does not know this expression. The fact that it is all these things is in some way connected with the fact that (like sin) it is alien to the divine nature and is no part of God's original intention in the creation. The Bible does not speculate upon the origin of death (or evil): the men of the Bible are not philosophers seeking rational explanations. How this alien thing (cf. I Cor. 15.26, 'the last enemy') found an entry into God's good universe we are not told; at best we come across mythological answers to such questions, and it is clear that the Bible does not set out to give us philosophical answers to them.

The insights of the OT are deepened in the NT. This is because a death has taken place which transforms all our thinking about death —the death of Jesus Christ. The incredible had happened: in Christ the immortal God had tasted death and in so doing had destroyed death (cf. Heb. 2.14f.). The Christian Church lived in the new and triumphant experience of victory over death; the common lot of humanity had been exchanged ('as in Adam all die') for the experience of resurrection through Christ ('even so in Christ shall all be made alive') (I Cor. 15.22; and cf. Rom. 5.12–21). The Christian had passed through death already at his baptism ('baptized into his death'; Rom. 6.3 and context, and cf. Col. 2.12). It was Jesus (not Paul) who first suggested the idea of his own death as a baptism (Luke 12.50) and declared that his disciples would share it (Mark 10.38f.). By baptism into the death of Christ the New Israel recapitulates the exodus of the Old Israel through the baptism of the Red Sea (cf. I Cor. 10.1f.)—Jesus himself speaks of his death as an *exodus* which he must accomplish in Jerusalem (Luke 9.31). Those who are baptized into Christ have their death already behind them, though their 'natural' death must still take place, because in this age the full glory is not yet revealed; our victory is still by faith. But now the Christians can look upon death as merely a sleep (I Thess. 4.13–18) from which there will be an awakening. Conversely, those who are still 'in their sins' are even now dead (Eph. 2.1,5, Col. 2.13, Rev. 3.1; cf. possibly Luke 9.60); they have no 'life' in them. The connexion between sin and death is now abundantly clear: 'the wages of sin is death' (Rom. 6.23); 'the sting of death is sin' (I Cor. 15.56), i.e. the real horror which attaches to death is the fact that death is the symbol in the natural order, in a fallen world (cf. Gen. 3), of rebellion and separation from God. This insight is deepened in the Johannine writings, where 'death' does not as a rule mean physical death, but the consequence of sin and alienation from God (contrast 'life', 'eternal life', and cf. John 11.25f., 5.24f., 6.50, 8.24). It should, however, be noted that, though the NT speaks of eternal life, it nowhere mentions eternal death; and we must not be hasty to embrace ideas about eternal extinction, etc., for which there is no clear biblical sanction. Possibly the 'second death' of Rev. 21.8 may refer to such final extinction, but the passage is not an easy one to interpret. In any case, the real terror of death does not consist in eternal destruction; to quote Dr. H. F. Lovell-Cocks (p. 57; see below): 'Once the God of religion had extended his rule over the dim lands beyond the grave, belief in an after life, so far from mitigating the dread prospect of death, intensifies its terror; Sheol is transformed into Gehenna. Epicurus, with more insight than some of his modern disciples, saw that what man fears is not that death is annihilation, but that it is not; that the horror of death is not extinction, but "the wrath to come".' (*V.* also DESCEND.)

BIBLIOGRAPHY

H. F. Lovell-Cocks: *By Faith Alone*, London (1943), V. J. S. Whale: *Christian Doctrine*, Cambridge (1941), VIII.

ALAN RICHARDSON

DEBT, DEBTOR

In ancient Babylon there was a highly developed credit system, but the Jews, who did not practise sea-going commerce or possess large trading centres, do not appear to have had any such system during most of the OT period. Passing exigencies, misfortune, extravagance or bad harvests (Neh. 5.3–4) led to the incurring of debts, which, however, were as a rule speedily redeemed (Gen. 38.18ff.). The richer members of the community were expected to help the poorer by loans without interest (Exod. 22.25, Deut. 15.7–11, Ps. 15.5). As a consequence, indebtedness was never accepted as natural and legitimate in Israel and there are comparatively few references to it in the OT. In I Sam. 22.2 debtors are among the outcasts of society who join David in the cave of Adullam, but the phrase used means literally 'he who has a creditor', with no distinct word for debtor. There was no provision in the law for recovery of debt, but non-payment was severely condemned (Ps. 37.21), and there were occasions when through sheer poverty men sold themselves and their families into slavery (Lev. 25.39–47, Isa. 50.1) in order to maintain life. The law did contain provisions for the humane treatment of such slaves as there were and their periodic release (Exod. 21.2). Further, such things as clothes and means of livelihood might not be taken away by the creditor as security for payment (Deut. 24.6,13,17, Job 24.3). The whole picture is of a community with wide differences between rich and poor, but where law and custom control the power which any creditor may exercise over a borrower.

In the NT, against a background of Roman commercial practice, it is evident that the ideas of credit, indebtedness and the power of the moneylender have become familiar. In two of his most striking parables our Lord makes use of this picture both to express the indebtedness of all men to God (and the consequent futility of attempting to put the relations of God and man on a business footing) and the fact that those who are aware of how great a debt has been cancelled for them by forgiveness, will express their gratitude (Matt. 10.8) by some dramatic act. In Rom. 4.4 the idea of debt is used as a figure for the obligation incurred by an employer in respect of work done for him by a labourer. A man's wages represent the discharge of a debt (payment for work done) and are in no sense a gift. In Rom. 13.6f. the Apostle urges Roman Christians to pay tribute readily (to pay back in full their taxes) as a return for benefits received from the State. Tax-paying is a Christian duty to be undertaken cheerfully and with a ready heart. The idea covers all kinds of obligations, moral as well as financial, so that in I Cor. 7.3 it is used for the personal relationship and mutual obligations of husband and wife. In the same way the obligation to obey the whole law or by default to become a law-breaker is expressed in terms of the debt to the law which is owed by every man (Gal. 5.3, Jas. 5.10–12).

The debt of love is the only debt that cannot be paid in full (Rom. 13.8) and which men should be proud to acknowledge as a lifelong obligation. A practical example of the outworking of this principle is to be observed in Paul's insistence on the Gentile churches acknowledging their debt to the Jerusalem church for the gift of the Gospel by raising a money contribution to relieve the necessities of the poverty-stricken mother church. To both parties it was a concrete expression (Acts 11.29–30, II Cor. 9.1–5, Rom. 15.26–7) of an indebtedness which could not ever be paid in full. Paul described himself (Rom. 1.14; cf. Rom. 8.12) as debtor both to Greeks and barbarians, and this recollection of what he owed both to his Lord and to men from whom he had received so much was the driving impulse of his evangelistic work. For the figure of repayment see Philem. 18, Rom. 2.16, 12.17. The same idea lies behind the common Pauline phrase 'bondservants of Christ' (Rom. 1.1), which expresses a profound obligation due to the Master who has set men free from the bondage of sin at the price of his own blood (Rom. 6.18–22, I Cor. 6.20, 7.23, Tit. 2.14). This is the nerve-centre of Christian ethics aptly summarized by St. Augustine in the phrase 'love God (responsive love, Rom. 5.5) and do what you will'. (*V.* also BOND.)

F. J. TAYLOR

DECEIT

In the OT this mainly renders words from a root *ramah*, meaning sluggishness, treachery. This is also translated GUILE, e.g. Ps. 34.13. One may speak deceit, imagine it, be full of it. It refers commonly to counsel, a witness, balances, and twice (Ps. 78.57, Hos. 7.16) to a bow.

It is not so common in the NT, and the fundamental meaning of the Gk. word (*planē*, *planao*), which it most frequently represents, is 'lead astray'—a rather different idea from the original Heb. one.

E. C. B.

DEFILE *v.* UNCLEAN

DELIVER, DELIVERER, DELIVERANCE

These words, which are closely allied in meaning to salvation (*q.v.*) and redemption (*q.v.*) and their cognates, express the dominant theme of the Bible—the activity of God in history directed towards the deliverance of his people from their troubles. In ordinary usage in the OT the word has the root meaning of snatch or take away and so to remove from the power of an enemy, as in Gen. 37.21, where Reuben persuades the brethren to spare the life of Joseph, or in II Sam. 19.9, when the people testify that David has enabled them to escape from all their enemies. The inability of men to save themselves from their enemies or from adverse circumstances (Amos 2.14) and the experience of the whole people of subjection to foreign domination led them to think of God as supremely the Deliverer and as the only one who could bring effective deliverance alike from the oppressor in Egypt (Exod. 3.8, 'I am come down to deliver my people'—a struggle between God and Pharaoh through Moses which ends in the deliverance of the people from Egypt and the discomfiture of their oppressors in the sea), from the menace of a cruel and mighty foe (II Kings 18.30–5, the scorn of Rabshakeh for those who would trust in the Lord to deliver Jerusalem from the Assyrian and the subsequent vindication of Hezekiah in II Kings 20.6 and Mic. 5.6 when the city was delivered), from fears and troubles of a personal kind (Pss. 34.4,17, 107.6, 120.2), and from condemnation and imminent danger or death (I Sam. 17.35–7, Pss. 22.20, 33.19, 79.9, Jer. 20.13, Ezek. 13.21, 34.10). Thus the word becomes virtually equivalent to redeem or to free (Job 33.28, Ps. 69.18). The final conquest and ruin of Jerusalem in 586 BC and the captivity of an important part of the population was interpreted by the great prophets of the time not as evidence for the indifference or weakness of God but as a sign of his inflexible will for righteousness (*q.v.*), which led him to deliver (or hand over) his people into the hand of the Babylonian rather than allow them to continue in an evil course (Jer. 20.5, 21.7, 24.9, 29.18, 43.3, Ezek. 11.8–9, 21.31; cf. Ezek. 25.4–7, 31.11).

In the NT the word most frequently used has the significance of handing over into the power of someone else—'the chief priests delivered him for envy' (Mark 15.1, Matt. 11.27, 18.34). It is used in the record of the Lord's own prophecies of his coming fate (Mark 9.31, 10.33, Matt. 20.18, Luke 9.44, 24.7). Another distinctive usage is in the handing down of a tradition where the tradition exercises a harmful influence (Mark 7.13; cf. Acts 6.14) and in the early missionary work of the Church for the preservation of the traditions about Jesus (Luke 1.2) and their formal delivery or handing over to a body of converts (I Cor. 11.23, 15.3). Here in primitive Christianity as in Judaism the word has a technical significance. In Rom.

6.17 the Apostle praises his readers for their obedience to the teaching delivered to them, inasmuch as they have ceased to be the servants of sin. The cutting off of an obstinate evil-doer from the living body of the church in Corinth is described (I Cor. 5.5) as 'delivering him to Satan' (cf. I Tim. 1.20), that is, removing from the sphere of Christ (the Church) into the sphere where Satan holds dominion.

St. Luke (4.18ff.) presents our Lord on the threshold of his public work as the reader and preacher in the synagogue of his own village on a Sabbath Day. The appointed reading was from Isa. 61, and Jesus appropriates the prophetic words as a manifesto of the aims and methods of his own ministry. He is to bring release to the captive, sight to the blind, freedom to the oppressed—in a word, deliverance to all who need it. The Gospel narratives depict him as the deliverer of men and women from the bondage of disease (Luke 13.16) which is interpreted as a visible token of the tyrannical sway exercised by the power of evil in human life. His healing ministry is presented as an assault on the kingdom of Satan, setting free multitudes of miserable captives (Luke 11.14–22) and enabling them to fulfil the purpose for which they were created. Although the title of 'deliverer' is not bestowed upon our Lord in the Gospels and is only twice used in the NT, once of Moses in Acts 7.35 and once in a quotation from the OT (Rom. 11.26; cf. Isa. 59.20) applied in a general way to Christ and his work, yet the purpose and result of his ministry, death and Resurrection is everywhere assumed to be the deliverance of his people from present distresses (II Tim. 3.11, persecutions and suffering, 4.17ff., from the mouth of the lion; cf. Heb. 11.35), from the power of sin (Rom. 7.18–25), from the threat of temptation (II Pet. 2.9; cf. Jas. 1.2), and from the tyranny of death (Heb. 2.15). Our Lord teaches the disciples to pray for deliverance from the power of the evil one (Matt. 6.13, Luke 11.4), and this notion of rescue is the primary meaning of deliverance in many passages, as in II Cor. 1.10, where Paul speaks of his rescue from death at Ephesus (cf. I Cor. 15.32). The rescue of man from his spiritual plight was achieved by the suffering and death of Christ, and it is often set forth in an eschatological context, as in Gal. 1.4 where the death of Christ is said to have delivered men out of the present evil age, or in I Thess. 1.10 where Jesus Christ risen from the dead bestows upon his people as a present reality, complete security from the destroying wrath of God which will be finally manifested in the day of judgment. (*V.* also DELIVER, REDEEM, ESCAPE.)

F. J. TAYLOR

DEMON *v.* ADVERSARY, SPIRIT I(*d*), MIRACLE

DENY

Mainly a NT word. The occurrences mostly worth noting are Mark 8.34 and pars. where it means 'deny oneself' for Christ's sake (*v.* FAST); and those passages where it signifies the ultimate sin of denying Christ. I Tim. 5.8 declares that to deny the faith is worse than having no faith; cf. also Mark 14.30f. (Peter), Acts 3.13f. (Peter's charge against the Jews), and Matt. 10.33, where the reference is more general. I John 2.22f. regards denial as the radical lie, and the word is more definitely moving towards the meaning 'refusal of assent to a proposition' (cf. I Tim. 5.8, 'faith') rather than rejection of a person.

The word 'deny' belongs in a context where fundamental attitudes are under consideration, viz. positive acceptance of Christ, which is faith, or positive rejection. As Christ himself affirms all the promises of God (says 'Yes' to them, II Cor. 1.20), men have the option of echoing that 'Yes', or of saying 'No', i.e. of denying. Ultimately, there is no other possibility. (Also *v.* CONFESS.)

E. C. B.

DERIDE *v.* LAUGH

DESCEND [DESCENT INTO HELL]

The earliest Christian teaching asserted that Christ really died; he went down into hell (*q.v.*), the abode of the departed, as other men do (Acts 2.27, Rom. 10.7, Eph. 4.9). By his conquest of death he became Lord of hell as well as of heaven and earth (Phil. 2.10, Rev. 1.18). While Christ's body lay in the tomb, he remained in Hades until the Resurrection. Two extremely obscure and difficult passages in I Pet. (3.18–20 and 4.6) seem to suggest the object of the descent into hell: it was to preach to the 'souls in prison'. PRISON here doubtless means Hades. The early patristic interpretation of the former passage was that Christ preached the Gospel to the souls of those drowned in the Flood—taken as typical specimens of sinners who had not had the opportunity of hearing the Gospel and thus repenting. Perhaps the legend (which was developed later into various and often beautiful stories of 'the Harrowing of Hell') arose as a result of speculation upon the question which is often asked to-day: What will happen to all those who have died without having heard of Christ? Will they in another life be given the opportunity of believing the good news? May we not hope that this is the motive of the author of I Peter, and that here we have biblical sanction for the belief that those who in this life have had no opportunity to repent and believe are not to be regarded as therefore necessarily deprived of salvation?

A. R.

DESIRE, CONCUPISCENCE, COVET, ENVY, LUST

These words belong to a cycle of ideas which is primarily psychological, and only secondarily ethical; and they express an intense emotional assertion of the self.

The Heb. words are bound up with the view that man is a soul (not simply that he possesses one; see Pedersen, *Israel*, I–II, p. 99). The soul, or total self, may properly seek to extend its influence over other persons or things (desiring, coveting) and to maintain itself against others (in a limited sense, trans. envy); and the strength with which it does so is a measure of the vigour of the soul. Desire (*'wh,hmd*) can be perfectly natural, e.g. for food and drink (Deut. 14.26), or of a king's desire to rule (II Sam. 3.21); and is only morally wrong when it is ungoverned and selfish, directed against God's goodness (Num. 11.4; with a ref. to idolatry: Isa. 1.29; what is dedicated to God: Josh. 7.21), or one's neighbour's possessions (Exod. 20.17, Deut. 5.21, Mic. 2.2). The disruptive effect of violent self-assertion (Jer. 6.13) is expressed by *bz'*, and it destroys the life of the man who indulges in it (Prov. 1.19). The eagerness of a soul to maintain itself (*qn'h*: Gen. 30.1) can be used of the zeal of men for God or of God for his people; but it easily turns into envy which destroys the harmony of society (cf. Isa. 11.13). The moral peril of trying to maintain oneself is expressed in Prov. 3.31, 'Envy not the man of violence and choose none of his ways'.

The Gk. word *epithumia* (with an equally wide range) normally expresses any intense longing, which is condemned only if it is (*1*) misdirected or (*2*) becomes excessive. (*1*) Thus it may be concentrated on money: Acts 20.33, I Tim. 6.9–10 (in vs. 10, and also in II Tim. 3.2 and Luke 16.14 is used the technical term for love of money—see RV); and Rom. 7.7f., though even here a wider meaning is possible; or on sexual experience (Matt. 5.28: it must be noted that 'lust' is seldom limited to this meaning). Desires misdirected produce disharmony; properly directed they produce harmony (cf. II Tim. 3.6 with 2.22). (*2*) But in this world, so often organized under the power of evil, desires tend to become excessive and to ruin human life (Mark 4.19; and I John 2.16,17, which includes both sensuality and covetousness). A power of control over the excesses of pagan society is expected of Christians (I Pet. 1.14, Titus 2.12). Warnings against excessive desire and lists of vices to be avoided were a commonplace of the popular Greek and Jewish moralists, and Christian teachers followed suit (Tit. 3.3, I Pet. 4.3, Col. 3.5, Rom. 1.24–7; and often in II Pet. and Jas). How impossible it is to confine 'lust' to sexual immorality is shown by the fact that in Rom. 13.14 'lusts of the flesh' sums up 'revelling, drunkenness, chambering, wantonness, strife, jealousy' (cf. Eph. 2.3, 'desires of the flesh and of the mind', and see esp. Gal. 5.16–23). But in contrast to Stoic morality Paul did not regard the flesh or the body as inherently evil: the body can indeed be the prey of lusts, but it can also be the instrument of righteousness (Rom. 6.12f.).

Hardly less restricted in its reference is *zelos*, an intense expression of being. It ranges from zeal for God (Rom. 10.2) and earnest desire for spiritual gifts (I Cor. 12.31) to anger (Acts 5.17) and jealousy. The last meaning appears in lists of vices, where it is often associated with strife (e.g. Gal. 5.20; cf. Jas. 4.2). The common synonym for envy (*phthonos*) appears only in a bad sense (e.g. Gal. 5.21).

One of the most interesting words in this cycle of ideas is *pleonexia*, which has a long history in Greek ethical writings. Its general connotation of ruthless, aggressive self-assertion is well illustrated in II Cor. 2.11, 7.2, 12.17f.; and when limited to money and possessions, in II Cor. 9.5, Luke 12.15. The same spirit may show itself in sexual relationships (Eph. 4.19), and the word, though never simply an expression for sexual immorality, is often closely associated with it in lists of vices. Since ruthless self-assertion is the very essence of idolatry (Eph. 5.5, Col. 3.5), the word forms a bridge between sexual vice and idolatry, and may in some quarters have been a euphemism for ritual fornication.

KENNETH GRAYSTON

DESOLATION *v.* ABOMINATION, ANTICHRIST

DESTRUCTION *v.* PERDITION

DETERMINATE, DETERMINE, PREDESTINATE (*AV*), FOREORDAIN (*RV*)

I. TERMS

The actual words occur with an infrequency surprising to anyone acquainted with the prominent position they occupy in Christian theology from the time of St. Augustine. In nearly half of their appearances, it is the word *determine* that occurs, used in a secular sense (e.g. II Chron. 2.1, 'make up one's mind', and Acts 19.39, of committee decision). The other and rather larger half of the occurrences connect Determination with God. It is tempting to suggest that the secular use influences the meaning of the words in their more supernatural employment. The Heb. and Gk. words, however, usually mark a distinction, and different terms are used to refer to human and to divine d. Yet one outstanding example (Acts 11.29, of the disciples; cf. 1.28, of God) of the use of the same word in both senses forbids too strict a distinction between the supernatural and technical and the secular and human employments. To offset the meagre appearance of the actual terms, there is a large number of terms so closely allied as to defy separation or even sometimes distinction (e.g. decree, reprobate, elect, ordained, providence, choose, know, foreknow; *q.v.* where appropriate). The *idea* of d. is in fact much more influential and pervasive throughout the Scriptures than the infrequent occurrence of the terms might suggest. The discussion here must deal with this *idea of d.* that overlaps the actual terms used, but it will be confined to *d. on the part of God.*

II. DEFINITION

By God's d. Holy Scripture means the ordering of events (Josh. 2.14,16, John 9.3), things (Job 37.15, Matt. 6.30*a*) and men (Isa. 41.25, 45.1ff., Acts 4.27f.) in accordance with his will (Ps. 115.3, John 6.39), for the fulfilment of his purpose (Isa. 42.6f., Matt. 1.21), and to the accomplishment of good (Gen. 45.8, Prov. 16.4, II Pet. 3.9).

III. OT

(*a*) *General D.* The thought that God really is the sovereign disposer of all that is belongs so essentially to the OT that its explicit expression is neither frequent nor required. The God who appears in its pages is almighty (Ps. 29.10); hence nothing falls outside his control. He is sovereign, or alone in the exercise of his almightiness (Ps. 89.6; and cf. the iterated question of Isa. 40.18,25, 45.6*b*, 46.5); i.e. he shares his authority and power with none outside himself. The inward expression of this entire sovereignty appears in the Name with which he names himself: 'I am that I am' (Exod. 3.14). Its outward or practical affirmation which concerns us here is found in the analogy of the potter (Isa. 45.9ff., Jer. 18.1ff.), and assumes almost violent form in Isa. 45.7 ('I make peace and create evil: I the Lord do all these things'; cf. Amos 3.6). All things are and remain in the hands of an absolute and almighty Sovereign. Related to his will and purpose, they fall under his disposal and determination. Chance and coincidence are quite ruled out. Thus when Abraham sends his servant to fetch a wife for Isaac, the whole venture is literally begun, continued and ended in reliance on God's d., and the servant finally cannot repress the conviction that 'the Lord hath prospered my way' (Gen. 24.56; cf. 24.52). Similarly, the concatenation of circumstances which culminates in Joseph saving his family from famine by the corn of Egypt is confidently referred to God's intention (Gen. 45.8; cf. 50.20).

Divine d. finds vivid illustration in the case of evil. It is not enough to say that in the above example (and, e.g., Ps. 76.10: 'Surely the wrath of men shall praise thee') God's sovereign might snatches victory out of virtual defeat, and, as it were, manages at the eleventh hour to make a good job of a bad business. A recurrent thought is not only that God redeems a situation but that the situation is itself precipitated by him according to his d. Not only the remedy, but the situation to be remedied, is run back into the d. of his will. The principle involved here is expressed by Isaiah (22.11, 37.26); illustrated in historical fact (Isa. 14.24ff.); applied to the details of life by the Psalmist (139.16), and to persons in such gracious words as Dan. 12.1 and Prov. 8.22.

Yet for all the force with which this unlimited sovereign d. is exercised, it is never held to exclude or suppress the reality of so-called 'secondary' or 'proximate' causes. These subserve his will (Ps. 104.3f., 148.8), but their independence is not thereby obliterated but rather affirmed (Gen. 8.22, Jer. 33.20,25, Ps. 148.6, Job. 38.33); and the real independence with which human agents are credited, even if they too minister to his good pleasure (Ps. 104.4, II Chron. 36.22, Isa. 44.28), appears in the testing to which they are subjected (Gen. 22.1, Exod. 16.4, Deut. 8.2), in the conversation which they hold with God (Exod. 20.22), and in the responsibility of choice which is fairly settled on their shoulders (Deut. 30.15).

(*b*) *Salvation D.* Man and things thus fall without remainder under the august and sovereign d. of God. Biblical interest in man at this point, though dominant, is not exclusive. According to Holy Scripture other things have an appropriate stake in the divine d.; cf. the no doubt rhetorical surprise manifested by the Psalmist that, in face of the wonders of the earth, man should occupy the attention of God at all (Ps. 8.3f.). Similarly, what God made was successively pronounced good before man appeared on the scene (Gen. 1.10, etc.), and 'the heavens declare the glory of God' (Ps. 19.1) in a manner not wholly dependent on the appreciative ear and eye of the human race. It is, however, indisputable that the chief concern of Scripture is to set forth the divine d. as it applies to man. God's d. is fundamentally a soteriological d.: his will is that men be saved, and his purpose is to save them. The knowledge that he has of all things lights upon man with special favour; a hierarchy of increasing familiarity is traceable: thus Job 28.23, of things; 21.27, of the devices of the wicked; and 23.10, of the way of the righteous; or even more vividly in Ps. 103.14, our frame; Ps. 138.6, the proud known 'afar off', but the faithful are 'searched' and 'known' intimately. The word for 'know' contains the suggestion of appointment; and God's d. is thus held to bear with increased strictness upon his faithful people, though without infringement of their genuine independence.

When brought to bear on men, God's d. takes firm shape and form. It is by the appointment of certain of the human race that both they and their fellows will enjoy the benefits of God's saving purpose. A determined or chosen group or person is employed to convey saving benefits to all. The fact of this discrimination is adverted to before history properly begins; in other words, it is lodged by the writers of the Bible to the earliest possible point of time. Thus Seth (=Sheth, 'appointed', marg.) is appointed to the place of Abel (Gen. 4.25); and Shem is preferred to Canaan (Gen. 9.26f.). The choice of Abraham is explicitly referred to the divine d. that 'all the nations of the earth shall be blessed in him' (Gen. 18.18), and is carried further in the successive choice of Isaac and Jacob (in preference to Ishmael and Esau; Gen. 21.12, 28.1ff.). Beyond the patriarchs, the initial choice of individuals for benefit of the race broadens out to the choice of their children, the people of Israel, for benefit of the nations of the world (Zech. 8.22f.) and then contracts again to the preservation of a 'remnant' for the good of the people (Joel 2.32).

Not only the purpose, but also the means for its execution belong to the d. of God. God's choice of instrument is grounded neither adventitiously nor empirically, but in his own d. Israel is chosen (Amos 3.2) not for any reason resident in the people chosen and extraneous to God (Deut. 7.7), but for reasons wholly internal to God himself (Deut. 7.8)—namely, 'because the Lord loved you' (cf. 10.15). The choice of Israel is made with superb independence, is grounded on the d. of God, and thus exhibits both the divine sovereignty and the divine grace.

IV. NT

The NT offers certain alterations of emphasis. But the same fundamental stress is laid on the sovereign might of God, by which all things are ordered and disposed. God is more evidently the heavenly Father, but there is no suggestion that things are less controlled by the Father's hand than by that of the Lord of hosts. The 'God and Father of our Lord Jesus Christ' (Eph. 1.3) is also 'the only Potentate' (I Tim. 6.15) and the 'Lord God omnipotent' (Rev. 19.6).

(*a*) *General D.* A pattern of thought identical with that of the OT is repeated in the NT: God's d. is apparent in his sovereign rule of things, his present direction of them for men's good, and his appointment of them to a final end. Thus, our Lord's teaching: God is the 'Father, Lord of heaven and earth' (Matt. 11.25), who absolutely knows his creation (Matt. 10.29), making present provision for the lower creatures (Matt. 6.26) and for men (Matt. 7.11), and who directs it to a determined end (Matt. 19.28, 25.31f.). Cf. St. Paul: all things are created not only by him but 'for him' (Col. 1.16), the visible presently serving to instruct men concerning the invisible (Rom. 1.20), and all eventually submitting to final subordination, that 'God may be all in all' (I Cor. 15.28); cf. also Acts 17.24f., 31 similarly.

(*b*) *Jesus Christ.* It would be unthinkable that the execution of this determined programme should be left to chance, or committed to the charge of fortuitous agents and means. In fact, with an insistence to which due weight has not always been allowed, Holy Scripture affirms that Jesus Christ is the means eternally appointed for its achievement. Matt. 11.3 carries forward into the NT the OT thought in the matter: 'Art thou he that should come, or do we look for another?' Here there appears both the expectation of a 'coming one' and the recurrent doubt concerning his identity (cf. the OT *passim* from Gen. 49.10 to Mal. 3.1, with Isa. 9.6 as key reference, and especially Isa. 62.11, Zech. 9.9, Ps. 118.26, Mal. 4.5, together with Isa. 42.19 indirectly, for the sending of a messenger to 'prepare a way'). When the disciples of John the Baptist ask this question, they hold hands with the men of the OT, and the event to which they refer is conceived by both to be grounded in the d. of God. The testimony of the NT is that the means foreshadowed in prophecy and popular expectation has now been supplied, and Jesus Christ is identified with the Coming One earlier discerned by prophecy as laid up in the d. of God for giving effect to his saving purpose.

This testimony is expressed in both dominical and apostolic words. In the hands of Jesus, the OT thought of the 'coming one' no doubt suffered drastic change. It would indeed have been impossible to fulfil without alteration all the diverse and conflicting conceptions of the bearer of this office. But that he laid claim to be this one cannot seriously be disputed. It is especially in the prosecution and fulfilment of this vocation that our Lord holds himself to be determined. Thus: 'truly the Son of Man goeth, as it was determined' (Luke 22.22); cf. the frequent reference to his appointed time or 'hour' (Matt. 26.45, Luke 12.40,46, and esp. John 7.30, 17.1, 12.27); also the more neutral reference to the 'will' of God (Matt. 26.39), and the 'cup' which in OT usage is invariably connected with divine appointment; and, further, Luke 13.33, Matt. 16.21.

The early apostolic witness sees throughout the whole career of Jesus the clearest evidence of divine d. Nothing seems to have impressed itself more deeply on the mind of the Apostles as, in the first momentous days of their mission to the world, they reflected upon the message which they were to proclaim: what had happened in the life, death, Resurrection and Ascension of Jesus had occurred by the inexorable decree and ordinance of God. God's general d. of all things (Acts 17.26) is narrowed down to the betrayal of Christ (2.23) with all that ensued therefrom, in which Herod, Pontius Pilate, the Gentiles and the people of Israel all play appointed parts (4.28); while the Judge at the end of time is seen through the medium of an ordained Incarnation (10.42), or more narrowly an ordained Resurrection (17.31). Anything less like the heroic redemption of a bad situation by some desperate and improvised measure can hardly be imagined. Every link in the whole historical sequence is, as it were, tested, and approved by the position it occupies in the divine d. What has happened is only the emergence into history of what was eternally laid up in the d. of God.

To this St. Paul adds little that is new. The early apostolic mind traced back the individual details of Christ's career to a place within the d. of God. Paul supplements the thought by attaching also the beginning, middle and end of the career to the divine d. Thus: 'When the fulness of time was come, God sent forth his Son' (Gal. 4.4); 'it pleased the Father that in him should all fulness dwell' (Col. 1.19); 'that in the dispensation of the fulness of times he might gather together into one all things in Christ' (Eph. 1.10). Cf. also Heb. 2.9, 10.10, 11.40, I Pet. 1.20.

(*c*) *Predestination.* In Holy Scripture p. is the special application of divine d. to man and his destiny. It can be rightly understood only as such a special case of the general principle. It is by no means an accident that in the NT, i.e. after the advent of Christ, the d. of the individual suddenly flares up into a prominence which it does not achieve in the OT. In Jesus Christ, God appoints and employs an instrument and means by which his saving purpose is with a new and evident efficacy and thoroughness applied to men; and in him the full consequences of the divine d. are with new clarity apparent. Final loss and gain are now determined in relation to Jesus Christ. As he on whom the final destiny turns belongs to the divine d., so too that final destiny of men, so far from finding itself at a loose end, is posited within the d. of God.

Outside the Pauline Epistles, p. finds expression in such varied writings as Heb. (3.1, 9.15), I Pet. (1.2) and Rev. (13.8, 17.8, as also in the more extended 20.12–15). The 'calling' of Heb. and I Pet. connects with the dominical use (Matt. 22.14), where 'calling' and 'choice' are contrasted. Whatever the exact meaning of this puzzling Matthean saying, the reference of those saved to the d. of God is unmistakable.

The three classic passages in which St. Paul outlines a doctrine of p. are Rom. 8.28ff., 9–11, Eph. 1.1–12. In the first passage, the writer's motive is to assure his readers, in face of the ambiguous and distressing circumstances of their earthly life, of a divine ordinance and providence by reminding them of its various moments. They who are the subjects of God's foreknowledge and predestination, the recipients of his call and justification, and the heirs of his glorification, may be certainly assured that 'all things work together for good to them that love God'. Their assured p. is almost adventitiously cited as the proof *a fortiori* of their providentia ldefence amid present perplexities.

In the second passage (Rom. 9–11) the welfare and future destiny of the faithful is taken up freshly from a different angle. It is the question of grounds that is now at issue. Salvation is freed from all dependence on vested racial privilege (9.7), or merit (9.16), and made to depend wholly and solely on grace (9.15f.). Thus the fact of salvation is run ruthlessly back to its ultimate grounds and found to be lodged, not in anything outside God, but in God's own sovereign will and purpose, in other words, in his d.

In the third passage (Eph. 1.1–12) the grace mentioned above is, as it were, identified. The grace of God is nothing but Jesus Christ. It is all one whether our election is said to be 'by grace' and 'not of works' (Rom. 11.6), or we are said to be 'chosen in Christ before the foundation of the world' (Eph. 1.4). That our p. is 'in Christ' means that our fate is not otherwise decided than by him, that we have nothing better or other to await from the hand of God than him, and that, if our destiny is run back to a 'determinate counsel' of God, it is one in whose determination Christ has a hand. The scriptural conception is that p. is strictly and solely in Christ, and any attempt to deprecate or mitigate its attachment to and its dependence on Christ involves a departure from the scriptural witness. 'This is my beloved Son' (Matt. 17.5)—if it is with this One that our p. is bound up, so that his destiny becomes our destiny in virtue of faith in him (Eph. 1.12), there is room for nothing but complete assurance.

(*d*) '*Double Predestination.*' The case of those who by the rejection of Christ fall outside the p. enjoyed by those who trust him is considered by Paul in the second passage cited, as a corollary of the doctrine of p. Such terms as election, call, choice, and so on possess a 'shadow side': if some enjoy the privilege, there are others who remain excluded from it; and 'chosen' means 'chosen from' and implies some not chosen. Paul realizes the logical drift of these conceptions. If the question be raised: What of those not chosen?, his reply is cautious. It consists of a warning: 'Nay, but, O man, who art thou that repliest against God?', deprecating the right of the creature to subject God to inquisition; and of a reference to the classes of the chosen and the rejected in the form of a supposition: 'what if God?' (Rom. 9.20,22). The implication of this is that though logic seems to point in a certain direction, detailed certainty at this point is outside our grasp. To put the matter in modern terms: though there appear *logically* to be two classes in a developed doctrine of p., that of the blessed and that of the reprobate, Paul is unwilling to assign *real* persons to these classes. They remain mere logical, and of course spiritual, possibilities, categories without assigned or assignable members.

In face of the Scriptural evidence that can be assembled (e.g. Ezek. 18.23, II Pet. 3.9), it is impossible to suppose that the Bible thinks of God as holding himself in stable equilibrium between good and evil, and indifferently consigning men to salvation and to reprobation. God's will inclines towards good, and his Son is sent 'for us men and for our salvation'. On scriptural testimony (Rom. 3.23, 'all have sinned'), we all stand under condemnation (cf. also Rom. 11.31). The cry of dereliction (Matt. 27.46) shows God's Son taking his place where we all are and bearing on his shoulders that reprobation which is rightly ours (Matt. 26.28, I John 2.2). He bears it, however, in order that we may *not* have to bear it (cf. the scapegoat, Lev. 16.8–10 and John 1.29), and that we 'in him' may enjoy blessedness. (Cf. Irenaeus: 'Jesus Christ, in his infinite love, became what we are, in order that he might make us what he wholly is.') If any then fail to come to the enjoyment of this blessedness, it will not be because by the p. of God they have been assigned another fate, but because they have turned their face away from the determined means of salvation proffered in Jesus Christ. That it should be possible for this to occur within the d. of all things by God is as finally mysterious as the existence of evil.

V. THE FRUITS OF D.

The interest that Scripture takes in d. and p. is practical and not merely speculative. D. and p. are declared to yield excellent moral fruit. Rom. 8.28 puts the whole doctrine of p. at the service of those hard pressed by circumstances of perplexity and hardship, so that they may rest confidently in a God who not only provides, but also determines. In Eph. 2.10, Paul adverts to the ethical results to be expected from those 'created in Christ Jesus unto good works'. D. and p. have thus a double fruit: they proffer a reliable assurance to the faithful believer, and they release an ethical vitality which issues in good works. (*V.* also CALL, CHOOSE.)

J. K. S. REID

DEVIL *v.* ADVERSARY, ANTICHRIST, SPIRIT I(*d*)

DEVOTE, ACCURSED, BAN

A 'devoted' (RV; 'accursed', AV) thing (Heb. *cherem*, Gk. *anathema*) in Semitic thought generally is something which utterly belongs to the deity and must not be touched or used by men. It is therefore 'most holy' (Lev. 27.28) and possesses all the contagion of a holy thing (*v.* under SAINT, SANCTIFY, UNCLEAN); hence Achan's sin infected the whole camp (Josh. 6.18, 7.1ff.). In early times the enemies of Jehovah (i.e. of Israel) were 'accursed' in this sense; their persons and property alike came under the ban. Hence arose the barbarous practice of 'devoting' them to Jehovah, i.e. utterly destroying them—men, women, children, cattle and goods (e.g. Josh. 6 and 7, Achan; I Sam. 15, the Amalekites). It was as though the enemies of the Lord were being sacrificed as a measure of thanksgiving for their defeat (cf. Num. 21.2f.). Thus warfare became 'holy war' (*v.* WAR), and no 'profiteering' could arise out of the spoils of victory, since all came under the ban. Similarly an Israelite who sacrificed to a strange god was to be utterly destroyed (Exod. 22.20, RV marg. 'devoted'; cf. Deut. 13.12ff.). Later to be 'devoted' meant not to be killed but to be excommunicated (Ezra 10.8) and to have one's property forfeited (RV marg., 'devoted'); and thus began the practice, continued through the Christian centuries, of interdiction and excommunication. A later Jewish modification of the ban was the practice of 'devoting' part of one's property as an offering to the Lord (Lev. 27.28);

hence arose the custom of *Corban* (Mark 7.11), for which *v.* SACRIFICE I(*b*)(1). (*V.* also CURSE.)

A. R.

DEVOUR *v.* EAT

DIE *v.* DEATH

DISCIPLE

'Disciple' is the Eng. form of Lat. *discipulus*, which is derived from *discere*, to learn, and so means 'learner', 'scholar', 'pupil', and, sometimes, 'apprentice' (cf. German *Lehrling*). The exactly corresponding Gk. word is *mathētēs*, also derived from the verb meaning 'to learn'. Also exactly corresponding is the Heb. *talmid*, from *lamad*, to learn; this is used in the OT only once, I Chron. 25.8 (EVV scholar), of the pupils in the music school of the Temple—an indication that 'learning' includes practice as well as theory. In the Eng. OT the word disciple also occurs only once, as the translation of another noun derived from the same verb, Isa. 8.16. This is a passage of special importance; the prophet, recognizing that his message had been rejected by his people, determined to entrust it to a band of followers who would not only preserve it, but make it effective in days to come. The likeness between Isaiah's disciples and those of Jesus is plain. In later Jewish usage the word 'disciples' (*talmidim*) was used especially of the pupils of the rabbis, the students and teachers of the law; *talmud*, learning, meant first this particular branch of learning, and then one of the great compilations in which were recorded the discussions and conclusions of the rabbis (the Talmud). But the word is also applied in a wider sense to those who accepted and practised the teaching of the rabbis, one of whose aims was to 'raise up many disciples'. The Talmud itself mentions the disciples (*talmidim*) of Jesus, but since it says that there were five of them it is clear that here the word has its narrower meaning.

In the NT the word 'disciple' is used only in the Gospels and Acts, but in these it occurs more than 250 times. In a few passages 'the disciples of John' (the Baptist) are mentioned. According to John 1.35ff., two among the first disciples of Jesus had been disciples of John, and transferred their allegiance to Jesus when John pointed him out as 'the Lamb of God'. From the account of John given in this Gospel it is difficult to understand why John himself and all his disciples with him did not forthwith become disciples of Jesus. But it is certain that in fact the disciples of John persisted as a definite religious group long after the death of their master. In the time of Jesus they were already distinguished by the observance of special fasts and the use of special prayers (Mark 2.18ff., Luke 11.1). Some of them were closely attached to the person of John, even when he was imprisoned (Matt. 11.2, Mark 6.29). Along with the disciples of John, 'the disciples of the Pharisees' are mentioned (Mark 2.18, Matt. 22.16), but probably this rather unusual phrase means no more than 'members of the Pharisaic party'; cf. Matt. 9.14, which speaks simply of 'the Pharisees' and the apparently synonymous phrase 'your sons' (i.e. sons of the Pharisees) in Matt. 12.27. In John 9.28 the Jews claim to be disciples of Moses; here the word is used in its widest sense.

But in most of the instances in the Gospels the word is used of Jesus' disciples, and it is to be noted that nearly always they are called, not 'the disciples', though that phrase would have been quite unambiguous, but 'his disciples'—'disciple' by itself does not yet mean, as it does in Acts, a follower of Jesus. Also, in the first three Gospels it is hardly ever used in the singular—never in Mark, and in Matthew and Luke only in four sayings of Jesus himself, Matt. 10.24f.=Luke 6.40, Matt. 10.42, Luke 14.26f. (not in the parallel in Matt. 10.37f.), Luke 14.33. None of these sayings refers to a particular disciple, but in John, in which the singular is used some 15 times, the reference is always to a particular individual (most often to 'the disciple whom Jesus loved'). It is not always possible to determine whether 'his disciples' means a small group living in close fellowship with Jesus, or the larger body of those who accepted him as their teacher or their leader. In Matthew and Mark it seems usually, if not indeed always, to mean the small group—small enough to go together into a house, Mark 9.28, or into a boat, Mark 6.45. But Luke speaks of 'a great crowd of his disciples', 6.17, and this just after he has told how Jesus chose the Twelve from the whole company of his disciples, 6.13—but cf. Mark 3.13f., Matt. 10.1 (not surprisingly, the inferior text on which the AV is based omits 'great' in 6.17, and the AV reduces 'crowd' to 'company'. In the next chapter, on the contrary, it is inferior MSS that add 'many' after 'his disciples' in vs. 11, and here the AV mistranslates, 'many of his disciples'). In 19.37 Luke similarly makes the whole crowd which hailed Jesus on his entry into Jerusalem consist of 'the disciples'. This wider application of the term is found also in John; cf., e.g. John 4.1, 6.60ff., 8.31, though usually 'the disciples' seems to mean the small group of those who were continually with Jesus, cf., e.g. 13.5, 18.1, 20.19,30.

In Acts 'disciples' is the most distinctive term for those who believed in Christ; cf. 6.1,2,7, 9.1, 11.26, 18.23, 19.1, 21.4,16. The derivative verb, which means 'to make disciples', is used in 14.21 (here the AV trans., 'had taught many', is mistaken). Only once is the word expressly connected with Jesus, 9.1, 'the disciples of the Lord'—an indication that the original sense has been almost forgotten.

It is surprising that in the other NT writings the word is not found at all, but in later Christian writings it is found in the same wide sense which it has in Acts. This raises the question whether Acts correctly reproduces the Christian usage of the apostolic Church, but we have no means of answering that question.

J. Y. CAMPBELL

DISEASE *v.* HEAL, MIRACLE, SUFFER

DISHONOUR *v.* SHAME

DISOBEDIENCE, DISOBEY *v.* OBEY

DISPENSATION *v.* TIME

DISTRIBUTE, DISTRIBUTION *v.* FELLOWSHIP

DIVINE *v.* SAINT

DIVORCE *v.* MARRIAGE

DRAGON *v.* ANTICHRIST

DREAD *v.* FEAR

DRINK *v.* WATER

DRINK-OFFERING *v.* SACRIFICE I(*g*)

DUST

Apart from the extensive metaphorical uses of 'dust' to denote multitude, death, mourning, dissociation (e.g. Num. 23.10, Isa. 47.1, Mark 6.11), the most striking use is in Gen. 2.7. A right understanding of this use can be fruitful for the understanding of Hebrew presuppositions about life. That man was shaped by God 'out of the dust of the ground', and life breathed into him, is a basic affirmation of Hebrew 'materialism'. Man is *not* a noble spirit temporarily imprisoned or entombed in the evil matter of the body; he is not a double creature of body or matter and soul or spirit: but in his primal state he is a natural, unified creation having life in the same way as all God's living creatures. The material life, the life of the senses, the temporal world, the world where we are now, with the life we have to live here and now, are man's habitat. Whatever else is added to the OT and NT conceptions of life, this can never be subtracted. (*V.* also ADAM, DEATH.)

R. G. S.

* * *

EAR *v.* HEAR

EARNEST *v.* INHERIT [NT (c)]

EAT, DEVOUR

Akal, the main Heb. word concerned, occurs *c.* 800 times in OT, usually trans. by 'eat', also 'devour', less often 'consume', occasionally by other words. In NT several Gk. words are concerned, which together occur *c.* 200 times.

(*a*) Very frequently of eating, as necessity for sustaining physical life. To feed the hungry an obvious duty (e.g. Job 31.17, Isa. 58.7, Matt. 25.34ff.). Connexion between working and the right to eat (e.g. Gen. 3.19, Matt. 10.10, II Thess. 3.10). To eat *with* someone—table-fellowship (e.g. I Sam. 9.19, Mark 2.16, Luke 15.2, Mark 14.18, I Cor. 5.11, Gal. 2.12). Eating and drinking sometimes stand for the passing pleasures of this world (e.g. Eccles. 8.15, Isa. 22.13, Luke 12.19, Matt. 24.49, I Cor. 15.32). In Mark 5.43, Luke 24.41ff., eating is a sign of being really alive.

(*b*) Often in connexion with cultus and ritual, e.g. blood and fat not to be eaten (I Sam. 14.34, Lev. 3.17, 7.23ff., Acts 15.20,29); 'clean' and 'unclean' animals (Deut. 14, Lev. 11, Acts 10.9–16ff.); the priests' share of victims and offerings (Lev. 6.16ff., 7.6, I Cor. 9.13, Heb. 13.10); eating the Passover (Exod. 12); eating 'before the Lord' (e.g. Deut. 12.7); various taboos with regard to eating (e.g. Gen. 32.32). Perhaps Gen. 2.17, 3.6 should be mentioned here.

When Gentiles began to enter the Church, OT ritual laws about eating became a burning problem. Were Gentile Christians to be bound by them? And Jewish Christians still? Jesus had shewn a certain freedom in these matters (e.g. Mark 2.26f., 7.1–23; also his running the risk of infringing ritual rules by eating with the disreputable, Mark 2.16, etc.). Early Church naturally interested in Jesus' attitude, as Mark 7.19 indicates. Cf. also Acts 11.1ff., 15, Gal. 2.12.

A related problem was whether one might eat meat that had been sacrificed to an idol. The Council of Jerusalem had forbidden it (Acts 15.29). But it was not easy to obey this decision. In a heathen city meat was seldom purely 'secular' Meat served in a heathen house would usually have been sacrificed first. Was the Christian then to be cut off from social intercourse with non-Christians? Even meat for sale in the market would often have been involved in a sacrificial rite first. St. Paul deals with this problem in I Cor. 8, 10.14–33 and Rom. 14. In Corinth there was tension between those who 'have knowledge' and those in whom 'there is not that knowledge', the former feeling quite free to eat because 'no idol is anything in the world', while the latter were troubled in conscience. Paul's decision is that fellowship with God does not depend on eating or not eating (I Cor. 8.8); but, whereas the man who has no scruple would not be hurt by giving up his freedom, the weak brother would be hurt by seeing him eat; therefore, though in itself there is nothing wrong in eating, in view of the weak brother's danger, to eat and so do violence to a brother's conscience is sin (8.11f.); better give up one's freedom than endanger one's brother. While Paul clearly sympathizes with those who 'have knowledge', he sees that knowledge needs to be counterbalanced by love. There was a certain amount of pride in the knowledge of these Corinthians (8.10, with its mention of eating actually in the heathen temple, suggests even bravado!). In 10.23ff. he recommends a kind of working compromise. In Rom. 14 the two parties appear as the *weak* and the *strong*. Paul clearly sympathizes with the strong; but again love will prompt the strong to give up his freedom voluntarily for the sake of his weak brother. Here Paul begins by laying down the general principle of Christian freedom and with it respect for the consciences of others: both the strong and the weak have been received by God, so both are to respect and refrain from criticizing each other. But in the nature of the case the strong can afford to sacrifice his freedom, while the weak cannot without hurt to his conscience give way to the strong. Consequently, it is the strong who have to be ready to give way for love's sake.

For not eating as a religious observance *v.* FAST. Jesus seemed to the Pharisees much too worldly to be a real man of God, because he came 'eating and drinking' (Matt. 11.19).

(*c*) Behm in *TWNT*, II, pp. 686ff. (to whom the present writer is indebted) mentions Exod. 24.11, Gen. 3.5f. and (a little far-fetched?) Ps. 34.8 as examples of the idea of a connexion between eating and drinking and seeing God, which certainly existed in other religions.

(*d*) In connexion with the Eucharist, *v.* THANK.

(*e*) Related to the tradition of the Eucharist is the teaching in St. John's Gospel about 'eating the flesh of the Son of Man', which is the same as eating of the bread of life, which Jesus is (John 6), i.e. believing in Jesus Christ.

(*f*) In connexion with the feast of the Lord, which plays a part in Biblical eschatology, as a figure of judgment and also of fellowship with God in the final perfection. In Zeph. 1.7 the Lord's judgment on his people is represented as a sacrificial feast. The victim is Judah. The guests have been sanctified in readiness to partake, but it is not said who they are. Ezek. takes up the figure and expands it (39.17ff., where the guests are beasts and birds of prey; cf. Jer. 46.10, Isa. 34.6). Rev. 19.17ff. is based on Ezek. 39.17ff. The OT origin of the use of the figure of the feast to represent the blessedness of the redeemed, fellowship with God in a restored world, is not so clear. Reference may be made to Isa. 25.6, and perhaps to such passages as Isa. 55.1f. In the NT it is quite prominent: Luke 14.15, 13.29 ('sit down'—at table), 22.16,30, and the parable of the Great Supper/Marriage Feast (Luke 14.16ff., Matt. 22.1ff.), and the marriage supper of the Lamb in Rev. 19.9. Matt. 26.29 makes explicit a connexion between this eschatological feast and the Eucharist. The earthly is a foretaste of the heavenly feast. (NB—how Matt. puts in the words 'with you', which are not in Mark 14.25 or Luke 22.16,18.)

(*g*) A special use is that in Jer. 15.16, further developed in Ezek. 2.8–3.3 and reappearing in Rev. 10.9f.

(*h*) Metaphorical uses: (1) to enjoy: Job 21.25 (RV, tasteth of); (2) frequently of destruction wrought by such things as fire, drought, frost, hunger, disease, the sword, the wrath of God, etc.; of the wicked devouring the poor, of false prophets devouring souls. These are mostly OT. In the NT see Heb. 10.27, Rev. 11.5, Jas. 5.3. The Heb. word *akal*, when used in this metaphorical way, is most commonly trans. devour, but also consume, eat up. (In this AV and RV sometimes differ. NB—'consume' in EVV sometimes represents a quite different metaphor from that of eating.) (3) To eat the fruit of—to bear the consequences of something: Prov. 1.31, Isa. 3.10. (4) To exhaust: Ps. 69.9.

C. E. B. CRANFIELD

EDOM, ESAU

The Edomites were an ancient tribe with whom the Hebrews were conscious of kinship, though unfriendly relations prevailed between them for centuries (Num. 20.18–21, I Sam. 14.27, II Sam. 8.13f., I Kings 11.14ff., etc.). Esau was their supposed ancestor, and he was the elder twin brother of Jacob, Israel's ancestor; the tradition that Jacob tricked Esau out of his birthright (Gen. 27) doubtless reflects a guilt-complex on the part of the Israelites, who are conscious of wrongs inflicted on their cousins. Nevertheless, Israel is convinced that Jehovah loved Jacob and hated Esau (Mal. 1.2f., Rom. 9.13), and the biblical-theological significance of Esau and Edom arises from the fact that they have thus become symbols of those whom God has *not* chosen as the instruments of his saving purpose. See discussion of divine election under CHOOSE, DETERMINATE. In NT times the country of the Edomites was known as Idumaea, and it was from among the Idumaeans that the Herod dynasty sprang—for the Jews a sufficient theological reason for denying the right of the Herods to rule over the true Israel. (*V.* also FIRSTBORN, HATE.)

A. R.

ELDERS (PRESBYTERS) *v.* MINISTER

ELECT, ELECTION *v.* CHOOSE, CALL, DETERMINATE, SAINT

ELIJAH, JOHN THE BAPTIST

The historical importance of Elijah in the development of Israel's religion cannot be exaggerated (*v.* W. A. L. Elmslie, *How Came our Faith* (1948), Chap. XI); as the champion of Jehovah's insistence upon social righteousness against the amoral Phoenician Baal, he became a great hero in the eyes of later ages. Yet we cannot entirely explain the dominating position which he assumes in the biblical theology merely by the fact that he had a hundred years' start over Amos. Perhaps the legend of his miraculous translation to heaven (II Kings 2) encouraged the belief in his return to the earth as the precursor of the Messianic judgment (Mal. 4.5); at any rate by NT times the current Pharisaic teaching was that 'Elijah must first come' (Mark 9.11) before the advent of the Messiah. In the synoptic tradition John the Baptist is explicitly identified with the *Elijah Redivivus* of popular expectation, and this identification is attributed to Jesus' own teaching (Mark 9.11–13, and esp. Matt. 11.13f. and 17.13). Mark's description of John's dress (1.6) is intended to remind his readers of the traditional picture of Elijah (cf. II Kings 1.8); and his detailed description of the Baptist's fate (Mark 6.14–29) is meant to recall the bitter struggle of Elijah against the wicked king and queen, with Herod playing the rôle of Ahab and Herodias that of the scheming Jezebel. It may well be that the identification of John the Baptist with Elijah in the Christian tradition arose first as an attempt to answer the Jewish objection that Jesus could not be the Messiah because Elijah had not yet come; to this it could be replied that Elijah had already come in the person of John. This apologetic might then have been read back into the teaching of the Lord himself. But perhaps it is more likely that John had himself deliberately acted (and dressed) the part of Elijah, in order to give point to his teaching that the day of judgment was at hand; perhaps he had come to believe that he actually was the Elijah. The emphatic words of Jesus, who identifies John with the 'messenger' of Mal. 3.1 and speaks of him as 'more than a prophet' (Matt. 11.9–15), suggest that the Lord himself regarded John as an eschatological symbol and event, a fulfilment as well as a bearer of prophecy, a portent as well as a herald of the Kingdom of God (*q.v.*). It remains to be noted that the Fourth Gospel, somewhat inexplicably, goes out of its way to deny the synoptists' view that John was the Elijah (John 1.21,25), while allowing that he was Isaiah's voice in the wilderness (1.23). In the synoptic story of the Transfiguration (*q.v.*) Jesus appears between Moses and Elijah—the representatives of the Law and the Prophets respectively (Mark 9.4, Matt. 17.3, Luke 9.36), of which he is the fulfilment. (For the connexion between John and Christian baptism *v.* BAPTISM I.)

ALAN RICHARDSON

EMMANUEL

This is the Gk. transliteration, used in Matt. 1.23, of a Heb. phrase more exactly transliterated 'Immanuel' in Isa. 7.14, where it first occurs. The prophet Isaiah had been sent by God with a message of encouragement to King Ahaz of Judah, when his land was invaded and his capital threatened by the allied Kings of Syria and Israel: let Ahaz keep calm; the attack would not succeed. When Ahaz refused to ask for a sign from God in confirmation of the prophet's message, Isaiah offered him one: a child would shortly be born whose mother would call him Immanuel, i.e. 'God (is) with us', and before that child was old enough to tell good food from bad the land of the two enemies so feared by Ahaz would be left desolate (Isa. 7.1–16). There is nothing in the Heb. of this passage to suggest that there would be anything unusual, still less supernatural, about the birth of the child. The Heb. *'almah*, usually here translated 'virgin', means only 'young woman', 'girl', and probably the word translated 'shall conceive' ought to be rendered 'is with child', since the value of the 'sign' depends upon its happening without any long delay. The name which the young mother is to give to her child is significant in the same way as that given to the prophet's own son, Maher-shalal-hash-baz, Isa. 8.4, is significant; it expresses that confident faith in God's care for his people which Ahaz lacked.

In the next chapter the Heb. phrase *immanu-el* occurs twice, vss. 8 and 10. In the second place, there is no doubt that it is an affirmation, 'for God is with us'; the plots of the enemies of Israel shall come to nothing, because God is with his people. It is therefore probable that the meaning is the same in the first place; though the armies of Assyria may overwhelm the land like the River Euphrates in flood, God's protecting wings will also cover the breadth of it, 'for God is with us'. In the Gk. version of the OT the phrase is so translated in both places, even though the second part of vs. 8, like the first, is taken to refer to the covering of the land by the hosts of Assyria, so that there is a rather violent change of metaphor.

In the earlier passage, 7.14, the same Gk. version transliterates the Heb. phrase as 'Emmanuel', and translates *'almah* by *parthenos*, which usually means 'virgin', though it is also used of young women who are not virgins. So the evangelist Matthew could find in the Gk. version, which he quotes in a form which differs slightly from that in the version as we now have it, a prophecy of the VIRGIN BIRTH of Jesus (Matt. 1.23, 'Behold, the virgin shall conceive and shall bear a son, and *they* shall call his name Emmanuel'). It has been held that it was this passage in Isa., in its Gk. form, which gave rise to the Christian doctrine of the virgin birth of Jesus Christ, or, alternatively, that it was at least an essential factor in the genesis of the doctrine. But the probability is that it was only because Matthew already accepted the doctrine of the virgin birth that he found a prophecy of it in this passage. It is significant that no other NT writer refers to the passage. Outside the NT, Justin Martyr (*c.* AD 150) is the first to do so; he uses it as an argument against unbelieving Jews. The use of it in this way led later Jewish translators of the OT into Gk. to remove the word *parthenos* from their versions of Isa. 7.14, and to use instead a word which meant only 'young woman'. But whatever may be said about Matthew's finding in Isa. 7.14 of a prophecy of the virgin birth, it is at least clear that the application of the title of Emmanuel to our Lord bears witness to the faith of the Church at the end of the first century that in the birth of Jesus a sign had indeed been given to the whole human race that God is with us (cf. John 1.14). (*V.* also VIRGIN (BIRTH).)

J. Y. CAMPBELL

END *v.* TIME

ENEMY *v.* ADVERSARY

ENLIGHTEN

This implies an activity of God. The metaphor is common in religious literature for the effect of truth or the knowledge of God which is for man's good, darkness being a ready metaphor for what is evil (cf. Eph. 1.17f.). The divine commandment, i.e. the moral law, is said to enlighten, Ps. 19.8. Life itself may be said to enlighten (Job 33.30), for death is darkness. (Also *v.* LIGHT, LIFE, DEATH, HELL.)

E. C. B.

ENVIOUS *v.* JEALOUS, DESIRE

ENVY *v.* DESIRE

EPHOD *v.* SACRIFICE III(*c*)

ERR *v.* SIN

ESAU *v.* EDOM

ESCAPE

The word occurs frequently both in OT and NT, and is often used untechnically (e.g. St. Paul's escape from Damascus in a fish-basket, II Cor. 11.33, or Acts 27.42). But in many passages the word acquires a peculiarly biblical quality against the background of the biblical sense of man's insecurity or predicament. All man's life is an escape from death, a just penalty that overhangs him; and in this sense every typically biblical escape is but the reverse aspect of an act of divine deliverance (*q.v.*). Lot's escape from the cities of the Plain (Gen. 19.17ff.) is symbolic of man's deliverance from the city of destruction into the city of refuge. The classic OT example of escape is that of the Exodus from Egypt, and every subsequent 'escape' from national destruction (cf. Ps. 124, esp. vs. 7) is interpreted in the light of this deliverance, which demonstrates Jehovah's power and his love for Israel. The NT parallel is, of course, the deliverance accomplished by God through the resurrection of Christ; in this connexion it is worth meditating upon the escape of Barabbas (though the word is not here used), whose other name is Everyman. Often the use of e. marks the sense of gratitude for deliverance (e.g. Isa. 10.20, 45.20f.); God offers a 'way of escape' from the 'trial' of this world (I Cor. 10.13); sometimes the note of warning is sounded (e.g. Rom. 2.3, Heb. 2.3: 'How shall we escape, if we neglect so great salvation?'). The biblical flavour of the word is well brought out by mixing two translations of Ps. 68.20: 'God is unto us a God of deliverances' (RV); 'God is the Lord by whom we escape death' (BCP version). (*V.* also DELIVER.)

A. R.

ETERNAL *v.* TIME

[EUCHARIST] *v.* THANK

EVANGELIST *v.* MINISTER

EVER, EVERLASTING *v.* TIME

EVIL

The Heb. term *ra'* conveys the factual judgment that something is bad (e.g. figs, cattle), displeasing (e.g. a woman in the eyes of her husband), or harmful (e.g. wild beasts, poisonous herbs, disease). Quite generally it means anything that causes pain, unhappiness, or misery, including the discipline of punishment sent by God. The context must determine the exact meaning; thus a man whose heart is evil may be sorrowful or vicious. In I Sam. 18.10 ('an evil spirit from God') it is purely descriptive, i.e. Saul was possessed by something that caused the violent prophetic frenzy, harmful to himself and his household. When God says: 'I make peace and create evil' (Isa. 45.7; cf. Job 2.10), what is meant is that he is the author of prosperity and adversity. The knowledge of good and evil (Gen. 2.9, etc.) does not imply the ability to make moral distinctions, but that perception of what is beneficial or harmful which cannot be expected of childish inexperience (cf. Isa. 7.15f.).

However, the development of a moral connotation is very natural; a harmful action, as viewed by the injured party, is a wicked one (Judg. 11.27, II Sam. 13.16). This equation is also made when an action injures the covenant between God and his people, particularly disobedience and idolatry (Jer. 13.10); but the close relation between the descriptive and moral meanings appears in the 'evil imagination' of Gen. 6.5, 8.21, and the choice between life and good, and death and evil in Deut. 30.15. This choice reappears in the Prophets with a typically moral emphasis (Amos 5.14f., Mic. 3.2, Isa. 5.20).

The Gk. words *poneria(os)* and *kakia(os)* have a similar double meaning which is usually made clear by the context. The moral meaning needs no comment. The descriptive meaning can include 'unsound' (cf. bad fruit, Matt. 7.17f., or a diseased eye, Matt. 6.23); 'malice'; and 'harmful', e.g. Matt. 5.39, 'the man who injures you'. In accordance with OT usage, 'the evil and the good' of Matt. 5.45 is an inclusive term for everyone. In NT times people firmly believed in harmful spirits (Matt. 12.45) or 'the evil one' (Matt. 13.19, Eph. 6.16), who could do great harm in 'this present evil age' (Gal. 1.4; cf. Eph. 5.16 and 6.12f., of the harmful planetary powers). Within this circle of ideas must be found the original meaning of, deliver us from evil' in the Lord's Prayer (Matt. 6.13). (*V.* also DEATH.)

KENNETH GRAYSTON

EXPIATION

This word occurs in EVV only in Num. 35.33 (*v.* SACRIFICE I(*b*)2, ATONE).

EYE

'Eye' predominantly occurs in the Bible in the literal sense of the organ of sight. Several special senses, however, are worth noting, which have only become familiar in English in so far as they have been taken over from biblical usage.

Ps. 19.8, for example, uses the word in a sense we should not expect, when it refers to the commandment of the Lord 'enlightening the eyes'. We may compare Luke 11.34, 'the light of the body is the eye', for a similar thought of the eye as the enlightener of the body in a moral sense. Notice, however, the enlightening of the eyes in a less exalted moral context, as due simply to bodily nourishment, I Sam. 14.27. The use of the word 'eye' does in fact illustrate how closely the ancient Hebrews related spiritual realities to the material embodiment or medium. Their conception of salvation is the prime example of this. Spiritual enlightenment was expected to show itself outwardly in bright eyes; conversely, dull eyes were a sign of weariness or depression (cf. Ps. 6.7, 38.10, Job 17.7, 31.16, Deut. 28.65). This interaction of soul and eye explains the expression 'evil eye', i.e. envy (Deut. 28.54, Prov. 28.22, Mark 7.22, Matt. 20.15) and its correlative, 'bountiful eye' (Prov. 22.9; Heb. *tob*=good) or 'single eye' (Luke 11.34). For pride the Hebrew could speak of a 'high eye' (Ps. 18.27; cf. Prov. 21.4, 'high look and a proud heart', Isa. 10.12); and in a poetic context the expression 'sharpen the eyes against' indicates the glance that means murder; for the Hebrew a fierce look, like a cursing word, had an objectivity and efficacy which are incomprehensible to modern readers.

In some cases where we should expect 'soul' or 'heart' or a personal pronoun, the Bible speaks of 'eye', e.g. Deut. 7.16 ('thine eye shall not pity'), Isa. 13.18 ('their eye shall not spare'), Ezek. 7.4, etc.; cf. also I Sam. 2.33 ('consume thine eyes'), I Sam. 12.3 ('bribe to blind mine eyes'), II Chron. 7.16 ('mine eyes and mine heart shall be there'). This is the distinctive vividness and concreteness of the Heb. language. The conception of character (soul) expressing itself through a particular part of the body is equally typical. 'When a man looks at something, the eye at that moment is the active part of the soul . . . the soul *is* at that moment eye' (Pedersen, *Israel*, I, p. 176). The phrase 'covenant with mine eyes' (Job 31.1) may be understood in the light of this; cf. also Matt. 5.28.

The phrase 'set eyes upon' means turn attention to, whether for blessing or punishment (Jer. 24.6, Amos 9.4). Other noteworthy phrases are 'find grace in the eyes of', and 'in the eyes of' generally, meaning 'in the judgment of' (cf. Ps. 11.4, Num. 15.39). To do what is right in one's own eyes is considered wrong (Deut. 12.8, etc.), man's own opinion being by implication contrasted with the judgment of God. The phrase 'apple of the eye' occurs 5 times in the OT, meaning 'pupil' and in the sense of 'that which is most precious'. The Pauline word 'eyeservice' (Col. 3.22, Eph. 6.6) is not distinctively Hebraic, but is very expressive for work which is only done when the eye of authority is upon it, or to curry favour. Among the anthropomorphisms of which the OT is not shy is that which attributes eyes to God. But God's seeing is conceived in a way which conserves his difference from man (cf. I Sam. 16.7, Job 10.4), and his omniscience (cf. Prov. 15.3). In particular, God's seeing means his awareness of man's predicament and readiness to succour him (cf. Gen. 6.5, Exod. 3.7). Perhaps most worth noting of all the 'eye' passages of the Bible are those which place emphasis on the opportunity of seeing the signs of God's saving activity, events which move a man to exclaim, 'This is the Lord's doing; it is marvellous in our eyes' (Ps. 118.23; cf. also Deut. 4.3, 11.7, II Kings 6.17, Job 42.5, and, on the culminating act of God in Christ, Luke 2.30, 10.23f., I John 1.1). (*V.* also MIRACLE.)

E. C. BLACKMAN

* * *

FACE *v.* PRESENCE

FAITH

The Biblical meaning of the noun, and of the associated verb 'to BELIEVE', deserves fuller exposition than is possible here. In Christian Scripture the words denote *the* criterion of right relationship with God, and in this sense St. Paul's doctrine of justification by faith has more than a polemical significance. The terms are most fully developed in the writings of St. Paul and in the Fourth Gospel (where the noun is deliberately avoided), but there is ample evidence from the Synoptic Gospels of their key role in the proclamation of Jesus (cf. Mark 1.15, etc.). In the Pastorals, James, and Jude, 'faith' has a more conventional meaning than elsewhere, and it has been noted that the verb is scarcely found at all. In I Pet. the words are used with full Christian meaning, but their use is coloured by the context of imminent persecution. This applies also to the use in Heb., but there the terms have a special nuance which brings them very close to the Pauline 'hope' (Heb. 11.1). To understand the Biblical use of the words, it is essential to realize that they contain no suggestion of an apprehension in some way inferior to reasoned knowledge, 'believing where we cannot prove'. The NT usage owes little or nothing to Plato. In some instances the noun means little more than the Christian religion, and the verb loyal adherence to it, but in the vast majority of cases the meaning goes back to a Heb. concept which was brought to full actuality in the relation with God established for Christians in Christ.

The core of this Hebrew concept is firmness, reliability, or steadfastness. To believe is to hold on to something firmly, with conviction and confidence. It is implied that steadfastness is sought in the object believed, and that in laying hold of the object, the believer himself will become steadfast. In Deut. 28.64–7 there is a vivid description of the unstable condition of men who cannot cleave in this fashion to the Lord. With this passage may be contrasted the summons to believe in Isa. 26.3f. Usually it is a person, rather than a statement, which is believed; and in the context of men's relation to God the verb always implies personal conviction and trust arising within direct personal relationship. The NT Greek reflects this point by introducing a preposition ('believe *in* . . .') in almost every instance where more is intended than mere credence.

If then a person 'holds sure in God', he may be said to 'have faith'. But the faith which he has, and exercises, has two aspects. From one point of view it is confident reliance on God. It is the act by which he lays hold on God's proffered resources, becomes obedient to what God prescribes, and, abandoning all self-interest and self-reliance, trusts God completely. This is the meaning which the noun 'faith' receives in St. Paul's writings, but it is virtually out of the question to give the noun this meaning in the OT. The most important instance there is the text cited by St. Paul from Hab. 2.4: 'The just shall live by his faith.' We are now, it seems, required to believe that St. Paul had no right to make this text refer to 'faith' in this first, active, sense. In the OT the noun always conveys the second aspect, viz. that a person who has faith is himself made firm and reliable. It is better, from this point of view, to speak of 'faithfulness'. He holds fast to his own integrity, like the righteous man of Ps. 15, and like the Christians in I Pet. It is never suggested, of course, that in the case of man, such faithfulness is a matter of self-reliance or independent achievement. But the suggestion lies very near when the words are used in contexts which obscure the divinely initiated personal relationship of man with God which is their true sphere of application. When, for instance, faith denotes assent to statements or loyalty to a religion, it quickly acquires the aura of a meritorious act. But the loyalty to God which is found in a man of faith, and all the derivative loyalties, are themselves created by *God's* act. On the basis of man's helplessness and instability, God makes the believer firm and trustworthy. The efficacy of faith for salvation and for right relationship with God is not to be sought in the act itself, but rather in that to which a man holds firm by believing. The Fourth Gospel, by the very fact of not using the noun, makes this plain. It is also, of course, the whole point of St. Paul's definition of faith as the criterion of right relationship with God, over against a doctrine of right relationship by works.

But it is not true to say that this act of utter reliance on God is a relapse into quietistic fatalism. The true nature of existence 'in faith' depends entirely upon that which is believed. And in the OT as in the NT that upon which the believer lays hold is the promised acts of God by which he is sustained and indeed recreated. Obedience (*v.* OBEY), conformity to what God prescribes, is the inevitable concomitant of believing. The faith of Abraham, with which St. Paul makes so much play in Rom. 4, is expectation in the presence of God 'who quickeneth the dead and calleth the things that are not as though they were'. The objections which are adduced in Jas. 2.14–26, apparently against argument of a Pauline kind from the case of Abraham, do not take account of the fullness of Pauline thought.

In the Synoptic Gospels, the faith to which Jesus summons men is confident conviction that God, through His Messiah, was able to do what he had promised through the prophets. It is decisive response to the proffered resources of God, directly present now in the flesh of his Son. And in faith the lame walk and the lepers are cleansed. It is not that their healing is a reward for accepting the claims of Jesus. To walk *is* the lame man's act of faith. He walks by directly cleaving to God. In this connexion it is noteworthy that faith, on the lips of Jesus, is often opposed to fear.

The writer to the Hebrews speaks of faith in a way which is fundamentally in harmony with these other writers. He is, however, more conscious of the opposition of faith to sight, and for him faith is confident trust in the *unseen* reality of God's present help, the title-deeds to the *unseen* prize promised to those who steadfastly endure. In St. Paul and St. John, the relation to God which the term 'faith' denotes has particular reference to what was done once for all in the flesh of Jesus. To believe, in the technical Christian sense, is to be related to God in trust and self-abnegation, *via* those historical events. The terms love and hope are used by St. Paul to supplement the description of our existence 'in Christ', and they express more particularly the present relationship with God and the forward look which are so strongly stressed in the faith-concept of Heb. But of course St. Paul makes it plain that the right relationship with himself to which God has brought Christians is a matter of faith 'from start to finish' (Rom. 1.17). And there is no ground for the suggestion that the relationship with God by faith is only a provisional one, to be superseded at some stage in the process of redemption by another one—sight, or unitive love. (*V.* also KNOW, OBEY, RIGHTEOUSNESS, TRUTH.)

BIBLIOGRAPHY

C. H. Dodd: *The Bible and the Greeks*, III, 3, and *The Epistle to the Romans*, on 1.16–17; W. F. Howard: *Christianity according to St. John*, VII; H. F. Lovell Cocks: *By Faith Alone*.

W. A. WHITEHOUSE

FALL

The word 'fall' in our EVV does not carry any special theological meaning. The expression 'the Fall', as applied to Adam's original transgression, is post-biblical; the nearest biblical usage is to be found in Rom. 5.15, where Paul speaks of Adam's *paraptōma* (RV, 'transgression'). This word literally means 'a slip or fall sideways', 'a false step', 'a lapse' (*v.* Sanday and Headlam, *Romans*, I.C.C., *ad loc.*). For treatment of 'the Fall' in this sense, *v.* ADAM, SIN, WORK.

A. R.

FALSE, FALSEHOOD

These words occur as renderings of the same Heb. and Gk. words as 'lie' and 'vanity', and esp. in the phrase 'false witness' (*v.* LIE, VAIN).

E. C. B.

FAMILY, FATHER, ABBA, MOTHER, SON, CHILD, BROTHER

I. THE HUMAN FAMILY

The *family* (*mishpahah*) appears in the later genealogical scheme of the OT as a link between the tribe and the father's house (*beth 'ab*), but in earlier writings no such distinction is made. These groupings are not limited by external rules, but are composed of those who are one FLESH and therefore of the same fundamental character. They extend as far as this unity is felt, i.e. they are homogeneous communities each with its own characteristics. The nucleus and centre of life is the father's house: first, the man as founder, then the wife who helps him to maintain the house, and then the children, i.e. all who call on the man as father. The family is all who claim kin with him. A family once founded lives and grows as long as there are any descendants, and it stretches back into the past to include all who have contributed to the strength of the family. Israel is a confederation of families (Jer. 31.1), the two kingdoms are two families (Jer. 33.24); indeed, the whole people (the widest extension of the community of kin) is one family among the families of the world (Amos 3.2). Whenever the Hebrew wishes to define a community, he speaks of a family (e.g. animals, Gen. 8.19; evildoers, Mic. 2.3) or a house (e.g. Rechabites, Jer. 35.18; artisans, Neh. 3.8).

The man's position in the family is expressed by his being its *ba'al* (possessor and master); his is the ruling will in the community. This does not imply one-sided sovereignty, but a much more intimate relation. The man is the centre from which strength and will emanate to the whole group which belongs to him and to which he belongs. The name FATHER means both kinship and authority—thus Naaman is the f. of his servants (II Kings 5.13), the priest is f. of the cultic community (Judg. 18.19), and Elijah is called f. by his disciple (II Kings 2.12). In late writings f. can mean ruler (I Chron. 2.24,42); and it can be used quite naturally for originator and patron (Gen. 4.20f., 'the f. of such as dwell in tents and have cattle . . . the f. of all such as handle the harp and pipe'). The f. is therefore the object of honour, obedience and love (Exod. 20.12, 21.15,17, Deut. 21.18f., Mal. 1.6); and his strength and authority may extend to an indefinitely large group (Job 29.16, 'a f. to the needy'; Isa. 9.6, 'everlasting f.' of the messianic King).

The complement of the father's authority is found in the meaning of SON, and it is entirely natural that Ben-hadad should call himself Elijah's son when he submits to the prophet's authority in order to be healed (II Kings 8.9); or that Ahaz should call himself the s. of Tiglath Pilezer in asking foreign help (II Kings 16.7). The father's strength is carried on in his sons (hence it is a wife's first duty to bear children to her husband: that is her function as mother—see MARRIAGE), and a s. is one who not only acknowledges the father's authority, but also bears his character (cf. Matt. 23.31, 'ye are sons of them that slew the prophets'; Matt. 5.44f., 'love your enemies, that ye may be sons of your F. . . . for he maketh his sun to rise on the evil and the good . . .'). Closely connected with this is the Hebraic method of describing character: thus, s. of might = strong man, s. of possessions = heir, s. of death = worthy of death. This idiom is not un-Greek, since it might well appear in impressive language, but the frequent NT expressions are clearly connected with Hebraic usage: sons of thunder, Mark 3.17; of comfort, Acts 4.36; of obedience, I Pet. 1.14, and disobedience, Col. 3.6; of peace, Luke 10.6. Apart from those obvious aspects of character, a man's inmost character reveals what kind of realm (psychic community, family) he really belongs to: hence the contrast in Luke 16.8 between 'the sons of this age' and 'the sons of light'; in Luke 20.34,36 between 'the ss. of this age' and 'ss. of the resurrection'; in Matt. 13.38 between 'ss. of the kingdom' and 'ss. of the evil one'. Matt. 8.12 shows that being a s. of the kingdom is not an immutable privilege, but depends on a continuous inner response to the call of God. The broad distinction is maintained throughout the NT: for the one side see Luke 7.35, John 12.36, I Thess. 5.5, Eph. 5.8, Gal. 4.28, Rom. 9.8; and for the other Matt. 23.15, John 17.12, II Thess. 2.3, Eph. 2.3.

A special Hebraic use of *son* is to be noted. 'Son of man' (*ben 'adam*) is a poetic synonym of 'man' (Num. 23.19, Ps. 8.4), i.e. a member of the community of mankind; and is so used with great frequency in Aramaic (cf. Mark 3.28, 'sins shall be forgiven unto the sons of men', where the parallel passage in Matt. has 'men'). In Ezekiel it occurs 90 times as the title by which God addresses the prophet. In Dan. 7.13, 'one like unto a son of man' means a figure in human form in contrast to the previous visions of incredible beasts, and in vs. 18 it is identified with the special community of 'the saints of the Most High'.

It is clear that Jesus put the weight of his authority behind the basic OT estimate of the family (Mark 7.10ff., 10.7,19) and presented his teaching in terms of the family (Luke 11.11, 15.11–32, Matt. 21.31); so that a transformation of the family relationship took place in the early Church (Eph. 6.1ff.). But he proclaimed a call that transcends and even breaks up the family (Mark 1.20, 13.12, Matt. 8.21f., 10.35ff.) just because a new community was now called into being (Mark 10.29f.—note the reward promised 'now'; 3.31–5). This naturally carries with it drastic criticism of every reliance on the fathers in the past (Luke 6.23ff.). Matt. 3.9 is the best commentary on Matt. 23.9: 'call no man your f. on earth, for one is your F. which is in heaven'.

II. GOD THE FATHER

In Semitic religion generally men and their gods form a social, political and religious whole, i.e. a family of which the god is father in a purely physical sense (cf. the 'sons of God' and the daughters of men in Gen. 6.2ff. For this name for supernatural beings, cf. Job 1.6, 2.1, 38.7, Ps. 29.1, 89.6). In the spiritual religion of the Hebrews, however, the idea of divine fatherhood (with its consequent sense of authority) is entirely dissociated from the physical. Man is created in the image of God, not begotten; God-sonship is a thing not of nature but of grace. Israel's creation by the Father-God (Hos. 11.1, Deut. 32.6) refers to a series of historical acts by which Israel was shaped into a nation. Of Israelites as a whole it may be said: 'Ye are the children of the Lord your God' (Deut. 14.1), but the individual Israelite (apart from the actual or messianic king, II Sam. 7.14, Pss. 2.7 89.26f.,) has no right to call himself God's son (W. R. Smith, *Religion of the Semites*).

The transition to the distinctive NT view may be found in Matthew's quotation (2.15) of Hos. 11.1: 'out of Egypt did I call my son'; for Jesus is not only the unique Son of God, but also he is obedient Israel. The works of Jesus meant that men inevitably passed beyond the plain fact of his human sonship (Mark 6.3 and birth narratives) to his messianic position as 'Son of David' (Mark 10.47f., Matt. 12.23, 21.9,15), though Jesus stamps this designation as unsatisfactory in Mark 12.35ff. Jesus' self-chosen designation, however, was 'Son of Man' (e.g. Mark 8.29ff., 14.61f.). This term may, as in the OT and in Aramaic, mean no more than 'man', though it would derive special force from its frequent application to Ezekiel; but it is closely associated in Dan. 7 with the transcendent Kingdom of God, and in the Similitudes of Enoch the symbolic figure of Dan. was invested with the full attributes of a pre-existent heavenly Messiah, combining features of the Davidic king and the Servant of the Lord (though it is not proved that Jesus' use depended on Enoch). The Gospel references to the S. of Man may be divided thus: (*a*) his coming in glory (e.g. Mark 8.38, 13.26, 14.62, Matt. 19.28, 25.31; cf. John 1.51, 3.13f., 5.27); (*b*) his suffering, rejection, death, and exaltation (e.g. Mark 8.31, 9.31, 10.33f., 14.21; N.B. John 6.53, 13.31); (*c*) his present activities (e.g. Mark 2.10,28, 10.45, Matt. 8.20, 11.19, Luke 12.10, 19.10). Hence 'S. of Man' seems to designate the Messiah from heaven who came to identify himself in utter compassion with sinful, suffering Israel, and thus manifested his glory as saviour and judge (for this, and the following discussion, see W. Manson, *Jesus the Messiah*). (*V.* also SON OF MAN.)

Behind Jesus' use of 'S. of Man' to designate his messianic mission, however, lies the name 'S. of God'. Although in a few OT passages, esp. Ps. 2, this was a title of Israel's anointed king, it had no place in official Jewish description of the Messiah. Gk.-speaking Christians, on the other hand, would be accustomed to interpreting all excellence and heroic achievement as manifestations of the divine (cf. Mark 15.39). But 'S. of God' is firmly rooted in the historical record of Jesus in Palestine—at the supreme moments of the Baptism and Transfiguration (Mark 1.11, 9.7), the Temptation and the Cross (Matt. 4.3ff., 27.40). Jesus is recognized as S. of God by the demons (Mark 3.11, 5.7) and his disciples (Matt. 14.33, 16.16), who alone could pierce his incognito.

For the origin of the title we must look to Jesus' own attitude to God. It is notable that he used the direct, intimate ABBA (Aramaic for 'father', Mark 14.36, as in the original version of the Lord's Prayer, Luke 11.2, RV—preserved as the distinctive Christian usage in Rom. 8.15, Gal. 4.6) instead of the customary Jewish sign of respect 'my F.' His unique revelation of the F. (Matt. 11.25ff.) springs directly from the knowledge that God is *his* F. This knowledge is not abstract but is embodied in action, first in the mission of Jesus (Luke 2.49, Mark 8.38, Matt. 10.32f., 25.34, Luke 22.29—the sayings are mostly eschatological), and then culminating in the passion and resurrection (Mark 14.36, Matt. 26.53, Luke 23.34,46, Matt. 28.19, Luke 24.49).

The theological relation of Jesus to God is further worked out by John and Paul. (*a*) The S. reproduces the activity characteristic of the F., i.e. he acts only because he sees the F. acting. The fact that the F. has life in himself makes possible the gift of life in himself to the S. So the S. raises the dead and judges as the F. does, and all proceeds, not from the Son's knowledge of the F., but from the Father's love of the S. (John 5.17–45; cf. Rom. 6.4). (*b*) The F. confers full authority on the S. (John 3.35, 5.22f., 16.15) and honours what the S. does (John 12.26, 14.21ff.). (*c*) The S. is the sole appointed mediator of the F. (John 14.6,9) and through him the gift of the Spirit is sent forth (John 14.16,26, 15.26). This involves a community belonging to the S. (John 6.37) and the reciprocal knowledge of Jesus and the disciples corresponds to the knowledge of F. and S. (John 10.15, 14.20, 17.11,21). (*d*) There is an essential unity of interrelation between F. and S. (John 10.30,38—expressed also in the metaphor of going to and coming from the F., 16.28), but the S. is wholly obedient to the F. (John 15.10), for 'the F. is greater than I' (John 14.28; cf. I Cor. 15.24ff.). This priority of the F. is expressed in the fact that the F. sent the S., i.e. in the priority of God's act (John 14.24; cf. Rom. 8.3,32, Gal. 4.4).

This profound Father-Son relationship is important, not only for the nature of Christ, but also for the nature of the Church; for God is F. of the disciples because he is the F. of Jesus. (*a*) The disciples are to reproduce the activity of God: 'ye shall be perfect as your heavenly F. is perfect' (Matt. 5.48; Luke has 'merciful'; cf. Mark 11.25, Matt. 5.9,45, 7.11). (*b*) The F. confers the Kingdom and the Holy Spirit on the disciples (Luke 12.32, Matt. 10.20). (*c*) The disciples mediate God to others: 'men may see your good works and glorify your F.' (Matt. 5.16). (*d*) There is a fundamental, secret relation of God to the disciples, who depend entirely on him for their very existence (Matt. 6). Hence, throughout the NT, F. is the distinctively Christian name for God, as in the Pauline epistolary salutations (cf. the frequent formula: 'blessed be the God and Father of our Lord Jesus Christ'); and in Eph. 3.14f. Paul speaks of 'the F. from whom all fatherhood in heaven and on earth is named'. It is to be noted that, apart from Matt. 23.9, the Gospels never show Jesus speaking of God as men's F., except to disciples. This corresponds to Paul's insistence that men are sons of God, not by right, but by adoption (Rom. 8.15,23, Gal. 4.5, Eph. 1.5); that men come to God as Father through Christ (Gal. 3.26); and that sonship is a consequence of God's gift of the Spirit (Rom. 8.14, Eph. 2.18: 'through Christ we both have our access in one Spirit unto the Father'). Because of this essential dependence of the sonship of Christians upon the Sonship of Jesus, Paul can say '. . . it was the good pleasure of God . . . to reveal his Son in me, that I might preach him among the Gentiles . . .' (Gal. 1.15f.), and 'the life which I now live in the flesh I live in faith, the faith which is in the S. of God, who loved me and gave himself up for me' (Gal. 2.20). The Epistle to the Hebrews expresses the same relation from the side of Christ's self-identification with the believer: the culminating revelation of God in his Son is worked out in Heb. 1–5 on the principle that 'it became him, . . . in bringing many sons unto glory, to make the author of their salvation perfect through sufferings' (2.10).

In a more general sense, various terms for *children* are used (*teknon*, *teknion*, *paidion*, and 'babe', *nepios*) to convey the sense of community, e.g. Jesus died 'that he might also gather together into one the children of God that are scattered abroad' (John 11.52). Hence, 'as many as received him, to them gave he the right to become children of God' (John 1.12f.). 'Children' therefore became a common term for Christians (e.g. Rom. 8.16f.,21, Phil. 2.15, Eph. 5.1), and Paul could think of them with affection as his children and himself as their father (I Cor. 4.14f.). The term has more than a conventional meaning when the word of Jesus is remembered: 'Whosoever shall not receive the Kingdom of God as a little child, he shall in no wise enter therein' (Mark 10.15; cf. 9.36f. and Luke 10.21: 'thou didst hide these things from the wise and understanding, and didst reveal them unto babes').

The universal, standard name for Christians, however, is *brother* (*adelphos*). In the OT, it is the most comprehensive term (*'ah*, alongside 'neighbour' and 'kinsman', Lev. 19.16–18) for a member of the Hebrew community of kin. It means, first, the one with whom a man has common parents, though in polygamous Israel there are many brothers who have only a common father. Brotherhood extends in fact as far as the feeling of consanguinity and corresponds with the idea of 'family' (Gen. 24.4,27,38). Thus the city community is a family and fellow citizens are brothers. The whole of Israel is a family; therefore all Israelites are brothers (Exod. 2.11, Lev. 10.6, Jer. 34.14)—a fact which is presupposed in Deut., e.g. 'Of a foreigner thou mayest exact it: but whatsoever of thine is with thy brother thine hand shall release' (15.3). Wherever there is social unity, there is brotherhood, e.g. David and Jonathan (II Sam. 1.26); and the pact may extend beyond the normal limits, as when Solomon and Hiram became brothers (I Kings 9.13), and whenever a foreigner was received as a residential guest.

In Acts and Rom. 9.3 the Jewish community is still addressed as brethren (12 times), but overwhelmingly this is the term for Christians (174 times). Jesus had said not only 'one is your teacher, and all ye are brethren' (Matt. 23.8), but also 'if ye salute your brethren only, what do ye more than others? do not even the Gentiles the same?' (Matt. 5.47), i.e. he was bringing men into a family which transcended the limits of blood relationship, because he was claiming them as *his* brethren (Matt. 25.40). Thus the status of a man is entirely changed by membership of the Church ('no longer a slave . . . but a brother beloved', Philemon 16), because he is 'the brother for whose sake Christ died' (I Cor. 8.11f.) and Christ is 'the firstborn among many brethren' (Rom. 8.29). The divine purpose in the work of Christ is just this fundamental unity with his brethren: 'for both he that sanctifieth and they that are sanctified are all of one: for which cause he is not ashamed to call them brethren (Heb. 2.11–18, taken up in the 'wherefore, holy brethren' of 3.1).

The outstanding emphasis on reconciliation in Jesus' use of 'brother' ('first be reconciled to thy brother', Matt. 5.21–6, 7.3–5, 18.15,21,35) is reflected in Paul's horror at finding brother going to law with brother before unbelievers (I Cor. 6.5ff.; cf. Rom. 14.10ff.), and in the conviction that sustains the whole argument of I John: 'he that loveth not his brother whom he hath seen, cannot love God whom he hath not seen' (4.20f., 2.9–11, 3.10–17). Hence brotherly love (*philadelphia*) is the accepted standard of Christian virtue (Rom. 12.10, I Thess. 4.9, Heb. 13.1, I Pet. 1.22, 2.17, 3.8).

KENNETH GRAYSTON

FAST, FASTING

In pre-exilic days fasting, which probably meant total abstinence from food, was practised as a spontaneous expression of strong feeling. It might denote mourning (I Sam. 31.13) or repentance (I Kings 21.27), or be used as a kind of reinforcement for urgent supplication (II Sam. 12.16). With the elaboration of the cultus after the Return, set fasts of religious obligation were appointed at special seasons (*v. HDB*), though the prophets could still call for solemn fasts as a mark of national repentance (Joel 2.12,15). By NT times the Pharisees regarded fasting as a work of merit, and devout Pharisees fasted twice a week (Luke 18.12). Apparently even the disciples of John the Baptist set considerable store by fasting (Mark 2.18). Jesus, while he condemned the ostentatious practices of the Pharisees, nevertheless assumed that his own disciples would fast, just as he assumed that they would pray; but he enjoined them to fast 'in secret', so that men would not know of it: such fasting would have its reward (Matt. 6.16–18). Moreover, he himself practised fasting on at least one important occasion (Matt. 4.2; it should be noted, however, that the words 'and fasting' in Mark 9.29, AV, are probably not a part of the original text; see RV marg.). But beyond his instruction that fasting should be done in secret, he seems to have left no rules upon the subject, and he justified his disciples' non-observance of a fast which the Pharisees and John's disciples were keeping (Mark 2.18f.): wedding-guests do not fast when the bridegroom arrives. The meaning of this saying would seem to be that there is no occasion for fasting in the Messianic Age. The interpretation of the next verse, however, is the key-problem in determining our Lord's attitude towards fasting in the Christian Church: 'The days will come when the bridegroom shall be taken away from them, and then will they fast' (Mark 2.20). If we regard this saying as historical, then it must be supposed that Jesus enjoined the practice of fasting; but some scholars have held that it has been read back into the narrative in order to justify the practice of observing regular fasts which had already arisen in the church for which St. Mark wrote. The NT, however, supplies no evidence that regular fasts were part of the normal life of the Church in the apostolic age. It seems, in view of the bulk of the advice contained in St. Paul's letters to Gentile churches, that exhortations to fastings were not a prominent part of the apostolic teaching; indeed Col. 2.16–23 would seem to deprecate any tendency to make rules on such matters. On the other hand, on special occasions of solemn moment the Church fasted spontaneously (Acts 13.2, 14.23), and Paul himself mentions his own fastings, though these may have been entirely involuntary (II Cor. 6.5, 11.27). More important than such passing references to fasting is the general NT teaching —including that of Jesus and Paul—concerning self-denial, self-control and the endurance of hardship. There is no value in these things as ends in themselves, nor are they to be practised (as in Stoicism) for the sake of the cultivation of one's own soul. There is for Christians a supreme end which makes them utterly worth while—the 'for my sake and the Gospel's' of Mark 8.36. The Christian life is a life of freedom from rules—'handle not, taste not, touch not' (Col. 2.21)—and yet it is comparable to the life of an athlete who is always in training. Thus St. Paul in Acts 24.16 uses the verb *askeō*, 'I train', as of an athlete's training (*askēsis*, whence our 'ascetic'); and in I Cor. 9.24ff. he develops the metaphor: the Christian athlete disciplines himself not for the sake of the victor's laurels, which will soon wither, but 'for the Gospel's sake' (vs. 23), and thus he wins an 'incorruptible crown'. Fasting, like all personal discipline, is but a means to an end; if it loses sight of the end, 'for the Gospel's sake', it becomes merely a 'work of law', an attempt to earn merit, and then it ceases to have any Christian value or sanction.

ALAN RICHARDSON

FATHER *v.* FAMILY

FAULT *v.* SIN

FAVOUR

There is rarely any particular religious significance in the use of this word in the EVV. It is one of the two words used in the OT for the Heb. *chen*, and signifies kindness and goodwill where there is no recognized tie between the two parties concerned. The important factor in the use of the Heb. word is that it is used, almost without exception, of the kindness shown by a superior to an inferior. It includes, therefore, the ideas of graciousness and condescension. The other word used in the OT for the Heb. *chen* is GRACE (38 as against 26 for 'favour'), and this latter word is used in cases where the idea of gracious condescension is more pronounced. There is no slightest obligation on the part of the superior to be thus gracious to the suppliant, and no blame can be attached to him if he is not thus gracious. The suppliant has no claim whatever on the goodwill of his superior, and there is nothing he can do to establish any claim. All the generosity of the superior is 'of grace', that is, of his absolute free will and complete freedom from any liability whatever. The idea of free, undeserved favour on the part of God reaches its fulness in the NT grace (*q.v.*) which is a development, partly from the loving-kindness of God (*q.v.*), and partly from this idea of unmerited favour. (Also *v.* GRACE.)

N. H. SNAITH

FEAR, AWE, DREAD

The 'fear of the Lord' is one of the dominating thoughts of the OT (see esp. the Psalms, and note the arresting personalization in Gen. 31.42, 'the Fear of Isaac'). Fear is to be recognized as one of the basic responses to God's demand on men. His holy otherness throws into relief man's sinfulness (Phil. 2.12). The situation is essentially a moral one—that is, it is God's purity which fills man with a sense of his own unworthiness. So the fear of the Lord is a permanent element in man's relation to God, and is the divine effect on man's anxiety, his uneasy conscience and divided loyalties. It transforms man's anxiety about himself and his world, leaving him with only this one fear, which is a trembling adoration of the transcendent Holy Lord (Ps. 103.11, 111.10). In the NT the situation is not changed (cf. Heb. 12.28), for the love of God which fills its pages is controlled by this thought of God's transcendent purity. I John 4.18 does not rule out this kind of fear, but only the anxiety which is not aware of God's initiating action of love in Christ. The meaning of the Cross can be seen only against the background of the sin of man and the fury of God's moral purpose—and thus in a context where he is feared as the transcendent Holy One. It is perhaps better to use the word 'awe' or 'dread' rather than 'fear' to describe this experience. (See R. Otto, *The Idea of the Holy*; S. Kierkegaard, *The Concept of Dread*.)

R. G. S.

FEASTS *v.* SACRIFICE IV: Day of Atonement (*e*); Passover (*a*) and esp. (*b*); Tabernacles (*a*) and esp. (*d*); Unleavened Bread (*a*) and esp. (*b*); Weeks (*a*) and esp. (*c*)

FELLOWSHIP, COMMUNION

OT: In EVV 'communion' never occurs in OT, 'fellowship' only once in RV, twice in AV; but the Heb. root *chabar*, which is sometimes, though by no means always, rep. in LXX by Gk. words of the *koinôn-* group (see below), occurs frequently. Its primary meaning is bind, join together. It is used of: joining curtains together (Exod. 26.6, couple; 26.4,10, coupling; 28.7, join); nations forming alliance (Gen. 14.3, joined together); house mutually shared or COMMON (Prov. 21.9, AV, RV, wrongly, 'wide'); bands of fishermen (Job 41.6); comrades (Eccles. 4.10, fellow); joining together for common task (II Chron. 20.35ff., join oneself with); fellow-shepherds (Song Sol. 1.7, 8.13, COMPANIONS); wife (Mal. 2.14, companion); bond uniting worshippers of the Lord (Ps. 119.63, companion); accomplices in wrong-doing (Isa. 1.23, Prov. 28.24, companion); Hos. 6.9, Job. 34.8, COMPANY); association with false gods (Hos. 4.17, join; Isa. 44.11, fellows); 'shall the throne of wickedness have f. with thee?' (Ps. 94.20).

The significant thing is that (with the possible exception of the last ref.) neither *chabar* nor *koinôn-* is used in OT of the relation of men to God. Though the men of the OT certainly experienced f. with God (one thinks at once of the evidence of Pss., Jer., the sacrificial meals, etc.), yet they avoided using the natural word to denote it. The reason for this was their consciousness of the distance between God and man, of the holiness of God. So, unlike the Greeks or even the Hellenistic Jew Philo, who freely talk of *koinonia* between God and men, they speak rather in terms which emphasize the fact of inequality and distance, e.g. 'servant', 'covenant'. So in Deut. 12, where the joy of communion is obviously present, the distance and inequality are underlined by the choice of preposition—'*before* the Lord' (12.7,12,18).

NT: Our main concern is the *koinôn-* group of words: (i) *koinonos* (10 times in NT), one who shares something with someone, partaker, PARTNER, companion; and *synkoinonos* (4), same meaning but stressing the *with* idea; (ii) *koinoneo* (8), (*a*) to have a SHARE in something with someone, (*b*) to give a share in something to someone, and *synkoinoneo* (3), same meaning, but stressing *with*; (iii) *koinonia* (20) sharing, having or giving a share, f.; (iv) *koinonikos* (1), ready to give a share. The whole group is derived from *koinos*—'common' (same root as *syn*=with). Partially synonymous with words of this group are *metecho* (=*koinoneo* in sense (*a*) above); *metochos*, *symmetochos* (adjs.=sharing, sometimes used substantivally); *metoche* (f.); *metalambano* (receive a share, PARTAKE). From the EVV it is impossible to tell whether it is one of these words or one of the *koinôn-* group that is used in a particular place, or whether it is verb, noun, or adj. The *koinôn-* words and synonyms are sometimes used in a merely general or secular sense (e.g. Luke 5.7,10); but in the great majority of instances they have a definitely theological meaning and refer to specifically Christian f., the foundation of which is the sharing together by Christians in Christ and his benefits. They occur most frequently in Pauline Epistles, but also elsewhere in NT.

(*a*) To express the fact that *Christians have a share in Christ and his benefits*. Of sharing in God's grace (Phil. 1.7), the gospel (I Cor. 9.23; cf. Phil. 1.5 (?)), the promise (Eph. 3.6), the glory that shall be revealed (I Pet. 5.1), the body and blood of Christ in the Eucharist (I Cor. 10.16; cf. 17), the Holy Spirit (Phil. 2.1,

II Cor. 13.14), the divine nature (II Pet. 1.4). (Cf. use of *koinos*='common', in Jude 3, Tit. 1.4). I Cor. 1.9 and Heb. 3.14 should be included here, if 'the f. of his Son Jesus Christ' and 'partakers of Christ' denote the *sharing in Christ* by Christians (but see below). The idea of sharing in Christ is not confined to passages where these words occur: it is implied, e.g. by the metaphors of vine (John 15) and body (Rom. 12.5, I Cor. 12.12ff.).

(*b*) In I Cor. 1.9, Heb. 3.14 it is not certain whether sharing *in* or sharing *with* Christ is meant. The latter idea is certainly present in NT. So in Phil. 3.10 'the f. of his sufferings' means sharing *with* Christ in his sufferings (cf. II Cor. 1.5,7, Col. 1.24). It is also expressed by the *syn-* (with) compound verbs, many of which are peculiar to Paul: die-, live-, crucify-, suffer-, glorify-, bury-, raise-, quicken-, reign-, make to sit-with, and the noun joint-heir with (see Rom. 6.4,6,8, 8.17, II Cor. 7.3, Gal. 2.19, Eph. 2.5,6, Col. 2.12,13, 3.1, II Tim. 2.11,12). These verbs often occur in pairs of contrasts, the present sharing with Christ in his sufferings being thought of as a pledge of a future sharing with him in his glory. Cf. I Pet. 4.13. Paul regards this sharing with Christ as so intimate and close that he can even say that, if there is no resurrection for us, then neither can there have been for Christ (I Cor. 15.13). The NT speaks not only of our sharing with Christ in the phases of his life, but also of his sharing with us (e.g. Heb. 2.14; cf. 17f., 4.14ff.). This f. *with* Christ (as distinct from sharing with other Christians *in* Christ) is most directly stated in I John 1.3, where the claim is also made that 'our f. is with the Father'. Note the contrast with the OT avoidance of *chabar* (see above) with ref. to God. In the meantime the supreme miracle of the Incarnation had taken place, the sheer grace of which so occupied the minds of the NT writers that they were in no danger of conceiving of their f. with God in terms of that presumptuous familiarity which the OT writers were concerned to avoid.

(*c*) But Christian f. consists of a twofold relationship. It is at the same time both a vertical relationship (the sharing together of Christians *in* and *with* Christ) and also a horizontal (the sharing *together* of Christians in and with Christ). So far we have been considering the vertical relationship. We must now look at the horizontal, the relationship that exists between Christians as a result of their common sharing in Christ and his benefits. Many passages might be cited to illustrate this, including those already cited under (*a*). (See also I John 1.3,7.) This relationship is expressed in love and unity, in mutual sympathy and service. It is of the utmost importance to realize that these two relationships are for the NT quite inseparable. The vertical is the origin of the horizontal, while the outward expression of the horizontal is at the same time the sign and pledge of the reality of the vertical. In exhortations to brotherly love, appeal is constantly made to the fact of the common sharing in Christ and his gifts (e.g. Phil. 2.1f.; cf. the connexion between I Cor. 1.9 and 10). So Christians are to love one another as Christ has loved them (John 13.34) and to wash one another's feet, because they have partaken in his washing of their feet (John 13.12ff.). Constant stress is laid on the importance of preserving *unity* (John 17.21–3, Eph. 4.1ff., Rom. 12.16, 15.5, II Cor. 13.11, Phil. 2.2, 4.2, I Pet. 3.8) and on the scandal of division (e.g. I Cor. 1.10ff., 3.3ff., 11.18ff.). In the Eucharist the two relationships are expressed (see esp. I Cor. 10.17).

The vitality of this f. is strikingly indicated by the remarkable number of *syn-* compounds in the NT used with ref. to what we have called the horizontal relationship (most of them different from those mentioned under (*b*) above); e.g. fellow-prisoner (Rom. 16.7), fellow-servant (Col. 1.7, 4.7, Rev. 6.11), fellow-worker (Rom. 16.21, Col. 4.11), fellow-citizen (Eph. 2.19), fellow-soldier (Phil. 2.25), of one accord (*sympsychos*, Phil. 2.2), elect together with (I Pet. 5.13), imitators together (Phil. 3.17), partaker with (Phil. 1.7), compassionate (*sympathes*, I Pet. 3.8, also the verb *sympatheo* in Heb. 10.34), suffer with (I Cor. 12.26), rejoice with (*ibid.* and Phil. 2.17f.), labour with (Phil. 4.3, also in 1.27 same Gk. word, where Weymouth translates 'fighting shoulder to shoulder'), find rest together with (Rom. 15.32), fitly frame together (Eph. 2.21, 4.16), build together (Eph. 2.22), comfort with (Rom. 1.12), and in Eph. 3.6, one after the other, fellow-heirs, fellow-members of the body, fellow-partakers. The fact that many of these *syn-* compounds first occur in the NT indicates the newness and uniqueness of this Christian f. Characteristic of the Church was a *togetherness* far deeper than any mere camaraderie.

In the early days of the Church in Jerusalem this f. found outward expression in a form of communism of material possessions (Acts 2.44f., 4.32ff.). The word *koinonia* (RV, fellowship) in Acts 2.42 is most probably a technical term for this having all things common (*koina*) mentioned in 2.44, 4.32. That is probably the significance of the definite article in the Gk., omitted by both AV and RV (but *v.* C. H. Dodd, *The Johannine Epistles*, p. 7). Acts 6.1–6 shows the development of the Church's *diakonia* or charitable work and the origin of the Diaconate. A charming glimpse is provided by Acts 9.36,39, of a timeless expression of

Christian f. In the Pauline Epistles great stress is laid on the collection for the poor saints in Jerusalem, and it is in connexion with this very practical thing that Paul writes one of his most beautiful sentences about the grace of Jesus Christ (II Cor. 8.9). He regarded it as an expression of f. between Gentile and Jewish Christians (Rom. 15.27). In I Cor. 16.1,2, the ordinary matter-of-fact word *logeia* (COLLECTION) is used, but in Rom. 15.26 and II Cor. 9.13, the word *koinonia* itself is used of the collection. AV renders once by CONTRIBUTION, once by DISTRIBUTION, RV in both places 'contribution'; thus EVV obscure the fact that the actual word f. is here used as a technical term for the collection, which was an expression of f. One could have wished that the RV had noticed this in a marginal note, or even rendered it by some such phrase as 'act of f.' In II Cor. 8.4 occurs the striking phrase 'the f. of the diakonia'. In Heb. 13.16 *koinonia* denotes not indeed a concrete collection, but the act of giving (EVV turn by a verb). Other *koinôn-* words are similarly used (Gal. 6.6, Phil. 4.14,15, I Tim. 6.18). See further F. Hauck in *TWNT*, III, pp. 789–810, to whom the present writer is much indebted.

C. E. B. CRANFIELD

FIGHT *v.* WAR

FIRE *v.* BURN

FIRMAMENT *v.* HEIGHT

FIRSTBORN, BIRTHRIGHT

I. *SPECIAL POSITION OF FIRST-BORN*

(*a*) The f. male, whether of man or beast, was regarded as belonging to the Lord. The f. of beasts were sacrificed, though the f. of an ass might be redeemed; the f. son was redeemed (Exod. 13.11–16, 34.19f., Deut. 15.19–23, Exod. 13.1). Exod. 22.29f. lays down that the f. is to be given to God on the eighth day from birth. Though the idea of the f. belonging to God probably goes back to primitive nomadic days, the practice is connected with the slaying of the f. of Egypt in Exod. 13.15, Num. 3.13, etc. It is possible that at one time f. sons were sacrificed (cf. II Kings 3.27, Mic. 6.7). (*b*) The f. possessed the *birthright*, which meant that he succeeded his father normally, and received the largest share ('a double portion of all that he hath') of the estate (Deut. 21.15–17). But the f.'s right was often passed over, e.g. Solomon, and cf. I Chron. 26.10. In the case of Esau and Jacob this was accounted for by Esau selling his birthright (Gen. 25.29–34).

II. *APPLICATIONS OF THE WORD FIRST-BORN IN OT AND NT*

(*a*) Israel is called the f. of the Lord (Exod. 4.22, Jer. 31.9), having a privileged position among the nations (cf. also INHERIT). (*b*) To the King of the house of David it is said, 'I also will make him my f., the highest of the kings of the earth' (Ps. 89.27). (*c*) In NT Christ is 'the f. among many brethren' (Rom. 8.29), 'the f. of all creation' (Col. 1.15), 'the f. from the dead' (Col. 1.18), 'the f.' (Heb. 1.6), 'the f. of the dead' (Rev. 1.5). (Cf. 'firstfruits' in I Cor. 15.20,23.) The application of the term to Christ expresses simultaneously his pre-eminent position (cf. 'the head of the body' in the same verse in Col. 1) and the fact that he shares the inheritance with his brethren. (*d*) The term is also applied to the faithful departed in Heb. 12.23 according to the most likely exegesis.

III. *THE BIRTHRIGHT OF ESAU*

In Heb. 12.16f. 'Esau, who for one mess of meat sold his own birthright' is a type of those who throw away their heavenly hope for the sake of temporal things.

C. E. B. CRANFIELD

FLESH, FLESHLY, CARNAL

The Heb. word *basar* has a wider meaning than animal flesh or the human body. Soul and flesh were distinguished (Isa. 10.18), but not as two fundamentally different forms of existence. Soul is more than flesh, but flesh is a perfectly proper manifestation of soul (Gen. 2.7), and therefore Job can say: 'horror taketh hold on my flesh' (21.6). Flesh means the entire human being. In Ps. 16.9f. heart, glory, soul, and flesh all mean the whole man in different manifestations. A ghost lacking flesh and bones has undergone psychic dissolution and has no real concrete existence (Luke 24.39). 'All flesh' means all souls displayed in bodies of flesh, i.e. the community of mankind (cf. Luke 3.6); and to be one flesh (by kinship, Gen. 37.27, and esp. by marriage, Gen. 2.24, Mark 10.8) is to have community of soul.

Man has a soul of flesh, i.e. a weak form of soul compared with divine souls, which are of less perishable substance. There is but one scale of existence with soul and strength at the top, flesh and weakness at the bottom; but this contrast is only made between men as a whole and God (Ps. 56.4, Isa. 31.3; cf. Matt. 16.17, John 1.13). A contrast is never made between weak flesh and strong soul within the individual.

The Gk. word *sarx* may simply mean the body (II Cor. 12.7, Gal. 4.13f.), and in I Cor. 15.39 clearly expresses the essence of a creature's nature. Paul can say indifferently that his spirit or flesh had no relief (II Cor.

2.13, 7.5). *Sarx* also means kinship (Rom. 11.14; and Eph. 5.29, where the meaning moves between 'his own actual body' and 'his own wife' because of the psychic unity established in marriage; cf. I Cor. 6.16). Hence it means the sphere of birth and natural descent (Rom. 4.1, 9.3,5,8, Gal. 4.23,29, II Cor. 11.18, Phil. 3.4, Heb. 7.16—in the Christological statement of Rom. 1.3 the Pauline antithesis of flesh and spirit creeps in; cf. I Tim. 3.16, I Pet. 3.18).

Therefore 'flesh' is used for observable, external things, e.g. Col. 2.1 means 'have actually seen me personally', and I Cor. 7.28 is equivalent to our 'practical difficulties'. In this sense there is often an implication of inferiority (Rom. 2.28) which arises from the standard contrast between mankind and God (cf. I Cor. 15.50, Gal. 1.16, Eph. 6.12). Flesh is therefore the sphere of imperfection: of knowledge, II Cor. 5.16, Rom. 6.19 ('because of your natural limitations'); of judgment, I Cor. 1.26; of will, II Cor. 1.17; and in I Cor. 3.1,3 'carnal' means defective in spiritual apprehension because of strife, etc. Because of this weakness, *sarx* is the sphere of sinfulness (Rom. 13.14, where clearly 'lusts of the flesh' are much more than sensuality, and 'flesh' means the whole personality wrongly directed; cf. Gal. 5.13, Eph. 2.3).

In Paul flesh and spirit are not contradictory modes of existence (II Cor. 7.1), though spirit is greater than flesh (Gal. 3.3) and the flesh may have to be sacrificed to preserve it (I Cor. 5.5). Although flesh is inevitably subject to dissolution, and spirit exists in the sphere of eternal life (Gal. 6.8), in principle flesh is morally neutral. However, there exists in fact a dynamic hostility between flesh and spirit, set out in Gal. 5.16–23, and more fully in Rom. 8.3–14, out of which the following points arise: (1) the flesh is weak and sinful, inevitably associated with death, and at enmity with God (cf. Rom. 7.14,18, and passages where the 'members' are the seat of sin). (2) It is contrasted with Spirit, which is associated with life and peace. Spirit is not a natural possibility for man, but depends on the Spirit of God indwelling him. (In John the new possibility is to be 'born of the Spirit', 3.6.) Hence arises the contrast between life in the flesh and in the Spirit. Paul does not here distinguish between life *in* the flesh and life *according to* the flesh, as he clearly does in II Cor. 10.2–5. In Rom. 7.5, 8.9, Col. 2.11 it seems to be implied that Christians are no longer 'in the flesh', but this impression is corrected by Phil. 1.22,24 and Gal. 2.20 (follow RV marg.). The wide range of meanings for *sarx* have not been reduced to a uniform terminology. (3) The positive value still given to the flesh is seen in Col. 1.24: Paul identifies himself with Christ's sufferings and completes that identification by suffering in his actual person, which belongs to the community of mankind in the flesh. When he refers to the manifestation of fleshly weakness in the individual he speaks of the sinful body. The body is dead because of sin (cf. the crucifixion of the flesh in Gal. 5.24), and its deeds must be put to death by the Spirit; but the Spirit can also make mortal bodies alive by the power that raised Jesus: cf. II Cor. 4.11, 'that the life also of Jesus may be manifested in our mortal flesh'. (4) Jesus came in the likeness of sinful flesh (in Eph. 2.15, Col. 1.22, where his meaning is not open to misunderstanding, Paul can speak without qualification of the flesh of Jesus) to condemn sin in the flesh, i.e. the victory was won on the ground where sin is strongest and man weakest; cf. Heb. 2.11ff., 10.5–20.

Johannine theology is quite clear that, in the Incarnation, the normally weak flesh becomes the perfect embodiment for the divine Logos (John 1.14). In the important passage, John 6.51–6, the flesh and blood of Jesus mean Jesus himself in his totality; to eat his flesh and to drink his blood means to take in his life. Those who do so *have* eternal life; they do not assimilate an alien 'soul' because it is the Logos which has become flesh. The primary reference is to faith in Christ and communion with him, though the realistic imagery also points to the Eucharist. The primacy of the *divine* transformation of flesh is therefore guarded by the statement of 6.63 that 'it is the Spirit that quickeneth; the flesh profiteth nothing'.

KENNETH GRAYSTON

FLESHLY *v.* FLESH

FLOOD *v.* NOAH

FOE *v.* ADVERSARY

FOLLY, FOOL, FOOLISH, FOOLISHNESS

In the OT several Heb. words denote 'folly', 'fool', etc. They do not usually imply mere stupidity or actual insanity, except in certain cases where the context makes this clear. There is generally a religious and ethical content in them. Folly is the opposite of wisdom (*q.v.*), which is always regarded as a gift of revelation. Hence the Gentiles, who do not possess revelation, are 'a foolish nation' (Deut. 32.21, etc.); when Israel disregards the divine revelation which she has received, she also is 'foolish' (Deut. 32.6, etc.). Since the content of wisdom is detailed in the Law, disobedience to the Law is the essence of folly; it leads to the denial of God—not so much theoretical atheism, but that overlooking of the divine righteousness which leads inevitably to disaster (Pss. 14.1, 53.1; Isa. 9.17, etc.). In Rom. 1.18–32 St. Paul shows how the corruption of such knowledge of God as the Gentiles should have possessed leads to every kind of superstitious, idolatrous and immoral foolishness: 'professing themselves to be wise, they became fools' (vs. 22). A special OT usage frequently employs 'folly' to denote sexual immorality (Deut. 22.21, etc.). It follows from the general OT use, described above, that amongst the Jews to call a man a fool is much more derogatory than merely to call him stupid or mad. This must be borne in mind when we come to explain the difficult Matt. 5.22: 'whosoever shall say, Thou fool, shall be in danger of the Gehenna of fire'. Jesus' meaning would seem to be: The rabbis say that if you say *Raca* (an expression of contempt) to a man, you are liable to punishment by the local council (Sanhedrin): but I say that, even if you so much as call a man a fool, you will be in danger of divine judgment and punishment (*v.* F. W. Green, *St. Matthew*, in the Clarendon Bible, Oxford, 1936, *ad loc.*). It is a serious matter to be a fool in the biblical sense, and the word virtually means 'apostate' or 'damned'. Hence folly is contrasted with that 'wisdom from the Lord' which is spoken of so highly in the NT as well as in the Wisdom Literature (cf. esp. Jas. 3.13–18). But there is a 'wisdom of the world' (Jas. 3.15) which is wise only in its own conceit (cf. Rom. 11.25, 12.16; cf. Prov. 26.5,12,16), and which is in truth folly in the eyes of God. This is the wisdom which confounds God's strength with weakness and its own weakness with strength (I Cor. 1.26–2.14). 'The wisdom of this world is foolishness with God' (I Cor. 3.19; cf. context, and cp. 4.10; II Cor. 11.16ff.). Paul is here using the language of paradox, but it is the paradox of the cross—'the divine foolishness'—which has inspired him to write in this way. He returns to the normal biblical usage in Eph. 5.15–17: 'Be ye not foolish, but understand what the will of the Lord is.' From this verse we may deduce the full biblical meaning of 'wise' and 'foolish'. (*V.* also WISE.)

ALAN RICHARDSON

FOOL *v.* FOLLY

FORBEAR, FORBEARANCE

In the OT the verb usually means 'cease, leave off', as in Exod. 23.5, where the meaning is 'refuse to help', and in the repeated phrase of Ezekiel 'whether they will hear, or whether they will forbear', where the meaning is 'whether they will obey or refuse to obey'. But in the NT the words, noun and verb, are used mainly of God's forbearance, by which he purposes to bring men to repentance. In this sense, the word is almost a synonym of long-suffering (*q.v.*).

The reference is to the suspension of the punishment which is due for sin, i.e. holding back, as in the OT in Prov. 25.15 and Jer. 20.9, not allowing the natural consequence to follow. The idea of suspension comes from the classical Gk. use of *anoche* (used in Rom. 2.4, 3.26) to mean an armistice, truce, temporary suspension of hostilities. God therefore calls a truce against sin; he does not retaliate forthwith in executing his judgment upon it; he delays the punishment. Thus the two words, 'forbearance' and LONG-SUFFERING, both refer to God's delayed action in respect of the punishment for sin, and are equally designed to suggest opportunity for repentance. The idea of delayed action is explicit in the word 'forbearance', but implicit in the word 'long-suffering', which emphasizes rather the patient endurance of God in spite of all man's waywardness and slowness in turning back to him.

Forbearance is required of Christians as being equivalent to long-suffering, Eph. 4.2 and Gal. 5.22. It involves readiness to forgive, and unwillingness to insist upon personal rights to the detriment of another.

N. H. SNAITH

FORE-ORDAIN *v.* DETERMINATE

FORGET

Sometimes the word is used in its everyday sense (e.g. Mark 8.14), but elsewhere a peculiarly biblical meaning emerges. Man forgets God: Deut. 4.23, etc., Ps. 9.17, 50.22, 103.2. God forgets man, or seems to, because of man's disobedience or unworthiness, e.g. Jer. 23.39. More commonly what a worshipper calls the forgetfulness of God is a temporary obscuring of his providence as it appears to man in suffering a persecution, e.g. Ps. 13.1. This, however, is not the final word of the OT; cf. Isa. 49.14f., which discerns that a bond stronger than natural affection unites God to his human worshippers and makes it impossible for him to forget them (cf. also Luke 12.6). (*V.* also MEMORY.)

E. C. B.

FORGIVE, FORGIVENESS

In the OT there are three words which are translated by 'pardon' and 'forgiveness' in the proportion of one to three, and with approximately the same relative frequency. From this we may judge that there is little difference between the meaning of the two words in EVV. The actual three Heb. words are *kipper* (probably meaning 'cover', once rendered 'pardon' and thrice 'forgiveness'), *nasa'* ('lift up, carry away', 4 and 13), and *salach* (possibly 'let go', but actually of wholly uncertain derivation, 13 and 35).

All three words are metaphors for the removal of sin. It is covered, so that it no longer obtrudes itself between man and God; it is carried away, so that it ceases to form a barrier; it is forgiven, so that there is no resentment or anger in the mind of the injured party. The first and the last of these three words are used only of God's forgiveness, e.g. for the first, II Chron. 30.18 and Deut. 21.8, Ps. 78.38, Jer. 18.23. The second word is used of forgiveness generally, whether of God to man, or between man and man. The more usual translation of the root *kipper* is 'atone' (*q.v.*).

Forgiveness is throughout conditional upon REPENTANCE, a word which quite clearly in its OT and NT equivalents involves a change of mind and intention. Its result is a restoration of the original relationship of good favour with its accompanying blessings. The sacrificial system provided a system of offerings (sin and guilt offerings) by which the taking away of sin involved in the forgiveness which follows repentance was symbolically set forth, the original 'magical' significance of the rite being doubtless spiritualized. Further, the giving of the gift was a token of the amends which the repentant sinner purposed to make. The prophets were insistent that no sacrifice of any type was of the slightest avail unless it was accompanied by sound ethical and humanitarian conduct, and to this, beyond question, the best of the priests would willingly subscribe. The prophets insisted, in season and out of season, on turning back again to God and a definite change of attitude.

In the NT there are three Gk. words translated 'forgiveness'; the word 'pardon' not being found in the NT of the EVV. These three words are *apoluo* ('loose away', twice only and both in Luke 6.37), *charizomai* ('be gracious', 11 times), and *aphiemi* ('send away', verb and noun 56 times). The last of these words belongs almost entirely to the Gospels and Acts, and the second is Pauline, being connected etymologically with his word for grace (*charis*). For Paul the idea of forgiveness is involved in his term 'justification' (*q.v.*), which includes all those elements which are concerned with a man coming into the right relationship with God.

For Jesus Christ, and therefore for the Christian, there is no limit to forgiveness, assuming always that there is true repentance on the part of the forgiven one. The rule is 'not once, nor seven times, but seventy times seven' (Matt. 18.20f.). This latter is a Rabbinic phrase for 'without limit'. There is another Rabbinic phrase used in connexion with forgiveness—namely, 'hath not forgiveness for ever'. It is used in the Talmud (*Jer. B. Qam.*, 6c) in a discussion concerning slander. This phrase lies at the root of the difficult sayings in Matt. 12.31f., in Mark 3.28–30, and in Luke 12.10, which is in part a repetition of the Matthean passage. The Mark passage, which looks like the original, is almost exactly the equivalent of the Rabbinic saying, and, as R. Travers Herford pointed out many years ago (*Pharisaism, Its Aim and Method*, 1912), the context is one of slander in that they said (Mark 3.30) that Jesus had an unclean spirit. This slander involved blasphemy against the Holy Spirit because it asserted that Jesus cast out devils by the prince of devils and not by the Holy Spirit. If the analogy with the Rabbinic saying is sound, then Jesus actually was talking about a human offence, and he meant that such slander was hardest of all to forgive. In this case, the idea of blasphemy against the Holy Spirit being the unforgivable sin is due to a misconception of the significance of the saying, for it is plain enough elsewhere that, given true repentance, there is no limit whatever to forgiveness. The 'sin to death' of I John 5.16 refers to that persistence in sin which so deadens the sensibility of a man that he cannot repent. It is therefore 'to death' because there can never be forgiveness without repentance.

The condition attached to forgiveness in the Lord's Prayer (Matt. 6.12, Luke 11.4) is that unless we ourselves forgive, then we have no hope of forgiveness from God. This is enforced vividly by the parable of Matt. 18.21–35, where the servant who would not forgive his fellow-servant a trifling debt is delivered to the tormentors till he shall have paid the enormous debt he was owing to his master. The moral is that he who does not forgive cannot repent (cf. also Mark 11.25f.).

The modern attitude tends to suggest that the restoration to full fellowship which is involved in the idea of forgiveness is a direct consequence of human repentance. This is part of that modern tendency which seeks to find rational and this-worldly reasons for the sequence of events, and so makes the restoration of fellowship automatic upon human action rather than upon the actual and personal immediate work of God. The Bible here, as elsewhere, regards God as actively busy in this matter in that he definitely and personally forgives every penitent, and this as a deliberate and separate act. (Also *v.* HEAL, SACRIFICE V.)

N. H. SNAITH

FORNICATION *v.* ADULTERY

FOUNDATION *v.* ROCK

FOUNTAIN *v.* WATER

FREE, FREEDOM, FREEDMAN, LIBERTY

(1) The plain, unmetaphorical idea of freedom as opposed to bondage or slavery is common throughout the Bible, e.g. Exod. 21.2, Jer. 34.9ff., I Cor. 12.13, Gal. 3.28, Rev. 13.16. The Ancient World knew slavery only too well. In the Bible its frequency is somewhat masked by the many instances where 'servant' would be better rendered by 'slave' (RV marg. freq. 'bondservant').

But (2) the OT Law, to which the Code of Hammurabi offers some parallel, provides for the unconditional *release* of slaves. Exod. 21.2 gives freedom to a Hebrew bondman after six years; Deut. 15.12ff. goes further, extending the release to female slaves and commanding the former owner to provide the ex-slave with capital resources for a new start in life. Lev. 25.10 'proclaims liberty' to all inhabitants in the year of jubilee.

The same phrase ('proclaim liberty') is used three times literally and once (17*b*) in bitter irony, in Jer. 34, a passage which shows that the Law was frequently disregarded. But the vitally important use of the phrase is Isa. 61.1, where the literal and metaphorical meanings are combined: 'the Lord . . . hath sent me . . . to proclaim liberty to the captives'. This passage leads straight to the theological conception of freedom in NT; for it was these verses which our Lord read in the Nazareth synagogue with the significant comment: 'To-day hath this scripture been fulfilled in your ears.'

(3)(*a*) This *fact* of realized freedom is echoed again in Christ's words to Peter, Matt. 17.26: 'the sons are free', and to the Jews, John 8.36: 'if the Son shall make you free, ye shall be free indeed'. It is insisted upon by St. Paul, e.g. Gal. 5.1: 'Christ set us free.' (The *fact* is not affected whatever reading and punctuation are adopted.)

(*b*) This freedom is a *present possession*, Gal. 5.1,13, Rom. 6.18,22; cf. I Pet. 2.16. Yet its *future perfecting* is also the subject of Christian hope, when it will be extended to the whole creation, Rom. 8.21. Even for the Christian, there is greater liberty still to come. 'Where the Spirit of the Lord is, *there* is liberty', II Cor. 3.17. The Spirit and his liberty are already truly, but still only partially, ours; cf. Rom. 8.23–5, II Cor. 1.22, 5.5, Eph. 1.14. The present is earnest of a still better future.

(*c*) In *content*, this freedom is not merely from ceremonial, and in themselves morally indifferent, regulations, though it naturally covers these, I Cor. 9.1,19, 10.29. It is freedom from the Law itself, and so from Sin and its wages Death, which are inextricably bound up with the Law. 'Sin shall not have dominion over you; for ye are not under law, but under grace', Rom. 6.14. Christian freedom is part and parcel of the new order of things inaugurated by God in Jesus Christ. The new relationship with God is a free gift to the believer, and it is to be enjoyed in perfect freedom. That is the theme of Galatians, worked out more fully in Romans. Thus the believer has been freed from the yoke of bondage to the Law, Gal. 5.1; cf. 2.4. He has been 'discharged from the Law', Rom. 7.6, and with the release comes also release from the authority of sin and death, Rom. 6.18,22, 8.2; cf. John 8.34–6. Thus the Christian is freed too from fear of condemnation, Rom. 8.1. In place of a spirit of bondage he now enjoys the spirit of adoption, and lives as a free son of God, Rom. 8.14–17; cf. Matt. 17.26.

Yet (*d*) *Christian freedom is neither anarchy nor autarchy*. St. Paul's teaching could easily be misunderstood or even deliberately misconstrued, Rom. 3.8, 6.1,15; cf. Jas. 2.14–26, and perhaps II Pet. 3.15f. The maxim 'Love God and do what you like' is always liable to abuse; the 'liberty' of II Pet. 2.19 is really licence. St. Paul's answer is in the form of a paradox. The Christian has exchanged one slavery for another, becoming (as the apostolic writers delight to describe themselves, Rom. 1.1, Jas. 1.1, II Pet. 1.1, Jude 1, Rev. 1.1) the bondservant of Christ in what St. James calls 'the perfect law of liberty' (Jas. 1.25, 2.12). 'Shall we sin because we are not under law, but under grace? God forbid.' That would, in fact, be a return to the bondage of sin and death, Rom. 6.15f. The Christian, on the contrary, is free from sin and has become the bondservant of righteousness, 6.18,22. Thus he *serves* in newness of spirit, 7.6,25, Col. 3.24. He is not his own; he has been bought with a price; he is, in fact, the Lord's freedman, I Cor. 6.20, 7.22f. That is, no doubt, the legal position. But his subsequent conduct will spring not from legal obligation but from overflowing gratitude. It is natural enough that the Christian has seen the position 'typified' in the law affecting the slave who refuses release from his master's service, Exod. 21.5f., Deut. 15.16f. 'I love my master. . . . I will not go out free; . . . and he shall serve him for ever.'

J. P. THORNTON-DUESBERY

FULFIL, ACCOMPLISH

In the EVV these words are used, without difference of meaning, to translate the same Heb. and Gk. words. They are used (1) of the completion of a fixed period of time, e.g. Gen. 25.24, 'when her days to be delivered were fulfilled'; Luke 2.6, 'the days were accomplished that she should be delivered'. Here, and in most instances of this particular sense, the corresponding Heb. and Gk. words mean, literally, 'to fill', and so *fulfil* (=fill full) and ACCOMPLISH (derived from a late Latin word with the same meaning) are very exact renderings. But where the Hebrews thought of the space of time which must elapse before something happened, we more naturally think of the point of time at which it must happen; it would therefore be more in accordance with English idiom to translate, 'when the time came for her to be delivered'. It was believed that the time of important happenings, if not indeed of all happenings, was fixed by God (*v.* APPOINT), and so Mark 1.15, 'The time is fulfilled', really means, 'The time appointed by God has now come'; the meaning is the same in Gal. 4.4, 'when the fulness of the time was come'. The time so appointed might be announced beforehand by prophets, and so both words are used (2) of the happening of things so predicted; thus in II Chron. 36.21 both senses of the word *fulfil* occur—'to fulfil the word of the Lord by the mouth of Jeremiah . . . to fulfil three score and ten years'. This second use is, however, infrequent except in the Gospels and Acts; cf. esp. the frequent occurrence in Matt. of some such phrase as, 'that it might be fulfilled which was spoken through the prophet saying'. In this sense several different Heb. and Gk. words are used, and are rendered by *fulfil* or *accomplish* in the EVV. Among these are the ordinary words which mean 'to do, perform'. So *fulfil* and *accomplish* are used (3) of the satisfying of a desire or request, or of the carrying out of a task or purpose, e.g. Ps. 145.19, 'He will fulfil [lit. "do"] the desire of them that fear him'; Isa. 55.11, 'it shall accomplish that which I please'. There are three Heb. words, and four Gk. words, which mean 'to bring to an end, finish, complete', which are occasionally rendered in the EVV either by *fulfil* or *accomplish*, in one or other of the senses noted.

There are a few passages in the NT in which the use of *fulfil* or *accomplish* may need some further explanation. In Luke 9.31, 'his decease [lit. "departure"] which he should accomplish at Jerusalem', the meaning is that the manner and the place of Jesus' death were foredetermined and foretold; cf. Acts 3.18, 'those things, which God before had showed by the mouth of all his prophets, that Christ should suffer, he hath so fulfilled' (the same Gk. verb, lit. 'fill(ed)', is used in both places). The thought is much the same in Luke 12.50 and 18.31, where the verb means, more exactly, 'to complete'. In Luke 21.24, 'until the times of the Gentiles be fulfilled', the idea probably is that a time has been appointed by God during which the Gentiles will dominate Jerusalem. In Luke 22.16, 'I will not any more eat thereof [the Passover] until it be fulfilled in the kingdom of God', the Passover is thought of as a prophetic 'type' of the kingdom of God—a common Jewish interpretation. When what is fulfilled is the will or the law of God, there is no suggestion that this is in any way the fulfilment of a prophecy. But, except in three instances in which *fulfil* is an over-translation (corrected in the RV) of the ordinary Gk. word meaning 'to do' (Acts 13.22, Eph. 2.3, Rev. 17.17*a*), the meaning is 'to do fully, completely'; cf., e.g. Rom. 13.10, 'love is the fulfilling of the law'. This is the meaning also in Matt. 3.15, 'to fulfil all righteousness', where 'all' emphasizes what is already expressed in 'fulfil'. But in Matt. 5.17, where 'fulfil' is the opposite of 'destroy' (=annul), it must mean 'to bring to completion, to bring out [its] full intention'; this our Lord did by his teaching. In the next verse, 'till all be fulfilled' is a mistranslation; the Gk. means 'till everything comes to pass'. Since this is a repetition in different words of the first clause, 'Till heaven and earth pass', it is probably a gloss which has somehow got into the text. (*V.* also PROPHECY I, TIME, DETERMINATE.)

J. Y. CAMPBELL

FULL, FULLNESS

The adjective *full* is often used in the EVV in senses not current in modern English, e.g. 'full of years', 'full of days' (=aged): 'I am full', Phil. 4.18 (=I have all I need or desire), but the context usually makes the meaning sufficiently clear.

The noun *fullness* sometimes means 'the state of being full', and so 'abundance', e.g. Ps. 16.11 ('fullness of joy'), Ezek. 16.49 ('fullness of bread'), but more often it means 'that which fills', 'content(s)', e.g. Ps. 24.1 =I Cor. 10.26, 'The earth is the Lord's and the fullness thereof'. Corresponding to the use of the adjective in such phrases as 'full of faith' is the use of the noun in John 1.16, 'of his fullness have all we received, and grace for grace' (better, 'from his fullness . . . grace upon grace'); he who was himself 'full of grace' has imparted that grace to others. Two passages in Colossians seem to express essentially the same idea: 'It was the good pleasure *of the Father* that in him [Christ] should all the fullness dwell', 1.19, and 'in him dwelleth all the fullness of the Godhead bodily', 2.9 (RV). Taken by themselves, these two sentences might be theological statements about the essential nature of Christ, closely parallel to John 1.14, 'the Word was made flesh'. But in both places Paul goes on to speak of what God has done for Christians through Christ: 'and through him to reconcile all things unto himself', 1.20; 'and in him ye are made full', 2.10.

So he seems to be thinking chiefly of the fullness of divine grace which is in Christ, and by him is made available for men. It is possible, however, that 'the Fullness' (Gk. *plērōma*) was a quasi-technical term used by the Colossian heretics whose teaching Paul is combatting; that would explain the use of it, without any qualifying addition, in the first passage. These teachers seem to have held that Christ was only one of many partial manifestations of the Deity ('Godhead'); 'the Fullness' was the totality of all such manifestations. But Paul insists that the whole fullness is in Christ alone; no supplementary manifestation is either necessary or possible. And since there is no real difference between the totality of the Deity and God simply, it is also possible that the first passage ought to be translated: 'In him all the fullness of the Deity was pleased to dwell.'

The use of the same word in three passages in Ephesians is different, and quite untechnical. In 4.13 the goal of Christian development is said to be 'mature manhood' (AV, 'a perfect man'; RV, 'a full-grown man'), or 'the measure of the stature of the fullness of Christ'. Probably the latter phrase means simply that the ideal of manhood is fully and perfectly realized only in Christ. But this is an ideal, not for the individual Christian, but for the Christian Church as a whole; the Church is to become a 'larger incarnation' of Christ, an organism through which he can work perfectly. The ideal will be realized only when all Christians are 'filled with all the fullness of God', 3.19, i.e. with the fullness which has its source in God, not the fullness which God has in himself, since neither individually nor collectively can men ever be filled with all the fullness of God in the latter sense. Much the same idea is expressed from a somewhat different point of view in 1.23, where the Church is said to be the body of Christ, and 'the fullness of him that filleth all in all'. Christ 'fills' the whole universe (cf. Col. 1.17, 'in him all things consist', or 'hold together'), but more especially he fills the Church, and makes it a living whole through which he effects his purposes, i.e. his 'body'. Another possible interpretation of 'fullness' as 'that which fills *up*, completes' (cf. Matt. 9.16, where the same Gk. word is used of a patch which is meant to 'fill up' a damaged garment) seems less appropriate in this context, though it is true that without his Church even Christ would not be 'complete'.

The other instances of 'fullness' in the NT are not difficult. 'The fullness of the time', Gal. 4.4, means the coming of the time appointed by God (cf. Acts 1.7); probably 'the fullness of the times', Eph. 1.10, means just the same, though the idea of the progressive infolding of God's plan in history may be in the writer's mind. In Rom. 11.12 'their fullness' means the ingathering of all Israel into the Church.

J. Y. CAMPBELL

* * *

[GEHENNA] *v.* HELL

GIFT(S) *v.* SACRIFICE I(*b*)1, SPIRIT VIII(*e*), MINISTER

GLADNESS *v.* JOY

GLORY *v.* PRESENCE

GOD, GODS

The materials may conveniently be arranged under four main headings:

I The Biblical Knowledge of God
II The Development of the Biblical Thought about God
III Names of God
IV Gods

I. THE BIBLICAL KNOWLEDGE OF GOD

At the outset it is essential to realize that according to the Bible the knowledge of God is not reached by abstract speculation, as in Gk. philosophy, but in the actual everyday business of living, of social relationships and of current historical events. God is known not by thinking out ideas about him, but by seeking and doing his will as made known to us by prophetic men and by our own consciousness of right and wrong (cf. John 7.17, Jas. 1.27, I John 4.7f., 12). No passage in the Bible better expresses this truth than Jer. 22.15f.: 'Did not thy father do judgment and justice? Then it was well with him. He judged the cause of the poor and needy; then it was well. Was not this to know me? saith the Lord.' God is made known to all men, even though they may not have learned to call him by his proper name, as moral demand in everyday life; disobedience to the known moral law is a degrading of our knowledge of God (Rom. 1.18ff.). It is because of the rebellious disobedience of those outside the Covenant that the knowledge of God amongst the heathen remains distorted and confused (*v.* Richardson, *Christian Apologetics*, Chap. V, esp. §4).

Essentially of a piece with this knowledge of God which comes to us in our encounter with his moral law in everyday life is the deeper insight of the prophets, by which the distinctively biblical understanding of God is brought to us; the significance of the work of the prophets is that they deepen, clarify and articulate our knowledge of God's character and purpose. It is they who interpret for us the action of God in history; they stand, for example, in the midst of a great historical crisis in their nation's life and interpret what God is doing in the events of their day. Thus it is true to say that the full development of the biblical understanding of God is due to the prophetic realization that he is the Lord of history, the controller of the rise and fall of nations and empires. This conception of God as the God of history is the differentiating characteristic of the biblical knowledge of God, marking it off from the God of Gk. philosophy on the one hand, and from the gods of the nature-religions of the surrounding tribes on the other (*v.* PROPHECY). This is what is implied in the Heb. characterization of God as *the living God*, the God who is active in history (cf. esp. Josh. 3.10, Hos. 1.10, I Tim. 3.15, Heb. 9.14, 10.31, etc.). From their encounter with 'the living God' in the events of history there follows inevitably the prophetic understanding of God as almighty, as sheer Power (*v.* MIRACLE . . . POWER). God's acts of power are grouped chiefly around three great crises in biblical history: the Deliverance of Israel from Egyptian bondage by the miracle of the Red Sea; the acts of divine Judgment and Mercy in the Exile and Restoration; and the raising of Jesus from the dead which brought the New Israel, the Church of Jesus Christ, in safety through the judgment of the present world-order, symbolized by the destruction of Jerusalem in AD 70. From this encounter with the Lord of History the biblical understanding of God's character as a God of judgment and of forgiveness, of righteousness and of love, is derived. Lastly, it was through the prophetic realization that God is the Lord of history that there came about the recognition of God as the CREATOR of the universe; this perception would not have arisen had not Israel's God been discovered to be the Lord of all history and of all nations. The necessary corollary ensued that nature, the theatre of history, was likewise subject to the creating, sustaining and directing power of the one God (cf. Jer. 27.5). Thus we arrive at the fully developed OT view of Jahweh as the Creator and Sustainer of the entire world, operating through his word, his *fiat*, which is at once the expression of his will and the executor of his power (cf. W. Grundmann in Kittel's *TWNT*, ii, p. 294; *v.* also WORK). The NT deepens this understanding in its even clearer recognition that the God of Creation is one with the God of Redemption, that the creative word was one with the redemptive word incarnate in Christ; the Apostles had learned from the Scriptures that God at the first creation had brought the world into existence through his word, but now they had themselves witnessed his mighty act in bringing into being through his incarnate Word a New Creation, the redeemed community, the Church of Jesus Christ. The doctrine of the God who creates the world by the word of his mouth is involved not only in the prophetic understanding of God as the Lord of history but also in the apostolic testimony concerning God as the Lord of the Church.

There is thus throughout the Bible a deep unity underlying all its various insights into the character and purpose of God. These various insights represent partial truths, and the differences between them must not be minimized. There is development, or perhaps we should rather say *deepening*, in the varying conceptions of God at different stages of Heb. history. These differences will be analysed more carefully in the next section. But the recognition of differences in viewpoint in the various strata of the biblical revelation should not be allowed to obscure from our eyes the essential unity of the biblical conception of God. Throughout the biblical records it is the *same* God to whom the testimony points, even though in places the testimony may be expressed in primitive and (in the light of later insight) distorted ways; this God is the God whose final and clearest revelation is seen in Jesus Christ. The same recognizable conception of God appears throughout the Bible, though under many forms and expressed in terms of widely different social, political and ideological conditions. In the far-off nomadic days, God is the Shepherd-King of his flock, ruling with severity but with goodness. If later he appears in the garb of a monarch of the 'oriental' type, he still nevertheless leads and feeds his chosen people. When, later still, he comes to be known as the Lord of the whole earth, he yet remains the faithful Keeper of the Covenant with Israel. When he manifests himself as the Judge of the nations—of Babylon or of Judea—he is still the loving God whose mercy is being exercised and revealed in the fulfilment of his purpose of salvation by means of his chosen instrument, the Old Israel or the New. There was in being a knowledge of God and a religious view of the world, when, 3,000 years ago, a slave-tribe came out of Egypt: that faith and that religious view remain to-day, vastly deepened and enlarged, as the faith of a world-wide Church throughout which the message of the Bible is proclaimed.

ALAN RICHARDSON

II. THE DEVELOPMENT OF THE BIBLICAL THOUGHT ABOUT GOD

Since the OT is a collection of writings which extend over many centuries, it is natural that its ideas about God should be very varied.

The early records of Heb. thought and history present naïve and primitive views of the divine action, of the manner in which God communicates with man, of God's nature, of his will and purpose. The oldest literary source of the Pentateuch, the so-called Jahwist, narrates, for example, that Adam heard the sound of the Lord God walking in the garden of Eden in the cool of the day. The same source also describes, in Exod. 4.24–6, a Jahweh of a very demonic sort who attacked Moses when the latter was at a lodging-place; Moses' safety was secured, we are told, by his wife Zipporah, who 'took a flint and cut off the foreskin of her son and cast it at his [Moses'] feet', saying, 'A bridegroom of blood art thou'. Of the same character, it is evident, is the deity who is associated with the festival of the Passover, who smote the firstborn of the Egyptians, but spared the Israelites when he saw the blood of the Passover offering on the lintel and side-posts of their houses (Exod. 12.23–7). In each case the averting power of blood in staying the deity's onslaught is to be observed. The carrying out of the *Herem* or ban, whereby, as a religious act, the whole population of a hostile city or district, men, women and children, were 'devoted to' or dedicated to Jahweh (cf. Deut. 2.34, I Sam. 15)—that is, in effect, exterminated—is at once one of the crudest features of the religion of old Israel and one of its best attested. At times also the character of God is compromised by narratives which rest upon widely spread primitive cult-concepts (cf. II Sam. 6.7) or upon the narrator's inability to make a distinction between the human actions which God permits and those actions for which God himself is directly responsible (cf. I Kings 22.21f.).

But in spite of the limitations which distinguish Jahweh as folk-God and God of the land and which present him as guardian of his people's rights and customs, but yet not as impartially or completely righteous, there attach to him, even in the early period of Heb. history, high moral qualities. He is an upholder of treaties and oaths. The Hebrews are visited with famine for the breach of an ancient bond which they had made with the Gibeonites (II Sam. 21). He is the protector of covenants (Gen. 31.49f., I Sam. 20.42). He is the avenger of the weak and oppressed as against the powerful despoiler, as in the story of Naboth's vineyard (I Kings 21), and, through the prophet Nathan, rebukes King David for the crime he had committed against Uriah the Hittite (II Sam. 12). In Exod. 34.14 (J) it is said that Jahweh 'whose name is Jealous, is a jealous God'. This means that Jahweh will not share with other gods the worship that is his due. He refuses to be one of a pantheon, a member of a hierarchy of deities. This character of Jahweh was to have far-reaching results of a moral and spiritual kind.

The development of deeper reflection upon God in Israel comes through the preaching of the prophets. Through them the idea of Jahweh as national deity and protector of the race was qualified, enriched and finally transformed by the conception of the divine transcendence, justice and holiness. Amos in his teaching clarifies and widens the whole ethical horizon. The impartiality of Jahweh's judgment and his justice are uppermost in this prophet's description of the divine nature. Jahweh is interested in justice as such and is offended by inhumanities that are perpetrated not only in Israel, but outside the national confines of Israel (Amos 1.3,13, 2.1). Amos indeed does believe that the relation of Jahweh to Israel is a special one, but by a turn of thought which reaches a high degree of subtlety he frees this special relationship of some of its power of prejudicing the idea of God's complete righteousness: 'You only have I known of all the families of the earth: therefore I will visit upon you all your iniquities' (3.2).

The thought of Jahweh's love of Israel runs throughout the Book of Hosea. Under the analogy of a woman's unfaithfulness to her husband, the prophet castigates the disloyalty of Jahweh's people to their God. The possibility of restoring the former ideal condition of affection in Israel's heart and mind is the problem with which Hosea wrestles. He balances the thought of the divine wrath (for Israel's conduct merits and will receive punishment) against God's desire for Israel's repentance and return to him. The prophet hears Jahweh saying: 'I will not execute the fierceness of mine anger, I will not return to destroy Ephraim: for I am God and not man; the Holy one in the midst of thee' (9.11). Hosea appears to be reluctant to let punishment be God's final word. The conceptions of Hosea are still nationalistic and particularistic, but the implications of the analogy on which his prophecy is based are of a distinctly soteriological character. It might quite fittingly be held that his representation of a God yearning and searching for Israel's love and obedience strikes a note which is recognizable again, though vibrating more strongly, in the NT doctrine of God's incarnation for man's salvation.

The consciousness of the majesty of God in Isaiah carries the spiritualizing of Israel's religious thought still farther. When Isaiah is called to his task, the vision of God sitting upon his throne and of the seraphim above the throne chanting 'Holy, holy, holy, is the

Lord of hosts: the whole earth is full of his glory' makes the prophet deeply aware of his insufficiency, that he is a man of unclean lips, a sinful creature (Isa. 6). He cannot be God's messenger till he be cleansed. There is a marked contrast here with the spirit of those psalms where some individual asserts before God his innocence and integrity (cf. Ps. 26, 17.3–5). Along with the fuller realization of what the divine nature implies there is drawn a humbler and more sober estimate of what man is and can do. Prophets who succeeded Isaiah express this same dual confession regarding God and man. The Deutero-Isaiah depicts God as incomparable in power, wisdom and holiness (40.12–31): 'To whom then will ye liken me, that I should be equal to him? saith the Holy One' (40.25). God is far exalted above human beings. 'For as the heavens are higher than the earth, so are my ways higher than your ways' (55.9). Yet he knows that God is accessible to man: 'Seek ye the Lord while he may be found' (55.6). 'The high and lofty One that inhabiteth eternity, whose name is Holy' indwells the man of humble and contrite spirit. Together with the recognition that this is the relationship of God and man there arises the deeper sense that God is omniscient, that man's inner disposition and thoughts are not concealed from him (Jer. 16.17, Ps. 94.7,9, Job 34.21–2) and that God is omnipresent (Ps. 139).

The dénouement of this trend of religious reflection is that there appears in some parts of OT literature a more profound realization of man's sinfulness: 'If thou, Lord, shouldest mark iniquities, O Lord, who shall stand?' (Ps. 130.3); and of the universal scope of sin (Ps. 51.5; cf. Job 4.17f., 14.4f., 15.14f.). We find therefore the view developing that man is not able to overcome evil unless he be given the help of God (Ps. 51.10, 143.10). Eventually God himself must provide the means of resisting the evil that is in man's heart—that is, God must himself provide the means of redemption from evil. Thus Jeremiah (31.31f.) conceives that the old covenant made at Sinai, and which had been broken and was thus cancelled, will be followed by 'a new covenant'. This covenant, which is made by God with Israel and Judah, will be obeyed because the law will be written in the inward parts of those with whom the covenant is made, and the knowledge of God will be given to them without the need of their receiving instruction from men. This 'new covenant', though it be not universal in its scope, being confined to the two tribes mentioned, presupposes the creation of a new humanity in a new world-age (cf. Volz, *Commentary on Jeremiah*, p. 294), and thus Jeremiah's prophecy has little to do with the present age except that it recognizes the failure of external law, stresses the need of God's grace to support man's effort to obey God, and foreshadows the NT teaching in regard to the necessity of a *new birth*. The influence which Jer. 31.31 had upon Christian thought is apparent in the Epistle to the Hebrews (*v.* PROMISE), where Jesus is called the mediator of a new (9.15) and better (8.6) covenant (cf. also 7.22, 12.24, I Cor. 11.25, II Cor. 3.6).

Long after the time of Moses the religion of Israel remained monolatrous—monolatry being the worship of only one God along with the belief that, or without denying that, other gods exist. The stage of monotheist belief, i.e. the belief which affirms that *only one* God exists, was only reached conclusively, as OT literature shows, in the time of Deutero-Isaiah (*c.* 538 BC), although monotheistic belief may be said to be in a state of becoming in all the prophets since Amos (*c.* 760 BC), though not unequivocally formulated. From the time of Elijah (*c.* 880 BC) to the time of Jeremiah there is no directly expressed denial of the existence of heathen gods, not even in Jeremiah, where some have held that monotheism is probably to be supposed (*v.* B. Balscheit, *Alter und Aufkommen des Monotheismus in der Israelitischen Religion*, Berlin (1938), p. 124). Nevertheless, it is the prophetism of this period which lays the basis of a speculative logical monotheistic faith. How tentative, however, is thought of a monotheistic tendency in the seventh cent. BC appears from the Book of Deuteronomy. Here it is said (4.35; cf. 4.39): 'The Lord, he is God: there is none else beside him'; while in 4.19 it is said of the sun, the moon and the stars, and all the host of heaven (i.e. the astral deities, against the worship of which Israel is warned) that Jahweh himself allotted these to 'all the peoples under the whole heaven' to worship. Then again in 6.13–15 the viewpoint is altogether monolatrous and represents Jahweh as jealous of the worship which Israel offers to other gods. In certain psalms (e.g. 82.1, 86.8, 135.5) it is admitted that there are other gods; while Ps. 96.5 denies their existence. But in the time of the exile in Babylon, at the lowest ebb of Israel's political life so far as this is portrayed by the OT, when the temple and Jerusalem had been destroyed and the representative mass of the people of Judah was hardly a nation, but rather a congregation of worshipping individuals, the harvest of the best seed of Israel's religious thinking came to fruition. The Deutero-Isaiah taught that Jahweh was the CREATOR of the world (40.12,22,26,28), the Lord of all nature (41.18–20), the director of history (40.23–4), the only God (43.10): 'that ye may know and believe me, and understand that I am he;

before me there was no God formed, neither shall there be after me'.

It might be thought that only with the clear emergence of monotheistic belief could the idea arise in Israel that Jahweh had created the world; and it is true that this idea as it appears in Gen. 1.1–24*a*, which belongs to the Priestly Code (P), of exilic or post-exilic origin, is enhanced by the monotheistic viewpoint of the writer. But polytheism is not an insuperable barrier to the belief in the creation of the world as the act of a single God. For in the Babylonian Creation epic, which assumes innumerable deities, the God Marduk, after overcoming the Goddess Tiamat, the representative of primeval chaos, creates the world and makes man. Also in the monolatrous period of the religion of Israel the old Jahwistic source (J) in Gen. 2.4*b*–4.26 says that 'Jahweh God made earth and heaven' (2.4*b*) and 'formed man of the dust of the ground' (2.7). Moreover, in the tradition of the flood (J; Gen. 7.22–3) and in the story of the Tower of Babel (J; Gen. 11.1–9) there are traits even of universalistic thought; for it is all mankind which God causes to perish in the flood, and the one language of all mankind which, in the Tower of Babel narrative, is changed by Jahweh into a confusion of tongues. But the notion of Jahweh as Creator-God in the J document and the elements of universalistic thought to be found therein are to be reckoned as remnants of the non-Israelite mythology from which that document derived (cf. Gunkel, *Commentary on Genesis* in *Schriften des Alten Testaments*, p. 113), remnants which remained dormant and sterile for centuries until awakened and touched with life by the pure monotheistic religion of Deutero-Isaiah and the Priestly Code.

From being a concept which had had but little (yet cf. Isa. 17.7) practical significance, the idea of God as Creator now becomes fraught with religious and ethical content. The Book of Job and the Proverbs show this when they speak of God as man's Maker (the present participle of the Heb. word *asah*=make); 'Shall a man be more pure than his Maker?' (Job 4.17; cf. 32.22, 35.10); 'he that oppresseth the poor reproacheth his Maker' (Prov. 14.31; cf. 17.5, 22.2). The Priestly Code in its account of creation in Gen. 1 had already given a certain theological quality to the notion of God's activity by using the word *bara*=create, a word which in the OT is only used of the divine activity. Significantly enough, this word is seldom used except in P and in Deutero-Isaiah (*v.* Oxford *Heb. Dict.*). P uses also the general word *asah*, 'make' in regard to God's works, e.g. 'Let us make man' (Gen. 1.26); but the divine action is not here described, as in J, as a forming or moulding of man from the ground. The God of P *speaks*, and what he proposes to create comes into existence. In effect, in Gen. 1, though it is only referred to indirectly, creation is through the divine word.

The full significance of this notion of a creative word was further developed in Judaism when the transcendent deity, who dwelt afar off in the heaven of heavens, was regarded as establishing his relationship with the earth and the world of men through intermediaries such as the spirit (Isa. 40.13, 48.16, Ps. 104.30, 139.7, Wisd. 1.5,7, 9.17, 12.1), and angels, wisdom (Prov. 8.22f., Ecclus. 24.3f.) and the word (Ps. 33.6, 107.20). Still later there emerged from this same movement of thought, and from the necessity of bridging the gap between God and the world, the Word (John 1.1, I John 1.1, Rev. 19.13) or *Logos* of the NT. This Logos, which in the full content of its meaning without doubt 'combines Eternal Reason with Eternal Revelation' (Curtis, *Jesus Christ the Teacher*, p. 6) and which in the Johannine literature is identified with Christ, nevertheless retains close affinity with the intermediaries that had preceded it, in that it possesses the same special function as had Wisdom (Prov. 8.30) and the word (Ps. 33.6) in the OT, namely, that of being an agent or an instrument in creation (John 1.3,10).

The universalism of Deutero-Isaiah may be held to have affected later literature, such as the Book of Jonah and certain of the psalms (e.g. Ps. 33.5, 96.10,13, 97.2, 98.2) which describe the interest of the Deity in all or other peoples. The high point of Deutero-Isaiah's prophecy is where the Servant of the Servant-Songs (Isa. 42.1,4, 49.6) receives the commission from Jahweh to be a light to the Gentiles, a missionary for the diffusion of true religion throughout the world. This idea of the universal character of the divine purpose constitutes, along with the heritage of the OT prophets' thought about God, the background of NT religion. Though Jesus limited his missionary effort to Israel (Matt. 15.24), he nevertheless declared that the gospel should 'be preached in the whole world for a testimony unto all the nations' and that many would come 'from the east and west and shall sit down with Abraham and Isaac and Jacob, in the kingdom of heaven' (Matt. 8.11). In John 10.15 he says that he has sheep other than those who are in the fold of Judaism.

Jesus' teaching about God was that he is the Father of all men—not merely of Christians—and God is often spoken of in such terms as 'the Father', 'your heavenly Father', 'the Father in heaven', 'our Father in heaven'. Consistent therewith, God's love and mercy extend to all men, even to bad men, for he lets his sun shine and rain fall on the just and the unjust (Matt. 5.45). The heavenly Father is ready to forgive any sinner who repents. His love, kindness and forgivingness are the subject of the parable of the prodigal son (Luke 15). In the OT the description of God as Father is not often met with. It appears in Deut. 32.6, Jer. 3.4,19, 31.9, Isa. 63.16, 64.7, Mal. 1.6, 2.10, where God is depicted as Father of the people of Israel, and in Ps. 68.5, 103.15, Ecclus. 23.1,4, in Wisdom and III Macc., where God is spoken of as Father of individuals. But in the teaching of Jesus the view of the Fatherhood of God receives an emphasis which makes it the chief mark of the character of God in his relationship with man. (*V.* FAMILY, II.)

Another aspect of the nature of God as this appears in the Synoptic Gospels is indicated by the expression 'Kingdom of God' or its equivalent 'Kingdom of Heaven' (*v.* NAMES OF GOD, KINGDOM OF GOD). The phrase signifies the sovereignty or rule of God over the minds of men and over all the relationships of men to men. This sovereignty is realized wherever God's will is obeyed, and implies that God is conceived of as King or Judge. Men should not fear their fellow men, who are only able to kill the body. Rather must they fear God who is able to destroy both soul and body in Gehenna (Matt. 10.28, Luke 12.4f.). They who do God's will are Jesus' brothers and sisters (Mark 3.35); and not everyone that says to Christ, 'Lord, Lord', shall enter into the kingdom of heaven, 'but he that doeth the will of my Father which is in heaven' (Matt. 7.21). But while the idea of God as Judge and Ruler is a substantial part of Jesus' teaching, as it is also distinctive of Judaism, it is secondary to Jesus' view of God as Father. Even in St. Paul's letters where the language, e.g. judge, judgment, justify, is so often reminiscent of the law-court, it is the love of God, who is willing to give man all things (Rom. 8.32), which forms the background against which the Cross is presented and explained. Nothing, no created thing, can separate the man in Christ from the love of God (Rom. 8.39). Also the Johannine literature in its emphasis on love as being the character of the divine mind—'God is love; and he that abideth in love abideth in God' (I John 4.16), 'God so loved the world that he gave his only begotten son . . .' (John 3.16)—certainly reflects what was the essence of the teaching of Jesus. That God is light (I John 1.5) and life (5.20) is also in the spirit of that teaching.

In all the Gospels Jesus occupies a unique relationship to God. Two most striking expressions of the conviction that the life and teaching of Jesus is a unique revelation of the mind and character of God are contained in Matt. 11.27 and John 1.18; and the Pauline description of God as 'the God and Father of our Lord Jesus Christ' (Rom. 15.6, II Cor. 1.3, 11.31, Eph. 1.3, Col. 1.3; cf. I Pet. 1.3) may be said to be that view of God which *par excellence* is presented by the NT. (*V.* also FAMILY, II.)

III. NAMES OF GOD

El and *Elohim.* (Cf. Bethel, house of God, Gen. 28.17–19, and Gen. 1.1, 'In the beginning God (i.e. *Elohim*) created the heaven and the earth'). It has been thought that these names derive from a Heb. word which means 'to be strong', or from a word which signifies 'to be mighty', or from a verb meaning 'to bind'. But these derivations have in no case any certitude. *El* and *Elohim* are from the earliest times the general names applied to the spirits or demons associated in popular belief with certain localities or natural objects such as trees, wells, rocks, stones, etc. Some of these numerous vague spirits attained in the course of time to a more definitely personal quality, advancing as the protective spirits of places and tribes to the stage of deity. An instructive passage is Gen. 33.20, 'And he [Jacob] erected there an altar and called it El-elohe-Israel'. *El* is here no longer a mere appellative, but has become a proper name, the name of the God of Israel, while at the same time it is the name of the altar itself, closely associated with the stone (cf. Gen. 28.18f.) of which the altar consists.

The word *Elohim,* which is a plural form, may be regarded as an abstract plural emphasizing the concept of deity. It can, for example, be used of the deity whom Israel worshipped or of Astarte, 'the goddess of the Zidonians' (I Kings 11.5), or of 'the other gods' as a simple plural (I Kings 11.4). It is the most commonly used and most general OT term expressive of deity. The source of the Pentateuch which is called the Elohistic source is called so because it employs the term Elohim (instead of Jahweh) for God practically exclusively. Also the author of the Priestly source, in describing the work of creation in Gen. 1, uses the wider and more general designation, Elohim, for the Creator.

Jahweh is the special name of the God of Israel. He appears from the descriptions that are given of him to have been a sky-God, a God of thunder and lightning (Exod. 19.16, 20.18, I Kings 18.38). Thunder is his voice (Exod. 19.19, Job 37.5, Amos 1.2), lightning flashes are his arrows (Ps. 18.14, Hab. 3.11). The sign of his covenant with all flesh is set in the heavens (Gen. 9.13). Consistent therewith is his association with the mountainous country. 'Their God', said the enemies of the

Israelites, 'is a God of the hills' (I Kings 20.23). He reveals himself on Sinai, a mountain in the north Arabian desert, and from this region he comes to help the Israelites when they do battle in the land of Canaan (Judg. 5.4f.). Moreover, fire is his manifestation, not only on Sinai, but in the pillar which by night guides the people on their exodus from Egypt (Exod. 13.21) and in the thorn bush (Exod. 3.2f.; cf. Deut. 33.16).

Since the name Jahweh occurs—in the form *Jau*—as a component in the names of two Aramaean princes of the eighth century, it would seem that this deity was not only worshipped by Israel but by Aramaean tribes also. In the time of David the cult of Jahweh was localized at Gibeon (II Sam. 21.6,9, I Kings 3.4) and at Shilo where the ark of Jahweh was kept. But at a still earlier time it would appear that the cult as practised by the Levitical priesthood had its centre at Kadesh (Num. 32.8, etc.). The tradition that Moses' father-in-law was a Kenite (Judg. 1.16) or a Midianite (Exod. 3.1) may indicate that the worship of Jahweh flourished among the Kenites or the Midianites or both.

Jahweh Zeba'oth (or SABAOTH) (Jahweh of hosts) or, more fully, *Jahweh elohe(ha)-zeba'oth* (Jahweh God of (the) hosts) is a special title of Jahweh. The *hosts* have been interpreted by some as referring to the armies of Israel (cf. I Sam. 4.4f., II Sam. 6.2; particularly I Sam. 17.45) and thus to Jahweh as God of war. Another view is that the hosts are the stars (cf. Judg. 5.20). But objection may be taken to the first interpretation on the ground that I Sam. 17.45 is a late passage and that the 'hosts' in the divine title usually appears without the definite article. And against the second view it has been pointed out that the stars are ordinarily called 'the host' (sing.) of heaven. Hölscher (*Geschichte der Israelitischen und Jüdischen Religion* (1922), p. 68) therefore thinks that the title specifies the hosts of spirits and demons, otherwise Elohim (cf. above), which accompany Jahweh or with which Jahweh is identified. Hölscher sees a possible allusion to these accompanying Elohim in Gen. 32.1,2: 'And Jacob went on his way and the angels of God [Elohim] met him. And Jacob said . . . This is God's host' (Heb. *mahaneh*, army). Eichrodt's view (*Theologie des Alten Testaments* (1933), Vol. I, p. 95) is very similar. He regards the 'hosts' as meaning the totality of all the earthly and heavenly beings, an interpretation which, he holds, corresponds to a rendering of 'Jahweh of hosts' by the LXX as *Kurios tōn dunameōn* (lord of the powers). In a secondary stage of its existence the title 'Jahweh of hosts' may have been applied, as in I Sam. 17.45, with reference to the armies of Israel, or to the stars, after its true and original significance had been forgotten. But that the title is not found in the Pentateuch or in Joshua and Judges, where so many of Israel's military exploits are recorded, is strong evidence against the interpretation of 'hosts' as armies of soldiers. Moreover, since the title is predominantly used in the oracles of the prophets where Jahweh is invoked as Judge of Israel and of the nations, it can hardly allude to Jahweh as commander of Israel's military forces.

BAAL (pl. BAALIM). With the settlement of the Hebrews in Canaan, their whole mode of life underwent a fundamental change, for they had to learn from the Canaanites the art of agriculture, and this was closely interwoven with the cult of the vegetation deities. The God of the desert, Jahweh, had originally nothing to do with the cultivation of the fields, the ploughing and the sowing, the culture of the olives and the vine, the festivals associated with the agricultural seasons, the cult that assured the fruitfulness of the earth. For the gifts of the earth, man offered thanks, prayers and sacrifices to the *Baals*, the deities who presided over particular areas of the land, each Baal being regarded as the owner (Baal = possessor) of the region with which he was associated. In Hos. 2.4f. we observe the prevalent concept that the Baal as lord of the ground had the function of fructifying the earth. Under such circumstances a natural result of the Israelites establishing themselves in Canaan was a coalescence of the cult of Jahweh with that of the Baals, and as time proceeded and Jahweh took over the various Canaanite shrines, this syncretism became deeper and more apparent. Jahweh himself became the lord or Baal of these shrines and was regarded as a vegetation deity. In the personal names of Hebrew individuals such as Jerubbaal (Judg. 6.32, 7.1f; cf. II Sam. 11.21, LXX), Ishbaal, Meribaal, the Baal to which reference is made is Jahweh. The paradox of Jahweh having his dwelling-place in the desert at Sinai while at the same time he was the Baal or deity of the local sanctuaries in Canaan was overcome by conceiving of his 'name' or 'face' (RV, 'presence'; cf. Exod. 33.12–15) being present at those latter sanctuaries. Later, in the course of the pre-exilic period, after a mingling of Jahwism with the religion of Canaan, which in many respects was salutary, there developed an antagonism of Jahwism to Baalism (cf. I Kings 18) which established for the former an existence upon a purer and more spiritual level. The prophet Hosea thus protests against the title Baal being given to Jahweh (2. 16).

JAH, *Jahu* (*Jaho*), JEHOVAH. The original

text of the OT was without vowels. Thus the divine name was represented by the four consonants JHWH (JHVH), the so-called tetragram. One of the consequences of the growth of monotheistic thought in Israel throughout the pre-exilic period, its coming to complete expression in Deutero-Isaiah (Isa. 40.55), its infiltration into the general consciousness of the people in the succeeding centuries, was that the proper name JHWH fell to some extent into disuse. At the stage of nationalistic, polytheistic thought it is natural that a God should have a personal name to distinguish him from other deities. But when religion reaches monotheism, the propriety of giving a name to the one and only deity becomes subject to doubt. Thus the tetragram does not appear in the poem of Job, nor in Ecclesiastes; from the second and the third book of Psalms it has practically been removed. In the late Hellenistic period the stage is reached when the use of the name JHWH was forbidden to the people on the ground of shielding it from irreverence. The name was still pronounced in the temple by the high priest when blessing or in prayer, but in the synagogue, in prayer and in reading from the OT, it was pronounced *Adhonai* (Lord). As a rule, the LXX translated the tetragram by *Kurios* (Lord) and the word Elohim by *Theos* (God). A consequence of this close association of the divine name with *Adhonai* was that, when the Massoretes (sixth to seventh centuries AD) supplied vowels to the Hebrew consonantal text, they gave JHWH the vowels of *Adhonai* except where, in particular circumstances, JHWH was given the vowels of Elohim.

From this procedure two notable results followed: (*a*) the real pronunciation of JHWH more and more receded from knowledge and became practically lost; (*b*) in the sixteenth century (1520) Christian theologians—not without the protest of certain scholars—combining the vowels of *Adhonai* with the consonants JHVH, produced the form *Jehovah*, a purely fictitious name which has become hallowed by four centuries of use. But the evidence of the pronunciation of the divine name as *Jahweh* is particularly good, for it is founded on the tradition handed down by Theodoret that the Samaritans pronounced the name as *Iabe* and upon Clement of Alexandria, who wrote of 'the mystic name of four letters' as *Iaoue*. The consonantal transcription of the tetragram as Iabe is also attested by the Egyptian Magic Papyri 'both directly and indirectly' (*v. Bible Studies*, by Deissmann, on 'Greek Transcriptions of the Tetragrammaton', pp. 322f.), and also the form presented by Clement receives there a measure of support (*ibid.*, p. 330). These Papyri date from, say, the end of the third century with a tradition that probably goes back a century earlier. Further, *v.* G. R. Driver: 'The Original Form of the Name *Yahweh*: Evidence and Conclusions' in the *Zeitschrift für Alttestamentliche Wissenschaft* (1928); also A. L. Williams, *Journal of Theological Studies*, Vol. XXVIII (1927), pp. 276f., on *Yahoh*, the abbreviated form which he takes to be the real name. On the question whether Jahweh, as the longer form of the divine name, has arisen out of the shorter forms, *Jah* (Exod. 15.2, Ps. 68.4, etc.; cf. Hallelu-jah) and *Jahu* (as in personal names, e.g. Jesha-jahu—Isaiah), Eichrodt (*Theologie des Alten Testaments*, Vol. I, pp. 91f.) is of the opinion that Jahweh is an expanded form of the other two names and is the archaic imperfect (*qal*) of the Hebrew verb 'to be'. The meaning of the word, if this derivation be accepted, is 'he that is', not in the metaphysical sense of absolute existence, but in the sense of 'he that is present', and thus ready to manifest himself as helper. This account of the history of the divine name Jahweh, Eichrodt connects with, and believes to be supported by, the story of the commission which Moses receives from God in Exod. 3.14 (from the Elohistic source), where there is certainly word-play upon the name Jahweh, and where God says to Moses, 'I am that I am'. The Sinai revelation begins under the ægis of a new name. Moses, the founder of a new religion, appeals to his people under the authority of this new and designedly constructed name, Jahweh, indicating the actively present God.

In criticism of this theory of the history of the divine name, it is difficult to believe that any appeal by Moses to the Israelites in Egypt, in preparation for their deliverance, could have rested on a philological variation of a divine name with which they were familiar. Since the form Jahu was not abolished by this supposed change, it does not seem that the new name had created a difference that was deeply appreciated. Great movements in religion and history do not as a rule originate in a nuance of philological character. Moreover, the oldest Pentateuchal source (the Jahwist) places the worship of Jahweh at the very beginnings of the human race (Gen. 4.26), and speaks of Noah calling upon Jahweh (Gen. 9.26) and of Abraham as building an altar to Jahweh (Gen. 12.8). The Jahwist does not apparently know of the special connexion of the name Jahweh with the Mosaic period. 'One thing at least seems sure', says A. Lods (*Israel from its Beginnings to the Middle of the Eighth Century* (1932), p. 323), 'namely, that this name did not appear for the first time in the Mosaic epoch, as E (the Elohist) and P (the Priestly Code) suggest, representing it as having been revealed for the first time to Moses.

If this were its true origin, it would have an intelligible meaning in Hebrew, the remembrance of which would have been preserved by the Israelites. It is apparently a much older name whose meaning the Israelites had already forgotten, and to which they attempted later to give a meaning conformable to their own religious conceptions'.

With the removal of the proper name, Jahweh, from ordinary use, there arose the need of supplying its place by substitutes, and so in Judaism many abstract descriptions of the Deity made their appearance. This must have taken place gradually throughout the post-exilic centuries. While in ordinary parlance God is popularly referred to as 'the Name', in contrast with heathendom God is called 'the living God' (cf. Jer. 10.10, Ecclus. 18.1, Dan. 6.20), 'the Eternal' (I Enoch 75.3, Jub. 12.29), 'the Immortal' (Sib. 111.10, etc.). The name given by Dan. 7.9 to the deity as 'the ancient of days' appears in several places in I Enoch (e.g. 46.1,2, 47.3). The title of 'the Highest' or 'the Highest God' (cf. *El Eljon*, Gen. 14.18f.), esp. the former, gained much currency. God's description as ALMIGHTY is frequent. The LXX often translates by *Pantokrator* (Almighty) the word 'HOSTS' in the expression 'GOD OF HOSTS' (cf. II Sam. 5.10); and where *(El) Shaddai* (cf. Gen. 17.1, where RV translates 'God Almighty') occurs in the poem of Job, the LXX offers the rendering Lord (*Kurios*) or Almighty (*Pantokrator*). But the LXX also had other renderings for the title *El Shaddai* (*v.* Eichrodt, *op. cit.*, p. 87). In the NT, except in the citation II Cor. 6.18, the title Almighty (*Pantocrator*) only occurs in the Apocalypse, and there eight times. 'The Heavens' as a title of God was a common one and is found in the NT. In Luke 1.18 and 24.49 we have in the words 'from on high' another, though less common, Jewish equivalent for 'from God'; *v.* Bousset, *Religion des Judentums*, 3rd edn. (1926), p. 311f. (Also *v.* REVELATION.)

IV. GODS

A good general description of the gods who were worshipped in the land of Canaan is given by the Book of Judges (10.6f.; cf. I Sam. 7.4): 'And the children of Israel again did that which was evil in the sight of the Lord [i.e. Jahweh], and served the Baalim, and the Ashtaroth, and the gods of Syria, and the gods of Zidon, and the gods of Moab, and the gods of the children of Ammon, and the gods of the Philistines.'

The words *El* (god), *Elohim* (god or gods) and *Baal* (lord, possessor) are general titles that are applied to various divinities; Jahweh himself at an earlier stage of Israel's history in Canaan could without offence be called Baal by his worshippers (see III, above). Other important Canaanite deities held this title. In Judg. 8.33 we are informed that as soon as Gideon was dead 'the children of Israel turned again and went a whoring after the Baalim and made Baal-berith their god'. This BAAL-BERITH (literally Baal of covenant, or of covenant-making) must be the same deity who is mentioned in Judg. 9.46 as El-berith and as having a sanctuary in Shechem. This sanctuary, together with the functions of the deity of covenant-making, appear later to have been taken over by Jahweh. It is at Shechem that Joshua is represented as making a covenant with the tribes of Israel regarding obedience to Jahweh: 'So Joshua made a covenant with the people that day and set them a statute and an ordinance in Shechem' (Josh. 24.25). Also Rehoboam, Solomon's son, sought ratification of his succession to the throne through a covenant made at this place: 'And Rehoboam went to Shechem; for all Israel were come to Shechem to make him king' (I Kings 12.1). Similarly, another deity, whose rivalry with Jahweh seems to have been keenly felt, was entitled Baal, viz. BAAL-ZEBUB, a god whose shrine was at Ekron in the Philistine country. Baal-zebub (literally fly-god) was, as we see from both the OT (II Kings 1.1–6) and the NT (Matt. 10.25, 12.24–7, Mark 3.22, Luke 11.15–19), a divinity whose healing powers were widely known and much sought after. Whether this Baal, 'the lord of flies', had the power of attracting flies (conceived of as demons) or of driving them away as harbingers of disease, cannot be said. In the NT he is called the prince of demons. The form of the name BEELZEBUL may be either a tendentious change of the word or a careless way of pronouncing it (*v.* W. Bauer, *Griechisch-Deutsches Wörterbuch zu den Schriften des Neuen Testaments*, 3rd edn. (1937)).

Among the deities worshipped by the Semitic neighbours of the Israelites were MILCOM of the Ammonites and CHEMOSH of the Moabites. It is reported in II Kings 23.13 that Solomon built 'high places' near Jerusalem for the cult of both Milcom and Chemosh. But in I Kings 11.7, where the same incident is recorded, we find the interesting variation that the high places were built for Chemosh of Moab and 'for Molech, the abomination of the children of Ammon'. From this latter passage it might seem that Milcom, who is the same as MOLEK of I Kings 11.7, is the same god as the Molek (LXX, Moloch) of II Kings 23.10 to whom children were made to pass through the fire in the rites which took place in the valley of Hinnom near Jerusalem (Lev. 18.20, 20.2–5). Both in I Kings 11.7 as referring to Milcom and in the other scriptural passages where Molek is mentioned, the form of the word Molek is best explained as being the word Melek, i.e. 'king' (as a title of divinity) furnished with the vowels of *Bosheth* (shame), a process which the name *Ashtoreth* (from a probable Ashtereth=Astarte) also appears to have undergone. Milcom is only an incremented form of the title Melek (*v.* the philological studies by L. Köhler in the *Theologische Zeitschrift*, Basel (June, 1945–February, 1946)). But the Milkom or Melek of the Ammonites (cf. LXX on I Kings 11.7) can hardly have been the Melek to whom the burning-rites in the Hinnom valley were paid. Lods (*Israel from its Beginnings to the Middle of the Eighth Century* (1932), p. 125) thinks that it is possible that these rites were paid to a particular Canaanite deity called *ha-Melek*, 'the king'. This view is not inconsistent with the suggestion of Volz (*v.* article on Moloch in the *Calwer Bibellexikon*) that the children were sacrificed to Jahweh as Melek. In which case a syncretism of Jahwism with the cult of the Canaanite deity who was associated with the Hinnom valley had taken place (cf. Ezek. 20.26). The purpose of these rites, Volz conjectures, was to obtain the divine favour and blessing of having many children through the sacrifice of the first-born. Noteworthy is the attraction of this cult for the Hebrews up to the time of the reformation in the days of Josiah.

Goddesses of vegetation and fertility known as *Astarte*, ASHERAH and *Anath* enjoyed a great reputation among the people of Canaan. For these divinities promoted the well-being and prosperity of the land, the increase of the crops and cattle. The phrase 'the Baalim and the ASHTAROTH', i.e. the Baals and the Astartes, which occurs in Judg. 10.6 (cf. above) is little more than a general expression for 'gods and goddesses'. But the goddess whose name in its Greek form is Astarte (Heb. probably Ashtereth; Accad. Ishtar) made, as we may see from Jer. 7.16–20, 44.15–30, a very deep impression upon the women of Judah. While Jeremiah traced the downfall of Jerusalem and the destruction of the state to the judgment of Jahweh upon the people's idolatry, the women of the colony of Jews who sought refuge in Egypt boldly told the prophet that all things had gone well with them in the days when they had performed the cult of Astarte. The sovereignty of Assyria over Judah had doubtless furthered the spread of this popular cult among the people of Judah. In the Babylonian-Assyrian religion, *Ishtar*, the mother of the gods, was the divinity of the star Venus and was called 'the mistress of the heavens and the stars'. Hence her title (Jer. 44.17), 'THE QUEEN OF HEAVEN'. The cakes that were baked (Jer. 44.19) in her honour or offered to her are possibly to be regarded as having the form of the goddess or as bearing the shape of a star, her symbol, in the same manner as the moon-shaped cakes offered to Artemis at Athens (*v.* Volz's commentary on Jeremiah, *ad loc.*, p. 99).

The two other deities mentioned above in association with Astarte—namely, ASHERAH and Anath—left traces upon Hebrew religion. Frequently the OT refers to the sacred tree or pole called *Asherah* (I Kings 16.33, II Kings 13.6, 17.16, etc., Judg. 6.26–31). This tree or pole, which was in proximity to a place of sacrifice, has been interpreted by some as a symbol of the goddess Asherah and by others (cf. Hölscher, *Geschichte der Israelitischen und Jüdischen Religion* (1922), p. 57) as a cult-object which gave rise to a goddess of that name. But it would seem that, whatever was originally the relationship between the symbol and the deity, long before Israel's entrance to Canaan the goddess was regarded as the deity to whose presence the pole witnessed. But the pole or tree as symbol of vegetation and fertility was evidently not confined solely to the goddess Asherah, for in Jer. 2.27 it represents a male deity.

That the female principle represented by the goddess of vegetation made stronger appeal to the Hebrews than is testified by the OT is clear from the Aramaic papyri of Elephantine in middle Egypt which date from the fifth century BC and which cast a light upon the Jewish military colony that lived there at that time. This colony seems to have been founded by emigrants from the northern kingdom of Israel in the seventh century. The papyri reveal that the Jews of Elephantine had a temple of Jahu and that, besides their god Jahu, they worshipped a goddess, a consort of Jahu, called *Anath-Bethel*, otherwise called *Anath-Jahu*. Another deity mentioned in the papyri who is named *Ashim-Bethel* has been thought by Kurt Galling (*Biblisches Reallexikon*, Tübingen (1937), p. 236) to be the same female deity as the Aramaic *Ashima* of II Kings 17.30. From the testimony of the Elephantine papyri it may be concluded that in pre-exilic Israel Jahweh had been commonly associated with a female partner or partners, just as we discover from the Moabite stone (*c.* 840 BC) that the Moabite deity Chemosh was partnered with an Ashtar-Chemosh. When Ezekiel (Chap. 23) depicts with scorn Samaria and Judah as the two unfaithful wives of Jahweh, there can be little doubt that the picture which the prophet draws is a conscious reflection upon the type of cult which the Jewish papyri reveal. This would appear to be the case whether we accept or reject the conclusion that the Ashim-Bethel of the papyri is a female divinity. Galling (*op. cit.*, p. 233) suggests that the description of Israel in the prophets as the wife of Jahweh was an indirect means of absorbing or rendering innocuous the tendency within Israel to be attracted by that particular religious element which in the Canaanite religion was supplied by the worship of the goddesses of fertility.

In Ezek. 8.14 reference is made to 'women weeping for Tammuz' near the northern gate of the temple. Only here is TAMMUZ mentioned by name in the OT. Tammuz is a dying and rising god, a personification of the *vis naturae*, who dies at the summer solstice when all vegetation is decaying and who revives again in the spring of the year. Of the worship which this divinity received, Dr. G. A. Cooke, in his commentary on Ezekiel (*ICC*, *ad loc.*, p. 96), says: 'It came from Babylonia and can be traced as far back as 3000 BC, so that it is one of the oldest forms of religious worship in the world.' When the god died with the withering of all vegetation, he was thought of as departing to the underworld, and this was celebrated by the ritual weeping of women. Tammuz is the beloved (son or husband) of Ishtar who, when he dies, descends into the underworld to seek for him. The Adonis-Astarte cult and ritual as practised in Phoenicia, Asia-Minor and Greece was similar to the Tammuz-Ishtar cult of Babylonia, reflecting the same religious hopes and background, even though it is not until the time of Origen that we actually find literary identification of Tammuz with Adonis. A reference to 'the desire of women' in Dan. 11.37 is probably rightly understood as an allusion either to Tammuz or Adonis. And the words of Isaiah (17.10): 'Therefore thou plantest pleasant plants, and settest it with strange slips' are best interpreted as alluding to the 'Adonis-gardens', i.e. the pots or vessels filled with earth and sown with seeds which quickly sprouted into plants that wilted again in the summer heat. These 'gardens' were prepared by the women celebrants. Gressmann (*Expositor* (1925), IX, Vol. VIII), on account of various features which the festival of Adonis had in common with the Hebrew festival of Booths (Tabernacles), held that the latter is derived from the Adonis festival as celebrated by the Canaanites. (See further Sir James Frazer, *Adonis, Attis, Osiris*; also O. S. Rankin, *Israel's Wisdom Literature*, pp. 185–90.)

Not only does the history of the religion of Israel show that influence, positive as well as negative, was exerted upon it by the religious ideas and cults of the people of Canaan, but the OT reveals, naturally to a lesser extent, that the Philistines too were not immune from that influence. Both Baal-zebub of Ekron and Dagon of Ashdod bear Semitic names. DAGON is undoubtedly (cf. Lods, *op. cit.*, pp. 59, 127) a Canaanite god of the corn (*Dagan*) who for centuries before the Philistines' arrival in Canaan had been worshipped in Babylonia and Assyria (*v.* S. A. Cook, *The Religion of Ancient Palestine*, p. 92). The tradition that Dagon had the form of a fish (Heb. *Dag*) is as old as the time of Jerome, but from the account given in I Sam. 5.4–5 seems very doubtful.

O. S. RANKIN

GOG, MAGOG *v.* ANTICHRIST

GOOD

The Heb. word (*tob*) which is commonly so rendered means pleasant, joyful, agreeable. It is used with ref. to sense perception, and also, derivatively, of aesthetic and moral judgments.

It occurs as descriptive of the creation in Gen. 1. It is often the opposite of evil: Gen. 3.5, Isa. 7.15, Jer. 24.2 (cf. in NT Matt. 5.45, Rom. 12.21); similarly it is often used almost synonymously with 'right'—a more definitely ethical term: cf. Deut. 6.18, 12.28, Josh. 9.25, I Sam. 12.23. The noun often carries the meaning of prosperity, benefit, as well as the ethical connotation: cf. Josh. 23.14f., I Kings 22.8, Job 2.10. God is referred to as good, e.g. Ps. 34.8, 145.9 (cf. Matt. 19.17); particularly to his covenant people (Exod. 18.9); and in his gift of the Law (Deut. 30.15ff.). The Rabbis of a later day referred to the Law as (the) good (cf. *Pirke Aboth*, 6.3: 'good simply means Torah'; and cf. also Rom. 7.12).

Thus *tob* is a very general word, needing to be made precise by the addition of such words as 'merciful', 'fearing God', 'innocent'. This is true also of the Gk. *agathos* (the commonest Septuagint rendering of *tob*) and *kalos* (which sometimes stands in the Septuagint for *tob*, but also renders *yapheh*, 'beautiful'). 'Good' in the Eng. NT represents almost without exception one of these two Gk. words, and they are practically synonymous. Their range of meaning is also wide, as is that of *tob* and the Eng. 'good' (e.g. in St. John's Gospel *kalos* is used both for 'good' wine and for 'good' shepherd).

The NT, generally speaking, carries on the OT conception of goodness, particularly in the theocentric character of its ethic, as contrasted with the anthropocentric or humanist ethic of ancient Greece and most moderns. But where the OT tends to assume that goodness is within man's power of attainment—there are some exceptions to this, notably in the Prophets—the NT in its deepest insights (cf. Rom. 7) realizes that this is not so apart from God. For the possibility of moral achievement in the NT see Matt. 5.16, Rom. 8.4,28, 12.2; Eph. 2.10 (*v.* also LOVE).

GOSPEL

To the saving acts of God which already in OT are the evidence of his goodness, the NT adds what God is doing in Christ. This is conceived as the coming of God's Kingdom. Ethically it may be described as the *summum bonum*, and then it corresponds to the Law in the OT as the standard by which the goodness of an act is judged. 'Good' works are those which are proper to a citizen of the Kingdom; cf. Mark 12.34, Matt. 5.16, 25.34ff. St. Paul does not use the phrase 'good works', but cf. Gal. 6.9 and Rom. 12.17 (where 'honest' is from the Gk. *kalos*, and might equally well be trans. 'good').

E. C. BLACKMAN

GOSPEL

The Eng. word *Gospel* (Anglo-Saxon, *godspell*, 'God-story') is used to translate the Gk. *euangelion*, 'good tidings'. The NT use of this word and of the verb *euangelizesthai*, 'to preach good tidings', derives from the LXX and witnesses to the belief that Christ is the fulfilment of the Scriptures. The key OT passage is Isa. 61.1: 'The spirit of the Lord God is upon me; because the Lord hath anointed me to preach good tidings to the meek [LXX, poor]. . . .' In his sermon at Nazareth Jesus explicitly referred these words to himself (Luke 4.18); and elsewhere he sees in his preaching of the Gospel to the poor the Messianic fulfilment of the Scriptures (Matt. 11.5=Luke 7.22, Q). The Gospel-writers leave us in little doubt that it was Jesus himself who first used the expression 'to preach the Gospel' of his own proclamation, and that he interpreted it as a fulfilment of Isaianic prophecy, even if such uses of 'gospel' as Mark 8.35 and 10.29 reflect its later technical connotation in a missionary Church. The content of the gospel which Jesus preached and which he sent out the Apostles on their mission to preach was that the kingdom or reign of God was at hand (Mark 1.15, Matt. 10.7f., Luke 10.9; *v.* KINGDOM OF GOD).

After the death and Resurrection of Jesus the content of the gospel, as it is understood by the apostolic Church, is Christ himself. It is no longer simply 'the gospel of the kingdom of God' (though, of course, that is involved), but is 'the Gospel of Jesus Christ, the Son of God' (Mark 1.1)—a phrase in which every word must be given its full significance. The word has now become a technical expression of apostolic Christianity. It is 'the Gospel of God' (Mark 1.14, Rom. 1.1), i.e. the saving message which God has addressed to the world, first by way of anticipation in the Scriptures (Rom. 1.1, Gal. 3.8), and now finally in the living word, Jesus Christ. It is therefore supremely the message of the cross and Resurrection, and it is 'the power of God unto salvation to every one that believeth' (Rom. 1.16). There can be no substitute for this one authentic gospel, even though such 'another gospel' were preached by an angel from heaven (Gal. 1.6–9). The Church itself is built upon this one gospel and is indeed a fellowship in the gospel (Phil. 1.5). Sometimes Paul speaks of 'my gospel' (Rom. 2.16), but he does not mean that his gospel is in any way different from that of the Church as a whole, but rather that he has had a personal apprehension—or, he would say, revelation—of the gospel (which is that of the whole Church) which authenticates its truth and constitutes him an Apostle (Gal. 1.1; cf. Rom. 1.1; and see esp. Gal. 1.11f.). The gospel must always be received personally by faith, for even though Christ crucified be 'placarded' before men's eyes, it will remain hidden (II Cor. 4.3), a 'mystery' (Eph. 6.19), until they appropriate it by the personal response of faith (Rom. 1.16). For those who thus receive it the gospel is always 'news', breaking in freshly upon them and convincing them afresh, though they may first have heard it and accepted it long ago.

It may perhaps be added that the word 'gospel' does not occur in the EVV of the OT; the phrase used to translate the Heb. equivalent of the LXX *euangelizesthai* is 'good tidings'. In the OT we notice a certain development from a purely everyday secular usage of this phrase (e.g. II Sam. 4.10, 18.27), through a kind of use which may easily be made to bear a deep parabolic significance (e.g. II Kings 7.9—a grand text for a missionary sermon), to the Isaianic sense of the proclamation of the 'day of salvation'—whether from Babylonian captivity or in a deeper Messianic sense (Isa. 40.9, 41.27, 52.7, quoted in Rom. 10.15; cp. Nah. 1.15, Luke 2.10).

The use of 'gospels' in the sense of 'the Four Gospels' is post-biblical (2nd cent.). (*V.* also PREACH.)

ALAN RICHARDSON

GOVERNMENTS *v.* MINISTER

GRACE

There is a sharp distinction between the use of the word in the two Testaments. In the OT it is one of two words which are used to trans. the Heb. *chen*, the other word being FAVOUR (*q.v.*). The word means kindness and graciousness in general—that is, where there is no particular tie or relationship between the parties concerned. Further, it is shown by a superior to an inferior, and there is no obligation on the part of the superior to show this kindness. The Gk. (Septuagint) equivalent is *charis*. Properly this word signifies that which gives pleasure, so that it stands both for that which gives pleasure and for the pleasure that is given, the kindness shown and the gratitude created in the giving. This use of the word is found in the NT (Luke 4.22) and, amongst other instances, in the greetings at the beginnings and the ends of the Epistles.

The main and characteristic NT use of the word grace (Gk. *charis*) is of God's redemptive love which is always active to save sinners and maintain them in proper relationship with him. In this sense the equivalent OT word is the Heb. *chesed*, normally trans. 'loving-kindness' (*q.v.*). This word stands for God's continued faithfulness to his covenant-people, and for his steadfast determination never wholly to let Israel go. The connexion with the OT use of the word 'grace' is to be found in the idea that God's favour is entirely free and wholly undeserved, and that there is no obligation of any kind that God should be favourable to his people. It was impossible for Paul, to whose vocabulary the word chiefly belongs, to use the normal Gk. equivalent for the Heb. *chesed*, because this is generally rendered by *eleos* (pity) in the Septuagint. This rendering he knew to be wholly inadequate. It did not emphasize the long-suffering (*q.v.*) of God, and his patience with which he so long forbears to punish sin. In any case, Paul's approach was through the idea of the covenant.

No one could be more sure than Paul of the wonder of that love of God because of which he chose Israel to be his special people. The Apostle realized the depth and wonder of the divine love all the more since the rejection of Jesus Christ had been the climax of a whole history of repeated apostasy. For Paul, the death of Christ had broken down the middle wall of partition between Jew and Gentile, with the result that all the wealth of God's covenant-love was now available for every man. Grace is God's covenant-love (*chesed*), which has broken down all barriers.

The idea of grace more than any other idea binds the two Testaments together into a complete whole, for the Bible is the story of the saving work of God, that is, of the grace of God. Without grace, there would never have been any chosen people, any story to tell at all. The first thing that we read concerning Noah after the introduction of his name and genealogy at the end of Gen. 5 is that 'Noah found grace in the eyes of the Lord' (Gen. 6.8). Here the word is *chen*, favour, necessarily here independent of any covenant between God and Noah, since that covenant was not yet made. This makes it all the more clear that the establishment of the covenant itself was due in the first place to God's favour, undeserved and unconditioned. This particular favour is bestowed upon the patriarchs, each in his turn, and it was by God's grace (EVV, 'mercy', but Heb. *chesed*) that he led forth from Egypt the people he had redeemed (Exod. 15.13). Again and again in Deut. it is made clear that God's choice of Israel from Egypt onwards was entirely of grace—that is, wholly undeserved on Israel's part (Deut. 7.7, 8.14–18, 9.4–6). The Song of Moses (Deut. 32) is the recitation of God's continuous forbearance towards the wayward Israel, whom he had chosen of his own free will. This motif is continued in later songs of the same didactic type, namely Pss. 78, 105, 106, 135, 136. The Prophets contribute their testimony also to the fact of God's continued loving-kindness towards a rebellious Israel (Isa. 43.2–15, Jer. 18.8–11, Ezek. 16). It may be that only a remnant will turn in repentance to God, but his grace is still strong towards the people of his choice (Isa. 10.21, Jer. 23.3, Mic. 2.12, 5.7f., etc.).

This grace of God in the OT is closely connected with the idea of the covenant, and the basis of the covenant is the Law. All the blessings which God is minded to bestow upon his people are dependent upon their fulfilment of the Law. God is full of anger (*q.v.*) against all manner of sin, whether regarded as transgression against the Law, or as rebellion (more often) against himself. At the same time he shows mercy and forbearance to his people, withholding from them the proper penalty for their apostasy until the time comes when the final and merited doom must be sealed. The reason for the continued existence of his people is to be found in the forbearance of his grace; otherwise they would have gone the way of the heathen and been lost in the welter of the nations. The condition of the enjoyment of his good favour is their fulfilment of the Law.

In the NT we find a new covenant which replaces the old covenant. Here we find the full revelation of that plan of grace which was implicit from the beginning in all God's dealings with Israel. It is the grace of the OT formerly manifest in God's dealings with his covenant-people, but now made manifest in the life and work of Jesus Christ. 'In him dwelleth all the fulness of the Godhead bodily' (Col. 2.9), so that we can speak of 'the grace of God', 'the grace of our Lord Jesus Christ', or 'the grace of God our Saviour', all of which is involved in the Pauline use of the word 'grace'. Paul says that the righteousness (i.e. salvation) of God, to which the Law and the Prophets gave witness, has now been declared and made clear to all without the Law. This salvation is found through faith in Jesus Christ, and it is for all who believe. There is now no distinction between the Law and not-the-Law, for all have sinned and fallen short, whether Jew or Gentile.

Now, all men can be 'justified (*q.v.*) freely by his grace through the redemption that is in Christ Jesus' (Rom. 3.21–4). It was through God's forbearance (Rom. 3.25) that the former sins were overlooked, but now is the time when his salvation is shown.

The NT emphasizes, at least equally with the OT, that this grace is the free gift of God (Eph. 2.4–9, Rom. 3.24, 11.6), and that it is not the outcome of man's deserving (II Tim. 1.9). Not only so, but Paul, for his part, is very sure that even his own response to the Gospel was due to God's good pleasure, and that he was called through the grace of God (Gal. 1.15). Further, the NT speaks generally of the grace of God as the determining factor in man's turning to God (Acts 5.31, 2.18, 16.14, Heb. 6.6). Even that faith which is the condition of salvation is due to the grace of God (Eph. 1.19, Phil. 1.29). Everything, therefore, from first to last is by grace, whether of redemption (Rom. 5.2, I Pet. 2.10) or of sanctification (I Thess. 5.23f.).

Since even conversion itself is the work of divine grace, how then comes it about that some are saved and others are not saved? Is grace irresistible? Paul speaks of the possibility, which is a very real one, of the grace of God being received in vain (II Cor. 6.1), by which, judging by the following verses, he means that there may be evident no fruits of the spirit. The Word of God, equally with the Law, can indeed be made powerless by man's stubborn refusal (Matt. 15.6, Mark 7.13, Rom. 3.3, 4.14, 9.6, I Cor. 1.17, Gal. 3.17). We are faced with the same dilemma as in the case of the idea of 'election' (*q.v.*). It is clear that men are saved by grace (Eph. 2.5), but equally clearly men themselves must choose (Phil. 3.17f.). At the same time Paul insists not that he apprehended, but that he was apprehended (Phil. 3.12f.). Here he speaks as though the beginnings of his Christian life were due wholly to grace, but that, having first been called, he himself must be persistent. The same double attitude is to be seen in Phil. 2.12f., where Paul urges his readers, 'Work out your own salvation with fear and trembling; for it is God which worketh in you both to will and to work, for his good pleasure'. Once again, the solution is to be found in Christian experience. The less a man knows in his own experience of the saving work of God, the more he emphasizes the human element; the more he knows of the grace of God, the more he speaks of it as being decisive in his own life. Everything, from first to last, is regarded as being the work of the Holy Spirit, whose function is the work of grace in the human heart. (Also *v.* FAVOUR.)

N. H. SNAITH

GRAVE *v.* HELL

GUILE *v.* DECEIT

GUILT *v.* SIN

GUILT-OFFERING *v.* SACRIFICE I(*f*)

* * *

HADES *v.* HELL

HARLOT *v.* ADULTERY

HATE, HATRED

Hatred is the opposite of Love, as Wrath—above all, God's Wrath—is the obverse of Love. But that which is most deeply opposed to Love is Indifference.

'Hate' is used in the Bible of men's hatred towards their fellow men, as when Esau hates Jacob, Gen. 27.41; of the ungodly hating the righteous, Ps. 34.21, and hating God, Ps. 139.21; of the righteous hating that which is evil, Ps. 97.10, and hating the ungodly, Ps. 139.21–2; of God hating evil, Prov. 6.16, and hating ungodly men, Ps. 5.5. So the disciples of Christ will be hated by men for his sake, Luke 6.22; the 'world' will hate them, because it hates him and hates his Father also, John 15.18–24. 'Hatred' in Gal. 5.20 is one of the 'works of the flesh'.

Such is the ordinary usage. There are certain more difficult phrases: (*a*) 'Jacob I loved and Esau I hated', Mal. 1.2,3, Rom. 9.13. Here 'hate' takes a more colourless sense; God's love is that of his election (or selection) of Israel for the working out of his saving purpose, as when in Deut. 7.7 his 'love' for Israel is coupled with his 'choosing' of them. Thus when God 'hates' Esau, it is that Esau is not 'chosen' (*v.* further under EDOM). (*b*) 'Ye have heard that it was said, Thou shalt love thy neighbour and hate thine enemy' (Matt. 5.43). This is not a quotation from OT, though as we have seen God's people do sometimes 'hate' their enemies. The phrase points the contrast with the Lord's teaching, 'Love your enemies', 'pray for them which persecute you' (Matt. 5.44), 'do good to them that hate you' (Luke 6.27). (*c*) 'If any man cometh unto me, and hateth not his own father and mother, and wife, and children, and brethren and sisters, yea, and his own life (soul) also, he cannot be my disciple' (Luke 14.26). It is the words 'yea and his own life also' that give the key to the meaning. The last person whom Jesus is likely to accept as a disciple is he who hates his relatives because he is eaten up with love of himself. He speaks of 'hating' the self in a similar sense to 'denying the self' (Mark 8.34), which means, not denying things *to* the self, but denying or removing the self itself, to the extent of being ready to go and be crucified. Similarly in the text before us, the next verse is, 'Whosoever doth not bear his own cross and come after me, cannot be my disciple' (Luke 14.27). Such discipleship, involving preparedness for martyrdom, can demand the leaving of home and family and all those whom the disciple naturally loves best. So Jesus himself had left the home which he loved. In this saying, then, he is sharpening up a paradox almost to the point of a contradiction, and demanding the 'hating' of those whom the disciple has not ceased to love most, in order to press home the paramount claim of the call of the Gospel.

A. G. HEBERT

HEAD *v.* BODY

HEAL, HEALING, HEALTH

The theological question here is that of the connexion between health (of mind and body) and salvation, or between sickness and sin. The Bible constantly implies that there is such a connection; the frequent metaphorical use of bodily diseases as a symbol of spiritual *malaise* (e.g. Isa. 1.5f.) points to a deep and mysterious inner relation. The crude but widespread view that all sickness is punishment for sin is rejected by Job (*v.* SUFFER) and by Jesus himself (Luke 13.1–5; John 9.1–3); but this must not be taken as a denial of any relationship between sickness and sin. Perhaps it was because of the dominance of the view that God alone can forgive sin and therefore heal diseases (cf. Ps. 103.3) that medical science did not develop amongst the Hebrews, and that it remained in the hands of the priests, who were the only physicians—or, better, accredited medical officers of health (cf. Lev. 14.2f.; Mark 1.44; Luke 17.14). Ben Sira, who was liberally minded in such matters, advises his readers not to despise the slightly foreign (Greek) profession of the physician (Ecclus. 38.1–15); 'The Lord created medicines out of the earth, and a prudent man will have no disgust at them' (vs. 4). This enlightened—almost Greek—viewpoint was not that of Palestinian Jews, who thought rather in terms of Satan's bondage (Luke 13.16) or divine retribution. Amongst the Jews of the Dispersion a more 'scientific' attitude towards medicine doubtless prevailed. St. Luke, 'the beloved physician' (Col. 4.14), was probably a Jew of the Dispersion; at any rate he noticeably tones down St. Mark's unflattering reference to his profession (compare Luke 8.43 with Mark 5.26). However easily it may lead to crude and superstitious ideas, the attitude of the Palestinian Jews did at least preserve a biblical emphasis, which all 'Greek' or 'enlightened' views are apt to disregard. There is a mystery here which is not solved by merely being overlooked. Even the words which we use everyday are evidences that the human mind is conscious of the connexion between suffering and sin—'affliction', 'blow', 'plague', and so on, like the NT word *mastix*, lit. a lash, used for 'plagues' (Mark 3.10, 5.29,34, etc.). Of much greater significance is the use of the word *sōzō*, to save, both in the religious sense of salvation and in the sense of healing a disease—'to make whole'. (Cf. the older Eng. use of 'health'.) Jesus is *sōtēr*, which means both 'Saviour' and 'Healer'. Although, as we have noted, Jesus denies the crude view that all illness is retribution, he nevertheless maintains that his power over disease is evidence of his power to forgive sin (Mark 2.1–12, the Paralytic). His healing miracles were not regarded by him as illustrations of a general law, such as that of the power of mind over the body; still less were they 'faith-healings' in the modern sense, though faith was often required. Just as his power over the demons demonstrated his conquest of Satan (Mark 3.27), so his power over sickness demonstrated his conquest of sin. The cleansing of a leper, since leprosy was defilement requiring priestly absolution, bore a significance which it is hard for us to-day to understand. The fact that the 'Messianic signs' of Isa. 35.5f., upon which Jesus fastened (Matt. 11.4f., Luke 7.22), are portents of healings is of the highest significance. Jesus as the Messiah was the bringer of 'health and salvation'. The Christian picture of Jesus as the Good Physician, the Saviour of both the body and the soul, is well-grounded upon the stories of the Gospels. That Jesus himself perceived the connexion between his healing ministry and his redemptive mission is obvious from such a saying as: 'They that are whole have no need of a physician, but they that are sick: I came not to call the righteous but sinners' (Mark 2.17). Or again, he speaks the same word to the Sinner-Woman (Luke 7.50) as to the Woman with an Issue (Mark 5.34): 'Thy faith hath saved thee.'

The apostolic Church preserved this sense of the connexion between salvation and healing. There appears to have been an order of 'healers' in the ministry of the NT Church (cf. 'miracles, then gifts of healings', I Cor. 12.28; cp. 12.9, where 'gifts of healings' are mentioned as among the gifts of the Spirit; and note Jas. 5.13–16, which stresses the connexion between forgiveness and healing, and which mentions the anointing of the sick with oil 'in the name of the Lord'; it is perhaps worth noting, too, that St. Paul attributes illness at Corinth to a sinful attitude towards the Eucharist, I Cor. 11.30). But upon this question of 'healings' in the Church we are given no further information, although we may note that throughout Acts it is implied that the power to heal was an apostolic gift. The success of Christianity as a missionary religion in the ancient world—and we may remind ourselves of the achievements of medical missions in the modern world—was in no small part due to its preaching of the Healer-Saviour, who satisfied a need which the old gods could not meet; and it is highly significant that the last of these gods to go down before Christianity was Æsculapius, a god of healing (*v.* Excursus ii. appended to his chapter on 'The Gospel of the Saviour and of Salvation' in Harnack's *Expansion of Christianity*, Eng. trans. 1904, Vol. I, pp. 121–51; also Alan Richardson, *The Miracle-Stories of the Gospels*, Chap. IV, London, 1941). (*V.* also MIRACLE, SAVE, SUFFER.)

ALAN RICHARDSON

HEAR, HEARKEN, EAR, LISTEN

The Hebrews regarded hearing as a serious matter involving the whole self. There was no conception of a central psychical centre (brain or mind) which could be a kind of clearing house to handle and sort all that passed through the various peripheral organs, nerves and senses. The whole body was the seat of the personality, indeed the body was the person, and every limb and organ was an integral part of the unity of personality. While a particular limb or organ was functioning the whole self might be, as it were, concentrated in it. When the EAR was engaged in hearing the whole psychical activity was acting in and through it. Thus Job can ask: 'Doth not the ear try words, even as the palate tasteth its meat?' (12.11; cf. 34.3). The ear may tingle at hearing of the extraordinary activity of God (I Sam. 3.11; cf. II Kings 21.12, Jer. 19.3). Jeremiah speaks of 'uncircumcised' ears (6.10), and Isaiah of the way his message will 'make heavy' his people's ears (6.10). There is an element of finality and irrevocability once the ears have accepted the message to which they have been opened: 'The Lord of hosts revealed himself *in mine ears*' (Isa. 22.14; cf. 5.9). 'He that hath ears, let him hear' (Matt. 13.43). 'Blessed are your . . . ears, for they hear' (Matt. 13.16). It is with the ear that words of command are heard, and therefore the slave who chooses to remain in his master's service has his ear bored with an awl to symbolize the life-long obedience he will render (Exod. 21.2–6).

In like manner, according to Hebrew psychology, we must regard hearing as a complex operation, exercising the whole attention and response, and yet as a single process which runs on from hearing to approval or disapproval, and then on to obedience or disobedience or any other response that may be involved (on this, see Pedersen, *Israel I–II*). Hebrew has no specific word for *obey*: the word of the Lord is uttered that it may be obeyed, and to speak of hearing it is to speak of obeying it (Jer. 17.24). In the hearing of God or of the word of God the whole personality is therefore brought into play (LISTEN and HEARKEN are kindred verbal ideas). We may distinguish four ways in which God is heard by men, but in so distinguishing we must not lose sight of the fact that there is no clear line of separation between them.

(*1*) DIRECT AUDITION. There seems reason to think that the prophets at times heard, as it were, an external voice, a voice from heaven. 'I will stand upon my watch', says Habakkuk, '. . . and will look forth to see what he will speak with me' (Hab. 2.1; cf. Jer. 23.18). The reality of such an experience is attested by the physical feelings that are stirred by it: 'Surely the Lord God will do nothing, but he revealeth his secret unto his servants the prophets. The lion hath roared, who will not fear? The Lord God hath spoken, who can but prophesy?' (Amos 3.7f.). Elijah was so constrained at hearing the gentle sound of Yahweh's voice that he wrapped his face in his mantle (I Kings 19.13). Prophetic inspiration is attributed as often to the coming of the dynamic word of Yahweh as to the inflowing of the spirit of God. In John 12.28–30 the voice from heaven was taken by some to be the sound of thunder and by others to be the voice of an angel.

(*2*) INDIRECT AUDITION. This term may perhaps be applied to instances of awareness of God where hearing is involved but where it is God's activity that is heard and not his speech. Job 37.2–5 carries us right into the workshop of God, and we are almost able to hear him at work (as the poet must have done) on his great and marvellous things (cf. Ps. 77.18f., where the deliverance at the Red Sea is heard). Ps. 29 is a magnificent hymn in praise of God who 'thundereth marvellously with his voice' (cf. also Ps. 68.33, of which Num. 7.89 could be regarded as a static representation).

(*3*) INTUITIVE PERCEPTION. Although the prophets could lay claim to hearing the voice from heaven, they also received the word of God through their own perception coupled with their understanding of the will of God. Amos is able readily to read the 'vision' of the basket of summer fruit (Amos 8.1f.) and Jeremiah that of the almond tree (1.11f.). Jeremiah was shown that he must exercise his own moral judgment in the reception and transmission of the word of God (15.19).

(*4*) MEDIATION BY PROPHETS. Ordinary, non-charismatic men and women are dependent for their knowledge and 'hearing' of the word of God on the inspired men of God. This is well expressed by the wish of the people concerning God's revelation on Mount Sinai: 'Go thou [Moses] near, and hear all that the Lord our God shall say: and speak thou unto us . . . and we will hear and do it' (Deut. 5.27). We are reminded of Paul's question: 'and how shall they hear without a preacher?' (Rom. 10.14).

L. H. BROCKINGTON

HEARKEN *v.* HEAR

HEART *v.* MIND

HEAVE-OFFERING *v.* SACRIFICE I(*h*)

HEAVEN(S) *v.* HELL, HEIGHT

HEIGHT, HIGHEST, HOSANNA, HEAVEN(S), FIRMAMENT, THRONE

When the people greeted Jesus on his way to Jerusalem with the words 'Hosanna in the highest' they were using a phrase which is capable of bringing together three things, the pious devotion of the OT, acclamation of Jesus as the Incarnate One, and God the Father who dwells in highest heaven. The word HOSANNA comes from Ps. 118.25, and is there addressed to God on behalf of the approaching pilgrims. It is an imperative form of the verb *y-sh-'*, 'to save', the same root as that from which the name Jesus comes. God alone has the prerogative of salvation. The prayer is to be heard 'in the highest'—that is to say, in the HIGHEST of the regions of heaven. Here, in striking contrast to the strong belief in God's personal presence on earth, is the idea that God is above the earth, both greater than it and removed from it. It is expressed poetically in Isa. 57.15: 'For thus saith the high and lofty one that inhabiteth eternity, whose name is holy.' The idea of height is also found in Isa. 6, where the prophet sees the Lord sitting upon a throne, high and lifted up. The figure of height, loftiness, may be deemed one of the proper symbols to express a truth about God for which we shall reach no more exact definition. It conveys the idea of something superior, of something immeasurably greater, something that men can look up to (see E. Bevan, *Symbolism and Belief*).

One of the things that make the Bible ring true is that it maintains a proper balance between the need for a God at hand to hear and answer prayer, a God to be apprehended by men, and a God afar off, greater than the world and having power to perform his will. The passage quoted above from Isaiah 57 fitly brings the two together, for it continues: 'I dwell in the high and holy place, with him also that is of a contrite and humble spirit.'

It is possible to trace back to a very early period the belief that God dwells in HEAVEN; it probably goes back to the early years of the monarchy when the connexion with Sinai was finally dissolved. There is often a touch of the superlative about the way it is expressed: The heaven of heavens cannot contain God (I Kings 8.27); Yahweh is in his holy temple . . . his throne is in heaven (Ps. 11.4); He that sitteth (or, is enthroned) in the heavens shall laugh (Ps. 2.4); he that sitteth upon the circle of the earth, and the inhabitants thereof are as grasshoppers (Isa. 40.22). Where and what is heaven? The passage from Isaiah last quoted goes on to say: 'that stretcheth out the heavens as a curtain and spreadeth them out as a tent to dwell in.' Strictly speaking, the thing stretched out was not heaven itself but the FIRMAMENT which supported it. According to its root the Hebrew word for firmament means something beaten out fine as one might beat out gold leaf. This solid substance formed a vault (sky) over the earth 'strong as a molten mirror' (Job 37.18), and the moon and stars had their courses set in it. The sun daily rode his chariot across it (Ps. 19.6). The heavens were above it, and the term often includes the firmament. There were windows in it, the windows of heaven, which may have been thought to pierce the firmament at intervals. Through these the rain, hail and snow would be released at God's pleasure; otherwise they were retained in large storehouses (Gen. 7.11, II Kings 7.2,19, Mal. 3.10, Job 38.22). Above the firmament was the permanent abode of God. There was his palace (or temple) in which he was enthroned (Ps. 11.4). Although heaven was thus regarded as his permanent dwelling place, he could communicate to men through the firmament or he could even leave it to come down on earth. More than once we meet with the prayer and wish, 'Oh that thou wouldest rend the heavens, that thou wouldest come down, that the mountains might flow down at thy presence' (Isa. 64.1; cf. Ps. 18.9, 144.5). After the baptism of Jesus, the heavens were opened and the spirit of God came down like a dove and a voice was heard speaking from heaven (Matt. 3.16,17). The THRONE is the natural symbol of kingship, one of the favourite attributes of God in the Old Testament, and was represented in the visions of Isaiah and Ezekiel. In the latter vision the essential feature of the throne was its mobility, symbolizing the omnipresence (and omnipotence) of Yahweh. In the vision of the elders (Exod. 24.10) and of Ezek. 1 the firmament seems to find a place as the pavement on which God stood or his throne rested. The psalms which celebrate Yahweh's kingship lead us to suppose that at some time the Israelites represented in the earthly temple the enthronement of Yahweh over the whole world. Ps. 47 describes the very act of enthronement: God is gone up with a shout (acclamation), Yahweh with the sound of a trumpet. The cherubim who figure either as the place of enthronement as in Pss. 80 and 99 or as the support for the throne (Exod. 25.18ff., Num. 7.89) are mythical figures which probably symbolize the heavy storm clouds.

In heaven God held his court, allusions to which we find in the prologue to Job, the vision of Micaiah ben Imlah (I Kings 22), the consultation of Yahweh with his counsellors in Isaiah's vision and the bold contention of Jeremiah that the true prophet, as distinct from the false, is one who has stood in the council of God (23.18). (*V.* also under HELL.)

L. H. BROCKINGTON

HEIR *v.* INHERIT

HELL, SHEOL, PARADISE, GEHENNA, HEAVEN (LIFE AFTER DEATH)

The Hebrews (like other ancient people) did not think of death as total extinction, a notion which is nowhere found in the OT or NT. Almost throughout the OT period it was held that the dead continue to exist in the underworld, a region of shadows, misery and futility; they lived on as unreal, half-material shades in a land of silence and forgetting. The name for this region was SHEOL (Heb.) or HADES (Gk.) (EVV usually 'HELL'; AV sometimes 'the GRAVE'). Another name was 'the Pit' (Heb. *bor*), a natural synonym (cf. Isa. 14.15, Ps. 28.1, etc.; cf. Rev. 9.1ff.). It was in Sheol that a man was 'gathered to his fathers'; the dead may not return to earth, but the living must eventually go to them (cf. II Sam. 12.23). It was held that upon occasion they could be called up to earth again for a season by the arts of necromancy (I Sam. 2.6), but these arts were regarded as impious and sternly denounced by prophetic religion (cf. Isa. 8.19, Deut. 18.9–11). There is no biblical sanction whatever for 'spiritualistic' experimentation, but rather an attitude of horror at the very suggestion of it, as an interference with the divinely appointed order of things. The dread of approaching death and the meaningless, desire-less existence which it entails is frequently expressed in the poetry of the OT, esp. the Psalter (e.g. Ps. 39, esp. vs. 13). But the real horror of death to the genuinely religious Hebrew mind lay in the fact that all intercourse with Jehovah was at an end; God's presence (or even interest) did not extend to Sheol (e.g. Ps. 88.4f., 10–12). Perhaps the conception of Jehovah as a sky-god made it impossible to think of him in connexion with the underworld. But with the deepening sense of God's omnipresence there seem to have arisen protests against this exclusion of Jehovah from what was coming slowly to be recognized as a part of his universe (e.g. Ps. 16.10f., 23.4, 139.8). There is little in the OT which even hints at a liberation or resurrection from Sheol; the AV of Job 19.25f. imputes to Job an affirmation of a bodily resurrection, but the Heb. says nothing at all about this. There are only two OT passages which speak clearly about life after death in a sense more real than existence in Sheol. Isa. 26.19 (an apocalyptic passage some 400 years later than the historical Isaiah) affirms that the righteous dead shall live to share in the coming deliverance. Dan. 12.2—at the very end of the OT period, *c.* 165 BC—affirms the resurrection of the righteous dead 'to everlasting life' and others 'to shame and everlasting contempt'.

By NT times belief in the resurrection of the dead was held by all Jews except the die-hard Sadducees, who argued that it could not be proved from the Pentateuch (hence the significance of Jesus' answer to their question in Mark 12.18–27). This belief had not evolved out of OT conceptions of Sheol; nor had it been imported from Mesopotamia or borrowed from Gk. philosophy. (This is not to say that no foreign influences had affected its growth or coloured its expression. Amongst philosophically-minded Jews of the Dispersion Gk. influence had been strong; cf. Wisd. 3 and 5.) The universality of the belief in the resurrection of the dead was due primarily to the growth of the apocalyptic point of view. God must one day vindicate and reward his faithful ones, who were suffering such cruel persecutions at the hands of the Gentiles (cf. the Maccabean struggle). When the oppressors' cup of wickedness was full to the brim, he would come to judge the earth; the righteous, though dead, would not lose their reward nor the wicked escape their penalty. In some quarters a doctrine of the resurrection of the body was taught in a grossly physical sense (e.g. the horrible story of Razis, II Macc. 14.46): the dead would have their limbs restored to them just as when they lived: for the Jew the idea of a real existence without a body was unthinkable: a man is a living body. It was natural that with the acceptance of apocalyptic ideas concerning a final Judgment there should arise the conception of Sheol as divided into separate quarters, so that the righteous and the wicked should be segregated even before the Judgment by impassable gulfs. Thus the Book of Enoch (22.1–14, *c.* 170 BC) mentions divisions occupied by the righteous who had been martyred, the righteous who had not been martyred, the wicked who had suffered for their sins in this life, and the wicked who had not as yet suffered at all. The parable of Dives and Lazarus (Luke 16.19–31) shows that Jesus (at least for teaching purposes) accepted the common rabbinic view, but we must remember that the aim of the parable is not to acquaint us with details about the life to come but to confront us with our duty in this life: Dives's fault arose from his misjudgment concerning what are in fact the 'good things' of this life (vs. 25).

The pleasant abode of the righteous dead was called PARADISE (Luke 23.43, II Cor. 12.4, Rev. 2.7)—originally a Persian word for a nobleman's park or garden; the term contains a reference to the Garden of Eden, in which was situated the tree of life. There seem to have been two Paradises in the thought of the rabbis—one in Sheol (perhaps that of Luke 23.43) and one in heaven (perhaps that of II Cor. 12.4). But the expression as used by Jesus (once only) is merely a conventional way of saying 'after physical death', and should not be held to constitute an endorsement of rabbinic theories. In post-biblical Christian theology the term came to be used interchangeably with 'heaven'. There is no support in the NT for rabbinic speculations (or later Christian ones) about Paradise as a place of purgation where souls are purified from sin and fitted for heaven. Jesus' word to the penitent thief must be understood as a striking application of the doctrine of Justification by Faith rather than as a metaphysical declaration about the condition of the departed.

The opposite of Paradise is GEHENNA, that part of Sheol reserved for the wicked. Gehenna was originally 'the Valley of Hinnom' near Jerusalem, where once child-sacrifice had been offered to Moloch by Ahaz (II Chron. 28.3) and Manasseh (33.6); it is thought to have become at a later date the city's refuse dump where rubbish was burnt, and so an appropriate symbol of punishment. Jesus seems to have accepted the conventional rabbinic term (Mark 9.43,45,47, etc., RV marg.) and emphasized it with great force. There is no need whatever to regard Jesus' use of the word as endorsing rabbinic (or medieval) notions of future punishment as physical torment; but on the other hand it is impossible to soften the severity of Jesus' warning against unrepented sin, and the sentimentalism which seeks to do so is a distortion of the teaching of Jesus and the NT as a whole. Whatever may be implied by the symbolism of 'unquenchable fire' (Mark 9.43) or 'eternal fire' (Matt. 18.8; cf. 25.41) or the casting of the wicked into the 'furnace of fire' (Matt. 13.42,50), we have no right to explain the symbolism away. From the destruction of Sodom and Gomorrah by the fires of judgment (Gen. 19.24) fire had been the biblical symbol of destruction, condemnation and punishment, and so it continues in the NT (*v.* BURN, FIRE). The NT does not answer the questions we like to ask about such matters as the nature of punishment after death, eternal retribution, and so on; and it is as much a mistake to erect its symbolic language into metaphysical answers to such questions as it is to ignore the solemnity of the warnings which that language conveys. The NT writers do not seek to satisfy our natural curiosity, but to awaken in us a sense of awed responsibility before God the Judge of all. Such tentative answers as we may propose to these questions must not be based on a few texts but on the total revelation in Christ of God as holy love.

HEAVEN, identified from primitive times with the sky (Jehovah was a sky-god), is essentially the place where God dwells (cf. Matt. 6.9). To be with God is therefore to be in heaven, and so both for rabbinic Judaism and for Christianity the redeemed shall dwell for ever in heaven. According to rabbinic teaching, the righteous now in Paradise will after the Judgment experience resurrection and be translated to heaven; sometimes it was taught that between the Judgment and the final exaltation to heaven would intervene the thousand years' reign of the saints on the earth (the Millennium) in the Messianic Kingdom. Such conceptions have left their traces in some parts of the NT (cf. Rev. 20.2–7; see commentaries). But the NT as a whole does not seek to give us an almanac of the end of the world, and the modern critical approach to the study of the Bible makes it obvious that it is just as foolish to look in Revelation for an account of the end of the world as it is to look in Genesis for a scientific account of its beginning. The final NT word concerning our questions about the life of the saints in heaven must surely be I Cor. 2.9 or else I John 3.2.

It must not be thought that the Christian conviction concerning the life after death was a mere borrowing or extension of the ideas of rabbinic Judaism. On the contrary, while it took over rabbinic terms and ways of expression, the Christian hope had an altogether new centre and ground: the Resurrection of Jesus Christ (cf. I Cor. 15.12–18). [See under RESURRECTION for treatment of the

Christian view of life after death as a 'being raised with Christ'.] It is St. Paul who discusses the Christian view of life after death as contrasted with any mere pagan (or OT) conception of that life as a 'ghostly' and unreal survival in Hades. The contrast between the two views is well symbolized by the transference of the *locus* of the blessed dead from the underworld, where God is not, to heaven (cf. I Thess. 4.17); and even more strongly by means of Paul's teaching about the bodily resurrection of the saints (I Cor. 15.35–54). Paul does not teach the crude rabbinic doctrine of the rehabilitation of these our present physical bodies: 'flesh and blood cannot inherit the kingdom of God' (vs. 50). Nevertheless, at our resurrection we shall possess what in the (literally to us inconceivable) world of spirit corresponds to our bodies in this material world—means of expression, identification, recognition, and so on. Straining language to breaking point, Paul calls this a 'spiritual body' (vs. 44)—if taken in a woodenly literal way, a contradiction in terms. By this expression Paul intends (*a*) to combat the pagan notion of existence in Hades as ghostly, incorporeal and unreal; (*b*) to assert the continuance of personal identity in the after life—with its necessary means of expression, recognition, etc.; and (*c*) to affirm the redemption of the physical order as well as of the merely 'spiritual', in opposition to the common Greek view that matter is evil and irredeemable. (All these things are asserted—not a crude rabbinic materialist view—by the clause in the Apostles' Creed about 'the resurrection of the body'.) (*V.* also HEIGHT, IMMORTAL.)

For Christ's Descent into Hell *v.* DESCEND.

ALAN RICHARDSON

HELMET *v.* ARMOUR

HELPS *v.* MINISTER

HENCEFORTH, HENCEFORWARD *v.* TIME

HERITAGE *v.* INHERIT

HIDE, HIDDEN

These words are employed in the EVV to represent about a dozen different words in the original. This amazing wealth of synonyms for 'hide' in the vocabulary of Heb. is an index of a distinctive attitude of mind: the mind of Israel was characterized by a profound sense of the hiddenness of things, in marked contrast to Gk. thought with its sanguine belief in the capacity of reason to probe the inmost secrets of reality.

No comment is required on the use of 'hide' for the ordinary and familiar act of men (e.g. Gen. 3.8, Josh. 7.22). The distinctively biblical usage appears where the subject of the verb is God: God hides certain things (II Kings 4.27, Prov. 25.2); he hides his face (Deut. 31.17, Ps. 13.1); and often he hides himself (Isa. 45.15, 57.17). (Cf. SECRET.) The hiddenness of God in the Bible must be carefully distinguished from agnosticism in the modern sense; it is correlative with revelation (cf. REVELATION); it is the obverse of the fact that God is known only when and where he chooses to reveal himself. And even in his revelation God remains hidden; for while he makes himself known, he does not explain himself to men. He is hidden in respect to his ways, which are 'past finding out' (Rom. 11.33, Isa. 55.9).

Revelation itself is a hidden process—hidden from all except those to whom it is given (Matt. 11.25, Mark 4.11, Luke 9.45, 18.34, 19.42). To them it brings a hidden wisdom (I Cor. 2.7), and it unites them by a hidden link with God (Col. 3.3). (*V.* also MYSTERY, REVEAL.)

G. S. HENDRY

HIGH PRIEST *v.* SACRIFICE III

HIGHEST *v.* HEIGHT

HITHERTO *v.* TIME

HOLY *v.* SAINT

HOLY OF HOLIES *v.* SACRIFICE II(*a*), (*b*) and esp. (*d*)

HOLY PLACE *v.* SACRIFICE II(*d*) and esp. (*e*)

HOLY SPIRIT *v.* SPIRIT

HONEST, HONESTY

This word occurs only in the NT. Six times it stands for the Gk. *kalos* (*v.* GOOD). In Phil. 4.8 the underlying Gk. *semnos* means rather honourable, proper; similarly the abstract noun *semnotes* in I Tim. 2.2 would appear more appropriately in Eng. as 'dignity', 'gravity' (RV and Moffatt). In Rom. 13.13 and I Thess. 4.12, 'honestly' renders an adverb which means decently, with propriety.

E. C. B.

HOPE

The use of this word in its full biblical-Christian sense is hardly found before we reach the Epistles, and this is not surprising, since Christian hope is grounded on the Resurrection of Christ: 'Blessed be the God and Father of our Lord Jesus Christ who . . . begat us again unto a living hope by the resurrection of Jesus Christ from the dead' (I Pet. 1.3). The noun does not appear in the

Gospels; and of the five occurrences of the verb in the Gospels, two carry the OT sense of 'trust' (Matt. 12.21, John 5.45) and the other three are non-technical (Luke 6.34, 23.8, 24.21). In the later OT books the word 'hope' is not infrequent, being used to translate several Heb. words ranging in meaning from 'trust' to 'expect', with a gradual development towards hope in an eschatological sense in the later books and passages. In general, we may say that the principal OT usage in a theological sense is that Jehovah is the h. of Israel and of the pious Israelite (e.g. Ps. 130.5,7, Jer. 14.8). In the NT we read of 'God our Saviour and Jesus Christ our h.' (I Tim. 1.1); broadly speaking, faith is placed in God's mighty acts for our salvation which he has wrought in the past, while h. is placed in the final consummation of our salvation in the future. The Resurrection of Christ is God's mightiest act; it has created our faith; and it is, as it were, an eschatological symbol in history of our ultimate salvation and therefore the ground of our hope (Rom. 5.1–5). In this sense, Paul can say 'by hope were we saved' (Rom. 8.24): our ultimate salvation is not yet apparent, and we must patiently wait for it (Paul does not mean that we are saved by hoping!)—no one hopes for what he sees (8.24f.). In this age we have only the 'earnest' (II Cor. 5.5) of our salvation, viz. the Spirit's testimony to Christ within us: 'Christ in you, the h. of glory' (Col. 1.27). Patience (*q.v.*) is therefore set beside h. in several Pauline contexts. It is Paul esp. who develops the NT idea of h., and it is he who describes himself, quite appropriately, as having been made a minister of the Gospel-hope (Col. 1.23). But the author of Hebrews can speak movingly of h. as 'the anchor of the soul' (6.18f.) and of 'h. unto the end' (3.6, 6.11; cf. 10.23); the author of I Peter connects our h. with the Resurrection of Christ (1.3,21) and exhorts Christians to be ready with an *apologia* for their h. (3.15); and the author of I John, setting h. in its usual NT perspective of the Parousia, puts it forward as a motive for purity (3.5).

It will be seen that the NT conception of h. has nothing at all to do with any this-worldly prospects; it is as far removed as possible from any notion of an earthly Utopia or any secular optimism. It is through and through eschatological, always bearing reference to the return of the Lord Jesus at the end of the age. This characteristic NT usage is perhaps most clearly seen in I Pet. 1.13: 'Set your h. perfectly on the grace that is to be brought unto you at the revelation of Jesus Christ', i.e. at the Parousia (*v.* REVELATION). (*V.* also FAITH, RESURRECTION.)

ALAN RICHARDSON

HORNS OF ALTAR *v.* SACRIFICE II(*c*)

HOSANNA *v.* HEIGHT

HOSTS, GOD (LORD) OF HOSTS *v.* GOD, GODS III

HOUR *v.* TIME

HUMBLE *v.* PRIDE

HUSBAND *v.* MARRIAGE

HYPOCRITE

It is *a priori* most improbable that Jesus used this word to mean 'one who acts a false part in life', i.e. 'one who pretends to be pious when he is not' (Plummer in *HDB*, II, 441); for the word *hypokrites* with the meaning of 'actor' belonged to the Greek drama, and so was alien to the Jewish tradition and the Aramaic language. The true meaning is deeper and more penetrating.

The Heb. *chaneph* is translated 'hypocrite' some 10 times in AV, and *hypokrites* twice in LXX, in Job 34.30, 36.13; elsewhere it alternates with *asebes*, impious, and *paranomos*, lawless; and the same synonyms occur in Aquila and Theodotion. The NT usage tells the same tale. Matt. 24.51, 'shall appoint his portion with the hypocrites', appears in Luke 12.46 as 'with the unbelieving' (*apiston*). Mark 12.15, 'Jesus perceiving their hypocrisy', has for parallels Matt. 22.18 'their wickedness' (*ponērian*) and Luke 22.23 'their craftiness' (*panourgian*); this shows that the evangelists recognized these words as synonyms. In Gal. 2.13 the derivative verb and noun, trans. 'dissimulation', 'dissembled', are used of the Jewish Christians, including even Peter and Barnabas, refusing to join (no doubt in the *agape*-eucharist) with the Gentile Christians, and thus dealing falsely with the principle already accepted, that the Gentiles were to be accepted as full Christians; plainly they are accused, not of playing a part, but of unprincipled action. It must be added, however, that when Luke is expressing himself in his own words, he can use *hypokrinomenoi* in Luke 20.20 of 'feigning themselves to be righteous'.

Hence the meaning with which Jesus used the word, speaking in Aramaic, cannot be that he accused the Scribes of deliberately acting a part or of conscious insincerity. The point was that while outwardly religious inwardly and in the sight of God they were profane and ungodly men; so in Mark 7.6 he calls them 'hypocrites' and quotes Isa. 29.13, 'This people honoureth me with their lips but their heart is far from me'. They are like whited sepulchres, outwardly whitewashed, inwardly foul, Matt. 23.27–8; more terribly still, in Luke 11.44, they are like sepulchres not whitewashed, so that people walking over them would become (spiritually) 'unclean', not suspecting that such outwardly religious men were really inwardly corrupt. Cf. John 5.42, 'I know you, that ye have not the love of God in yourselves'.

A. G. HEBERT

* * *

IDOL, IDOLATRY

To worship an idol was to the Hebrew an abomination (*q.v.*) because it meant worshipping another god than Jehovah, who could not be represented by any image whatsoever (Exod. 20.4f.); the second commandment of the Decalogue was a necessary corollary of the first. Therefore to worship idols was to go 'a-whoring' after false gods; and there begins thus early the equation of idolatry with adultery (*q.v.*). For the developed monotheism of Deutero-Isaiah all idols are empty stocks and stones, lifeless and useless (Isa. 44.6–20), and so it continued in later Judaism, when idolatry had come to be regarded as the worst of sins. It involved worshipping the created thing instead of the Creator, and this leads to every kind of corruption of religion and morals. In Rom. 1.20ff. Paul is doubtless following a usual line of rabbinic teaching about the immorality of the pagan world (see W. D. Davies, *Paul and Rabbinic Judaism*, London, 1948, pp. 29f.: 'In Rom. 1 Paul is describing the Gentile world, and in true rabbinic fashion finds the root of its evil in the most glaring of all the fruits of the evil impulse, idolatry'). Thus, in Gal. 5.20 Paul describes idolatry as one of the fruits of the flesh, and in I Thess. 1.9 he speaks of the conversion of the Gentiles as 'a turning unto God from idols'. See further under ABOMINATION, IMAGE.

A. R.

IGNORANT

Ignorance in the OT has a special ref. to the less culpable sins (cf. Leviticus and *v.* SACRIFICE I(*e*)). In class. Gk. and esp. among the Stoics, ignorance was used absolutely with ref. to the uneducated, and this usage has partly influenced the Septuagint, where it can describe the state of the heathen (Wisd. 14.22). This meaning also appears in the NT: Acts 17.30, I Cor. 15.34, Eph. 4.17f., I Pet. 1.14, 2.15. Elsewhere in NT we find the word in the ordinary sense of lack of knowledge, which partly excuses sin: Acts 3.17, I Tim. 1.13. In Rom. 10.3, however, ignorance of God is regarded as not excusable; cf. Rom. 1.19ff. See further under KNOW and FOLLY. For Acts 4.13 see under UNLEARNED.

E. C. B.

IMAGE

In the OT 'image' usually means an artificial representation of some object, designed to be used in worship. Commonly, though not invariably, such images were representations of some god, and in human form; cf. Isa. 44.9ff. Their use was forbidden to Israelites by the second of the Ten Commandments, Exod. 20.4. For this use of the word, *v.* IDOL.

According to Gen. 1.26f., God created man 'in his own image', 'after [his own] likeness'. It is a much discussed question whether this statement refers to man's bodily form or to his spiritual nature. The OT writers in general seem to have thought of God not as formless spirit but as having a form which could be seen (cf., e.g., Num. 12.8), and all the probability is that this form was supposed to be the same as man's own form. There is therefore no objection to taking the statement to refer primarily to man's bodily form. It accords with this that in Gen. 5.6 Adam, after his fall, when his spiritual likeness to God had been defaced if not destroyed, is said to have begotten his son Seth 'in his own likeness, after his image', and that later, in the story of Noah, murder is punishable with death because man was made in the image of God, Gen. 9.5f. But there is no reason why the likeness of man to God should not include also those spiritual qualities of which his bodily form is the symbol. The first clear statement of this spiritual likeness, however, is in the book of the Wisdom of Solomon, one of the OT Apocrypha, which is probably to be dated in the 1st cent. BC, and is strongly influenced by Gk. thought (it is extant only in Gk., and it is probable that it was originally written in Gk.). Here God is said to have 'created man for incorruption, and made him an image of his own proper being, but by the envy of the devil death entered into the world', Wisd. 2.23f. This plainly implies that man's likeness to God consisted in that original immortality which he lost at the Fall. And if the variant reading followed in the AV is correct, as it very well may be, 'an image of his own *everlastingness*'—the statement would be explicit. Yet this 1st cent. writing cannot safely be taken as a guide to the original sense of the passage in Genesis.

In the passages in Gen. just considered 'image' means a real likeness, but the same Heb. word is used twice in the Pss. in the sense of an unreal semblance—73.20, 'As a dream when one awaketh; so, O Lord, when thou awakest, thou shalt despise their image' (i.e. the illusory prosperity and arrogance of the wicked); 39.6, 'Surely every man walketh in a *vain show*' (i.e. his life is a mere appearance, lacking reality). Elsewhere in the OT the word always means a material representation of something, and usually an idol (cf. esp. Dan. 2.31–3.15, *passim*).

In the NT 'image' is the translation (except in Heb. 1.3) of the Gk. word *eikōn*, which is used in the Gk. version of the OT in most of the passages referred to above and in many others, e.g. Gen. 5.1, 'likeness'. In Matt. 22.20 =Mark 12.16=Luke 20.24 it means the likeness of the head of the emperor stamped on a Roman coin. In Rev. 13.14, etc., the 'image of the beast' is a statue of the emperor, used in the State worship of him as a god. In Rom. 1.23 the ref. is to the representation of the gods in human form (as among the Greeks and Romans) and even in animal form (as among the Egyptians). A statue, though it is only a representation of something else, is in itself solid and 'real', not a mere 'shadow'—it may itself cast a shadow; it is in this sense that the Law (which here means OT religion) is said to have only a 'shadow' of the good things to come, not the very 'image' of the things, Heb. 10.1. Here 'image' comes near to having the sense of 'replica', a copy, which, though it is not the original, is in other respects as good as the original. It is in this sense that we 'have borne the image of the earthy' man, Adam, and shall also 'bear the image of the heavenly' man, Christ, I Cor. 15.49—here 'image' connotes complete likeness; cf. also II Cor. 3.8, Rom. 8.29. In another connexion, Paul can say that 'man' (here distinguished from 'woman') is the 'image and glory of God', I Cor. 11.7, plainly with Gen. 1.26f. in mind. But since the Fall that likeness to God has been at best incomplete, and so the Christian is being 'renewed . . . after the image of him that created him', Col. 3.10; God's original purpose in creating him in his own image is now being progressively realized. In two passages Christ is said to be the image of God, II Cor. 4.4, Col. 1.15. In the context of the second passage particularly this seems to mean much more than that Christ as 'the heavenly man' is the image of God; it is in Christ that men know God who is himself invisible, Christ is God's representative. The same thought is expressed in different words in Heb. 1.3; here 'express image' (AV), 'very image' (RV), is in the Gk. *charactēr*, which means literally the impression made by a seal, and so has the more general sense of 'exact reproduction'. The contemporary Jewish theologian Philo similarly calls the divine *Logos* (Word, Reason) the 'impression of the seal of God', and the human reason an 'impression of the divine power'. (*V.* also SIMILITUDE.)

J. Y. CAMPBELL

IMAGINATION

In the OT this word renders 3 Heb. nouns. One of these is the noun from the root *chashab*, which is more commonly trans. 'thought'. Of the other two, one means strictly 'stubbornness', and, except for one place (Deut. 29.19), is confined to Jeremiah, who uses it 8 times and mostly in the phrase 'imagination of their (evil) heart', e.g. 3.17. The other word means lit. 'that which is formed' in the mind. We have it 3 times in combination with 'thought': Gen. 6.5, I Chron. 28.9, 29.18 (*v.* also THOUGHT). Cf. Gen. 8.21 and Deut. 31.21, where the sinister nuance of meaning is evident. Clearly the word does not signify fantasy, the free formation of mental images; but mental planning which is intended to result in some deed, and no well-intentioned deed at that.

The 2 NT occurrences of 'imagination' carry on this OT meaning, although the Gk. in each case is a word with a good philosophic background; cf. esp. Luke 1.51, Rom. 1.21, II Cor. 10.5. (Also *v.* THOUGHT.)

E. C. B.

IMMANUEL *v.* EMMANUEL

IMMORTAL, IMMORTALITY

This is not a very common word in the Bible, since the Apostolic preaching bore witness to an event which was described as the Resurrection (*q.v.*) and not as the survival of the soul of Jesus after bodily death. In the Gk. doctrine of immortality the body dies, but the soul, set free from the restrictions imposed by the body, continues its life. Immortality is held to be one of the distinctive qualities of a truly human life, so that there is no real death but only a discarding of the outworn envelope of the body. 'In the eyes of the foolish they seemed to have died' (Wisd. 3.2, showing Gk. influence). The Bible writers, holding fast to the conviction that the created order owes its existence to the wisdom and love of God and is therefore essentially good, could not conceive of life after death as a disembodied existence ('we shall not be found naked', II Cor. 5.3), but as a renewal under new conditions of the intimate unity of body and soul which was human life as they knew it. Hence death (*q.v.*) was thought of as the death of the whole man, and such phrases as 'freedom from death', 'imperishability' or 'immortality' could only properly be used to describe what is meant by the phrase the eternal or living God (*v.* LIFE, LIVING), 'who only hath immortality' (I Tim. 6.16). Man does not possess in himself this quality of deathlessness but must, if he is to overcome the destructive power of death, receive it as the gift of God, 'who raised Christ from the dead', and put death aside like a covering garment (I Cor. 15.53–4). It is through the death and resurrection of Jesus Christ that this possibility for man (II Tim. 1.10) has been brought to light and the hope confirmed that the corruption (Rom. 11.7) which is a universal feature of human life shall be effectively overcome. (*V.* also HELL, RESURRECTION.)

BIBLIOGRAPHY

A. E. Taylor: *The Christian Hope of Immortality*, London (1938). A. M. Ramsey: *The Resurrection of Christ*, London (1945). J Baillie: *And the Life Everlasting*, London (1934).

F. J. TAYLOR

INCENSE *v.* SACRIFICE II(*e*)

INDIGNATION *v.* WRATH

INHERIT, HEIR, INHERITANCE, HERITAGE: last 2 are synonymous in *EVV*

OT: These words represent 2 Heb. roots, *nachal, yarash* (once *cheleq*). Outside Bible characteristic ref. of these Eng. words is to hereditary succession, but not in OT. Inheritance in this sense was of course familiar among Hebrews, and *nachal, yarash* were used to denote it, as in most of following refs.: Gen. 15.3f., 21.10, 27.37, Num. 27.1–11, 36.1–12, Deut. 21.15–17, 25.6, Judg. 11.2, II Sam. 14.7, I Chron. 26.10, Job 42.15, Jer. 32.8; *v.* FIRSTBORN. But this is not the primary or characteristic meaning either of *nachal* or *yarash*, and Heb. has no special word for it. *Yarash* means, and is usually trans., 'possess'; *nachal* means primarily 'have divided out to one as one's share'. The 2 roots tend to be used as synonymous, in substantival form *nachal* being more frequent; in verbal forms *yarash*. *Nachal* is more important for us.

(*a*) *Canaan=Israel's nachalah* (n. below= substantive, *nachalah*). Fundamental ref.—Gen. 12.7 (J)—God's promise to Abraham. This promise constantly referred to through the Bible. But, because *nachal* means not just possess, but have divided out to one as one's share, this root is used only rarely until the actual allotment of land to tribes and families comes into the picture. In Deut. it is common (e.g. 1.38; cf. 3.28, 31.7, Josh. 1.6). Joshua's work culminates in the dividing out of the n. to tribes (Josh. 13.1,7). This is done by lot, i.e. regarded as done by God himself (Josh. 18.6,10). For the Hebrews' reverence for the divine sanction of this allotment *v.* Num. 36 (a tribe's n. must not be altered), I Kings 21.3, Mic. 2.2, Lev. 25.10,13,23,28,31. It was because this allotment passed from father to son that n. came to mean 'inheritance' in our sense; but allotment, not inheritance, is the primary idea.

For Canaan=Israel's n. outside Hexateuch *v.* I Kings 8.36, Neh. 9.8,15, etc., Amos 2.9f., Mic. 2.4, Jer. 3.18f., 11.4f., 7.7, Ezek. 20.5f.,42, 33.24, 35.15, 36.12, 37.25, 46.16ff., 47.13f. (reallotting of land after Exile foretold; cf. 45.1, 48.29), Isa. 49.8, 60.21, Zech. 8.12, Ps. 37.18, 44.2ff.,47.4,69.36,78.55,105.9ff.,135.12,136.21f. (Rare in 8th-cent. prophets, comes to fore with Jer., contemporary of Deut.)

N. used in this connexion served to emphasize 2 things: (i) that Israel's possession of Canaan rests on God's gift, not its own efforts or prowess; (ii) its security, permanence and legitimacy, because it originates not in a mere conquest, the result of which may later be reversed, but in God's deliberate allotting.

The idea undergoes a twofold process of narrowing and expansion. On the one hand, instead of the whole people, it is a remnant that is to inherit (finally, the promise is focused on the person of the Messiah); on the other hand, the inheritance expands to include not only Canaan, but 'the nations'. Cf. Isa. 54.3, Ps. 2.8, Dan. 7.14.

(*b*) *Canaan=Jehovah's nachalah*. The whole earth is his, but he allots himself this land specially; *v.* Exod. 15.17, Josh. 22.19, II Sam. 21.3, I Kings 8.36, II Chron. 20.11, Isa. 47.6, Jer. 2.7, Ezek. 38.16, Zech. 2.12, Ps. 79.1; cf. Joel 1.6, 2.18. But I Sam. 26.19 seems to reflect the idea that Jehovah was the *baal* of a particular territory and limited to it, an idea taken over from the heathen (cf. II Kings 5.17).

(*c*) *Israel=Jehovah's nachalah*. All peoples belong to him, but Israel is his special people. Exod. 19.5 (*segullah*), Deut. 7.6, 14.2, 26.18; his *nachalah*: Deut. 4.20, 9.26,29, 32.8f., I Sam. 10.1, II Sam. 14.16, 20.19, I Kings 8.51,53, II Kings 21.14, Isa. 19.25, 63.17, Joel 2.17,26f., Ps. 28.9, 33.12, 74.2, 78.70f., 94.5,14, 106.5,40, 135.4.

(*d*) *Nachalah* also used to denote a man's lot or destiny appointed him by God (Job 20.29, 27.13, 31.2).

(*e*) *Jehovah=the n. of the pious*. Ps. 16.5f.; cf. Ps. 73.26, 119.57, 142.5, Lam. 3.24. (Num. 18.20ff., Deut. 10.9, etc., not relevant here, as in those passages the ref. is quite material, viz. share in tithes, sacrificial meat, etc. cf. Josh. 13.14f.)

NT: Words of the *kleronom-* group (our main concern here) occur 52 times in NT: *kleronomeo* (inherit), 18; *kleronomia* (inheritance), 14; *kleronomos* (heir), 15; *synkleronomos* (joint-heir), 4; *katakleronomeo* (give for an inheritance), 1. We must also notice the word *kleros*, which in NT usually means 'lot', but twice is trans. 'inheritance' (Acts 26.18, Col. 1.12) and once by RV 'the charge allotted to you', where AV has 'God's heritage' (I Pet. 5.3), and the word *kleroo* (Eph. 1.11—'we were made a heritage').

The decisive idea of the *kleronom-* group in class. Gk. is 'inheritance by legal succession', though these words can denote simply 'possession'; but in LXX the hereditary idea is seldom present, *kleronomeo* usually representing *yarash*, and *kleronomia nachalah*. *Kleros* has 2 meanings (lot and allotment of land) both in class. Gk. and in LXX, where it represents Heb. *goral*, less often *nachalah*. In LXX both *kleronom-* and *kleros* express the conviction that Canaan was not won by any effort or merit of Israel, but was received as a gift, the portion allotted to Israel by Jehovah's free decision, and that it was only as a result of this divine allotting that Israel was able to take possession of the land. *Kleros* stresses the idea of dividing out, allotting, *kleronom-* that of permanence, security and legitimacy of possession.

(*a*) *The Heir and the Heirs*. The most interesting and significant fact about these words in NT is that the idea of hereditary succession or connexion between heirship and sonship, which is their decisive meaning in class. Gk., but is absent in OT (and also in Rabbinic writings, where *nachal* means merely 'obtain'), comes right to the fore and is their essential characteristic. The reason for this is not, as has been suggested, the hangover of the Gk. associations of the words. It is rather the use of the Aramaic equivalent of *nachal* by Jesus, behind which lies his own unique consciousness of being the Son of God. The clue to the NT significance of the *kleronom-* words is Jesus' consciousness of being *the* Son and Heir. The key passage is Mark 12.1–11 and par., where Jesus refers to himself as 'the heir'. This identification (Christ =*the* heir) is fundamental to the use of these words throughout the NT (apart from the few occasions like Heb. 6.12, 11.7, where *kleronom-* is used in the Rabbinic sense of 'obtain'). Cf. Heb. 1.2. Rom. 8.17 implies that Christ is the Heir, though Paul nowhere asserts it in so many words.

But Christians are also joint-heirs with Christ (Rom. 8.17). For them too heirship depends on sonship (contrast OT, which never connects Israel's *nachalah* with Father-Son metaphor). Hence connexion between heirship of Christians and ADOPTION. The word 'adoption' occurs in connexion with *kleronom-* in Rom. 8.15,23, Gal. 4.5, and the idea (implied by Father, sons, children) more frequently—Rom. 8.14,15,16,17,19,21, Gal. 3.26 (*kleronom-* in 18 and 4.1), 4.6,7. Christians are joint-heirs with Christ, because they have been adopted as sons by God. Their sonship is not physical, nor does it rest on any general use of the word 'Father' of God in the sense of Creator, nor does it depend on a physical descent from Abraham; but it depends on their faith in Jesus Christ (John 1.12f.).

(*b*) *The Inheritance* (=i. below). Our next question is: 'What is the i.?' What are the objects of the verb *kleronomeo* and the obj. genitives used with other words of this group? They are as follows: *kingdom of God* or *kingdom*, Matt. 25.34, I Cor. 6.9f., 15.50, Gal. 5.21, Eph. 5.5, Jas. 2.5 (cf. Matt. 21.43, where the i. is identified with the kingdom); *the earth*, Matt. 5.5; *eternal life*, Mark 10.17=Luke 18.18, Matt. 19.29, Luke 10.25, Tit. 3.7 (?); *salvation*, Heb. 1.14; *blessing*, I Pet. 3.9, Heb. 12.17; *incorruption*, I Cor. 15.50; *the promise(s)*, Heb. 6.12,17, 11.9; *the grace of life*, I Pet. 3.7; *glory*, Rom. 8.17f.; *a place* (i.e. Canaan), Heb. 11.8; *the world*, Rom. 4.13; *the righteousness which is according to faith*, Heb. 11.7; *all things* (of Christ), Heb. 1.2; *name* (of Christ), Heb. 1.4; *these things*, Rev. 21.7. So 'kingdom of God' or 'kingdom' is the most characteristic description of the i. The i. is 'the new world, in which God alone rules and rules completely' (W. Foerster in *TWNT*, III, p. 782).

(*c*) *Present or Future?* The heir of Mark 12.1ff. is not yet in possession of his i. In his earthly life the Son of God as the humiliated, suffering Son of Man, is Heir presumptive and not yet in possession of his i. Foerster (*op. cit.*, p. 782) suggests that it is because the Johannine writings lay such stress on the *present* glory and power of the Incarnate Word that they avoid the use of the *kleronom-* idea. For Christians too the i. is future: it is dependent on our adoption, which is future (Rom. 8.23). The i. is the object of hope (*v.* Rom. 8.24f., 5.2, Eph. 1.18, 2.12, 4.4, Col. 1.5,23,27, I Thess. 4.13, Tit. 1.2, 2.13; cf. I Cor. 13.9f.,12, II Cor. 5.7, Heb. 11.13, 13.14, I Pet. 1.3f., Rom. 8.17–18, I John 3.2f.). Throughout the NT there is a significant 'not yet'. Christians are heirs presumptive here; their entering into their i. is still to come. What they have here and now is not the i., but its EARNEST—'ye were sealed with the Holy Spirit of promise, which is an earnest of our i.' (Eph. 1.14; cf. II Cor. 1.22, 5.5). 'Earnest' (*arrabōn*) is a commercial term—the first part-payment that seals the contract. Jesus Christ entered on his i. at his Ascension, and sent the Holy Spirit to his followers as the pledge and guarantee of their also entering later into the i. (*V.* under SEAL.)

(*d*) *Continuity in OT and NT*. It is interesting and instructive to note both the continuity and the transformation of the OT ideas in NT. (i) Canaan=Israel's n. In the later parts of OT the n. became more and more eschatological, while in Rabbinic writings 'the age to come' replaces Canaan as the n. of the pious. In NT the n. is the kingdom of God, the new heaven and new earth (Rev. 21.1f.; cf. Heb. 11.13ff.). Moreover, it is now those who have faith in Christ who are to inherit (cf. Paul's polemic against the Judaizers, Gal. 3, 4, Rom. 4, esp. 13f., Eph. 3.6). The narrowing process, that we noted, was pointing forward to Jesus as *the* Heir, while the widening-out to include the nations finds its sequel in such passages as Eph. 3.6. (ii) Israel=Jehovah's n. Not Israel after the flesh, but the Church, the new Israel, is God's n. (I Pet. 5.3, for which *v.* note in E. G. Selwyn's commentary; cf. 2.9, Tit. 2.14, where the idea is present, but *kleronom-* not used). (iii) The idea that Jehovah is the n. of the pious remains and is enriched; for the eternal inheritance, the kingdom of God, eternal life, etc., are all ultimately summed up in the words 'to be with Christ' (Phil. 1.23; cf. John 14.3*b*). Jesus Christ himself is our future, our inheritance.

The present writer acknowledges great indebtedness to the article by W. Foerster and J. Herrmann in Kittel's *TWNT*, III, pp. 757–86.

C. E. B. CRANFIELD

INIQUITY *v.* SIN

INNOCENT, BLAMELESS, UNBLAMEABLE

The underlying Heb. word *naqi* comes from a root signifying clean, empty; thence means innocent in the sense of free from guilt. Innocence in the more positive sense would be another word, *tam*, which, however, is never rendered 'innocent' in EVV, but usually 'perfect'; it signifies wholeness, integrity. *Naqi* moves in this context of meaning, though it is far less common than *tam* (perfect) and *tsaddiq* (righteous). It is twice (Gen. 44.10, Josh. 2.17) trans. 'blameless'. Whereas 'innocent' is almost confined to the OT in our EVV, 'blameless' is more common in the NT. It corresponds to three practically synonymous Gk. words, and tends to acquire an eschatological sense, e.g. I Thess. 5.23, I Cor. 1.8, II Pet. 3.14; with Phil. 2.15 perhaps bordering on this sense. In the meaning 'beyond reproach' it is used with ref. to fitness for office in the Church: I Tim. 3.2,10 (AV), Tit. 1.6f.

The word 'unblameable' is identical in meaning. For the ordinary moral sense cf. I Thess. 2.10; and for the eschatological sense, I Thess. 3.13. In Col. 1.22 we have it again in the moral sense, and coupled with UNREPROVEABLE, a word of almost identical meaning. (The corresponding Gk. term is elsewhere 4 times trans. 'blameless'.)

E. C. B.

INSPIRE, INSPIRATION

Like certain other words which have figured prominently in the theological discussions of later ages (e.g. 'providence', 'dispensation'), the word 'inspiration' is hardly a biblical word at all. In the NT it occurs only in II Tim. 3.16, 'All scripture is given by inspiration of God' (AV; RV has 'every scripture inspired of God'); the word is doubtless intended to suggest that God has breathed life-giving truth into the scriptures just as he breathed into man's nostrils the breath of life and man became a living soul (Gen. 2.7; cf. Wisd. 15.11). (In Wisd. 15.11 and Job 32.8, AV, there is no reference to a written record.) This is a thoroughly biblical and illuminating use of the metaphor of 'in-breathing', but it bears little relation to the later use of the notion of inspiration which became Hellenized in the early centuries and led to the view that the Heb. prophets and Christian Apostles were inspired after the manner of Vergil's Sibyl (*Aeneid*, vi). Thus, Athenagoras represents the Spirit as a flute-player who uses the prophet as his instrument. As against all such unbiblical ideas the NT writers hold no theory of inspiration; they had inherited from Judaism the view that God had revealed his truth by 'showing' or 'speaking' it to the scriptural writers who had then written down what they had seen or heard. Thus the NT writers quote 'the scriptures' (usually the Gk. Bible, LXX) as the direct utterance of God himself (e.g. Eph. 4.8, 'He saith', Heb. 3.7, where Ps. 95 is cited: 'Even as the Holy Spirit saith, To-day if ye shall hear his voice'; cf. also Rom. 1.2, Luke 1.70, etc.). But the Bible itself gives plenty of evidence that to the writers themselves the reception and recording of divine revelation was not so simple a matter; e.g. St. Paul's experience was not that of being a mere pen in the hand of the Holy Spirit, for we can watch him as he determinedly thinks out his message (e.g. I Cor. 7.10,12,25,40). (*V.* also REVEAL, SCRIPTURE.)

A. R.

INSTRUCTION *v.* CHASTEN

INTERCESSION *v.* PRAYER

ISAAC

The traditions about Isaac (Gen. 24–8) are less colourful than those of Abraham and Jacob; but I. shares with them the status of being one of the three great patriarchs of the nation of Israel. It is even possible to call the nation by his name (Amos 7.9,16). By NT times the three patriarchs were looked upon as co-presidents at the feast of the faithful Israelites in Paradise (Matt. 8.11, Luke 13.28; cf. Mark 12.26). In the *Testaments of the Twelve Patriarchs*, there is a pregnant allusion (*Levi*, xviii. 6, 'With the Father's voice as from Abraham to Isaac') to Gen. 22.8 and the sacrifice of Isaac as a 'type' prefiguring the sacrificial obedience of the Messiah of the tribe of Levi. This appears to be the only allusion of its kind in a pre-Christian Jewish source, to a belief that the Messiah's obedience as a beloved son might involve the willingness to offer up his life in sacrifice, an idea which comes very close to that of Isa. 53.7, Jer. 11.19, and one that is in character in a priestly Messiah (cf. Mark 1.11 and John 1.29). The idea is developed in connexion with Christ in Heb. 11.17f. and Jas. 2.21; in medieval Judaism the sacrifice of I. was pleaded in the same kind of way that Christians pleaded the sacrifice of Christ; in I. the whole race of Israel had made its act of submission to God. In post-biblical times the Christian Fathers regarded the sacrifice of I. as a 'type' or pre-figuring of the sacrifice of the cross. This suggestion is first found in *Ep. Barn.* vii (Lightfoot, *Apostolic Fathers*, p. 251); it does not occur in the NT (but see Rom. 8.32).

MATTHEW BLACK

ISRAEL *v.* JACOB

* * *

JACOB, ISRAEL

With Abraham and Isaac, Jacob is regarded as one of the three great patriarchs of the Hebrews. The traditional stories (Gen. 25–50) present him as a scheming and deceitful character who defrauds his brother of his birth-right (*v.* EDOM, ESAU), but who nevertheless by discipline and spiritual discernment triumphed over his weakness and became a source of blessing to his posterity (Gen. 48f.; cf. Heb. 11.21). God's choice of J. in preference to the worthy Esau has always been regarded as a pointed illustration of the biblical doctrine of the divine election (cf. Rom. 9.13, Mal. 1.2; *v.* CHOICE, DETERMINATE, EDOM). J.'s determination to obtain a spiritual blessing, so powerfully dramatized in the story of his struggle with the angel in Gen. 32.22–32, has been regarded as symbolic of the spiritual tenacity of the Hebrew race: 'I will notl et thee go except thou bless me.' Having received the blessing, J. becomes a new person and receives a new name; he is no longer to be called 'Supplanter' (Jacob), but Israel—taken to mean 'Perseverer with God' (Gen. 32.28). The lesson of J.'s persistence is urged by Hosea upon the unstable Ephraimites (Hos. 12.2–4,12f.). It was held that God had entered into a covenant with J., as he had with Abraham (*q.v.*) and Isaac (*q.v.*) (*v.* COVENANT) (Exod. 2.24, Lev. 26.42; cf. Gen. 46.2–4). A common title for God was 'God of Jacob' (e.g. Isa. 2.3, Acts 7.46), and J. was often used as the title of the whole nation (e.g. Jer. 30.7,10,18). In NT times it was held by the rabbis that the patriarchs Abraham, Isaac and J. presided at the feast of the faithful Israelites in Paradise (Matt. 8.11, Luke 13.28; cf. Mark 12.26). The name 'Israel', however, was the one which above all others passed into common usage as the biblical title for the Hebrew nation (cf. 'Children of Israel', 'Israelites'). Israel was the chosen instrument of God's purpose (cf. esp. Amos 3.1f.) amongst the nations, but she failed to carry out that purpose, as the prophets so often lamented. Therefore they look forward to the day in which God shall fashion a new instrument, more adequate to his purpose. All the NT writers regard the Church of Jesus Christ as this new instrument, and see the true fulfilment of Israel's destiny in the new covenant which had been made and sealed through the death of God's Messiah. The Christian Church is, in fact, the New Israel, though this expression is not actually found in the NT (or for that matter in the OT). (*V.* also CHURCH, COVENANT.)

ALAN RICHARDSON

JAH (*Ps.* 68.4) *v.* GOD, GODS III

JEALOUS, ZEALOUS

The OT varies between 'jealous' 'zealous', and ENVIOUS in its renderings of the Heb. root *qana'* and its derivatives. This root originally means 'to be dyed dark red, black', a meaning which is to be found in Arabic and Syriac. In Heb. and other Semitic languages it is used of such deep personal emotions as customarily show themselves in a heightened colour. Thus the word can mean both 'envy against' (Num. 11.29) and 'zeal for' (Ps. 106.16). In such a case as that of the ordeal by jealousy (Num. 5.11–31) the trans. is obvious, but there are cases where it is far from easy to decide between 'jealous' and 'zealous'. In I Kings 19.10,14, Elijah says: 'I have been very jealous for the Lord of Hosts.' So both EVV, but the Douai Version has 'zealous'. This latter is because the Vulgate has in every case some derivative of the verb *zelo*. Similarly the Gk. Version (Septuagint) has regularly *zelos* and its derivatives, a word which in class. Gk. is used both for the ignoble passion of envy (cf. I Macc. 8.16) and for the noble passion of enthusiastic zeal (cf. I Cor. 14.12).

The double significance of the word is well illustrated in II Cor. 11.2, where Paul finds himself wanting to make it quite clear that he is using the word in a good sense, so he says: 'I am jealous over you with a godly jealousy.' On the other hand, in II Cor. 7.11

he makes the most of the double meaning when he declares that the godly sorrow of the Corinthian Christians engendered in them a zeal which was so intense that it looked like revenge.

For us the word 'jealousy' has usually a bad meaning, and this is why many find it strange that the word should be used of God. We do, however, legitimately speak of a man being jealous for his honour or for his wife's honour, and the word is frequently used in this sense of men jealous for God, e.g. in Num. 25.11,13 (Phinheas), I Kings 19.10,14 (Elijah), and II Kings 10.16 (Jehu). In the NT the rendering is usually 'zeal' when the sense is good and 'envy' when the sense is bad. Both of these words are used frequently in the OT, but the word 'jealous(y)' is rare in the NT, being found 4 times only.

The whole idea of the jealousy of God is a strong and bold anthropomorphism, on the analogy mostly of the jealousy of a husband concerning his wife. This works in two ways, both in the case of the husband and in the case of God. It appears as indignation against a wayward Israel (Ezek. 16.38, where the analogy of husband and wife is actually used), and as zeal on Israel's behalf against those who would harm her or lead her astray (Zech. 1.14, 8.2). The idea is most common in Ezek., a book which is so vivid in its anthropomorphisms that great care traditionally has been exercised in the study of it. The 'jealous God' (Exod. 20.5, 34.14, Deut. 4.24, 5.9, 6.15) is therefore a God who is 'a consuming fire' against all evil both within and without Israel, but full of zeal on behalf of the salvation of his people. In ordinary English speech the difference between the two ideas is shown by the prepositions which accompany the word. It is good to be 'jealous *for*' somebody or something; it is bad to be 'jealous *of*' somebody. Further, the whole idea of the jealousy of God is bound up with the idea of his covenant-people, the people of his choice. The husband is jealous concerning his wife partly because of what is right and wrong, but chiefly because she is his wife and no one else's, and because she therefore is in a special and peculiar relation to him. Similarly of God and Israel. The matter of right and wrong is involved, as it must always be involved in any matter where God is concerned, but the primary emphasis is on the fact that Israel belongs to God, and is therefore in a special and peculiar relationship to him. (*V.* also DESIRE.)

N. H. SNAITH

JEHOVAH *v.* GOD, GODS III

JERUSALEM *v.* CITY

JESUS

'Jesus' is the Lat. form of the name which in Gk. was spelt *Jesous* (the vowel combination ou does not occur in Lat.). *Jesous* is the form assumed in Gk. by the Heb. name Joshua, which in late Heb. and Aramaic had become *Jeshua*. So in the Gk. version of the OT the title of the book of Joshua is simply *Jesous*. In the two passages in the NT in which Joshua is mentioned (Acts 7.45, Heb. 4.8) this is the form used in the Gk.—which explains the rather misleading rendering 'Jesus' of the AV; RV has 'Joshua' in both passages. The name naturally was a common one among the Jews; one of the most important books in the OT Apocrypha, Ecclesiasticus, is the work of 'Jesus, the son of Sirach'; a Jesus who was the son of Eliezer occurs in Luke's genealogy of our Lord (Luke 3.29); Paul mentions 'Jesus who is called Justus' in Col. 4.11; and the historian Josephus mentions 4 (possibly 5) high priests during the Roman period who bore the name. The Heb. form Joshua was supposed to mean 'Jah (Jehovah) will save' or 'the salvation of the Lord' (so Philo), and so in Matt. 1.21 the choice of this particular name is explained—'for he shall save his people from their sins'. The parallelism between the Joshua who led the Old Israel across the Jordan into the Promised Land and the Lord Jesus who brings his New Israel through the waters of baptism into their heavenly inheritance did not escape the Fathers of the early Church.

J. Y. CAMPBELL

JOB *v.* SUFFER

JOHN THE BAPTIST *v.* ELIJAH

JOSEPH

The ancient traditions of the Hebrews contain no stories more vivid and unforgettable than those concerning Joseph (J and E; Gen. 37ff.), and it is small wonder that Joseph passed into Jewish history as an ideal figure representing faithfulness, obedience and forbearing love (cf. Acts 7.9–18, Heb. 11.21f.). The story of Joseph conveys in a form which children can apprehend the great biblical lessons concerning the divine election and compassion, man's sinful attempt to frustrate God's plan, and God's victory by means of suffering and forgiving love. These lessons, of course, are taught more directly and more profoundly in the later parts of the Bible, esp. in the NT; but there is about the Joseph-story a prophetic anticipation of or insight into the fundamental pattern of the biblical revelation which makes it easy to understand how Joseph has come to be thought of as a 'type' of Christ (*v.* PROPHECY I). This does not mean that we are to seek Christological interpretations of all the details of the Joseph-stories (e.g. Potiphar's wife!), but that, properly used, they can become the means of preparing the minds of children and adults alike for the reception of the Gospel of the cross and resurrection. We may sum up the lessons to be learnt as follows: (*a*) *God's Election.* Joseph is his father's favourite and wears the princely robe (Gen. 37.3); Jacob selects his youngest son, just as God surprisingly elects the less honourable and most unlikely people to be the instruments of his purpose. (*b*) *God's Compassion.* Jacob sends Joseph to see how his brethren are faring (37.13), just as later God sent his only Son into the world (cf. Mark 12.6, John 3.16). (*c*) *Man's attempt to frustrate God's plan* is illustrated by the treatment meted out by Joseph's brethren to the messenger of the father's love. (*d*) *God's victory* is nevertheless achieved: Joseph suffers, but lives to forgive and bless his brethren.

For a brilliant but highly conjectural attempt to discern a parallel between the Patriarch Joseph (who begged Pharaoh's permission to bury the body of Jacob, the Old Israel; Gen. 50.4ff.) and Joseph of Arimathea (who begged Pilate's permission to bury the body of Jesus, the New Israel), see Austin Farrer, *The Glass of Vision* (1948), pp. 144f.; if Dr. Farrer's conjectures are acceptable, he has come near to finding a Christological explanation even for the episode of Potiphar's wife!

ALAN RICHARDSON

JOY, REJOICE, GLADNESS

Throughout the OT and NT joy and gladness are specifically and consistently related to the whole life of Israel or the Church. Joy is not an isolated or occasional consequence of faith, but is an integral part of the whole relation to God. While it is possible to say of the well-known words in Phil. 4.4 that the Holy Spirit dwells only with joyful men, it is truer to see this joy as part of God's gift, proceeding from himself. Rom. 14.17 and 15.13 show this connexion clearly: it is 'in the power of the Holy Ghost' that joy arises. This source of joy in the life of God makes man's joy not only a gift derived from the joy of God, but also an anticipation of a final state. It is only in the fullness of the presence of God that joy is full: 'to enjoy God for ever', in the words of the *Shorter Catechism*, is possible only beyond this life, and this is the only fullness of joy. The typical OT ref., such as Isa. 12.3, 61.10, 65.18ff., Ps. 126, all have this anticipatory nature, i.e. they see joy as bound up with the fullness of salvation. The joy in the characteristic and most popular of the Jewish festivals, the feast of the tabernacles (cf. John 7.37), also has this eschatological reference. In the wedding metaphor, as used, e.g. in John 3.29, 17.13 and in Rev. 19.7, the idea of joy is thrown forward into the same almost ineffable situation of the presence of God. To sum up, joy in the Bible appears consistently as an eschatological reality which is proleptically, and partially, present in human life as an anticipation of the Kingdom of God.

R. G. S.

JUDGE, JUDGMENT

There are two senses in which the word 'judgment' is used in the OT: firstly, as a synonym for the statutes of God, his testimonies and his Law, and here generally in the plural; secondly, in the sense of God's judgments on the affairs of men and nations both in history and at the end of history. This latter is the sense in which the word is used in the NT.

The origin of the use of the word 'judgment' as a parallel to the statutes and the Law, is to be found in the custom in old Israel whereby men went to their local shrine when they needed any ruling of God on any matter of faith or practice. If the question was a new one, the cult official would seek an oracle from God. This he would do by sacrifice or by casting the sacred lot if he were a priest, or by dream and vision or in ecstasy if he were a prophet. This oracle would be a *torah* (instruction, law, *q.v.*). The next time the same question arose, the official would be ready with the answer, and he would now be able to give a ruling according to precedent. This ruling would be a *mishpat* (judgment). Gradually both words came to be used for the declared word of God, and as such both became synonyms for righteousness (that which conforms to the nature and will of God, *q.v.*) and for the testimonies, commandments, statutes; cf. Deut. 4.1, Neh. 1.7, and regularly, esp. throughout Ps. 119.

But the word is also used of God's judgment of men, whether during history or at the end of it. In Isa. 1.21 the prophet says that once the city 'was full of judgment'. He means, as the following phrase shows ('righteousness lodged in her'), that the city formerly was the home of right action which fulfilled the will of God. But in Isa. 1.27 the statement that 'Zion shall be redeemed with judgment' refers to a time in the future when the judgment of God shall have purged away the dross, and transgressors and sinners shall be destroyed. Isaiah is never weary of declaring that God will enter into judgment with his wayward people, for 'the Lord is a God of judgment' (30.18).

Gradually the idea grows of a great day of judgment, when righteousness shall be set on high. This consummation of history is called the DAY OF THE LORD, and it is the day of judgment upon all who are unfaithful to God whether within Israel or without. At first the Day of the Lord is to be a day of judgment within Israel, as in Amos and the pre-exilic prophets generally; but after the exile the returned exiles are regarded as being the faithful people of God, and so the tendency is for the Day of the Lord to be a day of rejoicing for Israel and of black darkness and doom for the heathen. In that day, judgment (the word is now *din*, strict justice, and not *mishpat*) shall be 'given to the saints of the Most High' (Dan. 7.22)—that is, to the Jews; 'and the kingdom and the dominion, and the greatness of the kingdoms under the whole heaven' (Dan. 7.27) shall be given to them. By this time a belief in the resurrection of the dead had developed (Dan. 12.2), and from this time onwards the belief in a great and universal judgment upon all men, both the living and the resurrected dead, grew more and more strong. This is the background of the larger part of the NT. Christ himself will come to judge both the living and the dead, and all men will stand before his judgment seat (Matt. 25.31ff., Acts 17.31, II Cor. 5.10).

The idea that God is judge is ancient, and is embedded in the earliest strata of the OT, e.g. Gen. 18.25. Just as an earthly king establishes his kingdom, and sits upon his throne to give judgment (II Sam. 8.15), this being the function of the king (Prov. 20.8, etc.), so God is king, higher than the kings of the earth (Ps. 89.27). Since God is king, he is also judge. He fixed the world firmly, and he shall judge the nations with equity, for he is coming to judge the earth with righteousness (Pss. 96.10,13; 98). Not only did he establish himself as king at the creation, but he establishes himself as king in every mighty act of salvation for his people (Exod. 15.18, Pss. 93, 95, 99, Isa. 52.7). And yet again, he will set up his kingdom at that great day when the consummation of history is accomplished, and the final judgments will be pronounced and sealed (Isa. 24–26). We have thus a triple time-content both for the Kingdom of God and for the Judgment of God. He has been both king and judge from the beginning; he becomes king and judge at every crisis in history; he will become king and judge at the great crisis which marks the end of history. And 'crisis' is nothing but the actual Gk. word for 'judgment'.

In the OT God delegates his function of judge on earth in part to the Messianic prince who is destined to establish the earthly kingdom. When therefore the idea of the Day of the Lord develops, we get parallel with it the idea that the Son of Man will be the judge of all men, so that in the NT and in the Creeds of the Church it is roundly declared that Christ will 'come again with glory to judge both the quick and the dead'. There can be little doubt but that this actually was the expectation of the NT writers generally, though in John the judgment is associated emphatically with his first coming (John 3.19,9.39, 12.31, etc.), and there is an equation of the gift of the Holy Spirit with the second coming of Christ. Such sayings as these have encouraged many moderns to think of the judgment of Christ in terms of the automatic working of history, and in the general evolutionary development which it is hoped will one day result in a Utopia. But this is not what the NT means by the Second Coming and the great Judgment Day. Nothing less than the end of history is involved, and with it a visible manifestation of Christ on this earth, and a demonstration of his eternal victory in the salvation of those who have faith in him and the destruction of those who persist in rebellion. To what extent such statements as these demand a literal interpretation is a matter for legitimate difference of opinion, but there is no justification for categorically denying any such dramatic finale. (*V.* also COMMAND, LAW, STATUTE.)

N. H. SNAITH

JUST, JUSTIFY, JUSTIFICATION

These words, apart from three cases in Prov., stand in both OT and NT for the words which are also translated by righteous, righteousness (*q.v.*). In both Testaments 'to be justified' means to be brought into right relations with a person. It can be used both of man to man, and man to God. In the case of man to man, justification is everywhere possible; but there is nothing man can do to secure justification before God. This is made clear in Ps. 143.2 and Job. 25.4. It is sometimes held that OT doctrine maintains that a man may be justified by his works, but this is denied, both in the OT (Isa. 57.12, 64.6) and by Paul (Acts 13.39, Gal. 2.16). By obeying the words of the Law, by sacrifices accompanied by true devotion, a man may continue in and maintain a right relationship with God, but the establishment of that relationship in the first place is by the good favour, that is by the grace (*q.v.*), of God.

The verb *dikaioo* ('justify') does not mean 'to make just', and indeed is not so much an ethical word as a word which belongs to the vocabulary of salvation. On man's part, the essential condition for justification is faith in Christ. This involves a complete trust in him, and a changing of man's attitude from that state of sin from which he desires to be saved.

On this condition every repentant sinner is brought by God into fellowship with him. This is the working of his grace, the undeserved favour with which God welcomes all who truly turn to him. Because of this relationship a man is 'created in Christ Jesus for good works' (Eph. 2.10).

Justification is the first step in the process of salvation, that first reconciliation to God which is the beginning of a steady growth in grace and in the knowledge of God (II Pet. 3.18). This is a process, but justification is that immediate setting-right with God which God himself accomplishes by his grace when man has faith. (*V.* further under SANCTIFY, III, IV.)

N. H. SNAITH

JUSTICE

It is noteworthy that this word is not found in NT, and rarely in OT. Where it is found in EVV, it represents the word translated 'judgment' (*q.v.*) once, and elsewhere (27 times) one of the two forms of the word usually translated 'righteousness' (*q.v.*). The Gk. *dikē* is found thrice only, and then of retributive justice (Acts 25.15, 28.4, Jude 7), of which the second only is true to the class. Gk. conception of that *dike* to which both gods and men are subject. The emphasis in much Christian teaching, which tends to put justice first and mercy afterwards, is due largely to the fact that in the Vulgate the Latin *justitia* is used most frequently where the EVV have 'righteousness', and the Latin *justus* where the EVV have 'righteous'. Compare the Douai Version, which regularly has 'justice' and 'just' in these cases.

N. H. S.

* * *

KIN *v.* KINSMAN

KIND, KINDNESS

The adj. is not found in the OT, and thrice only in the NT, where the meaning is 'good', 'pleasant'. The Gk. word (*chrēstos*) is used in class. Gk. largely of food, and is indeed used of wine in Luke 5.39. The noun is found rarely in the NT, twice of ordinary human kindness (Acts 28.2, II Pet. 1.7) and 4 times of Christian kindliness. In the OT it is used once of kindness in the sense of a good deed (II Sam. 2.6); and elsewhere (38 times) for the Heb. *chesed*, the covenant-word which Coverdale translated by loving-kindness (*q.v.*) in the Pss. and mercy outside the Pss. when the reference was to God and his people Israel, and by kindness when it referred to the relations between man and man.

N. H. S.

KING *v.* GOD, KINGDOM OF GOD, DAVID

KINGDOM OF GOD

'The K. of God' is the central theme of the teaching of Jesus, and it involves his whole understanding of his own person and work. His divergence from the outlook of contemporary Judaism concerned no mere question of interpretation or reform within Judaism itself; such a dispute would hardly have led to fatal consequences. The point at issue was the meaning of Jesus' work as a whole, which involved the setting up of himself as a rival authority to that on which Judaism was based, the Law. For example, in Mark 2.23–8, when his disciples were blamed for plucking and eating corn on the Sabbath, Jesus defends them by referring to 'what David did' (I Sam. 21.1–6) on an occasion when necessity overrode law. But the cases were not exactly parallel, since the disciples were not starving: the significance of the reference to David lies in the fact that David (*q.v.*) is the ideal king of Israel, always regarded as foreshadowing the Messianic King. If David could set himself above the Law, how much more could Jesus! Or again, in the discussion of divorce in Mark 10.2–12 Jesus does not take sides either with Hillel or Shammai: he goes back to the story of Creation and points out that God's original intention had been the life-long union of one man with one woman. This intention humanity had failed to realize, but Jesus made it clear that he was concerned with nothing less than the renewal of the world on the lines of God's original purpose.

Mark (1.15) summarizes the message which Jesus came into Galilee preaching: 'The time is fulfilled, and the K. of God is at hand: repent ye, and believe in the Gospel.' In general terms this means that Jesus proclaimed as good news the fact that God was setting about the task of putting straight the evil plight into which the world had fallen, or that he was beginning to bring to its fulfilment his original intention in the Creation. Mark's summary cannot be understood apart from its background of OT thought about the 'time' and its fulfilment (*v.* arts. TIME and PROPHECY, FULFILMENT OF), and also about the kingship of God (*v.* art. GOD, I). The Gk. word *Basileia* (like its Aramaic equivalent, *Malkuth*), rendered 'kingdom' in EVV, means strictly 'kingship', 'kingly rule', 'reign' or 'sovereignty', and the expression 'kingdom of God' thus basically denotes the sovereign Lordship of God over his people or over the world which he has made. (The alternative, 'kingdom of heaven', or 'of the heavens', common in Matt., means the same thing, since 'heaven' in this sense was merely a conventional Jewish usage whereby the taking upon one's lips of the name of God might be avoided, lest one inadvertently transgressed the 3rd Commandment.) Throughout the OT, whatever earthly rulers may rightly or wrongly be exercising sovereignty, the real King of Israel (and, later, of the world) is God; he may and does work through deputies, but no one can share his ultimate authority. Yet the frequent triumph of evil-doers and the misery of the righteous often made this fundamental Jewish conviction difficult to sustain. God must have put off some of his authority: he must one day assert his creative sovereignty again, and men longed for the coming of that 'day'—a day which the prophets declared would surely come. The fundamental message of Jesus' proclamation was that that day had now dawned. The things which many prophets and righteous men had long desired to see and hear are now present before the eyes and in the ears of Jesus' disciples (Matt. 13.16f., Luke 10.23f.). God's reign is here, or at least is so near at hand that already the signs of its activity are manifest; and men must make some response to the claims which it lays upon them. The signs of God's rule were present in the work and words of Jesus himself; they are proclaimed alike in his miracles and in his parables.

First, the reign of God was manifest in the deeds of Jesus, and this means principally in his miracles. (This theme is further dealt with in art. MIRACLE.) Thus, Jesus' power over the demons, attested by his casting of them out, could mean only that a decisive assault was being made upon the spiritual powers of evil. In Acts 10.38 Peter picks out the healing of 'all that were oppressed of the devil' as the significant sign that God was with Jesus; but the principal passages for the right interpretation of his exorcisms are those in the Gospels dealing with the 'Beelzebub Controversy' (Mark 3.20–30, Matt. 12.25–37=Luke 11.17–23, Q). Here Jesus derides the suggestion that he is in league with the devil: the struggle is not a civil war within the kingdom of Satan but a war of aggression against him. 'If I by the spirit' (Matt.; Luke, 'finger') 'of God cast out demons, then is the K. of God come upon you.' If the exorcisms wrought by Jesus are a sign of God's (and not Satan's) activity, then the K. of God is here (cf. Luke 10.9–11). The 'strong man's house' (i.e. Satan's kingdom) is being spoiled because the 'strong man' himself has been bound (Mark 3.27; cp. also Luke 10.18). The unequivocal assertion of his miracles as the signs of his Messiahship is given in Jesus' reply to the question of John the Baptist (Matt. 11.4f.=Luke 7.22, Q) (*v.* MIRACLE). The miracles are, as it were, enacted proclamations that the K. of God has come, and as such they call forth the response of repentance and faith; cf. Luke 10.13= Matt. 11.21, Q: 'If the mighty works had been done in Tyre and Sidon, which were done in you, they would have repented long ago, sitting in sackcloth and ashes.'

Secondly, the K. of God is the dominant theme of the recorded teaching of Jesus, most strikingly presented in his parables. Indeed, the parables of Jesus may be generally described as 'parables of the K. of God'. For example, in the Parable of the Seed Growing Secretly (Mark 4.26–9) the stress is on the fact that the germination and growth of a seed is a process with which man has nothing to do. The following parable, that of the Mustard Seed (Mark 4.30–2), contrasts the proverbially tiny mustard seed with the large plant that comes of it. The K. of God resembles these processes; there is the power of God behind it, like the elemental power which forces a blade of grass through the earth. The ministry of Jesus corresponds to sowing-time rather than to harvest; at present the K. of God is germinal rather than finished and complete. Its consummation is as sure as the harvest, but the consummation is not yet (cf. also the Parable of the Sower, Mark 4.1ff.). The presence of this germinal K. of God, as we may call it, challenges the men among whom it stands and calls for a decision while there is yet time, before it is too late, even though it may now be 'the eleventh hour' (cf. the Labourers in the Vineyard, Matt. 20.1–16). In the crisis which the arrival of the K. of God brings it is necessary to act quickly, like the Unjust Steward in the parable (Luke 16.1–8) or the Man Haled before the Magistrate (Luke 12.58f.). The costliness of the decision is emphasized (Luke 14.28–32), but the inestimable value of the possession of God's K. is also clearly taught (e.g. The Hidden Treasure, Matt. 13.44; the Pearl of Great Price, Matt. 13.45f.). The members of God's K. are not the 'righteous' (Mark 2.17), the proud and self-satisfied Pharisees, but repentant sinners (cf. the Great Supper, Luke 14.16–24, also 18.9–14, Matt. 21.28–31).

Thus, the K. of God as it is presented in the teaching and work of Jesus is essentially God's K. and not ours. It is something which God gives, not something which men 'build'. It is not a Utopia or new social order; and it is not a mere disposition within men's hearts (whatever the difficult saying of Luke 17.21 may mean, it cannot mean this: perhaps we should translate, with RV margin, 'The K. of God is in your midst'). It is an act of God himself; it is his initiative in breaking the power of evil. But, just because in the ministry of Jesus the K. was present in germinal rather than in finished form, men have still their part to play: they must make a response to God's offer of his K. Jesus is in his ministry engaged in making God's last offer, his last appeal to men (cf. Mark 12.1–12). In Mark 10.17ff., when asked the secret of eternal life by someone who was already living a better life than most men, Jesus said that he still lacked one thing: he must give up everything else to follow him. This challenge the questioner declined, and Jesus went on to say to his disciples how hard it was to enter the K. of God—not only hard but impossible, except with God. The K. of God has come so near as to provoke an unavoidable crisis: it is now for men to draw near to the K. of God, and their response to it is shown by their attitude to Jesus himself. For it is in the person and deeds of Jesus that God's reign has actively begun, that the assault against evil, physical and spiritual, has been launched. It is difficult to take up an attitude towards an abstract noun such as 'reign' or 'kingdom', but the issue is made concrete and personal in Jesus, who is the embodiment of the kingly rule of God, the only one who has done on earth God's will as it is done in heaven. Men's acceptance or rejection of God's K. is thus inevitably expressed by their attitude to Jesus. This truth was clearly seen by the Pharisees and by Caiaphas; no mere technical dispute or personal quarrel gave rise to their determination to destroy him. Jesus had come to do what their Law could never accomplish —to restore God's damaged and perverted creation to its original destiny in perfect obedience to his will.

There has been considerable discussion amongst scholars whether Jesus thought of the K. of God as present or future (cf. the phrases 'realized eschatology', 'futurist eschatology'). The dilemma is an unreal one, as we shall perceive at once if we recall that the K. of God means essentially God's reign, or, even less abstractly, God reigning. God is eternally regnant, but since the coming of Jesus he has begun to rule in a new way. In this sense God's K. has actually arrived—as we have noted that much of the recorded teaching of Jesus implies. But in another sense God's reign is still to be established, and it is in this sense that Jesus bids his disciples pray, 'Thy K. come'. In the absolute sense God's K. will not come until (in symbolic language) the return of the Lord at the 'last day'. It is generally in this latter sense that the expression 'K. of God' is used in the NT outside the Gospels, as denoting that Messianic K. which is the reward and goal in heaven of the Christian life here-below. The phrase is used several times by St. Paul, often in this sense, and it may be regarded as an echo of the familiar teaching of Jesus on the lips of the Apostle (e.g. Rom. 14.17, I Cor. 6.9f., 15.50, Gal. 5.21, Eph. 5.5, II Thess. 1.5). But in Paul (as with Jesus) the power of the K. of God is already manifested here and now (I Cor. 4.20), and we are already 'translated into the K. of the Son of his love' (Col. 1.13; cf. Heb. 12.28). In the Fourth Gospel the expression 'K. of God' is used (John 3.3,5; cf. 18.36), but in the Johannine reinterpretation of the teaching of Jesus the term 'life' in its peculiarly Johannine sense is usually employed to denote broadly what in the Synoptists is called 'the K. of God'; but that this equation of 'life' with 'the K. of God' is possible even in St. Mark (and perhaps therefore in the teaching of Jesus himself) is proved by a comparison of Mark 9.43 and 45 with 9.47.

BIBLIOGRAPHY

C. H. Dodd: *The Parables of the Kingdom*, London (1935), esp. Chap. II. Alan Richardson: *The Miracle Stories of the Gospels*, London (1941), esp. Chap. III. R. Newton Flew, *Jesus and His Church*, London (1938), esp. Chap. I. T. W. Manson: *The Teaching of Jesus*, Cambridge (1931). R. Otto: *The Kingdom of God and the Son of Man*, Eng. trans., London (1938).

ALAN RICHARDSON

KINSMAN

The words 'kin', 'kindred', 'kinsfolk', 'kinsman', 'kinswoman' in the EVV represent a number of Heb. and Gk. words of different roots, all expressing the same general idea, but focusing attention on different aspects, as mutual acquaintance, nearness, sharing in the same flesh, birth, family, tribe, race, or the rights and duties connected with such a relationship. The most interesting and theologically significant is the last—the Heb. root *gaal*, for which *v.* REDEEM.

C. E. B. C.

KNOW, KNOWLEDGE

OT: The Heb. *yada'* means know (whether person or thing), perceive, learn, understand, have skill; and also, with a wider sweep of meaning than our 'know', experience good or bad (including the sexual sense: Gen. 4.1, etc.). Knowledge for the Hebrews was not knowledge of abstract principles, or of a reality conceived of as beyond phenomena. Reality was what happens, and knowledge meant apprehension of that. Knowledge of God meant, not thought about an eternal Being or Principle transcending man and the world, but recognition of, and obedience to, one who acted purposefully in the world (Deut. 11.2ff., Isa. 41.20). This sometimes meant emphasis on the fact that God is one, and the later Hellenistic Judaism had to develop this in its Gentile propaganda (cf. Wisd. 12.27), adding a more intellectual element to the OT conception. For continuance of this emphasis in NT, cf. John 17.3, Rom. 1.18ff., I Cor. 8.4–6, Gal. 4.8f.

To know God is the chief duty of man: Deut. 4.39, 29.2–6, Isa. 43.10, Hos. 6.6, Ps. 46.10. In the case of God, knowledge means his providence and prosecution of his good purposes; and particularly his choice of a man or nation to play a part in those purposes: Amos 3.2, Jer. 1.5. For this thought carried on in the NT, cf. I Cor. 8.2f., Gal. 4.9. For the Rabbis of later Judaism, knowledge was primarily knowledge of the Law; cf. Rom. 2.20.

NT: In the NT generally the words used for 'know' and 'knowledge' have the various nuances of meaning which are familiar in Eng., and also contain the significance of the OT *yada'* which was mediated by the Septuagint; e.g. for 'know' in the sense 'have experience of', cf. the phrase 'know sin', Rom. 7.7, II Cor. 5.21. The phrase 'know the truth' is almost a synonym for 'become a Christian' or 'be converted'; it signifies not intellectual enrichment, but enlightenment which is a stimulus to a new way of life, viz. love: Phil. 1.9, Col. 1.9f., 3.10ff. This conserves the Hebraic use of know, which has in view conduct rather than theory; cf. Jer. 22.16: 'He judged the cause of the poor and needy. . . . Was not this to know me? saith the Lord.'

For the noun (*gnosis*) in an absolute sense, meaning religious knowledge, cf. I Cor. 8.7, 13.8. Some scholars regard this as due to Gnostic influence, together with Matt. 13.11 and Col. 2.2f., where we have also the word 'mystery', and Matt. 11.27, the most Johannine of the sayings recorded in the Synoptic Gospels. The use of words which had a vogue in non-Christian religious circles need not be denied, but it must be insisted that in the passages above cited such non-Christian terminology is used in the service of distinctively Christian ideas, not for the importation of alien ones. In the light of Phil. 3.8–15, it should be clear that the NT is trying to express the unique character of the believer's relation to Christ. This involves an element of knowledge. St. Paul's usage as a rule makes faith include this, but sometimes he allows himself the more intellectualist word. Johannine usage, which is worthy of more detailed examination than can be given here, distinguishes 'know' and 'believe' roughly as fruit and seed, and then connects 'know' with 'love' in a distinctive fashion. (Also *v.* SEE, PERCEIVE, UNDERSTAND.)

E. C. BLACKMAN

*   *   *

LABOUR *v.* WORK

LAMB *v.* PASSOVER, SACRIFICE V

LAST [LAST THINGS] *v.* TIME

LATTER [DAYS, etc.] *v.* TIME

LAUGH, MOCK, DERIDE, SCORN

In the Bible laughter does not denote amusement, and all the associations of l. serve only to emphasize the difference between the mentality of the ancient world and that of the modern, or between the East and the West. Most of the biblical associations of l. are unpleasant. Though the Preacher admits that there is 'a time for l.' (Eccles. 3.4), he disapproves of it (Eccles. 2.2, 7.3). L. occasionally denotes joy at good fortune (Ps. 126.2), but much more frequently denotes surprised incredulity (Gen. 17.17, 18.12, 21.6, Mark 5.40) or—most frequently of all—derision. Often in Pss. and elsewhere we read of the scornful laughter and derision of the wicked or of the enemies of Israel. When in Luke 6.25 Jesus says 'Woe to you that laugh now', he is denouncing the attitude of derisive unbelief; he does not denounce those who are merely cheerful. And when he says, 'Blessed are ye that weep now, for ye shall laugh' (Luke 6.21), he doubtless means 'laugh for joy' (as in Ps. 126.2). The Bible is not afraid of anthropomorphism, and God is sometimes depicted as 'laughing' at the wicked or the proud—not in amusement, but in righteous scorn (e.g. Ps. 2.4: 'He that sitteth in the heavens shall laugh; the Lord shall have them in derision'). The word 'mock', besides meaning 'deride', sometimes means 'deceive' (e.g. Judg. 16.10). To the men of the Bible unbelief, pride, blasphemy and irreligion are objects of ridicule because they are so patently things which only a fool could countenance.

A. R.

LAW

The word 'law' in the English Bible represents both the Heb. *torah* and the Gk. *nomos*, which were not originally equivalent (cf. C. H. Dodd: *The Bible and the Greeks*, Ch. II). *Torah* denotes the guidance or *instruction* which comes from God through the oracular utterances of the priests or through the prophets; it is the whole content of God's revelation of his nature and purpose, which incidentally makes clear man's responsibility before God. In so far as this responsibility is clarified by a collection of maxims into a legislative code, the term may be applied to such a code, and in this restricted sense it coincides with one meaning of *nomos*, a single enactment or the legal corpus of a given community, commonly esteemed among Gentiles as 'the invention and gift of the gods, the judgment of wise men, the correction of transgressions, and the common covenant of a state, in accordance with which all members of the state ought to live' (*Contra Aristogitonem*, 774, quoted by Dodd, *op. cit.*, p. 26). The LXX translators understood most of the OT references to *torah* in this sense, and supplied the translation *nomos*, which passed into NT thought and into our English Bibles as 'law', creating thereby a misleading impression of the way God had dealt with Israel to make them his people. It obscures the wider and more personal communication which is partly suggested by 'teaching', and implies that Israel is bound to God in a relation which is adequately expressed by strict obedience to a code of law. (The Lat. equivalent, *lex*, through which we have 'law' in the English Bible, reinforces this impression, and brings out a further implication in *nomos* —a clearly marked system of religion, or of social organization.)

In Matt., Luke, Acts, and Heb., the term 'law' is used in the LXX sense. In Paul and in John it has, for the most part, this meaning, but both writers show some understanding of the wider and more personal communication which is indicated by *torah*, and are ready to conceive it within the context of the Word of God, with which term *torah* is often used in parallelism in the OT. Paul and James sometimes use *nomos* in a characteristically Greek sense, which overlaps with OT categories only because of the context in which they write. The reference is to an underlying or immanent principle of life or action (cf. Rom. 8.2, Jas. 1.25). The primary NT reference, however, is to the legislation or legal system of a community, in particular of Israel according to the OT. It is in this sense that we shall evaluate its significance.

In what sense is this law peculiar to the people of the OT, and what part has it to play in the Christian understanding of life? NT teaching about this problem is shaped to a considerable extent by the controversy whether any man could be a good Christian unless he were first a good Jew. Paul's elaboration of the thesis that 'we are not under the law but under grace' (Rom. 6.15), which should be studied in Galatians and Romans, must be understood in the light of this controversy. The indiscriminate admission of Gentiles into the Church of the Messiah could hardly be resisted in face of the evidence that God had opened to them also the door of faith. The decision recorded in Acts 15.15–21 lays upon Gentile believers no other burden than certain simple precepts which must of necessity be observed if there were to be any fellowship at all between Jewish and Gentile Christians. The fundamental reality of the new dispensation is that men enjoy the favour of God irrespective of their past activities, without discharging any formal 'debt' or performing any specified 'work'. The favour of God was now being extended to those who previously were 'separate from Christ, alienated from the commonwealth of Israel, strangers from the covenants of promise, having no hope, and without God in the world' (Eph. 2.12). Here, as elsewhere, it is made clear that the Gentiles were being brought into a field of divine action which hitherto the Jews had alone occupied, and which they had *genuinely* occupied. 'Salvation is from the Jews. But the hour cometh and now is, when the true worshippers shall worship the Father in spirit and in truth' (John 4.23–4). But the possibility of this *rapprochement* rested in the fact that Christ had 'broken down the middle wall of partition, having abolished in his flesh the enmity, the law of commandments in ordinances' (Eph. 2.15). There can be no question then of setting up this law (or religion) as the essential pre-requisite of life by Christian faith. It proved necessary indeed to repudiate it, as a Law of commandments in ordinances, for thus conceived it was calculated to keep men out of the new dispensation. The 'grace' and 'truth' which the *torah* was to establish, according to many OT promises, did not come through the legislation attributed to Moses. They came by Jesus Christ who had been condemned as a result of that very legislation (John 1.17, 19.7).

Nevertheless, this new state of affairs, no less than the old, is being brought about through the operation of the efficacious 'Word of God', to which a unique witness had been given in the experience of Israel, in the documents of their history under the covenant, and therefore in the Law which those documents enshrined. To acknowledge this witness, and to affirm its unique character, were deemed indispensable to Christian faith for Gentile as well as Jew; a fact to which we owe the presence of the OT in our Bible. The grace of God in Jesus Christ cannot be understood apart from this background. This being so, there grew up a characteristically Christian estimate of the Law, which was worked out in the first instance by Christian Jews, Paul, James and John being our chief authorities for it. The command (*q.v.*) of God is as real in the dispensation marked by grace through Jesus Christ as it ever was, and the question is about the significance of law as such, in its incidence on Jews and Gentiles, as a mediator under Christ of that command. The term *nomos* meant something among the Gentiles quite apart from the particular *nomos* ascribed to Moses, and this fact influenced the new estimate of law, though biblical discussion is focused on the question of OT law as it now concerns both Gentiles and Jews.

What is the biblical interpretation of the presence among Gentiles of a valid awareness of God's command? There is a more ancient covenant of God with men than the covenant with Abraham which inaugurated the history of the Chosen People. That special covenant is taken to be a regulative fact of history by the biblical writers, and the priestly writer of Gen. 9 sees its pattern already traced in the new start to human history after the Flood. He makes explicit what is implicit in the earlier account of God's Word to Noah (Gen. 8.20–2), that a covenant was made with Noah and his descendants (i.e. all mankind) where the divine act of deliverance is proclaimed and the obligations of the covenant declared. All mankind, every living creature, the earth itself, are parties to it. This explains the regularities of nature (Gen. 8.22, Matt. 5.44–5) and the ordered life of the animal creation, which serve to rebuke men for their lawlessness and infidelity to the God with whom *they* are in covenant in a special way (Jer. 8.7, Isa. 1.3). Paul refers to the virtuous pagan who exhibits the effect of law written in his heart to which his conscience bears witness through his reasonings (Rom. 2.15), and estimates this as sufficiently impressive to shame the bad Jew. Addressing the Gentiles themselves on this matter in the previous chapter (Rom. 1.19–21), he reminds them of their ability to know God, which, had they not frustrated it by wrong moral choices, could have led to a much healthier state of things in pagan society than is actually the case. They are therefore responsible for its degradation although they have not had the privileges of the special revelation to Israel. The Noachian covenant is almost certainly his own warrant for these references to Gentile capacity to do by nature the things of the Law. It would also seem highly probable that the minimum requirements demanded of Gentiles in Acts 15.29 represent the primeval Law belonging to a primeval covenant and obligatory on all men.

That this awareness of the command of God on the part of the Gentiles is due to the revelation of the Word of God, is asserted in the prologue of the Fourth Gospel. This Word, equated with wisdom, and wisdom in turn with the *torah*, has brought into being all things, and a 'light that lighteneth every man' derives from it. John refuses to identify the Word with the Law of Moses, for which he reserves the term *nomos*. But he insists that in Christ, man is confronted with the Word, Wisdom, or Law which is the law of his being, and that the Law of Moses served to confront Israel with this same Law (John 5.30–47, 7.15–24). The difference between the two dispensations is discussed with the same effect in II Cor. 3, in Rom. *passim*, and in Gal. 3.15–29. The Law of Moses plays an indispensable role in the work which God has accomplished in Christ, and it is clearly implied that Gentile Christians must take account of this fact. The significance of their own, Gentile, experience of *nomos* can be evaluated only by reference to it.

'But now apart from the law a righteousness of God hath been manifested, being witnessed by the law and the prophets; even the righteousness of God through faith in Jesus Christ unto all them that believe' (Rom. 3.21–2).

How does the Law 'witness' to this new reality, and why, in its precise form as the Law of Moses, does this witness fail of its purpose? The Law was, in the first instance, an *offer* of life after a prescribed and blessed pattern. To men who cannot or will not accept what is offered in this Word of God, it becomes a stern command. The tragedy of the situation lies in the fact that men can only attempt to come to terms with this command by adopting it as the form which will give justification to their self-sufficient lives. That is to say, the relation with God which their obedience produces will be a distortion of that for which they were created (even a denial of it), and this alienation becomes graver the more successful they are in obeying the letter of the Law. To sinners, the Law presents itself as one more means of self-justification, and sin becomes more and more manifest, working death through that which is good (Rom. 7.13). But it is precisely for this reason that the law is seen to be holy, and the commandment holy, righteous, and good (7.12). God's operation through the Law is an indispensable concomitant of the supreme operation through which the offer of life to his people reaches them effectively, despite their sin. In more than a mere historical sense, the experience of Israel under the Law creates in unique fashion the situation where men must believe or disbelieve the Word which confronts them. When Jesus confronts men, in this crisis of faith or unbelief, they are identified with 'the Jews' of the Fourth Gospel, and their response will be that of men determined by life under the Law, whether or not they have been practising Jews. The purpose for which the Law was given to Israel becomes clear at that point, and we can speak of the Law as fulfilled (Matt. 5.17).

The Law is given within the one Word of God which is from the beginning good news of grace. It is given as a norm for the transformation of creaturely existence, innocent or sinful, into that righteousness which will fulfil the covenant God has established with mankind. The role which law fulfils in relation to the Gospel has traditionally been described in a scheme of three uses. (i) It serves to preserve the order of creation where there is no saving faith. (ii) By reason of fallen man's impotence to fulfil it, it drives him to realize the need for grace, and summons him to Christ the only Saviour. (iii) For believers it has a further use as a standard of obedience to God, by the guidance of which the fruits of the spirit may be brought forth. (It should be noted that the three main western traditions, Catholic, Lutheran, and Reformed, express their understanding of scripture on this point with somewhat diverse accents and emphases.) Since men do not cease to be sinners in this life, the Church has to be on constant guard against 'legalism', for concern with the law may always serve only to increase the pride and self-sufficiency of sinful men. Nevertheless, the purpose of the Gospel is not achieved apart from these political, paedogogic, and didactic, uses of the law. It *is* achieved where the law is written into the lives of God's people in whose hearts the love of God hath been shed abroad through the Holy Spirit which is given unto them (Jer. 31.31–4, Rom. 5.5, II Cor. 3.3).

As to what this law is with which Christians should be concerned (though it no longer has dominion over them), no distinction is drawn within the NT between ceremonial and moral elements, nor is it implied that the latter alone are still relevant. But the attention of Christians is directed to the OT Law in ways which are reflected in the characteristic attitude which the Church has adopted, notably the emphasis on the Decalogue and the Two Great Commandments of love of God and love of neighbour. This subject receives fuller treatment in the article on LAW-CODES. (Also *v.* COMMAND, COMMANDMENT, STATUTE, MOSES.)

W. A. WHITEHOUSE

BIBLIOGRAPHY

E. I. J. Rosenthal (Ed.): *Judaism and Christianity*, Vol. III, 'Law and Religion', London (1938). A. R. Vidler and W. A. Whitehouse: *Natural Law*, London (1946). R. H. Charles: *The Decalogue*, Edinburgh (1923). C. H. Dodd: *Natural Law in the Bible*, London (1947). A. R. Vidler: *Christ's Strange Work*, London (1944). A. J. Drewett: *The Ten Commandments in the Twentieth Century*, London (1941). *V.* also comms. on *Romans* by C. H. Dodd (Moffatt) and Sanday and Headlam (*I.C.C.*).

LAW-CODES

The material considered under this heading falls into the following groups:

The Decalogue, in two recensions, Exod. 20.1–17, Deut. 5.6–21 (*v.* COMMANDMENT).

The terms of Yahweh's covenant with Israel according to a primitive (and probably Southern) version, Exod. 34.10–26.

The Book of the Covenant (probably a Northern version), Exod. 20.22–23.19.

The Code of Deuteronomy, whose affinity with the legislation of the Northern kingdom and with the teaching of the northern prophets seems to be established, Deut. 12–26.

The Law of Holiness, and the related legislation in Ezekiel, Lev. 17–26, Ezek. 40–8.

The Priestly Legislation scattered throughout the Pentateuch. This should be considered, not so much in isolation, but rather in its function of amplifying and integrating the other codes which it incorporates into the unified Pentateuch.

The Precepts of Jesus included in the Gospels. Where these are grouped for catechetical purposes (as in Matt. 5–7), the significance of the grouping must not be ignored.

The Ethical Codes in the Epistles. (For recent research on this question, *v.* E. G. Selwyn, *The First Epistle of St. Peter* (London, 1946), Essay II, esp. pp. 419–39.) The instruction given in the Wisdom Literature, e.g. Proverbs, seems to be one of the sources underlying these codes, and should perhaps be included in a complete picture.

The Two Great Commandments in which the demands of 'the Law' are focused for Christians, Mark 12.28–31.

These codes should be understood first of all in their original reference. The OT codes indicate the pattern of Israel's religious and social life at different points of the national history. Their avowed purpose is to secure that the national life should show, in all its details, the characteristics of the people of Yahweh. In trying to understand how they served this purpose, it should be remembered that these codes regulated the life of an actual community, and, like all good law, their prescriptions did not go beyond the obedience which it was reasonable to expect. Further, they have concrete reference to the community of the Old Covenant living at a particular time and place. What they have to teach the Church about the life required of the people of God can only be discovered when they are studied with those two facts in mind. Such study will yield instruction when the significance of each code for securing these characteristics is appreciated in its own right, and attention is then given to the points at which it supersedes, or is superseded by, other codes. It does not follow that all the revisions represent a true discernment of the mind of the Lord (cf. the rejection of Deuteronomy as the effective Code at some stage of the history, and the high regard which Jesus seems to have had for it). Nevertheless, the process of community life which actually occurred did 'fill up the time' in a way which made possible the advent of the Messiah at a given moment, and a study of the Codes (illuminated by knowledge of the community life gained in other ways) helps to show what that involved. The purpose of the Codes was to shape the life of the people of God in preparation for the end of the age, and readjustment of the current Code was necessary from time to time as the events of the age took shape. They serve as a means of grace throughout the age which lasts from the creation to the consummation. That age has not yet ended, but the event (viz. the first coming of the Messiah) by which God closes it has already happened in a veiled form in the centre of history. What does this mean for a present estimate of the Code, both in regard to its function, and in regard to its content? In regard to its function, *v.* article LAW. In regard to its content we turn to the NT and its Codes.

The Precepts of Jesus, in the form of the Sermon on the Mount especially, are taken to be a proclamation of the Code in the final form which it must reach if it is to fulfil its purpose of regulating the life of the people of God in preparation for the advent of the Messiah in glory. For those who know that the Messiah has come, they are binding here and now. It is true that they are a human record of this proclamation, and serve only as a fallible witness to it. Their effective proclamation as the Word of God depends on the operation of the Holy Spirit in the believer's heart. These are the terms upon which men will be judged at the end of the age. And these are the terms upon which it is possible to enjoy here and now the life of the age to come. But, as will be seen by considering the revised estimate of the function of law, the intention of the covenant is not being secured by any 'righteousness of works', and so the hope of Christians is not bound up with a securing of adequate obedience to this or any other Code, except that obedience which has been secured for us in the person of Jesus Christ. The believer seeks to share that obedience—without expecting his sharing to be counted for righteousness in a meritorious sense—by allowing the life and words of Jesus to control his own behaviour.

The Ethical Codes in the Epistles indicate the way by which this end is promoted through the characteristic behaviour of men in the Church. They are peculiarly appropriate to 1st-cent. Christian communities in the Middle East, but they have that normative significance for Church life everywhere which is attributed to the whole testimony of the prophets and apostles.

Meanwhile, however, the life of the age goes on, and Christians are involved in it as much as anyone else. The question of what Code is appropriate at this given point in the age, in order that all mankind may be prepared for the end, is one which the Church has inherited from the old Israel. The NT hardly illuminates a situation in which Christians can press effectively for reformation of the society in which they live, but it contains three significant pointers to the direction in which such pressure should tend. In the first place, it is implied that the pattern of life in which OT legislation culminates has served its purpose and is not to be imposed on Gentiles who, it is hoped, will belong to Christ. Secondly, it is implied that the Decalogue safeguards in unique and adequate fashion the character of legislation in any community so as to make that community one in which the covenant can be achieved (*v.* COMMANDMENT). Thirdly, it is implied that the two commandments to love God and to love one's neighbour illuminate the direction in which all legislative reforms should take place, and that 'the law' for which Christians should contend in any given situation can be discerned by considering the experience of Israel from this perspective, keeping the while a firm hold on the realities of the situation for which legislation is necessary, as did those who originally framed the OT Codes. (Also *v.* COMMAND, COMMANDMENT, STATUTE, MOSES.)

W. A. WHITEHOUSE

LAYING ON OF HANDS

OT: Here the laying on of hands (or hand) implied (i) BLESSING, e.g. Gen. 48.14ff., Lev. 9.22 (here the hands are only 'lifted up toward' the recipients of the Aaronic blessing); (ii) Identification with a sacrifice, e.g. Exod. 29.10; (iii) transfer of gifts, and appointment to succeed in office, e.g. Num. 27.18,23, Deut. 34.9 (hands, pl. in second account).

NT: In NT Jesus uses the custom in blessing the children (Mark 10.13–16, and pars.) and in healing the sick (Mark 5.23). In Luke 24.50 he uses the same action as Aaron in blessing ('lifting up his hands he blessed them'). There are six important passages bearing on the usage in the Apostolic Age. (*1*) Acts 8.17,19. Here the Apostles lay hands on the newly-baptized Samaritan converts and the gift of the Spirit is received. As the leaders of the community, and perhaps as the original recipients of the gift (Acts 2.4; cf. John 20.22), the Apostles pass on the gift, as Moses had done in the case of Joshua. Here the laying on of hands follows baptism (*q.v.*) at an interval of time, and is done by persons of special status. (*2*) Acts 19.5,6. Here St. Paul baptizes *and* lays hands on the same people on the same occasion. The gift of the Spirit is given, but it is not stated that this is connected with one part of the initiation ceremony rather than another. (*3*) Heb. 6.2. 'Teaching of baptisms and of laying on of hands.' Though this might mean the laying on of hands in restoration (unlikely, in view of the rigorism of Heb.) or in ordination, it most probably means the laying on of hands which accompanied or followed baptism. (*4*) Acts 13.3. (*5*) I Tim. 5.14. (*6*) II Tim. 1.6. In all these cases, the ceremony carries with it appointment to office (though a similar passage in I Tim. 5.22 may refer to the restoration of penitents). There was precedent in OT and in contemporary Judaism for the laying on of hands in appointment or ordination. (The word *cheirotoneo* used in Acts 14.23 for 'appointing elders' means simply 'appoint', not 'laying hands on'.)

The imposition of hands was an integral part of baptism in the patristic period, and was only separated from it in the West from the 5th cent. onwards owing to the increase in the size of dioceses, and the fact that this part of the initiation ceremony was kept for the Bishop alone to perform. In the East, imposition of hands (in the form of anointing) has remained an integral part of baptism, but the episcopal contribution in this case is confined to the consecration of the oil which is used. As early as Tertullian, however, we find the idea that the gift of the Spirit is particularly associated with the laying on of hands, to which the washing in baptism is preparatory. (On this, see A. J. Mason, *The Relation of Confirmation to Baptism*; Gregory Dix, *The Theology of Confirmation in relation to Baptism*, Westminster (1946). Also *v.* BAPTISM, BLESS.)

R. R. WILLIAMS

LEARN

Heb. *lamadh* and Gk. *manthano* have nothing particularly distinctive about them. The use of *manthano* with Christ as direct object is noteworthy in Eph. 4.20; cf. Matt. 11.29.

E. C. B.

LEAVEN *v.* BREAD, PASSOVER

LEPER *v.* HEAL

LEVITE *v.* SACRIFICE III(*a*)

LIBERTY *v.* FREE

LIE

We may say generally that as truth (*q.v.*) is that which is the normal, permanent characteristic of the good man, so lying and cognate words mean by contrast what is abnormal, empty, lacking stability and permanence, disturbing of trust and harmony.

'Lie' renders in most cases the Heb. *kazab* and *sheqer*, which both signify deceit, falseness, as does the Gk. *pseudos*. Even a prophet may be guilty here, and prophesy lies instead of a true word of God: Jeremiah in particular denounces this, e.g. Jer. 14.14 (cf. 5.31, 'prophesy *falsely*'). The word 'lie' tends to mean 'idol', esp. when associated with vanity (*q.v.*); cf. Isa. 44.20, Jer. 10.14, Rom. 1.25. For lie as the opposite of truth in the more purely Gk. (and modern) sense, cf. I John 2.21. (Also *v.* DECEIT, VAIN.)

E. C. B.

LIFE, LIVE, LIVING

These words have first of all the ordinary meaning of existence, of physical life as opposed to non-existence or death. Thus 'Adam lived an hundred and thirty years' (Gen. 5.3; cf. Deut. 12.1). In the verbal forms they signify to give life (Job 33.4), to preserve it (Ezek. 13.18) or to restore it (II Kings 8.1, Isa. 38.10). In the earlier writings of the OT there is no distinction between the physical basis of life and the distinctive spiritual and moral attributes of human nature. The constitution of man is thought of as a body (cf. H. W. Robinson, *The Christian Doctrine of Man*) animated by a breath-soul (Gen. 2.7), and the whole body, flesh and blood, bones and organs, has a spiritual and moral significance. Thus one of the words most frequently used in the OT for life has the root-meaning of 'breath' as the very principle of life (II Kings 1.13, Ezek. 37.3–6). The cessation of breathing is the most noticeable feature of the end of life. In most passages in the Psalms translated 'soul' in AV and RV, the meaning is not soul as distinct from and perhaps superior to body, but life in contrast to death. The word is used to describe the full self-consciousness of human personality as in Gen. 23.7 where it is equivalent to 'will' or 'purpose' or in Job. 16.4 where it could be rendered 'understanding' or 'mind'. Another Hebrew word used for LIVE has the connotation of prosperity and good wishes. 'Let the king live for ever' (Dan. 11.4, Neh. 2.3).

There are, however, in the OT passages which indicate an awareness of the fact that man has open to him the possibility of a life which is higher than that physical life which he shares with the animal creation, a life which is nourished not by bread as is the body, but by the self-communication of God to his people signified by the utterance of his Word (*q.v.*). This is stated explicitly in Deut. 8.3, a text which the evangelists represent our Lord as using to resist the assault of temptation through the pangs of physical hunger (Matt. 4.1–4, Luke 4.1–4). The maintenance of this higher life is not achieved (as in some Gk. and Indian thought) at the expense of bodily existence, but is the development of that existence into the fullness of personal life. It is dependent upon men receiving the self-communication of God so that his very life is somehow active in them. 'In him is thy life and the strength of thy days' (Deut. 30.20, Ps. 30.5). In the OT this is commonly expressed in terms of the obedience which men must render to the revealed will of God (Deut. 30.20, Ezek. 20.11).

There is an important usage which though not prominent in the Scriptures is yet so characteristic of Hebrew ways of thought that it must receive some mention. The phrase 'the living God' puts into words the experience of God which lies at the heart of the faith of Israel. The people were proud to be called 'the sons of the living God' (Hos. 1.10), and no more solemn or characteristic oath could be sworn by an Israelite than 'as the Lord liveth' or 'by the life of Jehovah'. Such oaths occur frequently. The phrase 'the living God' marks first, the contrast between the true God whose reality is known by his acts and the dumb idols which do not see or hear or speak (I Sam. 17.36, I Kings 18.26–9, I Thess. 1.9). Secondly, God is called 'the living God' not only as the creator, but as the restorer of life in those that are his. 'My soul thirsteth for the living God: when shall I come and appear before God?' (Ps. 42.2, 63.1, 64.2). Thirdly, the phrase describes the providence of God, his ceaseless watchfulness, guarding and correcting, his care for the individual life even to the numbering of the very hairs of a man's head, and without whom not a sparrow falls to the ground (II Sam. 14.11, Ps. 18.46, Matt. 10.29–30). Thus the phrase also speaks of his redemptive activity in choosing (*v.* CHOOSE) and fashioning a people to be his instruments in dealing with other nations and thereby revealing himself in their history (Josh. 3.10) and through their life. 'Who is there of all flesh that hath heard the voice of the living God speaking out of the midst of the fire as we have, and lived?' (Deut. 5.26). In the four Gospels the phrase occurs only twice, in the Jewish Gospel of Matt., and both times n crucial Messianic passages (16.16, 26.63), where the attention of the reader is concentrated on the thought that the purposes of God depend on Jesus and his faithfulness. He is the faithful remnant through whom the living God will recreate Israel. The writer to the Hebrews uses the phrase 'the living God' four times (3.12, 9.14, 10.31, 12.22) and links the thought of the decisive self-communication of God, which man must receive to find his true life, with the Word of God uttered fully in the person of Jesus Christ (1.1–3). Thus in the presence of Jesus, men are in the presence of the living God (John 1.3–4) and are faced with the alternative of life with him or death apart from him (Matt. 18.8–9; cf. I John 5.12, Deut. 30.15–19).

In the Gospels two words are used for life which have the root meaning of activity and breath-soul respectively, but nowhere are body and soul set over against each other as though in conflict. Soul stands for the inmost life, the real ego. 'What shall a man give in exchange for his soul?' (Mark 8.37). 'What shall I do to inherit eternal life?' (Luke 10.25). In the fourth Gospel the word for life which emphasizes the activity of living is more frequently used. 'The words that I speak unto you . . . they are life' (John 6.63); and Jesus is represented as claiming to be the bread of life, the living water and the light of the world. He is indispensable to all true human life, even as bread and water are essential. The disciples acknowledge this in the words of their spokesman (John 6.68): 'Thou hast the words of eternal life', which means not descriptions of life hereafter but words which are living and effective to create and sustain eternal life. So the Christian and the Church are to have life in his name (John 20.31) by entering into a real and living relationship with him. Unbelief is a state of death even in life (John 5.24). The purpose of his coming and mission is summed up in the saying, 'I came that they might have life and might have it abundantly'. The powers of destruction are faced and overcome by the 'single unparalleled fact' (Westcott) of the life and death of Jesus; and through this life and death Christians have life, according to the will of God, measureless and unlimited.

F. J. TAYLOR

LIGHT, DARKNESS

In the Bible the words *light* and DARKNESS are used, oftener than not, in what are for us figurative senses. When we read, for instance, that 'God is light, and in him is no darkness at all', we understand this as a figure of speech, though a natural and helpful figure; the meaning is that God is altogether good, without any tincture of evil. And in this context (I John

1.5ff.) that is certainly what the writer is chiefly concerned to assert. But it is probable that for him the words were also true in their literal sense; in his very essence God is light—light in the simple physical sense of the word. So of the heavenly city, the new Jerusalem, we are told that 'there shall be night no more; and they need no light of lamp, neither light of sun; for the Lord God shall give them light' (Rev. 22.5). It is, in fact, not possible to distinguish clearly between the literal and the figurative senses of *light* and *darkness*, and other related words such as *day* and *night*. When St. Paul writes, 'It is God, that said, Light shall shine out of darkness, who shined in our hearts, to give the light of the knowledge of the glory of God in the face of Jesus Christ' (II Cor. 4.6), he makes the distinction clear by speaking of 'the light of the *knowledge* of the glory of God', but in such a passage as Luke 2.9, 'the glory of the Lord shone round about them', it is clear that 'the glory of the Lord' is conceived as light or radiance perceptible by human eyes. Similarly, 'the outer darkness' (better, 'the darkness outside') of Matt. 8.12, 22.13, 25.30 and 'the blackness of darkness' of II Pet. 2.17, Jude 13 (RV) are to be understood literally and symbolically at once.

In the OT *light* and *darkness*, when used figuratively, usually mean prosperity and happiness, and adversity and sorrow, e.g. Esther 8.16, 'The Jews had light and gladness, and joy and honour'; Amos 5.20, 'Shall not the day of the Lord be darkness and not light? even very dark, and no brightness in it?'; Isa. 45.6,7, 'I am Jehovah, and there is none other, The Maker of light, the Creator of darkness, The Maker of weal, the Creator of woe: It is I, Jehovah, that do all this' (translated by J. E. McFadyen). Instances in which *darkness* means wickedness are few (cf. Prov. 2.13, 'who forsake the paths of uprightness, to walk in the ways of darkness'), and a certain instance of *light* in the sense of moral goodness is hardly to be found. In the NT there are the usual figurative senses of the two words, and it is unnecessary to quote instances, but cf. esp. II Cor. 6.14, 'what fellowship have righteousness and iniquity? or what communion hath light with darkness? And what concord hath Christ with Belial?' It is remarkable how seldom, either in the OT or the NT, *darkness* means simply ignorance, and *light* knowledge and understanding. In Dan. 5.11,14 the 'light and understanding and wisdom' found in Daniel is knowledge of mysteries, of which most men are naturally ignorant. Probably the purely intellectual sense is primary when St. Paul speaks of those 'in whom the God of this world hath blinded the minds of the unbelieving, that the light of the gospel of the glory of Christ, who is the image of God, should not dawn *upon them*' (II Cor. 4.4); here the use of the word 'minds', which might more exactly be translated 'thoughts', is noteworthy. Yet even here the idea of *moral* insensitiveness is not far away; cf. also Rom. 1.18ff. The very difficult saying of Jesus which speaks of the possibility that the light which is in one may be darkness (Matt. 6.23, Luke 11.35) probably refers to moral and religious, rather than to purely intellectual 'darkness' or blindness.

In the religious thought of the first century of our era God, and everything associated with God, was often conceived in terms of light, and the power or powers of evil, and everything associated with evil, in terms of darkness. To this way of thinking many influences, from ancient sun-worship onwards, contributed; notable among these were the religion of Zoroaster and the philosophy of Plato. Some indications of it are to be found in Paul, e.g. Col. 1.11ff., 'the Father, who made us meet to be partakers of the inheritance of the saints in light; who delivered us out of the power of darkness'; Eph. 6.12, 'the world-rulers of this darkness, . . . the spiritual *hosts* of wickedness in the heavenly *places*'; the thought is that, apart from Christ, the world is under the control of spiritual powers of evil. But it comes to clearest and fullest expression in the Gospel and the First Epistle of John. It was suggested above that when the writer of the Epistle said, 'God is light', this was true for him in its most literal sense. But it was also true in a much deeper sense, which is not exhausted by saying that the meaning is that God is altogether good. Thought of this kind defies exact analysis, and cannot be fully expressed in any other terms. Nor are the expressions used always logically consistent. Thus it is to be noted that though in the Epistle God himself is said to be light, in the Gospel the life which was in the Word is said to be the light of men (John 1.4). Later in the Gospel, Christ declares that he himself is the light of the world (8.12, 9.5; notice that 'the light of this world' in 11.9 means simply the light of the physical world). But, taken by itself, 12.35f., 'Yet a little while is the light among you. . . . While ye have the light, believe on the light', would suggest that Christ is the light of the world only during his incarnate life—which is certainly not the evangelist's belief or intention.

J. Y. CAMPBELL

LIKENESS *v.* IMAGE, SIMILITUDE

LISTEN *v.* HEAR

LIVE, LIVING *v.* LIFE

LONG-SUFFERING

This word, like the word 'loving-kindness', has come into the EVV through Coverdale's use of it. He used it in Exod. 34.6 and Ps. 86.15, and he got the word from Tindale. The word is also found, so far as the OT is concerned, in Num. 14.18 and Jer. 15.15, where Coverdale has 'of long sufferaunce' in the one case and 'longe wrath' in the other. This latter rendering is an almost exact reproduction of the Heb., which is 'length of anger'. The meaning, as Tindale puts it in Num. 14.18, is 'the Lorde is longe yer he be angrye'. It describes that attitude of God whereby strict justice would long ago have swept Israel away in penalty for her sin and rebellion if it had not been that God is 'slow to anger and of great mercy'. This struggle between strict justice and mercy is admirably portrayed in Hos. 11.8f.

The word occurs 13 times in the NT. When it is used of God, it is used in the same sense as in the OT—that is, of God's continued mercy whereby Israel does not receive the full retribution which she undoubtedly deserves. An important passage indicating the purpose of God's long-suffering is II Pet. 3.9: 'The Lord . . . is longsuffering to youward, not wishing that any should perish, but that all should come to repentance' (cf. also Rom. 2.4).

When the word is used of man, it is used partly in the same sense of forbearance, not allowing anger to have place in order that men may continue in the fellowship rather than be cut out from it. In this respect, since this is an element of God's attitude to man, it is also an element in the Christian's attitude to his fellows, and is one of the fruits of the spirit (Gal. 5.22). But the word is also used in the sense of endurance, the 'patience' (Gk. *hupomone*) of Heb. 12.1. The word 'patience' is indeed actually used as the equivalent of long-suffering in Heb. 6.12 and Jas. 5.10. See also I Macc. 8.4, where the word is used of the steady endurance of the Romans in Spain, and is translated by 'persistence'. Examples of this use of the word are to be found in Col. 1.11, Heb. 6.15, Jas. 5.10. (Also *v.* FORBEAR, PATIENCE.)

N. H. SNAITH

LOOK

Notice I Sam. 16.7 for God's looking, i.e. judging, and cf. Isa. 66.2. More generally, for God's looking in the sense of surveying the earth, implying omniscience, cf. Ps. 33.13, 104.32. In the main the word is used of human sight. Under this heading notice particularly the use of 'look for', i.e. expect, with ref. to redemption (Isa. 5.7, 59.11, etc.). In the NT this is of course understood as the coming of Jesus (Matt. 11.3, Luke 2.38; also as the final redemption, Phil. 3.20, Tit. 2.13, Heb. 11.10). (Also *v.* SEE and EYE.)

E. C. B.

LORD

In the EVV 'lord' usually represents the Heb. word *adon*, the primary meaning of which is 'ruler', 'commander'; cf. Gen. 45.8. Often it means the 'master' of a slave (*'ebed*; EVV, servant), and is used especially by a slave in speaking of his own master; cf. Gen. 24, *passim*. Oftener still it is used as a term of courtesy in speaking to someone to whom one wished to show respect; cf. Gen. 44.18. The same word was used in speaking of, or to, God, but nearly always (some 130 times in the OT) in a special form, *adonai*. When the proper name of the God of Israel, written *JHVH*, became 'the ineffable name', which might not be uttered, *adonai* was spoken instead when the scriptures were read in public worship. (The form 'Jehovah' results from a combination of the consonants *JHVH* with the vowels of *adonai*, a device used in late MSS. of the OT; this was misunderstood by Christian readers.) (*V.* GOD, NAMES OF.) I thne Gk· version of the OT the word *kurios* (=lord, master) was substituted for the proper name; the EVV use LORD, printed in small capital letters. So for Greek-speaking Jews *Kurios* (usually the definite article, which would be expected in Gk. as in Eng., is omitted in this use of the word) became the ordinary designation of the God of Israel.

Like *adon*, the Gk. word *kurios* properly means 'ruler', 'one having authority'. Sometimes, though rarely, it has the sense of 'owner'; cf. Mark 12.9, 13.35. Still more rarely it is used in such expressions as 'lord of the harvest', Matt. 9.38; 'lord of the Sabbath', Mark 2.28. Very often it means the master of a slave; *doulos*, slave (EVV, servant) is the usual correlative; cf. Luke 12.46; but is seldom expressed. In NT times *kurios* was a common term of courtesy, especially in addressing a social superior, very much as 'sir' is in Eng.; cf. Matt. 21.30, 27.63, John 12.21 (EVV, sir).

Two special, closely related, uses of the word are to be noted. Kings are everywhere naturally styled 'lords', especially in addressing them; cf. I Sam. 24.8 (David to Saul). But in the ancient East, kings were supposed to be divine beings, even gods incarnate. So the title 'lord', when given to them, acquired a religious significance. In the 1st cent. BC the Gk. kings of Egypt were styled, in inscriptions, 'Lord King God'. The early Roman emperors refused such titles in Rome and the West, but had to accept them in the East. In Egypt, at the beginning of the Christian era, sacrifices were offered for 'the god and lord emperor', Augustus. In Acts 25.26 Festus refers to the emperor as 'the lord', but it need not be supposed that for him, a Roman, the title had any religious significance. From the 1st cent. BC onwards the title 'lord' was given, especially by their own worshippers, to gods of Eastern origin whose worship spread widely throughout the Roman empire, e.g. to the Egyptian god *Serapis*, and (in the fem. form) to the Egyptian goddess *Isis*. Thus in NT times there were literally 'gods many, and lords many' (I Cor. 8.5), and for pagans the two words had very much the same meaning.

But for Christians there was only 'one God, the Father', and only 'one Lord, Jesus Christ' (I Cor. 8.6). 'Jesus is Lord' was probably the earliest baptismal creed of the Church; cf. Rom. 10.9, Phil. 2.11. But though Christians acknowledged only one 'lord', they regarded the OT in Gk. as their Bible, and so they continued to call God the Father 'Lord' also, even when they were not quoting directly from the OT. Paul, however, boldly applies to Christ OT passages in which 'the Lord' meant God; cf., e.g. Rom. 10.13; and, except in OT quotations, it is doubtful whether in his letters 'the Lord' ever means anything but 'the Lord Jesus Christ'.

It is not difficult to understand how Gentile Christians came to give to Jesus Christ the title 'Lord'; it is very difficult to understand how Jewish Christians, trained in the strict monotheism of Judaism, ever came to do so. Paul, it is true, always maintains the subordination of the Lord Jesus Christ to God the Father; cf. Phil. 2.11, I Cor. 15.27f. Yet everything that a man may expect from God, Paul expects equally from Jesus Christ. Probably many factors, which cannot now be clearly distinguished, contributed to the development of the fully Christian use of the title. There seems no good reason to doubt that even during his lifetime his own disciples called Jesus 'Master and Lord', John 13.13, though it must be admitted that no instance is recorded in the earliest Gospel, Mark. In Aramaic they may have called him *Maran* (cf. I Cor. 16.22 and the translation of the phrase in Rev. 22.20). When this was translated into Gk. as (our) *Kurios*, Gentile Christians, for whom Christ was a saviour rather than a teacher and leader, naturally understood it in much the same sense as it had when it was used of pagan 'saviour-gods'. Then under the influence of developing Christian experience the title came to have the fullness of meaning which attaches to it as Paul uses it. But it must be added that this is at best only a plausible theory, which has not found acceptance with all NT scholars. (*V.* also GOD, III.)

J. Y. CAMPBELL

LOVE, LOVER, LOVELY, BELOVED, and (in AV of *NT*) CHARITY

OT: The Heb. root *aheb*, which occurs well over 200 times and is almost always represented by 'love' or deriv., denotes primarily passionate love between man and woman, but is also used of family affection, friendship, and sometimes with neuter object. In addition to its secular uses, it has a rich theological significance. Other roots sometimes represented by 'love' and deriv. are: *chashaq* (similar range to *aheb*, but much less frequent); *chabab* (in OT only Deut. 33.3); *'agab* (of doting); *dud* (esp. frequent in Song Sol.); *yadad* (e.g. Deut. 33.12, Ps. 60.5). The root *racham* is only once or twice represented by 'love', but is important for the understanding of OT idea of God's love: it denotes pity for someone in need of help, and is represented by 'tender mercies', etc. (*v.* MERCY). Other roots connected in meaning, though never represented by 'love', are *chaphets* (delight, etc.) and *ratsah* (accept, be pleased, etc.), which are probably technical terms of the language of sacrifice and of princely court; and, more important theologically, *chanan*, signifying the condescension of the rich to the poor (*v.* GRACE); and finally the word *chesed*, expressing loyalty and the conduct agreeable with it (*v.* MERCY). Apart from *chaphets* and *ratsah*, which indicate outward expression of approval rather than inward feeling, these roots are concerned with feeling and are strongly personal.

The theological use of *aheb*, etc., is threefold: of God's love to men, men's love to God, and love between men, seen as a religious duty.

(*a*) *God's Love to Men.* Already in the earliest strata of the Pentateuch, God's covenant with Israel is mentioned (Exod. 34.10,27f.—J, 24.1-11—JE). Amos too is clearly conscious of God's special choice of Israel (3.2, 7.15—'*my* people') and connects it with the Exodus (3.1, 2.10) as do the earliest sources of Pentateuch. We may with confidence trace back this sense of a special relation to Yahweh to the great formative event of Heb. history, the Exodus, and to Moses, the inspired interpreter of that event. But there is no occurrence of *aheb* in connexion with this Yahweh-Israel relationship in the OT that can be dated with certainty before Hosea. The avoidance of *aheb* in this connexion may be due to fear of blurring the distinction between God and man by ascribing such a very creaturely feeling to God (*v.* FELLOWSHIP, on *chabar*); or it may be because *aheb* played such a prominent part in the contemporary fertility cult—and that in the most crudely natural sense; or perhaps it was simply that the earlier OT writers were content with the fact of the covenant without asking about its motive. At any rate, as far as we can see, Hosea was the first in the true line of development of OT religion, who used *aheb* in this sense.

He introduced at the same time the marriage metaphor. It appears all through Hosea; in almost every chapter some expression suggests it. After Hosea it was widely used (e.g. Jer. 2.2,32f., 3.1,14, 31.32, Ezek. 16, 23, Isa. 50.1ff., 54.5, 62.4; and in NT, Mark 2.19f., Matt. 22.2, Eph. 5.22–33, Rev. 19.7,9, 21.2,9,22.17). The part played by Hosea's domestic life in determining the form in which he expressed his message is problematic. We cannot even rule out the possibility that the details of Ch. 1 and 3 are purely allegorical. It is noteworthy that Gomer is not referred to again after 3, and significant that in 3.1 Hosea does not argue from his own love to God's, but the other way round. Full weight needs to be given to the fact that he was not introducing an altogether novel idea: the notion of a divine marriage conceived in various ways was only too familiar (expressed in immoral worship, sacred prostitutes, etc.) both in the surrounding paganism and in Heb. syncretism, which tried to worship Yahweh by the methods of the fertility cult. In his attack on this syncretism Hosea was led (we cannot be sure how) to adopt as an effective metaphor the very relationship, which, understood in a crudely naturalistic sense as an actual reality, was central in what he was attacking. Perhaps it was because this was the most effective way of making his contemporaries aware of the tremendous contrast between the truth and their illusions.

We have not space to follow the idea of God's love through the OT, but must be content with noticing the main features: (*1*) Its *personal quality*. *Aheb* and the figure of marriage point behind and beneath the covenant to its motive and origin in the innermost personal being of Yahweh. His love is part of the mystery of his personality. In Hos. 11.9 the OT comes very near to saying that God *is* love. With the intensely personal quality of God's love is connected the daring use of anthropomorphic expressions, e.g. Hos. 11.8, Jer. 31.20, Isa. 63.15 (and 9, if Heb. text correct). (*2*) Its *selectiveness*. The root *bachar* (choose) occurs in connexion with God's love, Deut. 4.37, 7.6f., 10.15, Isa. 43.4 with 10, 20. It is a distinguishing, selecting love. Cf. Amos 3.2, Exod. 19.5, Deut. 14.2, 26.17f., Ps. 135.4, Mal. 3.17. (*3*) Its *voluntariness*. The emphasis on choice not only indicates that God distinguishes between peoples; it also is in sharp contrast with the naturalistic ideas of contemporary paganism, according to which a god was bound to a particular people by a natural and necessary solidarity. The heathen gods did not choose their peoples; for them the relationship was natural and inescapable. (*4*) Its *spontaneity*. It is not caused by any worth or attractiveness in its object, but rather creates worth in its object. The cause of God's love for Israel lies not in any qualities or potentialities of Israel but in the personal being of God himself. God's love has no cause prior to itself (Deut. 7.7f.). It is a mystery and a paradox (Deut. 9.4ff., Ezek. 16), which, when expressed in terms of the figure of marriage, must be indicated by a marriage that is to all appearance senseless and grotesque (Hos. 1.2, 3.1). But, while all the OT agrees that God's love for Israel was spontaneous in origin, there is observable a tendency to understand its continuance as conditional on Israel's behaviour (e.g. Deut. 5.10, Exod. 20.6, Deut. 7.9–13), and the possibility of regarding it as a reward for human merit arises. (*5*) Though God's love is undeserved, yet there is a sense in which Israel can claim it; for God has bound himself by his covenant. So Israel can claim it by virtue of God's faithfulness to his oath (e.g. Deut. 7.6ff.). This is why *chesed*, which means 'loyalty', is so prominent. Cf. Lev. 26.42, Exod. 2.24, 6.5, Ezek. 16.60, Ps. 105.8,42, 106.45, etc. (*6*) God's love *seeks moral fellowship* with Israel. It cannot be separated from his righteousness. It is not sentimental. Cf. the tremendous emphasis on knowing God in Hosea (*v*. esp. 2.20, 4.6, 6.6, 13.4; the root *yada'*='know' occurs 20 times in Hosea, *bin* ='understand' 4 times). The special position of God's 'peculiar people' goes together with the keeping of his commandments (Deut. 26.18). (*7*) Its *exclusiveness*. It demands Israel's undivided allegiance; cf. Exod. 20.3–5, Deut. 6.5, and (*b*) below. (*8*) Over against Israel's sin, God's love is expressed *in judgment and forgiveness*. God's punishment of sin is no contradiction of his love; it was precisely because he loved that he took Israel's sin so seriously (cf. the 'therefore' in Amos 3.2). His love was love in deadly earnest and could be severe. It was willing to hurt in order to save, to shatter all false securities and strip Israel of his gifts, if so be that in the end, in nakedness and brokenness, they might learn to know their true peace. But the severity was never separated from tenderness (cf. Hos. 11.8, Isa. 63.9, etc.). That God should go on loving this brazen-faced, stiff-necked people was sheer miracle and paradox. Justice and reason demanded her destruction, but God refuses to destroy (Hos. 11.9), and the ground for his refusal is in the mystery of his divine being—'for I am God, and not man; the Holy One in the midst of thee' (cf. Isa. 55.7f.). But neither God's tenderness nor his severity makes Israel repent; the fact is that Israel cannot repent. She is too far gone to respond to God's love. God must himself create repentance in her, if she is ever to repent; he must work a miracle in men's hearts (Jer. 31.33). The healing of Israel's sin will be like raising dry bones to life (Ezek. 37.1–14), it will be wholly God's work. In the OT the problem of sin is laid bare in its horror and hopelessness on the one hand, and on the other we have the promise that God will himself deal with it in his own time and way. We are left with the assurance that God's love is the very heart of his divine life, and that this love with which he has loved his people is everlasting (Hos. 2.19, Jer. 31.3, 35ff., Isa. 54.8). (*9*) The OT speaks mostly of God's love for Israel; not much is said directly of his loving individuals, though it is implied that the individual shares as a member of the people in God's love for Israel. Some of the Psalms unmistakably imply it, though we must make allowance for a collective meaning of the 1st pers. sing. in many Psalms. In Deut. '*thy* God' is like a refrain. It is difficult to decide how far it is collective and how far individual. 'The stranger' in Deut. 10.18 is collective, but again the individual's share as a member of the class is implied. In the sphere of God's relations with individuals the tendency to regard his favour as dependent on the person's goodness asserts itself strongly, and the common assumption was that prosperity is always the reward of goodness and adversity the punishment of evil-doing (cf. John 9.2). The Book of Job was a protest against the fundamental misunderstanding of the nature of God's love, which this doctrine implied (cf. *Expository Times*, Aug. 1943, 295ff.). (*10*) We do not find it explicitly stated that God's love reached beyond Israel to other nations, but it is hinted and implied (e.g. Amos 9.7, Ruth, *passim*—she is a Moabitess), and in some books the hints become specially clear (e.g. Isa. 19. 19–25, 42.1–6, 49.6, and Jonah, *passim*).

(*b*) *Men's Love to God.* This is not something independent, not the mystical quest of the religious *eros*, the upward striving of the human spirit towards the divine, such as is prominent in Plato, Plotinus, etc., but rather something dependent on God's prior love, the response of man to God's love, his gratitude. The initiative remains God's (cf. Deut. 4.5–40, Ps. 116.1ff., Exod. 20.1—appeal to gratitude). His love to God is the typical mark of the devout man of the OT (e.g. Isa. 41.8, where 'friend' rep. root *aheb*), and it is commanded in the Shema, the verses still regarded by Jews as the very essence of the OT (Deut. 6.5). This love is to be expressed in ethical terms, in obedience to God. Love to God is associated with keeping his commandments (Exod. 20.6, Deut. 5.10, 7.9, 10.12f., 11.1, I Kings 3.3, Dan. 9.4, Neh. 1.5), with serving him (Deut. 10.12, 11.13, Isa. 56.6), with walking in his ways (Deut. 10.12, 11.22, 19.9, 30.16, Josh. 22.5), and with fearing him (Deut. 10.12). Besides love to God, the OT also speaks of loving his name, the habitation of his house, his salvation, the place where his honour dwelleth, his commandments, law, precepts, testimonies. Deut. 30.6 seems to emphasize that this love is a miracle wrought in a man by God (cf. K. Barth, *Kirchliche Dogmatik*, 1/2, p. 410).

(*c*) *Love between Men, seen as duty before God.* This too is dependent on the prior love of God to men, part of man's response, his gratitude. It is theological, *pace* G. Quell, *TWNT*, I, pp. 22ff., who misleadingly deals with it under 'the profane and immanent idea of love'. It is commanded by God (Lev. 19.18). The 'neighbour' (sometimes 'brother') means first the fellow-Israelite, with special emphasis on those who need help, the weak, poor, the orphan, the widow; then it refers to the resident alien, the foreigner living within Israel's territory without civic rights and therefore specially helpless (Deut. 10.19, Lev. 19.34). Even the enemy, when he is in need of one's help, is included (Exod. 23.4f.; cf. Deut. 22.1–4; also Prov. 25.21); he is to be helped, though it is not directly stated that he is to be loved. The OT commandment to love the neighbour is thoroughly unsentimental and practical. It starts at home, but works outward, and it is to be shown by deeds, though it is a matter of the heart (Lev. 19.17 with 18). Though Deut. 23.6 (the passage referred to in RV margin to Matt. 5.43*b*) forbids the Israelite to seek the peace of an Ammonite or Moabite, the neighbour did come to have an universal significance for men like the authors of Jonah and the Servant Songs (e.g. Isa. 49.6), who saw in the Gentile peoples neighbours to whom Israel had a God-appointed mission.

NT: Class. Gk. has several words for love: (*1*) *erao, eros*: sexual love, but also spiritualized (e.g. in Plato, esp. *Symposium*, *Phaedrus*; Aristotle, *Metaphysics*, 1072.a.27f.) of the upward striving and quest of the human soul toward the supra-sensual and divine. Both in its primary and metaphorical sense it always denotes a love that is called forth by the inherent worth of its object, and desires to possess and enjoy its object. It is essentially egocentric, seeking its object for the sake of its own satisfaction and self-fulfilment and self-enhancement. (*2*) *phileo, philia*: social love, affection of friends. (*3*) *stergo, storge*: very rarely of sexual love, characteristically of family affection. (*4*) *philadelphia*: love between brothers, sisters. (*5*) *philanthropia*: humanity, kindness, courtesy. (*6*) *agapazo, agapao*:

etymology unknown, has neither the warmth of *phileo* nor the intensity of *erao*. A colourless word, often meaning merely 'be content with', 'like'. Its sense is not at all sharply defined, so that it can serve as a synonym for both *phileo* and *erao*, when a synonym is required for the sake of euphony; but it does evidently refer to the will rather than to the emotion, and often conveys the idea of *showing* love by action. The substantive *agape* is almost entirely absent from pre-Biblical Gk.

LXX almost always translates *aheb* by *agapao*, *ahabah* by *agape*. This root was presumably chosen, because it was free from erotic associations and conveyed the idea of a love that showed itself by helping its object rather than by desiring to possess and enjoy it, and also because its very indistinctness of range fitted it to receive the OT associations of *aheb*. LXX avoids *erao* and *phileo*. Even in Hosea, where the marriage metaphor is prominent, *agapao*, not *erao*, is used. It is still more striking that this is so in Song Sol.

In NT *erao*, *eros* do not occur. *Agapao*, *agape* are the main words, with *phileo* used occasionally as a synonym (with the suggestion of a certain warmth of endearment). *Philia* is only used once. (*3*) is rare (Rom. 1.31, II Tim. 3.3, Rom. 12.10). (*4*) is used with a new meaning—of Christian brotherhood. (*5*) occurs Acts 28.2, Tit. 3.4.

(*a*) *God's Love to Men.* All that the NT—and for that matter the OT too—has to say about the love of God to men is expressed in the two words, 'Jesus Christ'. What we know truly of God's love we know through his self-revelation, not by the intensification or idealizing of the love in our own hearts. Its character is to be seen in the Incarnation of the Eternal Son of God. Reference to the classical texts, John 3.16, Rom. 5.8, will suffice here, though many others could be added. Jesus reveals God's love by what he says, does and is. According to the Synoptic Gospels he does not use *agapao*, *agape*, *phileo* or *philia* of God's love to men (though Matt. 5.45 is in a context where *agapao* is used), but only in senses (*b*), (*c*) and (*d*) below. Instead, he speaks of God's mercy, pity, etc., or depicts God's love in action (as in Luke 15). But by his deeds he reveals the divine love again and again, in works of compassion and by being the friend (*philos*) of sinners (Luke 7.34). Only after Pentecost did the full significance of his person become clear to the disciples; then they had to confess that 'God was in Christ reconciling the world to himself' (II Cor. 5.19), and to recognize 'the love of God . . . in Christ Jesus our Lord' (Rom. 8.39). For Paul, the love of God and the love of Christ are one.

We shall get an idea of the NT picture of God's love if we go over the 10 points noted under OT(*a*) to see how these features appear in the NT. (*1*) See below under (*b*): God's love is grounded in the mystery of his triune being. (*2*) For its selectiveness cf. Mark 7.24ff., and in Matt. par., esp. 15.24, Matt. 10.5f., Rom. 9.13 and 8.28; the parallelism of *elect* and *beloved* in Col. 3.12 (cf. Rom. 1.7); and the connexion between God's love and election in Rom. 9.11ff., 11.28, Eph. 1.4f., I Thess. 1.4, II Thess. 2.13; and refs. to Israel and the new Israel (e.g. Gal. 6.16), the people of God (I Pet. 2.9), and Christ's love *for the Church* (Eph. 5.25). God's love is for the world (John 3.16, etc.), but works through a chosen people. For (*3*) cf. the NT distinction between Israel after the flesh and Israel after the spirit; God is not dependent on Israel (cf. also Matt. 3.9). For (*4*) (the spontaneity of God's love) cf. Matt. 5.45 and the parable of the labourers in the vineyard (Matt. 20.1–16), the purpose of which is to expose the wrongness of thinking of God's relations with men in terms of book-keeping. See also Rom. 5.6–8, I John 4.10,19, etc. (*5*) The NT carries over the idea of covenant—the new covenant (Mark 14, I Cor. 11.25). Cf. the refs. to God's promises (II Cor. 1.20, Heb. 10.23, I John 2.25). For (*6*) there is no need of refs., the ethical seriousness of NT being everywhere apparent. (*7*) The exclusiveness of God's love is indicated by Jesus' demand for full, undivided, absolute allegiance to himself (Matt. 10.37f.=Luke 14.26f., Matt. 12.30=Luke 11.23), to his Father (Matt. 6.24, Mark 12.29f., etc.). (*8*) The whole emphasis of NT is on forgiveness of sins, reconciliation, redemption, with the cross and resurrection of Jesus central. One or two classical passages will suffice for reference here (Mark 10.45, Matt. 26.28, I Cor. 15.3, Rom. 3.23ff., Heb. 9.28, I Pet. 2.24, 3.18). (*9*) Gal. 2.20, Luke 15.7,10, Matt. 18.10,14 are enough to show the NT position with regard to the individual. Cf. Jesus' attitude to individuals generally. But it would be quite false to the facts to stress a contrast here between OT and NT, as though there were a development from an OT collectivism to an NT individualism; the truth is rather that in the NT both the individual and the corporate find clearer expression. For a useful discussion of this whole question, see C. H. Dodd, *The Bible To-day*, pp. 146–63. (*10*) For the reaching out of the divine love beyond Israel see Mark 7.24ff., Matt. 8.5ff., Eph. 2.5,11ff.; and 'world' in Johannine writings, e.g., 3.16, I John 4.14, 2.2; also II Cor. 5.19, Gal. 3.28, and Acts 10 and the Gentile mission.

(*b*) *God's Love apart from, and independently of, Men.* We have already noted that the ground of God's love for us is altogether in himself. He loves us, because he *is* love. In loving us, he has also revealed himself to us as being in himself, and apart from us, love. The statement in I John 4.8,16 is true quite independently of our being there to be loved. God is eternally love prior to, and independently of, his love for us. In the process of revealing his love to us he has given us a glimpse into his inmost personal being. So in the NT we hear of love within the triune life of God from all eternity. Most frequently of the Father's love for the Son: Mark 1.11=Matt. 3.17=Luke 3.22, Mark 9.7=Matt. 17.5=Luke 9.35 (cf. II Pet. 1.17), Matt. 12.18, John 3.35, 5.20 (*phileo*), 15.9f., 17.23f.,26, Col. 1.13. Cf. Mark 12.6=Luke 20.13. Of the Son's love for the Father: John 14.31. Of mutual intimacy of Father and Son: Matt. 11.27. For the mutual intimacy of the Holy Spirit with the Father and Son: John 16.13–15, I Cor. 2.10–13. Barth sums this up admirably: God is Love, before he loves us and without his loving us. He is Love as he is everything that he is, as the triune God in himself. Even without us and the world and its reconciliation he would suffer in himself no lack of love (*Kirchliche Dogmatik*, 1/2, p. 417).

(*c*) *Love to God* in NT sense is not natural to men; for we are 'by nature inclined to hate God' (with this phrase of the Heidelberg Catechism cf. 'enemies' in Rom. 5.10, Col. 1.21; 'hate' in John 3.20, 7.7, 15.18–25, and also Mark 12.7, Luke 19.14; and the supreme manifestation of this hatred in the crucifixion of Christ). It is a miracle only conceivable in the context of the twofold divine initiative of Christmas and Whitsun, man's response to the prior love of God in Christ (I John 4.10,19, John 15.9; and implied throughout NT), a response itself the creation of the Holy Spirit (Gal. 5.22 of love both to God and neighbour; Rom. 5.5 if 'of God' is here an obj. gen.). It is a love that has no kinship with the spiritual *eros*, natural to man and egocentric, which seeks in God its own satisfaction and self-enhancement, familiar in mysticism.

The classical passage for love to God is Mark 12.29f. (and par.), where Jesus takes up Deut. 6.4f. The love here commanded is the response of a man in the totality of his being to the prior love of God. The whole man is the object of the divine love and the whole man is thereby claimed by God for himself. The command forces man to a radical decision (e.g. Matt. 6.24).

It is clear that 'love to God' and 'faith' largely overlap. Both denote the response to the divine love. It is noticeable that, though often speaking of the divine love and of love between Christians, Paul rarely speaks of the Christian's love to God. Nygren argues from this that Paul avoided using 'love' in this sense on principle, because he was fixing *agape* as a technical term for the spontaneous, uncaused love (God's love to men and its 'extension' in our love to neighbours), and so did not want to use the same term of our love to God, which is essentially *caused*, not spontaneous. Nygren's view is that Paul used *pistis* (faith) to denote what in the Synoptics is love to God. However, Paul does use the verb *agapao* in this sense, as Nygren admits, in Rom. 8.28, I Cor. 2.9, 8.3, Eph. 6.24; and we may add *phileo* in I Cor. 16.22; and in the case of the noun *agape* it is not certain that this sense is excluded in Rom. 5.5, II Thess. 3.5, I Cor. 13.8,13. Though undoubtedly right in his general thesis, Nygren is perhaps rather doctrinaire in pressing this distinction between Paul and the Synoptics. In this connexion it is interesting that Barth (*Kirchliche Dogmatik*, 1/2, pp. 435f.) can see a similarity between God's love to us and ours to him, that makes the use of the same term for both appropriate.

For love to God see also John 5.42, Jas. 1.12, 2.5; for love to Christ, John 14.15,21, 21.15ff., I Pet. 1.8. For the connexion between love and obedience, John 14.15, etc., I John 5.3. And for the priority and absolute pre-eminence of the divine love over the human response, see further the play on active and passive in Rom. 8.28, Gal. 4.9, I Cor. 8.3, 13.12, Phil. 3.12.

(*d*) *Love between Men.* Jesus, following Jewish tradition, sets after the 'great' commandment a second commandment—to love one's neighbour as oneself (Mark 12.31=Matt. 22.39; cf. Rom. 13.8ff., Gal. 5.14, Jas. 2.8). The two commandments cannot be separated—love to man is dependent on love to God, and love to God is proved by love to man (I John 4.20f.); but the two remain two, and are not identical. In NT 'love' in this sense (both noun and verb) is very frequent, much more frequent than in senses (*a*), (*b*) or (*c*).

This love too is wholly dependent on, and conditioned by, God's prior love. In exhortation to love the brethren the ground of appeal is that God has loved us (I John 4.11; cf. Rom. 12.1). This dependence is indicated variously. So Christian love is *imitation* of the divine love (Matt. 5.43ff., Luke 6.35f., John 13.34, 15.12, Rom. 15.7, Eph. 4.32–5.2, 5.25ff.). It is also *the work of the Spirit* (Gal. 5.22; cf. II Tim. 1.7, Rom. 5.5). In Rom. 5.5 another thought seems to be suggested—that the love with which we are to love one another is actually the divine love itself poured into us and overflowing into the lives of others, an 'extension' of God's love for us, so that Luther speaks of 'faith and love, by which a man is placed between God and his neighbour as a medium, which receives from above and gives out again below, and is like a vessel or tube through which the stream of the divine blessings must flow without intermission to other people' (*WA*, X,1.1, p. 100, quoted Nygren, *Agape and Eros*, II,2, p. 517). Nygren says (*ibid.*, I, p. 96): 'The love which he [the Christian] shows to his neighbour is God's *agape* in him' (cf. Matt. 10.8 and the way 'love of God' is used in I John 3.17f.). A rather different way of indicating the dependence is implied in Rom. 14.15 and I Cor. 8.11: love means the refusal to see, think of, or deal with, one's neighbour except in the light of what Christ has done for him, as the brother for whom Christ died. Still another way is seen in Matt. 25.31ff., according to which the neighbour is to be understood 'christologically', as Christ's representative or envoy, who comes in Christ's name to receive from us the love and service we owe to Christ; in our neighbour we meet Christ. From the foregoing it should be clear that this *agape* is not a diluted form of ordinary liking or passionate love, as is sometimes sentimentally imagined, but is something altogether unique.

We may notice further the eschatological association in Rom. 13.8ff. (the 'this' in 11 referring back to the duty enjoined in 8–10), I Pet. 4.7f. To see the other man already lit up by the reflection of the light of God's new day is to be enabled to love him. Moreover, love belongs to the new day; when other things pass away, love will endure (I Cor. 13.8–10). Those who are children of the day, of the new age, must live accordingly in love.

Love is the badge by which Christ's disciples may be recognized (John 13.35), the sign that they are God's children (I John 4.7), that they have passed from death to life (3.14). Love is the mark of the Church. Failure of this love is a denial of the very nature of the Church. Cf. the tremendous stress on unity (John 17.21ff., Eph. 4.1ff., Rom. 12.16, 15.5, II Cor. 13.11, Phil. 2.2, 4.2, I Pet. 3.8) and on the scandal of division (e.g. I Cor. 1.10ff., 3.3ff., 11.18ff.). This love is to be expressed quite practically (I John 3.17f.).

It is noticeable that the object of *agapao* in this sense (*d*) is usually 'the brethren', or some other expression pointing to fellow-members of the Church. In fact, it is not easy to find passages where *agapao*, *agape* in this sense can definitely be shown to have a wider ref. than the Church. But in the Synoptic Gospels there are the very clear passages, Luke 6.27f.,32–5, Matt. 5.43–8; and the fact that the Christian's love is to be modelled on, and flows from, God's love necessarily implies the wider range (cf. Rom. 5.6ff., John 3.16, etc.). That the Apostles thought in wider terms is clear—if not from their words—at least from their deeds; it is implied by the fact of their missionary labours. See also Gal. 6.10, I Thess. 3.12.

See further: G. Quell, E. Stauffer, in *TWNT*, I, pp. 20–55; G. G. Findlay in *HDB*, pp. 554–6; on OT, W. Eichrodt's *Theologie des Alten Testamentes*, I, chapter on 'Die Liebe Gottes'; on NT and subsequent history, A. Nygren, *Agape and Eros*, Part I, trans. by A. G. Hebert, Part II, trans. by P. S. Watson (in I, p. 165, there is a useful table of contrasts between *agape* and *eros*); J. Moffatt, *Love in the New Testament*; on men's love to God, incl. exegesis of Mark 12.29f., K. Barth, *Kirchliche Dogmatik*, 1/2, pp. 408–42; cf. also THANK, NT(*b*); for love to neighbour, incl. exegesis of Mark 12.31, K. Barth, *ibid.*, pp. 442–504; also R. Bultmann in *Scottish Periodical*, I, 1, pp. 42–56.

C. E. B. CRANFIELD

LOVING-KINDNESS

This is a biblical word, invented by Miles Coverdale, and carried over into the EVV generally. It is one of the words he used in the Pss. (23 times, plus Hos. 2.19) to translate the Heb. *chesed* when it refers to God's love for his people Israel. Otherwise he used 'mercy', 'goodness' and 'great kindness' in the Pss. for God's attitude to man; and, outside the Pss., such words as 'mercy', 'goodness', 'favour' for God's attitude to man, and 'kindness' for man's attitude to man. It is important to notice that Coverdale takes pains to avoid using the word 'kindness' of God's attitude to man, though he is not followed in this respect by AV and RV. There is one case in the Pss. (141.5) where the word *chesed* is used of man's attitude to man, and even here Coverdale avoids 'kindness' (so AV and RV), but has 'friendly'. The nearest NT equivalent to the Heb. *chesed* is *charis* (grace, *q.v.*), as Luther realized when he used the German *Gnade* for both words.

The word is used only in cases where there is some recognized tie between the parties concerned. It is not used indiscriminately of kindness in general, haphazard, kindly deeds; this is why Coverdale was careful to avoid using the word 'kindness' in respect of God's dealings with his people Israel. The theological importance of the word *chesed* is that it stands more than any other word for the attitude which both parties to a covenant ought to maintain towards each other. Sir George Adam Smith suggested the rendering 'leal-love'. The merit of this translation is that it combines the twin ideas of love and loyalty, both of which are essential. On the other hand, it does not sufficiently convey the idea of the steadfastness and persistence of God's sure love for his covenant-people. His other suggestion, 'troth', is better in this respect, but the etymological core of the word is 'eagerness, keenness', and, whilst there is considerable development from this, the word never belies its origins. In Isa. 40.6, for instance, the word *chesed* is used to describe man's steadfastness, or rather the lack of it. The EVV have 'goodliness', following some of the ancient versions, but the Targum (old Jewish Aramaic paraphrase) was right when it said 'their strength'. The prophet is contrasting man's frailty with God's steadfast reliability. He says that all man's steadfastness is like the wild flowers, here to-day and gone to-morrow, whilst the Word of the Lord is steady and sure, firm and reliable.

God's loving-kindness is that sure love which will not let Israel go. Not all Israel's persistent waywardness could ever destroy it. Though Israel be faithless, yet God remains faithful still. This steady, persistent refusal of God to wash his hands of wayward Israel is the essential meaning of the Heb. word which is translated loving-kindness. In Jer. 2.2 the word *chesed* is rendered 'kindness', the reference being to 'the kindness of thy youth', and this phrase is paralleled by 'the love of thine espousals'. The meaning is not that Israel was more tender in her attitude towards God or in her affections, but that in the first days after the rescue from Egypt she was faithful to the marriage-covenant with God. The charge of the prophets is that Israel's loyalty to her covenant with God (Hos. 6.4: EVV, 'goodness') is 'as the morning cloud, and as the dew that goeth early away', a regular feature of the Palestinian climate when once the spring rains are past.

The widening of the meaning of the Heb. *chesed*, used as the covenant word and especially of the covenant between God and Israel, is due to the history of God's dealings with his covenant-people. The continual waywardness of Israel has made it inevitable that, if God is never going to let Israel go, then his relation to his people must in the main be one of loving-kindness, mercy, and goodness, all of it entirely undeserved. For this reason the predominant use of the word comes to include mercy and forgiveness as a main constituent in God's determined faithfulness to his part of the bargain. It is obvious, time and again, from the context that if God is to maintain the covenant he must exercise mercy to an unexampled degree. For this reason the Gk. translators of the OT (3rd cent. BC onwards) used the Gk. *eleos* (mercy, pity) as their regular rendering, and Jerome (end of 4th cent. AD and beginning of 5th) followed with the Lat. *misericordia*.

The loving-kindness of God towards Israel is therefore wholly undeserved on Israel's part. If Israel received the proper treatment for her stubborn refusal to walk in God's way, there would be no prospect for her of anything but destruction, since God's demand for right action never wavers one whit. Strict, however, as the demands for righteousness are, the prophets were sure that God's yearnings for the people of his choice are stronger still. Here is the great dilemma of the prophets, and indeed the dilemma of us all to this day. Which comes first, mercy or justice? Rashi (11th-cent. AD Jewish commentator) said that God gave 'precedence to the rule of mercy' and joined it 'with the rule of justice'. But this much is clear: when we try to estimate the depth and the persistence of God's loving-kindness and mercy, we must first remember his passion for righteousness. His passion for righteousness is so strong that he could not be more insistent in his demand for it, but God's persistent love for his people is more insistent still. The story of God's people throughout the centuries is that her waywardness has been so persistent that, if even a remnant is to be preserved, God has had to show mercy more than anything else. It is important to realize that though the Heb. *chesed* can be translated by loving-kindness and mercy without doing violence to the context, yet we must always beware lest we think that God is content with less than righteousness. There is no reference to any sentimental kindness, and no suggestion of mercy apart from repentance, in any case where the Heb. original is *chesed.* His demand for righteousness is insistent, and it is always at the maximum intensity. The loving-kindness of God means that his mercy is greater even than that. The word stands for the wonder of his unfailing love for the people of his choice, and the solving of the problem of the relation between his righteousness and his loving-kindness passes beyond human comprehension.

BIBLIOGRAPHY

N. H. Snaith: *Distinctive Ideas of the Old Testament*, London (1944).

N. H. SNAITH

LOWLY *v.* PRIDE

LUST *v.* DESIRE

* * *

MAGNIFY

The Heb. and Gk. words so translated may mean either (*a*) to make great or (*b*) to make to appear great—to extol, to glorify. Commonly in an *evil sense* (Pss. 35.26, 55.12, etc.)

—to boast oneself, to make oneself (appear) great at another's expense.

In a *good sense*, (*1*) of men: see Josh. 3.7, Acts 5.13, where the senses of real and apparent greatness are combined; (*2*) of God and Christ: God is said to magnify himself by his acts (Ezek. 38.23); and to be magnified by the deeds and praises of men (Ps. 34.3, Luke 1.46, Acts 19.17, etc.).

In a sense, God's greatness is absolute and cannot be increased or diminished by human action or omission. But compare the parallel conception of God's glory which is at once something which he possesses absolutely as the manifestation of his own holiness (Isa. 6.3), and something which he possesses relatively to men, as his 'fame' among them, i.e. something which increases and diminishes relatively to man's recognition (Ps. 79, etc.). This is the paradox of God's grace, that though he needs nothing from men, he yet condescends to receive glory from them. So with his greatness: there is a real sense in which to magnify God is to make him great.

J. S. MCEWEN

MALEFACTOR *v.* SIN

MAN *v.* ADAM

MAN OF SIN *v.* ANTICHRIST

MANIFEST

A predominantly NT word, whose meaning needs no definition, but which becomes more distinctive when it renders the Gk. adj. *phaneros* and Gk. verb *phanerō*. It then indicates the eternal purpose of God which has been hidden, but is now made known as part of his saving work, set in motion by the ministry of Jesus, e.g. John 1.31, I John 1.2, 3.5,8, 4.9, Rom. 3.21, 16.26, Col. 1.26, Tit. 1.3, II Tim. 1.10, I Pet. 1.20. There are eschatological implications in Mark 4.22, I Cor. 3.13, Eph. 5.13. (Also *v.* REVEAL.)

E. C. B.

MARRIAGE, HUSBAND, WIFE, BRIDE, BRIDEGROOM, VIRGIN, CONCUBINE, BETROTHAL, DIVORCE, WIDOW

In Hebrew society the family (*q.v.*) is central, and its character and maintenance is determined by marriage. The creation stories show that the order of the world is crowned by the creation of man and woman, so that on their union are laid the blessings to which later generations owe their existence. The closeness of the marriage relation is somewhat differently expressed in the two accounts. The Priestly account (Gen. 1.1–2.4), describing the creation of various genera, regards man-woman as one genus in contrast to others. Hence man and woman together make 'man' ('*adam*); not until they are united do they form a whole human being. 'God created man in his own image, in the image of God created he him; male and female created he them' (1.27). The Yahwist account (Gen. 2.4–25), describing the world in which man lives and the distribution of power within it, naturally makes man prominent because he is the ruler. He provides bread and makes the soil yield its wealth. Woman is dependent upon him, but not like the animals. She is part of him, of his flesh (*q.v.*); and must be there for him to be man wholly. When a son leaves his father's house and unites himself to a woman he becomes man wholly. Thus in the Yahwist account, when God has created 'the man', he perceives that he lacks something and so woman, his help-meet, is created out of something taken from man (2.18,21–4). It is notable that the only direct teaching of Jesus on the fundamental nature of marriage draws on insights from both these accounts (Mark 10.6–9).

In the actual marriage practice of the OT, a man must normally choose as his wife a woman not so far removed from his own family as to introduce new and strange elements which he cannot assimilate. Thus when Abraham was living among Canaanite strangers he found it necessary to seek a bride for his son Isaac among his father's house in his native land (Gen. 24, and cf. the theme of Tobit). But Lev. 18 and 20 show that there are limits to the closeness of the related group from which the wife may be drawn. These are not primitive eugenic rules based on the observation that marriages between near relations produce unhealthy children, for the observation is itself uncertain, and in any case would not cover all the prohibitions. The rules arise naturally from the intimate character both of family relationship and of marriage, so that difficult psychic disturbances would take place if the two were to clash. Thus it is said: 'The nakedness of thy father, even the nakedness of thy mother, shalt thou not uncover. . . . The nakedness of thy father's wife shalt thou not uncover: it is thy father's nakedness' (Lev. 18.7–8). This means that between the father and his wives the feeling of shame has been abolished; they form a psychic unity, and the women have thereby entered into one particular intimate relationship with the father's sons which cannot be reconciled with the different intimate relationship of being the son's wife. The same principle applies to numerous relations, more or less close; e.g. it prevents marriage with the wife of brother or father's brother because, through her marriage, the woman bears the impress of her husband and her nearest male kin, and she cannot stand in two different intimate relations to the same man. But the penalties enjoined depend on the closeness of the relation: the man who marries his mother or daughter-in-law is to be put to death, whereas if he marries the wife of his brother or father's brother the marriage will simply prove childless. Marriage with the wife of the mother's brother is not excluded because the relationship through the mother is weaker than through the father. (It is surprising that marriage of a man with his daughter is not mentioned, and it must be presumed to have slipped out of the text.) Marriage with niece or cousin is permitted; indeed, the cousin is a man's natural bride, being of the same kin yet far enough away for marriage to be possible. It is forbidden to marry a woman and her daughter or a woman and her sister (while the woman is living) because marriage to one man would make them related in a way that would destroy the relation already existing through their mutual kindred. It is to be noted that the system of Lev. does not always represent the facts of Israelite life, neither as early as the patriarchs' days nor as late as the time of Ezek. (22.10f.). The story of Amnon and Tamar presupposes that they could marry if the father's permission had been obtained (II Sam. 13.13); and marriage with non-Israelites was certainly practised (e.g. Jud. 3.6 and cf. the reaction to this in Exod. 34.16, Deut. 7.3).

The law of Levirate marriage (Deut. 25.5–10; cf. Ruth 4; presupposed in Mark 12.18ff.) conflicts with the prohibited degrees, and was interpreted by later Judaism as a device by which a man could rid himself of his brother's childless wife whom he inherited with the property. But originally the law ministered to the overriding importance of maintaining the dead man's family by providing a son for him.

When a marriage was contracted it concerned two families (hence the choice was often made and the first steps taken by the parents). The bride's family gave of their own flesh and blood, and so the bridegroom's family must also give something (the 'bride-price', *mohar*)—not merely as a material compensation, but as a kind of mental balancing of the relations. Thus one family were not wholly givers nor the others wholly receivers, and so the bond was strengthened. The marriage ceremony was a legal formality rather than a religious rite (its main feature involved fetching the bride from her father's house); but betrothal was far more important. Unfaithfulness during the period of betrothal was adultery, punishable with stoning.

In the marriage relation, the husband had the dominating position (*v.* FAMILY). He was *ba'al*, the possessor and master of his wife, the domestic animals, and all his property, the centre from which strength emanated to the whole family. It was the man's duty to support his wife, though she might have her own property and generally received a gift from her family to form a link with her father's house and to give her a certain independence of her husband. She did not belong wholly to her own or her husband's family, and if the husband died she would return to her own family (Ruth is mentioned as an outstanding exception to this custom).

The wife is first and foremost a sexual being; her duty is to multiply her husband's family, so that death is the penalty for unfaithfulness (though the man was entitled to intercourse with another woman so long as he did not infringe another husband's rights). Since everything centred on the man, polygamy was the natural type of marriage for Israelites, for several wives do more than one to satisfy the demand for children. If a wife gave her husband insufficient children he might take secondary wives and concubines and be encouraged by his wife to do so (Gen. 16.1ff., 30.1ff.). A concubine was a slave captured in war or bought from traders, or even an Israelite sold for debt. Since a slave lacked the protection of her kindred and could not maintain her rights against her husband, the law attempted to regulate her status (Exod. 21.7–11 for an Israelite, Deut. 21.10–14 for a foreigner).

Israel worked out its view of marriage as the way of maintaining the People of God in contrast to the practices of the surrounding Canaanites. The earliest Christians worked out their view of marriage as the way of maintaining the Church of God until the coming again of her Lord in contrast to surrounding hellenistic practices. Examination of the ethical sections of the Epistles shows that a common catechetical system was in general use, presumably for candidates for baptism (for detailed treatment, see E. G. Selwyn, *First Epistle of St. Peter*, Essay II). It contained a section dealing not with the status of women, but with the concrete life of the home, in the form: 'Wives, be in subjection to your husbands, as is fitting in the Lord. Husbands, love your wives, and be not bitter against them' (Col. 3.18f., I Pet. 3.1ff.; expanded in Eph. 5.22–33, where Paul uses the familiar relation of husband and wife to illustrate the relation of Christ and the Church; cf. Tit. 2.4f.). The pattern, though hierarchical, is reciprocal (husband and wife are 'joint heirs of the grace of life') and the determining motive is Christian love. This complex relation is expounded in I Cor. 11.2–16, where 'the head of every man is Christ; and the head of the woman is the man', and also 'neither was the man created for the woman, but the woman for the man'—a reinterpretation of the creation story in the light of the fulfilment in Christ.

The problems of maintaining Christian marriage in the midst of pagan society appear in I Cor. 7, where Paul answers the questions of Christians who, reacting violently from contemporary lasciviousness, were proposing not to marry or (if married) to give up intercourse. Paul's fundamental position is this: in view of the imminent consummation of all things, it is better to be unmarried, because marriage makes people anxious about the wrong things (vss. 1,7,29–35). Yet the best plan is for Christians to remain exactly as they are: if they are unmarried, to stay so (vs. 8); if married, not to separate (this is Christ's command against divorce), and if the wife departs she must either remain unmarried or be reconciled to her husband (vss. 10–11; Paul carefully distinguishes his own commands from the Lord's). Even if one partner is an unbeliever, there is to be no divorce unless the unbelieving partner insists, when it is permitted (vss. 12–17). Yet it is certainly not sin to marry (vs. 28; Paul could have married as Peter and other Apostles did, I Cor. 9.5), and in fact it may be imperatively necessary because of the temptations to incontinence (vss. 8–9; cf. I Cor. 5.1). If marriage is undertaken, the partners must accept their proper mutual responsibilities to the full (vss. 2–6). Finally, Paul advises couples who are attempting a purely 'spiritual marriage' (vss. 36–40—the RV translation is misleading).

As expectation of the immediate Parousia weakened, the situation changed and the post-Pauline author of the Pastoral Epistles had to take strong action against heretics who were forbidding marriage (I Tim. 4.3). He had also to advise young widows to remarry, instead of applying for enrolment in the special class of church workers (I Tim. 5.3–16). In I Tim. 3.2,12, 5.9, Tit. 1.6 it is laid down as a qualification for office that a bishop, elder, or deacon must each be 'the husband of one wife', and a widow 'the wife of one husband'. This is commonly explained as referring to remarriage after the death of the first partner; but more probably it refers to Christians who had used the permission to separate from a non-believing partner, and had then married a Christian partner (pagan epitaphs give the meaning of 'husband of one wife' as 'undivorced').

It is clear both from Paul and the gospels that there is little direct teaching of Jesus on marriage, though it is true that what he said and what he did in his followers gave marriage a wholly new status. In returning to the original purpose of marriage, he repudiated divorce as a concession to human weakness (Mark 10.2–12 appears to be original as against Matt. 19.3–9—in fact, Matt. 19.10–12 presupposes the stricter rule—and Luke 16.18 as against Matt. 5.32. That a man may divorce his wife (though not a wife her husband) is taken for granted in Deut. 24.1f., especially if the wife is childless, though it is strongly condemned by Mal. 2.14,16). Jesus therefore reaffirmed the function of marriage in the divine plan of salvation and did the first of his signs at a marriage feast (John 2.1–11); but he denied that it has an absolute status both in this age and in the age to come (Luke 20.34ff.), and conceived that men, moved by the crisis of his proclamation of the Kingdom, might voluntarily renounce marriage (Matt. 19.10–12).

More prominent in the teaching of Jesus is the marriage metaphor (see C. Chavasse, *Bride of Christ*). From the time of Hosea onwards (Hos. 2.19f., Isa. 54.5, Ezek. 16) the nature of God and his attitude towards Israel had been expressed in terms of marriage. God's love was in the foreground, refusing even to divorce Israel for her adultery; and the mutual knowledge of God and Israel is mirrored in the intimate relation of man and wife. In the NT this metaphor is transferred to Christ and his Church: in Mark 2.18–20 Christ is the bridegroom (cf. John 3.29) and the Kingdom is pictured as a marriage feast (Matt. 22.2–12, 25.1–13, Luke 12.35ff.). In Revelation the Church is the Bride (19.7ff., 21.2,9, 22.17). Paul gave the metaphor normative expression in Eph. 5.23–33, where he stresses the indissoluble real unity of Christ and the Church with all its members, the love of Christ which cannot be set aside by human sin, and the mutual knowledge of Christ and his Church. The Church is presented to Christ as a pure virgin (II Cor. 11.2) whose pattern is the mother of Jesus, by reason of her purity of heart and her willingness to bear shame according to the command of God. To the evangelists the divinely wrought birth of Jesus was both a historical fact and a symbol of Israel of whom the prophets had spoken. This significant use of the marriage metaphor reflects back upon human marriage itself, giving it the status of something which can represent not unworthily God's relation to his people, and providing the basis of that hierarchical and reciprocal relation of which Paul speaks. (*V.* also FAMILY, VIRGIN BIRTH.)

KENNETH GRAYSTON

MARVEL *v.* ASTONISH

MARY *v.* VIRGIN (BIRTH)

MEAL-OFFERING *v.* SACRIFICE I(*g*)

MEDIATOR

The word appears only in Gal. 3.19f., I Tim. 2.5, Heb. 8.6, 9.15, 12.24 (verbal form in Heb. 6.17), but there is in Job 9.33 an equivalent translated as 'daysman'. 'Day' was sometimes used to signify a day appointed for hearing causes and giving judgment (cf. I Cor. 4.3–5 and the apocalyptic use of 'the day' (*q.v.*) or the 'day of the Lord'), and the word 'daysman' (cf. herdman, craftsman) was formed to describe the judge, arbiter or umpire who settled the dispute or brought the parties together (cf. Abraham in Gen. 18.22ff.). In the NT the word has the meaning of one who stands in the middle, a go-between or intermediary who in some way intervenes between two parties who are separated from each other. This intervention may have as its purpose the reconciliation (*q.v.*) of those who hitherto have been at enmity with each other (Rom. 5.10, Col. 1.21) or the drawing together of two parties by a compact or covenant (*q.v.*) without the necessary implication of a previous quarrel. The passages in Heb. convey this latter meaning. In the passage in Gal. Paul is expounding the inferiority of the Law to the Promise of God made to faith. The Law reached men at two removes from God, since according to Jewish tradition it was instituted through angels, who being many were in turn obliged to employ an intermediary, Moses, to communicate it to men. The Promise was given to Abraham direct from God, who being one had no need to employ a mediator. In I Tim. 2.5 the word is used in its distinctive Christian context as a description of the office and work of Christ in bringing together God and man hitherto kept apart by reason of human sin (Isa. 59.3, Rom. 3.23).

Although the word does not occur very frequently, it should be observed that the idea of mediation is essential to the biblical understanding of the relations between God and man. Thus Moses (and after him the prophets) represents what may be called 'descending' mediation (from God to man), for he was the agent by whom God spoke to his people and delivered them from bondage (*q.v.*) and through whom the law as the expression of the divine will was delivered. God dealt with the community by dealing with Moses as a friend (Exod. 33.11, Numb. 12.6–8) and Moses stood in the midst between God and man (Deut. 5.5, a cognate adverbial form in the LXX). He also acted as the representative of the people in their approach to God (ascending mediation), seeking on their behalf the forgiveness of their sins (Exod. 32.11–14, 30–32). At a later period 'ascending' mediation came to be concentrated in the priesthood (but cf. Judg. 17.10–13 for a belief in the mediatorial efficacy of the presence of a priest) of the Levites (Deut.) and then of the house of Zadok (Ezek.) and was fulfilled by means of the offering of sacrifice (*q.v.*). The prophetic mediation characteristic of the ministry of Moses was continued both in the proclamation of 'thus saith the Lord' (descending mediation) and in the intercessory work (ascending mediation) of Jeremiah (32.16ff.), the Suffering Servant (Isa. 53.4,5,12) and Ezekiel (11.13ff.).

In the NT the doctrine of mediation is concentrated on Christ, who is God's representative to man, and who also, as perfect man (Heb. 4.15) is man's representative to God. This is set forth in the Gospels in the description of his work, his prophetic intercession for the faithful remnant (*q.v.*; cf. John 17.9ff.) and in the sacrificial giving of himself in death for many (Mark 10.45; cf. I John 2.2, Mark 14.24, Luke 22.19–20, I Cor. 11.24–5). Heb. expounds as its central theme the mediatorial functions of our Lord by a deliberate comparison with the similar functions of the Jewish priesthood. He was sent by God to reveal divine truth (Heb. 1.1–3), to execute the divine will (10.7–9), to bring deliverance to men from sin and ruin (2.15), and to confer the gift of eternal life (2.10, 10.14, 12.28). The efficacy of his mediation compared with that of angels (1.4, 2.5 ; cf. Gen. 16.7ff., 21.17ff., 28.12) or of Moses (3.1–19) rests on the fact that he is the Son of God, able to represent God perfectly, and also partaker of flesh and blood and therefore a merciful and faithful high priest. His sacrifice of himself is able to achieve what the Jewish priesthood professed to be able to do but in fact could not accomplish, as the necessity of continual repetition clearly demonstrated (9.25–8), namely, the cleansing of conscience (9.14), the redemption of transgression (9.15) and the remission of sins (10.17,18). Thus his people were enabled to come into the very presence of God, and Jesus could be described as the mediator of a new and better covenant (8.6, 9.15, 12.24), which really does bring together God and man (Rom. 8.3) on the basis of sin dealt with. (*V.* also ATONE, RECONCILE.)

F. J. TAYLOR

MEDICINE *v.* HEAL

MEDITATE

The word is practically confined to the Psalter. Of the two NT refs., Luke 21.14 means rather 'to premeditate', and I Tim. 4.15, AV, is a mistranslation. Of the OT refs. outside the Psalter, Gen. 24.63 is textually doubtful. The two remaining refs. are noted below. In the Psalter the subjects of meditation are: *God*, 63.6; *God's Law*, 1.2, 119.15,23,97, etc., cf.

Josh. 1.8; *God's works*, 77.12, 143.5, cf. Isa. 33.18. Although the word is absent from the NT, the practice is certainly enjoined in Phil. 4.8.

From the refs. cited, it appears that meditation means active contemplation, not wandering reverie. It depends on purposeful concentration of the mind on the subject of meditation and deliberate expulsion of discordant thoughts and images. Later mysticism describes a further stage of meditation in which personal activity is inhibited, rational thought transcended, and the individual is carried on a current of contemplative feeling into a state of ecstasy which marks the summit of religious experience. Of this there is no trace in the Psalter: prophetic religion meant reasonable intercourse between God and man, and nothing higher than this was conceivable. In the NT ecstatic states are not uncommon. St. Paul glories in them (II Cor. 12.1–7), yet refuses to assign to them the highest place (I Cor. 14.1–19).

J. S. MCEWEN

MEEK *v.* PRIDE

MELCHIZEDEK

In the strange story of Gen. 14 Abraham is blessed by Melchizedek, who is described as 'King of Salem' (probably Jerusalem, since that title appears as early as 1400 BC in the Tell-el-Amarna letters; cf. Ps. 76.2, where Salem means Jerusalem) and 'priest of God Most High' (Gen. 14.18); to him (for some unexplained reason) Abraham pays tithes (14.20). There is no other ref. to M. in the OT except in Ps. 110.4, a psalm in honour of Simon Maccabeus, who had been acclaimed King and High Priest in Jerusalem; the writer wishes to confer a title to these offices (which the Maccabean dynasty did not rightly possess) by suggesting that Simon stood in the lineage of a kingship greater than David's and a priesthood more honourable than Aaron's: 'Thou art a priest for ever [i.e. the high priestly office is to become hereditary in Simon's family] after the order of M.' Abraham, the ancestor of Israel and therefore of the Aaronic priesthood, was blessed by M. and paid tithes to him, and therefore M.'s claims were higher than those of the regular Aaronic or Levitical ministry. Essentially the same argument is developed at length in the NT by the writer to the Hebrews, but he applies it not to the Maccabees, but to Christ; M. is for him a type of Christ. Christ's is a royal priesthood, as Aaron's was not, and Ps. 110.4 is cited as a prophecy concerning Christ (Heb. 5.6; Jesus himself had cited this psalm as concerning himself, Mark 12.36.) Christ's eternal priesthood holds a blessing which even Abraham must accept (Heb. 6.16 in its context and 7.7). The writer translates M. as 'King of Righteousness' and Salem as 'peace', and hence M. is the type or foreshadowing of Christ as the true King of Righteousness and King of Peace (Heb. 7.2). From the fact that nothing is said in Gen. 14 about the ancestry or fate of M., the writer concludes that he fittingly symbolizes the eternal priesthood of Christ (7.3), 'after the power of an endless life' (7.16). To us this reference to an obscure OT passage may seem odd, but we must remember that the writer to the Hebrews was striving to commend the Gospel to those who had been conditioned to rabbinic ways of thinking. The truth he is trying to convey to them in their own categories is the truth which he states more straightforwardly towards the conclusion of Chap. 7: 'Relays of priests have had to be ordained, because being mortal they cannot go on for ever; but Christ's eternal priesthood never changes. Hence he can completely save those who approach God through him, since he is for ever there to pray for them' (7.23–5).

ALAN RICHARDSON

MEMORIAL *v.* MEMORY

MEMORIAL-OFFERING *v.* SACRIFICE I(*g*)

MEMORY, MEMORIAL, REMEMBER, REMEMBRANCE

In this article the attempt will be made, first, to indicate the difference between the Biblical and the modern uses of these words, and then to interpret the words of the eucharistic institution, 'Do this in remembrance of me'.

The Heb. verb is *zakar*, with the nouns *zeker*, *zikkaron*, *'azkarah*; the Gk. verb is *mnaomai* and cognates, with the noun *anamnēsis*.

The modern notion of 'remembering', psychologically viewed as the act of an individual human mind, is quite alien to the Heb. conception, which is in the first place communal, and closely related to the idea of the 'name'. (See, for this, Pedersen, *Israel*, I–II, pp. 245–59. He says: 'One makes a name alive by remembering it; the name immediately calls forth the soul it designates; therefore there is such a deep significance in the very mention of a name. . . . The man wants to be remembered; thus his name is made to live. The substance of his soul must be so strong that it does not perish, but works through the generations. If he has no sons, then he may seek compensation in setting up a memorial, into which his name has been laid so as to be preserved' pp. 256–7). So, in II Sam. 18.18, Absalom, who has no son to keep his name in remembrance, has set up a pillar in the king's dale 'and it is called Absalom's monument, unto this day'. Similarly, bitter hatred of enemies expresses itself in the desire that their name should be blotted out, like that of Amalek, Exod. 17.17, Ps. 109.13. The name will be forgotten, when the tribe, or family, ceases to exist. 'The extermination of the name is the strongest expression of annihilation. The Israelites in their anguish beseech their God that their enemies may not succeed in exterminating their name from the earth; even if he deserts them, and they are struck by misfortune, he cannot surely let it go thus far (Josh. 7.9, II Kings 14.27). . . . In the name lies the whole substance of the man's soul; if it is killed, there is only absolute emptiness' (*ibid.*, p. 255). Hence the connexion of the remembrance of the name with progeny, which the Israelite desires more than anything else. Further, memory is not thought of as a mere mental activity, but in close relation to the activity to which it gives rise. When in Mal. 4.4 the people are bidden, 'Remember ye the law of Moses my servant', the meaning is that they must obey it. The '*azkarah*, the sacrificial 'memorial' of the Priestly code, Lev. 2.2,9, etc., is an action.

The verb 'to REMEMBER' is however used in a majority of instances with God as subject. He remembers persons, to show mercy, protect, deliver them: as Hannah in her childlessness, I Sam. 1.11; Jeremiah amidst his adversaries, Jer. 15.15; afflicted Israel in its distress, Lam. 3.19; those who make offerings and burnt sacrifices, Ps. 20.4; those who intercede, Jer. 18.20. He remembers the sin of his people in judging them, Hos. 7.2, Jer. 14.10. He remembers his Covenant, Gen. 9.15,16, Exod. 2.24, Ps. 105.8,42; his mercy, Pss. 25.6, 98.3, Hab. 3.2; and his 'remembrance' is one with his action in judgment and salvation. So far is the idea from that of a mere psychological remembering, that the widow of Zarephath can say to Elijah, 'Art thou come hither to bring my sin to remembrance, and to slay my son?' (I Kings 17.18). Yet Elijah has said no word to her about her sins. She means that the coming of the holy man has set in motion spiritual forces, so that the guilt of the sins, which would otherwise have lain dormant (covered, as it were, in layers of dust), now awakes to activity and pounces on the life of her child. Here the 'remembering' is objective and concrete; much as the word of peace to be spoken by Jesus' disciples, Luke 10.6, is no mere 'good wish', but something substantial, like Noah's dove, which if it finds no resting-place must return back. So the sins come back, out of the past into the present, in living power. Another instance is in Num. 5.11–31, where a 'meal offering of memorial, bringing iniquity to remembrance' is prescribed as a kind of trial by ordeal for a woman suspected of adultery. A curse is written out for her, that if she has committed adultery, her thigh is to fall away and her belly to swell; her hair is let down, she takes the sacrifice into her hand, and is made to drink of water into which the ink of the document containing the curse has been blotted. If now she is guilty, something is going to happen; the sin has been 'remembered' in the sense of being concretely brought back.

When therefore Jesus said, 'Do this in remembrance of me' (I Cor. 11.24f.), he was assuredly not planning merely to keep before his disciples' minds that which they could anyhow never forget; it was to be a 'concrete remembering', a bringing back out of the past into the present—of what? Not of sins, for by his Sacrifice they are taken away. But of the Sacrifice itself, or rather of *him*, crucified, risen from the dead, victorious through death. As he at the Last Supper, taking *his* bread and wine, identified them with his Body and Blood, as the liturgical emblems of his Sacrifice: so they, afterwards, taking *their* bread and wine, would do with them what he had done 'in objective-remembrance of him'. Then he, in the power of his accepted Sacrifice, would be present in their midst in living power. The Sacrifice offered once for all and unrepeatable, would be continually renewed and become newly present. Such would be his *anamnēsis*.

A. G. HEBERT

MERCY

This word stands in the OT chiefly (148 times, two-thirds of them in the Pss.) for the Heb. *chesed*, the word which Coverdale frequently (23 times) rendered in the Pss. by loving-kindness (*q.v.*). It thus signifies that continued forbearance of God by which he 'keepeth covenant' (Deut. 7.9) with Israel, even when Israel is slow to keep his commandments and is wayward to a degree. It also represents, especially in such phrases as 'show mercy', 'have mercy', two other Heb. roots, namely *racham* (34 times) and *chanan* (16 times). The former of these has to do with God's tender compassion, that pity which he has for man in his weakness and misery and helplessness. The latter refers to God's generous and kindly disposition.

The word 'mercy', therefore, has nothing to do in the OT, except accidentally, with the question of the forgiveness of sin. The use of the word in the NT is similar, where the Gk. word is almost invariably *eleos* (pity, mercy). For God's mercy towards repentant sinners, *v.* FORGIVE, ATONE, etc.

There are two instances in the OT where the word 'merciful' is used in connexion with the forgiveness of sin. These are Deut. 21.8 and 32.43, where the Heb. word is *kipper*, the regular word for atone, atonement (*q.v.*). Parallel with this use is the word MERCY-SEAT (Heb., *kapporeth*), lit., the place of covering, the propitiatory, with reference to the space just above the Ark in the Holy of Holies, between the over-arching cherubim where the Presence of God was supposed to be most intensely located. The word 'Mercy-seat' is from Tindale, who got it as a rendering of Luther's *Gnadenstuhl.*

NT exceptions to the statement that 'mercies', 'merciful', etc., have no reference to the forgiveness of sin are Luke 18.13 and Heb. 8.12. In each case the Gk. has a word belonging to the Propitiation group.

N. H. SNAITH

MERCY-SEAT *v.* ATONE, MERCY, SACRIFICE II(*b*)

MESSIAH *v.* CHRIST

MIGHT, STRENGTH, POWER, PRINCIPALITY

It is not possible to distinguish nicely between the meanings of these three English words, still less between those of the Heb. and Gk. words so rendered in the EVV. STRENGTH represents some thirty different Heb. words, and there are six Heb. words which are rendered, now by *strength*, now by MIGHT, and now by POWER, and two Gk. words of which the same is true. In the RV some inexact renderings in the AV have been corrected, but no attempt has been made to render the same Heb. or Gk. word by the same English word throughout.

The plural POWERS, which occurs only in the NT, means (except in Heb. 6.5) the holders of power, whether human, rulers and magistrates, as in Luke 12.11, Rom. 13.1, Tit. 3.1; or superhuman, as in Matt. 24.29, Mark 13.25, Luke 21.26, Rom. 8.38, Eph. 3.10, 6.12, Col. 1.16, 2.15, I Pet. 3.22. The superhuman 'potentates' are maleficent angelic beings who were believed to exercise power both on earth and in 'the heavenly places', but who in principle, if not yet in actual fact, have been overcome by Christ. In Mark 13.25 and the parallel passages in Matt. 24.29, Luke 21.26, 'the powers in [of] the heavens shall be shaken' is an (inexact) quotation of the Gk. version of Isa. 34.4, 'all the host of heaven shall moulder away'. The 'host of heaven' means the stars, which were supposed to be spirits or at least animated by spirits. These spiritual beings had their power from God, but they misused it for evil. They are variously designated in the NT (see Rom. 8.38, I Cor. 2.6, 15.24, Col. 1.16, 2.15, Eph. 1.21, 3.10, 6.12, I Pet. 3.22), but the precise difference of meaning, if any, between the terms used cannot be defined. (*V.* also AUTHORITY, MIRACLE.)

J. Y. CAMPBELL

MILCOM *v.* GOD, GODS IV

MIND, HEART

In our EVV of the OT 'mind' generally rep. one of three Heb. words: *nephesh* (soul), *ruach* (spirit), and *leb* (heart). The precise distinction between these three is hard to determine and can be more easily felt than defined. 'Man in his totality *is* a *nephesh,* but he has a *ruach* and a *leb*' (Pedersen, *Israel,* I, p. 104). In this matter modern usage does not correspond, and it may easily obscure the meaning of a scripture passage. In particular, the widely-held distinction between mind as seat of thinking and heart as seat of feeling (esp. tender feeling) is alien from the meaning these terms carry in the Bible.

SOUL (*nephesh*) means the living being. We might render it 'person' or 'personality', so long as we remember that in Heb. thought even an animal is a *nephesh.* In passages of dignified or poetic diction the word is used instead of the personal pronoun (my soul=I or me); or to give a reflexive sense (his soul=himself, etc.). Roughly speaking, it means mind as distinct from matter (to quote the terminology of a once familiar dualism), but always indicates more than mind in the limited sense of the reasoning faculty. It includes feelings, interest and inclination; cf. Jer. 15.1. Ezek. 23.17f. is also illuminating here: Heb. has *nephesh,* which RV translates 'soul'; but the AV 'mind' is to be preferred, provided it is understood in the inclusive sense above mentioned. I Chron. 28.9 speaks of 'perfect heart and willing mind'.

SPIRIT (*ruach*), lit., wind, and in a person, BREATH, means that which is the mark of the living as opposed to the dead. This, however, does not distinguish it from soul (*nephesh*), and one would be tempted to make a distinction by calling *ruach* the whole non-physical aspect of man were it not that it is difficult to say that the Hebrews did not conceive both *ruach* and *nephesh* as in some way physical and having substance, modern notions of immateriality being beyond them. Pedersen differentiates thus: '*Ruach* is the motive power of the soul' (*op. cit.,* p. 105), and illustrates from Ezra 1.1: 'The Lord stirred up the spirit of Cyrus', i.e. moved Cyrus to do something; similarly Hag. 1.14. *Ruach* is frequently used of mental processes, esp. vivacity, impulse, anger. See Isa. 40.13 (AV though, not RV) for an example of its trans. 'mind'. (*V.* SPIRIT.)

Heart (*leb*) is 'the soul as an operating force' (Pedersen, *op. cit.*, p. 104). Cf. Exod. 35.21, where, however, 'whose heart stirred him up' and 'whom his spirit made willing' seem practically synonymous; similarly in Ps. 78.8 a 'prepared' (RV margin) heart seems synonymous with a steadfast spirit, in each case the distinction of *ruach* and *leb* from *nephesh* being more tangible than their distinction from one another. It may be doubted whether Pedersen's definitions of *ruach* and *leb* as just quoted suffice to make clear what differentiates the two, and it is perhaps wrong to attribute even to the OT writers themselves a clear idea of the functions of either in relation to the other.

The phrase 'prepare the heart' occurs again in I Sam. 7.3 and implies what we should call an act of will. (The same verb is found with *ruach* in Ps. 51.10, where 'steadfast (prepared) spirit' is balanced in the parallel clause by 'clean heart'.) Hebrew has no separate word for will. For this sense cf. also Exod. 14.5, Jud. 9.3, I Sam. 14.7. Sometimes heart means nature or character. Samson told Delilah 'all his heart' (Jud. 16.18). God gave Saul another heart, in preparation for kingship (I Sam. 10.9). God promises Israel a new heart in preparation for better living (Ezek. 11.19). In I Sam. 16.7 heart means the true worth as contrasted with outward appearance, however imposing.

Heb. says 'come into the heart' where we say 'come into the mind', Jer. 19.5, Deut. 30.1. 'Call to heart' is one way of saying 'remember'. 'To set one's heart on' means to give attention (I Sam. 9.20); and the phrase 'with the whole heart' (often plus 'with the whole soul') means full and undivided attention and devotion. For the meaning 'judgment', 'good sense', cf. Jer. 5.21, Job 12.3. For the heart thinking see Gen. 6.5, Deut. 4.39, Isa. 10.7; and cf. the phrase 'say to my heart', i.e. to myself, inwardly. Acc. to Heb. ideas, soul and spirit also think. The phrase 'speak to the heart' signifies speaking kindly, cheerfully, reassuringly (Ruth 2.13, Isa. 40.2, etc.). For heart as equivalent to our conscience see Job 27.6; where we talk of conscience pricking, Heb. talks of the heart striking, I Sam. 24.5.

The Septuagint mostly renders *leb* by *kardia*, which is the ordinary Gk. word for heart in the physiological sense. Sometimes it realizes the variety of Heb. senses of *leb* and renders by *dianoia* (mind) or *psyche* (soul, more exactly corresponding to *nephesh*). Very occasionally it chooses the Gk. *nous* (mind), or *phrēn* (mind in the more inclusive sense, wider than ratiocination).

The NT reproduces the OT meanings of *leb*, and, like the LXX, makes the Gk. word *kardia* take on a wider range of meaning than it was accustomed to bear. It is interesting to note that the Jewish writers Philo (*c.* 20 BC–AD 49) and Josephus (AD 37–100) use *kardia* in its stricter physiological sense. But in the NT as in the OT the heart is the seat of the reason and will (cf. Mark 7.21) as well as of the emotions; that is, NT follows OT, both in the specific senses of the term 'heart' and in the general meaning of 'inner man' (cf. I Pet. 3.4).

To summarize: 'The heart is above all the central place in man to which God turns, where religious experience has its root, which determines conduct' (*TWNT*, III, p. 615). Cf. further, for NT usage, Mark 12.30, Matt. 13.19, Acts 16.14, Rom. 5.5, Eph. 3.17.

The other words which NT uses for mind are chiefly *dianoia* and *nous*. (For *phronema*, the noun cognate with the verb *phroneo*, *v.* under THOUGHT.) Both of these are good class. Gk. words, and potentially introduce philosophical associations which are very different from the Hebraic thought world. But the influence of the LXX must not be forgotten, and by the time these words were at the disposal of NT writers they had picked up certain Hebraic colourings through their usage in the LXX and its influence upon NT writers, even upon Luke, who perhaps came to Christianity from a non-Jewish background, and upon Paul, who could read his OT in Heb. but in fact relied very much on the LXX version. Neither *dianoia* nor *nous* is very common in the NT (*dianoia* occurs 12 times and *nous* 24 times); *kardia* (heart) is overwhelmingly more common (*c.* 150 times). This corresponds broadly with the usage of the three words in the Septuagint (*kardia* some 700 times, *dianoia* about 45 times and *nous* only 11 times).

Nous meant in class. Gk. intellect or reason (esp. in the philosophers), and also mind in a more general sense, including feeling. *Dianoia* was not extended to include feeling, but could mean intention or purpose; and also was used for a specific thought, as *nous* was not. In the Septuagint *nous* is used 6 times out of its total of 11 occurrences to translate the Heb. *leb* (heart); and once to translate *ruach* (spirit), viz. in Isa. 40.13. The influence of this isolated instance on Paul is notable, for he quotes this verse of Isaiah twice (Rom. 11.34, I Cor. 2.16); and particularly in the second case he would have served his context better if he had used the Gk. word *pneuma* which would be a more accurate equivalent of the original Heb. of Isaiah; instead however he relies on the Septuagint. The other occurrences of *nous* are of no significance in the present connexion.

Dianoia in the Septuagint mostly stands for *leb* (heart)—38 out of 45 times; 3 times it trans. the noun connected with the verb *chashab* (think). The Heb. *leb* most frequently (over

600 times) becomes *kardia* in the Septuagint, and its significance obviously determines the meaning of *kardia* in the NT, as has been pointed out above. The comparative infrequency of its trans. by the other two words should not obscure the fact that their meaning becomes affected by the meaning of this Heb. term. The possibility at least must be kept in mind when the relevant NT passages are considered. Thus Rom. 7.25, 14.5, seem to preserve the original Gk. meaning of *nous*, and Mark 12.30 of *dianoia*. But Hebraic influence has made itself felt in Eph. 2.3, 'desires . . . of the mind' (*dianoia*), and in Col. 2.18 'mind (*nous*) of his flesh'. Probably only a Heb. could think of a mind being renewed, Rom. 12.2, Eph. 4.23 (*nous*). (Also *v.* THOUGHT.)

E. C. BLACKMAN

MINISTER, MINISTRY

In NT times the ministry of the Jewish priests was confined to the sacrificial worship of the Jerusalem Temple. Prophecy of the kind familiar in OT days had ceased altogether in Judaism (but cf. John Baptist). In spite of their importance as the professional interpreters of the Law, the scribes had no special place in the worship of a Jewish SYNAGOGUE in which any member of the congregation might be invited to lead the prayers and expound the scriptures, as Jesus was at Nazareth (Luke 4.16ff.) and Paul frequently in Acts. The judicial and administrative business of each local synagogue was in the hands of a body of elders (in Gk. *presbyteroi*). In Jerusalem the Sanhedrin of seventy-one members controlled the affairs of the Temple, but the priests alone ministered.

The Christian ministry derives its essential nature directly from the person and work of Christ and only indirectly from anything in Judaism, though some of its organization and outward forms were taken over from that source. The whole priestly and sacrificial system of Judaism was abrogated by its fulfilment in Christ's priesthood and sacrifice (cf. especially Heb.); the Mosaic Law ceased as a ceremonial code to be binding on Christians, and therefore needed no professional scribes to expound and interpret it. On the other hand the Christian rite of the Eucharist was a memorial of our Lord's sacrifice and comparable to the Jewish sacrifices (cf. I Cor. 10.18), and this eventually, though not in NT, gave rise to an explicit association of the Christian ministry with our Lord's priesthood. Already in NT priestly language is used of the Church as a whole (I Pet. 2.9). Again, though scribal interpretation of a Law was superseded, the work of preaching the Gospel and instruction in Christian living was essential in the Church. With the outpouring of the Spirit, prophecy revived in a new Christian form. There is thus some continuity of function between the Christian and the Jewish ministry, but the revelation and work of Christ transformed the character of the ancient ministry as it did that of the CHURCH (*q.v.*).

A reference to certain characteristic terms reveals the fundamental ideas of Christian ministry. The *Apostles* (deriv. from Gk. *apostellein*, to send) were men appointed and sent by Christ with authority to continue his own mission (cf. 'As the Father hath sent me, even so send I you', John 20.21). They bear witness to the facts of the Gospel; they teach, give decisions on discipline, and provide for the needs of the expanding church by 'sending' other ministers. For a full treatment *v.* APOSTLE. In Apostleship we clearly see as fundamental to Christian ministry the idea of *mission*, of being sent to continue and participate in that movement of God towards man which began with the mission or sending of Christ and of the Holy Spirit (cf. Acts 13.4, I Pet. 1.12). The idea of authority is inherent in such a mission, but another important word, viz. 'ministry' itself, expresses an essential aspect of this authority: 'minister' and 'ministry' in EVV almost always represent the Gk. word *diakoneia* (with *diakonos* and other deriv.), which in everyday speech meant generally 'to serve', especially in a personal capacity, and particularly 'to wait at table', as in Luke 17.8. Jesus uses this particular meaning of the word in Luke 22.25–7 to enforce a paradoxical lesson that greatness in the community of his disciples is to be measured in terms of willingness to *serve*. Similarly, in Mark 10.45 the same principle is derived from the character of his own mission. He, the Son of Man, the predestined universal ruler and judge (cf. Dan. 7.13,14) 'came not to be ministered unto, but to minister (*diakonein*) and to give his life a ransom for many'. In the Christian community, therefore, any conspicuous position, office or work was essentially a 'ministry', a 'service' to God and to the brethren, which might culminate in a total sacrifice like that of the Lord himself. Thus the exercise of the apostolic commission is a 'ministry' (cf. Rom. 11.13, II Cor. 6.3f., Acts 20.24), and so is also St. Paul's collection for 'the saints' in Jerusalem, Rom. 15.25, II Cor. 8.19,20, and the provision of meals for the poor in Acts 6.1,2. (Towards the end of NT times this word *diakoneia* and its derivates acquire a special meaning in reference to a particular office, that of *deacon*, *q.v.* below.)

Other general terms describing the functions of the ministry emphasize the aspect of *responsible authority*. *Episcopein* (from which derives *episkopos*, bishop, overseer), meaning 'to have the oversight', and *poimainein* (with *poimēn*, SHEPHERD, PASTOR), meaning 'to tend or feed as a shepherd', are characteristic. In Acts 20.28, 'the flock in which the Holy Ghost hath made you *bishops*, to *feed* the church of God', the two ideas appear together, as they do in I Pet. 5.2–4 and 2.25, where God or Christ is 'the Shepherd and Bishop of your souls'. For Christ as shepherd see also John 10.11ff., Heb. 13.20 and I Pet. 5.4. Peter is commissioned in John 21.16 to 'feed' or 'tend' Christ's sheep. The pastoral oversight to be exercised by the Christian ministry is thus closely associated with our Lord's own office as shepherd and overseer of his people, and behind this again lie passages in the OT where God or the responsible leaders of the Jewish Church are its shepherds or overseers (*v*. especially Ps. 23, Ezek. 34 and 37.24). The Oriental shepherd was responsible for his flock in the widest sense; he gathered the sheep together, searched for the lost, tended the sick, guarded them from attack and led them into the fold or to good pasture. *Episkopos*, 'bishop' or 'overseer' (*q.v.* below), ultimately, like *diakonos*, 'minister', 'deacon', became the title of a particular office, but 'shepherd', 'pastor', did not.

The NT is clear that all the various ministerial functions by which the life of the Church is maintained and extended are 'gifts' (in Gk. *charismata*='grace-gifts') of Christ to the Church through the presence and operation of the Holy Spirit within it. This was true whether a man received a particular office by some human method of appointment (cf. Acts 20.28, 'the Holy Ghost hath made you bishops'), or whether the 'gifts' appeared spontaneously in unofficial individuals as in some instances of 'prophecy' (*q.v.* below). In this connexion two passages containing lists of 'gifts' or functions deserve special consideration, viz. I Cor. 12.28 and Eph. 4.7–12. In the former passage St. Paul begins the list with what appear to be three *offices*, apostles, prophets, teachers. This has led to the view that in the early Church there were three chief orders of ministers, apostles, prophets, teachers; that these were 'charismatic' ministries, depending for their authority simply on the manifest inspiration of the Spirit and not originating from any human appointment or ordination; and that these ministries, being confined to no particular locality and being recognized as manifesting the presence of the Spirit, were regarded in apostolic times as superior to the local and *appointed* ministry of elders or bishops and deacons (*q.v.* below). This view rests on a misunderstanding of I Cor. 12.28. In spite of the first three items in the list, St. Paul is not here enumerating ecclesiastical *offices*, but is describing the variety of *functions* and kinds of service in the one body (cf. vss. 12–27), which all contribute to its corporate life and arise from the diverse operation of the one Spirit within it (cf. vss. 4–11). One man might exercise all these functions (as indeed St. Paul himself would have claimed to do) or one of them only or more than one. I Cor. 12.28 (and the same applies to the parallel passage Rom. 12.5–8 and to Eph. 4.7–12) does not therefore give us evidence about the organized ministry of the early Church, though it tells us much of the forms of activity ('diversities of gifts') in it. (*V*. SPIRIT, VIII (*e*).)

We now consider in more detail the list of functions in I Cor. 12.28, with illustrations from other parts of NT. For MIRACLES, HEALING, TONGUES, *v*. arts. HEAL, MIRACLE, SPIRIT V. The gift of PROPHECY which is second in St. Paul's list is particularly prominent in I Cor. because its use at Corinth needed regulation. Acts mentions a number of individuals who prophesy or are PROPHETS (Agabus, 11.28, 21.10; Judas and Silas, 15.32; Philip's daughters, 21.29), and this activity ensues when the apostle's hands are laid on some ordinary Christians after baptism in Acts 19.6. It appears to be assumed both by St. Paul and Acts that any Christian might be expected to exercise this gift from time to time (cf. I Cor. 14.29–31). Some, however, had the gift in a permanent and intense form, and these were called 'prophets'. St. Paul describes the content of prophecy as 'edification, comfort and consolation' (I Cor. 14.3), which means that we might generally describe it as 'inspired preaching'. A clear example of prophecy is provided by the letters to the seven churches in Rev. 2f., in which the Spirit speaks to the churches through the prophet in words of exhortation, encouragement, judgment and warning. At times, as in Acts 13.1,2 and 11.28, a prophet might utter in the name of the Spirit a specific command or a foretelling of the future. Perhaps fervent extempore prayer was also included under the term 'prophecy'. St. Paul carefully distinguishes the inspired utterance of the prophets from 'speaking with tongues' (*v*. SPIRIT V). It is the main point of I Cor. 14 (which should be read in close connexion with 12 and 13) that 'prophecy' is to be preferred to 'tongues' because it is intelligible and edifying to the hearers, and may even strike home to the conscience of the unbeliever who happens to be present (14.24,25). Although it is the result of the Spirit's inspiration, the prophetic gift can be controlled and used in an orderly way (vss. 29–33); it is subject to 'discernment' on the part of the hearers (vs. 29), i.e. they must actively understand and interpret the message; and the content of the message must be consistent with the Gospel if it is to be recognized as emanating from the Holy Spirit (cf. I Cor. 12.3). In I John 4.1–3 a doctrinal test (the recognition that Jesus Christ is come in the flesh) is prescribed to distinguish the true prophet from the false and real from apparent inspiration. Thus St. Paul and St. John, while regarding 'prophecy' as a supernatural gift, will recognize it as genuinely present only when its utterances conform to the general faith of the Church. The outward marks of inspiration, such as emotion or impressiveness, do not by themselves guarantee that the Holy Spirit speaks in a 'prophetic' utterance. Other spirits (cf. I John 4.1), i.e. evil spirits, can inspire in their own way.

Third in the list in I Cor. 12.28 are 'TEACHERS'. The NT appears to draw a general distinction between 'preaching' and 'teaching'. The proclamation of the fundamental facts of the Gospel (e.g. the coming, death and resurrection of our Lord) with a view to creating or strengthening belief in them is 'preaching'. But Christian converts needed constant instruction in the practical duties of the Christian life; it was also necessary to ground them in knowledge of the (OT) scriptures, especially if they were Gentiles, and to answer problems raised in their minds by points of Christian belief. All this was included under 'teaching'. For examples in the NT itself, see Rom. 12ff. (ethical instruction), Gal. 3 (the meaning of Abraham's faith), and I Cor. 15 (questions about the resurrection). We can therefore see why St. Paul puts the work of the 'teacher' third after that of the apostles and prophets. The apostle proclaimed the Gospel and converted people to belief in Christ; the prophet by his inspired utterance renewed and deepened conviction, repentance, and hope; to the teacher fell the task of building up the daily thought and life of the local community of Christians by expounding points of belief and conduct. In Eph. 4.11 he is coupled with the pastor or shepherd who attends to the daily needs of his flock. Though the teacher did not speak with the outward marks of inspiration which were expected in the prophet, his function implied authority; he was not expounding his own opinions, but interpreting the revelation of God in Christ. Sometimes he could appeal to the tradition of Jesus' own words (cf. I Cor. 7.10); sometimes (cf. I Cor. 7.25 and 40) he would speak explicitly as one who had the Spirit's gift of teaching. On some points, too, there rapidly grew up a formulated tradition in the Church, which teachers could use and adapt for particular audiences. Thus a comparison of Eph. 5.22–6.9, Col. 3.18–4.1 and I Pet. 2.18–3.7 shows that there was a recognized pattern of teaching about the domestic duties of husbands and wives, parents and children, masters and servants, which appears in varying forms in these passages. Traces of similar formulations or summaries of doctrinal and ethical teaching appear in other parts of the epistles. Many of those who had to perform the function of teaching in the early church would need the guidance afforded by such formulations; in most local churches there would be few, if any, Christian *documents* to appeal to. The work of teaching, except in so far as an apostle, like St. Paul, had time for it on occasional visits or in letters, must have been done by local ministers (see below).

Two other unusual words in I Cor. 12.28—namely, HELPS and GOVERNMENTS—call for brief comment. 'Helps' seems to refer to those engaged in various works of charity, especially the relief of the poor and the sick, which formed a prominent part of the 'ministry' of Christians to one another, and 'governments' to those who administered the affairs of the local churches, perhaps specifically to one aspect of the work of the presbyters or 'elders' (see below). Both functions are, like the others in the list, 'gifts' of God to his Church and endowments of the Holy Spirit.

In Eph. 4.7–12 the list of ministerial functions is slightly more elaborate than that in I Cor. 12. A fresh term, EVANGELISTS, follows 'prophets', and 'pastors and teachers' (see above) are coupled. The title 'evangelist' is given to Philip in Acts 21.8, and perhaps in this Eph. passage the word denotes travelling missionaries of a lower status than that of an apostle (cf. Philip's missionary journey in Samaria, Acts 8, where the apostles come down to complete the work begun by him). In any case the function of the 'evangelist' is to preach the *euangelion,* the good news or gospel of Christ. We note in Eph. 4.12ff. the statement of the purpose for which Christ has bestowed these gifts of ministerial functions on his Church. Their purpose is (to give the most probable meaning of vs. 12) 'the full equipment of the saints (i.e. all Christians) for the work of service, for the building of the body of Christ'. The apostles, prophets, etc., by *their* ministry prepare those to whom they minister to do their part in serving the whole body, and thus by the 'ministry' or service of all, according to their vocation and grace (cf. vs. 7), the body of Christ is built or grows (vs. 16) to its full stature in him. (*V.* GOSPEL, PREACH.)

So far our consideration of the NT evidence has been concerned mainly with some of the general functions included under the term 'ministry'. We must now consider the ministers themselves and how they were organized in relation to the Church and to one another.

The interpretation of the NT evidence on this point is a matter of some controversy. We do not possess all the information we should like to have, and what there is needs to be discussed in relation to other evidence belonging to the period immediately following the NT. For example, we know what was the normal organization of the clergy throughout the ancient church from the 2nd cent. onwards. A single BISHOP was the chief minister and ruler of the Christian people in a city or district. He alone was qualified to exercise *all* the functions of the ministry, and, in particular, he alone ordained others to the ministry by prayer and the laying on of hands. Associated with him, but without his power of ordaining others, were a body of PRESBYTERS (ELDERS) who as parishes multiplied became local parish priests, and again there were DEACONS, recognized as a third order, who assisted the bishop and his presbyters. It is a matter of dispute how far and in what sense the beginnings of this three-fold ministry of the bishop with his presbyters and deacons can be found in NT. In this article we present the NT evidence as simply as possible, leaving open some questions which could not be properly discussed without bringing in outside evidence.

Acts gives some valuable information, though it is only incidental. The small Christian community in Jerusalem began with the Twelve in a position of unquestioned authority. (At least St. Paul and James the Lord's brother, and probably others who had seen the risen Lord, were later recognized to be full apostles.) In Acts 6.1–6 St. Luke describes what he probably meant to be a typical ordination of new ministers. The people chose seven men and presented them to the apostles, who ordained them to a new office with prayer and the laying on of hands. The particular office is not named, but it is clear that the Seven did not confine themselves to the 'serving of tables' (vss. 1,2) which is given as the original reason for their appointment (cf. the subsequent activities of Stephen and Philip in Ch. 6–8). Traditionally the Seven have been regarded as the first 'deacons', but in fact it is not easy to co-ordinate their office with any of the later forms. They clearly remained subordinate to the apostles. Later on, in Acts 15, when Paul and Barnabas go up to Jerusalem to get a settlement of the question of the obligations of Gentile Christians, we find a reference to the *apostles and elders* (15.4,6,22,23), who now evidently constitute the governing body of the church in Jerusalem. Among them James, the Lord's brother (cf. Gal. 1.19) seems to be in a special position. He sums up the debate in Ch. 15, and St. Paul on his last visit to Jerusalem presents himself to *James and the elders*, 21.18. Perhaps James had become the only apostle permanently resident in Jerusalem and so was recognized as the local head of that church. (He thus provided an important precedent for the single 'monarchical' bishop in each church, which eventually became the normal rule.) With him are associated the elders (*presbyteroi*). We note also that in the churches newly-founded by Paul and Barnabas they appointed elders, 14.23, and in 20.17 Paul addresses the elders of a particular church, that of Ephesus, founded by himself.

From Acts we can therefore form a reasonably clear picture of the way in which the Apostles provided for the ministry of the local churches, as these were founded by missionary effort. A body of ELDERS was appointed to exercise authority in each place. (Probably, at least in the earliest days, they were literally senior men, and often heads of families who could provide in their houses a place of meeting for the local congregation or part of it.) In this the Christian Church was following the organization of the Jewish Church all over the Roman Empire. The affairs of the local Jewish synagogue were in the hands of a body of elders who conducted its business and exercised discipline in accordance with the Mosaic Law. There is evidence that these Jewish elders were appointed to their office by the laying on of hands. Such evidence as there is in NT (Acts 6.6, I Tim. 4.14, II Tim. 1.6), together with the universal practice of later times, would lead to the conclusion that laying on of hands with prayer was also the method of ordination to ministerial office in the Christian Church. How far did the *functions* of the Christian and the Jewish elders resemble one another? In a Jewish community its elders were responsible for seeing that the Law was observed, and they could excommunicate those who persisted in breaking it; they also, when necessary, represented their community in dealing with the local Roman magistrates. But they did not, in addition to these judicial and administrative functions, act as pastors of their people or conduct the worship of the community assembled in the synagogue. Acts 20.28 suggests that the Christian elders had much wider functions; they are exhorted to 'feed' or shepherd the Church of God, in which the Holy Spirit has made them 'overseers' or 'bishops'. In order to get further light on this point we must now notice evidence from other parts of the NT and other titles used of Christian ministers.

Jas. 5.14,15 refers to the elders as exercising the pastoral function of visiting, praying for, and anointing the sick. In Rom. 11.8 and I Thess. 5.12,13 the same Gk. word lies behind 'he that ruleth' and 'them that are over you in the Lord'. In the second passage these persons 'admonish', i.e. teach and exhort. It is natural to identify them with the 'elders' of Acts. The same Gk. word 'to rule' is used explicitly of elders in I Tim. 5.17, where some of them are said to 'labour in the word and in teaching'. In Heb. 13.7,17,24, where another Gk. word is used for those who 'rule' or 'guide', the author of the epistle alludes to the fact that these rulers 'spoke the word of God' to his readers and 'watch in behalf of their souls'. The combination of 'ruling' with preaching, teaching, and pastoral responsibility is entirely in line with the general ideas of Christian 'ministry' discussed earlier in this article. The teaching, example, and redeeming work of Jesus Christ necessarily made the functions of the Christian elders towards their brethren different from those of Jewish elders, who administered a Law and not a gospel of redemption. Responsibility to God for the welfare of the souls of the flock was inseparable from any exercise of ruling authority in the Church of Christ. St. Paul's own example alone would have impressed this lesson upon the elders of the churches he had founded.

Two other important titles of Christian ministers in NT call for consideration, namely *episkopoi* (OVERSEERS, BISHOPS) and *diakonoi* (DEACONS). We have already noticed earlier in this article the fundamental meaning of the word *episkopos* and its deriv., and the way in which it is associated with the pastoral work of 'shepherding'. How are these *episkopoi* related to the elders? In Phil. 1.1 St. Paul mentions *episk.* and *diakonoi* at Philippi, but does not refer to elders. On the other hand, in Acts 20 the elders (vs. 17) of Ephesus are referred to in the speech as *episk.* (vs. 28). This would suggest that elders and *episk.* are interchangeable terms for the same officials. (It is most unlikely that the *diakonoi* were included in the elders, since both their name and their later history indicate that they were subordinate ministers.) A similar conclusion may be drawn from Tit. 1.5–7, where the command to appoint elders is immediately followed by a list of qualifications for the office of an *episk.* Again in I Pet. 5.1–4 the verb *episkopein* ('exercising oversight') is used in connexion with elders as though they all acted as *episkopoi.* In spite of this apparently strong and consistent evidence, the conclusion is not certain. We know that in the first half of the 2nd cent., if not earlier, one *episkopos* emerged in each local church as the chief minister to whom the *presbyteroi* or elders ranked second. At Antioch and in some of the churches of Asia Minor, e.g. Ephesus, Smyrna, this position was already settled as early as 110 AD. This development is hard to explain if originally *all* the elders were also *episkopoi.* It is therefore possible to hold that among the body of elders in each church only *some* were *episkopoi,* with special functions, though they could be spoken of by either title. Acts 20.28 and Phil. 1.1 show clearly that in St. Paul's day there were a number of *episkopoi* in each local church. On the other hand, the evidence of the Pastoral Epistles (I and II Tim. and Tit.) is best interpreted as implying a *single* bishop in each place or district, with a number of elders and deacons. If as is probable, these epistles are not in their present form St. Paul's, but were composed just before or just after AD 100 in one of the churches of Asia Minor, this agrees with other evidence for this area about AD 110. The 'episcopal' function had become concentrated in the hands of *one episkopos* in each place. Before referring further to this development it will be convenient to say something of *diakonoi.*

As pointed out above, *diakonos* and its deriv. are in use in the NT for any kind of 'ministry' or service. But in Phil. 1.1 the noun has become the title of particular officials, 'DEACONS'. In this passage and in I Tim. 3 the deacons are associated with the *episkopoi,* and clearly exercise a subordinate ministry. This corresponds entirely with the subsequent history of the office in the early centuries; deacons were the personal assistants of the bishop both in the conduct of public worship (especially at the Eucharist) and in the administration of church affairs. The two NT passages do not by themselves give a clear idea of the functions of deacons, but the list of qualifications for the office in I Tim. 3.8–13, as well as the general meaning of the word *diakonos,* suggests that among their duties, as in later times, was the administration of the charitable funds of the church. Perhaps the 'attendant' in the Jewish synagogue (cf. Luke 4.20) supplied the model of the Christian deacon. More probably we should assume that the Church, under the guidance of the Apostles, created the subdivisions of its ministry in forms adapted for its mission to the world. It transformed whatever it took from other sources, and gave to words like *episkopos* and *diakonos,* which had no technical religious meaning in ordinary Gk., a new significance related to its own work as the Church of Jesus Christ.

[Note on DEACONESS. This word occurs in RV margin at Rom. 16.1, where Phoebe is called the *diakonos* (masculine form) 'servant' of the church at Cenchreae. (In I Tim. 3.11 it is quite uncertain whether the 'women' or 'wives' are deaconesses or the wives of deacons.) Since the next certain reference to deaconesses occurs in the 3rd cent., and since the word *diakonein* and its deriv. were used with such wide meaning in the NT period, it is doubtful whether Phoebe was regarded as holding any particular office. More probably she was one who performed notable 'service' to her local church by various labours and works of charity (vs. 2).]

We must now consider some more general questions relating to the ministry in the NT. How far were ministerial functions restricted to the elders or *episkopoi* and *diakonoi*? An extreme view would be to suppose that these officials dealt mainly with the administrative side of local church life, particularly matters relating to organization and finance, while the spiritual activities, particularly public worship, were led by any members of the congregation who were recognized to have the 'gifts' of prophecy, teaching, etc. (*v.* above, on I Cor. 12.28). But any such restriction of the function of the elders, etc., would be incompatible with evidence already discussed; 'oversight', 'shepherding', and 'teaching' were spiritual and pastoral activities, however much they might also involve dealing with funds and organization. At the same time it is clear that at least at some times and in some places (e.g. Corinth) unofficial individuals recognized as possessing special gifts of the Holy Spirit, such as prophecy and teaching, were allowed to exercise these gifts in public worship or at other meetings. (Often, however, the possession of such gifts would mark a man out as a natural candidate for the office of elder or *episkopos*.) On the whole we may conclude that, during the earlier part of the NT period, i.e. that covered by St. Paul's lifetime, while general control of all activities was exercised by the appointed ministry in each local church, a considerable contribution to its spiritual life was also made by the ministrations of spontaneous prophets and teachers who held no office. In later NT times, i.e. the last forty years of the 1st cent., the dangers of false claims to inspiration were becoming more apparent, and the ordained ministry was in a more exclusive way conducting worship, preaching, teaching and exercising discipline. As the Church grew in experience and consolidated its tradition, it relied less upon the emergence of special personal gifts of the Spirit among its members and more upon its appointed ministers, who were believed to have received the endowment of the Spirit at their ordination (cf. I Tim. 4.14, II Tim. 1.6). In particular, at the celebration of the Eucharist one person must have presided and have pronounced the thanksgiving and blessing over the bread and the cup, in accordance with our Lord's example at the Last Supper. The evidence of the 2nd cent. would lead us to conclude that from the first, in the absence of an apostle, the person presiding would have been one of the *episkopoi*. The conduct of the chief act of Christian worship would in itself ensure to the ordained ministry a pre-eminence in spiritual things.

Christian ministry is exercised within the Church. How does NT conceive the relation of the ministry to the Church as a whole? St. Paul in I Cor. 12 (cf. Rom. 12.4f.) thinks of the Church as forming in Christ one body, animated by one Holy Spirit, who produces in its different members the variety of gifts which sustain and enrich its life. The body, by virtue of this divine power within it, produces the organs of its own activity, by a process similar to that which takes place in our natural bodies when their limbs and organs develop. Starting from this description we should be led to think of the Church as the Spirit-filled body able to produce, vary and adapt its ministerial and other organs under the guidance of the Spirit. The ministry on this view is essential to the Church, but no more essential than other organs or functions which, like the ministry, derive from the vocation and gift of the living Spirit operating in all its members. Some scholars regard this as the fundamental teaching of NT about the relation of the ministry to the Church and infer that no principles of permanent and binding validity can be derived from NT about particular forms of ministry or modes of ordination. There are, however, certain other points in NT teaching which deserve attention and have led to a different view. In the first place the description of the Church as the body of Christ occurs again in Eph. 4 with a different emphasis. Christ is now the *head* of the body, who gives to his Church apostles, prophets, etc., in order that the Church may be built up. The suggestion of this passage is that the ministry is the organ or channel formed by Christ through which the life flows down from him, the head, into the body as a whole. There is also the position of the Apostles in the NT Church to be taken into account. Their ministerial power and authority were derived from their personal appointment by Christ himself. The Church did not begin as an undifferentiated mass of believers, and then produce its own ministry for itself; it grew as a body around the apostles whose position was determined by the act of the historical Christ. They then 'sent' other ministers to carry forward their work and similarly to teach with authority in the name of Christ. This view, in contrast to that summarized at the beginning of this paragraph, makes the ministry of the apostles an original constituent, and essential element in the life of the Church by the direct institution of our Lord, and leads on to the view that their supreme ministry was intended to be handed on to others so as to endure permanently in the Church as the only supreme ministry and the only source of lesser ministries. If we adopt this view that our Lord intended the ministry he once gave to the Apostles to be transmitted to others, does the NT show us how this transmission took place and who were their 'successors'? In the course of the 2nd cent. there came to be a single bishop in each city or district, who was recognized as a 'successor' of the apostles, and as alone possessing, like the apostles, *all* the powers of the Christian ministry. Each bishop was himself consecrated to his office by other bishops, and he alone ordained others to the lesser ministries or 'orders' of presbyters and deacons. In the NT the local ministry of elders or *episkopoi* is still under the supervision of the apostles or of their personal representatives, such as Timothy and Titus, who seem to be in charge of a large number of local churches. Also, generally speaking, there is not yet a single supreme *episkopos*, bishop, in each church. It must suffice to say that there is no agreed view as to the precise steps by which this situation developed into that which prevailed everywhere by the end of the 2nd cent. In the NT we see the apostles supervising the local churches and ordaining men to other ministries by the laying on of hands with prayer. When the apostles and their personal representatives were dead, the ancient church, in the course of time, recognized that the apostolic work of supervision and ordination had been inherited by the bishop of each community. To discover the stages of this development in the different parts of the Church, and how this apostolic authority was transmitted, would involve the discussion of evidence lying outside the NT; even then a number of points would remain obscure. (*V.* also TWELVE, THE.)

BIBLIOGRAPHY

K. E. Kirk (ed.): *The Apostolic Ministry*, London (1946). T. W. Manson: *The Church's Ministry*, London (1948). J. B. Lightfoot: *Philippians* (1868), containing his classical *Dissertation on the Christian Ministry*. B. H. Streeter: *The Primitive Church*, London (1929). F. J. A. Hort: *Christian Ecclesia*, London. A. C. Headlam: *Doctrine of the Church and Reunion*, London (1920). H. B. Swete (ed.): *Early History of the Church and Ministry*, London (1918).

H. J. CARPENTER

MIRACLE, WONDER, SIGN, POWERS

The three principal NT words for miracles are *dunameis* (lit. 'powers' or 'acts of power', 'mighty works'), *terata* ('wonders') and *sēmeia* ('signs'). The first of these words emphasizes the essential biblical notion of miracles as the result of the operation of the *dunamis* (power) of God, who is the source of all power and with whom all things are possible (Gen. 18.14, Jer. 32.17, Mark 10.27). In Jewish literature 'the Power' was used as a name for God (Dalman, *Words of Jesus* (1902), pp. 200f.; cf. Mark 14.62 and pars.). Disbelief in the miracles is usually the result of disbelief in the biblical conception of God as the source of all power or in Christ as the veritable incarnation of the *dunamis* of God (cf. I Cor. 1.24: 'Christ the *dunamis* of God'). The God of the Bible is he of whom alone it may with propriety be said: *panta dunata*, 'all things are possible'. The reluctance of the Bible to dwell upon the merely marvellous character of the *dunameis* (though they are indeed wonders) is evinced by the fact that *terata* is never once used in the NT except in conjunction with *sēmeia* ('wonders and signs').

A miracle in the biblical sense is an event which happens in a manner contrary to the regularly observed processes of nature. We must not say 'contrary to nature', but 'contrary to what is known of nature' (St. Augustine, *De Civ. Dei*, Bk. XXI, Ch. viii). It may happen according to higher laws as yet but dimly discerned by scientists, and therefore must not be thought of as an irrational irruption of divine power into the orderly realm of nature. Once this has been thoroughly thought out, a good deal of the so-called 'scientific' objection to the conception of miracle will be found to disappear.

OT: The credibility of a miracle (from the standpoint of those who accept the biblical conception of God as *dunamis*) depends upon (*a*) the sufficiency of the evidence for it, and (*b*) its congruity with the total biblical picture of God's action. In the OT there are two main groups of miracles: (i) those associated with the Exodus from Egypt (the Ten Plagues, Exod. 8–12; the Red Sea, Exod. 14.21ff., etc.); and (ii) those associated with Elijah and Elisha in I and II Kings. (The Books of Jonah and Daniel are not nowadays regarded as histories, but as stories with a meaning.) With regard to (ii) it may be doubted whether they can pass either of our two suggested tests, and opinion will doubtless vary concerning the historicity of these narratives. But as regards (i) the position is very different. It is true that there is no contemporary evidence for any of the OT miracles (unlike the NT); the accounts of the Exodus were written down centuries after the events recorded. Hence we cannot hope to reconstruct anything like a reliable historical account of what happened. But it must be said that something quite remarkable must have taken place. It is historically probable that the distinctively biblical recognition of God as the Lord of history took its origin in those events, deeply impressed upon the racial memory of the Hebrews, by which their national existence was determined—the Exodus from Egypt and the deliverance at the Red Sea. The biblical religion was not evolved from some theory concerning God's power, but arose through an actual historical manifestation of that power; in the OT the decisive event, which became for the Hebrew mind the symbol and type of all God's deliverances in history, is the miracle of the Red Sea. It is to the OT what the resurrection of Christ is to the NT. Without the sign of the Red Sea there would have been no Jehovah-religion, no Israel and no OT, just as without the sign of the Empty Tomb there would have been no Christian religion, no Church and no NT. God's action at the Red Sea became the theme of subsequent Jewish literature (cf. esp. the Psalms), worship (cf. the Passover) and hope for the future, just as God's action in raising Christ became the theme of Christian writing (all the NT books), worship (the Eucharist; cf. I Cor. 5.7) and hope. In these two acts the power of God is revealed supremely as decisive action for our salvation in the concrete events of history. The Heb. mind dwells not so much upon the *being* of God as upon his *activity*; God cannot be known to us in his inner being, but only in so far as he reveals himself to us through his acts. It is only through the things he does or makes that we have knowledge of his 'everlasting power and divinity' (Rom. 1.19f.).

NT: As has been suggested, the supreme miracle in the NT is the resurrection of Christ. It is the keystone of the whole biblical revelation, the strongly attested and utterly congruous sign of God's character of power and love. (*V.* RESURRECTION.) Had there been no resurrection, not only would we never have heard of the other Gospel-miracles: we should never have heard of the name of Jesus of Nazareth. God's mighty act in raising him from the dead is the sign of who Jesus is, and when we know Jesus to be in very truth the 'strong Son of God' we will no longer doubt his power to work wonders and signs as the Gospel-records testify of him.

The Miracles of the Gospels. First, it should be noted that there is strong contemporary evidence of these. All the people who knew Jesus best believed that he worked miracles; even his enemies believed it (Mark 3.22). But, secondly, it should also be noted that he rejected the temptation to work miracles to dazzle people or to seduce them into believing in him (cf. the refusal to cast himself from the pinnacle of the Temple in his parable of the Temptation; Matt. 4.5–7, Luke 4.9–12). He refused to give the sceptical Pharisees a 'sign from heaven': 'There shall no sign be given to this generation' (Mark 8.12; cf. Matt. 12.39, Luke 11.29, Q); he even suggests that it is reprehensible to seek after a sign (cf. I Cor. 1.22). It was not as a wonder-worker that he desired to be sought after, as his various commands to silence after a cure make abundantly clear.

Yet the miracles of Jesus are SIGNS; they are never mere *terata* (wonders), but *terata* and *sēmeia* (signs). But they are signs only to those who have eyes to see, those to whom it is given to understand the mystery of who Jesus is. To the rest (whether first-century Pharisees or twentieth-century sceptics) they are 'mere wonders'—and Jesus does not expect or desire such people to be impressed by them. They will have meaning only for those whose eyes have been opened to the truth of Jesus' person; there is deep significance in the miracle-stories of the opening of the blind eyes. Thus, the opening of the eyes of the Blind Man of Bethsaida (Mark 8.22–6) is, if one might so speak, a symbolical 'curtain-raiser' to the story of the opening of the blind eyes of St. Peter and his fellows in the following *pericope* (Peter's Confession, Mark 8.27–30). When Blind Bartimaeus had his eyes opened (Mark 10.46–52), he 'followed Jesus in the way' (of discipleship). To penetrate the mystery of Jesus' *incognito* is to understand that his miracles are the acts of the Messiah; to fail to see who Jesus really is—as the fellow countrymen of Jesus did when he visited his own locality (*patris*) and they mistook him for one of themselves, a 'native'—means that Jesus can there perform no *dunamis* because of unbelief (Mark 6.5f.). The faith which Jesus demands of those who come to him to be cured is not, of course, faith in the modern sense of 'faith-healing'—such a notion is utterly foreign to the Gospel atmosphere—but a believing relation and attitude towards his own person as Messiah and Son of God, even though those who came to him to be healed could not have articulated their belief in so precise a formula as this.

The Gospel writers present the true significance of the miracles as consisting in the fact that they are *gesta Christi*, the works of the Messiah, as these were foretold by the prophets of Israel. They are the 'miracles of the Kingdom of God', 'the *dunameis* of the age to come' (Heb. 6.5). Thus Jesus had himself regarded them. 'If I by the finger of God cast out demons, then is the Kingdom of God come upon you' (Luke 11.20, Matt. 12.28, Q). They were the signs that the Messianic Age had dawned. Thus, to the question of John the Baptist, 'Art thou he that should come (i.e. the Messiah)?' Jesus replies: 'Go and shew John those things which ye do hear and see; the blind receive their sight, the lame walk, the lepers are cleansed, the deaf hear, the dead are raised up, and the poor have the Gospel preached to them' (Matt. 11.4f.; cf. Luke 7.22, Q). These words reflect the language of Isa. 35.5f., 61.1, and other Isaianic prophecies, and it is clear that Jesus sees in his mighty acts the signs that the Messianic predictions of the OT are being fulfilled. The things which many prophets and righteous men had desired to see and hear are now presented to the eyes and ears of Jesus' disciples (Matt. 13.16f., Luke 10.23f.). The working of miracles is a part of the proclamation of the Kingdom of God: as such they are designed to awaken, not wonder, but repentance; the sin of Chorazin and Bethsaida is spiritual blindness: 'If the *dunameis* had been done in Tyre and Sidon, which were done in you, they would have repented long ago' (Matt. 11.21, Luke 10.13, Q). Even the heathen, who did not know the prophets' teaching, would have understood the meaning of the mighty works and would have repented. Jesus does not upbraid anyone for not showing astonishment at his miracles but for not repenting: 'Then began he to upbraid the cities wherein most of his mighty works were done, because they repented not' (Matt. 11.20). Those form-critics (Dibelius, Bultmann, etc.) are as far as possible from the truth who have imagined that the miracle-stories of the Gospels are to be classed as fabulous. The mighty works of Jesus are the miracles of the Kingdom of God, and the appropriate response to them is 'repent and believe the good news'.

All the miracles of Jesus are signs to those who have eyes to see, revealing who Jesus is. His power over the 'demons' is a sign that Beelzebub's kingdom is being cast down, that the 'strong man' is being bound (Mark 3.22–30, Matt. 12.25–37, Luke 11.17–23). His power over physical disease (which was believed by all his contemporaries to be punishment for sin; cf. John 9.2) is the sign of his power to forgive sins (Mark 2.1–12, the Paralytic). His power over the forces of Nature is the sign of his unity with the God of OT religion, 'who maketh the storm a calm, so that the waves thereof are still' (Ps. 107.29) and who rules the pride of the sea (Ps. 89.9). Mark expects his readers to know the answer to the question: 'Who then is this, that even the wind and the sea obey him?' (4.41). Every miracle in the Gospels may be regarded as the fulfilment of some OT conception of God and his Messiah. The Barren Fig-tree (Mark 11), for example, is just as much an enacted fulfilment of prophecy as is the riding into Jerusalem on an ass, which was a dramatized representation of Zechariah's 'King meek and lowly' (9.9): the fig-tree, which had a fine show of leaves, but no fruit (like Pharisaic Judaism), represents the barren religion of the Jewish Temple (cf. the parable of the Barren Fig-tree in Luke 13.6–9, which clearly represents Judaism): the Messiah, though he loves Jerusalem and weeps over it, must pronounce God's curse upon the faithless city. (In the OT the fig-tree is often used as a symbol of Judaism, and we find metaphors of judgment upon it, e.g. Jer. 8.13, Joel 1.7.) The miracles likewise reveal the functions of the Messiah. For example, the two Feeding Miracles (Mark 6.33–44, 8.1–9) show Christ as the dispenser of the Bread of Life—to the Jews (the five thousand) but also to the Gentiles (the four thousand). As Moses had dispensed bread from heaven in the wilderness, so Jesus, the 'prophet like unto Moses' (Deut. 18.15ff., John 6.14, 31–3, 49f., 58; cf. Acts 3.22) sustains his people and gives them the sign of the Broken Bread: note the Eucharistic interpretation of the five thousand in John 6 and St. Mark's insistence upon the mystery of the broken loaves (6.52, 8.14–21). Whatever we make of the historicity of the Raising of Lazarus (John 11), it is clear that John intends us to understand from the story that the actual reason why Jesus was put to death was that he demonstrated not merely in words but through his mighty acts the truth of his claim to be the resurrection and the life (cf. esp. 11.47f.: 'This man doeth many signs; if we let him alone all men will believe on him . . .'). The Lazarus story contains the truth of history—namely, that Jesus was crucified not merely because he preached about the love of God and the brotherhood of men, but because he showed by his works of power that he was indeed the Christ of Israel's expectation. The realistic rulers of the Sanhedrin knew well enough the impotence of sermons and ethical ideals; they would not have crucified an ethical teacher: their action bears the clearest historical testimony to the truth of the miracle stories of the Gospels.

It may be noted that in the Fourth Gospel the mighty acts of Jesus are never spoken of as *dunameis* or as *terata*; they are *sēmeia*, 'signs' which show forth his *doxa* (glory). But St. John's attitude is precisely the same as St. Mark's; the signs are understood only by those who have faith, and the *doxa* of Jesus is always veiled, except from the eyes which have been opened to the true Light. Only men of faith can say 'We beheld his glory', and they alone can understand the meaning of his *sēmeia*. 'The world knew him not' (1.10; cf. 14.22).

'This beginning of *semēia* did Jesus in Cana of Galilee, and manifested his *doxa*, and *his disciples* believed on him' (2.11; cf. 11.40).

THE NT OUTSIDE THE GOSPELS. The whole of the NT regards Jesus as the *dunamis* of God (cf. I Cor. 1.18, Acts 10.38), and the apostolic Church is thought of as sharing in Christ's power. God's *dunamis* is delegated through Christ to those who believe on him: the power of Christ works in his community (I Cor. 5.4, Col. 1.11, Eph. 1.19, 3.16, 6.10, etc.). The community itself is enabled to work miracles (I Cor. 12.10,28, Gal. 3.5, Heb. 2.4), though it is implied in I Cor. 12.29 that this power is not the possession of all Christians. St. Paul claims that he has worked miracles (Rom. 15.18f., II Cor. 12.12), and several miracles are, of course, attributed to him and to other apostles in Acts (*passim*). In his earthly life Christ had delegated his power to his apostles (Mark 6.7, Matt. 10.1,8, Luke 9.1, 10.19), and after his resurrection he had not withdrawn it from them (John 14.12, Acts 1.8). Everywhere in the NT miracles are regarded as evidences, not of any inherent powers in the Church, but of the presence of the divine power in it; and the discussion of miracles must always be conducted from the standpoint of the biblical conception of the power of God. In other words, the biblical miracles must be discussed not merely *historically* (did they happen?), but also theologically (what is their meaning?). Disregard of the biblical theology leads inevitably to the attempt to explain away the power of God and the apostolic testimony: 'Is it not for this cause that ye err, that ye know not the Scriptures, nor the *dunamis* of God?' (Mark 12.24). (*V.* also HEAL.)

BIBLIOGRAPHY

Alan Richardson: *The Miracle-Stories of the Gospels*, London (1941); *Christian Apologetics*, London (1947), Chap. VII. C. S. Lewis, *Miracles*, London (1947).

ALAN RICHARDSON

MISCHIEF *v.* SIN

MOCK *v.* LAUGH

MOLECH, MOLOCH *v.* GOD, GODS IV

MOMENT *v.* TIME

MONTH *v.* TIME

MOON, NEW MOON *v.* TIME

MORTAL *v.* DEATH

MOSES

Biblical writers regard Moses as the unique law-giver to Israel and as the founder of OT religion. The historical question of who he was and what he did is exceedingly difficult, because of the lack of contemporary documents, and because his figure acted as a magnet accumulating the credit for much which happened long after his time. It is safe to say, however, that a people was created under his leadership, through the establishment among them of a religion whose characteristic features persisted through all the recorded history. In particular, he inaugurated the tradition of jurisprudence, whereby the national life was ordered according to the decisions of its divine head, and displayed in all its detail the characteristics of the people of Yahweh (cf. Exod. 18.13–16, 33.7–11).

The priests, guardians of the Law in Israel, deliberately refer every promulgation of law to the work done once for all by this man, and this must be understood as a perfectly natural process under the circumstances. In respect of law, at any rate, the Hebrews were interested in *what* actually happened, and did not consider the *order in which* it happened of any significance. Consequently, the developments of law could appropriately be gathered up and put into the hands of one outstanding figure whose reputation would serve to make clear the meaning of what had been done throughout. In particular, the authority which the law should have in Israel had to be expressed in the concrete authority of a commissioned agent of God, and it is precisely as such that Moses dominates the traditions of Israel. Again, the promulgation of a divine decree through human lips can take place only where the spirit of the Lord has established the human agent in communion with God, and the spirit which was upon every true law-giver was the same spirit which was upon Moses (Num. 11.16–17). Provision had been made, in the divine wisdom, for the work of Moses to be continued (Deut. 18.15–18), and as this happened entirely by the grace of God, the emphasis should rightly be placed on the intrinsic content of what is given and not on the actual compilers of successive strata.

The account given of Moses in Stephen's speech (Acts 7.20–50), and the reference to him in Heb. 3.1–6, imply that what Christ is to the new dispensation, Moses was to the old. He was 'a faithful servant, giving testimony of those things which were afterward to be spoken'. In this role he appears, with Elijah who is the comparable figure for prophecy, at the transfiguration of Jesus. Leaving on one side the questions which arise about the abiding significance of the old dispensation now that Christ has come (*v.* LAW, LAW-CODES), there is in John 1.17 a clear statement of the place to be assigned to Moses and his work by the Church of Jesus Christ. According to various OT passages, the Law had, as its outstanding attributes, 'grace' (or mercy) and 'truth' (*q.v.*). Taking up these terms, the Fourth Evangelist says that what was given by Moses was 'the law' only in a restricted sense; a precipitate of the divine command (*q.v.*) which in itself lacks 'grace' or 'truth'. The command, in its saving power, is not given apart from the person of Jesus Christ. He discusses this theme fully in John 5.30–47, 7.15–24. 'If ye believed Moses, ye would believe me; for he wrote of me. But if ye believe not his writings, how shall ye believe my words?'

The Christian tradition has always considered Moses the Deliverer (cf. Acts 7.35, *lutrōtēs*, 'redeemer', RV margin: the only instance of this word in NT) as the forerunner and 'type' of Christ. Moses delivered the Old Israel, Christ the New. Moses left the palace of the King to identify his destiny with that of his enslaved nation: 'it came into his heart to visit his brethren' (Acts 7.23; cf. Heb. 11.24–6); Jesus, though he was rich, became poor for our sakes (II Cor. 8.9; cf. Phil. 2.5–7). Moses delivered his people by revealing to them the name (character) and command of God; in a deeper sense Jesus delivers mankind by the same means. The 'baptism' of the Red Sea (cf. I Cor. 10.2) foreshadows baptism into the Church of Christ, as the Old Covenant and the Passover foreshadow the New Covenant and the Eucharist. Yet Moses had been the helpless babe in the bulrushes (Exod. 2.3): Jesus the babe in the manger; Moses was mistrusted by those he came to save (Exod. 16.2f., Acts 7.24–8,35): Jesus came unto his own, and his own received him not (John 1.11). God had used the weak to bring to nought the things that are strong (I Cor. 1.26–9). Cf. also Moses and Jesus as the givers of 'bread from heaven' (cf. John 6.14 with Deut. 18.15,18). (Also *v.* LAW and LAW-CODES.)

W. A. WHITEHOUSE

MOTHER *v.* FAMILY

MOUTH

The most noteworthy usages are with ref. to: (i) speaking truth, wisdom, etc., with the mouth, e.g. Prov. 8.7, Luke 6.45; cf. Rom. 10.9f. for a function of the mouth which takes precedence over all others; profession of faith in Jesus, cf. Phil. 2.11; for prophetic speaking, cf. Exod. 4.12ff., Deut. 18.18, I Kings 17.24, Isa. 6.7, Jer. 1.9, Ezek. 33.7; (ii) praising God, e.g. Ps. 34.1, 51.15; (iii) the anthropomorphic conception of God speaking, e.g. Deut. 8.3 (cf. Matt. 4.4), Josh. 9.14, Isa. 1.20, 55.11, Lam. 3.38, Acts 3.18; God's mouth may emit judgment like a weapon of punishment: Isa. 11.4, Rev. 2.16; (iv) the need to watch the mouth, lest it speak lies or folly or anything hurtful: Prov. 21.23, Ps. 63.11, 144.8, Matt. 15.11, Col. 3.8. (Also *v.* SPEAK.)

E. C. B.

MURDER *v.* BLOOD

MUSIC *v.* WORSHIP

MYSTERY

The word occurs only in the NT, and there principally in the Epistles of Paul. The sense it bears is rather different from that of 'mystery' in modern English. In modern usage, a mystery may be defined as a secret or riddle to which the answer has not been found. Thus a crime is a mystery so long as the author of it has not been discovered, but when he is discovered, it is no longer a mystery. In the NT a mystery is a secret which has been, or is being, disclosed; but because it is a divine secret it remains mystery and does not become transparent to men. Thus the kingdom of God is a mystery (Mark 4.11 and pars., the only occurrence of the word in the Gospels) just because it is the kingdom *of God*, and its knowledge is only for those to whom it is 'given', like the knowledge of Christ (Matt. 16.17). (*V.* PARABLE.)

It is Paul who uses the term most frequently, in ref. to God's purpose or plan of salvation disclosed in his revelation. In the Pauline terminology mystery is correlative with revelation. The substance of revelation is the mystery of the gospel (Eph. 6.19), or the mystery of God (Col. 2.2), the divine purpose which was kept hidden from former ages and has been made known in the fullness of the times through Christ (Rom. 16.25f., Eph. 1.9f.). For Paul *the* mystery relates to the inclusion of the Gentiles as well as the Jews in the divine purpose of salvation (Rom. 16.26, Col. 1.27, Eph. 3.3–6). This is mystery, not because it offers so little to our understanding, but because its superabundant wealth overwhelms our understanding (Col. 2.2; cf. Phil. 3.8).

The word is employed in a derivative sense in other passages where it is applied to objects which have a revelationary significance. The man of sin (II Thess. 2.7), the scarlet woman (Rev. 17.5–7), the institution of marriage (Eph. 5.32) are all mysteries, because they have a significance in the framework of the divine plan which is made known only by revelation.

Mystery is a term which had been familiar to the Greek-speaking peoples of the Mediterranean world for centuries before Christ. The mysteries were the secret rites into which the worshippers were initiated in the so-called Mystery religions. The adoption of the term by Paul does not indicate, as was once supposed, that he himself was influenced by these cults. Paul borrowed the term unashamedly as a convenient means of imparting to the Greeks the gospel of Christ, in accordance with his avowed principle of accommodation (I Cor. 9.22). And it was not inappropriate; for the gospel of Christ brings to men the fulfilment of that aspiration for communion with the divine which was the concern of the Mystery religions.

The application of the term to the Christian sacraments is post-biblical. (*V.* also HIDE, REVEAL, SECRET.)

BIBLIOGRAPHY

J. Armitage Robinson: *Ephesians*, pp. 234–40. E. F. Scott: *The New Testament Idea of Revelation*, pp. 147–53. A. G. Hebert: *The Authority of the Old Testament*, London (1947), pp. 77f.

G. S. HENDRY

* * *

NAME

In the thought of the ancient world a name does not merely distinguish a person from other persons, but is closely related to the nature of its bearer. Particularly in the case of such powerful persons as deities, the name is regarded as part of the being of the divinity so named and of his character and powers. The name therefore is conceived of as possessing an infinitely greater degree of reality and substantiality than has a mere sign of identification. The Hebrews shared in this estimation of the name common to the thought of the peoples among whom they lived. The OT exhibits various aspects of this appreciation of the divine name. In the OT the sanctuary where the deity is worshipped may be spoken of as the place where God has recorded his name or made his name to be remembered (Exod. 20.24), but it is also described as the place which God has chosen 'to cause his name to dwell there' (Deut. 12.11). The name here is a sort of double of the deity. The priestly blessing as described in Numbers is not only a petition to God on behalf of Israel, but is the means of conveying a power to the people or an influence upon them. For when the priests say the blessing 'they put my name upon the children of Israel' (Num. 6.27). The name of Jahweh is often used as a mere circumlocution to indicate Jahweh himself, e.g. 'Let them that love thy name be joyful in thee' (Ps. 5.11; cf. Ps. 7.17, 9.2,10, 18.49, etc.). But in other places it reaches independent or hypostatic character, e.g. it is said of the angel which Jahweh sends before the Israelites to guide them, 'Take ye heed of him and hearken unto his voice . . . for my name is in him' (Exod. 23.21). The name here signifies the presence of God. In the late Hellenistic period 'The Name' (*ha-shem*) *par excellence* becomes one of the popular substitutes for the special name Jahweh when the latter is forbidden to general use (*v.* GOD III).

The ideas concerning the name of the deity which have their root in primitive conceptions and are prevalent in the OT make their appearance also at later stages of religious thought. In the NT in such phrases as 'hallowed be thy name' (Matt. 6.9), 'blaspheme his name' (Rev. 13.6), 'hope' in his name (Matt. 12.21), 'call on the name' (Acts 2.21), 'sing unto the name' (Rom. 15.9), the name has little more than pronominal value and has hardly an independent character. But in John 17.6: 'I manifested thy name unto the men whom thou gavest me' (cf. vs. 26), the name implies God's nature and will, while 'a chosen vessel to bear my name' (Acts 9.15) must mean to represent God's mind and purpose. To believe in the name of someone signifies to believe that the person to whom reference is made is worthy of trust or, more specifically, that he bears his name appropriately or rightly and can perform that which his name or title implies (cf. John 1.12, 2.23). Thus St. John says of Jesus as Son of God: 'He that believeth on him is not judged; he that believeth not hath been judged already, because he hath not believed on the name of the only begotten Son of God' (3.18). Christian prayer must always be prayer in the name of Jesus, i.e. in the character, spirit and attitude of Jesus; it is this kind of prayer which will be answered (cf. John 14.13f., 15.16, 16.23f., 26). In many cases in the NT the expression 'in the name of God' (or Jesus) is associated with the idea of calling upon God to act or of invoking divine help, e.g. Mark 9.38: 'We saw one casting out devils in thy name'. In the sentence (Matt. 18.20), 'Where two or three are gathered together in my name', the force of the last three words is equivalent to 'because of me', 'on my account' or 'thinking upon me' (*v.* Heb. 6.10). The significance of 'baptized into the name of' (I Cor. 1.13,15) is probably that the baptized person is thought of as the property of, or under the protection of, the bearer of the name. Cf. Isa. 63.17, where 'as they that were not called by thy name' is parallel to 'as they over whom thou never bearest rule'. Israel, as the people who are called by Jahweh's name, are for that reason under Jahweh's rule and protection. In Phil. 2.9–11 'the name' which is 'above every name' and which is given to Jesus, is signified in vs. 11 as being 'Lord' (Gk. *Kurios*). It is applied to God himself, and it is also applied to Jesus Christ in the Christian confession of his divinity (cf. I Cor. 12.3). (*V.* also names of God, under GOD III.)

BIBLIOGRAPHY

B. Jacob: *Im Namen Gottes* (1903). W. Heitmüller: *Im Namen Jesu* (1903).

O. S. RANKIN

NECROMANCER *v.* HELL

NEIGHBOUR

In the OT 4 distinct Heb. words (*rea'*, *shaken*, *amith*, and *qarob*) are represented, though not exclusively, by 'neighbour' in the AV. Of these the main one is *rea'*. In the NT 3 different Gk. words are represented by n.—*geitôn*, *perioikos*, and the adverb *plêsion* (near) used as a noun, the last being the most important.

(*a*) In the OT n. sometimes simply stands for a reciprocal pronoun (e.g. Jer. 22.8, 23.27,30, 31.34, Ps. 12.2). Cf. the use of 'brother' (e.g. Heb. of Gen. 13.11, where RV, 'the other'). Sometimes *rea'*, when used in this way, is not translated n. (e.g. Gen. 15.10, 'the other', where it refers to a thing, not a person).

(*b*) In the OT n. generally means a fellow-member of the Covenant-people (cf. similar use of 'brother'). It has moral associations, and implies reciprocal obligations and rights. (NB its use in the Ten Commandments (Exod. 20) and very frequently in Deut.)

(*c*) These moral obligations are most fully expressed in the command to love one's n. (Lev. 19.18), which is taken up in the NT (Mark 12.31 and par., Gal. 5.14, Jas. 2.8); *v.* LOVE.

(*d*) Of special importance is Luke 10.25–37. There is an interesting discussion of this passage in K. Barth's *Kirchliche Dogmatik*, 1/2, pp. 457–74, the substance of which is as follows: One would have expected Jesus' application of the parable to have run something like this: 'The Samaritan did not stop to ask, as you have done, "Who is my n.?"; but recognized his n. in the man who had fallen among robbers, and treated him accordingly. "Go, and do likewise!" ' In other words, the point which we naturally expect to be made is that one's n. is the man who needs one's help. But that is not the point that Jesus actually makes. Though he does finish with 'Go, and do thou likewise', he actually comes to it by a quite different way. In vs. 36 the question he puts is: 'Which of these three (i.e. priest, Levite, Samaritan), thinkest thou, proved n. unto him that fell among the robbers?' So the point of the story is that it is the man who showed compassion (not the one who needed it) who is the n. The lawyer has to recognize himself in the wounded man needing help and his n. in the hated and despised foreigner, who gives help. Barth sees a significant hint of the lawyer's real difficulty in the phrase in vs. 29, 'desiring to justify himself'. The reason why the man, who can so admirably recite the law of love, still does not know who his n. is, and so does not love him, and so does not (as a matter of fact) love God either, is that he refuses to live by God's compassion, and is determined to live by his own righteousness. If only he could now be made to see himself reflected in the wounded victim of the robbery, and so see himself as the *recipient* of compassion, he would be set free from his self-righteousness, set free to accept God's compassion, and so to love God and his n. But the lawyer does not see, and the story once more takes an unexpected turn—at least, unexpected after vs. 36. Instead of trying to drive home the moral of his question in this verse, Jesus tells the lawyer simply to go and be the helping compassionate n. himself, implying that, if he obeys, he will at the same time find his own n., who will help him.

The ancient exegesis was right in seeing in the Good Samaritan a picture of Christ himself—the compassionate, helping n. *par excellence*. In fact, the n. in the Bible can only be rightly understood if understood christologically. My n. is the one who stands forth from the ranks of my fellow-men to do me good. To the question, 'How does he do me good?' Barth answers: 'By proclaiming Christ to me, reminding me of him.' To do this, it is not necessary that he should know what he is doing. Someone quite outside the Church can be n. to me in this sense. My fellow-man becomes my n. when he is seen in the light of the manhood of Jesus Christ and so by his humanity reminds me of the humanity of the Son of God and summons me to be grateful to God. My fellow-man who is in distress is pre-eminently fitted to become my n.—for in his need he can do me good, can be to me the helping n.; for the first thing he does is not to make a demand on me for my help, but rather to *give* me something. His gift is that in his need he sets before my eyes the real humanity of Christ, which was not a triumphant, but a suffering humanity. The reality of this gift by my n. does not depend on whether I recognize it or not. In Matt. 25.31ff., which should be carefully compared, it is noteworthy that neither those on the left nor those on the right have recognized Jesus Christ in the brother in need. Here the encounter with, and the decision about, the n. precede the recognition in him of Jesus Christ. But the significance of the encounter and the decision lies in the fact that it really was Christ who met them in the n.

C. E. B. CRANFIELD

NEW, OLD, RENEW, REFRESH

These words are, of course, frequently used in the Bible in their ordinary everyday sense. But the word 'new' acquires its distinctively biblical meaning whenever it takes on an eschatological significance and implies the passing away of the old order—this present world-age—and the breaking in of the new, 'the world to come'. Thus the OT looks forward to the making of a 'new covenant' (Jer. 31.31; cf. Ezek. 34.25, 37.26), the imparting of a 'new spirit' (Ezek. 11.19, 18.31, 36.26), the making of new heavens and a new earth (Isa. 65.17, 66.22), and so on. The NT claims that the 'new age' has already broken in and has manifested itself in Jesus and his Church (cf. Heb. 6.5); the new covenant has been made and sealed in the death of Jesus the Messiah (Mark 14.24, Heb. 9.15); the 'new Spirit' has been given and brings 'seasons of refreshing from the presence of the Lord' (Acts 3.19); the new creation has been achieved (II Cor. 5.17, Gal. 6.15, Eph. 2.15, 4.24, Col. 3.10). There is thus a very distinctive Christian meaning in the word 'new' in the 'New' Testament: Christians have a new song (Rev. 5.9, 14.3) and a new commandment (John 13.34, I John 2.8); in their baptism, being new persons, they receive a new name (cf. Rev. 2.17). The very proclamation (*kērugma*)—the message heralded—is *news*, good news (*euangelion*). Religious truth always strikes one afresh and is always news, however often we have previously experienced or heard it (cf. Lam. 3.23: 'Thy mercies are new every morning'), and this is supremely true of the news of Jesus' Resurrection. But over and beyond this in-breaking of the new age, which was manifest in Christ and the Kingdom of God which he proclaimed, the NT looks forward to a full and utter realization of the eschatologically new—at the end of this age, the Parousia or Second Coming of Christ. The word 'new' can be used in an absolute sense only in respect of the Parousia. The new heavens and new earth will then be revealed (II Pet. 3.12f., Rev. 21.1,5), and the New Jerusalem will be established (Rev. 3.12, 21.2); until this time comes, the heavens must receive Jesus—'until the times of the restoration of all things' (Acts 3.21).

A. R.

NINEVEH *v.* CITY

NOAH, FLOOD

The primary theological significance of Noah and the myth of the Flood (Gen. 6–9) lies in its teaching concerning God's covenant-relation with the whole human race. All the race is corrupt before God, and the earth is full of violence (Gen. 6.11f.); mankind deserves to perish. But the Bible does not teach 'total depravity' without qualification (*v.* ADAM): 'Noah was a righteous man' (6.9), and in the myth he represents man's 'original righteousness': the image of God in man (Gen. 9.6) is defaced but not obliterated. Noah (like Adam) is the ancestor of the whole human race, and in entering into a covenant with Noah God is making a covenant with mankind as such. On his part God guarantees the stability of the natural order and the continuing supply of human needs (Gen. 8.21f.)—of which the rainbow is the abiding token or mercy-sign. Man for his part must observe certain divine laws (the so-called Noachic Code), very primitive in their expression (Gen. 9.1–7), but nevertheless a sure recognition that there is a divinely established 'natural law' or 'order of creation' which imposes moral obligations upon man as such. Here is the biblical affirmation of the fact of a general revelation that is prior to God's covenant with Abraham or Israel and that is vouchsafed to man as man. (See C. H. Dodd, 'Natural Law in the Bible', art. in *Theology*, Vol. XLIX, Nos. 311, 312, May and June, 1946, subsequently published as a pamphlet by S.P.C.K.)

A secondary theological meaning in the episode of the Flood is detected in I Pet. 3.20f., in which Noah's salvation through the ark is regarded in some sense as an 'antitype' of Christian baptism; for the exegesis of this difficult passage, see the commentaries, esp. E. G. Selwyn; also *v.* BAPTIZE IV. A third meaning is suggested in Heb. 11.7, where Noah is presented as an example of saving faith. Also *v.* BOW, COVENANT.

A. R.

NOW *v.* TIME

* * *

OATH, SWEAR

(*a*) *Oaths made by God.* In the OT these words are mainly used of God's sure promises to his people: (1) These promises, in the tradition of Israel, are those which God 'sware unto Abraham, Isaac and Jacob' (Gen. 50.24, Ps. 105.9ff.)—promises which decreed to them and their families a divinely appointed and guided destiny among the nations. The outward symbol of this sure promise and covenant was for many years the possession of the holy land, 'the land which God sware unto their fathers to give them' (cf. Deut. 6.18,23, 7.13); but it included all that was signified by the 'Covenant which he sware' (Deut. 4.31), 'the mercy which he sware' (Deut. 7.12), and 'the blessing which he sware unto the fathers'. (2) The promises to

David's house ('the sure mercies of David') are confirmed by oath, Ps. 89.35,49 and frequently. In the psalm referred to there is the notable complaint of Israel that the Lord has broken the promises and cast David's crown to the ground; and it must have seemed so at the Exile. (3) But God's sure promises remain steadfast through judgment, and are reaffirmed by the exilic prophets, Ezekiel and Deutero-Isaiah. The oath here clearly includes a promise to admit the Gentiles to the worship of the one true and living God of Israel, Isa. 45.18–22, and also a renewed covenant of peace with Israel, Isa. 45.9–10. (4) Lastly, in the OT the priest-king of Ps. 110 is appointed to his office by an oath, 'The Lord sware and will not repent, Thou art a priest for ever after the order of Melchizedek' (Ps. 110.4).

In the NT these oaths of God are fulfilled: 'The Lord God of Israel . . . has visited and redeemed his people . . . to perform the mercy . . . to remember his covenant, the oath which he sware to our father Abraham' (Luke 1.68–73, 2.6ff.). Christ by his Resurrection and by his being seated on the throne of God has fulfilled the 'oath to David' (Acts 2.30); as priest-king he has been appointed by the oath of God, after the eternal order of Melchizedek (Heb. 7.20,21,28). In her Messiah Israel has fulfilled her destiny, and God has made good his promises which were confirmed by oath with Israel, though with Christ it looked as if the oath had been broken, that God had forsaken his Anointed and cast his crown to the ground (Ps. 89.38–9; cf. Mark 15.34). See CURSE, ii: the curse attached to crucifixion.

(*b*) *Oaths made by Men.* Oaths such as were made by men before the time of the New Covenant, to confirm their own words, are in principle unnecessary or presumptuous in the Kingdom of Christ, whose members must show the same faithfulness to truth as God has shown by the keeping of his word. In their conduct with one another, God's truth must prevail, without the need of guarantees. 'Swear not at all', our Lord says, 'but let your speech be, Yea, yea, or Nay, nay' (Matt. 5.34,37)—or as is perhaps the original form of the logion, 'Let your Yea be yea and your Nay nay' (Jas. 5.12)—the repeated 'yea' or 'nay' was considered by the rabbis to be so strong an affirmation of one's word as to be in effect an oath. As with most of the absolute commands of the Sermon on the Mount, there has been a tradition among a minority of Christians to refuse all requests to speak an oath. It is perhaps worth noting that our Lord replies to the adjuration of the high priest (Matt. 26.63)—though the Marcan account omits this detail (Mark 14.60); and St. Paul calls God to witness to the truth of his words and actions (e.g. I Thess. 2.10). Certainly one of the evils among the religiously-minded people in our Lord's day was not only a needless use of oaths, but also a foolish casuistry which took no account of the real order of things in the Divine Service: 'Whether is greater', asks the Lord of them, 'the gift or the altar which sanctifieth the gift?' (Matt. 23.16ff.). (*V.* also PROMISE.)

R. C. WALLS

OBEY, OBEDIENCE

In the OT this word is used by translators to bring out the full meaning of the verb 'to hear'. It indicates the right response to 'the voice' or 'the word' of God. To receive the utterance of God in a noncommittal or merely passive fashion is virtually out of the question. 'To hear' is to be persuaded (as the LXX and NT words suggest), and so to obey. The only other possibility is active resistance, for which the translators have used the words 'REBEL' and 'REVOLT' in the OT, and 'disobey' in the NT. The terms must be understood against the background of God's covenant-transaction with men. The fitting response to God's initiative is humble acquiescence, a combination of active obedience and unconditioned trust. The word 'obey' and its associates are used in the closest possible association with 'BELIEVE' and its associates (*v.* FAITH). The actions denoted by these two groups of words are almost indistinguishable. But it would seem that where this covenant-response is explicitly referred to, or explicitly required from men, the OT usage gives priority to the term 'hear' or 'obey', whereas the NT on the whole prefers the term 'believe'. This may to some extent be accounted for by the special reference given to 'obedience' in the NT to denote the work of Christ upon which salvation rests. By 'believing' men come to participate in the accomplished obedience of Christ, so where this is established, the primary demand on everyone else is to *believe*. In the OT, where it has not yet been established, the primary demand is precisely for *obedience*. This difference in the circumstances of the old and new dispensations may also account for the distribution of the negative terms in the English versions, to which reference has already been made. 'DISOBEDIENCE' (almost confined to NT instances) means now rejecting the obedience of Christ; and this, it is suggested, is the grievous reality which was foreshadowed in the 'revolts' and 'REBELLIONS' of those who broke the old covenant.

To obey is to conform in humility to that which God prescribes by way of claim or of promise. The close association of 'faith' and 'obedience' is clear in the case of Abraham. St. Paul refers to his having '*believed* God'

(Rom. 4.3; cf. Gen. 15.6), but in the words attributed to God himself, Abraham '*obeyed* my voice' (Gen. 22.18, 26.5). In a later passage in Romans, which has a peculiarly Hebrew background, St. Paul possibly has in mind the relation of the two acts. In Rom. 10.17 faith is by 'hearing', and 'hearing' through the word of Christ; and he goes on to expose the tragedy of Israel, a people who apparently 'heard', but are reproved by God as a '*disobedient* and gainsaying people'.

The demand that Israel should 'hear' stands at the head of the primary law-codes, notably in Exod. 19.5, where God offers his covenant to those who 'will obey my voice indeed', and in Deut. 6.4 and elsewhere throughout the book. From this latter passage it is also clear that 'obedience' was never construed in a mechanical or impersonal fashion. It is the response of love to the gracious initiative of God. And though obedience is the *sine qua non* on the human side for the fruition of the covenant, its effect is never explained by a calculus of merit (Deut. 11.27f., Isa. 1.19, Jer. 7.23, 11.1–8, Zech. 6.15). There is no place for the notions of merit or reward, for obedience, conformation to that which God prescribes, is itself an end, and not just means to an end.

The disobedience (rebellion) of Israel is a continuing theme of prophecy from Hosea to Stephen (Hos. 13.16, Isa. 1.2, Ezek. 2.3, Neh. 9.16f., Isa. 63.10, Acts 7.39,51). Yet the writers of the NT were persuaded that the covenant of God had been brought to fruition by the adequate and representative obedience of Jesus Christ. The life, passion, death, and resurrection of Jesus comprise the required covenant obedience (Phil. 2.8). To achieve it is beyond the powers of fallen men. But 'the obedience of the one' (Rom. 5.19) counteracts the rebellion of the rest. It is an act done *for* the many; an act of complete self-offering to God the Father in which the rebellious many are included. This mode of description (obedience) underlies other descriptions of how men have been reconciled to God. It is an obedience in which their sins are expiated. It is an act of obedience in which the true role of High Priest is fulfilled (Heb. 5.8f.). Sacrifice at last fulfils its function because adequate obedience, which OT writers sometimes saw as its only *rationale*, was the very substance of Christ's sacrificial death (Heb. 10.5–7). The 'odour of a sweet smell' (Eph. 5.2) obliterates the 'bitterness' which is suggested by the Hebrew word for rebellion (*marah*).

Therefore, under the new covenant, 'obedient' becomes almost a technical term for those who are joined to Christ. In them the covenant is being surely fulfilled, not in virtue of their own achievement but in virtue of his (Rom. 15.18, 16.19, I Pet. 1.2). They hear, and are conformed to, 'the teaching' (Rom. 6.17), 'the truth' (Gal. 5.7), 'the word' (I Pet. 3.1), 'the gospel' (II Thess. 1.8). And this description of their condition serves to explain the injunctions to manifest obedience, slaves to their masters, children to their parents, wives to their husbands, which are prominent in the codes of conduct (*v.* LAW-CODES).

It is true that the terms under discussion are used throughout the Bible in a 'secular' context, as well as to denote men's reaction to the utterance of God. But in the NT especially, obedience to other men always has theological significance. The case of 'kings and those in authority' calls for special comment. At the heart of the OT tradition of the earthly kingship established in Israel, there is the incident of Saul's usurpation of divine prerogatives (I Sam. 15). Verses 22–3 are a *locus classicus* in the OT for the supreme importance of obedience. And the tradition of earthly kingship is coloured throughout by Hosea's judgment that what happened at Gilgal was gross rebellion against the Lord, a rebellion into which Israel were led precisely by their king (Hosea 9.15–17; cf. 13.9–12). The lesson was not forgotten, and its fruits were quickly manifest in the Christian Church (Acts 4.19, 5.29): 'We must obey God rather than men.' There is an appropriate trust and obedience among the members of the Christian household and the Christian church (Heb. 13.17), and it manifests, in its own way, the obedience which lies at the heart of Christian existence. It should be extended, wherever possible, to 'the powers that be', in conformity with Christ's own submission to Pontius Pilate. But in all this, Christian action cannot go beyond humble participation in the obedience which Christ has rendered to God on their behalf, an obedience which has secured for them the covenanted blessings of God. (Also *v.* ADAM, SIN.)

W. A. WHITEHOUSE

OBLATION *v.* SACRIFICE I(*b*)1

OFFENCE *v.* SIN

OFFERING *v.* SACRIFICE I(*b*)1

OIL *v.* SACRIFICE III(*d*)2

OLD *v.* NEW

ORDINANCE *v.* STATUTE

OVERCOME *v.* VICTORY

OVERSEER *v.* MINISTER

* * *

PARABLE

The study of this word falls into two parts: (i) the parable-form, in itself beautiful, simple, and effective; and (ii) the perplexing difficulty of Mark 4.11–12, where it seems to be said that the parables hide the truth instead of revealing it, and the difficulty is explained by the Heb. meaning of 'parable'.

(i) In the parable-form we have a more or less developed exposition of some spiritual truth by means of a simile or likeness drawn from earthly things. The *Parable proper* is a consistent story, such as the Labourers in the Vineyard, Matt. 20.1–16, or the Prodigal Son, Luke 15.11–32; cf. in OT, Jotham's fable of the Trees in Judg. 9.7–15, Nathan's Ewe Lamb in II Sam. 12.1–6, or Isaiah's Song of the Vineyard in Isa. 5.1–7. The argument of Jesus in the 'parable proper' is that of Analogy: because one God is the author of the kingdoms of nature and of grace, the growth of vegetables can illustrate the growth of souls, as in Mark 4.29–31; and if an earthly father loves his son, *a fortiori* does the heavenly Father, Luke 11.11–13. His parables are sometimes deliberately one-sided: if a callous and cruel judge will yield at last to persistent entreaties, how much more God, Luke 18.1–8! Here it is taken for granted that God is *not* like an unjust Judge; but since on the other hand he is not like a fond and indulgent father, we must go on praying even when he seems to refuse to hear; only so can prayer be answered, and only so can it be proved that we really care.

While, however, the *Parable proper* is consistent as a story, in the *Allegory* a detailed correspondence is suggested between particular points in the simile and the application, which can sometimes tear the story to pieces; thus in Matt. 22.6–8 the Feast is prepared and the dinner cooked; the guests refuse; a military expedition is undertaken and their city is burnt; yet at the end of all this the dinner is still cooked and ready. Cf. John 10.11, where the Shepherd gives his life for his sheep, a thing which it would not be right for an earthly shepherd to do.

Both Parable proper and Allegory are found in the gospels: the former, where the teaching is of the spiritual life in general, as e.g. about prayer; the latter, where the parable directly illustrates the Messianic Kingdom. In the two parables of the Lost Sheep in Matt. 18 and Luke 15, Jesus is plainly the Shepherd; that he did so speak of himself is attested by Mark 14.27. In Mark 4.3 he is the Sower, and the seed (the divine word) combines with the soil (human nature) to produce what we call the fruits of grace; the problem is, why are the fruits in many instances not forthcoming? Mark 12.1–9 is an allegory of God's dealings with Israel, sending first the prophets, and last his only (*agapētos*) Son; the question is: When the Son has been rejected, what will the Lord of the Vineyard next do? This allegorical element constantly tends to come in, as even in the Unjust Judge; but not in the twin-parable of the Importunate Friend, Luke 11.5–8, where there is no allegorical counterpart to the 'children in bed'.

In the traditional interpretation of the parables the allegorical method has often been pushed to unwarranted lengths; Jülicher's book, *Die Gleichnisreden*, was an attempt to escape from arbitrariness and subjectivity to objectivity of interpretation. But Jülicher's chilly rationalism, which found in them only the demonstration of universal truths of religion and morals, is deservedly satirized by Nygren in *Agape and Eros*, I, pp. 59f.

It must be added that in the gospels there are numerous instances of less developed similes, e.g. the New Patch and the New Wine, Mark 2.21,22, or the so-called Parable of the Leaven, Matt. 13.33. Mark 13.34 contains in germ the parable of the Talents, Matt. 25.14–30.

(ii) But the Heb. for 'parable', *mashal*, means a 'proverb'. 'The words of the wise and their dark sayings', Prov. 1.6, may be difficult to outsiders, but plain to the wise man's disciples. 'Parable' is thus used in the Gospels, of pithy sayings, in Mark 3.23, 7.17, Luke 4.23; cf. John 16.25–9. Mark 4.9–11 has been wrongly dismissed as unauthentic (e.g. by Rawlinson, *St. Mark*, pp. 47–8). The difficulty is to see how he could have told the parables in order that the outsiders seeing might see and not perceive, lest haply they should turn again and it should be forgiven them; for did not he come to seek and to save that which was lost? The passage however is quoted from Isa. 6.9–10. Running through the Bible there is the mystery of rejection; in each generation there is unbelief and rebelliousness, side by side with faith and receptiveness. There was something which caused the meaning of his teaching to be hidden from the wise and prudent, Matt. 11.25; yet it was not any sort of obscurity in the teaching, but rather its divine simplicity. The man who as good as asked him for a parable about a Wedding-feast, Luke 14.15, was not expecting one which compelled him to search his own conscience to see whether he himself were not one of those who were making excuse. Those who built the tombs of the prophets, Matt. 23.29–31, were quite sure that if they had lived in the days of the prophets they would not have been guilty of their blood; of course they would have been on the right side. He told them, 'Wherefore ye witness to yourselves that ye are sons of them that slew the prophets'; your very self-confidence makes it certain that you would have been on the wrong side. The terrible word 'lest', Mark 4.12, signifies that which prevents men from believing and being saved: the self-centredness, the love of the Ego, which can cause a man to applaud loudly the faultless beauty of the parable of the Prodigal Son, and fail to see where he himself comes into it: if not as the Prodigal Son, then as the Elder Brother. (*V.* also SIMILITUDE.)

A. G. HEBERT

(PARACLETE) *v.* SPIRIT IX(*d*)

PARADISE *v.* HELL

PARDON

The word does not occur in the NT of the EVV. In the OT it is, with one exception, equivalent to forgiveness (*q.v.*). The exception is Isa. 40.2, where Jerusalem is told that 'her iniquity is pardoned', or, as in the RV margin, 'her punishment is accepted'. The verse is important for two reasons: first, because the word used is properly 'iniquity', but it is used, as in Gen. 4.13, for the consequences of iniquity, these being inevitable; secondly, because, forgiveness or no forgiveness, the consequences of sin have to work themselves out. The price of sin must always be paid, a fact which is of the utmost importance in the doctrine of the atonement. The verb translated 'pardon', 'accept', involves the idea of the restoration to full favour. It is the verb used in Ps. 44.3, where the translation is 'because thou hadst a favour unto them'. It stands for the full fellowship existing between a loving God and a faithful people. This is indeed the message of the prophet in Isa. 40.2. Jerusalem has paid a double penalty for her iniquity. The debt is more than paid; the faithful Israel is about to return from exile, and the full favour of the forgiving God is to be enjoyed.

N. H. SNAITH

PARTAKE *v.* FELLOWSHIP

PARTNER *v.* FELLOWSHIP

PASSION

The word has first the meaning of emotion or feeling as in Gal. 5.24, Col. 3.5, I Thess. 4.5, and in each of these references passion is closely connected with the disorderly forces of unredeemed human nature and identified with uncontrolled appetite which must be compelled to submit to the rule of the Spirit or to the reign of Christ himself. In Acts 14.15, Jas. 5.17, the reference is to the weakness and creatureliness of man without special emphasis on appetite. In one passage only (Acts 1.3) is the word used as an equivalent for the suffering and death of our Lord Jesus Christ. The English word 'passion' is derived from the Gk. word to suffer (there are close links in sound) and in such passages as Rom. 8.18, Heb. 2.9, 10.32, I Pet. 1.11, 4.32 in the Wycliffe and other earlier EVV the word 'passion' was used for the sufferings of Christ and of believers, but was retained by AV and RV only in Acts 1.3. In Gk. the word has also the idea of being subject to pressures and wounds from without, and therefore could never have been applied to a divine being by a Gk. thinker, for to him a god was a remote self-sufficient being.

F. J. TAYLOR

PASSOVER

Probably the greatest of all Jewish festivals and the one which has endured over a longer period than any other, the origin of the Passover is lost in the dim mists of the past. It is generally believed that it goes back far beyond the time of Moses, and in this remote origin consisted of two spring festivals, pastoral and agricultural, merged into one in historical times. The agricultural feast of unleavened bread and bitter herbs was combined with the primitive nomadic feast of the firstborn of the flock sacrificed at the same vernal season. Other features of the ritual in the earliest surviving account (Exod. 12) have the appearance of survivals from these primitive customs. The association of the feast with the time of the full moon nearest to the spring equinox may be a relic of moon-worship, as also the command that all must be eaten and nothing left to the morning. The prohibitions in the ritual very probably were directed against the primitive nomadic habit of eating the whole of the fresh carcase raw—flesh, blood and bones. Whatever meaning these associated festivals may have had in earlier ages, from the time of the Exodus the memory of that great divine act of redemption was stamped upon this annual festival and the details of the ritual were given a new historical justification. It served as a solemn reminder of the fact that Israel was a redeemed people: for 'it shall be when thy son asketh thee in time to come, saying, what is this? that thou shalt say unto him, By strength of hand the Lord brought us out of Egypt' (Exod. 13.11–15). Thus the Passover gained a new significance as a memorial of the deliverance from Egypt and the subsequent covenant with God; and in the title of the feast alike in Heb. and in the EVV there is a play on words. Though some of the domestic features of the celebration were retained, in the later Jewish centuries and in apostolic times the feast was observed at the central sanctuary in Jerusalem. The evidence of Josephus (*Antiquities*, 17.9.3, 20.5.3) supports the witness of the Gospels that Jerusalem was overcrowded at Passover-time and that there was great danger of seditious outbreaks.

In the NT three points of importance call for some comment. (1) There is a connexion between the Passover and the Last Supper of the Lord, although the evidence is uncertain and the interpretation of the documents a matter on which there is divided opinion among scholars (*v.* THANK, NT(*d*)(3). The Synoptic Gospels apparently present the Supper as a Passover Meal, but the Fourth Gospel implies that it was eaten before the Passover (John 18.28, 19.14), and that Jesus was crucified on the day of which the same evening was Passover night. There is some confusion in the Synoptic narratives, and it may be that the Supper was a hurried anticipation of the Passover meal (cf. Luke 22.15–18). Nevertheless, whatever the decision reached about the dating of the Supper, it is indisputable that the incident took place at the Passover season and that Paschal ideas and associations must have filled the mind of Jesus at such a time. The new feast, like the old (*v.* THANK), pointed to a definite date in history and an event in history; and thus it commemorates the deliverance effected by Christ. The deliverance commemorated by the Passover was purchased by 'the divinely offered sacrifice of him who represented the new Israel of God. In all the complex of ideas that gather round the Last Supper and the Crucifixion the Passover had no little place' (H. H. Rowley, *The Rediscovery of the OT*, p. 214). As the old deliverance was followed by the covenant (*q.v.*) of Sinai, sealed by sacrificial blood, so the new deliverance in Christ is linked with the new covenant promised in Jer. 31; and the Supper instituted at Passover-time was linked to that covenant in the blood of Jesus, by which the redeemed would pledge themselves in loyalty to God every time it was repeated. (2) Reference to the Passover elsewhere in the NT occurs as a note of time (Acts 12.3, 20.6), indicating something of the importance it held in the observances of the year as a significant moment; cf. refs. to other festivals in the same way—Tabernacles (John 7.2), Pentecost (Acts 2.1, 20.16, I Cor. 16.8). (3) There was also a theological exposition of the death and resurrection of Christ in terms of the Passover ritual (I Cor. 5.6–8, 15.20,23). (*a*) Christ in his sacrificial death for men is described as 'our passover sacrificed for us', which appears to be a recollection of the ceremonial slaying of the lambs for use in the feasts (cf. the use of LAMB OF GOD, John 1.29, Rev. 5.9). Possibly there is here a recollection of the tradition, embodied in the Fourth Gospel, that Christ was dying upon the cross, a victim without blemish, at the same time as the lambs were being slaughtered in the temple (John 19.36), and certainly a reference to the power of the shed blood (*q.v.*); cf. Exod. 12.22,23, I John 1.7. Note, however, that in Hebrews the ritual of the Day of Atonement and not of the Passover is used to interpret the death of Christ. (*b*) The association of the feast of unleavened bread with the Passover lamb and the diligent care with which every household removed all vestiges of leaven is used as a symbol for the new life which Christians should possess and in which they should rejoice as a new leaven working in their lives (I Cor. 5.7–8). (*c*) The accompanying ceremonial of offering the first fruits of barley-harvest in the temple at Passover-time is used to describe the significance of Christ's resurrection (Lev. 23.10, I Cor. 15.20, 23). As the gathering of first fruits and presenting them is a pledge that the whole harvest shall be reaped, so the resurrection of Christ is a pledge of the resurrection of the human race (cf. I Cor. 15.22). (*V.* arts. SACRIFICE, IV(*b*), THANK, NT(*d*)(3.)

BIBLIOGRAPHY

G. Dalman: *Jesus-Jeshua*, London (1929). W. O. E. Oesterley: *The Jewish Background of the Christian Liturgy*, London (1925). G. H. C. Macgregor: *Eucharistic Origins*, London (1929). G. Dix: *The Shape of the Liturgy*, pp. 48–102, London (1945). J. Jeremias: 'The Last Supper' (*JTS*, No. 197–8, Jan.–April, 1949, pp. 1–10).

F. J. TAYLOR

PASTOR *v.* MINISTER

PATIENCE

In the OT patience might seem to mean simply the endurance or long-suffering of evil and wickedness (Job). In Isa. 53, however, where, characteristically, the word itself is not used, patience has sacrificial power to transform the evil. But patience, in the OT, is less a distinctive quality than the very nature of God's rule. Such basic passages as Exod. 34.6 and Num. 14.18 show that patience is primarily God's own character. The patience of men has in it therefore, besides endurance, the quality of expectation, waiting for something to happen, for 'someone to help'. The message of God's patience in and through the prophets makes for a quickening of patience. God's patience breeds men's patience.

In the NT there is the same wide range and underlying scope of the thing beyond the mention of the word. (There are many Gk. words used to express aspects of patience, and one word in I Tim. 3.8 has at least eight possible English versions.) The 'patience of God' (Rom. 15.5) has still the same broad sense as in the OT, but now human endurance is quickened by more than expectation: patience in the midst of tribulation is now one link in a chain which leads through to triumphant faith in the love of God (Rom. 5.3–4). For now the 'patience of Christ' (II Thess. 3.5) is communicated to believers as the gift of his victory. The 'patience of the saints' (Rev. 13.12 and elsewhere) is thus more than endurance of persecution or passive acquiescence in temporary evils. It is a lively outgoing power of faith, an active energy rather than a passive resignation. For it is an expectation which has been fulfilled in Christ, and is thus perfected and also continually merging into hope and faith in the coming Christ. (See W. Meikle, 'The Vocabulary of Patience in the OT and NT', *Expositor*, March and April, 1920.) (*V.* also LONG-SUFFERING, HOPE.)

R. GREGOR SMITH

PEACE

The word *eirēnē* (peace) in classical Gk. is primarily negative, denoting absence or end of war. So occasionally in OT (Judg. 4.17, I Kings 4.24, Eccles. 3.8; *v.* REST) and NT (Acts 24.2). Also of a treaty (I Kings. 5.12, Acts 12.20). But generally the biblical sense of 'peace' is determined by the positive conception of the Heb. word *shalom* (rendered almost always in LXX by *eirēnē*, and only *shalom* so rendered).

Shalom is a comprehensive word, covering the manifold relationships of daily life, and expressing the ideal state of life in Israel. Fundamental meaning is 'totality' (the adjective *shalem* is translated 'whole'), 'well-being', 'harmony', with stress on material prosperity untouched by violence or misfortune. Peace is 'the untrammelled, free growth of the soul [i.e. person] . . . harmonious community; the soul can only expand in conjunction with other souls . . . harmony, agreement, psychic community; . . . every form of happiness and free expansion, but the kernel of it is the community with others, the foundation of life' (Johs. Pedersen, *Israel*, I–II, pp. 263–335). This well-being is manifested in every kind of good for man, bodily health (Ps. 38.3 RV marg., Ecclus. 38.8), strengthening and security (Dan. 10.19, Judg. 6.23), a long life of happiness ending in natural death (Gen. 15.15), prosperity and abundance (Lam. 3.17, Ps. 37.11, Zech. 8.12, Job 5.19–26, Lev. 26.6ff.; cf. 'is it well with?'; marg., 'is there peace to?'), successful issue of an enterprise (Judg. 18.5f., I Sam. 1.17), victory in, not cessation of, war (Judg. 8.9, I Kings 22.27–8). Peace is the normal and proper condition of men in relationship with one another, enjoyed most intimately in the family (Gen. 13.8), and extended to others by a covenant (I Sam. 20.42) which determines relationships and is so a 'covenant of peace'. To greet with peace, send away in peace, is to confer a benefit and to admit to mutual confidence and inviolability (Gen. 43.23, Judg. 19.20); hence the question, 'Is it peace?' (I Sam. 16.4f.). Enjoyed in Israel as a single and harmonious community (II Sam. 17.3, Exod. 18.23, Ps. 125.5), to which others may be admitted if subservient (Deut. 20.10–12), but not if they threaten to corrupt Israel (Deut. 23.6, Ezra 9.12). The good as opposed to the evil (Prov. 12.20, Ps. 28.3), the fruit of righteousness (Ps. 37.37) denied to the wicked (Isa. 48.22). The source of peace in all its forms is Jehovah, the God of peace (Judg. 6.24, Isa. 45.7), who overcomes the forces of disharmony in the heavens (Job 25.2), who blesses Israel (Lev. 26.6, Num. 6.26, Ps. 29.11, 85.3–12), the house of David (I Kings 2.33), the priesthood (Mal. 2.5), the faithful Israelite (Ps. 4.8) with peace.

Peace is central to the preaching of the prophets, who from Micaiah to Ezekiel engage in conflict with false prophets on the question of Peace or No Peace (I Kings 22, Micah 3.5–11, Jer. 6.13f., 14.13–18, 23.16ff. Ezek. 13.1–16). They interpreted the political and social turmoil as the necessary judgment of God, in the face of which to prophesy security is to pass over sin. Only after the judgment has taken place can Jeremiah write to the exiles that Jehovah now cherishes thoughts of peace towards them (Jer. 29.11). II Isa. announces the deliverance from Babylon as a gospel of peace (Isa. 52.7, 55.12, 57.19); Jehovah will make a covenant of peace with the restored community (Ezek. 34.25–30, 37.26, Isa. 54.10). Peace is thus brought into relation with salvation, and although it does not lose its underlying meaning of prosperity (Isa. 49.22-6, 60.12–14), it is closely conjoined with righteousness and truth in the prophetic teaching (Jer. 33.8–14, Isa. 54.11–17, 57.19, 60.17, Zech. 8.16–19, Ps. 85.9f., 119.165). The suffering Servant brings peace to the nations (Isa. 53.5). A final peace as the gift of God in the coming age is a constituent of OT eschatology, and is envisaged either as the abolition of war and the rule over the nations of Israel's messianic king (Isa. 9.2–7, Zech. 9.9f., Micah 5.5, Haggai 2.7–9), or as a paradisal existence in which all forms of strife will have been removed (Isa. 11.1ff., 2.2–4, 65.25, Ezek. 34.25–28).

This long-awaited gift of the last days (Rom. 2.10), which is deliverance from the enemies of life and the establishment of righteousness, begins to be a present fact with the birth of the Baptist (Luke 1.79,71) and of Jesus (Luke 2.14,29–30). It is the coming of the Kingdom of God, recognized by disciples (Luke 19.38), unrecognized by the nation which thereby rejects its salvation (Luke 19.42). The mission of Jesus brings no easy harmony but division

(Matt. 10.34, Luke 12.51), which will be reproduced in the mission of the Twelve as his representatives to announce the Kingdom as a gift to be accepted or taken back (Matt. 10.12–15, Luke 10.5–9). Those who make peace between warring parties reproduce the character of God (Matt. 5.9), and the disciples must combine obedience to the severe demands of the Kingdom with harmony amongst themselves (Mark 9.50). Miracles are signs of the Kingdom in removing disorder and creating wholeness (Mark 5.34, Luke 7.50, John 7.23), but the peace of unbroken union with the Father in the midst of adversity, which is the supreme gift of Jesus to the disciples and which is to be distinguished from all forms of worldly security (John 14.27), is dependent upon his final victory over the chief enemies, sin and death (John 16.33). Hence it is that after the resurrection the Lord greets his disciples with 'Peace', shows them the marks of the passion and passes on to them his own mission and victory over sin (John 20.19–23,26). The life, death and resurrection of Christ can be called God's gospel of peace for all men (Acts 10.36: cf. Isa. 52.7, Eph. 6.15, 2.17; cf. Isa. 57.19, possibly of the exalted Christ). Although the greeting 'peace', found in all the NT Epistles except Hebrews, James and I John, is a conventional Jewish (not Gk.) usage (cf. Ezra 4.17, Dan. 4.1), it is given deeper content by its conjunction with the grace and mercy of God (I Tim. 1.2, II Tim. 1.2, II John 3), mercy and love (Jude 2) and grace (the remainder of the epp. except III John; cf. Rev. 1.4), and is determined by the theological statements with which the epistles open, where it is said to be the gift of God (Col. 1.2), of God and Jesus Christ (Rom. 1.7, I Cor. 1.3, II Cor. 1.2, Gal. 1.3, Phil. 1.2, II Thess. 1.2; *v.* J. Moffatt, *Grace in the New Testament*, pp. 140ff.; E. de W. Burton, *Galatians*, I.C.C., p. 425).

God is called the God of peace in that through the resurrection he establishes the death of Christ as the sacrifice of the eternal covenant which he makes with men and which enables the doing of his will (Heb. 13.20f.), and in that he will finally destroy Satan (Rom. 16.20) and is able to preserve men blameless at the Parousia (I Thess. 5.23; cf. II Pet. 3.14). As a development of this, peace describes the removal of estrangement and the new relationship with God secured through the obedience, righteousness and death of Christ for those who respond (Rom. 5). Peace is thus almost synonymous with eternal life, in contrast to the sinful life of the flesh which leads to death (Rom. 8.6–11), is the calling and present possession of Christians, arbitrating in favour of decisions and actions which produce freedom and love (I Cor. 7.15, Col. 3.15), is to be pursued in company with fellow Christians (Heb. 12.14, II Tim. 2.22) and beggars description because it mounts guard over them and preserves them in their inner being until the Parousia (Phil. 4.7).

In Eph. 2.14–17, the law exposes a double estrangement, viz. between God and man and between Jew and Gentile, which is abolished in the Cross by Christ, who both makes peace and is peace (cf. Heb. 7.2 for Melchizedek, king of peace, as a type of Christ), in that he reconciles Jew and Gentile in a single body to God. This is God's act; its intended scope is the restoration of the whole creation to its proper harmonious life in Christ (Col. 1.19–22), its present embodiment is the Church and its mode of life (Col. 1.18). Life in the Church and the calling of peace are coincident (Col. 3.15). In the Church, which is the sphere where the powers of the Kingdom are operative through the Spirit (cf. Gal. 5.22 for peace as a fruit of the Spirit), there is to be a harmony of righteousness and joy because the weaker brother is not grieved by the overriding of his conscience (Rom. 14.15–17). To pursue peace is to build up one another (Rom. 14.19). God is called the God of peace principally where the unity and harmony of the Church is felt to be threatened (Rom. 15.33, 16.20, I Cor. 14.33, II Cor. 13.11, Phil. 4.9, II Thess. 3.16, Heb. 13.20). Peace is that by which the spiritual unity of the corporate life of the Church is to be maintained (Eph. 4.3), to be pursued, along with righteousness, faith and love, as the wholesome condition of the Church in the face of strife engendered by foolish disputes (II Tim. 2.22–3) or the jealousy and faction engendered by worldly wisdom, in contrast to the heavenly wisdom, which is itself peaceable, the seed from which righteousness grows as a fruit being the ministrations of peacemakers (Jas. 3.16–18; cf. Heb. 12.11 for peace as an attribute of righteousness as a fruit). In such passages (cf. Rom. 12.18) peace approximates to love (II Cor. 13.11). Of inward peace of soul (Rom. 15.13). (*V.* also REST, RESTORE, SABBATH, WAR.)

C. F. EVANS

PEACE-OFFERING *v.* SACRIFICE I(*d*)

PENTECOST, FEAST OF: *OT v.* SACRIFICE IV(*a*) and esp. (*c*); *NT v.* SPIRIT V

PERCEIVE

Apart from the ordinary verb for see (*ra'ah*) there are two Heb. verbs underlying 'perceive' in EVV of the OT. These are *bin* (e.g. I Sam.

3.8) and *yada'* (e.g. Isa. 6.9). For the meaning of *bin* see UNDERSTAND; of *yada'* see KNOW. Similarly in NT 'perceive' represents *ginōskō* and its associates. (See KNOW and SEE.)

E. C. B.

PERDITION

This and the word DESTRUCTION are the two renderings in the NT (8 and 5 respectively) for the Gk. *apoleia*. RV has 'perdition' for AV 'destruction' in Phil. 3.19; whilst in II Pet. 3.7 the contrary change is made. The word 'perdition' is not found in the OT, though 'destruction' is common enough, representing as many as 34 different Heb. words. In John 17.12 it is clear that Judas Iscariot is meant by 'the son of perdition', but in II Thess. 2.3 the phrase refers to Antichrist. The other six passages deal with the fate of the wicked in general, including that of Antichrist, and the same applies to the five instances where the word 'destruction' is found.

There is considerable division of opinion concerning the ultimate fate of the wicked. Jesus himself used two figures in the main, one of outer darkness and the other of the ever-burning rubbish heaps in the Valley of Hinnom (Gk. *Gehenna*) outside Jerusalem. The idea of unending torment and punishment is being recognized more and more as being incompatible with the character of God. Equally, it is clear that Jesus envisaged a definite time when the doom of the wicked would be irrevocably fixed; he spoke, for instance, of the door being closed fast with those outside for ever shut out. Whether there is opportunity for repentance beyond the grave or whether all opportunity ceases at death is much disputed. Jesus certainly spoke as though some would be lost, and these passages which speak of 'perdition' and 'destruction' clearly portray an annihilation that is complete and final.

N. H. SNAITH

PERFECT

Our modern use of the word is closely associated with ideas of moral betterment and development. 'Perfect' is vaguely understood to mean the last state in a progression. It is possibly because Luke perceived such a possible connotation in *teleios* (Gk.=full-grown, whole, perfect) that he replaced it with *oiktirmōn*, merciful (Luke 6.36; cf. Matt. 5.48).

In the LXX the word is frequent, usually as a translation of *tamim*. Three typical usages are Deut. 18.13, I Kings 8.61 and 11.4. In these passages *tamim* is used as an expression of the cult, and means whole, or sound, or unblemished, like the sacrificial offering. To be perfect means, therefore, to be whole or sound or true; and to be perfect as the heavenly Father is perfect (Matt. 5.48, the main NT reference) means to be wholly turned, with the whole will and being, to God, as he is turned to us. This is a response of obedience and of effort carried out *in faith*. It is the call to purify our heart and to will one thing. The command falls within a religious situation, not simply a moral situation of improving our conduct by ever more strenuous efforts or the like.

'Perfect' in the Bible, then, does not have a legalistic background. Nor does it have a pietist authority as though perfection could be achieved by some kind of technique of 'imitation' of Jesus. Nor do we find in the Bible any authority for speaking of perfection as the end-state of an ever-increasing goodness spreading through the individual or society. 'Be perfect' is the command of God, springing from his own life, which can strike from our hearts only one response, that of faith. Our obedience in faith is not the beginning of some vague progress on a shadowy moral way, but is the acceptance of grace, which is always whole, complete, perfect; and in the strength of this encounter our life is lived. 'Perfect' is something belonging to God and coming to us by our contact with God, not as a possession but as a gift. All that God has, and is, is perfect: it is never partial or unfulfilled. Our relation to him determines our share in this kind of wholeness. (*V.* also SANCTIFY.)

R. GREGOR SMITH

PERISH

Three uses can be distinguished: (1) Purely physical: destruction in (or from) this world, without any idea of judgment or punishment (II Sam. 1.27, Job 4.11, Matt. 8.32, John 6.27). (2) Much more frequently, however, the destruction (while still purely physical and 'this-worldly') is regarded as the consequence of, or punishment for, wrong-doing. This is the typical OT usage; cf. esp. Deut. 4.26, 8.19f., 11.17, etc. Luke 15.17 ('I perish with hunger') is an interesting NT example. 'Perish' here translates the same Gk. word as that used for the 'lost' sheep and the 'lost' coin (vss. 4,6,8,9), and the 'lost' son himself (24,32). But the son is 'perishing' as the result of his self-will in a sense which can only be very partially applied to the sheep and not at all to the coin. (3) The distinctive NT use: a 'perishing' which affects not only the physical body (Matt. 5.29,30), but a man's whole ego, being, or soul (Matt. 10.28, where 'destroy' renders the same Gk. word). 'Perishing' is the antithesis to 'having eternal life' (John 3.16, 10.28), or 'coming to repentance' (II Pet. 3.9), or 'being saved' (II Cor. 2.15f., II Thess. 2.10). It is unthinkable for those 'who are fallen asleep in

Christ' (I Cor. 15.18). This idea of 'next-worldly' perishing naturally developed along with that of personal survival and immortality. But the physical applications of the usual term (Matt. 5.29f., 9.17=Luke 5.37) suggest the annihilation of the soul rather than its continued punishment in the world to come. (*V.* also DEATH, LIFE, PERDITION.)

J. P. THORNTON-DUESBERY

PERSECUTION *v.* SUFFER

PERVERSE *v.* SIN

PETER *v.* ROCK

PHYSICIAN *v.* HEAL

PIT *v.* HELL

PITY, PITIFUL

The word occurs but once in the AV of the NT (Matt. 18.33) where the RV has 'mercy'. The adj. 'pitiful' is found twice in AV, Jas. 5.11 and I Pet. 3.8, but the RV avoids the word because of the change in its meaning since the 17th cent., having 'full of pity' in one case, and 'tender-hearted' in the other. The word stands generally for that compassion which precludes the strict exercise of merited punishment. The most outstanding instance is Isa. 63.9: 'In his love and in his pity he redeemed them', speaking of God's saving work for Israel in the early days before Canaan. There are about 40 instances altogether; half of them are of that compassion for men, whether of God or of other men, which is altogether commendable; the other half occur in contexts where compassion is deprecated lest sin should be condoned (e.g. Ezek. 5.11, etc., of God; Deut. 7.16, etc., of men).

N. H. S.

PLAGUE *v.* HEAL

PLEAD

Seldom if ever in the sense of earnest appeal or prayer. Practically always in legal sense of maintaining a cause as in a court of law. In RV sometimes 'contend', e.g. Job 13.19; in Moffatt sometimes 'argue', e.g. Hos. 2.2. The basic conception is best seen in Isa. 1.18, though the word is not used there. God *reasons* with men. Religion is *reasonable* intercourse between God and man, an affair therefore of mind and conscience, not of blind ritual and sacrifice. This is the prophetic as against the priestly conception of religion, and it is not surprising that the word occurs almost exclusively in the prophetic books of the OT and in Job.

J. S. M.

POOR, RICH, POSSESSIONS, WEALTH

The Bible does not teach that the possession of wealth is evil in itself, but that cupidity, greed and the desire to become rich are sources of spiritual danger and of social misery. 'The love of money is a root of all kinds of evil' (I Tim. 6.10). Rich men are almost always bad men: so the prophets had discovered. Perhaps the simple eudaemonism of the older Hebrew point of view contributed to this result, for had it not long been taught that the possession of wealth was evidence of the divine favour (e.g. Ps. 1.3f.)? Against such a view the Book of Job protests, and the Psalmists generally are perplexed by the success of the wicked and the misfortune of the godly (e.g. Pss. 37, 49, 73; cf. Job 21.7ff.). Worldly success leads to pride, self-esteem and contempt for the unsuccessful, as well as to lust for even greater riches and power. Thus, in the Pss. the expression 'the poor' has acquired a sort of religious significance, and may often almost be equated with 'the godly' (*Hasidim*)—the humble as contrasted with the arrogant rich, those who trust in God as against those who trust in their material wealth. It is important that we should understand that the words 'poor' and 'rich' have in many contexts a religious and an ethical content rather than an economic one. This meaning is carried over into the NT, and underlies such sayings of Jesus as 'Blessed are ye poor' (Luke 6.20), which Matt. rightly paraphrases as 'poor in spirit' (5.3). Jesus means 'the poor' in the sense in which the term is used as a technical expression in later Jewish literature, as denoting the class of pious, hard-working, humble folk who look to God for redemption and who do not put their trust in political schemes or material prosperity: theirs, says Jesus, is the Kingdom of God. In the situation of Jesus' own day, the 'rich' would be represented by the wealthy Sadducean high-priestly families, a worldly set of men who made a splendid profit out of their control of the Temple; while the 'poor' would be simple, devout folk—whether in the lower priestly classes (like Simeon in Luke 2.25—'righteous and devout, looking for the consolation of Israel') or in the rank and file of the working-class (like the family or the disciples of Jesus themselves). But the distinction between the two classes was religious rather than economic: Joseph of Arimathaea, though a rich man (Matt. 27.57), was 'a good man and a righteous' (Luke 23.50). The publicans, who were Jesus' 'friends', were wealthy men, and Zacchaeus promised to give up only *half* his goods (Luke 19.8)! It was not so much the possession of riches as one's attitude towards them and the use which one makes of them which was the special object of Jesus' teaching; and this is true of the biblical teaching as a whole. Jesus does not condemn private property, nor is he a social reformer in any primary sense; he is concerned with men's motives and hearts: 'Make purses which wax not old, a treasure in heaven which faileth not . . . for where your treasure is, there will your heart be also' (Luke 12.33f.). He did not call the rich man who built larger barns a wicked capitalist but a fool; his folly consisted in thinking that his wealth was a permanent and ultimate source of satisfaction: 'a man's life consisteth not in the abundance of his possessions' (Luke 12.16–21). In the parable of Dives and Lazarus the point of the condemnation of Dives lies not so much in the fact that he was rich as in the fact that he had regarded his riches as his 'good things' (Luke 16.25): it is to be noted that when Lazarus dies he rests in Abraham's bosom (*v.* ABRAHAM)—and Abraham was the very type of the wealthy Jew (cf. Gen. 13.2)! Jesus teaches indifference to possessions: 'Consider the ravens . . .', etc. (Luke 12.22–34); anxiety about food and clothing betrays lack of faith in God: trust in riches is practical atheism. He teaches his disciples to look to God for their daily bread (Luke 11.3). It is because they have such a tempting alternative to trust in God that rich men are in mortal danger. One rich man at least was counselled by Jesus to give away all that he had (Mark 10.17–22); when he refused, Jesus said: 'How hardly shall they that have riches enter into the Kingdom of God' (17.23), but he explains to the amazed disciples that he really means 'those that trust in riches' (17.24). 'Who then can be saved?' ask the disciples. All of us have a defective faith in God; we all trust in our 'riches', whatever they may be, to some extent. No one can be saved by human effort, however rich or poor he may be, says Jesus, in effect; but happily things which are impossible with men are possible with God (17.27). Jesus repeats the usual Jewish emphasis on the value of ALMSGIVING (Luke 12.33), an activity which presupposes the institution of private property; and again he stresses the factor of motive as being of greater importance than the sum involved (Matt. 6.2–4, Luke 21.1–4). The NT bears plenty of evidence that the apostolic church possessed at least some well-to-do members, and was willing to accept their gifts and their hospitality and support. The use of the word 'communism' in connexion with the spontaneous and voluntary act of sharing in the early Jerusalem church is highly misleading, in view of the modern associations of that word (Acts 2.44f., 4.34–7); the experiment does not seem to have been copied elsewhere, and some scholars have held it to have been in part responsible for that state of economic distress which necessitated Paul's collections from his Gentile churches. More significant is Jesus' own poverty and renunciation of worldly goods; he and his disciples used a common purse and were supported by the voluntary offerings of a wider circle of disciples and well-wishers. It is Jesus himself who embodies the biblical ideal of 'the poor man' who trusts only in God, and herein lies the real theological significance of his poverty: 'Ye know the grace of our Lord Jesus Christ, that, though he was rich, yet for your sakes he became poor, that ye through his poverty might become rich' (II Cor. 8.9; cf. 6.10).

ALAN RICHARDSON

POSSESSIONS *v.* POOR

POWER(S) *v.* AUTHORITY, MIGHT, MIRACLE

PRAYER

Etymology. Owing to lack of fixity in their usage, there is comparatively little to be gained from a study of the etymology of the dozen Heb. and Gk. words used to denote aspects of prayer. See article on Prayer in *HDB.*

Attitudes of Prayer. In OT commonly *standing*, and see also Mark 11.25, Luke 18.11,13. *Kneeling* is common in OT and NT, e.g. Ps. 95.6, Acts 21.5. In abasement or emotion, the worshipper might bow from the kneeling posture until the forehead touched the ground, thereby *'falling on his face'*, e.g. Josh. 5.14, Mark 14.35. The hands might be spread forth, Isa. 1.15; or lifted up, I Tim. 2.8.

I. PRAYER IN OT

In its most primitive forms prayer is akin to magic and charming. The worshipper seeks to gain his ends by enlisting or even compelling the aid of supernatural powers by the utterance of their magical sacred names. Traces of this may be found in the early parts of the OT especially where importance is attached to 'calling on the name of the Lord' (Gen. 4.26, 12.8, 13.4, II Kings 5.11). But these are mere traces. Prayer in the OT is far removed from magic. It involves personal dealing with a personal God. This is so much the case that the prayers of such men as Abraham and Moses are represented as conversations or even arguments between man and God (e.g. Gen. 18.23ff., Exod. 32.7ff.).

The patriarchs exercise also a ministry of *intercession.* By virtue of their covenant relationship to God, their prayers find special favour in his sight. Therefore their intercessions are sought by those outside the covenant relationship (e.g. Abimelech in Gen. 20.7). This intercessory function is further developed by the prophets. The underlying conception is that the prophet possesses the spirit of God and is therefore specially fitted to be a channel of communication between God and man. As God speaks to man, through the Spirit, by the prophet, so man may speak to God, by the Spirit, through the prophet, who thus becomes an intercessor both for the individual and for the nation (I Kings 13.6, I Sam. 12.19, Jer. 14, 15). This intercessory function, however, is not altogether restricted to the prophets. Kings may pray for their people (II Chron. 32.20), and righteous men for unrighteous friends (Job 42.8). Intercession benefits those who offer it (Job 42.10), and refusal to intercede is a sin against God (I Sam. 12.23).

The Exile is a landmark in OT prayer. The sacrificial worship of the Temple being suspended, prayer became the sole effective means of worship. The Jew became noted among his neighbours as a man of prayer (Dan. 6). Compare the prominence of prayer in Nehemiah and Ezra. Nehemiah opens his book with prayer for the nation and closes it with prayer for himself. Note also Neh. 2.4, 4.4,9, and Ezra 8.21. Another Exilic passage, Isa. 56.7, describes the future Temple as not only a place of sacrifice, but a house of prayer for all nations.

Between the Exile and the Maccabaean period the PSALMS were collected for use in the Temple liturgy. They abound in prayers of all types and of various spiritual quality. As the hope of immortality developed late among the Hebrews, the average Jew expected to see the goodness of the Lord in the land of the living, and his prayers tended to be for temporal rather than spiritual blessings. This is reflected in the Psalms. But although (with one doubtful exception) they have no outlook beyond this earthly life, not a few rise beyond all thought of material blessing to a spiritual longing for God for his own sake (e.g. Pss. 42,51, 63,119) and can be uttered without alien feeling by Christian lips. It should be noted that with few exceptions the Psalms represent corporate rather than individual worship.

The SYNAGOGUE played a vital part in fostering prayer in the hearts and homes of the people. At first its function was probably only instruction in the Law; but gradually prayer was added to instruction, and the synagogue became a place of worship, with prayer as a substitute for the sacrifices of Temple worship. By the influence of the local synagogues prayer began to permeate the daily life of the people. Every Jew (ideally at any rate) prayed thrice daily (Ps. 55.17, Dan. 6.10). There were family prayers at the beginning and ending of the Sabbath, before and after meat, at the Passover, and a general custom of invoking God's name before any special task or enjoyment. By Christ's time the life of the people was thus pervaded with the atmosphere of prayer—but how far vital, and how far merely formal, it would be hard to decide.

II. PRAYER IN APOCRYPHA

The Apocryphal books reflect the post-Exilic emphasis on prayer, together with one or two interesting developments and some significant links with the NT. Thus, PRAYER FOR THE DEAD is found in II Macc. 12.44, a conception impossible in the OT, where the dead are regarded as beyond the care and interest of God, and past praying for. PRAYER BY THE DEAD FOR THE LIVING is suggested in II Macc. 15.12ff.; but its value is denied in II Esd. 7.45. Connections with the NT may be traced in the following examples: Matt. 6.7—Ecclus. 7.14; Matt. 6.14—Ecclus. 28.2–4.

III. PRAYER IN NT

THE LORD'S PRAYER must take first place in discussion of NT prayer as the model given by our Lord in response to the request by the disciples for instruction in the art of prayer. In its actual phrasing there is perhaps little that is original: Klausner in his *Jesus of Nazareth* quotes plausible parallels in various Jewish sources for most of the petitions. The originality lies rather in their choice and arrangement. As regards choice, only one petition refers to a material blessing; it takes a subordinate place, and is not for merely private and individual benefit. As regards order, it is remarkable that prayers for God's Glory and Kingdom precede all other requests. The meaning is plainly that all requests must be subordinated to the eternal purpose of God to establish his Kingdom among men (see also Matt. 6.33).

It should be noted that the instruction which, according to the Fourth Gospel, was given by Jesus that all prayers were to be offered in his name (John 14.13, 15.16, 16.23f.) is already implicit in the Lord's Prayer. For, as we have just seen, all requests are subordinated to the request for the coming of God's Kingdom. Now, the life, death and resurrection of Jesus Christ are the sole means to the realization of that Kingdom. It is therefore through him alone that man's will is brought into line with the divine purpose. To pray with true understanding for the coming of God's Kingdom is therefore inevitably to pray 'through Christ' and 'in his name'. To add such a phrase at the end of the Lord's Prayer would therefore be tautologous. One further remarkable feature of the Lord's Prayer should be noted: it is universal, not Jewish. Its phraseology may be drawn from Jewish sources, yet the prayer is at home on the lips of men of any age or race.

THE PARABLES ON PRAYER: Luke 18.9–14 forbids profession of ritual holiness in prayer as a piece of spiritual unreality, i.e. hypocrisy. In the publican's prayer, note, in addition to its spiritual reality, its brevity; and compare Matt. 6.5–7 where 'vain repetition' is forbidden, i.e. unthinking repetition of formal prayers as if the mere repetition had magical efficacy. On the contrary, prayer must be an act of personal communion with God, and therefore requires mental concentration and the shutting out of all distractions (Matt. 6.6; and cf. Mark 1.35, etc.). Luke 18.1–8 and 11.5–10 teach importunity in prayer, not because God is unwilling, but because 'faith needs to find some resistance before it can be called out in any strength'. (Cf. Christ's treatment of the Syrophenician woman in Matt. 15.22–8. The need for UNQUESTIONING FAITH in prayer is stressed in Mark 11.24 and Luke 17.6. But these strong statements should be read in the light of John 15.7,16. Answer is certain if the prayer is in the name and spirit of Christ and thus in line with God's will (see also I John 5.14).

INTERCESSION: The warrant for this is found not only in the example and teaching of the Master (Luke 6.28, 22.32, 23.34, John 17.9–26, etc.), but also in the Lord's Prayer itself which, being cast in the first person plural, is necessarily an act of intercession throughout. In the Pauline epistles the duty of intercession for the Christian brotherhood is stressed. Not only does Paul constantly pray for his converts, but he begs them to intercede for him (Rom. 15.30, II Thess. 3.1, etc.). He does not stress intercession for the heathen (cf. John 17.9), but this is really implicit in his prayers for the success of the Gospel. The doctrine of THE HEAVENLY INTERCESSION OF CHRIST is developed most fully in the Epistle to the Hebrews, where it is shown that, although his act of propitiation was completed once for all on the Cross and needs no repetition, his very presence at the right hand of God is an eternal act of intercession on man's behalf (cf. Rom. 8.34, I John 2.1). The doctrine of THE INTERCESSION OF THE DEAD FOR THE LIVING, and the practice of the INTERCESSION OF THE LIVING FOR THE DEAD, are not found in the NT, unless the pious wish in II Tim. 1.18 be taken as an example of the latter.

THE INTERCESSION OF THE HOLY SPIRIT: The chief passage is Rom. 8.26f. We saw that the prayers of the prophets had special power because they were spirit-filled men. Now all Christians have the same spirit, and so may pray with the same power. The indwelling spirit is distinct from man's spirit, yet in so intimate a relationship with it that he is able to interpret even its most inarticulate longings to God. The difficulty of shaping the prayers of the sinful human mind into a form acceptable to God is suggested by the unutterable groanings of the spirit. The necessity of this work of intercession is to be found in human ignorance. While we know in a general way that God's will for us is the perfecting of our salvation, we are ignorant of what this may involve in daily living, so that we might easily pray contrary to God's will. The Spirit, however, knows not only our mind but also the mind of God, and is therefore able to frame our prayers in accordance with the divine purpose. Thus, every human prayer offered with right intention is supported by a double intercession—that of the indwelling Spirit, and that of the glorified Christ. But the NT does not seem to suggest that either of these ministries of intercession is available save to believing Christians.

BIBLIOGRAPHY

While much has been written on prayer in general, the literature on biblical prayer is scanty. For the most part the student must search commentaries and books of biblical theology for himself. The best book on the whole subject is probably still *The Prayers of the Bible*, by J. E. McFadyen, London (1906).

For special aspects of the subject see: R. M. Woolley: *The Liturgy of the Primitive Church*, Cambridge (1910). A. J. Tait: *The Heavenly Session of Our Lord*, London (1912). W. Milligan: *The Ascension and Heavenly Priesthood of Our Lord*, London (1901). H. B. Swete: *The Holy Spirit in the New Testament*, London (1909). J. H. Srawley: *Early History of the Liturgy*, Ch. I, Cambridge (1947). Old, but still quite useful, is J. Buchanan: *The Holy Spirit*, Part 3, Ch. 3, Edinburgh (1856). A popular treatment of Pauline prayer is W. H. G. Thomas's *The Prayers of St. Paul*, Edinburgh (1914).

See also articles on Prayer and Intercession in *HDB* amd *ERE*.

J. S. MCEWEN

PREACH, TEACH

We hear little of preaching in the OT (Jonah preached to Nineveh, Jonah 3.2), though we come across the idea of proclaiming good tidings; the most significant ref. is Isa. 61.1. For this OT usage, *v.* under GOSPEL.

In the NT we find three words used: *euangelizesthai*, to preach good tidings (*v.* under GOSPEL), *katangellein*, to declare, announce, and *kērussein*, to proclaim as a herald. The fundamental idea of these words is the telling of news to people who had not heard it before —'evangelization'. In the NT preaching has nothing to do with the delivery of sermons to the converted, which is what it usually means to-day, but always concerns the proclamation of the 'good tidings of God' to the non-Christian world. As such, it is to be distinguished from TEACHING (Gk. *didachē*), which in the NT normally means ethical instruction, or occasionally apologetics or instruction in the faith (*v*. C. H. Dodd, *The Apostolic Preaching*, pp. 3–6). When the preachers (originally the Apostles, later the accredited evangelists) had attracted 'hearers' by their proclamation in the market-place of the gospel of the cross and resurrection, they handed them over to the accredited 'teachers' for further instruction in the faith and for preparation for baptism. Evangelists and teachers seem to have been distinct 'ministries' in the early church (Eph. 4.11, and *v*. MINISTER).

This distinction between preaching and teaching is found within the ministry of Jesus himself. (For the content of his preaching, *v*. under GOSPEL.) Jesus preached (i.e. proclaimed the Kingdom of God: John the Baptist had likewise 'heralded' the Kingdom of God, Matt. 3.1, though his proclamation was rather a warning of judgment than 'good news'); and he taught (note the distinction which occurs twice in Matt.: 4.23, 9.35). The instruction which he gave to his disciples in, for example, the Sermon on the Mount, is *didachē* (teaching) rather than preaching.

The apostolic church possessed a definite *kērugma* (lit. 'thing preached', 'proclamation', from *kērussein*). This *kērugma* underlies every book in the NT; it is the apostolic gospel. It is the Church's saving proclamation, even though it seems foolish in the eyes of the world: 'it was God's good pleasure through the foolishness of the thing preached [RV marg.] to save them that believe' (I Cor. 1.21). This *kērugma* may be summed up in a word as the message of the cross and resurrection of Jesus Christ. The earliest Christian preachers went out to the world with this *kērugma*, not with a *didachē*: Christian ethics follows, and is built upon the essential Christian message of what God has done in Jesus Christ. The Gospel-tradition of the teaching of Jesus was built up during the oral period of its formation in the decades in which the preachers were proclaiming the unchanging *kērugma*, which was and is the foundation on which the Church stands. C. H. Dodd, in his important book *The Apostolic Preaching*, has shown how the content of the earliest Christian proclamation can be reliably discovered in the recorded sermons of St. Peter in the early chapters of Acts. He thus sums up the content of the *kērugma* in these speeches: (i) the age of fulfilment has dawned—the 'latter days' foretold by the prophets (cf. Acts 2.16, 3.18,24); (ii) this has taken place through the life, death and resurrection of Jesus: the evidences of his Messiahship are recounted, great emphasis being laid on the fulfilment of scriptural prophecy; (iii) by virtue of the resurrection Jesus has been exalted at the right hand of God, as Messianic head of the new Israel (Acts 2.33–6, 3.13, 4.11): scriptural proofs are again recited; (iv) the Holy Spirit in the Church is the sign of Christ's present power and glory (Acts 2.33, 17–21; cf. Joel 2.28–32, Acts 5.32); (v) the Messianic Age will shortly reach its consummation in the return of Christ (Acts 3.21); and, lastly, (vi) the *kērugma* always closes with an appeal for repentance, the offer of forgiveness and the gift of the Holy Spirit, and with the promise of salvation. This fundamental preaching, as Dr. Dodd shows, underlies the whole of the NT. (*V*. also GOSPEL, MINISTER.)

ALAN RICHARDSON

PREDESTINATE *v*. DETERMINATE

PRESENCE, SANCTUARY, FACE, COUNTENANCE, ARK, CLOUD, GLORY (SHEKINAH)

PRESENCE

A lively sense of the presence of God on earth runs through the OT from beginning to end, and is continued in the NT, where it is strengthened and enriched by the Incarnation. There is a rich variety in the forms of expression, but it is mostly couched in simple, anthropomorphic terms; and it is this directness and simplicity that has helped, almost more than anything else, to keep the experience of God's presence real and vivid. It has been rightly said that 'Unprejudiced appraisal of Old Testament anthropomorphism leads to the recognition that the basis of the Old Testament's faith in God is not God's spirithood, but his full and living personality, or his personal vitality, which is conceived, involuntarily, as human' (Eichrodt, *Theologie des Alten Testaments*, i. 105). This is not to deny that the Israelites also recognized a supra-mundane dwelling-place of God, nor that there were times of crisis when it seemed that God had withdrawn himself from amongst his people. The Exile in Babylon was chief of such crises and became the occasion of spiritual despair in at least two directions. First, there was despair in some quarters because the fall of Jerusalem deprived the Jewish people of the Temple, the focal point of worship, the dwelling-place of God on earth. God no longer had a habitation on earth. It was Ezekiel who combated this by recounting his experience of the glory of God in Babylon (see GLORY below); God had removed *with* his people. In the second place, there developed a strong tradition that, though the Temple was rebuilt (516 BC) and worship restored, God never again took up his residence in the Temple. The second temple was said to lack five things of which one was the *shekinah* (see below). (The other four are: the Fire from Heaven, the Ark, the Urim and Thummim, and the Holy Spirit. This is based on Rabbinic exegesis of Hag. 1.8.) This may well have been the *theory* of God's presence, but it cannot be said to be in accord with religious thought and practice of post-Exilic days. 'Even after the destruction of the Temple, it was maintained by Eleazar ben Pedat that God's Presence still abode on the ruined site in accordance with his promise, "My eyes and my mind will be there perpetually" (I Kings 9.3)' (G. F. Moore, *Judaism.* i. 369). 'If two sit together and words of the Law [are spoken] between them, the Divine Presence rests between them' (*Pirke Aboth,* iii. 2). Jesus ben Sira could scarcely have written such a generous eulogy on his contemporary the High Priest Simon (Ecclus. 50) if the worship in which Simon engaged had not sometimes achieved the communion with God towards which it was directed. Perhaps the best and richest testimony to the continued presence of God is Ps. 22.3: 'Thou that art enthroned upon the praises of Israel.'

The belief, then, was that wherever God's ultimate dwelling might be he could be found on earth and dwelling amongst men. For the ancient Hebrew there was no problem as to what form God took to appear on earth. Man was made in God's image as a son is born in the image of his father (cp. Gen. 1.27 with 5.3). God was thought of in human terms without question. He came down to visit the pair in the garden, to see the gigantic tower men were building or to defeat the Egyptians at the Red Sea. Being thus conceived, he was spoken of as having a bodily presence and bodily parts. At no place do we, or ought we to expect to, find a detailed verbal portrait. Such features, limbs or organs were spoken of as were necessary to describe experiences of God which came to men through the senses of sight, hearing and (but very rarely) touch. Moses was allowed to see God and the story speaks of God's FACE, but later thought so revolted from the simple anthropomorphism that, though he was not entirely deprived of the privilege of vision of God, he was made to see only the 'back parts' of God's retreating figure (Exod. 33.17–23). Moses was also accredited with speaking to God face to face (Exod. 33.11). It is this idea of God's physical presence that underlies the old phrase used in connexion with attendance at the sanctuary to worship: 'to come and see the face of God'. It was, indeed, this very fact of God's presence at the spot which constituted a sanctuary.

SANCTUARY

Places became holy or sacred by virtue of God's presence, and were resorted to as places of worship or of asylum. They became *sanctuaries.* The prophetical narratives of the Pentateuch (J and E) were interested in associating a theophany with each of the traditional sanctuaries in Canaan (Shechem, Gen. 12.6,7; Beersheba, Gen. 21.33; Bethel, Gen. 28.10ff.; Peniel, Gen. 32.24ff.). Many of the sanctuaries in use in ancient Israel were probably taken over from the Canaanites and were adapted for the worship of Yahweh in this way. The strength of holiness at a sanctuary may be seen in the story of Moses at the place of the burning bush. Horeb, or Sinai, where it is said to have taken place, was probably a long-established sanctuary. Hills and mountains were favourite places among the Semites for sanctuaries (see Robertson Smith, *Religion of the Semites*). It has, indeed, been suggested that the name Sinai may be connected with that of the moon god, Sin. In any case, the bush (Heb. *seneh*) incident was almost certainly associated with it through the partial play on the name. When Moses approached he heard the command: 'Put off thy shoes from off thy feet, for the place whereon thou standest is holy ground' (Exod. 3.5). With so strong a sense of the presence of God in a *place*, it was inevitable that worship should be localized—eventually in one central sanctuary (as demanded by the Deuteronomic code)—until such time as the presence of God, spiritually conceived, could be entirely divorced from an earthly dwelling (John 4.23). The Deuteronomic writer's definition of the sanctuary is the place which God chose out of all the tribes to 'put his name there' or 'to cause his name to dwell there'. There is still insistence on the immediate presence of God, as also in the fragment of verse ascribed to Solomon at the dedication of the Temple: 'The Lord hath said that he would dwell in the thick darkness. I have surely built thee an house of habitation, a place for thee to dwell in for ever' (I Kings 8.12f.).

FACE

Men went to the sanctuary to 'see God's face' and thus to have some kind of 'audience', as we would say, with him. Ultimately the phrase was almost uniformly converted into the less anthropomorphic form 'to appear before God', whereby nothing of the sense of coming into God's very presence has necessarily been lost, but the impropriety of speaking so simply of God's face was shed. One result of this anthropomorphism is that the Hebrew word *face* is very frequently used in speaking of God's relation to men, but mostly in a prepositional use (in front of, before, over against). There are three places, however, where it is used as a strong personal pronoun and conveys the idea of God himself in person (Exod. 33.14, Deut. 4.37, Isa. 63.9, in the LXX, 'it was no messenger or angel, but he himself saved them'). Clearly the idea of bodily presence clings to it, and the usage is consonant with Hebrew psychology which permitted the Hebrew to speak of the whole man in terms of the part of the body involved in, or affected by, the activity at the time of speaking. Our EVV employ the word presence in a number of instances where *face* is used prepositionally in the Hebrew, but it should be borne in mind that the word 'presence' in this connexion does not, or should not, imply any sort of *representation* of God, God himself is present, *in person.* Such anthropomorphism gave rise to several expressions which have come into metaphorical use and are still charged with deep spiritual meaning. The priestly benediction calls upon God to 'make his face shine upon thee' and to 'lift up his countenance upon thee' (Num. 6.25f.). The shining of the face is a mark of joy and favour (Ps. 31.16), and the directing of the face implies the concentration of the whole will upon an object. If God were to 'hide his face' it would mean withdrawal of his favour (Pss. 27.9, 102.2, etc.) and of his creative power (Ps. 104.29). True worshippers 'seek' Yahweh's face (Ps. 24.6, 27.8). As with 'face' so also, but less frequently, with other parts of the body: eyes, mouth, arms, hands, right hand, voice, were all ascribed to God as experience and articulation of it demanded.

In course of time such simple anthropomorphism became inadequate to represent the full power and transcendence of God and the Hebrews were constrained to devise, probably without conscious endeavour at first, some means of speaking of God's earthly presence whilst safeguarding his majesty and his omnipotence. Even a cursory reading of the OT will reveal that, however much the Hebrews 'represented' God's presence, they never really lost the sense of God's own personal presence on earth. Whilst writing of the angel of Yahweh, a writer could drop the figure of the angel and leave Yahweh as the central actor.

ARK

One of the earliest ways in which the presence of God was represented was that of the *Ark.* In origin it seems to have been a portable shrine such as the primitive camel-Bedouin tribes used when campaigning in order to carry their god into battle with them. In the course of its use in Israel it must have suffered modification, for it seems to have been capable of at least two functions, that of a receptacle for the sacred stones and that of a throne for God himself. The ark belongs essentially to the crisis-period of Israel's history and religion, the stage in which God was still a storm-and-battle God, a God of crisis. 'And it came to pass, when the ark set forward, that Moses said, Rise up, O Yahweh, and let thine enemies be scattered; and let them that hate thee flee before thee. And when it rested, he said, Return, O Yahweh, unto the ten thousands of the thousands of Israel' (Num. 10.35f.). During the Philistine wars its habitual home was the sanctuary at Shiloh, and thence it was taken into battle. Its loss was grievous, and the only name that came to mind for a new-born child was Ichabod, 'the glory is departed' (I Sam. 4). The story of its ultimate removal to Jerusalem shows the strength of the belief in God's presence and power in it. When Uzzah touched it he defiled its holiness and was punished by death. Its very removal to Jerusalem and ultimately to the new Temple shows that the Temple could not have become the dwelling-place of God if the sacred ark bearing his presence had not been brought within it. Later on, when it had fulfilled its function as a palladium, and when other conceptions of the manner of God's presence had gained currency, it was housed in the sanctuary and used as a safe place of deposit for the tables of the Law. It thus became a national treasure embodying the history of the nation in its pristine, nomadic days. The presence of God was still closely linked with the restored ark in the second Temple, and the Priestly tradition was that the Voice of God spoke to Moses from the Mercy-seat that was upon the ark of the testimony (Num. 7.89). It furnished the Holy of Holies into which the High Priest entered once a year only and then with the utmost precaution, enveloped in a cloud of incense to veil the brightness of God's glory (Lev. 16.12).

CLOUD

So strongly did the ark mediate the presence of Yahweh that one of the early narratives (E) represents it as the effective guide of the Israelites through the wilderness (Num. 10.33; cf. Josh. 3.3f.). How, then, did the other historians represent Yahweh's presence in the desert? The J narrative records the pillar of smoke by day and of fire by night which guided the Israelites to Sinai (Exod. 13.21f.). This is clearly dependent on the tradition that Sinai was once volcanic. After the Israelites had thus been guided to the sacred mount and had joined Yahweh there, they would naturally expect him to accompany them into Canaan (Exod. 33.1,3); but there seems to have been some hesitation about this in J's mind, and he finally records that Hobab was asked to guide the Israelites (Num. 10.29–32). His acceptance of the task is not recorded, having probably been displaced in favour of material from another source.

The Elohist has woven two, if not three, different conceptions into his story. First, there is the belief that Yahweh himself in his own person (face) led his people (Exod. 23.14f.); in the second place, there is the angel who was Yahweh's personal representative (Exod. 33.20, 32.34; cf. 14.19) and who bore Yahweh's name (Exod. 23.21). Finally, Yahweh came down in the pillar of cloud and went inside the tent of meeting to talk with Moses face to face while the cloud remained at the door. The people recognize the cloud as the visible sign of God's presence (Exod. 33.7–11). The cloud thus came to be both a symbol of God's presence and a veil to hide the brilliance and strength of it.

GLORY

The Priestly writer seems to have taken over the conception of the *glory of Yahweh* from Ezekiel. The glory was veiled from human sight, except on the rarest occasions, by the cloud. The cloud, which was over the tent and not at the door of it, was the visible sign of Yahweh's presence; but the presence itself was veiled by it. The 'glory of God' is, in effect, the term used to express that which men can *apprehend*, originally by sight, of the presence of God on earth. It was Ezekiel who first used it and described by it the brilliant appearance of God when he came to renew the prophet's call to prophesy amongst the exiles in Babylon after the fall of Jerusalem. It was a second inaugural vision (the first was experienced on Palestinian soil) in which Ezekiel saw God. In describing what he saw in detail, when he comes to the divine majesty seated on the throne he says: 'This was the appearance of the likeness of the glory of God' (Ezek. 1.28). Later we are told that Ezekiel saw the glory of God move out of the Temple eastward to the Mount of Olives, presumably on the way to Babylon where his people were exiled (Ezek. 11.23). *Glory* (Heb. *Kabod*) seems to have been a peculiarly happy word to choose, not only for its Hebrew antecedents, but for the way in which its equivalent in translations could readily take over the new Hebrew content. Its primary meaning is that of weight and substance. A man of wealth is a man of substance, of *kabod*. His external appearance and bearing would, in nine cases out of ten, reflect his wealth, and also be called *kabod*. His wealth and dignity demanded and compelled respect and honour from his fellows, and this too was called glory or honour (*kabod*). Hence weight, substance, wealth, dignity, noble bearing and honour all contributed to its meaning. To these fundamental meanings Ezekiel added that of brightness, the dominant element in the chariot vision. As already noted, the word and idea were taken up by the Priestly writer (Ezekiel himself was a priest) to whom we owe the description of it as 'like devouring fire on the top of the mount in the eyes of the children of Israel' (Exod. 24.17). In P the idea is used in two ways. First, the appearance of the glory established the fact of Yahweh's presence on the mount and later in the sanctuary (Exod. 24.16f., 29.43, 40.34f.); and, second, it vindicated the rights of Moses and Aaron when the people murmured against them (Exod. 16.10, Num. 14.10, 16.19,42, 20.6). To God's enemies it was an ominous appearance, verily a *devouring* fire. Outside Ezekiel and P it is found in Zechariah (2.5), Isaiah (24.23, 59.19, 60.1f., all late passages) and Psalms (97.6, 102.16). In the non-priestly passages there is a notable reorientation. The glory is no longer conceived as an actualized or potential experience in this life but as an element in the messianic age.

This new direction of thought came to stay, and glory slowly became eschatological, so that in the NT we find it as an integral part of the life of the Kingdom of God, both realized now and expected in the future. The actual and the eschatological elements come together with dynamic certainty in the person of Jesus Christ. The *doxa* (glory) of God, who dwells in light unapproachable (I Tim. 6.16), shone about the shepherds when Christ's birth was announced. On earth the glory of God was made known in him, and men apprehended through him the presence of God. At death he was 'glorified' and sat down at the right hand of God, thus pioneering in a path that men of faith might tread after him and through him share in the glory of God. Henceforth vision of Christ came in the same form as did formerly the vision of God (Acts 22.6,7): the glory of Christ is identifiable with the glory of God. It is in the face of Christ that the light of the knowledge of the glory of God shines in our hearts with creative power (II Cor. 4.6).

Throughout the NT Christ is presented as the glory of God made visible on earth to those whose eyes are opened to see it; but it is perhaps in the Fourth Gospel that this conception is most strongly stressed. Behind the Johannine *doxa* (Gk., glory) we must recollect the full biblical richness of the word, as we have described it above. 'We beheld his *doxa*, glory as of the only-begotten from the Father' (John 1.14). The miracles of Christ manifested his *doxa* (2.11). His *doxa* is not the glory of men but of God (5.41, 17.5,22). The great high-priestly prayer of Jesus (John 17) is dominated by the idea of *doxa*, and the entire Passion of Jesus is presented to us as his 'glorification' (17.1): he goes to the cross not as a helpless martyr to his agony, but as a victorious king to his crowning. In the Passion and Resurrection of Christ the utter glory of God is revealed.

SHEKINAH

Much of what has been said of glory is true also of the rabbinical term *shekinah*. Underlying the use of the term 'glory' is the belief in Yahweh's personal presence on earth. He dwelt among men or caused his name to dwell in the Temple. The Hebrew root for dwell is *sh-k-n*, from which the post-biblical word *shekinah* is derived. The use of the term naturally carries with it the idea of God's presence among men. 'A heathen asked R. Joshua b. Karha: Why did God speak to Moses from the thorn bush? R. Joshua replied: If he had spoken from a carob tree or from a sycamore, you would have asked me the same question. But so as not to dismiss you without an answer, God spoke from the thorn bush to teach you that there is no place where the Shekinah is not, not even a thorn bush' (quoted in Montefiore and Loewe, *Rabbinic Anthology* (1938), p. 13). Those who live a devout life are worthy to see the face of the shekinah; but there are four classes of men who do not see it—mockers, hypocrites, slanderers, liars. The phraseology sometimes suggests that it is thought of as something distinct and distinguishable from God: 'I have caused my shekinah to descend because of Israel.' Alongside the dominant idea of presence there remains also that of brightness. It is explained that the brightness on Moses' face as he descended the mount was because he had shared in the brightness of the glory of the shekinah whilst on the mount. Its light is said to be more intense than that of the midsummer sun. But although in these ways it continued to express the apprehended presence of God, like the term glory, it was also used as a circumlocution for God himself; it was simply a reverent equivalent for God, and is frequently so used in Rabbinic literature. (*V.* also TRANSFIGURE. See A. M. Ramsey, *Glory of God and Transfiguration of Christ*, London, 1949.)

L. H. BROCKINGTON

PRIDE, BOAST, MEEK, LOWLY, HUMBLE

A distinctive feature of biblical religion is its teaching about pride and its converse, humility; this is unparalleled in other religions and ethical systems. According to the Bible (and to the classical Christian moral teaching), pride is the very root and essence of sin. Sinfulness consists essentially in the rebellious pride which attributes to self the honour and glory that are due to God. Pride was the sin of Adam (*q.v.*); and throughout the OT the condemnation of the proud and the commendation of the lowly (esp. in Pss. and Wisdom lit.) form a remarkable anticipation of the revelation in Christ. Boasting, and the pride which trusts in oneself or in any human prince or army, are constantly contrasted with the true humility which trusts in God alone (e.g. Pss. 118.8f., 146.3f.); the proper attitude for man in the presence of the Lord is self-abasement and trustfulness (e.g. Ps. 123, 131). In the NT the lowliness of the incarnate Son of God is fittingly anticipated in Mary's Song (Luke 1.46ff.); indeed, the Magnificat may be said to sum up the biblical teaching in general. Christ agrees with John the Baptist in condemning p. of race (Luke 3.8, Matt. 8.10–12, Luke 10.33, etc.). He likewise condemns the p. of the Pharisees—spiritual p. which resulted in ostentation (Matt. 6.5, 23.5, Luke 18.9ff.)—and all forms of social pride (Matt. 23.6f., Luke 14.7ff.). He enjoined upon his followers the humility of children, and bade them refuse all titles of honour (Matt. 23.8,10) and positions of privilege (Mark 10.35–45). The washing of his disciples' feet was the perfect symbol of his life of lowliness (John 13). It was indeed even more by his life and deeds than by his words that he introduced a new virtue—Christian humility—into the world. St. Paul perceived the theological significance of the lowliness of the Son of God in his incarnation: he who was in the form of God emptied himself and humbled himself (Phil. 2.6–8): he who was rich became poor for our sake (II Cor. 8.9, 13.4). The wonder of the divine humility, revealed in the manger at Bethlehem, in the life of a working man in Nazareth and on the cross on Golgotha, has led men in every succeeding age to 'pour contempt on all my pride'. Paul, the converted Pharisee, constantly warns us against spiritual p. (e.g. I Cor. 4.6ff.); neither Jew nor Gentile has grounds for boasting (Rom. 2 and 3). The Christian may boast of one thing and one thing only—the cross of Jesus Christ: for the rest, he will be content simply to 'glory' in his weaknesses, out of which through the power of Christ he is made strong (cf. II Cor. 11–13).

BIBLIOGRAPHY

R. Niebuhr: *Nature and Destiny of Man*, I, Chap. vii.

ALAN RICHARDSON

PRIEST *v.* SACRIFICE III

PRINCIPALITY *v.* MIGHT

PRISON (I Pet. 3.19) *v.* DESCEND

PROBATION *v.* SUFFER

PROFANE *v.* UNCLEAN

PROMISE

Of the various assurances given in the OT to individuals or to the community of Israel in the name of God, there are some which have been interpreted by the NT as having been fulfilled by Christ. These are those which the NT esteems to be of high apologetic importance for the presentation of its teaching, and comprise the promises recorded in the OT as made to David; to the houses of Israel and Judah concerning a New Covenant; in regard to the outpouring of the Spirit of God upon all flesh; and, in particular, to Abraham. The principle of the interpretation of these assurances from the point of view of the NT writers is quite plainly stated by St. Paul in II Cor. 1.20, where he says: 'For how many soever be the promises of God, in him [i.e. in Christ] is the yea.'

St. Peter in his speech at Pentecost (Acts 2.30) bases upon David's knowledge of the promise which God had made to him—namely that 'of the fruit of his loins he [God] would set one upon his throne' (Ps. 132.11; cf. I Kings 8.25, 9.5, 11.36)—the belief that David in Ps. 16.8–11 speaks with foreknowledge of the resurrection of the Messiah, who was to be of his line. St. Paul also (Acts 13.23; cf. Luke 1.32) speaks of God as having 'according to promise' raised from David's seed a Saviour, Jesus (cf. also Acts 13.35f.). The manifestations at Pentecost which are mentioned in Acts 2 are explained by St. Peter as the fulfilment of the prophecy of Joel (2.28–32). The Apostle affirms that such as repent and are baptized in the name of Jesus will receive the gift of the Holy Spirit. St. Peter further (Acts 2.39) characterizes this gift as 'the promise' made to his hearers and to their children and to as many as God shall call. The same description, viz. 'the Holy Spirit of promise', appears in Eph. 1.13 together with the additional observation that the Spirit is 'an earnest of our inheritance' (vs. 14), which means that the Spirit is a pledge or guarantee of the heavenly benefits of salvation which have yet to be bestowed in the future (cf. II Cor. 1.22, 5.5), or, in other words, that the Spirit which Christians have now been given is 'the firstfruits' (Rom. 8.23) of the age to come. In regard to the promise of the Spirit, the nature of its content, the question of who receives it and of the conditions of receiving, these are made sufficiently clear in the passages to which reference has been made. 'The promise of the Spirit' is, according to St. Paul (Gal. 3.14), 'through faith' and not by the works of the law (Gal. 3.5). In the early Church the Holy Spirit was generally conceived as being communicated to the believer at baptism (*v.* W. Bousset in his Commentary on Galatians, p. 52, and on I Corinthians, pp. 171–2, in *Die Schriften des Neuen Testaments*, Vol. II, Göttingen, 1908).

The author of the Epistle to the Hebrews (8.6) describes Christ as 'the mediator of a better covenant, which hath been enacted upon better promises'. He defines these promises as those mentioned in Jer. 31.31–4, which excel the promises on which the Old Covenant given on Sinai was established. That which the new and better Covenant holds out to man is the forgiveness of sins and a full and inward knowledge of God's law and of God himself. The contrast in the author's mind is between the law with the temple-cult for which the Old Covenant stood (but which are unable to remove guilt from the conscience) and the 'better hope' which brings nigh unto God (7.19) and which is given through Christ.

In Rom. 4 and Gal. 3 prominence is given by St. Paul to the promises which the OT narrates were made by God to Abraham (Gen. 12.2–3,7,13.15–17,15.18,17.4–8,16,19,22.17–18) —namely, in short, that Abraham should have an innumerable posterity who would possess the land of Canaan, and that in his seed all nations of the earth should be blessed. In Rom. 4.13 St. Paul refers to the content of the promise made to Abraham as being that Abraham's descendants should inherit 'the world'. The land of Canaan alone was promised in scripture, but Jewish theology had explained this promise as containing an assurance of God that his elect people would have world dominion in the Messianic end-time (*v.* Jülicher, Commentary on Romans, *Die Schriften des Neuen Testaments*, Vol. II, p. 247). St. Paul accepts this interpretation held by contemporary Judaism except that he interprets 'Abraham's seed' as signifying Christ (Gal. 3.16). But in Rom. 4 the Apostle is not so much concerned with the content of the promise as with the conditions of its fulfilment. He wishes to show that the heirs of the promises are those who follow the example of Abraham's faith, in particular those who believe on 'him that raised Jesus our Lord from the dead' (Rom. 4.24). In Gal. 3 St. Paul pursues the same theme. The promise made to Abraham which is here mentioned is that in him 'shall all the nations be blessed' (vs. 8). These words in Rabbinic exegesis had reference to the bliss of the Messianic inheritance which should be enjoyed by all people who had connexion with Abraham through circumcision (cf. Bousset, *op. cit.*, Epistle to Galatians, p. 50). But St. Paul holds that the mark of the descendant of Abraham is faith, not works of the law;

that the blessing of Abraham comes upon the Gentiles (vs. 14) and that those who are Christ's are Abraham's offspring, heirs according to promise (vs. 29).

The Epistle to the Hebrews more persistently than any other NT writing lays emphasis on God's promises as a means of exhortation to loyalty and belief. Though the writer may speak both of 'the promises' (cf. 11.13) and of 'the promise' (11.39), he is ultimately only thinking of one promise—namely that of the soul's salvation in the Kingdom of God. He extracts (3.11, 4.6) from the oath which, in Ps. 95.7–11, God takes with reference to the unbelieving Israelites in the wilderness, viz. 'they shall not enter into my rest', evidence of a promise that still remains open to Christians of entering into God's rest (4.1,7–9). In the Psalm the 'rest' which the unbelieving generation in the wilderness forfeited means entrance into Canaan. But the promise which remains to Christian believers in the interpretation of the Epistle is the heavenly rest in which God, since the finishing of the works of creation, now dwells (Gen. 2.2) and into which the Christian pilgrim may enter and have fellowship with God. Also in 12.26f. the promise there spoken of has the same content. Here the author cites a prophecy of Haggai (2.6) about the convulsion of the earth and of the heaven and applies it as signifying a promise made by God to inaugurate 'a kingdom that cannot be shaken'. In his retrospect on the heroes of faith (Heb. 11.39–40), of whom he has spoken at some length, the author says that though their faith was 'well attested' (ARSV) they did not receive 'the promise, God having provided some better thing concerning us, that apart from us they should not be made perfect'. The thought of the writer is that God's purpose for the pious who lived in the period of the Old Covenant was that they should not enter into the blessedness of the Messianic kingdom without the Christians. Had the consummation of history taken place under the old dispensation, then the later generations of men would not have been born. But God's purpose was that the Messianic kingdom, in effect the second coming of Christ, should come at the end of the times so that apart from the believers in Christ they, the faithful persons of old, should not be made perfect. This conclusion is led up to by the statement of 11.9–16 that Abraham was 'a sojourner in the land of promise' along with Isaac and Jacob, and that they and other 'strangers and pilgrims on the earth' (vs. 13) sought a 'heavenly' country. But this vision of the promise had to tarry because of the reasons given in vss. 39–40.

The content of the promises (1.4), or promise (3.13), of which mention is made in the Second Epistle of Peter, is the second coming of Christ and world renewal which are preceded by a world destruction. This renewal is regarded by the author as the fulfilment of the divine assurance made in Isa. 66.17: 'For, behold, I create a new heaven and a new earth' (cf. 66.22f.).

O. S. RANKIN

PROPHECY, PROPHESY, PROPHET, SEER

For convenience of treatment, this art. will be divided into two sections, dealing respectively with the biblical understanding of prophecy as such and with the actual origins and development of the prophetic function as these may be traced in the Bible.

I. PROPHECY

Although in its origins Heb. prophecy is doubtless akin to various phenomena amongst other peoples (*v.* next sect.), there develops a peculiarly *biblical* conception of prophecy and its fulfilment. The NT everywhere presupposes that 'all the prophets from Samuel and them that followed after, as many as have spoken' (Acts 3.24), foretold the events of the life, death and resurrection of Jesus Christ. Especially had they predicted the passion of Christ (Luke 24.25–7, Acts 3.18, I Cor. 15.3, etc.); it may be noted how the evangelists particularly stress those details of the passion story which appear to fulfil the 'prophecies' (e.g. Ps. 22 and Isa. 53): 'the Son of man goeth even as it is written of him' (Mark 14.21; cf. 14.49). But the whole life of Jesus in every part is presented as a fulfilment of the scriptures, which testify of him (John 5.39). Sometimes in their desire to find fulfilments of prophecy the Gospel writers seem to us to overreach themselves (e.g. Matt. 2.15,17f.; cf. Hos .11.1, Jer. 31.15). But whatever we may think of the details of their application of it, there can be no doubt about the principle which the evangelists and indeed all the NT writers affirm: that in Christ all the prophecies are fulfilled.

Thus, there was developed from apostolic days the view that the importance of OT prophecy consisted chiefly in the element of *prediction* which it contained. Christian missionaries like Apollos, a converted Jew at work in Ephesus, 'publicly shewed by the Scriptures that Jesus was the Christ' (Acts 18.28); and in the later history of the Church, from the days of Justin Martyr (*c.* AD 150) to those of Bishop Butler (1692–1752), the 'argument from prophecy' was one of the most telling weapons in the armoury of the Christian apologist. But since the rise of biblical criticism in the nineteenth century there has been a tendency to lay stress upon the element of 'forthtelling' rather than upon that of 'foretelling' as the more significant factor in the work of the OT prophets. The prophets, it is rightly said, were concerned not so much to foretell a distant future but to tell forth the will of God in the crisis of their own days; and historical criticism has wonderfully made the prophets 'come alive' for us by exhibiting them as real men, struggling with the real problems of government and politics, of invasion and resistance, of public morality and social justice. The value of such historical rehabilitation of the life and work of the prophets cannot be overestimated.

Nevertheless, it would be false to the standpoint of the NT if we were to say that the significance of OT prophecy consists solely in 'forth-telling' and to discount the element of 'foretelling' altogether. The 'argument from prophecy' is still impressive when it is restated in the light of modern knowledge. We can indeed no longer imagine that the OT writers were given a miraculous 'preview' of the events of the life and death of Jesus, or that detailed predictions of his ministry and passion were divinely dictated to them; nor shall we look for precise fulfilments of particular OT texts, as writers in the pre-critical period have done ever since the days of the author of St. Matthew's Gospel (e.g. Matt. 1.22f., 2.5f.,15,17f.,23, etc.). We shall notice rather that the prophets, standing in the midst of the stirring events of their times, discerned therein the character and purpose of God, more particularly his judgment and mercy. The pattern of his action, both for judgment and salvation, was discerned and forth-told by them in their declaration of his will. As their sense of God's unfolding purpose deepened, they came increasingly to look forward to a *dénouement*, a climax of Israel's history, a 'day of the Lord' in which those things which were now but partially revealed should be fully and finally made manifest. The writings of the prophets are eschatological in this sense, with the result that it is often difficult to determine with certitude whether they are referring primarily to the events of their own day, or whether they are looking forward towards an end or 'goal' of history, of which the crisis of the prophets' own time is but the foreshadowing or 'type'. In this sense, the apocalyptic writers are themselves developing or extending an essential aspect of the prophets' work; they are more concerned with the future than with the present, whereas the prophets are immersed in the present, yet are able to discern in it the signs of the ultimate triumph of God's purpose, which shall bring history to an end.

Beneath the apologetic attempts of the NT writers to find proof-texts to demonstrate from the Scriptures that Jesus is the Messiah there lies a deeper and (for us) more convincing argument. They seek to show that every significant insight of the prophets into the purpose of God has been fulfilled in the coming of Jesus and his Church. To the NT writers, says R. V. G. Tasker, 'the whole story of the people of Israel, their divine call, their redemption from Egypt, the giving of the Law on Mount Sinai, the triumphant establishment of the worship of Jehovah in the Holy Land, the building of the temple, the tragedy of the exile, and the subsequent resurrection and return of the remnant to Zion—are all foreshadowings of the greater and final salvation given in the life, death and resurrection of Jesus, apart from which they have in themselves no abiding significance and are not fully comprehensible' (*The OT in the NT*, p. 12). The whole pattern of the OT history is prophetic of the Christ who should come. The Jews had long expected that there should appear 'a prophet like unto Moses' (Deut. 18.15,18, John 6.14), that he would deliver his people from a bondage more terrible than Pharaoh's, that he would give to them a new law and make for them a new covenant (Jer. 31.31). The prophetic remnant had declared that Israel would become a light unto the Gentiles, that God would raise up a new Israel which should be a fitter instrument for the achievement of the divine purpose than the old rebellious Israel had ever been. In their moments of deepest insight the prophets had foreseen that the Servant of the Lord could accomplish God's will not by trampling down those who resisted but by suffering humiliation and rejection (Isa. 53). The NT writers teach that all these insights (and many more) had been fulfilled in the coming of Jesus and his Church. The Church was the spiritual seed of Abraham; it inherited the promises (*q.v.*) and the commission of the Old Israel; it was the new People of God, the royal priesthood and holy nation (cf. I Pet. 2.9f. with Exod. 19.5f.); it was Isaiah's faithful remnant, Ezekiel's resurrected Israel, Jeremiah's people of the New Covenant, Daniel's people of the Saints of the Most High. The pattern of the divine salvation which the OT had adumbrated was now made manifest in the events to which the NT contains the apostolic witness. As St. Augustine said, what was latent in the OT was patent in the NT. Both Testaments are witnesses to Christ, the OT by way of prophecy, the NT by way of fulfilment. Christ is the theme of the OT no less than of the NT, and thus the Christian Bible is necessarily a book of two Testaments, not of one. In the words of the judicious Hooker: 'The general end both of the OT and the NT is one; the difference between them consisting in this, that the Old did make wise by teaching salvation through Christ that should come, the New by teaching that Christ the Saviour is come, and that Jesus whom the Jews did crucify and whom God did raise again from the dead is he' (*Ecclesiastical Polity*, Bk. I, Chap. XIV). The unity of the whole Bible is deeply impressive when Christ is seen to be the key which unlocks all the Scriptures. The prophets anticipate the proclamation of the apostles; the apostles corroborate the witness of the prophets; and thus the biblical criterion of the truth of prophecy is itself fulfilled: 'when the word of the prophet shall come to pass, then shall the prophet be known, that Jehovah hath truly sent him' (Jer. 28.9; cf. Deut. 18.22). Cf. W. Vischer: 'The Bible in its entirety witnesses under the attestation of the Holy Spirit that Jesus of Nazareth is the Christ. That is why it is the Holy Scripture of the Christian Church. For the Christian Church is the community of those who on the basis of the biblical witness recognize and believe that Jesus is the Christ, the Messiah of Israel, the Son of the Living God, the Saviour of the World' (*Das Christuszeugnis des A.T.*, I, p. 7). (See also PROMISE, TIME.)

BIBLIOGRAPHY

R. V. G. Tasker: *The Old Testament in the New Testament*, London (1946). Alan Richardson: *Christian Apologetics*, London (1947) (esp. Chap. VIII). W. Vischer: *Das Christuszeugnis des Alten Testaments* (1946), Band I, Zurich, 7th edn.

ALAN RICHARDSON

II. PROPHET, SEER

The limitations of our knowledge of the functions of the seer in Israel are indicated by the statement of A. B. Davidson (*HDB*, Vol. IV, on 'Prophecy and Prophets', p. 108) that 'there may have been a class of "seers" in the time of the Judges whose methods may not have been greatly unlike those in use among other Semitic peoples. But we know nothing of them. Samuel is the only "seer" known to history'. Nevertheless, though the clues are few, there are some which shed light upon the position which the seer held in relation to both the priest and the prophet. Excluding references which the late Book of the Chronicles contains, the word *hozeh* (seer) occurs six times in the OT and *ro'eh* (seer) seven times. The priest at Bethel (Amos 7.12) says to Amos: 'O thou seer, go . . . into the land of Judah, and there eat bread and prophesy there.' The prophet Gad in II Sam. 24.11 is referred to as a prophet and also as David's seer. The word 'seers' appears parallel to the word 'prophets' in II Kings 17.13 and Isa. 29.10; and to 'diviners' (Heb. *qosemim*) in Micah 3.7. Samuel is called a seer (*ro'eh*) thrice in I Sam. 9, where the interesting archaeological note appears (in vs. 9): 'Beforetime in Israel, when a man went to inquire of God, thus he said, Come and let us go to the seer; for he that is now called a prophet was beforetime called a seer.' In II Sam. 15.27 King David says to Zadok the priest: 'Art thou not a seer?'

While the data upon which a judgment must be founded are not abundant, it would seem that the term 'seer' is the widest and most general title given to those who were able to interpret 'signs', i.e. unusual occurrences (Gen. 25.22f.) or ordinary but perplexing events (I Sam. 10.2f., the question of the whereabouts of Saul's father's asses), or to explain dreams (Gen. 40.8), or to have dreams (Deut. 13.1f.), or to answer enquiries by giving an oracle. The profession of seer under this interpretation includes the whole class of diviners whose particular differences of method are specified under the Heb. verbs *nahash, qasam, lahash, halam*, together with the priest (*kohen*) and the prophet (*nabi*). The reason for the very infrequent mention of the seer may appear when we consider the office of the priest. The Levitical priesthood, being in possession of a technical method of oracle-giving, namely, the Urim and Thummim, and being available at all the shrines and holy places where the deity dwelt, must have become in course of time the chief practitioners in answering those who came 'to enquire of God'. The non-priestly diviners or seers doubtless still managed to make a living or a reputation by special methods of divination, but the priesthood and prophecy would tend to become the chief sources of oracle-giving; and the activities of priest and prophet belonging to the main stream of religious interest would be reflected in the literature which has come down to us to the almost entire exclusion of the activities of other kinds of seers. That in early times the close relationship of priest and seer was a popular commonplace may perhaps be seen in II Sam. 15.27 and be inferred from the fact that the Arabic *Kahin*, which is the same word as the Heb. *Kohen* (priest), has the general significance of soothsayer (*v.* Hölscher, *Geschichte der israelitischen und jüdischen Religion*, § 34). So far it seems clear that the priest and the prophet (e g. Samuel) may be called seer, but that every seer is not necessarily a priest or a prophet. Both these offices had functions which distinguish them from each other (even though, as in the case of Ezekiel, a man might be both priest and prophet) and which no less distinguish them from other seers.

The archaeological remark in I Sam. 9.9 shows that its author was aware that the prophet's vocation was of more recent date in Israel than the other vocations to which had been given the title seer. This title had probably dated from the nomadic period of Israel's history. In regard to the profession of prophet, Hölscher (*op. cit.*) holds that Israel must first have come into contact with prophets in Canaan, to which land the prophetic movement had spread from Asia Minor. For *ecstatic* prophecy, he says, was not known to Arabs, Egyptians, Assyrians or Babylonians, but was widespread in Syria, Asia Minor, Thrace and Greece. Hans Schmidt (*RGG*, Vol. IV, Cols. 1,536f.) also remarks that, while the prophetic garb seems to be best explained as the protest of the desert against the civilization of cultivated lands, the prophetic ecstasy points to an origin in the Near-Eastern nature religion with which Israel came into contact in Canaan.

If the prophet had a religious origin which was different from that of all others who with him could bear the title of seer, he yet shared with the seer in general the power of beholding in the ordinary events of human life and nature what the ordinary person does not see and fails to interpret. The prophet has visions and auditions, even though it be that the latter are for him the more important. The prophet and other seers may be conceived of as alike possessed by the spirit of Jahweh and thus enabled to interpret signs (cf. Amos 7.1f.). But the distinctive mark of the prophet, at least in the early days of the movement in Israel, was certainly the ecstatic state into which he fell and in which he was able to declare the will of God. The prophet therefore is subject to a particular kind of inspiration. 'It is in every case a strong subconscious experience of an ecstatic kind in which a superhuman power comes upon the man whom it calls and compels, with or without his will, to do its service' (Hauer, *v.* Bertholet, *RGG*, IV, *Propheten*). The band of prophets whom Saul meets (I Sam. 10.5f.) as they come down the hillside with a psaltery, a timbrel, a pipe and a harp, and who are 'prophesying', exhibit that which is characteristic of prophecy—namely its ecstasy, at least in the time of the non-writing prophets, and which continues in a lesser degree in most of the pre-exilic writing prophets. Amos, though disclaiming any connexion with the prophetic guilds, yet prophesies and feels the compulsion to prophesy to be irresistible (3.8). Hosea (cf. 9.7), Isaiah (8.11, 22.14), Jeremiah (4.19–21, 23–6, 6.11, 10.22, 23.9) seem to be the subjects of ecstasy. Ezekiel in his experiences of a more frenzied kind appears to revert to the violent form of behaviour known to the early prophetic guilds. As to the presence or absence of ecstasy among these writing prophets, it is natural that there should be much difference of opinion. But more recently the ecstatic nature of the mentality of the great prophets has been emphasized by Hölscher, Gunkel, Hertzberg, T. H. Robinson and Lods (*v.* A. Lods, *The Prophets and the Rise of Judaism*, pp. 56f.). With time the high afflatus of prophecy faded and vanished. In the fifth century the prophets Haggai, Zechariah, Joel and Malachi are men of ordinary proportions. The promise of the outpouring of the spirit of God is for the future (Joel 2.28f.). The religious cultus which the great prophets attacked comes into its own again (Hag. 1.4,8, Zech 1.16, Joel 1.9,13, Mal. 3.10). In I Chron. 25.1–3 the music of the temple choir is called prophesying—a memorial at least of the part which music had played in the early days of the prophetic guilds.

'*Nabi*' (prophet), says Guillaume (*Prophecy and Divination*, p. 113), 'always meant one subject to the inspiration of a god or demon, and the behaviour associated with a prophet in a particular age (whether ecstatic speech and action or measured and authoritative pronouncements) determined the meaning of the verb (to prophesy). . . . Thus it was that the word "prophet" could be applied to the great exponents of ethical religion . . . and to the savage devotees of Baal who gashed themselves with knives on Carmel.' Prophecy, being in early times an utterance in the state of ecstasy, could be of the wildest sort, without any apparent ethical content, though not without religious fervour. Ecstasy, as we may judge from what is told of the guilds of the non-writing prophets, was valued for its own sake, and this is no doubt the reason for these prophets assembling in groups. The presence of their settlements in the neighbourhood of shrines suggests that they performed certain offices (giving oracular guidance? music?) in connection with the cultus (*v.* A. R. Johnson, *The Cultic Prophet in Ancient Israel* (1944), pp. 25f., 53f.). But two excellent descriptions of these ecstatics are given in I Samuel: first, the band of prophets whom Saul met as they came down from a high place (i.e. a shrine) playing music and 'prophesying' (I Sam. 10.5); and, secondly (I Sam. 19.20), another company in a high state of ecstasy performing religious exercises with Samuel as leader. This company too is said to be 'prophesying'. The prophets of Baal, who in the scene on Carmel (I Kings 18) call out 'O Baal, hear us' from morning till noon and who lacerate themselves, are likewise described as prophesying. In all these cases probably the prophecy tended toward, or consisted in, the making of unintelligible sounds or raving, to which level ecstasy might on occasion descend (cf. I Cor. 14).

The prophecy of the writing prophets, as this appears to us from the time of Amos onwards, takes the form of a declaration of the will or thought of Jahweh. A common introduction to what is said is: 'Thus saith Jahweh'; for the content of what is said is not primarily a discourse of the prophet to the people but rather the words of Jahweh addressed to the prophet. Jahweh reveals his counsel (RV, secret) unto his servants the prophets (Amos 3.7). The announcements which are made in the name of Jahweh (e.g. on such topics as the impending punishment of Israel's sin and infidelity; the political situation and the call to dependence upon God; true religion contrasted with the cult and sacrifices; social injustices; the oppression of the poor by the wealthy and the powerful) are for the most part of a religious and moral content, without any very strongly predictive element. In Isa. 1, for example, there are six oracles (vss. 2–3, 4–9, 10–17, 18–20, 21–8 and 29–31), only the last two of which are predictive. But no hard and fast distinction can be drawn between prophecy as forthtelling and prophecy as foretelling, since very frequently God's future mode of action, on account of Israel's or her oppressor's sin, is foreshadowed. It is impossible to declare the will and purpose and judgment of God without reference to the future. The prophets threaten, and every threat involves the future. They may be distinguished as prophets of weal or of woe, and both of these terms imply the future. Indeed, the OT itself (Jer. 28.9, Deut. 18.22) defines a false prophet as one whose predictions do not come to pass. The prophets of the OT—even as John the Baptist and Jesus in the NT—though they make references to God's judgment, aim at bringing religious influence to bear upon their own generation.

In the NT (cf. I Cor. 12.14, Eph. 4.11), prophets along with apostles and teachers held a spiritual office in the Christian community and till about the end of the second century they exercised their ministry within the Church. There is an account of a visit (Acts 11.27) made by prophets of the Church at Jerusalem to Antioch, on the occasion of which a prophet called Agabus made a prediction about a famine which, he said, was to be world-wide. The function of the prophet in the early Church appears from the use of *propheteuein* (to prophesy) in the NT. This verb is employed in the sense of: (1) to announce as a revelation made by God: Matt. 7.22 ('Many will say . . . Lord, Lord, did not we prophesy by thy name?'), Acts 19.6, 21.9, I Cor. 11.4f., 13.9, 14.1,3–5 (vs. 3, 'He that prophesieth speaketh unto men edification, and comfort, and consolation'), 24,31,39, Rev. 11.3; (2) to reveal that of which the evidence has been hidden: Matt. 26.68 ('Prophesy unto us, thou Christ: who is he that struck thee?'); (3) to foretell the future: Matt. 11.13, 15.7, I Pet. 1.10.

The claim that Jesus fulfils the prophecies of the OT is best established when taken as referring to the prophets' teachings and ideals rather than to predictions that may be extracted from their writings or from the OT in general. There is ample and legitimate ground for speaking of a preparation for Christ in the OT, and the account of Jesus' thought and life in the NT sufficiently confirms this, without there being any need of doing violence to the character or exegesis of the OT such as the early and medieval Church was guilty of when it rested Jesus' claim as Fulfiller upon a fulfilment of predictions. The highly artificial nature of these so called proofs from prediction and their harmful result may well be judged by the collection of them made by the learned monk Isidore of Seville (7th cent.) in his work *Contra Judaeos*. (See L. Williams, *op. cit.*, pp. 216f., 282f.) (*V.* also MINISTER.)

BIBLIOGRAPHY

A. Lods: *The Prophets and the Rise of Judaism*, London (1937). Guillaume: *Prophecy and Divination*. A. R. Johnson: *The Cultic Prophet in Ancient Israel*, London (1944). J. M. Powis Smith: *The Prophets and their Times*, Chicago (1924). L. Williams: *Adversus Judaeos*, London (1935). Essay by N. W. Porteous in *Record and Revelation*, ed. H. W. Robinson, Oxford (1938).

O. S. RANKIN

PROPITIATION *v.* SACRIFICE II(*b*), MERCY-SEAT under MERCY, ATONE

PROVIDENCE

This is not a biblical word at all, since in the OT and NT it occurs only on the lips of a heathen orator (Tertullus) as a conventional flattery of a Roman procurator (Felix) (Acts 24.2, where it means 'foresight'). The idea of divine providence was a Stoic commonplace, and we may surmise Stoic influence behind the use of the word in Wisd. 14.3. Later Christian usage has applied the word to the Fatherly love and care of God, his beneficent providential control of all that happens. This, of course, is an essentially biblical conception, and it is prominent in the teaching of Jesus himself (cf. Matt. 5.45, 6.25–34, 10.29–31). There is dominical authority for the view that the laws of nature reveal to God's children the loving purpose of their heavenly Father 'whose never-failing providence ordereth all things both in heaven and earth' (*BCP*, Collect for Trinity VIII; cf. also Collect for Trinity II).

A. R.

PRUDENT, PRUDENCE

The OT acquaints us with words which signify prudent in a good sense, e.g. Amos 5.13. But there is another word, fairly common in Prov., which gives it a slightly bad sense: crafty, self-regarding, e.g. Prov. 12.23, 14.15. This adj. is used of the serpent, Gen. 3.1 ('subtil'). The NT words rendered prudent, prudence have a good sense, cf. Matt. 11.25, Eph. 1.8 (of God).

E. C. B.

PUNISH, PUNISHMENT

The OT speaks frequently of punishment for sin, the NT rarely, the proportion in AV being 54 as against 8. At first sight this suggests that the OT has more to say about punishment and the NT more about forgiveness. This view is superficial and erroneous, since both Testaments are strong in judgment for sin and forgiveness for the penitent. See especially Isa. 40–55, where the prophet never speaks of the sins of Israel without immediately talking of forgiveness. The NT uses the words 'condemn', 'condemnation' (*q.v.*), and this group is represented more than twice as often in the NT as in the OT.

There are, in the main, three aspects of punishment in the OT. First, we find the idea of retribution, expressed in the *lex talionis* of Exod. 21.23–5. These verses are concerned with wrongs done between man and man. Where Israel is stubbornly apostate in spite of correction, she is threatened with a sevenfold punishment (Lev. 26.18,24). Jesus deprecated the insistence on 'an eye for an eye and a tooth for a tooth' (Matt. 5.38–42) and definitely advocated forgiveness and no retaliation between man and man, advocating forgiveness up to 'seventy times seven' (Matt. 18.22). On the other hand, he is in some respects stricter in his judgment upon sin even than the Law. He extended the commandment against murder to include even anger and abuse, and that against adultery to include lustful thoughts and looks (Matt. 5.21–32).

Secondly, there is the great majority of cases where the verb is used, and it stands for the Heb. *paqạd* (visit, attend to). This use shows the reaction of God to sin. Whenever he comes into contact with it, he is violently hostile to it. His only possible attitude to sin and to the persistent, unrepentant sinner is one of condemnation and punishment. This is true both in the OT and in the NT.

The third type comprises the majority of cases where the noun is found in the OT. Here the actual word used is a Heb. word for sin itself. For instance, in Gen. 4.13 Cain is represented in the EVV as saying 'My punishment is greater than I can bear'. The Heb. word is '*awon*, which actually means 'iniquity' and is generally so translated. It is clear, however, that Cain means the consequences of his sins. There are altogether 9 cases of this, and in addition 3 cases where other Heb. words for sin are found. This usage shows how closely the Hebrews connected the ideas of sin and its consequences. They knew that sin has its inevitable sequel in pain and suffering and death, and so they connected the two indissolubly in thought and word. This idea is seen in Isa. 53.12 where the phrase 'he bare the sin of many' means that he bore the consequences of the sins of many. When, therefore, we say that Jesus bore our sins on the Cross, we mean, not that he was guilty of them, but that he suffered the consequences of our sins. (Also *v.* CHASTEN, CORRECT.)

N. H. SNAITH

PURCHASE *v.* REDEEM

PURIFY *v.* UNCLEAN

PURPOSE

In scripture the concept of purpose is conveyed in a variety of words and phrases. In I Cor. 4.5 the writer says that Christ at his coming will bring to light the hidden things of darkness and make manifest 'the counsels of the hearts' of men. God's desire that 'Israel should walk in my ways' was thwarted so that Jahweh had to let his people 'go after the stubbornness of their heart, that they might walk in their own counsels' (Ps. 81.12–13). God, says Amos, does nothing without revealing his resolve (Heb. *sod*; *Oxford Heb. Dict.*, secret, counsel) to his servants the prophets (3.7). And in regard to the divine counsels, Deutero-Isaiah (55.8–9) states that these transcend the counsels of men in a degree that is immeasurable: 'For as the heavens are higher than the earth, so are my ways higher than your ways and my thoughts than your thoughts.' Dr. Skinner (*Cambridge Bible, ad. loc.*) comments that the contrast here does not concern the moral quality of the divine thoughts but that the prophet means that the thoughts and ways of Jehovah are his purposes of redemption, which are too vast and sublime to be measured by the narrow conception of despairing minds (Isa. 40.27f.).

The OT is not at all shy of the idea that God can change or modify his purpose. In the Book of Jonah, God is described as altering his intention of punishing the city of Nineveh and as displeasing Jonah by this reversal. The principle of divine action in regard to God's purposes with men is clearly stated by Jeremiah (18.8) when he makes Jahweh say: 'If that nation concerning which I have spoken turn from their evil, I will repent of the evil that I thought to do unto them.' Sometimes, however, a prophet may speak with great certainty of God's purpose of acting in a particular manner as immutable (Isa. 14.24–7).

As the conception of the character of the deity as supreme in wisdom and power developed, and according as he was conceived of as having an interest not merely in the welfare of Israel but in other nations, the view appears that God judges the other nations also and that those judgments accomplish moral ends (cf. Amos 1.3–2.16) or support such ends. Jahweh comes to be thought of by the prophets as the lord of history. The nations and empires are the mere instruments of his will. Israel's political misfortunes are Jahweh's disciplinary measures, the punishment of his people's unfaithfulness. But God's purpose may also be revealed in grace and favour. Thus the prophet of the exile, Deutero-Isaiah (40–55) interprets the political situation of the times in terms of God's intention to liberate Israel from the Babylonian captivity through the rise of Cyrus. The prophet announces Jahweh as saying of this event: 'My counsel shall stand and I will do all my pleasure: calling a ravenous bird from the east, the man of my counsel from a far country' (Isa. 46.10–11). In continuance of the eschatological teaching of certain prophecies and of the prophetic idea of world-history as being guided and controlled by the purpose of God, the apocalyptic literature, of which the Book of Daniel in the OT is an example (cf. ch. 7), took upon itself the task of describing the events of history as leading to a glorious consummation, a Messianic age of peace and prosperity in which Israel should have freedom from all her enemies.

Christianity adds to the ideas of the OT on the purpose of God the specific teaching that God's purpose for the world is bound up with the life and teaching of Jesus. Eph. 3.11 speaks of 'the eternal purpose which he [God] purposed in Christ Jesus our Lord'. This purpose is conceived of in the NT as a sending by God of 'his only begotten son' into the world that "whosoever believeth on him should not perish, but have eternal life' (John 3.16; cf. vs. 17). The supreme purpose of God, then, is the salvation of all men through belief in Christ. In regard to this plan of salvation, St. Paul in Rom. 8.28–9 indicates that, for the recipients of salvation, the plan involves a process of five stages, one of which is their *fore-ordination* by God and another their *calling* by him (cf. Eph. 1.3–11). The Gospels variously represent Jesus' mission to be the fulfilling of God's intention to give 'a light for revelation to the Gentiles' (Luke 2.32), i.e. to fulfil the mission of the Servant mentioned in Isa. 42.6, 49.6: 'to preach good tidings to the poor . . . to proclaim release to the captives and recovering of sight to the blind, to set at liberty them that are bruised, to proclaim the acceptable year of the Lord' (Luke 4.18–19 from Isa. 61.1–2); 'to minister and to give his life a ransom for many' (Mark 10.45). The expression which is perhaps most pregnant with the concept of purpose in the NT might be said to be 'Kingdom of God', since it signifies that condition in which God's sovereignty has been realized.

O. S. RANKIN

* * *

QUEEN OF HEAVEN *v.* GOD, GODS IV

QUICK

There are several passages in both AV and RV where the word is used merely to signify the living in contrast to the dead (Num. 16.30,33, Acts. 10.42, II Tim. 4.1, I Pet. 4.5), so that the phrase 'the quick and the dead' has passed into the Apostles' Creed and thence into common speech. Elsewhere the word has the extended meaning of lively, forcible, or acute. In Wisd. 7.22, wisdom itself is described as having 'a spirit quick of understanding . . . subtil, freely moving, clear in utterance'.

Shrewdness of understanding and power to utter penetrating judgment is noted in Wisd. 8.11, while in Ecclus. 31.22 the meaning is equivalent to active. In Heb. 4.12 quick means living, but the rest of the verse describes the sense in which the Word of God can be described as quick or living. It is 'active, sharper than any two-edged sword', piercing to the very heart of the truth, and thus able to lay bare the secret thoughts and motives of a man. In the verbal form 'to quicken', the word signifies to give or restore life either in physical recovery or spiritual renewal. In John 5.21 both ideas are strikingly combined, but in Eph. 2.5 and Col. 2.13 believers are described as quickened or raised from spiritual death by the life-giving power of the Father, whose characteristic exercise of power was demonstrated by the raising of Christ from the tomb of death to the power of an endless life (Heb. 7.16). (*V.* also LIFE, LIVING.)

F. J. TAYLOR

* * *

RAINBOW *v.* BOW

RANSOM *v.* REDEEM

REBEL(LION) *v.* OBEY

REBUKE *v.* CORRECT

RECOMPENSE *v.* REWARD

RECONCILE, RECONCILIATION

Reconciliation is the word used in the NT to describe the changed relations between God and man which are the result of the death and resurrection of Jesus Christ. To reconcile is the distinctive activity of God himself, and the world of men is the object of reconciliation. The noun and the two verbs which express the idea of reconciliation are found only in the Pauline Epistles and have no direct OT ancestry. Apart from I Cor. 7.11 (cf. Matt. 5.24, where a different word is used for being reconciled to a fellow man), which refers to the reconciliation of a wife to her husband (passive form of verb used, but active co-operation implied), there are twelve occasions on which the words are used (Rom. 5.10f., 11.15, II Cor. 5.18–20, Eph. 2.16, Col. 1.19–22) with a primary reference to God's act in history through Christ. The root meaning of the word is an exchange of equivalent values, and then, through the ideas of exchange of sympathy and mutual understanding, the notion of a thorough or radical change. Thus reconciliation has the significance of a new stage in personal relationships in which previous hostility of mind or estrangement has been put away in some decisive act.

In Rom. 5.10f. reconciliation is set forth as the work of God; it is man who is reconciled to God through the death of Christ, who has thus inaugurated a new era in the relationships of God and man. But, as Sanday and Headlam remark (*ICC*, *Romans*, 5th ed., p. 130), 'the natural explanation of the passages which speak of enmity and reconciliation between God and man is that they are not on one side only but are mutual'. The paradox which Paul is proclaiming is that, although God looks upon sinful men as enemies, yet he reconciles them to himself and has done this by the one decisive act of the cross of Christ. In II Cor. 5.18–20 the Apostle again refers to the reconciling act of God and describes it as having been accomplished in Christ and especially through his death and resurrection. This reconciliation is effected by God 'not reckoning unto men their trespasses' and 'having committed unto us the word of reconciliation', that is, by the exercise of divine forgiveness and the proclamation of the Gospel message intended to elicit a response of faith on the part of the hearers. The passage reveals the very great importance which St. Paul attached to this message and his profound conviction that he had been divinely commissioned to declare it. A sense of urgency pervades the whole paragraph. In Eph. 2.16 the immediate concern of the writer is with the bringing together of Jew and Gentile in the one household of God; but the reconciliation of those who hitherto had been at enmity with one another is declared to be the result of both parties having peace with God in the blood (*q.v.*) of Christ. By his death Christ has taken away the barriers which kept God and man (Eph. 2.18) apart and the middle wall of partition (Eph. 2.14) which estranged Jew from Gentile. As in the other passages the source of reconciliation is the love of God, and the sphere in which reconciliation is an experienced reality is the new divine community being built up by the activity of the Spirit of God. The Ephesians passage (as also Col. 1.19–22) presents reconciliation not merely in terms of an individual transaction but as a fact of corporate and universal significance. Thus in Col. 1.19–22 the essentially personal work of reconciliation is revealed as having a universal scope, for through the death of Christ all things (earthly and heavenly) are to be reconciled to God. Reconciliation is thus an act rather than a process by which men are delivered from a condition of estrangement and restored to fellowship with God; the act is accomplished by God through the power of the sacrificial death of Christ. It includes other blessings such as peace (*q.v.*) with God (Eph. 2.14–17; cf. Acts 10.36, Rom. 5.1, Col. 3.15), freedom (*v.* BONDAGE; Rom. 6.22, 8.2, Gal. 5.1), and sonship or adoption (*q.v.*) (Rom. 8.15, Gal. 4.5, Eph. 1.5); it issues in fellowship with God and man (I Cor. 1.30, Phil. 4.1, I Thess. 3.8) and has as its goal the sanctification of believers in a life of ethical and spiritual progress (Gal. 5.22ff., Col. 3.4, I Pet. 1.2, I John 3.3–6). (*V.* also ATONE, MEDIATOR.)

F. J. TAYLOR

REDEEM, REDEEMER, REDEMPTION, RANSOM, PURCHASE

The word 'redemption' and its cognate forms, like most of the important words of the Bible, is not derived from abstract philosophical thought, but is based upon the distinctive Heb. way of thinking in concrete terms. It is derived from the practice of buying back something which formerly belonged to the purchaser, but has for some reason passed out of his possession (as in redeeming a pledge from pawn) or of paying the price required to secure a benefit (the money paid for acquiring or freeing a slave) and comes from the same root as the word ransom. When used figuratively in the Bible, it emphasizes the fact that in the saving activity of God, supremely manifested in Christ, something of decisive import has been done for the salvation (*q.v.*) of mankind.

In the OT the terms 'redeem', 'redeemer', 'redemption' occur some 130 times as the translation of two Heb. roots, while the related term 'ransom' occurs (as noun or verb) 13 times. The fundamental idea of the first word is the payment of an equivalent for what is released or secured, the price paid in compensation for a life forfeited (Exod. 21.30), as when Jonathan unwittingly broke the taboo laid by Saul on the eating of any food and was condemned to death, but saved by the popular demand and the probable provision of a substitute (I Sam. 14.24ff.); or in the purchase of release for Israel from captivity in Babylon, when God paid the ransom to Cyrus of giving him an empire in Africa (Egypt, Ethiopia and Seba) in exchange (Isa.43.3; cf. Job 33.24). It was believed by ancient Israel that the first-born (*q.v.*) both of man and beast belonged to God and must therefore be redeemed or ransomed from him (Exod. 13.12,13, 34.30) if the owner or parent desired to retain it. Thus, while the idea of a price paid is an essential feature of the term, the emphasis is more frequently laid upon the result, the deliverance or release which is secured by the payment. This is particularly evident when the redeeming activity of God is described, in relation both to the nation (Deut. 7.8) and to the individual (Job. 33.28). With the exception of Ps. 130.8, the redemption is always from some physical suffering or political menace, and ransoming signifies escape from actual calamities and restoration to prosperity as the tangible evidence of restoration to favour with God. To the men of the OT material prosperity was closely linked with spiritual status, so that redemption could be understood only in a material context.

The word redeemer (Heb. *go'el*) was derived from the fact that, if a man had sold himself into slavery, the obligation to buy back his freedom for him rested upon a kinsman, unless 'he be waxen rich' (Lev. 25.48f.), which would be very unlikely to happen. In Ruth (4.1–11) the duty of the kinsman to redeem the land of Naomi was held to include the obligation to marry Ruth. The kinsman was not willing to do this, and formally passed over his responsibility to Boaz in the presence of the elders at the city gate. Boaz thus became a redeemer, and the duties fell upon him. The right and duty of a kinsman to be a redeemer (or vindicator) was particularly important in the discharge of that primitive justice by which 'an avenger of blood', being a near kinsman of the slain man, could claim an equivalent life from the family of the murderer. The well-known passage in Job 19.25, 'I know that my redeemer liveth', refers to one who will avenge his shameful death and vindicate him in the eyes of men. When God is described as redeemer, the same term is used, implying that he acts on behalf of Israel as a worthy kinsman would do for the honour of his kin. This usage is very frequent in Deutero-Isaiah, occurring more frequently there than in all the rest of the OT. 'Fear not, for I have redeemed thee; I have called thee by thy name, thou art mine' (Isa. 43.1; cf. 41.14, 44.6, 47.4, 60.16, 63.4,9, etc.). The primary reference is to the exercise of that divine right and power for the people (comparable to the right and duty of a kinsman) by which the poor and feeble exilic community is to be restored to its rightful land (cf. Isa. 52.12 for a comparison of the return from Babylon with the redeeming acts of God in the Exodus from Egypt). But the idea of payment is not wholly forgotten—'As ye were sold for nought ye shall be redeemed without money' (Isa. 50.1, 52.3,5). This OT evidence may be summarized by saying that (1) the theme of redemption is embodied in every part of the literature and informs the whole course of Israel's history; (2) emphasis is laid upon the divine initiative in redeeming and ransoming man; (3) redemption is primarily from material perils and hardships, but these usually have a spiritual reference; (4) the redemptive activity is usually directed towards the whole people, though in Jer. 31.29–34 and Ezek. 18.4–28 there is apparent some concern with the relation of the individual to God.

In the NT the words redeem, redemption, occur some 22 times (redeemer not at all, but *v.* SAVIOUR) and ransom 3 times, translating two Gk. words, one denoting primarily the ransom or price paid for the emancipation of a slave and the other denoting purchase in the market (cf. 'purchased' in Acts 20.28, used of Christ shedding his blood to make the Church his own, and in I Tim. 3.13 of deacons gaining a good standing in the Church through devoted service).

Perhaps the most important passage to consider (cf. F. J. A. Hort, *The First Epistle of St. Peter*, p. 75, on I Pet. 1.19: 'the starting point of this and all similar language in the Epistles is our Lord's saying in Mark 10.45') is Mark 10.45=Matt. 20.28 (cf. Luke 22.24–7 and John 6.51, the Son of Man giving his flesh for the life of the world, 10.11 the good shepherd laying down his life for the flock, and 15.13 the master giving himself for his friends), which reads: 'the Son of Man came not to be ministered unto but to minister and to give his life a ransom for many'. Rashdall in *The Idea of the Atonement* devoted a long discussion to the thesis that the text was not authentic, but the arguments of V. Taylor, *Jesus and His Sacrifice*, present a convincing reply. 'It is better to conclude that Jesus has furnished a theme for later Pauline developments rather than that Mark has introduced a Pauline sentiment into the words of Jesus' (p. 105). The verse as a summary of the character and purpose of the ministry of Jesus asserts (1) the voluntariness of the act as a deliberate sacrifice of self; (2) the costliness of it, using the word employed to describe the price to be paid for the release of prisoners or the manumission of slaves; (3) something done for the many which they could not do for themselves but must have done if they were to have hope; the use of the preposition 'for', requiring the ordinary meaning of 'in place of the many', suggests a substitutionary idea which is elsewhere expressed by reference to what Christ bore for men (Rom. 3.24, Gal. 3.13, II Cor. 5.21); (4) the scope of redemption which is for many; this word does not conflict with the idea that it is for all men (cf. I John 2.2) and not merely for a select few. Behind such a saying lie the ideas and language of the Suffering Servant passage in Isa. 53 and possibly Ps. 49.7–9. The language in Mark 10.45 is distinctly sacrificial in tone, and it is to be observed that in two important NT passages, Rom. 3.24f. and I Pet. 1.18f., ransom and sacrifice are brought together in the effort to elucidate the meaning of the redemption that is in Christ (Eph. 1.7) and to show how God can forgive sin without compromising his righteousness.

Many other NT references emphasize the costliness of the redemption wrought by Christ (Gal. 1.4, 2.20, Eph. 5.2,25, Col. 1.14, Tit. 2.14), his precious blood being compared favourably with the ineffectual offering of the blood of bulls and goats (Heb. 9.12) or the money payments to release slaves (I Pet. 1.18f.). As in the OT the word denotes the objective atonement in Christ and the results which follow in the lives of believers. It is the sheer unmerited love of God which has been manifested in the suffering and death of Christ (Rom. 5.5, Gal. 2.20, II Cor. 5.14,19).

Three other points call for some comment. (1) The results of redemption, on which so much emphasis is laid especially in the Epistles, are to cleanse men from the guilt and power of sin (Heb. 9.14, I John 1.7,9), to make effective the knowledge of forgiveness (Acts 2.38, 13.38, Eph. 1.7), to deliver from futility (I Pet. 1.18) and alienation from God (Rom. 5.8, Eph. 2.12), to set men free from servitude to the assumptions and activities of the present world order (Gal. 1.4, Tit. 2.14), and to make of the redeemed a kingdom and priests unto God (Rev. 1.5), so that they shall reign even upon the earth (Rev. 5.10). (2) The recollection of the price paid by Christ to secure the redemption of men is set forth as the dynamic of Christian service (Gal. 2.20, I Pet. 2.21–3). The declaration twice repeated, 'ye are bought with a price' (I Cor. 6.20, 7.23; cf. II Pet. 2.1), is used as an incitement to Christian effort and loyalty. Because Christians belong to Christ by virtue of the price he has paid they must live worthily of the Master. He has established his claim to ownership of the Church by the shedding of his blood (Acts 20.28, Rev. 5.9) and the blood (*q.v.*) of the Lamb is the triumph song of the redeemed (Rev. 14.3,4). In Gal. 3.13, 4.4ff., the same ethical motive is described under the figure of slavery. Those who formerly were in a state of slavery have been purchased and set free and now live as sons in the divine household (*v.* BOND). (3) The term 'redemption' is sometimes used explicitly in an eschatological context, and is commonly to be interpreted against that background. The day of redemption (often proclaimed as near at hand) is a symbol for the completion of that redeeming work inaugurated by Christ (Eph. 1.14, 4.30). The experience of redemption which Christians now possess is but the first-fruits (a foretaste of the genuine article) of that full redemption whose scope will embrace all history and nature (Rom. 8.19–23). To summarize the evidence of the NT, the stress (as in the OT) is on the divine initiative in redemption, and the presupposition of all the writings is that in Christ full redemption has already entered into the world but awaits its final consummation. (See A. Deissmann, *Light from the Ancient East*, 4th ed., pp. 318–38). (*V.* also ATONE, DELIVER, RECONCILE, SAVE.)

F. J. TAYLOR

REFRESH *v.* NEW, WATER(IV)

REFRESHMENT *v.* REST

REFUGE *v.* ROCK

REGENERATION *v.* BIRTH

REJECT

In the OT the Heb. word (*ma'as*, meaning despise) is used for man's rejection of God, i.e. refusal to obey his commandments, and also for God's rejection of Israel (I Sam. 15.23ff. (Saul), Jer. 6.30, etc.). In the NT it is the rejection of Christ which is chiefly in view where the word 'reject' occurs (cf. Mark 8.31, 12.10). The Gk. word (*apodokimazo*) properly means 'set aside as unfit after examination', and so the thought is of the tragic mistake of human judgment, typified in the Jews, blinded by their own theories of the purpose of God and of what constitutes true religion, and as a consequence unable to realize that the purpose of God was being worked out in Christ and that true religion henceforward consisted in acknowledging him as the supreme agent of that purpose. (Also *v.* DENY.)

E. C. B.

REJOICE *v.* JOY

RELIGION, RELIGIOUS

The word 'religion' (Gk. *thrēskeia*) found in Acts 26.5 (RV) and Jas. 1.26f. does not mean 'religious belief', but rather 'cultus' or 'system of worship'. Thus St. James is saying what the OT prophets from Amos had reiterated, that the outward practice of religion is worthless apart from works of righteousness, or perhaps that 'good works' are the only form of cultus that God desires. In Acts 26.5 Paul is affirming that he had been a practising member of the most rigorous type of Pharisaic discipline; in Col. 2.18—the only other use of *thrēskeia* in the NT—Paul is referring to some cult of angel-worship at Colossae, but the word 'religion' is not here used in EVV. For 'religion' as a translation of the Gk. *deisidaimonia* ('fear of the gods') in Acts 25.19 (and cf. 17.22), *v.* SUPERSTITION. The phrase 'the Jews' religion' in Gal. 1.13f. represents the single Gk. word *Ioudaïsmos*, i.e. 'Judaism'. Thus, the word 'religion' as used to-day can hardly be said to be a biblical word at all; it does not occur in the OT, and in the NT there is no sanction for the modern usage. The faith of Christ is not presented as one of the 'religions' of the world, but as the unique and final truth with which no 'other gospel' may be compared (cf. Gal. 1.6ff.). (*V.* also SUPERSTITION.)

A. R.

REMEMBER, REMEMBRANCE *v.* MEMORY

REMNANT

The Bible presents the idea of the Remnant in two ways: first through the Hebrew words for the idea, and secondly in those passages where the idea of the remnant occurs but in which the terms are not employed. The 'remnant' terminology in the OT is represented mainly by the four roots, *srd*, *plt*, *ytr*, and *sh'r*. The first word describes mainly survivors from disaster (Josh. 10.28,30,37,39,40), or what is left over in regard to possessions (cf. Job. 20.21), esp. in J,E,D and prophetic usage. The second word, *plt*, describes deliverance, the noun being rendered 'escape' or 'deliverance'. When it is rendered 'remnant' the emphasis is on an 'escaped remnant', and is thus used of things (cf. Exod. 10.5), of persons (cf. Judg. 21.17, Isa. 15.9, etc.), of Judaeans who have escaped from the Assyrian invasion (cf. II Kings 19.30f.=Isa. 37.31,32, etc.), of the escaped of the nations (Isa. 45.20), and from Jehovah's final judgment (cf. Isa. 4.2, Obad. 17, Joel 2.32). The third root, *ythr*, means 'remain over', 'leave over', 'save over', 'show excess' and reveal 'pre-eminence'; the noun is similarly mainly used for remainder, and there are cases where it may be translated 'superiority', 'excellence' (Gen. 49.3), 'abundance' (Job 22.20), and in adverbial phrases 'abundantly' (cf. Isa. 56.12). As a remainder, it is used of 'the rest of the affairs of' in summary statements concerning the reigns of Israelite and Judaean kings (cf. I Kings 11.41), of the remainder of pastures (Exod. 10.15), of breaches in Jerusalem's walls (Neh. 6.1), of the Passover lamb (Exod. 12.10), of widow's oil (II Kings 4.7), of land (Ezek. 48.15), of temple vessels (I Kings 15.18, Jer. 27.18), of manna (Exod. 16.19) and other things; and of various types of people, of the king's sons (II Sam. 13.30), of sons of Aaron (Lev. 10.12,16), of David's army (I Sam. 30.9), of the Syrian army (I Kings 20.30), of the people, etc. (II Sam. 10.10) and of a remnant of Israel or Judah (*v. infra*)—altogether to describe the remainder of more than forty things or persons or peoples. The fourth term, *sh'r*, means to 'remain', 'be left over', 'leave' or 'keep over'. Similarly, the noun means 'rest', 'residue', 'remainder', 'remnant'. Again these words are employed to describe the remainder of nearly forty objects or persons as above. One of the nouns, *sh'erith*, can mean 'posterity' (Gen. 45.7), and is thus used closely with 'name' (II Sam. 14.7). From these, more than 430, recurrences of these roots in their various forms, the following account of the Remnant, in the theological sense of the term, may be derived.

The first root gives one reference only, Joel (2.32; cf. Heb. 3.5), 'and it shall come to pass that whosoever will invoke the name of Jehovah shall be delivered (*Plt*): for in Mount Zion and in Jerusalem shall be a deliverance (*Plt*) as Jehovah has said, and in the remnant ("survivors", pl. of *srd*) whom Jehovah shall call'. This reference shows that the remnant is called by Jehovah, is connected with Zion, is a future entity and is a place (or possibly a nucleus) of deliverance.

The remnant designated by *plt* will survive the sword (Ezek. 6.8), will announce Jehovah's vengeance (Jer. 50.28), will remember Jehovah (Jer. 51.50), will be blessed by God's presence (II Chron. 30.6), will have a fruitful destiny (II Kings 19.30=Isa. 37.32), will have a holy character (Isa. 4.2, Obad. 17), will be a nucleus of life (Ezek. 9.8), and will maintain life (Gen. 45.7). The *sh'r* root may be here used to illustrate the varying identity of the remnant. Thus the remnant is the remnant of all Israel (Deut. 4.27, 28.62, Isa. 46.3), or the remnant of the northern kingdom (II Kings 17.18, 21.14, II Chron. 30.6, Isa. 10.20, 28.5, Jer. 30.7), or the remnant of Judah (II Kings 19.30=Isa. 37.31, Jer. 40.11,15, 42.15,19, 43.5, II Chron. 36.20), or the remnant of Judah and Jerusalem (II Kings 19.4=Isa. 37.4, Jer. 8.3, Ezek. 5.10), or the remnant of Zion (Isa. 49.21, Ezek. 9.4,8), or of Jerusalem (Jer. 24.8, 38.4, 52.15, Neh. 1.2,3), and the remnant of Mizpah (Jer. 41.10) and the remnant of the remnant of Mizpah (Jer. 41.16, 44.7,12,28).

The idea of the remnant, however, is more widely employed in the OT than the terminology would suggest. The story of Noah clearly illustrates the remnant idea. He and his family are the survivors from the flood, and so of the first humanity, Noah at least is righteous (Gen. 7.1, 6.8,J, 6.9,P); the little group in the Ark maintain life through the crisis, and they become the founders of the new humanity. All the essential remnant ideas are present in that story. There is an approach to the remnant idea after the dispersal from Babel (Gen. 11). Here the 'second humanity' is not destroyed but scattered over the earth, and the story is concentrated in Shem, Eber and Abram. As interest centres in Abram to the neglect of other branches of the line of Shem and Eber, we see how the future is concentrated in Abraham (Gen. 20.1–3). This narrowing process is probably part of J's theory of history (cf. Exod. 33.16), and certainly of P's.

In the Exodus stories Moses is presumably the only man child saved from the slaughter in Egypt (Exod. 1.15–2.10,JE), and after many years he becomes the leader. Later in the story, when Jehovah is confronted with the idolatry of his people by their worship of the golden calf, he proposes to destroy the people and make of Moses alone a great nation (Exod. 32.10). Moses persuades Jehovah to desist, but the intention is quite clear. Jehovah would have destroyed the people, but one of their number would have been preserved, and he, i.e. Moses, a remnant, would have founded a new Israel. Finally, the wilderness generation does die in the wilderness, though Caleb and Joshua of that generation alone enter the promised land (Num. 14.30,P), apart presumably from the house of Aaron (cf. Josh. 24.33,E and 14.1, 17.4,P). Here a generation has to perish for its sins, though the life of the people is continued through their children. Samuel, future leader of Israel and inaugurator of the monarchy, was a survivor of the priestly community of Eli which tended the Ark.

It should also be borne in mind that from one point of view the idea of election contains the idea of a remnant. This is clearly seen in the choice of Noah to be the survivor from the flood. It is also implied in the call of the prophets. The prophets are called to proclaim the doom of their contemporaries, though not only is there the possibility that a small part will repent and be saved, but also that as possessors of Jehovah's word and believers in it, they will not perish, but form part of the remnant. This connection of election and remnant is to be seen notably in Isaiah. Whether Chapters 6 to 8 have an original connexion or not, Isaiah is called to be a prophet, and he and his family are to form the nucleus of the remnant mentioned in Isa. 8 whose leader is to be no other than Immanuel. More individually Jehovah promises Jeremiah his life when Jerusalem does fall (Jer. 39.18).

Since election (*v.* DETERMINE) is the prior and positive context of the idea of the remnant, it will be seen that, logically speaking, the remnant is not at first a saved remnant which becomes a saving remnant, but both functions of the remnant are original, the remnant survives and is therefore saved just as it also seeks to save others. Thus the prophets who predict the end also hold out the hope of life even if that is only for a remnant. Further, since election is really God's answer to human sin which deserves destruction or to human need which unless remedied may bring about the end of life, election throws into high relief the elect and the non-elect, or the remnant and the 'many'—the 'others'. Thus when election is presupposed, as in the Davidic king, the prophets, the Messiah, the Servant of the Lord, the Danielic Son of Man, and the Saints of the Most High, we have also to reckon with the idea of the remnant.

From the study of the Hebrew terms and from the appearance of the idea in the OT apart from the terms, the following characteristics of the idea of the remnant should be noted: (1) The remnant is made up of survivors from a great catastrophe, which is often regarded as a punishment for sin. The meaning of the Hebrew words and the consistency of this idea in the OT make examples superfluous. (2) Though the identity of those who have thus survived or will do so is left uncertain, there is a tendency to insist upon the righteous character of the remnant (Isa. 4.2, Obad. 17, Zeph. 3.13, Ezek. 9.4,8), or the faith of the remnant (Isa. 10.20, 28.16), or to claim the poor of the land as the remnant (II Kings 25.12,22, Jer. 39.10, 52.16, Zeph. 3.12; and cf. Isa. 11.4). (3) The surviving remnant survives the catastrophe, not only that its members may live, but that through them, and indeed in them, the life of the people to whom they belong may go on. In that sense the remnant is a 'depository' of that life which is destroyed in the majority. Thus Gen. 45.5,7 and Ezra 9.8, however late these passages may be, are especially instructive, because of the connexion between the 'posterity' and 'deliverance' mentioned and the root 'to live'. Joseph, for example, is described as a 'Mihyah', i.e. a place where life is to be found, a nucleus of life (Gen. 45.5). So in Isa. 4.2 the remnant consists of all those 'who are written for life in Jerusalem'. After the restoration the children of Israel will be known as the children of the living God (Hos. 1.10=Heb. 11.22). The connexion of the idea of the remnant with the idea of life is fundamental, and, indeed, may be of greater importance than its connexion with the idea of righteousness in the ethical sense of this word. (4) It is Jehovah who leaves a remnant. He is the Deliverer who causes seven thousand to remain in Israel (I Kings 19.18), and who remainders the daughter of Zion as a remnant in Israel for Judah (Isa. 1.8; and cf. Joel 2.32=Heb. 3.5, Zeph. 3.12). Hence prayer may be offered to God for the remnant (I Kings 19.4=Isa. 37.4, Jer. 42.2; and cf. Ps. 79.11). (5) If it may be said that sin is the real background or presupposition of election, and if election, thus the manifestation of God's grace as the divine response to sin, or indeed to human need, is the 'upper' or 'divine' side of remnant, then it also follows that separation is also a mark of the remnant. The separated character of the remnant is seen in the fact of its survival, in the qualities of righteousness that it possesses, and, especially, in its relationship to the presence of God. Thus the grace of God and his presence with his people, and their resultant separation, is clearly shown in Exod. 33.16. The eschatological reunion of presence and remnant is shown in Isa. 28.5 and II Chron. 30.6, and especially in Micah 2.12f., 4.4,7. The presence of the king with the remnant receives concrete expression in that destiny of the remnant whereby they too shall exercise the overlordship (Micah 5.8). The remnant is to enjoy world dominion. This application of kingship ideology (cf. Ps. 2, esp. vss. 7–8 and Ps. 110) to the remnant is noteworthy, and though this kingship ideology finds its proper sequel in the kingdom of God and his Christ, there is a similar extension of the thought in such passages as I Cor. 6.2 and Rev. 1.6, for example.

In the light of the foregoing evidence the question arises whether there are any marked stages in the development of the idea of the remnant in the OT. It may fairly be claimed that the OT writers represented by the symbols J and E saw in Noah the remnant of the first humanity descended from earth's first human pair. Taking into account the idea of election as the upper and divine side of the remnant, it is possible to discover in these same early writers the idea that Abraham and his seed are also a remnant. It is the scattering of mankind from Babel which is here the background catastrophe, and interest is concentrated in the line of Shem, and within Shem, in the line of Terah. It is not in mankind, scattered to the four winds, that progress lies, but henceforward in Abraham and his descendants the purpose of God is active. In a manner of speaking, then, Abraham and his seed are the remnant of the second mankind sprung from the house of Noah.

In the days of Moses and for many centuries thereafter there can be no thought of a remnant in national terms. The history of Israel from Moses to the monarchy is the history of the achievement of the idea and the fact of Israel. The idea of remnant reappears in the decline of the nation. The fall of the northern kingdom before the Assyrians in 722 leaves Judah as the remnant of Israel. In II Kings 17.18, 'and Jehovah was very angry with Israel, and removed them out of his sight; there was none left but the tribe of Judah only' (cf. II Kings 21.14, Ps. 78, esp. vss. 67–8, Hos. 1.7, Isa. 1.8, 28.5, Micah. 2.12, etc.). Such passages show that Judah was regarded as the remnant of Israel. The prophetic denunciation of Judah leads us in turn to expect a further shrinking in the remnant. In this way begins to emerge the idea of a remnant of Judah (Isa. 4.2ff., 37.31,32, Zeph. 2.7, Jer. 40.11,15. Ezek. 11.13, 14.22, Obad. 17), though the remnant which survives the exile and is considered to have a future is variously described (cf. Jer. 3.11–14, 31.2–6,7–9, and Zech. 8.6,12, Ezra 9.8,13,14,15).

These passages reveal the dwindling of the remnant from Israel to Judah, and to smaller units within them both. This dwindling process may thus be briefly outlined. From the first humanity to the family of Noah; from this second humanity to a family again, that of Abraham; from the nation of Abraham's descendants and related groups, that is Israel, to Judah, and still smaller groups.

Further study of the idea of the remnant will inevitably concern itself with this question of the identity of the remnant, and thus with the question whether the remnant in the OT is merely to be regarded as an idea, and not also as a historical fact. The line of prophets and especially Isaiah and his group of disciples confirm the view that the OT remnant is not merely an idea, but is a historical fact. If this be the case the question of the identity and function, of the person and work of the remnant, will continue to be of the greatest importance for christology. Further, the idea of the remnant is inevitably a nexus for much biblical theology, and its proper study calls for this wider context, not merely in the OT and NT, but also within Judaism.

Strictly speaking, the Resurrection of our Lord is the end of the remnant idea. Here he who is truly the righteous remnant 'survived' the ultimate catastrophe, 'death', by resurrection. In that survival life was maintained and indeed made available by the act of God, and thereafter the Presence and Kingship of God are manifested in and bound up with the resurrected Lord. The Resurrection was like a fly-wheel to the purpose of God in his remnant.

They who participate in this new life are the new Israel, the heirs of the people of God, the colony of heaven, and the 'remnant according to the election of grace' (Rom. 11.5). But the very paucity of references to the remnant in the NT shows that the resurrection has put the remnant into reverse. Henceforth it is the destiny of the 'Christian Remnant' not to dwindle, but to expand, though, of course, the warning in Matt. 7.13,14 should not be forgotten. (*V.* also DETERMINE, SERVANT, SON OF MAN.)

BIBLIOGRAPHY

T. W. Manson: *The Teaching of Jesus*, London (1931), Chap. vii.

G. HENTON DAVIES

RENEW *v.* NEW

REPAY *v.* REWARD

REPENT, REPENTANCE, CONVERT, CONVERSION, TURN, RETURN

The word 'repent' is infrequent in the OT, and in many cases is used of Jehovah, not of men: 'the Lord repented that he had made Saul king' (I Sam. 15.35); 'he repented according to the multitude of his mercies' (Ps. 106.45). This usage shows that the word can be used in a morally neutral sense, with the meaning of 'change one's mind' or 'reverse one's former judgment'. The Heb. mind is not afraid of thus speaking about God anthropomorphically, yet such language is only superficially inconsistent with the idea of God's changelessness: his purpose remains the same, but when it encounters human obstinacy or fickleness it seeks to achieve itself by changing its former attitude or policy. Cf. Num. 23.19, 'God is not a man . . . that he should repent'; I Sam. 15.29, 'he is not a man that he should repent'; Ps. 110.4, 'the Lord hath sworn and will not repent'. Furthermore, it should be noted that repentance in biblical usage is not always 'godly repentance'; Judas 'repented himself' (Matt. 27.3, *metamelesthai*), i.e. changed his mind.

In the OT the idea of repentance is often expressed by such words as 'turn', 'return'. The fundamental idea behind the use of these words in a religious sense is that of subjects who had rebelled coming back to serve their rightful king, or of a faithless wife returning to her husband, or of those who had been seduced by the baals (*v.* under GOD, IV) returning to the worship of Jehovah. In this sense 'turning' means much more than a mere change of mind, though it includes this; it represents a reorientation of one's whole life and personality, which includes the adoption of a new ethical line of conduct, a forsaking of sin and a turning to righteousness. That this was the fundamental call of the prophets to Israel can be seen by a casual glance at a concordance under 'turn', 'turn again' (contrast 'turn aside') and 'return'. It will be noted that the contemporary prophets (Deutero-Isaiah, Haggai, Zechariah) hoped that the Return (from the Exile) would prove in this deep sense a return unto the Lord. The sacrificial system of the Old Covenant (*v.* SACRIFICE) was not closely connected with penitential longings, and this side of its use is certainly ignored by the prophets even where they do not openly assert its ineffectiveness; what the Lord requires is not sacrifice but a clean heart. At the deepest level of OT religion it is perceived that all that men can offer to God is not their righteousness but their contrition (Ps. 51, esp. vs. 17); though elsewhere it seems to be suggested that man can, if he wills to do so, fulfil the Lord's requirements of mercy, justice and humility (Micah 6.6–8). But this must be balanced by other passages in which we find a deep insight into the truth that it is God himself who must give to men repentance and a clean heart (Ps. 51.10, Ezek. 36.26, Jer. 31.33; cf. Ps. 19.7).

In the NT the prophetic requirement that repentance should be sincere—'rend your heart and not your garments' (Joel 2.13)—is deepened and made a *sine qua non* of entry into the Kingdom of God in the teaching of our Lord. This was in strong contrast to the current attitude of Pharisaic religion (Mark 7.6 and context, Luke 18.9–14), which stressed outward observances rather than inward 'turning'. But it was John the Baptist who had first revived the prophetic call to repentance, making the latter the condition of escape from the judgment at hand (Matt. 3.1ff.). Jesus makes 'repent and believe' the key-note of his Galilean preaching (Mark 1.15), thus indicating the integral connexion between repentance and faith. The encounter with Christ produced both these things in men's hearts (cf. Zacchaeus, Luke 19.1–10), and both of them are God's gifts, not men's achievements (cf. Acts 5.31, 11.18, Rom. 2.4, II Tim. 2.25). To awaken to repentance is part and parcel of the awakening to faith; repentance means turning from sin just as faith involves turning to God. Repentance thus means much more than being sorry for one's misdeeds; it involves the active acceptance of God's gift of faith. Jesus' supreme teaching on this matter is found in the parable of the Prodigal Son (Luke 15); and the adjacent parables of the Lost Sheep and the Lost Coin stress the 'joy in heaven over one sinner that repenteth'. Indeed, the whole mission of Jesus is represented under the figure of the Good Shepherd going out to seek and to save that which is lost, to lead to repentance those who have gone astray (cf. Mark 2.13–17). Small wonder, then, that the earliest apostolic *kērugma* (preaching) always included the call for repentance (*v.* PREACH), since without it faith itself is impossible. Thus, though the Gk. word *metanoein* is often used for 'repent', in its NT usage it implies much more than a mere 'change of mind'; it involves a whole reorientation of the personality, a 'conversion'. The NT does not teach that conversion to faith is either a rapid or a dateable process; indeed, long after Peter's confession the Lord says to him, 'when thou art converted . . .' (Luke 22.32, AV). The word 'convert' is rare in EVV, and RV usually prefers the literal form, 'turn again' (*epistrephein*, to turn). The word 'conversion' occurs in EVV only in Acts 15.3, 'the conversion of the Gentiles'. (*V.* also FORGIVE.)

ALAN RICHARDSON

REPROOF, REPROVE *v.* CORRECT

REQUITE *v.* REWARD

REST

(*i*) To desist (Isa. 62.1, Rev. 4.8). Of temporary cessation from labour with a view to further activity (Mark 6.31); of sleep (Mark 14.41). Hence connected with REFRESHMENT (Gen. 18.4), given by Jehovah to those who trust in him and not in foreign powers (Isa. 28.12), enjoyed through the SABBATH (*q.v.*) (Exod. 23.12), by God himself (Exod. 31.17), by Christians through the exchange of love and fellowship (I Cor. 16.18, II Cor. 7.13, Philem. 20 (Gk. 'cause to rest'). For Acts 3.19 *v.* RESTORE.

(*ii*) Connected with peace (Ps. 38.3 marg.) in its negative aspect. PEACE (*q.v.*) is positive, consisting in the fullest expansion of life through covenant or victorious warfare; rest is security and undisturbed possession, esp. of the Promised Land (a favourite conception of Deuteronomy, and of books edited from the Deuteronomic standpoint: Deut. 3.20, Josh. 1.13–15, Judg. 3.11, etc., II Sam. 7.11, I Kings 8.56), the absence of enemies and cessation of war (Josh. 21.44, II Chron. 14.6). This became the ideal of later Israel. Hence David, in earlier tradition a man of peace because successful in war (II Sam. 19.30), is later characterized as a man of war in contrast to Solomon, who through despotic rule ensures security (I Chron. 22.7–10). Rest, the opposite of turmoil of spirit (Job 30.27, Ps. 55.6, Jer. 45.3), the reward of tranquil trust in Jehovah (Isa. 30.15), denied to the wicked (Isa. 57.20), equivalent to death as the final cessation from strife (Isa. 57.2, Job 3.13–17).

(*iii*) Positively, satisfaction, in the sense that there is a limit to the expansion of life, and a goal which is divinely appointed. Jehovah gives rest (Exod. 33.14), causes to rest in the land which he has promised (Deut. 12.9), which thus becomes the symbol of man's true home; disobedience to Jehovah forfeits secure possession of it (Deut. 28.58–68, Ps. 95.11, Neh. 9.28, Mic. 2.10; cf. Jer. 6.16), deliverance from the consequences of disobedience will be entry into a new Promised Land (Jer. 31.1–9, of the N. Kingdom, Isa. 14.1–3, 63.7–18, Ezek. 34); the sabbath (*q.v.*) a sign of the attainment of this goal through divine deliverance (Deut. 5.14f.), of God's own attainment in the finished work of Creation (Exod. 20.8–11, Gen. 2.2f.). Rest is the gift of the Wisdom of God to those who seek her (Ecclus. 6.28, 51.27).

(*iv*) Resting place (Gen. 8.9, Matt. 12.43), home (Ruth 3.1), permanent abode, esp. of Jehovah in Zion (I Chron. 28.2, Ps. 132.8–14, Isa. 66.1), of the Messiah (Isa. 11.10), of the Spirit of God possessing the elders (Num. 11.25f.), abiding with the Messiah (Isa. 11.2, with Christians who suffer for Christ (I Pet. 4.14); of the abode of the divine Wisdom in Israel (Ecclus. 24.7–11).

In Matt. 11.28–30, which is closely related in form to Ecclus. 51 (cf. also Jer. 6.16), 'to give rest', in the double sense of relief from fruitless labour and of permanent satisfaction, describes the saving work of Jesus. Those to whom the Pharisaic law is burdensome and oppressive are invited by Jesus (who may be identifying himself with the divine Wisdom) to come to him, and to receive the true knowledge of God which he alone possesses as Son and the obedience which the presence of the Kingdom makes easy.

Heb. 3.7–4.11 expounds the salvation in Christ, and the faith which appropriates it, in terms of rest. The commission to Joshua (LXX, Jesus) to lead Israel into the Promised Land implies a divinely appointed goal for the people of God (the heavenly Jerusalem, Heb. 12.22, a heavenly country, 11.16, the city whose maker and builder is God, 11.10), which is, to share God's own sabbath rest, i.e. his purposeful, creative activity and the satisfaction which belongs to it. This was not achieved by the entry into Canaan because of unbelief, and in the OT it remains in the sphere of promise, as is indicated by the reference to another day (Ps. 95). This rest belongs to the last days, which have become 'To-day' through the final revelation in Christ, who conducts into the heavenly places, and it is entered upon by those who are partakers of Christ, if they maintain faith to the end. For rest as the final state of the elect, in the cessation from strife with evil and in the harvesting of good works, *v.* Rev. 14.13. (*V.* also PEACE, PROMISE, RESTORE, SABBATH, SLEEP, WORK.)

C. F. EVANS

RESTORE

Connected with peace (*q.v.*) in the sense of WHOLENESS (cf. Mark 3.5, 8.25, John 7.23, etc., for restoration to wholeness through acts of healing), and with righteousness which maintains harmony within a community and equilibrium between communities. Breaches of harmony by violence and fraud constitute serious wrong (Ezek. 18.5–13, II Sam. 12.5–6) which must be made good (I Sam. 12.3, Judg. 11.13, Luke 19.8: 'to make restitution', 'redeem', 'avenge'). Israelite law laid down compensation for such (Exod. 22.1–7, Lev. 6.1–5, Deut. 22.1f.; cf. Neh. 5.11f., Prov. 6.31), and required the next of kin to intervene as restorer (*goel*) in the case of a man who dies without issue (Ruth 4.14f.), or who is so poor that he sells family possessions (Lev. 25.25), or who falls into slavery (Lev. 25.47–54). Jehovah is the *goel* or restorer of Israel from the wretched state consequent upon sin into a blessed and harmonious life (Jer. 30.12–22, Isa. 42.22–43.6, Joel 2.25), from captivity into the enjoyment of its former possessions upon repentance ('to bring again', 'to turn the captivity', Jer. 15.19, 16.15, 24.6, 31.23, Deut. 30.2f.) and who refreshes with strength the pious Israelite (Ps. 23.3).

The question in Acts 1.6 reflects Jewish expectation that the Messiah would restore the supremacy of Israel; Jesus does not reject the belief itself, but its political form, and links it to the progress of the Gospel through the Spirit (1.7f.). In the Gospels restoration is the function ascribed to Elijah as the forerunner of the Messiah. The belief in the return of Elijah, derived from Mal. 4.5 (which identifies him with the messenger of the covenant, the forerunner of God, cf. Mal. 3.1), developed in Ecclus. 48.10 and by the Rabbis (Mark 9.11), for whom he was the forerunner of the Messiah, was widespread (cf. Mark 6.15, 8.28, John 1.21–5), and was accepted by Jesus (Mark 9.12), who identifies him with the Baptist (Matt. 11.14, Mark 9.13). The restoration of 'all things' (Mark 9.12) is probably to be understood, with reference to the form of this expectation, as meaning the establishment of harmonious relations between Israelites, and the preparation through repentance of a whole people ready to receive the salvation of the last days (Mal. 4.4ff., Luke 1.16f.; Ecclus. 48.10 adds 'to restore the tribes of Jacob', i.e., probably, to bring back the Dispersion), possibly with reference to Elijah as the restorer of the covenant (I Kings 19.10). Acts 3.19–21 (if the correct translation is not 'until the times of the establishment of all things which God spake . . .') refers to a wider renewal of the whole earth, and a restoration to a paradisal existence in the last times (cf. 'regeneration', 'new creation') as the content of prophecy (Isa. 11.1–9, 65.17), to be realized in the coming of Jesus, the risen and ascended Messiah, with power in response to the repentance of Israel (cf. Amos 5.15, etc.); 3.19 refers either to the subjective aspect of this as 'revival' (cf. Isa. 57.15–21), or the present anticipation of it in the forgiveness of sins (cf. 3.26). (*V.* also NEW, PEACE, REST, SABBATH.)

C. F. EVANS

RESURRECTION

This art. deals with (*a*) the resurrection of Christ, and (*b*) that of those who are 'in Christ'. For treatment of the general idea of resurrection and of life after death in OT and rabbinic theology, *v.* under HELL. Also *v.* concluding para. of art. HELL for treatment of the resurrection of the body. (*V.* also IMMORTAL.)

(*a*) *The Resurrection of Christ.* Every book in the NT declares or assumes that Christ rose from the dead. This event took place 'on the third day' (acc. to Jewish ways of reckoning), i.e. on the Sunday morning after Jesus was crucified on the Friday afternoon. The narratives which describe this happening in all four Gospels are late in date, since none of them could have been written (as we now have them) less than fifty years afterwards. [For a consideration of the historical evidence which they present, *v.* art. 'The Evidence of the Resurrection' by E. G. Selwyn in the S.P.C.K. *New Commentary on Holy Scripture* (Part III, pp. 301ff.).] Much earlier documentary evidence is supplied by St. Paul in I Cor. 15. The main evidence for the r. of Christ, however, is provided by the existence and growth of the Church itself, if we have regard to the circumstances in which the earthly mission of Jesus ended on Good Friday in utter catastrophe. That the Apostles within a few weeks of the crucifixion should have boldly confronted those who had condemned Jesus and proclaimed his r. and lordship—this is the real evidence for the r. as a fact of history (cf. Acts 2.23f.,32, 3.14f., and esp. 4.10). Full weight should be given to the fact that from the earliest days the characteristic act of worship of the apostolic community was 'the breaking of bread' (*q.v.*)—surely a memorial of unbearable sadness except for the knowledge of the Risen Christ: 'he was known of them in the breaking of the bread' (Luke 24.35). Luke's Emmaus story (24.13–35) implies that the Risen Lord was made known in his Church in two ways: in the expounding of the Scriptures (*q.v.*) and in the breaking of bread, i.e. through the ministry of the Word and Sacraments. In both these ways still to-day is the power of Christ's r. made known in his Church.

The NT writers regard the r. of Christ as the fulfilment of scriptural prophecy (cf. esp. I Cor. 15.4). Like his passion and death, the r. was a part of the predetermined divine plan for our salvation; but, since the gravamen of the Jewish objection to the Messiahship of Jesus lay in their inability to believe that the Christ should suffer rather than that he should triumph over death, the NT writers are found more frequently arguing that the passion had been foretold by the prophets (e.g. Luke 24.46). Nevertheless, the apostles firmly held that the r. had been predicted in the Scriptures (e.g. Acts 2.25–36); it was no mere afterthought or attempt to make the best of a bad job: it was (like Christ's death) a part of God's eternal purpose. The r. of Christ shed a new light on the ancient scriptures; they could now be read with a fresh understanding which illuminated many obscure and unexplained prophecies and mysteries. [The problem whether Jesus himself predicted his r. (Mark 8.31, 9.31, 10.34, etc.) or whether these predictions have been read back into his life-time by the evangelists raises difficult critical and Christological questions which probably admit of no conclusive answer.]

The NT writers are concerned to proclaim the r. of Jesus, not to explain it. It is a mystery beyond human comprehension, and the Apostles are its witnesses, not its psychologists. It has come to them as a fact, not as a philosophical explanation. The earliest recollections of the apostolic proclamation (e.g. the sermons of St. Peter in Acts) give no rationale or account of the mode in which it took place. St. Paul does not seem to have been called upon to explain to the Corinthians the nature of Christ's resurrection body. It is not until we reach the later stages of the tradition (the stories in the Gospels) that we find definite teaching concerning the bodily r. of the Lord. The Gospel accounts teach or imply that Jesus rose in the body (Luke 24.39–43, John 20.6f.,27), though it is implied that his risen body possessed capacities not shared by our ordinary bodies (John 20.26). The tomb was empty—and indeed the strongest evidence for the physical r. consists in the fact that the Sanhedrin did not produce the putrefying corpse of Jesus to disprove the preaching of the r., although it had been buried in the garden of one of their own number; the slander that the disciples themselves had stolen and hidden the body is at least as old as the first century (Matt. 28.13)—but it is notoriously difficult to dispose of a dead body! Towards the end of the first century AD there were many teachers of strange doctrine, including docetists who taught that Jesus Christ had not come in the flesh at all (I John 4.1f.), so that his incarnate life was only an apparition and his r. the ghost of an apparition. Against all theories that the Risen Christ was merely a kind of ghostly appearance the Church taught that his r. was real, objective, palpable—bodily. His presence to the Apostles after his r. was as 'real' as his bodily presence in Galilee had been. Against all modern attempts to explain the r. as something natural and comprehensible (e.g. a case of spiritualistic survival, such as might be the subject of a piece of psychical research, as with other such reported phenomena), it is necessary to insist that the r. of Jesus is *miracle*, mysterious and irreducible, from the biblical point of view. Despite (or, rather, because of) the advances of modern physical science, we now know that we know so little about the properties of bodies that we must not dogmatize about what the body of the Lord could or could not have done; and the Christian mind will be slow to set aside the apostolic witness in favour of any changing modern hypotheses. Without committing ourselves to any crudely materialistic notions or any over-simple explanations of the mode of the r., we may maintain that the doctrine of the physical r. conserves more of the unfathomable truth behind the mystery than does the denial of it. It is a fitting symbol of the truth that the redemption wrought by Christ includes the whole natural order, including the physical world, and is not limited to any merely 'spiritual' elements: the material realm is the vehicle and sacrament of the eternal order. The 'whole creation' is to be redeemed (Rom. 8.22f.).

The NT writers affirm that the r. of Christ was God's act (Acts 2.24,32, etc., Rom. 6.4, I Cor. 15.15, Heb. 13.20, I Pet. 1.21, etc.) in the same sense that the OT writers had taught that the redemption of Israel from Egypt or Babylon was God's act. The r. too is connected with redemption; St. Paul esp. connects the r. with the atoning work of Christ—not merely his passion and death ('raised for our justification', Rom. 4.25; cf. 8.33f., Phil. 3.9–11). It is the sign vouchsafed by God of the ultimate victory over sin, death and the devil (Rom. 6.9, I Cor. 15.26, etc.), but in this age the victory is discerned only by faith (*v.* HOPE): the Risen Christ appeared to none save believers, nor will he be seen save by the eye of faith till the Parousia (Rev. 1.7). In this sense the r. of the Lord must be viewed as an eschatological sign or symbol in history of the ultimate consummation of God's purpose 'beyond history'—the final triumph of God (I Cor. 15.20–8).

(*b*) *The Resurrection of Christians 'in Christ'.* The Christian hope of resurrection is not based on any speculation—philosophical or apocalyptic—but on the fact of Christ's r. If Jesus had been a man like us, of whom it had been credibly reported that his survival had been demonstrated, the matter would have no Christian significance: what of it if a man's spirit had succeeded in making contact with the earth from 'the other side'? Such things are reported at every 'spiritualistic' rally. The point is that Christ was not merely a man, but Man, representative humanity, in whom the human race in principle triumphed over death. 'Since by man came death, by man came also the r. of the dead. For as in Adam all die, even so in Christ shall all be made alive' (I Cor. 15.21f.). Christ is the 'last Adam' (15.45), who finally crushes the serpent's head (Gen. 3.15; *v.* ADAM). Those who are 'in Christ' partake of the New Humanity of the Second Adam (cf. II Cor. 5.17, I Pet. 1.3). At their baptism into Christ they die and are raised in him to share in his risen life. 'All we who were baptized into Christ Jesus were baptized into his death. We were buried therefore with him through baptism into death: that like as Christ was raised from the dead through the glory of the Father, so we also might walk in newness of life' (Rom. 6.3f.; see the whole passage, 6.3–14). Christian baptism is no mere service of 'reception and blessing'; it is incorporation into the body of Christ, a new birth ('regeneration') out of sin into righteousness. For the baptized death is past: they have died, and now they live the eternal life. Although the natural phenomenon of physical death must still take place, the mortal crisis of spiritual death and judgment is a thing of the past (*v.* DEATH): henceforward they are 'alive unto God in Christ Jesus' (Rom. 6.11). But Christian baptism is for the NT no merely magical rite, since faith is always required of the candidate for baptism (*v.* BAPTISM). We have died and been raised again in our baptism, but in this dispensation we live the risen life by faith; we walk by faith, not by sight (II Cor. 5.7). As the Risen Lord appeared only to believers, so he appears to us in this life only by faith; if we have not faith, we shall not know him, and our baptism will be an empty ceremony. Thus it comes about that the Church is both the company of those who are baptized and the fellowship of those who believe; there can be no antithesis between sacrament and faith. The NT conception of our resurrection life is thoroughly eschatological; it is stressed (esp. in John's Gospel and I John) that here and now Christians have eternal life (*v.* LIFE), but they have it by faith; in principle they have passed from death to life (I John 3.14). Their assurance of this results from the convincing work of the Holy Spirit within them—the 'earnest' (II Cor. 5.5) of their ultimate salvation (I John 4.13). The Spirit, given in baptism, is the mode of Christ's indwelling in his disciples (*v.* SPIRIT) and in them he works according as he will (I Cor. 12). 'If the Spirit of him that raised up Jesus from the dead dwelleth in you, he that raised up Christ Jesus from the dead shall quicken also your mortal bodies through his Spirit that dwelleth in you' (Rom. 8.11). The Spirit is the agent by which we come to faith (I Cor. 12.3), and his presence is the assurance of him in whom we have believed, until after our physical death we shall see him as he is. We must never forget that, though even now we know Christ 'by faith', nevertheless, 'to die is gain', since that is 'to be with Christ, which is far better' (Phil. 1.21,23; cf. the whole context). The Church must continue till the end of the age to bear her apostolic witness to Jesus and the resurrection, and this she must do—paradoxically and gloriously—by 'shewing forth the Lord's death till he come' (I Cor. 11.26).

BIBLIOGRAPHY

A. M. Ramsey: *The Resurrection of Christ*, London (1945).

ALAN RICHARDSON

RETURN *v.* REPENT

REVEAL, REVELATION

Reveal means literally to unveil, to remove the covering by which some object is hidden and so to expose it to view. In the Bible, however, it is scarcely ever employed in this general sense. It might have been expected to occur in II Cor. 3.13ff. (cf. Exod. 34.33–5), where the cognate word is used of the veil that covered Moses' face, or in I Cor. 11.5f., where Paul speaks of the covering of the woman's head, but in both passages he employs different compounds to describe the removal or absence of the covering. 'Reveal' and 'revelation' in the Bible are used almost exclusively in reference to God and divine things, and may thus be described as technical-theological terms. They are of fundamental importance for the understanding of the Bible, which consists of recorded testimony to *the* revelation of God. (The Gk. word for 'revelation' is APOCALYPSE.)

I. THE REVELATION OF GOD

The proper subject of revelation is God, God himself in his being and works. God reveals himself, and we are dependent on his revelation of himself for all our knowledge of God. Had we no revelation, God would remain absolutely hidden (John 1.18, I Tim. 6.16). All human endeavours to obtain knowledge of God by independent inquiry are vain (I Cor. 1.21), and those who pretend to a knowledge of God otherwise than by his revelation of himself are impostors; such pretended knowledge of God is to revelation as the chaff to the wheat (Jer. 23.28).

Revelation is essential because the realm of God is exalted above this world (I Tim. 6.16); he dwelleth on high (Isa. 33.5); he is the high and lofty one that inhabiteth eternity (Isa. 57.15); he is in heaven, and we upon earth (Eccles. 5.2). In modern language, God is transcendent. He is not an object accessible to our observation in the world. He cannot be 'imaged' in the categories at our disposal (Exod. 20.4). The knowledge of God must be given to us by God himself. Faith comes by hearing (Rom. 10.17).

Ideas of revelation are common to all religions (with the possible exception of Buddhism); nowhere is the divine conceived as directly accessible in the same way as objects of sense and human beings. But only in the Bible is revelation asserted in the strict and absolute sense. Here God himself is at once the subject and the object of it. It does not consist in the impartation of supernatural knowledge or the disclosure of the future. These may indeed occur (e.g. in I Sam. 9.9 we read of a custom observed 'when a man went to inquire of God'); but they are secondary and incidental to the main theme, which is God's revelation of himself—as, in the instance cited, when Saul came to Samuel to inquire about the asses, the answer concerned God's purpose with his people. So also, while the earlier strata of the OT show that the technical means of procuring revelation, familiar elsewhere, were employed in Israel (lots, dreams, auspices, etc.), these were realized to be survivals of heathenism incompatible with the spiritual faith of the prophets (Isa. 8.19), and they were roundly condemned in the Deuteronomic legislation (Deut. 18.9–12). Revelation is not a thing to be procured from God by any technique; it is living encounter with God himself, and it is to be received only by *waiting* upon him (Ps. 123).

The content of revelation is the living God. This is the new and unique revelation to Israel (Jer. 10.10). God reveals himself as the living and personal God. His revelation is therefore fraught with mystery; for he reveals himself as the Lord, whose ways are higher than our ways, and whose thoughts are higher than our thoughts. Even in his self-disclosure he remains a hidden God (Isa. 45.15).

The personal character of God's revelation is expressed in the language of the OT by the NAME OF GOD. The name bears a fuller connotation than we associate with it in modern speech and probably comes nearer to our conception of person or personality. It is by the communication of his name that a personal being makes himself known to another. Thus when God makes known his name to men, it means that he makes himself personally known to them. Something resembling a formal introduction is recorded in Exod. 3.11–15 (cf. 6.2f.), where the mysterious divine name is communicated to Moses. But the thought is more often of what the knowledge of the name of God means for those to whom it is given: they have access to his presence in prayer. This is particularly true of the temple in Jerusalem as the place of which God said, 'My name shall be there' (I Kings 8.29). To know the name of God is to have a sure refuge (Ps. 9.9f.). There is nothing in which the personality of God is more clearly expressed than in the fact that he has a name which he imparts to men as the means of establishing a personal relationship with them.

II. THE MANNER OF REVELATION

God reveals himself in his acts on the plane of history. The fundamental fact of OT faith is the liberation of Israel from the house of bondage (Exod. 19.4, 20.2, Amos 2.10, Hos. 11.1, Ps. 81.10); it is by this act that God made himself known to Israel (Exod. 6.7). For God acts in history, and through all that he does he makes himself known (Deut. 3.24, 11.2–7). The creed of Israel consists of a rehearsal of the acts of God, and the books of the OT which we call 'historical' were described in the Jewish Canon as 'the earlier prophets'; for the history they record is not that of the people of Israel, but the mighty acts of the Lord (Ps. 106.2).

God's mighty and gracious acts, however, often failed to achieve their revealing purpose because of the blindness and obtuseness of his people (Isa. 1.2f.). So God raised up a special class of men to speak for him and to be interpreters of his work (Amos 3.7, Hos. 6.5, 12.10, Jer. 7.25, 25.4, II Kings 17.13). These men, the prophets, became by an act of grace (Deut. 18.15–18) the great agents of God's revelation of himself by his word. Yet the word is never to be thought of in an intellectualistic sense as the communication of abstract truth. The Heb. term for 'word' means also thing, act, event, and with God word and work are one (Gen. 1.3, Ps. 103.7); the word of God is the speaking or significant side of his work.

The revelation of God by his word exhibits its character as an essentially personal transaction; for word, as rational and intelligible address, is the proper means of communication between person and person. The Bible knows of 'theophany', where God appears in his overwhelming majesty in a manner terrifying to behold (Exod. 33.12–23, 19.16, Heb. 12.21), but such occurrences are rare. The 'numinous' has no independent place in the Bible; it is never more than an accompaniment of revelation. Revelation is essentially a dialogue, in which God speaks his word, addresses it to man's understanding, and seeks to elicit an understanding response (Isa. 6). It is of the grace of God that he chooses to reveal himself to men, not as the 'wholly other', but by 'one of thy brethren, like unto me [Moses]' (Deut. 18.15). He comes to meet us where we are, on our own level. 'The word is nigh thee' (Deut. 30.14, Rom. 10.8); there is no need to scale the heights or plumb the depths.

The revelation of God achieves its consummation in Jesus Christ, in whom all that was scattered and fragmentary in the former dispensation is gathered into unity and fullness (Heb. 1.1–2). The NT revelation is sometimes contrasted with that of the OT as the final with the provisional, the permanent with the transient, the perfect with the imperfect, the substance with the shadow (II Cor. 3.7–11, Heb. 7–10), but more often it is set in direct continuity with it as the fulfilment of the promise and the realization of the hope (Luke 1.54f., 68–75, 4.21, Acts 2.16, I Pet. 1.10–12). For the revelation of God in the OT was prospective; it pointed beyond itself to a future consummation to which the men who received it looked forward—and already saw (Matt. 13.17, John 8.56, Heb. 11.13, I Pet. 1.10f.). It is the revelation of God in Christ that discloses the meaning of the OT revelation (Rom. 3.21, II Cor. 3.14); the NT is the definitive exposition of the OT (Luke 24.27, John 5.39). Christ stands at the convergence of all the perspectives of the OT. In him all the diverse strands and fragments of revelation are gathered up into a single, significant pattern; in him the Scriptures are fulfilled.

The revelation of God is not confined to the words of Christ which are merely the 'running commentary' upon his work (the NT lends no countenance to the modern practice of isolating the Sermon on the Mount as the essence of Christianity); revelation is to be found in the whole fact of Christ, his person and work, his life, death, resurrection, ascension and promised advent in glory.

III. IS THERE A 'NATURAL REVELATION'?

Is the revelation of God, however, confined to his 'mighty acts' recorded in Scripture? Is no trace of him to be discerned in the world around us? Is there not a natural revelation, i.e. a knowledge of God which is always and everywhere available to men? Such was the teaching of the Stoic philosophers. The idea was taken up by the Alexandrian Jewish philosopher, Philo, and it was accepted by the writer of the apocryphal Book of Wisdom (Wisd. 13). Many have supposed it to be present also in the famous passage in Rom. 1.19f. and in some of the so-called 'nature psalms' such as 19, 29, 104. The thought can only be read into these passages, however, when they are detached from their biblical context. It is impossible to conceive of the Psalmist contemplating nature in an abstract way as a second or alternative source of the knowledge of God, if only because the idea of 'nature' as something abstracted from God is entirely unknown to him (cf. H. Wheeler Robinson, *Inspiration and Revelation in the Old Testament*, p. 1). It is creation he contemplates, and the source of his inspiration is clearly shown in Ps. 19: what he celebrates is the reflection in creation of the light which has been given to him in the law (vs. 7) and by which his eyes have been enlightened (vs. 8) to see this reflection. As Dr. E. F. Scott has written: 'The 19th Psalm is paraphrased in Addison's well-known hymn as if it were nothing but a statement of the argument from design. The stars address themselves to "reason's ear", and are forever singing "the hand that made us is divine". But the Psalmist never doubted the existence of God, and requires no proof of it. Neither was he concerned with anything that the stars might say to "reason's ear". His mood is one of sheer rapture, and this is always the mood of those Hebrew poets. They do not argue from nature, but exult in it. . . .' (*The New Testament Idea of Revelation*, p. 39.) The interpretation of Rom. 1.19ff. as an erratic block of Stoic speculation in the midst of the apostle's testimony to the gospel of Christ is untenable for similar reasons. It is impossible to suppose that Paul should here be asserting the reality of a 'natural' knowledge of God among the heathen, antecedent to and independent of his revelation in Christ: for in other passages he expressly denies such a thing (I Thess. 4.5, I Cor. 1.21). What he is concerned to assert is that a knowledge of certain invisible attributes of God by inference from his works in creation has been given by God to men, but that men have rejected the inference and so forfeited this knowledge. The knowledge of God in creation remains an objective possibility, as it were, but the subjective condition for receiving it has been lost. And the consequence is that when man, alienated from God, yet haunted by the lost knowledge of God, attempts to recover it by himself, he reaches only distortions and perversions (Rom. 1.21–5).

IV. THE END OF REVELATION

The end or purpose of revelation, as has been said above, is more than intellectual enlightenment; it is the establishment of a personal relation between God and men: 'I will be your God, and ye shall be my people' (Lev. 26.12). Thus its characteristic form is that of a call (Isa. 6) or an invitation (Matt. 11.28). In revelation, God promulgates his covenant by which he binds himself to men and men to himself (Gen. 17.1–8) or, as some of the prophets illustrated it in a bold figure, he proposes marriage (Hos. 2.19). It may be noted that traditionally the Bible is variously entitled 'the word of God', and 'the old and new covenants'—so inseparably is form wedded to content here.

Jesus Christ, the mediator of the new covenant, is the definitive revelation of God. In him the purpose of God receives its full and final expression, as the NT emphasizes again and again (Heb. 1.1f., II Cor. 1.20, Eph. 1.10). Yet at the same time the covenant-relation with God through Christ is itself provisional; it points forward to a consummation, the nature of which exceeds our power to conceive (I Cor. 13.12, Phil. 3.12). Christ's revelation in the form of a servant (Phil. 2.7) will be completed by his revelation in glory (Col. 3.4). When the NT speaks of the 'revelation' or 'appearing of Jesus Christ', it is to this ultimate goal of faith and hope that it refers (I Pet. 1.7,13, II Thess. 1.7). And 'The Revelation' is the title given to the book which describes the dramatic conflicts that will accompany this final appearing.

V. THE RECEIVING OF REVELATION

Jesus Christ is the key to the understanding of the revelation of God: its essential nature and conditions are paradigmatically exhibited in him. Revelation is God's personal communication of himself to men. As such, it involves the necessity of God's approach to men, God's entry into the sphere of men, i.e. the world (John 3.17,19, 6.14, 11.27, 18.37, I Tim. 1.15, I John 4.9); for God is the Creator, and man is the creature. 'God is in heaven, and thou upon earth' (Eccles. 5.2); in order to reveal himself, therefore, God must 'come down' from heaven (John 3.13); he must enter into the sphere of creation. Now God could do this in such a way 'that the nations might tremble at his presence' (Isa. 64.2)—and 'even thus shall it be in the day when the Son of man is revealed' (Luke 17.30). But it is of the grace of God that he has chosen to reveal himself, not in his naked divine majesty, but clothed in the vesture of humanity (John 1.14), 'in the likeness of sinful flesh' (Rom. 8.3); 'he emptied himself, taking the form of a servant, being made in the likeness of men' (Phil. 2.7). God in his revelation has accommodated himself to our creaturely capacity.

It is precisely this accommodation, however, which renders revelation ambiguous and paradoxical. The revelation of God is at the same time by its very thoroughness a veiling of God. The incarnation, as Kierkegaard said, is the assumption of an incognito, which obscures the person of the Incarnate, and lays it open to misinterpretation. He who is the Word incarnate speaks our language so perfectly that no trace of a foreign accent is discernible, and he can readily be mistaken for one of ourselves, a native (Mark 6.3).

How then is revelation received by men? The knowledge of the mystery is only for those to whom it is given (Mark 4.11) by God (Matt. 16.17). Human intelligence and acumen are of no avail here; rather they constitute a disqualification (Matt. 11.25, I Cor. 1.19–25). Revelation is in fact so absolute that it can only achieve its own reception. Indeed it is not so much man that receives revelation as revelation that receives him. For man, as he is, is incapable of receiving it (I Cor. 2.14); he must be taken up into revelation. It is not something that happens to him, but *in* him (Gal. 1.16); he must be transformed if he is to know it (John 3.3, Rom. 12.2). The knowledge of revelation is not so much a knowing as a being known (Gal. 4.9).

This unique knowledge, which is at once knowing-and-being-known, is faith. Faith is at once absolute passivity (John 6.44f., Eph. 2.8), and absolute activity, the supreme act of decision and self-committal (Luke 9.62, 14.33, II Tim. 1.12, I Pet. 4.19). But faith is more than knowledge, as revelation is more than disclosure of truth. Revelation is the manifestation of life (I John 1.2); to receive it is to pass from death unto life (John 5.24, I John 3.14).

The Spirit of God is frequently named as the agent of this transaction (Rom. 8), and thus also the Spirit is the agent of revelation (Eph. 1.17). It is the Spirit that gives life (John 6.63, II Cor. 3.6). No man can say that Jesus is Lord but by the Holy Spirit (I Cor. 12.3). God gives man his Spirit when he enters into personal converse with him and establishes a living relation with him. The Spirit is the Spirit of sonship or adoption (Rom. 8.14f., Gal. 4.4–6), and as such the creator of that affinity which is the indispensable condition of personal knowledge (I Cor. 2.10–16).

VI. THE CONTINUANCE OF REVELATION

The Spirit is the agent of the extension and continuation of revelation; for by the work of the Spirit the apostolic witness to Christ has itself the virtue of revelation (Luke 10.16, John 13.20, Rom. 1.16f., I Cor. 1.18). And the Spirit is promised as the Paraclete who is to abide for ever (John 14.16), thus ensuring that revelation shall be continued in perpetuity. Yet the continuing revelation of God by the Spirit will conform in all essentials to that to which the prophets and apostles bore testimony. There will be no 'new revelations' of such a nature as to render us no longer dependent on the original. The 'truth' into which the Spirit of truth will guide (John 16.13) is not general or abstract truth, but the truth which came by Jesus Christ (John 1.17), the truth which liberates (John 8.32) and sanctifies (John 17.17). The work of the Spirit is to give life to the truth which is in Jesus: 'he shall glorify me; for he shall receive of mine, and shall show it unto you' (John 16.14).

The promise of the continuance of revelation through the oral testimony of those who were its original witnesses applies with equal validity to the Bible; for the Bible is that same testimony recorded in writing for the benefit of later generations. The written words of the Bible are not to be identified directly with revelation any more than the spoken words of the original witnesses. But they are in a sacramental sense the instruments of revelation; they point beyond themselves to the word of God which is living (Heb. 4.12), and which alone is able to effect that personal encounter with God which is the end of revelation. The words of the Bible have no revealing virtue in themselves; in themselves they are 'the letter which killeth', but as testimonies of faith they can become the media of the life-giving Spirit (II Cor. 3.6).

Such testimonies, it is clear, may be indefinitely supplemented, but the testimonies of the Bible possess an unique status as standing in an original and immediate relation to the revelation of God, while all subsequent testimonies are in fact, if not always confessedly, dependent on them. The testimonies of the Bible are primary, and form the Canon or rule of faith. The existence of the Canon of Scripture represents the truth that revelation is already completed in principle, as it were, and it provides the norm or criterion by which the authenticity of any supposed revelation may be tested (I John 4.1–3).

VII. THE TRUTH OF REVELATION

The question of the truth of revelation is not raised in the Bible in the modern, abstract form: Is such a thing as revelation at all credible? The occurrence of revelation is 'taken for granted', naïvely, as it seems to modern, rationalistic thought, in which the non-occurrence of revelation is taken for granted, perhaps no less naïvely. Yet this apparently naïve and unquestioning acceptance is the most appropriate response to revelation and accordingly the most convincing 'proof' of its real occurrence.

This is not to say, however, that the critical question does not arise at all. While revelation is a problem to the modern mind because of its supposed rarity or non-occurrence, it was 'the abundance of revelations' (II Cor. 12.7) which presented problems to the men of the Bible and obliged them to ask, How is true revelation to be distinguished from false? It may be regarded as another 'proof' of revelation that the Bible knows no sure and infallible criterion. A number of tests are employed, but their variety and occasional inconsistency show that they are only in the nature of working hypotheses and do not yield conclusive results in every case. Thus the fulfilment or non-fulfilment of prophecy is used as evidence of truth or falsity in the prophet in Deut. 18.21 and frequently in 2nd Isaiah (Isa. 41.22, 43.9, 45.21, etc.). But against this, a true prediction may be given by a false prophet (Deut. 13.1–5), and the word of an undoubtedly true prophet may fail of fulfilment—to the sore dismay of the prophet himself (Jer. 20.7–18); and the application of this rule is still further complicated by the paradoxical fact that false revelation is also traced back to God (I Kings 22.19–28). A test of a more subjective nature was sought in the absence of ulterior motive (Amos 7.14, Mic. 3.11), and the sincerity of a prophet could be gauged by the overwhelming compulsion under which he spoke (Amos 3.8, Jer. 20.9, I Cor. 9.16), but this too could be ambiguous (Jer. 20.7). A more reliable criterion is found in the content of the prophetic word, according as it speaks weal or woe. It is accepted almost as a general principle that prophecies of good (I Kings 22.13), of smooth things (Isa. 30.10), of peace (Jer. 6.14, etc.) are false, while prophecies of war, evil and pestilence (Jer. 28.8) are true. A true word from God must be consonant with the judgment of God upon the sin of men; a prophecy which disregards moral realities is unquestionably false (Isa. 1.18–20, taking vs. 18, with many commentators, as an ironical question). Yet neither is this rule infallible; for judgment is not the last word from God: 'For I know the thoughts that I think towards you, saith the Lord, thoughts of peace, and not of evil, to give you a future and a hope' (Jer. 29.11, last phrase as rendered by Peake in *Century Bible*). God also sends his word of comfort (Isa. 40.1), of healing (Hos. 14.4), of restoration (Amos 9.11), while his greatest word of all is of him who is the Prince of Peace (Isa. 9.6).

The provisional character of all these tests bears witness to the truth that there is no criterion of revelation apart from revelation itself. At the most, it can be examined in regard to its own internal self-consistency (Deut. 13.1–5, I John 4.1–3, II John 7), but there is no external test by which it can be authenticated; for revelation is by its nature unique and incomparable; it cannot be explained or proved, it can only be received (John 3.11) in faith and humility.

BIBLIOGRAPHY

Baillie and Martin (ed.): *Revelation*, London (1937). E. F. Scott: *The New Testament Idea of Revelation*, London (1935). C. H. Dodd: *The Authority of the Bible*, London (1928); *The Apostolic Preaching*, London (1936); *History and the Gospel*, London (1938); 'Revelation' (*Expository Times*, Vol. LI, pp. 446ff.); *The Bible To-day*, London (1946). F. W. Camfield: *Revelation and the Holy Spirit*. H. Cunliffe-Jones: *The Authority of the Biblical Revelation*, London (1945). A. G. Hebert: *The Authority of the Old Testament*, London (1947); *Scripture and Faith*, London (1947). H. Wheeler Robinson: *Inspiration and Revelation in the Old Testament*. E. Brunner: *Revelation and Reason*, London (1946). K. Barth and E. Brunner: *Natural Theology*, London (1946). Alan Richardson: *Preface to Bible Study*, London (1943); *Christian Apologetics*, London (1947). G. S. Hendry: 'The Rediscovery of the Bible' (in *Reformation Old and New*, London, 1946); 'The Exposition of Holy Scripture' (*Scottish Journal of Theology*, Vol. I, No. 1).

G. S. HENDRY

REVOLT *v.* OBEY

REWARD, RECOMPENSE, VENGEANCE, AVENGE

In the OT the idea of reward is part of the more fundamental premiss that life is dependable, that the world is governed by reason and morality, and is not subject to blind fate or the fickle activity of unjust deities. The rule governing life is constant, and it is man's task to discover its nature and to live in accordance with it. Man, therefore, seeks to search out the norm by which life is tested and rewarded, and for Israel it was Jehovah who was the guarantor of the norm.

The justice of the Law depended upon an equivalence between service or disservice rendered and its corresponding recompense. The classic Heb. outlook is that it fares well with the good and ill with the wicked, that those who obey Jehovah will be rewarded—whether as individuals or within the structure of the society of which they were members. God is sovereign, and God is dependable. The corollary is that a purpose can be found in human history, and particularly in the history of those whom Jehovah had called to be his people. In later Jewish thought, however, there is also present the more pessimistic outlook of those who doubt the existence of a rational and moral order in the universe, or who feel that man, at any rate, is incapable of discovering its nature well enough to regulate his life accordingly. In Ecclesiastes we have the chief rebel against the commonly accepted position. 'For Ecclesiastes life is just futile. The writer has almost ceased to worry about the brevity of life and about man's return to the dust whence he came. Man's frailty is epitomized by the cosmic ignorance to which he is forever doomed; for God has decreed that man shall not know his work' (Rylaarsdam, *Revelation in Jewish Wisdom Literature*, p. 80).

The classic OT statement is that in Deut. 28 (cf. Lev. 26), where divine reward and retribution are perceived in the material well-being of the nation or in national disaster. Deut. was produced under the influence of the prophets of the 8th cent. BC, who held that God was active in Israelite history. The Deuteronomic historians (especially in Kings) hold that national history should be interpreted on the basis of the doctrine of rewards, whilst the Priestly tradition in Chronicles clings even more closely to the view that 'the stone a man sets rolling will recoil upon him' (Prov. 26.27). Jeremiah feels that life is disordered if 'evil be recompensed for good' (Jer. 18.20).

Divine vengeance, then, is part of the OT writers' belief in the moral order of the universe. (N.B. Jer. 51.56: 'For the Lord is a God of recompense, he shall surely requite.' Ezekiel, too, is insistent that divine requital is sure: 'As

I live, surely mine oath that he hath despised, and my covenant that he hath broken, I will even bring it upon his own head' (Ezek. 17.19). For his distinctive phrase—'upon his own head'—cf. Ezek. 9.10, 11.21, 16.43, 22.31.) The destruction of Jerusalem is seen as an act of divine vengeance for the sins of Manasseh's reign. But it might happen that Israel was innocent and yet suffered. Where, then, was the morality? In the experience of the exile Israel was thought to have suffered 'double for all her sins' (Isa. 40.2). The solution was that God would act on her behalf. In ancient Israel there was current the practice whereby a man was avenged by his next of kin, if he suffered a wrong (e.g. murder) which he could not avenge himself (cf. Deut. 19.6,12, Josh. 20.5,9). It is the rôle of 'avenger' that God takes upon himself, when he vindicates the righteousness of his servants. Israel can turn to Jehovah: 'O Lord, thou hast seen my wrong; judge thou my cause' (Lam. 3.58)—in the knowledge that that judgment will be according to deeds (cf. Isa. 59.18: 'According to their deed, accordingly he will repay, fury to his adversaries, recompense to his enemies'). The enemies of Israel become the objects of divine vengeance (cf. Jer. 46.10, 50.28, 51.6,11). At times the OT writers were so convinced of their own innocence and of the divine vengeance that they looked forward with confidence to the overthrow of their tormentors (cf. Ps. 58.10: 'The righteous shall rejoice when he seeth the vengeance'). The 'Day of the Lord' is spoken of as a 'day of vengeance', when requital is made to all in judgment (cf. Isa. 61.2, Mic. 5.15).

In the Book of Enoch the moral ideal is conceived of in terms of uprightness and righteousness (cf. 91.5, 92.1,2, 93.1,10). 'Love righteousness and walk therein; for the paths of righteousness are worthy of acceptation, but the paths of unrighteousness are suddenly destroyed and vanish. . . . Seek and choose for yourselves righteousness and a holy life, and walk in the paths of peace, that ye may prosper' (Enoch 94.1,4). It is in the Messianic Age that the righteous will be vindicated, and receive their due reward: 'I know this mystery, and have read it on the heavenly tables—that manifold good shall be given you in recompense for your labours, and that your lot is abundantly beyond the lot of the living' (103.1–3). II Esdras also pictures the reawakening of the world (7.31), when rewards shall be duly apportioned: 'And the work shall follow, and the reward shall be shewed, and good deeds shall awake, and wicked deeds shall not sleep. And the pit of torment shall appear, and over against it shall be the place of rest; and the furnace of hell shall be shewed, and over against it the paradise of delight' (II Esd. 7. 35f.). (Cf. the picture in Rev. 14.13: 'And I heard a voice from heaven saying, Write, Blessed are the dead which die in the Lord from henceforth: yea, saith the Spirit, that they may rest from their labours; *for their works follow with them.*')

The NT standpoint reflects that of the OT, although the Gospels protest against the rigid externalization of the concept of obedience to the Law, which was apparent in the Pharisaism of the 1st. cent. AD. The covenant was held by the Pharisees to be strictly a legal one, by which the contracting parties were mutually bound. The people, for their part, were to observe the Law given them by God, exactly, accurately and conscientiously, while God was bound to pay in return the promised recompense in proportion to their performances. The man who did much was to expect from God's justice the bestowal of much reward; while, on the other hand, every transgression entailed its corresponding recompense of ill. (The working-out of this rigid system may be seen in the Mishnah: 'Seven different plagues came into the world on account of seven chief transgressions. (1) If part of the people tithe their fruits and part do not, such a famine arises through drought that part of the people are in want and part have enough. (2) If no one tithes, there follows a famine from the devastations of war and from drought. (3) If nowhere the heave-dough has been separated, a famine consuming all arises. (4) A pestilence rages when such crimes gain the upper hand as have in Scripture the penalty of death pronounced upon them, but whose perpetrators are not delivered up to justice for its execution. (5) War devastates the land because of delay of sentence, turning aside of the law and illegal interpretation of Scripture. (6) Wild beasts get the upper hand on account of perjury and the desecration of the divine name. (7) Carrying away into foreign lands is the punishment for idolatry, incest, murder, and neglect of the Sabbatic year' (*Aboth* v. 8–9).) The full pattern of reward would not be witnessed in this present life; it remained for the 'coming age' to witness the reconciling of all seeming inequalities. The righteous man who still experienced sorrows in this life would receive a fuller reward hereafter. It was recognized that the present world was still a world of imperfection and evil; in the future world all weakness would cease (cf. Schürer: *The Jewish People in the Time of Jesus Christ*, Part II, Vol. II, p. 92).

It was held that good works here and now were a kind of capital reserve for the after-life, although the interest might be drawn upon in this present life. 'An index of this conception,' writes Bultmann, 'is the absurd dispute in which several rabbis engaged: what will become of the men whose good and bad deeds are equal?' (*Jesus and the Word*, p. 71). (Not only did a man gain merit for himself; the old notion of corporate personality meant the solidarity of all the members of the community of Israel. W. D. Davies suggests that here is to be found the background for the Pauline view that the merit of Christ as the new Adam, can be imparted to the whole of the new race that finds its life in him (*v.* Rom. 5.17–19). He points out that it was commonly held that by obedience to the Torah a man gained merit—cf. 'In keeping of them [*sc.* the laws] there is great reward' (Ps. 19.11). 'These merits, however, benefited not merely the person who by his obedience had acquired them, but also his contemporaries, and in addition, because of that solidarity of all the members of the community both past, present and future . . . , they would also avail for those who preceded him and those who would follow him both here and hereafter' (*Paul and Rabbinic Judaism*, p. 269); cf. Rom. 9.5, 11.8).

There were those who stressed that Israel had to serve God without reward (e.g. Antigonus of Socho, quoted in *Aboth* i. 3), but it was generally felt that, though God's reward may be the result of his activity of grace, he was bound to keep to the system he had himself initiated. (Cf. G. F. Moore: *Judaism*, Vol. II, p. 90: 'God does not *owe* him a recompense for doing his duty. But God has put himself under obligation by his promise of reward, and in this sense man, in doing what God requires of him, deserves recompense.')

In the Gospels Jesus, whilst at times corroborating the Jewish view, also makes a demand for radical obedience, which is irrespective of reward (cf. Luke 17.9f.: 'Doth he thank the servant because he did the things that were commanded? Even so ye also, when ye shall have done all the things that are commanded of you, say, We are unprofitable servants; we have done that which it was our duty to do'). This idea that service is a mere duty which cannot merit reward is quite foreign to contemporary Jewish thought. It follows from it that any reward must be a free and unmerited recompense, given by God (cf. the Pauline insistence that 'works' cannot give a man status with God). The notion of reward is still permitted—but mainly in the sense that conduct has its consequences. The reward is not set forth as the motive for right conduct; the position is that a certain type of conduct will bring its own reward (*v.* Creed: *Commentary on St. Luke's Gospel*, p. 92; Plummer: *Exegetical Commentary on St. Matthew*, pp. 91, 158). Altruistic action in this life will find its true recompense 'in the resurrection of the just' (Luke 14.14). But, whilst it may be said that particular conduct has its own consequence (e.g. Rom. 1.27: 'Receiving in themselves that recompense of their error which was due'), the over-all theocentric approach to life meant that this 'recompensing' must be referred to God (cf. Heb. 2.2: 'Every transgression and disobedience received a just recompense of reward'). There is also apparently a place for works: 'The Lord shall render to him according to his works' (II Tim. 4.14; cf. Matt. 16.27, Rev. 18.6).

It was the presence of persecution in the Church which strengthened the conviction that God would avenge the suffering of the faithful witnesses (cf. Luke 18.3–8). Both St. Paul and the author of Heb. quote the Deuteronomic dictum: 'Vengeance is mine, and recompense. . . . I will render vengeance to mine adversaries. . . . For he will avenge the blood of his servants, and will render vengeance to his adversaries' (Deut. 32.35,41,43; cf. Rom. 12.19, Heb. 10.30). (*V.* also JUDGE, CHASTISE.)

R. J. HAMMER

RICH *v.* POOR

RIGHT *v.* UPRIGHT

RIGHTEOUS, RIGHTEOUSNESS

The twin Heb. words *tsedeq* and *tsedaqah* are regularly translated by 'righteousness' in EVV, though occasionally the rendering is 'justice'. Originally they signified that which conforms to the norm, and for the Hebrews this norm is the character of God himself. The idea conveyed by the words is certainly ethical, but there is a steady tendency towards the idea of salvation. This is due, in the first instance, to the writings of the 8th-cent. prophets.

It is true that these 8th-cent. prophets, Amos, Hosea, Isaiah and Micah, were ethical prophets, for they insisted with the utmost firmness and resolution upon right action and fair dealing between man and man. They all make charges of glaring injustice, bribery and corruption, in the courts, and Micah even goes so far as to charge the rich with 'skinning' the common people (3.2f.). All four prophets are unanimous in condemning the fulsome ritual in the worship of the period because it is accompanied with glaring misconduct and sheer wickedness (Amos 5.22f., Hos. 6.6, Isa. 1.10–15, Micah 6.6–8, which is from the same period if not actually from Micah himself). Nevertheless, to say that they were ethical prophets and no more is to say less than the truth, because they showed a marked bias in favour of the poor and the needy, and this bias is indissolubly bound up with their notions of righteousness. In Deut. all these poor and needy who have no helper, emerge as the poor, the widow, the orphan, and the resident alien ('the stranger that is within thy gates', Deut.

5.14). It may well be, and doubtless it is the case, that their emphasis on behalf of these unfortunates had its origin in the fact that here most of all there was need for emphasis. However that may be, this emphasis works out from the 8th cent. onwards in making it more and more clear that if God is going to see righteousness established in the land, he himself must be particularly active as 'the helper of the fatherless' (Ps. 10.14) to 'deliver the needy when he crieth; and the poor that hath no helper' (Ps. 72.12).

Righteousness involves the establishment of equal rights for all, and to this extent 'justice' is a sound equivalent. The word is actually used in the sense of giving judgment, and God does judge righteously (Ps. 7.8–11), though at the same time it is remarkable how, even in passages where God is spoken of as judge, there is the reference to the poor and the needy on one side and 'the person of the mighty' on the other (cf. Lev. 19.15). All this means that if justice be taken to mean no more than strict equality, then the word in the main is inadequate. If, for instance, the Lat. *justitia* (the regular equivalent in the Vulgate, whence the 'justice' of the Douai Version) is to be regarded as a sound translation of the original words, then it must be understood sometimes to mean 'clemency', 'compassion', as occasionally in Julius Caesar and in Cicero.

The original Heb. words, therefore, include the idea of God's vindication of the helpless, with the result that already in the OT (Ps. 112.9, Dan. 4.27) they are closely connected with 'shewing mercy to the poor'. In Isa. 40–55 the full meaning of salvation and redemption must frequently be allowed, notably in Isa. 45.8,23, 46.13, 51.5,6. When Pharaoh says to Moses and Aaron (Exod. 9.27) that 'the Lord is righteous, and I and my people are wicked', he is not using the words in a truly ethical sense. He means that God has proved himself to be the stronger and Pharaoh and his people the weaker—that is, God has won the victory in the contest of the plagues. In Zech. 9.9 the Messianic King is described as being 'just and having salvation'. The meaning is that he is victorious and has been given the victory, the two words being not very distinguishable in meaning.

But later developments of the words stress the aspect of generosity and benevolence to the helpless. There are four cases in the OT where the Gk. translators have 'pity' (Ezek. 18.19,21, Dan. 4.27, Ps. 33.5). In Rabbinic writings the Heb. *tsedaqah* (or its Aramaic equivalent) mostly means almsgiving, benevolence. A well-known illustration of this tendency in NT times is to be found in Matt. 6.1 where the AV has 'alms', following the Received Text, and the RV has 'righteousness', following the Alexandrine Text, but both evidently go back to the same Aramaic original, the equivalent of the Heb. *tsedaqah.* When Jesus used this word he did not mean ethical righteousness; he was following the development which the word had reached in his day, and he meant benevolence, almsgiving. Indeed, in one Rabbinic writing (*Tosephta Sanhedrin*, i.3) the Aramaic word is actually contrasted with justice. The history, therefore, of the twin words usually translated 'righteousness' in the OT shows that, whilst they mean ethical uprightness, they have also a wider content than the ethical, and that they gradually develop this emphasis towards the meaning benevolence, salvation.

In the NT the word regularly translated 'righteousness' is *dikaiosune*. The corresponding verb is, with two exceptions (Rom. 6.7, AV, Rev. 22.11), translated 'justify' (*q.v.*). The question arises: Does this word always mean righteousness in the ethical sense, or has it anything of this wider salvation-meaning which we have seen to be involved in growing measure from the 8th cent. BC onwards, and especially in Isa. 40–55 (Deutero-Isaiah)? The words, noun, adjective and verb, are chiefly used by St. Paul. He uses the noun in the double sense, sometimes in a truly ethical sense and sometimes practically as the equivalent of salvation. When he writes of the law of righteousness (Rom. 9.31), he is referring to the ethical demands of the Mosaic Law, but when he uses the phrase 'the righteousness of God', he means that salvation which God accomplishes through Christ (Rom. 3.21). Similarly, the 'belief unto righteousness' of Rom. 10.10 is more accurately 'faith unto salvation'. In Rom. 6.16 'sin' is contrasted with 'obedience' after the fashion of the prophets who generally think of sin as rebellion against God, and 'death' is contrasted with 'righteousness'. The presumption here is that the Gk. word means something to do with life, that is, in the terms of Paul, with salvation. In the remainder of Ch. 6, the meaning of the word translated 'righteousness' actually varies between salvation and that standard of Christian ethics which is the outcome of it. We thus see that in the Pauline Epistles the word righteousness is used in three main senses: first, of that ethical conduct which is demanded by the Mosaic Law; second, of the salvation which is the gift of God through Christ; third, of that ethical conduct which is demanded of the Christian, that which involves as its minimum ethical demands all that is included in turning the other cheek and going the second mile, or that which is contained in the statement that we are unprofitable servants even though we have done that which it was our duty to do (Luke 17.10). The connexion of the Gk. *dikaiosune* (EVV, righteousness) with the idea of salvation is to be seen further in the use of the word 'justify'.

BIBLIOGRAPHY

H. Wheeler Robinson: *Inspiration and Revelation in the Old Testament*, Oxford (1946). N. H. Snaith: *Distinctive Ideas of the Old Testament*, London (1944).

N. H. SNAITH

ROCK, FOUNDATION, REFUGE, STRENGTH, PETER

In the OT Jehovah is often called 'Rock' (e.g. Ps. 18.1f.,46, 19.14, 31.2f., 62.2,6f., etc., Isa. 17.10, 26.4: 'in Jah Jehovah is an everlasting Rock'—RV marg., 'a Rock of ages'; 30.29, 44.8, Hab. 1.12), though this is often obscured in AV and BCP Psalter, where such renderings as 'strength' and 'refuge' are found. Thus, we are less familiar with RV: 'O Lord, my R. and my redeemer', Ps. 19.14. The title (*zur*, rock), says Driver, 'designates Jehovah by a forcible and expressive figure as the unchangeable support or refuge for his servants, and is used with evident appropriateness where the thought is of God's unvarying attitude towards his people. The figure is, no doubt, like *crag*, *stronghold*, *high place*, etc., derived from the natural scenery of Palestine' (*ICC.*, *Deuteronomy*, p. 350). On this latter point, cf. Isa. 32.2: '. . . a hiding place from the wind . . . the shadow of a great r. in a weary land'. The key OT passage, however, for the study of this word is the so-called 'Song of Moses' in Deut. 32.1–43, a very fine poem written probably towards the end of the Exile. Its theme is God's unchanging quality, his faithfulness to his covenant and promise, his care for and protection of Israel (vss. 10f.), his fatherhood (vs. 18), his salvation. God's faithfulness is contrasted with Israel's faithlessness. In this poem, which marks one of the high levels in the development of OT religion, the title 'Rock' is used several times and emphasizes God's constancy, changelessness and protection.

It is against the background of this OT usage that we should understand the uses of *petra* (Gk., 'rock') in the NT. Here the qualities of Jehovah which are denoted by R. in the OT are transferred to Christ. In the NT we do not find R. as a name for God; this may be due to the influence of the LXX, which translates Heb. *zur* by 'God' or some equivalent—doubtless wishing to avoid any suggestion of idolatry (the worship of stone or r. images, etc.). But of course in the NT God still retains those qualities denoted by *zur*. And these qualities are now revealed in Christ and reflected in his Church. Christ himself is the foundation upon which the whole edifice of Christian faith and life must be built (I Cor. 3.11). The man who builds his house upon the r. of Christ's words is indeed the wise man (Matt. 7.24–27=Luke 6.48). Faith in Christ is the foundation upon which St. Paul builds (I Cor. 3.10–15); it is the r. upon which the Church itself is built, for Christ is the foundation of the Church. This is the probable explanation of Matt. 16.18: 'Thou art *Petros*, and upon this *petra* I will build my Church; and the gates of Hades shall not prevail against it.' In Gk. *petros* means a fragment of *petra*, rock; it is a translation of the Aramaic *Kephas*, the name given by Jesus to Simon (Symeon). The saying can hardly mean that Peter is the r. on which the Church is built, since in the NT the foundation-r. of the Church is Christ (or faith in Christ). Rather is it Peter's rock-like faith in Christ which is to be the foundation of the Church. The old Jerusalem built on Zion's r. faced squarely the valley of Hinnom (*v.* HELL); so the new Jerusalem stands upon the r. of Christ, four-square against the powers of Hades; it is 'the city which hath foundations' (Heb. 11.10), for which faithful Abraham had looked. Thus the ancient fathers interpreted the passage; Origen, for instance, says: 'If thou hast Peter's faith, thou art a r. like him; if thou hast P.'s virtues, thou hast P.'s keys.' The Church in every age is stayed upon its 'rock-men'; they are rocks—Peters—because they rest upon the one *Petra*, Christ himself. In the NT there is little sign of the growth of a 'Petrology', and later notions should not be read back into this Matthaean passage. Peter appears as the natural leader of the apostolic band, but he takes second place to James at the Council of Jerusalem (Acts 15) and is subject to the rebuke of Paul (Gal. 2). (*V.* also APOSTLE, MINISTER.) In I Cor. 10.4 Paul explicitly calls Christ *petra*: here Christ is identified with the r. by which (acc. to non-biblical rabbinic *haggadah*) the Israelites were constantly refreshed in the desert on their pilgrimage towards the Promised Land. The water in the desert becomes for St. Paul the symbol of baptism, and he affirms the pre-existence of Christ and his guidance of Israel in the past: Christ has all along been the R. of Israel. We must not dismiss the profound symbolism of this great passage (I Cor. 10.1ff.) as mere barren *haggadah*. It emphasizes several of those leading ideas which are associated with the biblical conception of the 'Rock' and which have been finely gathered together in A. M. Toplady's famous hymn, 'Rock of Ages'.

ALAN RICHARDSON

* * *

SABAOTH (Rom. 9.29, Jas. 5.4) *v.* GOD, GODS III

SABBATH

From root 'to desist'; but the original etymology, relation to Babylonian *shabattu*, and origins, are still debated: *v.* arts. in dictionaries, and N. H. Snaith, *The Jewish New Year Festival*, pp. 103ff. Conjunction with New Moon (II Chron. 2.4) suggests that it was a lunar festival in early Israel, a day of abstention from normal business (Amos 8.4–6), of joy and mirth (Hos. 2.11; throughout Hosea Sabbath is associated with joy, and may not be a fast day), of religious activities (Isa. 1.13, II Kings 4.22–3). Uncertain when it became a weekly observance to mark the close of seven day week and one of the days called *shabbathon* (Exod. 31.15, etc.; EVV, 'sabbath of solemn rest'), to be observed by complete abstention from any kind of work. The fact that it is first in the list of holy seasons in Lev. 25, the only one to be mentioned in the Decalogue (Exod. 20.8–11) and to be given a mythological basis (Gen. 2.2f.), shows that in later Judaism it had, with circumcision, become the fundamental observance of the religion of the Jews, distinguishing them from aliens. From Jeremiah onwards (if Jer. 17.21–7 is his), its maintenance is stressed by the prophets as a delight, as part of the law of righteousness, and as the hallmark of devotion to Jehovah, guaranteeing Israel's permanence and prosperity (Ezek. 20.12–20, Isa. 56.2–8, 58.13f.). This is reflected in the Law. The Sabbath is God's (Exod. 20.10), a day blessed by Jehovah, and thereby charged with the vitality which comes from holiness (Exod. 20.11), a token of his covenant-relation with Israel (Exod. 31.13; cf. Gen. 17.11–13, of circumcision), by which time is hallowed, and the community and the land gain strength and refreshment (Exod. 23.10–12, Lev. 25.1–7). Profanation of the Sabbath, as of circumcision, is a breach of the covenant-relation and of the holiness of Israel, punishable with death (Exod. 31.14f., Num. 15.32–6, Gen. 17.14). In D it is connected characteristically with Israelite concern for subordinates, and is a memorial of deliverance from bondage (Deut. 5.12–15); in P it is connected with the rest and refreshment of God after Creation, and is a memorial of his finished work (Exod. 20.11, Gen. 2.2f.). In J and P it is connected with the divine gift of manna sufficient for two days (Exod. 16.22–30). The above, as also Neh. 10.31, 13.15–22, show that need was felt of enforcing Sabbath observance as a distinctive mark of Judaism, with the result that the negative aspect of total abstention from work became uppermost (contrast II Kings 4.22–3 with I Macc. 2.34–41, and see Jubilees 1.6–13, Matt. 24.20, John 5.10). *Tractate Shabbath* is a rabbinic treatise on what may or may not be done on the Sabbath; plucking corn contravened the third and fifth prohibitions, i.e. of reaping and threshing.

Jesus claimed freedom from Sabbath restrictions for himself and his disciples (Mark 2.23–8; cf. Col. 2.16 for a similar freedom for Christians), but in itself this is insufficient to account for the fact that he went out of his way to heal on the Sabbath (Mark 1.21,29, 2.23–3.6, Matt. 12.11, Luke 14.5 (Q?), 13.10–16 (L), John 5.1–18, 9.10–16), or for the violent opposition which this action aroused (Mark 3.6, Luke 13.14, John 5.16–18, 7.23). (See Israel Abrahams, *Studies in Pharisaism and the Gospels*, First Series, Chap. XVII, for the comparative humanity of the rabbinic view, and for parallels to 'the Sabbath was made for man and not man for the Sabbath'.) In reply to the ruler of the synagogue who states the Pharisaic ruling that healing is only permissible on the Sabbath if it is to save life, Jesus claims the Sabbath as the necessary day for that healing which is the rescue of a member of the chosen race from the bondage of Satan (Luke 13.14–16). The Sabbath, being a memorial of the peace and rest which is God's, is pre-eminently the day for the performance of those works which constitute its fulfilment, inasmuch as they are signs of the advent of the Messianic order of peace (wholeness, cf. John 7.23, contrasted with the partial healing of circumcision), life (Mark 3.4) and merciful deliverance (Matt. 12.11, Luke 14.5). Something greater than the Temple is here (Matt. 12.5f.); before his presence, and that of his disciples, Sabbath restrictions must yield, as before that of David, the type of the Messiah, in flight with his companions, the Son of Man determines the Sabbath (Mark 2.23–8). It is from Jesus and not from the Law that those who are burdened will receive the true Sabbath rest and refreshment (Matt. 11.28–9). (The remarkable addition of MS D at Luke 6.5 seems to mean that the man working on the Sabbath is blessed if he does so in knowledge that the Messianic Age has come; otherwise he remains under the jurisdiction and curse of the old order.) The fourth evangelist, therefore, interprets the Sabbath healings as involving a claim by Jesus to be the Son of God who is performing God's life-giving work of creation (John 5.16–18). The author of Hebrews has probably coined the word *sabbatismos* (4.9) to indicate that the life entered upon by Christian faith is a Sabbath existence of consummation and satisfaction (not merely 'rest'; cf. 4.4f.), secured by the saving work of Jesus in fulfilment of the OT hope of a divine rest for the people of God. Whether such an interpretation of the

Sabbath as a foretaste of the world to come had already been developed in Judaism on the basis of such passages as Ezek. 34.14–16, Isa. 14.3, or was a creative interpretation of Jesus himself, is uncertain. (*V.* also REST, RESTORE, PEACE, WORK.) C. F. EVANS

SACKCLOTH

The word is itself of Semitic (? Phoenician) origin, and denotes a rough textile of goat's or camel's hair. Originally worn as a sign of mourning for death or disaster (e.g. Gen. 37.34), it naturally came to be used as symbol of mourning for sin in repentance and contrition. So I Kings 21.27, Dan. 9.3, Jonah 3.5,6,8, Matt. 11.21=Luke 10.13. J. P. T.-D.

SACRIFICE

The purpose in the OT sections of this article is not to outline the history of the Jewish sacrificial system, but to describe it in its developed form in the closing centuries BC. At the same time it will be well, occasionally, to say something about the history of a particular institution. This will help the reader to get a stereoscopic view of the subject, instead of seeing everything, as it were, on a flat surface. By far the best way to study OT sacrifice is to read the Book of Leviticus with a good commentary. The materials may be conveniently arranged under five main headings:

I Classes of Sacrifices
II The Place where Sacrifices were offered (Temple, Altar, etc.)
III The Ministers of Sacrifice (Priests)
IV The Festivals (Feasts in EVV)
V The New Testament Fulfilment (cf. G. B. Gray, *Sacrifice in the Old Testament*, 1925, the standard English work on the subject)

I. CLASSES OF SACRIFICES

The Heb. noun translated 'sacrifice' (*zebah*) means literally 'slaughter', all slaughter of domestic animals (the only animals it was permissible to offer as sacrifices) being in early OT times sacrificial slaughter.

(*a*) *Motives underlying Sacrifice*. The motives which prompted early man to offer sacrifices were complex. Three are fairly easily discernible, though it is by no means easy to decide, in a particular class of sacrifice, which of them was uppermost in the intention of the offerer. (Sacrifices might be either public, i.e. offered on behalf of the community, or private.) They are, sacrifices as (*1*) gifts to God, (*2*) means of entering into communion with God, (*3*) means of releasing life, whether for the benefit of God himself, or of the worshipper (cf. W. O. E. Oesterley, *Sacrifices in Ancient Israel*, 1937). In regard to this third motive, it should be clearly understood that the object in offering a sacrifice was never to present the dead carcase of an animal, but to release its potent life. This 'life' was conceived to be resident in the blood (cf. Gen. 9.4 and margin refs.), which was dashed against the altar.

(*b*) *Sacrifices as* (*1*) *Gifts*, (*2*) *Atonement*

(*1*) GIFT: OFFERING: OBLATION. By the later centuries BC all sacrifices had come to be thought of as in some way gifts to God. The two Heb. words covering all classes of sacrifices, *minhah* ('offering' in the early passage Gen. 4.3, though in later times it came to denote specifically 'meal-offering', cf. Lev. 2.1, RV, see below, I(*g*)), and *qorban*, Lev. 1.2, RV, 'oblation'; both signify a gift, *minhah* being used of a present (Gen. 32.13) or tribute (II Sam. 8.6) from man to man, and *qorban* (cf. Mark 7.11), literally 'something brought near', always, in the Bible, of a gift to God.

(*2*) ATONEMENT: EXPIATION. By the close of the OT period, too, all sacrifices were believed to have atoning value. This is stated not only of sin-offerings and guilt-offerings, but even of the burnt-offering (Lev. 1.4). The verb rendered 'to make atonement' in the EVV is *kipper*. Its original meaning is uncertain: the cognate word in Arabic means to cover, hide; in Aramaic, to wipe away. The former of these senses seems the more prominent in OT. Gray would render 'make expiation'. The 'expiatory' character of *all* sacrifice is a comparatively late development, due to the deepened sense of sin occasioned by the Babylonian exile. The general theory, though it is nowhere elaborated in the OT, would seem to have been that God accepted the gift of the sacrifice as an expiation (*v.* ATONE).

(*3*) BURNT-OFFERING. The most regular offering was the burnt-offering, best spelt with a hyphen, since it represents one word (*'olah*) in Hebrew. *'olah* means 'that which ascends', either to the altar, or in smoke from the altar. The ritual governing it is prescribed in Lev. 1. The burnt-offering was most commonly a public sacrifice, and the occasions when it was offered on behalf of the community as a whole are listed in Exod. 29.38–42 and Num. 28f. They included the regular morning and evening offerings, which were supplemented on the Sabbath, at New Moon, and at various anniversaries. Because of its regularity and frequency the burnt-offering was called the *tamid* ('continual', Exod. 29.42). Another name for it was the *kalil* ('whole burnt-offering', 'holocaust', Ps. 51.19), because it was entirely consumed by fire, no part of the flesh being available for human consumption. The original gift-idea is more transparent in the burnt-offering than in any other sacrifice; cf. the 'sweet savour unto the Lord' of Lev. 1.9,13,17, also Gen. 8.21. A relic of the ancient belief that the sacrifice actually nourished the god is contained in the phrase 'food of the offering' (RV margin, 'bread', Lev. 3.11 and marginal refs.). Private burnt-offerings might be offered at any time by individuals so disposed, whether in fulfilment of a vow ('votive-offering') or as 'freewill offerings' in recognition of some particular mark of divine favour (Lev. 22.18, Num. 15.3). Such offerings had to be unblemished males, and might be taken from the herd or the flock, according to the means of the offerer. Provision was made for the poor, who might bring turtle-doves or young pigeons.

(*4*) PEACE-OFFERING. The Heb. word for this offering (in early times often called *zebah*, 'sacrifice', 'slaughter' simply) is *shelem*. It is translated 'peace-offering' in the EVV because of its obvious relation to the word *shalom* (peace), as of an offering that promoted peaceful relations with God. It may, however, in some passages equally well be rendered 'recompense-offering', and this is supported by the fact that the three classes of *shelem* (thank-offering, votive-offering, and freewill-offering; cf. Lev. 7.11–16, 22.21) are clearly in the nature of recognitions of benefits received or expected. The ritual of the *shelem* is prescribed in Lev. 3. It was for the most part a private and family sacrifice, the only public peace-offerings (in post-exilic times) being at Pentecost (Lev. 23.19) and at the consecration of priests (Lev. 9.4). That it was regarded as of less sanctity than the burnt-offering is evident from the fact that female as well as male animals were eligible, while for the freewill-offering, which was an offering additional to anything that the Law prescribed, even an animal not physically perfect was accepted (Lev. 22.23). The choice of animal depended upon the means or disposition of the offerer. The intestinal fats were burnt upon the altar; certain portions of the flesh went to the priest who conducted the sacrifice; the rest was eaten by the offerer and his friends. Of all the sacrifices the peace-offering retains most clearly the characteristics of the ancient communion sacrifice, since God and the worshipper were thought to share a common meal.

(*5*) SIN-OFFERING (Heb. *hattath*). This offering, as its name implies, had a closer relation to sin and its expiation than either the burnt-offering or the peace-offering. Even so, the only sins for which it could atone were those committed in ignorance (RV, 'unwittingly'). For deliberate or 'presumptuous' sin (Ps. 19.12f.) there was no remission by sacrifice (Num. 15.30f.). The significance of this is emphasized by the Epistle to the Hebrews (Heb. 10.26–31). It should be explained that in a community which gave great prominence to the due performance of a complicated ritual, and laid the main emphasis upon actions themselves rather than upon their underlying motives, it was easy to 'sin unwittingly'. The sin-offering was intended to expiate such unwitting sins, whenever they were later discovered. The ritual prescribed is detailed in Lev. 4.1–5.13. The costliness of the offering, and the procedure to be followed, depended upon the rank of the offender. If he were the High Priest, the whole community incurred guilt, and a costly sacrifice was required. This was a young bullock. Some of its blood was taken by the High Priest into the sanctuary, and sprinkled upon the veil which separated the Holy Place from the Holy of Holies. The fat pieces were dealt with in the manner of the peace-offering, while the flesh was burnt, not upon the altar, but outside the sanctuary precincts. Sin-offerings for the community as a whole, for a ruler, and for a layman, were prescribed according to a descending scale of costliness and solemnity of ritual. In addition to the sin-offering for unintentional trespass, similar offerings were required at the consecration of a High Priest (Lev. 8), and from persons emerging from such conditions of ceremonial uncleanness as child-birth (Lev. 12; cf. Luke 2.22ff.) and leprosy (Lev. 14.19; cf. Mark 1.44). All the OT evidence appears to indicate that it was not until post-exilic times that the sin-offering came into prominence, the usual offerings in pre-exilic times being the burnt-offering and the peace-offering.

(*6*) GUILT-OFFERING (Heb. *asham*). This, like the sin-offering, though not perhaps unknown before the exile, only became important in post-exilic times. The ritual relating to it will be found in Lev. 5.14–6.7, 7.1–7, Num. 5.5–8. The difference between it and the sin-offering is not entirely clear, and it would appear that in some circumstances the two had features in common (cf. Lev. 5.1–6, where in vs. 6 both are mentioned together). Its main purpose was to make expiation for dues withheld from God (Lev. 5.14–19) or from man (Lev. 6.1–7). A due withheld from God is defined as neglect to pay at the proper time what was due to the sanctuary. Dues withheld from man included such unneighbourly acts as robbery, or a man's neglecting to return at the appointed time property deposited with him for safe keeping. Such acts appear to be anything but 'unwitting', and the provision of the guilt-offering to make 'atonement' or 'expiation' (Lev. 6.7) for them might seem to negative the assertion that sacrifice never atoned for deliberate sin. On the other hand, it should be noted that nothing is said about the matter being referred to the law-courts; the offering was intended to put matters right as between parties who settled their dispute amicably, without resort to litigation. The general principle governing the guilt-offering was that the offender had to repay what he had withheld, plus one-fifth of its value, and in addition offer a ram as a sacrifice. It may be noted that in the passage relating to the Suffering Servant (Isa. 53.10), 'when thou shalt make his soul an offering for sin', the Heb. word is *asham* ('guilt-offering', so RV margin).

(7) MEAL-OFFERING: DRINK-OFFERING: MEMORIAL-OFFERING: SHEWBREAD. The Heb. word for meal-offering (*minhah*), as already explained, means literally 'gift'. In early times it embraced both vegetable and animal offerings (Gen. 4.3–5), but after the exile it came to be confined to non-animal offerings (Lev. 2.) Such meal-offerings might be offered alone, but it was usual to offer them together with a flesh offering (Lev. 7.11ff., Num. 15). The idea obviously was that since no civilized man ever ate a meal consisting only of flesh, it would be highly indecent to offer only flesh to God. The materials of the meal-offering comprised fine flour, olive oil, and frankincense. Another accompaniment of flesh offerings, usually of the burnt-offering, was the 'drink-offering' (*nesek*), which consisted of wine (Num. 15.5). Another term (used only 7 times) associated with the meal-offering is 'memorial' (see Lev. 2.2 and refs.), properly 'memorial-offering' (Heb., *azkarah*). This was a small part (handful) of the flour and oil, together with all the frankincense, of the meal-offering, which the priest was to burn upon the altar. The rest of the meal-offering was consumed by the priests. Similar to the meal-offering was the 'shewbread' (literally 'presence-bread', Exod. 25.30, RV margin), which goes back to very early times (I Sam. 21.1–6) and is evidently a survival of the idea that a god was actually nourished by the offerings brought to him by his worshippers. In later times it was unleavened (leaven being symbolical of corruption), and in Lev. 24.7 the frankincense that accompanied it is called a memorial-offering. It was to be renewed on the Sabbath of each week, the old bread, which was 'most holy', being eaten by the priests within the sanctuary precincts (cf. Mark 2.26).

(8) *Other Sacrificial Terms:* HEAVE-OFFERING, WAVE-OFFERING. These were not separate offerings. Heave-offering (Heb. *terumah*) comes from a root meaning 'to be high', and denotes, usually, a specific part of an offering, which was 'lifted off', and so set apart, generally for the priests as their portion; e.g. the 'heave thigh' of Lev. 7.34. Similar to it was the 'wave-offering', the 'wave breast' and the 'heave thigh' being mentioned together in Lev. 7.34 as perquisites of the priests. The Heb. word (*tenuphah*) conveys the idea of moving to and fro. It would appear that the priest took his own portion of the offering and 'waved' it in the direction of the altar, as a symbol that it was offered to God, and then 'waved' it back from the altar in token that God had assigned it to the priests as his representatives.

(9) *Sacrifices as 'Holy'*. All sacrifices belonged to the class of 'holy' things. Although they were not graded in any strict order of sanctity, some were more holy than others. Among the 'most holy' (*qodesh haqqodashim*, lit. 'holy of holies', a Heb. way of expressing the superlative) were naturally the sin-offerings and guilt-offerings (Lev. 6.25, 7.1). This meant that their flesh was only to be eaten by male members of priestly families, and by them only within the sanctuary precincts (Lev. 6.26, 7.6). The lower grades of sin-offerings and guilt-offerings came within this category. The higher grades of sin-offerings, viz. of those animals whose blood was sprinkled on the veil between the Holy Place and the Holy of Holies (Lev. 4.1–21), were not eaten at all (Lev. 6.30). Holiness as it related to sacrificial offerings was thought of not so much as a moral quality, but according to the antique conception of it as quasi-physical, what in recent years we have learned to call *tabu*. As such it was contagious and needed to be insulated if it was not to do damage. This is the reason why the most holy offerings had to be disposed of in the Temple court, and is confirmed by the directions about the vessels in which their flesh was boiled. If it was boiled in a metal vessel—boiling, not roasting, being the prescribed method of cooking (cf. I Sam. 2.15)—the vessel had to be thoroughly scoured and rinsed in water after use; but if an earthenware vessel was used it had to be broken, presumably because the 'holiness' of the flesh would get too closely into its texture to be purged by any process of lustration (Lev. 6.28).

II. THE PLACE WHERE SACRIFICE WAS OFFERED: *Temple, Altar*

In early times and until almost the close of the period of the monarchy, sacrifice was offered at any place where God was believed to have revealed himself, at the so-called 'high places'. In practice it was found impossible to control the worship at these local shrines, where much that was heathenish was carried on. In 621 BC, not long before the exile, King Josiah attempted to confine sacrifice to the Jerusalem Temple; but although his reform broke down, it was taken for granted after the exile that the Temple was the only place where sacrifice might be offered.

(*a*) THE TEMPLE: *General Description.* The Temple proper was not a large building. Like other temples in ancient times it was intended as the earthly dwelling-place of God, not as a place for congregational worship. The Heb. word for it (*hekal*) is literally 'great house'. It can also mean 'palace', the Temple being the palace of God. Herod's Temple was a rectangular structure, 90 ft. long, 30 ft. wide, and 90 ft. high. It stood within an enclosure known as the Priests' Court. Outside that, again, was the Court of Israelites. Still farther removed from the central sanctuary was the Women's Court. The whole was bounded by a large Outer Court, to which Gentiles were admitted, but beyond which they might not go on pain of death. The conception was of a HOLY OF HOLIES standing, though not exactly geometrically, at the centre of a series of concentric rectangles which were arranged according to a decreasing scale of sanctity as they became farther removed from the most holy place. This symbolism of degrees of sanctity was repeated in the persons of those who were allowed access to the several courts, from the High Priest at the one end, who once a year went even into the Holy of Holies, to ordinary priests, Levites, lay Israelites, women, and finally Gentiles. It was also maintained in the materials of which the Temple buildings were constructed: pure gold in the sanctuary, the ordinary gold of commerce, silver, and finally bronze.

(*b*) TEMPLE *and* TABERNACLE. There were three temples in the course of Jewish history: (*1*) The Temple of Solomon, (*2*) The Second Temple (Zerubbabel's), (*3*) The Temple of Herod. In addition, the OT contains descriptions of two ideal structures: Ezekiel's Temple (Ezek. 40–48) and the wilderness Tabernacle (Exod. 25–30, 35–40), which was conceived as a kind of shadow Temple. Since we have no full, or at any rate entirely clear, descriptions of any one of them, except of the Tabernacle, which was largely an ideal creation, the picture of the Temple which we frame in our minds is bound to be somewhat composite. It is reasonably certain that not all of the elaborate symbolism of the Tabernacle was ever reproduced in any of the temples that were actually built. For example, in the second Temple there was no ark, and if there was no ark there could hardly have been a MERCY-SEAT (Heb. *kapporeth*, 'propitiatory'), which is described as a slab of gold, covering the ark (Exod. 25.17–22), and surmounted by two golden cherubim. In point of fact, the Holy of Holies in the post-exilic Temple was empty, and yet the full symbolism of the sacrificial ritual is largely based upon that of the Tabernacle, which is said to have been copied from a heavenly pattern delivered to Moses on Mount Sinai (Exod. 25.40). So important was the Tabernacle symbolism that its 'mercy-seat' even figures in the NT (Gk. *hilasterion*, in Rom. 3.25 rendered PROPITIATION, and in Heb. 9.5 'mercy-seat'), and the whole is followed with close attention to detail by the writer of the Epistle to the Hebrews (*v.* ATONE).

(*c*) *Priests' Court:* ALTAR. The sacrifices were offered in the Priests' Court, to which laymen were admitted when they had private sacrifices to offer, since they were required to lay their hands on the victim (Lev. 1.4). The intention of this manual act does not seem to have been that the animal was slain as a substitute for the man who offered it, but as a token that it was his and that he thereby solemnly dedicated it. An animal sacrificed privately was usually slain by its offerer, the priest's part being to dispose of the blood, which he dashed against the altar (Lev. 1.5). The altar (Heb. *mizbeah*, lit. 'place of sacrifice') of burnt-offering was situated below the steps that led up to the sanctuary proper. It was furnished with ALTAR HORNS, i.e. projections, at its four top corners. The origin and significance of the horns are obscure. One or two examples of horned altars have been unearthed by the spade of the archaeologist. In early times, before the centralization of worship at the Jerusalem Temple and the consequent provision of cities of refuge (Deut. 19.1–13), altars provided sanctuary for fugitives suspected of murder, who 'took hold of the horns of the altar' and were safe pending their trial (cf. I Kings 2.28).

(*d*) SANCTUARY: HOLY OF HOLIES. The sanctuary or *hekal* proper was divided into two compartments, the 'Holy Place' and the 'Holy of Holies'. In the description of Solomon's Temple this latter is called the *debir* (lit. 'hindmost chamber': EVV, 'oracle', I Kings 6.5, etc., is based on a wrong etymology). The floor space of the Holy of Holies was 30 ft. square, that of the Holy Place 60 ft. by 30, just double the size of the former. The two were separated, not by a wall, but by—so it is said in the Mishna—a double VEIL, the curtains of which were a cubit (18 in.) apart. The outer curtain was loose on the south side, the inner on the north. On the Day of Atonement (see below IV(*e*)) the High Priest entered by the outer curtain at its open end, passed along between the two curtains, and thence by the open (northern) end of the inner curtain into the Holy of Holies.

The *debir* of Solomon's Temple had contained the ark, but, as already indicated, this was apparently destroyed at the exile, and no attempt was made to construct a new one. The ark still figures in the idealized Tabernacle of the post-exilic Priests' Code, with even the addition of the 'mercy-seat'. But in the Temples of Zerubbabel and Herod the 'Holy of Holies' was empty. There were neither windows nor roof-lights to the Temple, and since the only inside light was that of the lampstand in the Holy Place, little or no light could have penetrated the veil into the Holy of Holies.

(*e*) SANCTUARY: THE HOLY PLACE. In the centre of the Holy Place was the altar of INCENSE, with the seven-branched lampstand on its south side, and the table of shewbread on its north side. The altar of incense was a costly replica in miniature of the altar of burnt-offering (Exod. 30.1–10), even to being provided with horns. Only pure incense was burnt upon it, and its fire was provided from the main altar in the Priests' Court. The fragrance of the incense, in contrast with the heavy smoke from the larger altar, was symbolical of the prayers of the faithful. The service of the Holy Place was the duty of the priests according to their courses (Luke 1.8f.). No layman was ever allowed inside the sanctuary. It is all but certain that the descriptions of the incense altar are among the latest passages in the OT, and the first historical reference to it dates from the time of the Maccabees (I Macc. 1.21). There is of course no doubt that the custom of burning incense in worship goes back to quite early times, but it should be stated that in some early OT passages which speak of 'burning incense' the meaning is no more than to offer sacrifice. Such a passage is Jer. 11.12f. The Heb. word for incense (*qetoreth*) originally meant SMOKE. Such smoke might be the thick smoke of burning fat, or the more refined smoke of incense. The corresponding verb meant 'to make sacrifices smoke', and it was only in comparatively late times that it began to take on the specialized meaning 'to burn incense'.

III. THE MINISTERS OF SACRIFICE (PRIESTS)

(*a*) *Orders of Priests.* In post-exilic times the priesthood was divided into three orders: (1) the HIGH PRIEST, (2) ORDINARY PRIESTS, (3) LEVITES. The members of all three orders were, at least in theory, descended from Levi, one of the twelve sons of Jacob. All priests were therefore Levites, in that they were descended from Levi; but by no means all Levites were priests. The priesthood proper was confined to those members of the tribe of Levi who were descended from Aaron, one of Levi's grandsons. These were known as SONS OF AARON, or AARONITES. But Levi had other descendants than those who could trace their genealogy back to Aaron. These non-Aaronite Levites became, in post-exilic times, a lower order, whose duties were to minister as acolytes to the priests proper (Ezek. 44.14, I Chron. 23.28–32). (For the genealogy of the Aaronites and Levites, see I Chron. 6, and for the duties of the Levites, as prescribed for the Tabernacle, Num. 4.)

(*b*) *Historical Summary.* In early Israel priesthood was not confined to Levites. Micah, an Ephraimite, consecrated one of his sons to be his domestic priest (Judg. 17.5). David's sons were priests (II Sam. 8.18—RV text is the only legitimate translation). It was not considered wrong for a layman to offer sacrifice: Gideon did so (Judg. 6.26), and the Danite Manoah (Judg. 13.19). But already by the end of the period of the Judges the Levites were beginning to become cultic specialists, and Micah was highly pleased when he secured the services of a 'Levite of the family of Judah' (Judg. 17.7–13). This last passage is one of several indications that the Levites were originally a professional guild, not a secular tribe. The origin of the Levites is obscure, and the OT has preserved divergent traditions. The question is of considerable interest, but so far no solution of it is forthcoming. There is no need to pursue it here, since it is not important for the purposes of this article. It must suffice that in post-exilic times all Levites were supposed to be descended from the tribal ancestor, Levi.

In the Book of Deuteronomy, which reflects the usage of the later period of the monarchy, all Levites are priests, the term for priests being 'the priests the Levites', i.e. the levitical priests (Deut. 18.1). Ezekiel complained that the Levites had been unfaithful to their charge (Ezek. 44.10), and therefore proposed to confine the priesthood to the guild of ZADOK, which ever since the reign of Solomon had been in charge of the worship in the Jerusalem Temple (Ezek. 44.13–15). Zadok's descent was traced to Aaron (I Chron. 6.3–8), but Aaron had other descendants than the Zadokites. After the exile, Ezekiel's programme was partially adopted, but modified, so far as membership of the priesthood was concerned, to include all descendants of Aaron, as well as those of Zadok, as eligible for the priesthood.

(*c*) *Functions of the Priesthood.* In early Israel, when laymen were competent to offer sacrifices, one of the functions—perhaps the chief function—of the priest was to ascertain the will of God, which was usually done by means of the EPHOD (I Sam. 23.6–12). This is partially confirmed by the fact that in Arabic the word *kahin*, which corresponds to the Heb. word for priest (*kohen*), has degenerated into meaning 'diviner'. Even as late as post-exilic times, one of the duties of priests was to deliver *toroth* (plur. of *torah*, lit. 'instruction', in later times coming to be hardened into 'law': see Hag. 2.11–13). (See also JUDGMENT.) It was only gradually that the priests came to be concerned mainly with the offering of sacrifices. By the closing centuries BC the interpretation of what was now written 'Scripture' was largely the work of the scribes, and the priests had come more and more to specialize in the sacrificial ritual.

(*d*) CONSECRATION OF PRIESTS. The order for the consecration of priests is set forth in detail in Exod. 29, a chapter repeated almost word for word in Lev. 8, which tells how the instructions were carried out. As they stand, these chapters have reference to the consecration of the original High Priest, Aaron, and his sons, and we may be disinclined to read them as 'history'. They are, however, important historical sources in that they certainly embody the ritual performed at the consecration of a High Priest at the close of the OT period. The word 'consecrate' in Lev. 8.33 means literally 'fill the hand of' (so RV margin, and cf. Judg. 17.5, RV margin), and may possibly refer to the placing in the hand of the newly ordained priest of something that was the symbol of his office, somewhat as a Bible is delivered to ordinands to-day (though see below under (*3*)).

(*1*) VESTMENTS. The garments worn by the High Priest were of regal magnificence (Exod. 28.3–5, Lev. 8.7–9), as befitted one who, so far as the condition of the Jews as subjects of an imperial power (of Persia, Greece, or Rome) permitted, was the successor of the pre-exilic kings. It is consistent with this that in pre-exilic times we never hear of the 'High Priest', except in one or two passages (II Kings 12.10, 22.4,8, 23.4), where the text has probably been expanded.

(*2*) ANOINTING. Like the kings, too, the High Priest was anointed with OIL, some of which (Lev. 8.10f.) was also applied to the 'tabernacle' and its furniture in the course of the consecration ceremony. It would seem that 'Aaron', i.e. the High Priest, alone was anointed, not the ordinary priests, his 'sons' (Lev. 10.7 might seem to say that they were, but it should be read in the light of 8.30. Oil was poured upon the head of the High Priest, but only sprinkled upon the garments of the other priests).

(*3*) *Consecration sacrifices.* These included a sin-offering (Lev. 8.14–17), a burnt-offering (vss. 18–21), and a consecration offering proper (vss. 22–32). The sin-offering differed from a sin-offering for high-priestly inadvertence (Lev. 4.3–12) in that none of its blood was taken inside the sanctuary. The burnt-offering was dealt with according to the usual ritual (Lev. 1). The consecration offering, a ram, closely resembled an ordinary peace-offering, except that some of its blood was applied to the right ears, thumbs, and great toes of Aaron and his sons, thus symbolizing the consecration of the priests in their whole persons to the service to which they were dedicated. The Heb. word for consecration in the passage is literally 'fillings' (cf. what has been said above), and it may be that it refers to the 'wave-offering' which was placed 'upon the hands of Aaron, and upon the hands of his sons' (Lev. 8.27). In effect, the offering was an installation sacrifice.

IV. THE FESTIVALS

(*a*) *Historical summary.* The Heb. word for festival is *hag*, generally translated FEAST in the EVV. It is cognate with the Arabic *hajji*, a title given to anyone who has made the pilgrimage to Mecca. To attend a *hag* involved the making of a journey. Before the centralization of sacrificial worship at the Jerusalem Temple the journey required would be short, perhaps no farther than to the local sanctuary or 'high place'. The three great annual festivals were originally related to farming and agriculture, and the dates on which they were held would depend upon harvest conditions in the locality, and were therefore not fixed according to a definite calendar. When, after the exile, the only altar was at the Jerusalem Temple, it became necessary to fix the dates of the festivals, which thus came to some extent to be dissociated from agriculture, and to be related instead to the decisive events in Israel's history. Thus, Passover and Unleavened Bread commemorated the Exodus; Weeks—or Pentecost, as it came to be called in NT times—the giving of the Law on Mount Sinai, and Tabernacles the wilderness wanderings.

(*b*) PASSOVER *and* UNLEAVENED BREAD (Deut. 16.1–8). These were originally distinct. Passover was a lambing festival, nomadic and even pre-Mosaic in origin. Unleavened Bread was agricultural, and was held at the beginning of the barley harvest (our March-April). It was so called because at it bread (in the form of flat cakes) was baked without leaven, partly, perhaps, because of the haste imposed by the harvest labours, and partly in order once a year to break off the use of the highly fermented dough of the year preceding. After the settlement in Canaan the two festivals, the one nomadic and the other agricultural, became practically one, because they fell at about the same time. The paschal lamb was eaten with unleavened cakes. The date in the fixed calendar was the first full moon after the spring equinox (Lev. 23.5f.), a date which still determines Good Friday and Easter in the Christian calendar. Passover was essentially a family festival, but since it was a sacrifice belonging to the category of peace-offerings, it could after the exile be celebrated only in Jerusalem. (*V.* also under PASSOVER.)

(*c*) WEEKS, *or* PENTECOST (Deut. 16.9–12). This originally marked the end of the wheat harvest. In the later fixed calendar it was reckoned seven weeks, or, to be exact, fifty days from the Sabbath following Passover (Lev. 23.15f.); hence the name Pentecost in NT times.

(*d*) TABERNACLES (Deut. 16.13–15). This festival marked the end of the agricultural year, and was the general 'harvest home'. It took place in the autumn, when the fruit harvest had been safely gathered in. In Exod. 23.16 it is called the 'feast of ingathering, at the end of the year'. A better translation than 'end' would be the 'beginning' of the (new) year: the Heb. word means 'going out', and properly describes the 'going out' or start of a new year rather than the end of the old (in Exod. 34.22 the word used is 'revolution', see RV margin). The old year ended with the conclusion of the harvest, and a new year forthwith began. There is some apparent confusion in the fixed calendar date of the festival, which is given as in the seventh month (Lev. 23.34). The explanation is simple: in ancient Israel the new year began in the autumn; but the Babylonian new year was in the spring, and after the exile the Jews adopted the Babylonian calendar for the *ecclesiastical* year. The *civil* year began, as it still does among the Jews, in the autumn, and in Lev. 23.24 the blowing of trumpets, which marked the (original) new year, is now ordered to be 'in the seventh month, in the first day of the month'.

The word Tabernacles in the EVV is not a good translation. The Heb. word (*sukkoth*) has no relation to the wilderness tabernacle (Heb. *mishkan*). Its proper meaning is BOOTHS (so Lev. 23.34, Deut. 16.13, RV margin), the booths being made of the leafy fronds of trees. During the festival, which lasted seven days (Deut. 16.15), everyone lived in the open air with no more shelter than was provided by these temporary structures. This they did for sheer gladness of heart, rejoicing in the safe garnering of the harvest (cf. 'Thou shalt be altogether joyful', Deut. 16.15). Even after the festival came to be kept in Jerusalem, the booths were erected in the streets of the city. Their true origin was forgotten, and the festival came, quite appropriately, to commemorate the wanderings in the wilderness. In pre-exilic times the festival of booths was associated with a good deal of drunkenness and sexual licence.

(*e*) *The* DAY OF ATONEMENT. After the exile the festivals lost much of their originally joyous character, and became solemn anniversaries of the historical events they had come to commemorate. The deepened consciousness of sin was largely responsible for this change. In particular, a few days before the festival of booths the Day of Atonement was kept, on the tenth day of the seventh month. This was properly a fast, not a feast, and in NT times it was called 'The Day' or 'The Fast' (cf. Acts 27.9) simply. It was the most important day in the ecclesiastical year. The prescribed ritual is found in Lev. 16, and more fully in the Mishna tract *Yoma* ('The Day'). Outside Lev. 16 and one or two other brief passages (Exod. 30.10, Lev. 23.27–32, 25.9, Num. 29.7–11) in the latest document of the Pentateuch, there is no mention of it in the OT, and it would seem that it was not celebrated until well on in post-exilic times. It therefore marks the latest stage in the OT economy of sacrifice. At the same time, certain parts of the ritual go back to remote antiquity, particularly that part of it which relates to the SCAPEGOAT.

On the Day of Atonement special sacrifices were offered, for the High Priest and his colleagues the priests in particular, and for the people collectively. The former consisted of a young bullock for a sin-offering and a ram for a burnt-offering, the latter of two he-goats for a sin-offering and a ram for a burnt-offering. The garments worn by the High Priest were of linen, not the regal garments worn on festive occasions. On this one day in the year the High Priest took the blood of the sin-offerings through the Temple veil into the Holy of Holies, and sprinkled it upon the mercy-seat. (The directions in Lev. 16 presuppose the ark and mercy-seat, but it will be remembered that in post-exilic times the Holy of Holies was actually empty—see above, II(*b*).) The blood of an ordinary sin-offering, even that of a High Priest, was not taken any farther than to the veil which stood before the Holy of Holies (see above, I(*e*)).

Of the two he-goats of the people's sin-offering, only one was actually sacrificed; the other—the choice between them being made by lot—was designated 'for Azazel' (so RV text; AV, 'scapegoat'; RV margin, 'for dismissal', is based upon a wrong etymology). Azazel was a wilderness demon of popular imagination, and there is no doubt that the ideas associated with him were very ancient. In the apocalyptic book of Enoch he is said to have been the leader of the fallen angels who married the daughters of men (Gen. 6.1–4). After the sin-offerings had been completed, the High Priest placed both his hands on the head of the goat, and confessed over it 'all the iniquities of the children of Israel, and all their transgressions, even all their sins' (Lev. 16.21).

Here we have a clear example of the conception of guilt transferred from the human beings who have contracted it to an animal which is guiltless, and it is significant that the guilt so transferred was guilt incurred by the commission of real sins, not merely the sins of inadvertence which were all for which any sin-offerings, even those on the Day of Atonement, could make expiation. But the 'scapegoat' was not properly a sacrifice. It was not offered upon the altar, but led out into the wilderness, where, according to the Mishna tract *Yoma*, it was thrown over a precipice. The purpose of the sin-offerings on the Day of Atonement went no farther than to make expiation for such sins as might have been committed unwittingly during the year preceding, but of which the community, notwithstanding careful scrutiny, was unaware.

V. THE NT FULFILMENT

(*a*) *The Inadequacy of the Sacrificial System.* When the Epistle to the Hebrews declares that 'it is impossible that the blood of bulls and goats should take away sins' (Heb. 10.4), it is only saying what the Law frankly acknowledged, viz. that the only sins for which even the sin-offering could make expiation were breaches of ritual committed in ignorance. It may well be that in actual practice a man would offer a sacrifice in the expectation that his known sins would thereby be forgiven. But, if he did so, he was assuming something for which the Law gave him no justification. The OT has, it need hardly be said, much to say about forgiveness. FORGIVENESS was a real thing to the Jew, but he did not, if he read his Scriptures aright, think of it as a *quid pro quo* for sacrifice. It was the free gift of God, dependent only upon repentance and confession (cf. Ps. 32.5). Forgiveness cannot be purchased, or it would not be forgiveness.

In the pre-exilic prophets there are a number of passages in which animal sacrifice is condemned so roundly (Amos 5.21–5, Hos. 6.6, Isa. 1.11–15, Mic. 6.6ff., Jer. 7.21ff.) that it has been plausibly argued that the prophets condemned sacrifice *as such*, and not merely the abuse of it. However that may be, there are in the Psalms a few passages (probably post-exilic) in which the attitude to sacrifice is not so much the negatively hostile attitude of the prophets as that of men who have come to realize that animal sacrifices, even with the best intentions, are less acceptable to God than the offering of a pure and holy life (Pss. 40.6ff., 50.7–15, 51.16f.). This, indeed, had come to be the attitude of the most spiritually minded Jews by the beginning of the Christian era, and there is in Philo a famous passage (quoted by Gray, *op. cit.*, p. 146) which compares the bloody sacrifices which were offered on the altar of burnt-offering with that of the offering of incense, which symbolized the prayers of the faithful, much to the disparagement of the former (cf. Prov. 15.8). But if to obey was better than sacrifice (I Sam. 15.22, Prov. 21.3), the problem for an eager soul like St. Paul was that with the best will in the world he found it impossible perfectly to obey (Rom. 7.7–25).

(*b*) *The Death of Christ as a Sacrifice.* In the early years of the present century much emphasis was laid upon the contrast between the prophetic and priestly ideals in the OT. It was frequently assumed that the priestly ideal, together with the sacrificial system that went with it, was the fossilized remains of antique conceptions, and therefore more or less irrelevant to spiritual religion. This attitude was usually associated with the denial of any substitutionary, or even 'objective', element in the Christian doctrine of the ATONEMENT. To-day it is generally agreed that the idea of substitution, even if it is present at all in OT sacrifice, is by no means prominent, so that a recognition of the relevance of sacrifice to the gospel of the Cross need not commit us to any acceptance of crude theories of substitution. There is also greater readiness than there was to study the sacrificial system sympathetically, as something that embodied ideas and aspirations which are of permanent value and significance for religion. Moreover, it is coming to be realized that what the NT says about the Cross cannot be interpreted without violence to its plain meaning, if we read it without reference to ideas about sacrifice (see especially Dr. Vincent Taylor's books, *Jesus and His Sacrifice* and *The Atonement in New Testament Teaching*). Such a passage as I Pet. 1.18f., 'knowing that ye were redeemed, not with corruptible things, with silver and gold . . . but with precious blood, as of a lamb without blemish and without spot, *even the blood* of Christ', was evidently written with the sacrificial system in mind (cf. also passages like John 1.29, Rom. 3.24f., Rev. 5.6–9).

At the same time it should be recognized that in the very passages which embody the language of sacrifice, the thought is often associated with ideas which belong strictly to a different category, viz. that of redemption or ransom from slavery and bondage. This is so in I Pet. 1.18f., Rom. 3.24f., Rev. 5.6–9. Jesus, too, with reference to his approaching sufferings, said that he 'came to give his life a ransom for many' (Mark 10.45). As it stands this need have no reference to sacrifice as such. Yet it is clearly reminiscent of Isa. 52.13–53.12 (note the word 'many' which recurs in the passage, 52.14f., 53.11f.), where the Servant is said to give his life as a guilt-offering (*asham*, 53.10, RV margin). It would seem therefore that the NT, when it speaks of the Cross, draws upon metaphors from two categories, without always attempting to distinguish clearly between them.

(*c*) *The Consummation of Sacrifice*. The most elaborate and consistent attempt in the NT to interpret the Cross in terms of the sacrificial system is that of the writer of the Epistle to the Hebrews (see especially Chs. 9–10). To understand his reasoning it is necessary to keep in mind the plan of the Temple (or Tabernacle) and the general pattern of the sacrificial system, particularly the ritual of the Day of Atonement. When the writer relates the Cross to the sacrificial system, his argument is not invalidated by the fact that the latter was never intended to deal with any but venial transgressions, with what in fact was not really 'sin' at all. He knew very well that sacrifice could not atone for deliberate sin (Heb. 9.9, 10.1,4,11), but he insisted that what the Temple sacrifices were unable to do, Christ could do and had actually done. For him the law was but 'a shadow of the good things to come' (10.1). The Tabernacle, according to Exod. 25.40, 26.30, had been modelled upon a 'pattern' revealed to Moses. What the writer of the Epistle to the Hebrews had in mind was this heavenly original of the earthly fane (9.24). Another contrast is that between the High Priest and Christ. Christ is without peer: even the angels are but servants, he is the Son (Ch. 1). High priests are 'many in number, because that by death they are hindered from continuing'; but Christ 'because he abideth for ever, hath his priesthood unchangeable' (7.23f.). He is 'a high priest for ever after the order of Melchizedek' (5.10, 6.20). The High Priest, too, must make expiation for his own sins as well as for the sins of those to whom he ministers (5.3).

The argument of the Epistle reaches its climax in 10.19ff.: 'Having therefore, brethren, boldness to enter into the holy place'—he means the Holy of Holies—'by the blood of Jesus, by the way which he dedicated for us, a new and living way, through the veil, that is to say, his flesh; and having a great priest over the house of God; let us draw near with a true heart in fullness of faith. . . .' Clearly this must be set against the background of the Temple-Tabernacle and the ritual of the Day of Atonement. There are obvious similarities to Jewish rites in what the writer of the Epistle has in mind, and equally obvious differences. The chief difference is that the Epistle thinks of the earthly Tabernacle as but an imperfect copy of another and greater Temple, a Temple eternal in the heavens. As he says elsewhere: 'Christ entered not into a holy place made with hands, like in pattern to the true; but into heaven itself, now to appear before the face of God for us' (9.24). Christ, then, entered into the heavenly sanctuary. The veil through which he entered was his flesh, the idea being that by his dying upon the Cross he broke through the limitations of his earthly life. His earthly life is thought of as a veil or curtain which separated him for a time from perfect fellowship with God, a veil which was rent asunder by his death. Further, the High Priest had to enter the Holy of Holies once every year. The virtue of the sprinkled blood which he took with him lasted for only twelve months. Also the blood with which he entered was not his own, but the blood of an animal. 'Nor yet that he [Christ] should offer himself often; as the high priest entereth into the holy place year by year with blood not his own; else must he often have suffered since the foundation of the world: but now once at the end of the ages hath he been manifested to put away sin by the sacrifice of himself' (9.25f.). Lastly, the death of Christ effected what the ritual of Jewish sacrifices could never do. The only Jew who could ever enter into the Holy of Holies on earth was the High Priest. Laymen were never allowed even into the earthly sanctuary. But Christ opened up and dedicated a way, a new and living way, for all the children of men, including—we must assume—laymen, women, and Gentiles, who come to him with a true heart and in fullness of faith, into the very sanctuary of God in the heavens. (*V.* also ATONE, MEDIATOR, RECONCILE.)

BIBLIOGRAPHY

G. B. Gray: *Sacrifice in the Old Testament*, London (1925); W. O. E. Oesterley: *Sacrifices in Ancient Israel*, London (1937); *Jewish Background of the Christian Liturgy*, London (1925). A. C. Welch: *Prophet and Priest in Old Israel*, London (1936). C. R. North: *Old Testament Interpretation of History*, London (1946). N. H. Snaith: Essay on 'The Priesthood and the Temple' in *A Companion to the Bible* (ed. T. W. Manson), Edinburgh (1939). W. J. Phythian-Adams: *The Way of At-one-ment*, London (1944). A. R. S. Kennedy: *Leviticus* (*The Century Bible*), Edinburgh (n.d.).

C. R. NORTH

SAINT, HOLY, DIVINE

Hasidim (a plural) is translated by AV as 'saints' in I Sam. 2.9, II Chron. 6.41, Prov. 2.8 and in sixteen verses in the Psalms. (For these latter passages, *v.* Young's *Analytical Concordance to the Bible*, under 'Saint'.) In all three verses the RV follows the AV except in I Sam. 2.9, where the RV has 'holy ones'. *Hasidim* means kind, godly, or pious persons, either indicating their 'duteous love' (so Cheyne) towards God, or that 'kindness is prominent in the godly' (*Oxford Heb. Dict.*). The singular of the word, viz. *Hasid*, is not translated by AV or RV as 'saint' (e.g. Ps. 4.3, 12.1, 32.6, where AV and RV have 'godly', while in Ps. 86.2 AV has 'holy', RV 'godly'), although there can be no valid reason for differentiating in this way between the singular and the plural.

Qadosh=holy. The plural of this word is rendered by AV as 'saints' in nine places, in five of which (viz. Ps. 89.5,7, Job 5.1, 15.15. Zech. 14.5) RV renders 'holy ones', apparently reserving the term 'holy' to designate angels, and 'saints' to denote mortals of high spiritual worth. In two passages where the singular *Qadosh* appears, i.e. in Ps. 106.16 and Dan. 8.13, AV has 'saint'—in each case inappropriately, since in Dan. 8.13 the reference would seem to be to a heavenly being (hence RV 'a holy one') and in Ps. 106.16 Aaron is better described in virtue of his priestly office as 'the holy one of Jahweh' than as 'the saint of Jahweh' (*v.* Num. 16.3f. and Oesterley's *Psalms*, Vol. II, *ad loc.*). RV, however, follows here AV. *Qaddish* (Biblical Aramaic), 'holy', is, in the plural, used in the Book of Daniel of deities and angels where AV and RV translate 'holy ones' (cf. 5.11, 4.13). Throughout Chap. 7, where the word is used of Israel, both versions render 'saints', viz. 'the saints of the Most High'.

The root significance of *Qadosh* and its Aramaic equivalent is that which is *separate*, and thus in a religious sense the word implied that which, being associated with a deity, was cut off from all profane contact or use. Contacts with a deity are very varied. Hence in the OT such things are described as holy as: garments, vessels, places, the temple, the temple mount, the city of Jerusalem, tithes, waters. The priest and the Nazirite are holy persons quite apart from any consideration of their possessing moral eminence. Male and female temple prostitutes (*Qedeshim* and *Qedeshoth*, wrongly called harlots and sodomites by RV, cf. Deut. 23.17,18, II Kings 23.7) were, as their titles proclaim, sacred ministrants. They were attached to the Canaanite cult of the deity of fertility, but the fact that, though not without interruption, they flourished in Israel down to the time of Josiah's reformation of religion shows how tenaciously the early notion of 'holiness' persisted.

Hagios, the term most frequently used in the NT to signify 'holy'—much more often than *hosios* (used four times) and *hieros* (twice) —has a history similar to the Hebrew *Qadosh*, for originally it was a cult concept indicating that which is consecrated or devoted to a deity or deities (*v.* W. Bauer, *Griechisch-Deutsches Wörterbuch zu den Schriften des Neuen Testaments*, 3rd edn. (1937), on *hagios*). In the NT it is predicated of things, men, angels and God. It is applied to the scriptures (Rom. 1.2), to the Christian calling (II Tim. 1.9), the faith (Jude 20), sacrifice (Rom. 12.1), the prophets (Luke 1.70), to John the Baptist (Mark 6.20), to pre-Christian saints (Matt. 27.52), to Christians as 'holy brethren' (Heb. 3.1), to the children of Christians (I Cor. 7.14), to Christ (Acts 4.27,30), to angels (Mark 8.38), and to God (John 17.11). Christians as persons who are consecrated to God, professing Christ and sanctified by the Spirit, are described as 'holy' in many passages where the EVV render 'saints'. The members of the Christian community in Jerusalem are the 'saints at Jerusalem' (Acts 9.13, cf. 9.32, Rom. 8.27, 12.13, 15.25, I Cor. 6.1f., etc.).

The prophets of the OT were not the inventors of ethics in Israel, but their ethical teaching deepened and widened the concept of holiness, so that its ritual and external aspects, without being eliminated, yet occupied a position of importance secondary to that of its moral and spiritual content. As the ideas of the divine justice, compassion and wisdom took firmer root, the notion of Jahweh's holiness also grew. For Isaiah a title of Jahweh is 'the holy one of Israel'. Eventually in two passages in the OT (Isa. 63.10,11, Ps. 51.11) there emerges the expression 'holy spirit' (*q.v.*).

Not only in the prophetic writings does a deep appreciation of the moral quality of the divine character develop. In the Psalms too the same phenomenon is to be observed, for example, in the sense of sin, humility and penitence of the writer of Ps. 51, and in the stress laid upon keeping the moral law in Ps. 15 and Ps. 24.3–4. In the so-called 'Law of Holiness' (namely, Lev. 17-26: according to Oesterley and Robinson, *An Introduction to the Books of the Old Testament*, p. 61, this law is of seventh century BC) we read the exhortation given to Israel (19.2): 'Ye shall be holy; for I the Lord your God am holy.' This sentence is of significance, for it belongs to the literature of the priestly legislation and by no means inculcates a purely external holiness (cf. 19.11–18). But it must not be misunderstood as if its implications had no reference to the religious cultus. The legislative portions of the OT place side by side cultural and moral requirements, regarding both as a part of one whole. The 'Law of Holiness' is an example of the close cohesion of both elements. Indeed, the particular aim of this document is, as Haller (*Das Judentum*, 1914, p. 196) says, 'to separate that which belongs to the cult from that which is profane and to place the whole congregation of Israel in the sphere of the former'. In the NT, where there is no considerable growth of ritual practice, the idea of holiness is practically entirely of a spiritual sort, and St. Paul wages a virile polemic against the cult notions of sacred and impure, the observance of 'days and months and seasons and years' (Gal. 4.10) and ordinances of 'handle not, nor taste, nor touch' (Col. 2.21).

A term of infrequent occurrence, appearing only in the NT, is the word 'divine' (*theios*) in the sense of from, of, or like God. The writer of II Peter in 1.3,4 speaks of Christ's 'divine power' having granted Christians all things that pertain to life and godliness and of their being enabled through the promises (of Christ's second coming and of the world-end) to escape from the corruption that is in the world and 'become partakers of the divine nature'. (With the thought of the passage, cf. II Cor. 3.18, Rom. 8.21,23, Phil. 3.21, I John 3.2.) G. Hollmann, in his commentary *ad loc.* in *Die Schriften des Neuen Testaments*, takes the view that the phrase 'divine nature' in this letter, together with the belief that this immortal nature can be partaken of in this present life, reveals the author to have been a Greek theologian of the second century. The neuter form of the word used in II Peter as adjective, meaning divine, is found in Acts 17.29 in the sense of Godhead, who, it is affirmed, is not 'like unto gold or silver or stone graven by art and device of man'; while in Rom. 1.20 the substantive (*Theiotes*) occurs in the statement that God's 'everlasting power and divinity' are 'perceived through the things that are made'.

In Heb. 9.1 the translation 'ordinances of divine service' renders by the two last words one single Greek word *latreia*, which means service in the sense of worship (cf. *A.R.S.V. ad loc.*, 'regulations of worship'). In all other passages where *latreia* appears AV and RV have 'service' (cf. John 16.2, Rom. 9.4, 12.1, Heb. 9.6).

The proverb, 'A divine sentence is in the lips of the king' (Prov. 16.10), means, as literally translated from the Hebrew: 'A divination is on the lips of a king', i.e. a diviner's oracle is on a king's lips. (*V.* also SANCTIFY.)

O. S. RANKIN

SALVATION *v.* SAVE

SANCTIFY, SANCTIFICATION

The form of the words implies the making of something, i.e. a process complete or incomplete, but not in any event the finished product itself. 'Sanctify' evidently means to make *sanctus* or holy, and s. means the process of being made or becoming holy. Whatever is meant by *holy* will naturally throw light on the process of becoming holy. It may be noted here that in the Gk. s. and 'holy' come from the same root. If we had such a word as 'holify', it would serve to mark the connexion. It is therefore with a reference to holy and holiness that the start is here made.

I. HOLY AND HOLINESS (*v.* also under SAINT). The constant witness of Scripture is that holiness belongs properly to God alone.

(*a*) in the OT, God is holy (Ps. 99.9), or equivalently his Name is holy (Ps. 99.3, 111.9), and may not be profaned (Lev. 20.3). If anything else is called holy, it is in a sense derivative from him and dependent upon him or upon his will. Things are not by nature holy; rather by s. they become holy. It is not the cult or 'religion' that imparts holiness; on the contrary, the cult or religion has holiness imparted to it in virtue of its relation to God himself. Thus the 'ground' of Exod. 3.5 and Josh. 5.15 is 'holy', though it has had no contact with the cult; its holiness is an acquired characteristic in virtue of its 'nearness' to God, or more simply its employment by God. The apparatus and observances of the cult enjoy a similarly derivative holiness, since their employment and practice bring them into relation with God. Hence the ark is holy (II Chron. 35.3), and the vessels (I Kings 8.4), and the place where they rest (I Kings 8.6); while those that minister these things are also holy (II Chron. 35.3). Similarly, sabbaths are holy (Exod. 20.8,11) or the seventh day (Exod. 35.2); and garments (Exod. 28.2), feasts (cf. Isa. 30.29, 'holy solemnity' or 'festival night', Moffatt), and of course God's house (*passim*). These things, or certain of them, are themselves held to impart holiness. Our Lord mentions with apparent approval that the temple sanctifies the gold, and the altar the gifts brought to it (Matt. 23.17,19). But this is evidently in a derivative sense, since things are also sanctified without and apart from the temple.

This direct dependence upon God for holiness and for the power to confer holiness is of the greatest importance in determining the meaning of the terms. First, since God is the Author of holiness, there is a personal conception of holiness implicit at the source, a germ capable of development into full moral significance. It is not by cult, ritual, observance or ceremonial that holiness is imparted; on the contrary, all holiness derives from the personal God who is himself holy. Since holiness is thus personal, ethical meaning is easily read into it; e.g. the Levitical idea regards holiness at times as bare severance or separateness (Lev. 20.26), as obtained through ritual performance (21.8), as maintained by avoidance of ceremonial defilement (11.44f.), and as arising absolutely from direct relationship with God (19.2). But already through this conception, almost ready to burst into view, there dimly appears a personal holiness with ethical qualities, which it was left to the prophets fully to express (cf. Hab. 1.13 and Isa. *passim*, esp. 6.3,5, where the recognition of triple holiness in God inspires dismay at personal uncleanness).

The personal character of this holiness is sometimes obscured by a more naturalistic view. (Cf. the baleful influence of the ark as recorded I Sam. 5f., II Sam. 6; 'the ark is loaded as with a holy electricity, whose shock strikes profane things like lightning' (Procksch in Kittel's *TWNT*).) But this is a temporary concealment and by no means a cancellation of the prevailing personal conception of holiness. The strongly personal character of the idea in the OT enables it to be carried over into the NT without violent alteration.

The second lesson to be learned from the OT thought of holiness is allied with what has been said. Holiness has an objective character. It is not something that is worked up, but something that is rather sent down—conferred upon those things and persons that are brought into relation with God. Nor is holiness a quality naturally possessed, but one supernaturally granted from the underived holiness which belongs to God alone. Holiness is not so much acquired as conceded, though the concession is ordinarily made through certain regular channels (cf. citations from Lev., *supra*). It follows that it is less an activity than a status. This lesson too has been learnt as the idea is transferred to the NT, so that the holiness and s. that appear there retain a strongly objective character.

(*b*) In the NT, the emphasis is transferred almost exclusively to the personal aspect and implications of holiness. S. is not withdrawn from things. According to dominical teaching, the temple and the altar are able to sanctify (Matt. 23.17,19); the rigours of sabbatarianism are checked, but the Son of Man still retains his lordship over the day (Luke 6.5); and the defilement of the temple by traders (Matt. 21.12ff.) implies a sanctity violated. But the emphasis is now elsewhere. The temple now regarded as holy is the 'household of God', with all the saints, Jesus Christ being the chief corner stone (Eph. 2.20f.); the 'holy sacrifice' demanded is the living sacrifice of men's bodies (Rom. 12.1). In Heb., one would expect a more formal and ceremonial employment of the idea, and the expectation is indeed not disappointed. But this reversion to OT usage is evidently made for purposes of analogy. The whole sanctifying apparatus of sacrifice is employed to set forth the work of Christ and its fruits in holiness of living (Heb. 9.13f.); and in this employment it finds its completion and its only remaining legitimate use.

II. SANCTIFICATION. That holiness of this personal and objective kind should be induced is the object of scriptural s. Rom. 12.1 bids Christians 'present your bodies a living sacrifice, holy acceptable unto God, which is your reasonable service'. The demand made here is for a personal offering of the body to the will and disposal of God. This offering is represented as a sacrifice, and covert reference is thereby made to the Jewish OT sacrificial system. In this new and spiritual sacrifice, purity is demanded, just as it was expected in the sacrificial system. The cult demanded a ceremonial purity in the sacrifice; Paul here demands an ethical or personal purity; and the purity of the cult colours with objectivity the personal purity required. In sacrifice it is not the practice of holiness that is primarily required, but an objective status of holiness. The analogy with this ceremonial purity imparts an objective quality to the personal purity demanded by Paul. He thinks, that is to say, not only of a more or less close approximation to holiness in the sacrifice made, but of a holiness already realized and enjoyed. (Cf. the realized and objective character of the 'cleanness' and 'purity' claimed in Acts 18.6, 20.26.)

S. in the NT is thus not something that remains wholly to be achieved. In fact, the word is used in a double sense, but the two senses are by no means incompatible with each other and indicate aspects of the same thing. From one point of view, s. is complete—a *fait accompli*; from another it has still to be achieved, or, if begun, to be completed. To illustrate: when Christ is said to have loved the Church and to have given himself for it, 'that he might sanctify and cleanse it' (Eph. 5.26f.), something has already been accomplished and imparted by his work. S. is so far a completed thing, which has only to be enjoyed. S. is already possessed: 'Ye are washed, ye are sanctified' (I Cor. 6.11); it belongs not to the sphere where the race is still to be run, but to the eternal predisposition of God, who has 'from the beginning chosen you to salvation through sanctification of the Spirit' (II Thess. 2.13), now manifested and applied in Christ. Cf. also I Pet. 1.2, where s. is traced back to the divine foreknowledge.

On the other hand, s. is also something held out as in some sense a goal to be reached and an end to be accomplished. Thus the Corinthians are exhorted to rid themselves from all uncleanness of flesh and spirit, 'perfecting holiness in the fear of the Lord' (II Cor. 7.1). The

Thessalonians are warned that their s. consists in abstinence from fornication (I Thess. 4.3); and Timothy that a man is sanctified only if he 'purge himself' (II Tim. 2.21); while Rom. 6.19 suggests that s. is something to be achieved by 'serving righteousness'.

It need hardly be added that other passages appear neutral to this distinction, e.g. I Thess. 3.13, where Christ's work in increasing his people in love is said to be to 'stablish your hearts unblameable in holiness before God'.

III. GROUNDS OF SANCTIFICATION. Different grounds are clearly to be sought for the two aspects of s. that have become evident. The s. already possessed by Christians is unambiguously traced to Jesus Christ and his work. The passages where the strongly objective character of s. especially appears usually name him as its ground. Christ's love and sacrifice for the Church has as end its s. and cleansing (Eph. 5.25f.; cf. also I Cor. 1.2). Cleansing, justification and s. are all attributed to 'the name of the Lord Jesus' (I Cor. 6.11). In this sense, Christ's work guarantees, achieves and even applies to us a s. which is already to become ours.

On the other hand, where s. is regarded as something still to be achieved, Christians are exhorted to bestir themselves for its accomplishment. The completion of s. lies ahead as a task to be discharged 'in the fear of God' (II Cor. 7.1). 'Righteousness' is the means of its attainment (Rom. 6.1), and its negative conditions are abstinence from fornication (I Thess. 4.3) and purgation (II Tim. 2.21). The repeated emphasis on negative conditions is noteworthy. They are more prominent than positive conditions such as righteousness. The reason for this is to be found, not in any narrowly ascetic view of the Christian life, but rather in that other aspect of s., the fact that it is in a sense already achieved and may therefore be regarded as the Christian's possession unless forfeited.

IV. THE NATURE OF SANCTIFICATION. Certain things therefore become clear. The proper subject of s. is not man but God. It is God that sanctifies, and s. is of him. This will be no surprise to those who remember where the OT emphasis lies. Whether it is himself (John 17.19) or the Church (Eph. 5.26) that is sanctified, Christ effects it in virtue of the equality with God which he enjoys. The constant disposition of God to sanctify things and persons for his purposes comes to a head in Christ, and it is from him that we have such s. as is ours.

This s. is conferred on and appropriated by those that are in Christ: 'both he that sanctifieth and they who are sanctified are all of one' (Heb. 2.11). S. has ethical corollaries; but the relation of ethics to s. is not, according to Scripture, that of cause and effect, means and end. S. that has Christ as ground has no need of supplementary assurance or guarantee. If it really is conferred upon us, it is not something primarily achieved by us. It may indeed be fortified, as Paul's constant exhortations are designed to impress on those to whom he wrote; but it is not a thing to be won.

Thus s. is less an activity than a status. The purity which characterizes the 'reasonable service' of the 'living sacrifice' is not one that has hazardously to be attained. It is already theirs who have in Christ appropriated it. While, however, s. is not an activity, it can legitimately be described as a practice or exercise. It is to the practice of their s. that Paul adjures his readers: they have to conduct themselves as those that are sanctified. This is the force of the 'unblameable' of I Thess. 3.13. The natural order may be held to be reversed. In the sphere of the Gospel, it is not 'handsome is as handsome does', but with fair accuracy just the reverse: those that are sanctified will give no occasion for reproach.

The principle that s. once laid hold of will issue in ethically worthy deeds and conduct is a self-evident commonplace, but one which must always be held before the eyes of Christians. S. stands at the beginning of the Christian moral life, not at its end. If the idea of progress is to be linked to s. at all, it is a progress *in* s., not a progress towards s., of which we must speak. As one restored from death to life might be expected to be capable of progress from sickness into health within the life to which he has returned, so with s. The decisive transition has been made: the Christian is sanctified; but he has still to live this status out. The final term in progress of this kind is identical with love; and here God's work begun finds completion in a 'bond of perfectness' that ties the Christian equally with his neighbour and his God.

It appears, then, that s. stands nearer to Justification than is often supposed. If, as must be the case, it be rescued from immersion in bare moralism, it will occupy a position nearer to the initiation of the Christian life, and *ipso facto* to JUSTIFICATION (*q.v.*). It is tempting for the sake of logical neatness to make a clean division between the two; but the temptation must be resisted, if in fact the division is absent from Holy Scripture. The definition of terms at this point is eased if Justification be given a declaratory, imputed or forensic ('reputed', Luther) character. The way is then open to regarding s. as the real status thereby conferred, which in its turn awaits exemplification, practice or exercise, just as from the newly accoladed nobleman one expects noble deeds. It is in such practice that the status is maintained. There is a certain inevitable looseness of definition in the case of a conception in which God in Jesus Christ must be held to do all, and yet men must nonetheless be exhorted to 'improve' (as the Westminster Confession of Faith says of our Baptism) that in them which he has already accomplished (cf. Phil. 1.6). (*V.* also SAINT.)

J. K. S. REID

SANCTUARY *v.* PRESENCE, SACRIFICE II(*d*) and (*e*)

SATAN *v.* ADVERSARY, ANTICHRIST

SATISFY, SATISFACTION

These words, which have had so considerable a place in the theology of the atonement, have (except for the literal meaning of fulfilling an appetite) very little place in the Bible. They are used in Num. 35.31,32 in AV as an equivalent for atonement in the sense of covering sin (*v.* COVER, ATONE), but in RV they are rendered ransom (*q.v.*). The idea of ransom does, however, suggest an equivalent or satisfaction for a life forfeit through sin but bought back, and for the redemption (*q.v.*) of all first-born males claimed by the Lord (Exod. 13.12, 34.19). From this original conception the idea was extended to include what could be accepted as an alternative to punishment and a ground for cancelling the penalty demanded by the moral law. It is largely through Anselm (derived from Cyprian) that the term came to dominate Western thought on the atonement.

In the NT the term satisfaction is not used in the sense of Christ's having been punished for us, although several passages speak of him having borne our doom ('the wages of sin is death', Rom. 6.23) for us. In II Cor. 5.14f. the death of Christ has a substitutionary and inclusive significance—'one died for all (so then all died) and died for all that they who live . . .' The end of the same paragraph in II Cor. 5.21 reads, 'He [God] made him [Christ] who knew no sin to be sin on our behalf, that we might become the righteousness of God in him'—that is, God made him die that death which is the wages of sin, as our substitute. In Gal. 3.13, 'Christ redeemed us from the curse of the law, having become a curse for us'; he made our curse (i.e. death as the doom pronounced on sin) his own, giving himself up to death on the accursed tree (cf. I Pet. 2.24, 'who his own self bare our sins in his own body upon the tree, that we having died unto sins, might live unto righteousness'). There are divine necessities as well as human, to be satisfied in any genuine atonement or reconciliation. God must be true to himself and to the moral order he has established in the world, and sin must not only be forgiven but be borne away. (*V.* also ATONE, RECONCILE, REDEEM.)

F. J. TAYLOR

SAVE, SALVATION

In the OT salvation is expressed by a word which has the root meaning of 'to be wide' or 'spacious', 'to develop without hindrance', and thus ultimately 'to have victory in battle' (I Sam. 14.45). To save meant to be possessed of the necessary strength and to act upon it so that it became manifest. David gained salvation when he reduced the surrounding peoples to obedience (II Sam. 8.14). Any chieftain who had sufficient strength to gain victory over the foes of the people could be described as their saviour (Judg. 2.18, 6.14), but as it was God who had raised up the saviour (Exod. 14.30, I Sam. 10.19), he was pre-eminently their Saviour. The word salvation came to receive a definite content as attention was focused on the result of the victory. He who needs salvation is one who has been threatened or oppressed, and his salvation consists in deliverance from danger and tyranny or rescue from imminent peril (I Sam. 4.3, 7.8, 9.16). To save another is to communicate to him one's own prevailing strength (Job 26.2), to give him the power to maintain the necessary strength. Only God is so strong that his own arm obtains salvation (victory, security, freedom) for himself (Ps. 98.1, Job. 40.14), and everybody else, including the king (Ps. 20.5,6,9), must rely on a stronger than himself (i.e. God) for salvation. In Deutero-Isaiah the conception of salvation is very closely linked with the earlier prophetic idea of divine righteousness. The mighty work of God, in which his righteousness is manifested, is in saving the humble (cf. the contrast with Babylonian idols which have to be carried and cannot even save themselves; Isa. 40.18–20, 44.9–20, 46.6–7), the poor and the dispirited. The last of the Servant Songs (Isa. 53) suggests that this saving work can be carried out only through suffering. The history of Israel is thus the history of the saving activity of God in the corporate life of the people through the agency of appointed leaders. Salvation is thus a distinctively divine accomplishment: 'salvation belongeth unto the Lord' (Ps. 3.8; cf. 47.9, 62.11); the phrase 'God saves' or 'God is salvation' (I Sam. 14.39, I Chron. 16.35, Ps. 20.9, 68.20, Isa. 33.22) could almost be likened to a primitive creed.

In the later centuries before Christ, men came to despair of salvation in the present order, which was so evil that it could only come under condemnation; and they began to look for the coming of that day when God would interpose his mighty arm in the affairs of the world and out of judgment bring full salvation to those who were acquitted at that judgment. Evil and all disobedience to the sovereign rule of God would be utterly destroyed (cf. KINGDOM OF GOD). Thus the concern of men was to be assured of acquittal in the day of judgment; and about one-fifth of the 150 instances in the NT of the words 'save' and 'salvation' refer to a salvation to be consummated at the last day (Rom. 13.11, 'now is our salvation nearer', I Pet. 1.5, 'salvation ready to be revealed in the last time', I Thess. 5.8, where the hope of salvation is like a helmet to be put on during the present stage of struggle; cf. also II Tim. 4.18, Heb. 1.14). Nevertheless, the future destiny of a man is determined by his present standing before God, so that it is possible to speak of a man as already saved—that is, accepted of God and secured against condemnation in the final judgment (Rom. 8.24, II Tim. 1.9, Tit. 3.5; cf. justification (*q.v.*) and its eschatological significance; *v.* Taylor, *Forgiveness and Reconciliation*, pp. 57–62).

In the synoptic Gospels the definitions given of the purpose of Christ's ministry, to save people from their sins (Matt. 1.21), to seek and to save those who are lost (Luke 19.10), imply the possibility of salvation being accomplished in the present. In like manner, a preacher is said to save his hearers, or God saves them through man's preaching (I Cor. 1.21, Rom. 11.14, I Cor. 9.22), and Christians may save their unbelieving partners by faithful witness (I Cor. 7.16). In the Fourth Gospel the present possession of eternal life is offered to men, and there is evident the thought of a definite transition from darkness to light, from death to life (John 5.24, 12.35, 17.2; cf. I John 5.12).

Nearly a third of the NT references to salvation (and its verbal forms) denote (as so frequently in the OT) deliverance from specific ills, such as captivity, disease and devil possession (Matt. 9.21, Luke 8.36), eschatological terrors (Mark 13.20), or physical death (Matt. 8.28, Acts 27.20; cf. Heb. 2.15). It is through faith that men receive salvation (Eph. 2.8) to which they contribute nothing, as it is accomplished by the grace of God (Eph. 2.5). The Gospel itself can be briefly comprehended as the saving power of God at work in the world (Rom. 1.16), and available for all men who will receive it into their hearts by faith (Rom. 4.16, 10.9, I Pet. 1.5). Only in one passage (Matt. 1.21) is salvation explicitly stated to be from sin, but the close connexion of specific troubles and dangers with disobedience to God means that this particular text does express the meaning of the NT as a whole. Salvation is from darkness to light (I Pet. 2.9), from alienation to a share in divine citizenship (I Pet. 2.10, Eph. 2.12–13), from guilt to pardon (Eph. 1.7, Col. 1.14; cf. Luke 1.77), from slavery to freedom (Gal. 5.1, II Cor. 3.17), from fear of hostile powers to liberty and assurance (I John 4.18, II Tim. 1.7; cf. Eph. 6.12), and all these definitions carry a strong moral content. (*V.* also DELIVER, HEAL, REDEEM.)

F. J. TAYLOR

SAVIOUR

In the OT the word is used as a title applied to successful captains (Judg. 3.9), kings (II Kings 13.5), and in a general way to leaders and deliverers of the people in the course of their history: 'thou gavest them saviours who saved them out of the hand of their adversaries' (Neh. 9.27). Since it was God who raised up saviours for the nation in time of need and in many historical crises, he was thought of as *the* Saviour. In relation to his people he was known in the character of Saviour (Ps. 106.21, Isa. 43.3,11, 60.16), and in comparison with him there was no one else who could justly claim the title of Saviour. In the LXX the word is used as a divine title about 30 times. The name is a marked feature of the vocabulary of Deutero-Isaiah (45.15,21, 46.26).

In the NT there are 24 instances of the use of the word, and its distribution is significant. Only Luke among the Gospels has it: in 1.47, 2.11 (both examples in the Nativity material which is strongly Hebraic in tone); cf. also Acts 5.31, 13.23. The first reference continues the OT usage of applying the word as a title for God, as in I Tim. 1.1, 2.3, 4.10, Tit. 1.3, 2.10, 3.4, Jude 25; the other three use it as a title for Christ, as do all the remaining references in the NT. The word occurs only twice in Paul (Eph. 5.23, Phil. 3.20) and twice in the Johannine writings in the phrase 'the Saviour of the world'. No less than 10 examples (out of the total of only 24) occur in the Pastoral Epistles, generally acknowledged to be among the latest writings included in the NT. In a recent study, B. S. Easton (*The Pastoral Epistles*, pp. 230f.) has drawn attention to this distribution of the word and suggested that the title was widely adopted by a later generation than the apostolic age as a protest against the abuse of the word as an honorific epithet in the emperor-cult. 'Not Caesar but Christ [or God] is the true Saviour'; and about one-third of the references to the title in the NT (all, except Acts 5.31, in Pastorals and I Pet.) speak of Christ as a saviour from man's worst enemy, his own sin. (*V.* also DELIVER, REDEEM, SAVE.)

F. J. TAYLOR

SCAPEGOAT *v.* SACRIFICE IV(*e*)

SCORN *v.* LAUGH

SCRIPTURE(S)

The word 'scripture(s)' in the NT broadly refers, of course, to what we now call the OT. The Jews of Palestine did not formally define the canon (or authoritative list) of s. until after the fall of Jerusalem (AD 70), when they were driven to make a book rather than a place (the Temple) the focus of their religious unity. This they did at a council of rabbis known as the Synod of Jamnia (*c.* AD 90), and their list was the equivalent of our OT. But outside Palestine the Greek-speaking Jews of Alexandria and elsewhere did not, as the Palestinian rabbis did, limit their list of sacred s. to works written in Heb.; the Gk. version of the s. (begun in the third century BC) and known as the Septuagint (LXX) was claimed by them to be of equal authority with the Heb. s., and this claim was supported by means of the legend of the miraculous identity of the versions made by all the seventy translators working independently. Accordingly the Alexandrian canon or 'Greek Bible' includes several works, many written originally in Gk., which are not found in the Palestinian canon; these are the books now found in our Apocrypha. (The Christian Church took over the Alexandrian canon as its OT, not without certain misgivings; but at the Reformation the reformers decided to limit the canon of the OT to the Palestinian or Heb. Bible, and so it has continued to this day in the churches of the Reformation. The Church's canon of NT scriptures was not finally determined until the fourth century AD, and so the subject falls outside the scope of this volume.)

The NT writers inherit the Jewish view of scriptural inspiration along with the scriptures themselves. The latter are quite simply the record of what God has shown or spoken to the men of faith who lived under the Old Covenant (*v.* INSPIRE). But these records cannot be properly understood apart from their fulfilment in the New Covenant of Jesus Christ. The events of Heb. history, no less than the words of the Heb. s., are the preparation for and foreshadowings of God's great and final act in the redemption of the world by the death and resurrection of his Messiah. To this coming redemption all the prophets had borne witness (Luke 1.70, 24.25–7, John 5.39, Acts 3.24, 18.28, Rom. 1.2, etc.); it was indeed the primary function of the s. to bear witness to Christ. Christ was the key that unlocked the s., and the Heb. s. were a Christian and not a Jewish book. The OT taught that the Christ should come; the task of the Christian evangelists was to proclaim that Jesus of Nazareth was he. Henceforward the s. must be read in the light of Jesus' resurrection; the Spirit of the Risen Lord would interpret to the Christian reader the things in all the s. concerning himself. This is the meaning of St. Luke's Emmaus story (24.13–35): our pilgrimage through the s. becomes an Emmaus walk with Christ by our side. Our hearts 'burn within us' and we are convinced by the testimony of the Spirit that the witness of the s. is true. This is the basis of the doctrine of the *Testimonium Spiritus Sancti internum*—the inner witness of the Spirit, who guides into all truth (John 16.13). St. Luke is, perhaps surprisingly, the NT writer who most strongly and clearly brings out the apostolic doctrine of Holy S., both in his Gospel and in Acts (cf. esp. Luke 24.44–7, as well as the Emmaus story, and also the similar passages in Acts). (*V.* also REVEAL, PROPHECY, INSPIRE.)

BIBLIOGRAPHY

Alan Richardson: *Christian Apologetics* (1947), Chaps. VIII and IX. A. G. Hebert: *Authority of OT* (1947). H. Cunliffe-Jones: *Authority of Biblical Revelation* (1945). W. Vischer: *Das Christuszeugnis des AT*, Band I (Zürich, 7th Edn., 1946), esp. pp. 7–41.

ALAN RICHARDSON

SEA *v.* WATER

SEAL

Heb. *chotham*, the noun; also trans. signet 10 times in EVV; *chatham*, the verb; Gk. *sphragis* and *sphragizo*. The literal meanings are plain, the metaphorical meanings often difficult and doubtful.

First there is *the seal itself*, a treasured article, worn round the neck (*Ox. Heb. Lex.*, p. 368), Gen. 38.18, or on the right hand, Jer. 22.24; sometimes set in gold, Ecclus. 32.5,6, with lifelike designs, Ecclus. 38.27; the stones on the high-priestly vestments are 'engraved like a signet', Exod. 28.11,21,36, 39.6,14,30, Ecclus. 45.11,12. Metaphorically, Zerubbabel will be the Lord's signet, Hag. 2.23 (i.e. as being *precious*); Ecclus. 49.11. So, 'Set me as a seal upon thine heart', Song Sol. 8.6; while in Ecclus. 17.22 the word is used of alms as being meritorious.

Then its uses:

(i) To *secure* by a seal: so, to *close up* the lions' den, Dan. 6.17; money-bags, Tob. 9.5; the sepulchre of Christ, Matt. 27.66; the abyss, Rev. 20.3. Metaph. Job's transgressions are 'sealed up in a bag', Job 14.17; the stars, so that they cannot rise, Job 9.7; a chaste woman is compared to 'a sealed fountain', Song Sol. 4.12. Vengeance is sealed up among God' treasures, Deut. 32.34. Perhaps the idea of *closing-up* explains Job 37.7, where human strength is seen to be powerless; perhaps also Job 33.6, with the added thought of 'making firm' or secure. The metaphor of *closing* reappears in the 'seal upon my lips' of Ecclus. 22.27; the close keeping of goods, Ecclus. 42.6; and the stoppage of the physical issue, Lev. 15.3. In Ezek. 28.12, the king of Tyre is said to 'seal up the sum' of wisdom and beauty, i.e. to be perfect. In Rom. 15.28, the words 'when I shall have accomplished this [the delivery of the great Collection to St. James at Jerusalem] and have sealed to them this fruit', have nothing to do with the sealing of the money-bags, which would have been done months before, but describe (as we say) the setting of the seal on an accomplished work.

(ii) To seal up a book, because *it is finished and nothing more is to be added*; so vision and prophecy are sealed up, Dan. 9.24, 12.4,9, because the last prophecies have been made and nothing remains but to await the Day. A sealed book cannot be opened and read, Isa. 29.11; similarly in Isa. 8.11 his teaching is 'sealed' as regards the general public, and handed on by his disciples. Hence when in Rev. 5.1,2 we meet again the 'sealed book' of Daniel, the Seer is found weeping (vs. 4), because the prophecies are complete, but there is no fulfilment. But the Lion of the tribe of Judah looses the seals and opens the book, vs. 5, because in him the Day has arrived and the eschatological expectation is fulfilled. After this in Rev. 6.1–12 and 8.1 a whole series of seals is loosed; and in Rev. 22.10 the Seer is told not to seal up anything, for the Fulfilment is in process.

(iii) To seal documents, and so *confirm* and *attest* them. Letters about Naboth are sealed with Ahab's seal, I Kings 21.8; similarly Jeremiah's legal documents, 32.10,11,14,44; the Covenant of Ezra's reform, Neh. 9.38, 10.1; royal letters, Esth. 8.8,10; some prize proverbs, I Esdr. 3.8; a document, Tob. 7.14. Metaph. we get the 'seal of circumcision' as the attestation of Abraham's faith, Rom. 4.11; the existence of the Corinthian Church is the attestation of St. Paul's apostolate, I Cor. 9.2. In John 3.33, he who having previously refused to receive the witness of Christ, vs. 32, turns and receives it, sets the seal of his personal experience to the truth and faithfulness of God, who has saved him out of his unbelief through Christ whom he has sent. In John 6.27 Christ is 'sealed', attested, by the Father.

The same meaning governs some passages which readily fall into a baptismal context. In Rev. 7.1–3, the convulsions of the earth cannot begin till the 144,000 have been sealed in their foreheads. In Rev. 14.1 we see them again, on Mount Zion, with the Name of the Lamb and the Name of his Father written in their foreheads. We are reminded of the mark (*tau*) set on the foreheads of the faithful in Ezek. 9.4. In II Cor. 1.22 St. Paul speaks of an anointing, and a sealing, and a gift of the *arrabon* or first instalment of the Spirit in our hearts, and in Eph. 1.13 of a sealing with the Holy Spirit of the Promise, and in Eph. 4.30 of a sealing by the Holy Ghost unto the Day of Redemption (for even if the dockyard metaphors which Moulton and Milligan find in this passage are valid, yet surely the Biblical allusions must be present to St. Paul's mind). If then there is sometimes an echo of the metaphor of sealing goods for transit, the sealing is primarily an attestation, a marking of the persons with the Owner's Name. Whether there existed already in the baptismal rites of the apostolic age some sort of anointing on the forehead, is a question which cannot be answered from the NT evidence, since the writers nowhere describe the rite which was used. The words under discussion describe a theological fact, and we are not told in detail how it was ritually symbolized. (*V.* also INHERIT, NT (*c*).)

A. G. HEBERT

SEASON *v.* TIME

SECRET

Both noun and adjective occur in the ordinary sense. A secret is something which has been confided in a man and which he ought not to disclose (Prov. 20.19, 25.9), or it may be anything whatsoever that is concealed from public observation (e.g. Mark 4.22). By a natural extension of usage the Bible speaks also of the secrets of wisdom (Job 11.6). Generally, however, the thought is of the secrets which are concealed behind the closed doors of the council chamber, either of men (Gen. 49.6) or, more often, of God. The idea of a 'privy council' in which the Lord holds secret converse with the 'sons of God' is dramatically represented in the prologue of Job, and it is echoed elsewhere in the Bible (e.g. Isa. 40.13, Jer. 23.18, Rom. 11.34). It is above all the privilege of the prophet to be admitted to the secret of God (Amos 3.7).

The great secret is the purpose of God concerning the future. God reveals it only to those whom he chooses (Dan. 2.18ff.). The secret of the future, and its unravelling, is the main theme of the apocalyptic literature.

The thought of the secret council of God is sometimes widened to that of the intimate friendship and protection of God, which is the privilege of the faithful (Ps. 27.5, 91.1, etc.). To dwell 'in the secret place of the Most High' is to have a shelter from the storm and a refuge in time of trouble.

From God himself, on the other hand, nothing can be kept secret. He sees in secret (Matt. 6.4). He is the God 'to whom all hearts be open, and from whom no secrets are hid' (Ps. 139, Rom. 2.16, I Cor. 4.5). (*V.* also HIDE, MYSTERY, REVEAL.)

G. S. HENDRY

SEE

Cf. article on EYE, esp. the last par. with which the foll. passages should now be considered: Exod. 14.31, Ps. 98.3, 107.24, Isa. 9.2, 52.10, Mark 2.12, Luke 19.37.

Attention is claimed by a group of passages which may be labelled *responsible* seeing, viz. Isa. 6.9 (quoted several times in NT, e.g. Mark 4.12, Acts 28.26), Matt. 5.16, Luke 7.22, 11.33, 23.47, John 9.39, 20.5, Acts 4.20. Man is responsible for making himself aware of what God is doing for his salvation. Good deeds without confession of faith in Christ may be a fulfilment of his command and as such tantamount to 'seeing' him (Matt. 25.37ff.). By contrast, cautious orthodoxy confuses seeing a sign with discerning the work of God, and this demand for signs is repudiated by Christ (Mark 15.32, Matt. 12.38, Luke 23.8, John 4.48). In two places Luke (19.3f., 23.8) mentions a desire to 'see Jesus', in one case genuine and praiseworthy, in the other case due to base motives. This is much emphasized in the Johannine writings, where the word 'see' is made to mean (by the use of more than one Gk. term), not only physical sight, but also spiritual perception (John 14.19, 16.16ff.). This is the achievement of faith (John 20.29; cf. I Pet. 1.8 on discipleship without actual sight of Jesus, and Heb. 12.2 for thought of Christ as 'pioneer and perfecter of faith'). The mark of a disciple is this awareness that there is more in Jesus than is revealed to the eyes, or is to be found in ordinary men. The truly opened eye discerns in him the Son of God and the King of Israel (John 1.46); he is the one who takes away the world's sin (1.29); he is 'a man who told me all things that ever I did . . . the Messiah' (4.29). The request, 'We would see Jesus' (12.21), implies that the enquirers are on the brink of this revelation, and the possibility is open to all men, for the question is placed on the lips of Greeks, i.e. people without the advantage of the Jews in the matter of revelation. A more systematic statement of what seeing Jesus can mean is found in I John 1.1–3, 4.14f.

For the thought of present sight as imperfect and to be contrasted with the vision of God and enjoyment of the Kingdom of God which is the privilege of the redeemed, cf. Matt. 5.8, Mark 9.1, John 1.50f., I Cor. 2.9, 13.12, II Cor. 4.18, Heb. 11.1. On visionary seeing, cf. I Kings 22.19, Isa. 6.1, Jer. 1.11, Ezek. 1.1, Zech. 1.8 (also *v.* VISION). In the NT the appearances of the risen Christ would come in this category.

With regard to the vision of God, the Bible is in general very reticent, and some passages deny the possibility of any man seeing God, e.g. Exod. 33.20, Deut. 4.12, I Tim. 6.16, John 1.18. This is a conservation in the realm of serious theology of quite primitive notions which are common to many religions. On the other hand, the personalizing of the concept of God and the affirmation that he does make his will known to man forced the admission that a few privileged persons had been honoured with the vision of God, and we find this attributed to Jacob (Gen. 32.30), Moses (Exod. 33.11,23), Moses together with Aaron, Nadab and Abihu and seventy elders (Exod. 24.10f., where, however, note that the Septuagint reads 'they saw the place where the God of Israel was standing' instead of 'they saw the God of Israel'), Isaiah 6.1,5, Amos 9.1, the Psalmist (Ps. 63.2). The Christian revelation maintains that no vision of God has been vouchsafed to mankind except in Jesus Christ (John 1.18, 14.9); at least this is the intransigent claim made by the Johannine writer. On the whole, the Bible speaks more readily of men seeing God's glory than of seeing God himself (Exod. 16.7, Isa. 35.2, 40.5, Luke 9.32, John 11.40, Acts 7.55); *v.* GLORY.

E. C. BLACKMAN

SEER *v.* PROPHECY II

SERAPH *v.* CHERUB

SERPENT *v.* ADAM, ANTICHRIST

SERVANT

The ordinary Heb. word for *servant*, *'ebed*, which occurs nearly 800 times in the OT, properly means simply 'worker'. But in Biblical times servants were usually slaves, the property of their masters or lords. So *'ebed* sometimes means 'slave'. In ancient Israel, however, the condition of a slave was normally neither ignominious nor irksome—the servitude of a whole people, like that of the Hebrews in Egypt, 'the house of bondage' (literally, 'of servants') was, naturally, something very different—and a slave might hold positions of trust and responsibility in his master's household, as Eliezer did in Abraham's household (Gen. 15.2; cf. Chap. 24). He might even hold high offices of state, as Joseph did in Egypt. It is therefore seldom that *'ebed* is used in a derogatory sense, as in Eccles. 10.7, Jer. 2.14, Lam. 5.8. The subjects of a king are his *servants*, esp. those subjected by being defeated in war, cf. I Chron. 21.3, II Sam. 8.6f. But officers of state are also the king's *servants*, just as in English they are still the king's 'ministers' (e.g. I Kings 20.23). As a mark of deference or courtesy to the person addressed, a speaker often refers to himself as 'thy servant' (e.g. Jacob speaking to Esau, Gen. 33.5). (*V.* also BONDAGE.)

The worshippers of a god are called his *servants*—the worshippers of Baal and the worshippers of Jehovah (the Lord) alike, though where the Heb. text speaks of 'the servants of Baal', the EVV render this, 'the worshippers of Baal', II Kings 10.19–23. But the singular form of the phrase, 'the servant of the Lord' is a title of distinction and honour, given to individuals who have shown special devotion or rendered distinguished service to Jehovah—Abraham (Gen. 26.24), Moses (Exod. 14.31), and David (II Sam. 3.18) are the most notable 'servants of the Lord' in this sense. In some of the later books of the OT this title becomes 'the servant of *God*' (e.g. I Chron. 6.49), without difference of meaning, though it happens that all the passages refer to Moses (cf. also Rev. 15.3). It is in this special sense that 'Israel' or 'Jacob' (meaning the people, not the patriarch) is called, by God himself, 'my servant' in some passages in Isaiah (e.g. 41.8f.), Jeremiah (e.g. 30.10) and Ezekiel (e.g. 28.35); Israel is 'my servant' because it is the chosen people of God. In the latter part of the Book of Isaiah there are four passages (42.1–4, 49.1–6, 50.4–9, 52.13–53.12), which are concerned with 'the servant of the Lord', and which are easily distinguishable from the context in which they stand. In these 'Servant-poems' (of which the last and longest is also the greatest and most notable) the Servant is one who fulfils his divine mission, which is not to Israel only but to the world, through suffering and death borne for the sins of others, and then is raised from death and exalted by God so that those who had rejected him are constrained to recognize that he had suffered for their sins and their salvation. The identity of the Servant is a much discussed question (cf. Acts 8.38), and scholars still differ widely in their opinions. In spite of the fact that the way in which he is described suggests that he is, as the Ethiopian eunuch supposed, either the prophet himself or some other man, the opinion most widely held is that he is a personification of Israel, though of an ideal rather than of the actual Israel. But whatever the prophet may have intended, the Christian Church has from the beginning found in these passages an impressive prophetic foreshadowing of Jesus Christ, and many NT scholars hold that our Lord himself was deeply influenced by them in his thought about his own mission and person (*v.* SUFFERING).

The nearest Gk. equivalent for Heb. *'ebed* was *doulos*, but this meant 'a slave', and even, strictly, one born a slave. So in ordinary Gk. it could hardly be used of a servant who was not a slave. Nevertheless, *doulos* is freely used in the old Gk. version of the OT as a translation of *'ebed*. But just as often another Gk. word, *pais*, which properly means 'a child' (whether in age or by parentage), but was often used of a servant (cf. French *garçon*), takes its place. (In the phrase, 'the servant of the Lord', the Gk. translators usually avoid *doulos*; in the Servant-poems in Isaiah they use *pais*, with obvious appropriateness.) In the NT *doulos* is much more frequent than *pais*, which does not occur at all outside the Gospels and Acts. In Matt. 12.18, the first of the Servant-poems in Isaiah is quoted as a prophecy fulfilled in Jesus—'Behold, my servant (*pais*) whom I have chosen'. It is almost certainly in this sense that Jesus is called the *pais* of God in Acts 3.13,26, 4.27,30, where the AV, wrongly, rendered the word by 'son' and 'child' (cf. the use of the same word of David in 4.25, where it is correctly rendered 'servant'). Nowhere is Jesus called the *doulos* of God, although in Phil. 2.7 it is said that he took upon himself 'the form of a *doulos*'. But Christians are frequently called the *servants* (*douloi*) of Christ, and, less frequently, of God. Paul, especially, often uses the word in this way, both of himself and of others; the primary significance is that Christians, having been 'bought with a price' (I Cor. 6.20, 7.23), belong to their masters. At the same time Paul insists that Christ sets men free from every other kind of bondage, so that they are no longer 'slaves', but sons of God (Gal. 4.7). But the precise meaning of the noun *doulos* and the corresponding verb varies according to the context; thus in one context Paul says that Christians must not become slaves of men (I Cor. 7.23), in another he bids those who are slaves (in the literal sense) to be obedient in all things to their earthly masters (Col. 3.22), and in yet another he enjoins all Christians to serve (be slaves to) one another in love (Gal. 5.13). And in more than one passage he insists that 'in Christ' there is no distinction between slaves and free men (Gal. 3.28, I Cor. 12.13, Col. 3.11, Eph. 6.8; cf. also I Cor. 7.21ff.).

Of the other Gk. words for *servant* used in the NT little need be said. *Oiketēs*, used 4 times only, means properly 'a domestic servant', who was normally a slave (Luke 16.13, Acts 10.7, Rom. 14.4, I Pet. 2.18). A *misthios* (only Luke 15.17) or *misthōtēs* (Mark 1.20, John 10.12f.) is 'a hired servant', and therefore a free man. *Hupēretēs* usually means a subordinate official or 'attendant' (so often in the Gospels), but is used in Acts 13.5 of John Mark as the 'minister' of Paul and Barnabas; and in Acts 26.16 of Paul; and in I Cor. 4.1

of Paul and his fellow Apostles, as 'ministers' of Christ. *Therapōn* (only Heb. 3.5) and *diakonos* both mean simply one who renders service; in the AV the latter is usually rendered by 'minister', but sometimes by *servant* (e.g. Mark 9.35), and 5 times, where it means an official of the Christian Church, by its English form, 'deacon' (e.g. Phil. 1.1)—the precise nature of the office cannot be determined. (*V.* also MINISTER, SUFFERING, BONDAGE.)

J. Y. CAMPBELL

SERVICE

The Gk. word *leitóurgein* (whence our 'liturgy') in class. lit. means service rendered to the State. In the LXX it denoted the s. of priests and Levites in Tabernacle and Temple (Num. 8.22,25, 18.4, etc.). This usage is found in NT (Luke 1.23, Heb. 9.21: RV 'ministry'). It is used also of the worship of the Church (Acts 13.2) and of works of charity (II Cor. 9.12, 'the deaconing of this liturgy', Phil. 2.17,30). From the 5th cent. AD onwards it came primarily to denote the central rite of the Christian Church, the Eucharist (*v.* J. H. Srawley, *Early History of the Liturgy*, p. ix). In Rom. 13.6 Paul speaks of the rulers in the State as God's *leitourgoi* (ministrants). Thus, God's s. is not to be narrowly interpreted: it is rendered not only in prayer but in life, in deed as well as in rite: the faithful s. of God in public life is 'liturgy' as truly as is the 'divine service' in church. The conception of s. implied in such phrases as 'cabinet *minister*', 'civil *servant*' is one of the finest flowers of a Christian civilization. In Rom. 15.16 Paul speaks of himself as the sacrificing priest (*leitourgon*) of the Gospel of God offering up the oblation of the Gentile Church; this vs. brings out clearly the priestly aspect of Christian 'liturgy' which can never be far distant from the use of the word in view of its LXX associations. (*V.* also MINISTER, SERVANT, WORSHIP.)

A. R.

SHAME

1. 'Shame' in biblical language is frequently *objective*='ignominy', 'disgrace', e.g. Ps. 35.26, 'Let them be ashamed and confounded together that rejoice at mine hurt: let them be clothed with shame and dishonour that magnify themselves against me', 69.19: 'Thou knowest my reproach, and my shame, and my dishonour.' This is an extremely common OT usage, esp. (but not exclusively) in the Psalms and Prophets. The frequent coupling of 'shame' with such words as 'dishonour', 'confusion', 'mockery', 'defeat', 'destruction', etc., makes the objective meaning quite clear. Very commonly, as in the first quotation sup., the 'shame' is regarded as a judgment sent by God. 'Let them be ashamed' is a prayer constantly on Hebrew lips, a prayer primarily for the outward ruin of the foe, and only secondarily for the *subjective feeling* of shame which it will rouse in him.

This use is carried over in the NT, but, apart from quotations, is not common there; cf., however, Phil. 3.19, of those unnatural beings who glory when they are disgraced, and Heb. 12.2, of Jesus who despised the ignominy of the Cross (*q.v.*). Further, in grand contrast with the judgment of the OT, Christian hope never puts a man to shame by failing or deceiving him (Rom. 5.5; cf. 9.33, 10.11—both quotations from Isa. 28.16).

2. *Subjectively,* (i) a sense of shame may act in a good sense as a deterrent from wrongdoing. Such is the 'shamefastness' of I Tim. 2.9. On the other hand, some shrink back from right conduct for fear of what may be said or thought about them, such are those who are 'ashamed of the Son of man' (Mark 8.38= Luke 9.26). Very different was St. Paul: 'I am not ashamed of the gospel of Christ' (Rom. 1.16), and he pays similar tribute to Onesiphorus who 'was not ashamed of my chain' (II Tim. 1.16). God himself is not ashamed to call men brethren and to be called their God (Heb. 2.11, 11.16). (ii) More commonly, however, a sense of shame *follows* shameful action. (*a*) Occasionally, this is shame for a wrong *suffered*, as those men were ashamed who had been misused by Hanun the Ammonite (II Sam. 10.5). But (*b*) usually it is shame for a wrong *done*, and where this is a first step towards contrition and repentance, it is frequently praised (and its absence blamed) in Scripture. Examples in which there is no necessary suggestion of moral consequence are II Chron. 32.21 (of Sennacherib) and Luke 14.9 (the discomfited guest). Repentance (or failure to repent) is involved in such passages as Ezra 9.6, Jer. 6.15, 8.12, Zeph. 2.1, 3.5, Rom. 6.21 (cf. II Cor. 4.2, 'the hidden things of shame'). In I Cor. 6.5, 'I say this to move you to shame', the Gk. word implies that the readers will be 'turned in upon themselves'; so also I Cor. 15.34, II Thess. 3.14, Tit. 2.8.

3. By a special Heb. usage, *bosheth* (shameful thing) not infrequently stands for Baal (lord, as a Canaanite title of God, *q.v.*), e.g. Jer. 11.13, 'Ye set up altars to the shameful thing, even altars to burn incense unto Baal'; cf. 3.24, Hos. 9.10. Similarly, 'Baal' as an element in compound proper names was changed to 'bosheth', e.g. Esh-baal (I Chron. 8.33, 9.39) becomes Ish-bosheth (II Sam. 2.8), and Merib-baal (I Chron. 8.34) becomes Mephibosheth (II Sam. 4.4).

J. P. THORNTON-DUESBERY

SHARE *v.* FELLOWSHIP

(SHEKINAH) *v.* PRESENCE

(SHEOL) *v.* HELL

SHEPHERD *v.* MINISTER

SHEW

Common in the obvious meanings, 'make visible', 'present', 'explain', rendering a variety of Heb. and Gk. verbs, including (in Heb.) the causative forms of the verbs, 'know', 'see', 'hear'. Worthy of special notice are the phrase 'shew mercy' (Exod. 20.6, of God; II Sam. 9.1, of man), and the usage for God declaring his will, salvation, etc. (Ps. 25.4, Mic. 6.8, etc.; and esp. John 14.8, 'shew us the Father'). We find the sense of revelation of the future in Isa. 48.5, John 16.13 and Rev. *passim.*

E. C. B.

SHEWBREAD *v.* BREAD, SACRIFICE I(*g*)

SHIELD *v.* ARMOUR

SIGN *v.* MIRACLE

SIMILITUDE, LIKENESS

By its derivation from Lat. *similis* (like), 'similitude' is an exact synonym of 'likeness'. It occurs 9 times in the OT (AV); the RV alters it 6 times, 4 times to 'form', Num. 12.8, Deut. 4.12,15,16, once to 'likeness', Ps. 106.20, and once to 'fashion', Ps. 144.12. The change to 'likeness' might equally well have been made in II Chron. 4.3, and in Dan. 10.16 'one like the similitude of the sons of men' means simply 'one who was like a man'. In Hos. 12.10 'similitudes' means 'parables' (whether spoken or acted), but the passage is difficult, and the Heb. text may be corrupt. In each of the 3 NT passages in which the word occurs in the AV, Rom. 5.14, Heb. 7.15, Jas. 3.9, the RV changes it to 'likeness'.

'Likeness' occurs in the OT (AV) 29 times, 15 of which are in Ezekiel. Twice the RV changes this, rather needlessly, to 'form', Deut. 4.23,25, and in Ezek. 23.15 it substitutes 'likeness' for AV 'manner'. In Ps. 17.15 the parallelism between the two parts of the verse shows that 'likeness' means practically the same thing as 'face'; it is God himself that the Psalmist hopes to see, not any mere likeness of God; cf. Num. 12.8. In Gen. 1.26, 5.1,3 'likeness' is clearly a synonym of 'image' (*q.v.*).

In the NT the AV has 'likeness' 4 times and 'similitude' 3; the RV has 'likeness' in all 7 places. The only passage that causes any difficulty is Rom. 8.3, where Paul says that God sent his own Son 'in the likeness of sinful flesh'. This does not mean that Christ only appeared to come 'in the flesh', but that in his ease the flesh in which he came was not 'sinful flesh'. By 'sinful flesh' Paul means human nature as we know it in ourselves and other men, fallen human nature. Christ took upon himself human nature as God meant it to be, though so far as his purely physical nature was concerned he was like other men; cf. Phil. 2.7, 'was made in the likeness of men', where also it is the reality, not the unreality, of the humanity of the incarnate Christ that is expressed by the phrase. But in Acts 14.11 'likeness' means outward appearance only. In Rom. 5.14 men from Adam to Moses are said to have 'sinned', but not, like Adam, to have 'transgressed', because they did not disobey any commandment of God of which they were aware; here the likeness or similitude (which did not exist) is a real, not merely an apparent, likeness. (*V.* also PARABLE.)

J. Y. CAMPBELL

SIMPLE, SIMPLICITY

The Heb. word *pethi* (simple) is used in both a good sense (Ps. 116.6, God guards them; Ps. 19.7), and a bad sense, i.e. silly, the opposite of prudent (Prov. 8.5, etc.). It is not, however, so bad as *nabal,* which comes near to meaning impious, immoral (Ps. 14.1), or *kesil* (Prov. 10.23). The good sense of *pethi* is paralleled by the Gk. word *akakoi,* trans. 'simple' in Rom. 16.18. In the next verse 'simple' stands for another word, *akeraioi* (innocent), which is also trans. 'harmless', Matt. 10.16, Phil. 2.15. This meaning is equivalent to that of the Heb. trans., 'in their simplicity', II Sam. 15.11.

One other Gk. word is worth notice here, viz. *haplotes,* lit. 'singleness' (and so rendered, Eph. 6.5, Col. 3.22, in the phrase 'singleness of heart'). We have it as 'simplicity', Rom. 12.8, II Cor. 11.3. In II Cor. 8.2, 9.11,13, it appears as 'liberality'. The essential meaning is absence of ulterior motives, artlessness, transparent honesty. The opposite is the adj. *diplous* (the noun is not found), 'double', which can have a moral sense of treacherous, doubleminded. Cf. Jas. 1.8, 4.8, which, however, translates another Gk. adj., *dipsychos,* lit. 'double-souled'. A more instructive parallel is the use of 'hypocrisy' in the Gospels (*q.v.*).

E. C. BLACKMAN

SIN, SINNER, ERR, FAULT, GUILT, INIQUITY, OFFENCE, MALEFACTOR, MISCHIEF, PERVERSE, TRANSGRESS, TRESPASS, WICKED, WRONG

OT: Despite the variety of these words which denote something central in the religious consciousness, they are inadequate to express the corresponding Heb. terms. Nor has the English

Bible any consistent way of translating one Heb. word or group of words by one English word. The Heb. usages may roughly be classed according to derivation thus: (1) Deviation from the right way: *h t'*, to miss a goal or way; e.g. among the Benjamite warriors there were men 'who could sling stones at an hair-breadth, and not *miss*' (Judg. 20.16). Hence sin is failing to do something in relation to man or God. The same idea underlies *'awon* (iniquity), *shagah* (err), and *'wl* (wicked). A group of seven words is represented by 'perverse', meaning any deviation, distortion, crookedness of what is properly upright. In the Wisdom literature, perversity becomes a consciously arrogant attitude which inevitably leads to strife and disharmony. Its opposite is 'the fear of the Lord', i.e. the true religious life. (2) Words denoting the changed status of the agent: *rasha'*, used of the guilty as opposed to the innocent; and *'asham* (guilt, guilt-offering). Lev. 4.1–6.7 sets out the consequences for anyone who sins unwittingly in any of God's commanded things. Neither the sin-offering (the root is *h t'*) nor the guilt-offering is known before the exile, and they are not clearly distinguished; though the guilt-offering seems to apply to offences against God or man that could be estimated and so recovered by compensation (e.g. a ram as sacrifice, restitution, and one-fifth the value as penalty). The sin here in question is not deliberate disobedience of moral laws but ritual and ceremonial mistakes, and defilements by inadvertence and ignorance. It follows from Hebrew psychology that a man is responsible for all his actions, for every action has its effect on the soul of the person who acts. This state of 'answerableness' for something done is expressed by *'asham*; and unless some atonement is made it poisons the soul from within. Unless it is laid down that a man bears his own sin, 'guilt' spreads and infects the group to which he belongs. (3) Rebellion against a superior or unfaithfulness to an agreement (*pasha'*—inadequately translated 'trespass', 'transgress'). 'Israel rebelled against the House of David' (I Kings 12.19) gives the secular sense, and 'Thy first father sinned, and thy interpreters have rebelled against me' (Isa. 43.27) the religious sense. Cf. Isa. 1.2, 'sons have I brought up and reared, and they have rebelled against me'. The force of this word is shown by Job 34.37: 'he addeth rebellion (*pesha'*) unto his sin (*hatta'th*)'. Together with associated terms it describes sin as a personal, voluntary act; rebellion against a superior, not withdrawal from co-operation with an equal. (4) A wide group of words characterizing sin as badness, violence, destructiveness, trouble, worthlessness, vanity, folly, and senselessness.

No difference of any importance is discoverable in the OT use of the three commonest roots, *h t'*, *'awon, pesha'*, i.e. behind the diversity of derivation there is a fundamental, unified conception of sin characterized in part as failure, in part as irregularity or crookedness, in part as infringement of the psychic totality of the soul. In the old Israelite view of life, good actions are normal and must produce good results. Sinful actions are abnormal, preying on the positive forces of life. The righteous soul is upright; the sinful soul is crooked. Sin means dissolution of the soul, and the soul entirely sinful is no longer reckoned a human soul.

All life is upheld by covenant (*q.v.*); and the essence of sin is breach of covenant, e.g. injuring one's brother: 'forgive . . . the transgression of thy brethren, and their sin, for that they did unto thee evil' (Gen. 50.17; note how widely this extends in Amos 1.6,9,11). Every violation of marriage is sin, because taking another man's wife violates a covenant (e.g. Gen. 39.9, 'how then can I do this great wickedness, and sin against God?'). So also is incest as violating one's own covenant (Lev. 20); the deed at Sodom as violating hospitality towards strangers (Gen. 19); and not at once giving a hired labourer the wages due to him by covenant (Deut. 24.15). Every deed which injures the community is sin: thus Hezekiah offended by failing in his vassal duties to Sennacherib (II Kings 18.14). In Gen. 43.9 (RV marg.). Judah, who has taken responsibility for Benjamin, says to Israel: 'if I bring him not unto thee . . . then I shall have sinned against thee for ever'. Thus one man may be a sinner in relation to another, by virtue of the obligation between them; and *rasha'* often means the man who is wrong in a particular case. In Exod. 23.1 assistance to the wicked is forbidden (i.e. to the guilty party in a lawsuit), for that is equivalent to 'justifying' him (Exod. 23.7, Deut. 25.1, Prov. 17.15, Isa. 5.23). If the wicked man does not fulfil the duties of fellowship, the righteous man who maintains them does not get his due from the community. The violator of the covenant becomes the debtor of the righteous who can claim recompense and vengeance.

But sin also means that the soul itself is diseased, to a degree determined by the consideration: did the action arise in the centre of the will, or did it merely lie on the circumference? A man may sin unknowingly (Balaam sinned *because* he did not know that God's angel stood before him, Num. 22.34), and none can avoid such actions (*shagag*, to err); but the infringement of rights can be healed by restitution and the mental hurt that threatens the sinner by sacrifice. But more deeply seated sin cannot be so removed: it spreads like a poison, issues in violence and mischief (Ps. 55.9–11), is allied with the curse (Deut. 28.15ff.) as righteousness is allied with the blessing, and finally must come out and destroy the doer. 'The wicked are like the troubled sea; for it cannot rest, and its waters cast up mire and dirt. There is no peace . . . to the wicked' (Isa. 57.20f.). The frequent descriptions of sinners reflect this point of view; though in the Psalms 'sinners' represent a definite religious type which lacks the fundamental devotion of the righteous to the Law. The term is applied as a result not of individual sinful acts but of an attitude comprising a man's life as a whole.

The sinner counteracts the positive forces which uphold the community and have their root in God. All sin, not only cultic transgression and direct apostasy, is violation of God because he is the soul of every Israelite covenant (II Sam. 12.13). As a result of the work of the eighth-century prophets, sin centred more and more on disobedience and rebellion against God, and gave strength to belief in God's imminent intervention in judgment upon sinners. 'But I will not be always wroth: for the spirit should fail before me, and the souls which I have made' (Isa. 57.16). God is merciful (Mic. 7.18ff.) and keeps his covenant with the fathers; and the soul dominated by consciousness of sin trusts in him and is maintained in life. Confession of sin (Ps. 32.5, 38.18), not only in the cult but face to face with God (Ps. 51), wins forgiveness and so the soul is restored to wholeness; 'thou hast in love to my soul delivered it from the pit of corruption; for thou hast cast all my sins behind thy back' (Isa. 38.17).

NT: There are few direct references to sin in the Synoptic Gospels, but the writers display Christ's work in relation to it (as does John, e.g. 1.29): so in the birth story (Matt. 1.21). The Baptist heralds the forgiveness of sins (Mark 1.4f.), and Jesus' proclamation of the Kingdom involves repentance (Mark 1.15). The forgiveness and healing of the paralytic has a prominent position (Mark 2.5ff.—as in the OT the two are connected, though indirectly: cf. Luke 13.2, John 5.14, 9.2f.). Parables explain the work of Jesus as the rescue of sinners, according to God's will (Luke 15.7,10). Matt. 26.28 directly connects the death of Jesus, and Luke 24.47 the proclamation of the gospel, with remission of sins. Repentance and remission of sins were a feature of the earliest preaching to Jews and Gentiles (Acts 2.38, 3.19, 5.31, 10.43, 13.38) and an element in Paul's conversion (Acts 22.16).

Jesus neither speculated about sin nor explained what he understood by it. He simply reckoned with its reality. The Gospel teaching may best be studied in the word sinner (*hamartolos*). (*a*) In the OT sense of 'godless', i.e. one living in conscious contradiction of the law: so, 'publicans and sinners', where 'sinners' are murderers, robbers, etc., and members of dishonourable professions, such as harlots (Luke 7.37). They are therefore distinguished from both Pharisees and ordinary people. (*b*) The '*am ha-'arets* (people of the land) who are sinners, not because they transgress the law, but because they do not hold the Pharisaic interpretation of it. Almost everybody fell into this class, and so 'sinners' were the daily company of Jesus (Mark 2.15ff., Matt. 11.19, Luke 15.1f.). (*c*) The heathen (Mark 14.41, Luke 24.7, viz. Roman soldiers; Luke 6.32ff., where Matt. has 'Gentiles'). (*d*) Those who are separated, consciously or not, from God (Luke 5.8, 18.13, here only as a self-designation; Mark 8.38; cf. Matt. 17.17, where we see the upright one in the hands of faithless and distorted men). Jesus neither rejected nor suppressed the current distinction of righteous and sinner. Sinners did not expect to be drawn to him (Luke 19.7), but precisely because they needed him, Jesus drew them (Mark 2.15ff.). He did not call men to self-contempt and condemnation, but to stand before the whole reality of God. There is no confession of particular sins, though Jesus was clearly aware of them (Mark 7.21ff.) and knew that there were 'offences' (*skandalon*: a cause of stumbling) and treated them with the utmost seriousness (Mark 9.42ff.). He himself was exposed to them (Matt. 16.23), and knew that the disciples would also be (Mark 4.17, Matt. 13.41). It may be that Jesus spoke of specific sins (for which the usual word is *paraptoma*, Mark 11.25) only to the community of disciples (Matt. 18.15,21, Luke 11.4, with the OT idea of claim prominent). He himself was an 'offence' to disciples (Mark 14.27ff.), as he certainly was to the righteous (Mark 6.3, Matt. 11.6, 15.12) to whom he spoke of the *state* of sin, because he regarded them as needing God. He did not count their righteousness as sin, but condemned it for its self-centred confidence, arrogance, and lack of compassion (Matt. 7.23, 23.28: in this context Matt. 12.31 must find its meaning). Jesus overthrew the idea that sinners are special men or groups: all are involved. John 8.46 rightly interprets the synoptic evidence that Jesus was not conscious of sin in himself; yet he identified himself with sinners in his Baptism and his Death (Luke 22.37, 23.32), and would rather accept the name of 'sinner' (John 9.16,24,31f., 18.30) than forgo his divine commission.

The fundamental passage for Paul's view is Rom. 3.23: 'all have sinned (*hamartano*: missed the mark), and fall short of the glory of God', i.e. sin is the objective condition in which men lack the image of God (cf. I Cor. 11.7) whether or not they know it or are responsible for it. This condition is demonstrably universal (Rom. 3.9–18); and sin is regarded almost as a personified power external to man which reigns over him (Rom. 5.21, 6.12) and enslaves him (Rom. 6.17,20, 7.14,23) so that he experiences conflict between his own inclinations and the power by which he is possessed (Rom. 7.17,20). There are in fact two laws in conflict: the law of life and the law of sin and death (Rom. 7.25, 8.2; the conflict is also described as sin-grace, Rom. 5.20, righteousness-iniquity (*anomia*), II Cor. 6.14). Death (*q.v.*) is a comprehensive term for the physical and spiritual results of sin's dominion (Rom. 6.23, 7.5, I Cor. 15.56, sin goads men on to death, Eph. 2.1). This state of affairs is accounted for in two ways: (*a*) sin and death entered the world by Adam's fall (Rom. 5.12,19)—regarded not purely as a 'historical' fact, but as expressing a mystical unity of mankind in Adam (cf. I Cor. 15.22, 'As in Adam all die, so in Christ shall all be made alive') (*v*. ADAM). (*b*) Men have turned away from whatever of God is manifested to worship idols and so have come under demonic principalities and powers. Hence they perceive God only as wrath against all ungodliness and wickedness (Rom. 1.18ff., 2.8). The primary seat of sin is the flesh which, though morally neutral, is weak and easily passes under the domination of sin (*v*. FLESH).

It is the function of the law to show up sin for what it is by laying down commandments (Rom. 7.13), so that 'through the law cometh the knowledge of sin' (Rom. 3.20). To recognize that the law is holy, just, and good is to recognize that men are sinful by the fact of their actual trespasses (*paraptoma*, Rom. 5.20, Gal. 6.1) and transgressions (*parabasis*, Rom. 2.23, 4.15, Gal. 3.19). From Adam to Moses sin was in the world and there were transgressions, but men were not guilty before the law (Rom. 5.13f.). Man's situation is such that the law gives sin occasion for fresh attacks (Rom. 7.7–11; cf. the mystery of lawlessness in II Thess. 2.3,7f.). This close association of sin and transgression or trespass makes it possible for 'sin' also to be used occasionally of specific acts of wrongdoing.

Paul expresses the primitive proclamation of the Church in 'Christ died for our sins' (I Cor. 15.3; cf. Rom. 4.25, Gal. 1.4, II Cor. 5.19, Rom. 5.8, 'while we were yet sinners Christ died for us'—Paul always includes himself in the word 'sinners'; unlike Jesus, he cannot look away from himself; cf. I Tim. 1.15). Christ entered the sphere which sin had claimed as its own and won the verdict there, not in theory, but in fact (Eph. 2.1; cf. I Cor. 15.17). The corporate unity of men with Christ in redemption (Rom. 5.15ff.) is expressed in II Cor. 5.21 by a paradoxical interchange between Christ and sinners. Rom. 6 sets out the complete liberation of men from domination by sin when in baptism they share in Christ's dying and rising again. The Christian is free to present himself to God or to sin. Paul repudiates the view that men living in the spiritual state of grace need not be concerned about transgressions, for if a man sins against the brethren he sins against Christ (I Cor. 8.12). The practical ethical advice of his epistles and the lists of virtues and vices (Rom. 1.29f., 13.13, I Cor. 5.10f., 6.9f., II Cor. 12.20f., Gal. 5.19ff., Eph. 4.31, 5.3ff., Col. 3.5,8; cf. I Tim. 1.9f., II Tim. 3.2ff., I Pet. 4.3, Rev. 21.8, 22.15) spring directly out of the nature of Christian love (I Cor. 13.4ff.).

The Epistle to the Hebrews restates the primitive proclamation in terms of the OT priestly ritual which is only a shadow of the perfect sacrifice that can remove sins once for all. This Christ accomplished by the sacrifice of himself, having been identified with men in all respects except sin (1.3, 2.17, 4.15, 5.1ff., 7.26ff., 9.26ff., 10.2ff.). On the surface 'sins' here mean 'acts of wrongdoing'; but the profounder OT sense underlies the whole treatment.

In the Fourth Gospel sin is a quality of life expressing itself in thought, word and deed (John 8.21,24,34) and its nearest definition is lack of faith in Jesus (John 16.8f.; cf. 15.22,24). In the First Epistle of John 'sins' are acts of wrongdoing. John deliberately adopted this definition (*anomia*—lawlessness, *adikia*—unrighteousness, I John 1.9, 3.4, 5.17) because he was combatting the belief that Christians in communion with God had been given a new nature so that nothing they did would be sin. This was akin to John's own position (I John 3.4ff.; cf. I Pet. 4.1); but he did not believe that Christians were so changed that the need for moral striving was removed (I John 1.5–2.2). This could mean that Christians may in fact commit sins but cannot be habitual sinners; but the apparent contradiction must probably be resolved by saying that in one place he was writing against complacency and in the other against laxity. A Christian may indeed sin and be forgiven (cf. Jas. 5.15f.), though there may be some sins (perhaps apostasy) which place men beyond fellowship with God (I John 5.16f.; cf. Heb. 10.26). To deny that Christians have sins is to deny the gospel (cf. I John 2.12, 4.10, Rev. 1.5) and to make Jesus, advocate and expiation for us and the whole world, of none account.

KENNETH GRAYSTON

SINCERE, SINCERITY

Very rare in OT. The adverb in Judg. 9.16 is better rendered 'uprightly' (RV). From the same Heb. we get the rendering 'in sincerity', Josh. 24.14 (both AV and RV). The Heb. *tamim* signifies integrity, perfection in the sense of nothing being lacking. 'Sincerity' is thus inadequate as a translation. The word moves in a realm of ideas which includes purity, innocence, simplicity, and is contrasted with duplicity, deceit, hypocrisy.

In the NT 'sincerity' is slightly more common. In Phil. 1.10, I Cor. 5.8, II Cor. 1.12, 2.17, the Gk. is *eilikrinēs* (or its abstract noun), which signifies 'pure'. The underlying Gk. of II Cor. 8.8 means 'genuineness'. Eph. 6.24 should be rendered 'in uncorruptness' (RV). (Also *v.* SIMPLE, DECEIT.)

E. C. B.

SIN-OFFERING *v.* SACRIFICE I(*e*)

SLEEP

(*i*) Bodily rest and refreshment (John 11.12, Jer. 31.25f., Ecclus. 31.1f.). Peaceful and secure sleep is the gift of Jehovah who never sleeps (Ps. 121.4; cf. I Kings 18.27) to the godly who trust in him (Pss. 4.8, 127.2; cf. Mark 4.38–40), to Israel through redemption (Ezek. 34.15f.,25). A special significance attaches to sleep in that dreams and visions which are given in sleep are a means of revelation (Gen. 15.12; 28.10ff., I Sam. 3.1ff., Jer. 23.32, Dan. 7.1ff., Joel 2.28, Matt. 1.20).

(*ii*) In a condemnatory sense, of sloth (Prov. 6.10, etc.), and esp. of unreadiness for the crisis of the last days and its sudden approach (Mark 13.36; cf. 14.37–41). The life of unredeemed humanity is a sleeping life, akin to death, in the darkness of night (cf. Eph. 5.14, possibly of baptism); those who by faith already belong to the Age to Come are awake and fully alive in the light of the Day, by which they ought not to be surprised (I Thess. 5.4–8), their close relation to which invests their actions in the world with urgency and importance (Rom. 13.11f.).

(*iii*) A synonym for death (John 11.11–13, Job 14.12, Jer. 51.39) not confined to the Bible. Incorrectly called a 'euphemism', since it is 'peace' or 'rest' which denotes the death of the righteous (Isa. 57.2, Wisd. 3.3), while 'sleep' denotes the absence of strength and vitality which is brought by death, the great enemy of the vigour of the soul (person). The dead 'lie down' in the dust (Job 21.26), in the grave (Ps. 88.5), which is also Sheol (Ezek. 32.19–32), the communal grave—hence the phrase 'he slept with his fathers'; and cf. Judg. 2.10. The sleep of death is not non-existence, but insubstantial existence; it is originally unrelated to the idea of resurrection and is not derived therefrom, but when the idea of resurrection arises it can be presented, with reference to the earlier conception, as an awakening to full life and activity (Dan. 12.2f.) In NT the conception is taken over—it is the usual term in Paul for the death of believers—but, as in NT eschatology generally, the determinant factor is not the Jewish imagery, but the relation to the Lord, whose presence and power make death temporary (Mark 5.39, John 11.4,11f.—which may have the secondary meaning 'if he is dead he shall be saved'), and whose resurrection is the pledge of the resurrection of his own (I Cor. 15.18–20; cf. Acts 7.59f.). Believers who sleep in death do so in, or through, Jesus (I Thess. 4.14); nothing is said about an intermediate state except that it is 'in Christ', and that death cannot bring the believer into any situation which means separation from him (I Thess. 4.13–18). At the Parousia they will be brought, together with those who are awake (i.e. the living), to be 'with' Christ in fullness of life (I Thess. 5.10, I Cor. 15.51). (*V.* also DEATH, PEACE, REST.)

C. F. EVANS

SLING *v.* ARMOUR

SMOKE *v.* SACRIFICE II(*e*)

SODOM AND GOMORRAH *v.* CITY

SON, SON OF GOD *v.* FAMILY

SON OF MAN

The Heb. phrase *ben adam*, literally, 'son of man', means simply 'member of the human race', 'human being'. In the OT it occurs infrequently, except in Ezekiel, and usually as a synonym for the ordinary word for 'man', *ish* or *enosh*, used in a parallel phrase in the same sentence, e.g. 'What is man, that thou art mindful of him? and the son of man, that thou visitest him?' (Ps. 8.4, quoted Heb. 2.6). In such passages it is English idiom which requires the use of the definite article, '*the* son of man'; it is not used in Heb., nor yet in the Gk. rendering. In Ezekiel the phrase is used very often by God in speaking to the prophet, e.g. 'Son of man, stand upon thy feet, and I will speak with thee', 2.1. This form of address seems to emphasize at once the littleness and insignificance of the prophet by contrast with the majesty of God, and the dignity which God gives him by choosing to speak with him and through him.

The corresponding Aramaic phrase, *bar ᵉnash*, occurs once in the OT, in the part of the Book of Daniel which is in Aramaic, not Heb.: 'I saw in the night visions, and, behold, there came with the clouds of heaven one like a son of man, and he came even to the Ancient of Days. . . . And there was given to him dominion, and glory, and a kingdom' (Dan. 7.13f.). Here the figure 'like a son of man' symbolizes the kingdom of the saints of the Most High which is to be established, just as the figures like four great beasts seen earlier in the vision symbolize four pagan kingdoms (cf. vs. 17). There is nothing to suggest that the man-like figure had any real existence, outside the vision, any more than had the beast-like figures. In late Aramaic the same phrase, in the form *bar-nash*, is the ordinary expression for 'man', and it is often used (as 'a man' is in English) as the equivalent of an indefinite pronoun, 'one', 'someone'. This use seems to have been well established in the second century AD, and there is no good reason to doubt that it already existed in the time of Jesus. It is commonly supposed that the Aramaic for 'the [particular] man' would be *bar-nasha*, but this form is seldom found in the scanty Aramaic writings which are extant, and when it does occur it does not seem to differ in meaning from *bar-nash*.

In the NT the Gk. phrase, 'the son of [the] man', which must have sounded even stranger in Gk. than it does in English, occurs 81 times in the Gospels, always as a self-designation of Jesus, and only once elsewhere, Acts 7.56. (In Rev. 1.13, 14.14, and in the OT quotation in Heb. 2.6, neither noun has the definite article and the correct rendering is 'a son of man'.) Although in the Gospels the phrase is never used by anyone except Jesus himself, it is clear that the evangelists sometimes omitted it in reporting his words, substituting for it the pronoun 'I' or 'me', and sometimes inserted it in place of the pronoun (cf. Mark 8.31 and Matt. 16.21, Mark 9.1 and Matt. 16.28). Neither Jesus himself, nor the evangelists, ever explain the meaning of the phrase or the reason for his use of it, and none of his hearers ever asks for an explanation—even the question of the 'crowd' in John 12.34 seems to refer to the application of the term rather than to its meaning. This is also the only occasion on which Jesus' use of the phrase is reported to have caused any remark whatever. These facts present a problem for which no altogether satisfactory explanation has yet been found.

Until recent times the usual explanation was that, just as the title 'the Son of God' expressed the divinity of our Lord, so 'the Son of Man' expressed his humanity; he, uniquely, was at once God and Man. Recently, however, the prevailing view among NT scholars has been that 'the Son of Man' was a messianic title in use among the Jews in Jesus' time. The only evidence for this is found in a strange apocalyptic book, the *Book of Enoch*, which is now extant as a whole only in an Ethiopic version; here several different Ethiopic phrases, which are reasonably regarded as variant renderings of *bar-nasha* in the supposed Aramaic original, occur sixteen times in all. The history of this book is exceedingly obscure. The Ethiopic version was certainly made, by Christians and for Christians, long after the time of Jesus. It is therefore possible that the references to the Son of Man are Christian additions to the original text. Further, the book is not a unitary work, but a compilation of writings of many different dates; there is no certainty whatever that the part in which these references occur existed at all in the time of Jesus. So it is exceedingly doubtful whether 'the Son of Man' was, in fact, a messianic title current in Jesus' day. It is still more doubtful whether, if it was, it was a title which Jesus would have wished to claim for himself.

But if the phrase was a messianic title used by Jews in Jesus' time, then probably it was derived from the passage in Daniel (7.13f.) referred to above. It is therefore possible that Jesus himself took the title directly from Daniel, and that by using it of himself was claiming to be that Son of Man to whom had been given, or would be given, the everlasting kingdom foretold in the prophet's vision. But in Daniel the 'one like a son of man' represents, in the symbolism of the vision, 'the people of the saints of the Most High' (cf. Dan. 7.18,22,25,27). So it is an attractive suggestion that by 'the Son of Man' Jesus meant, to begin with, not himself alone, but the holy community which would have come into being if the Jewish people had responded to his preaching. They did not respond, and so at the end of his ministry Jesus alone was, or at least represented, 'the Son of Man' in this sense. The end which he had hoped to achieve by his ministry was achieved, but in a larger sense, only after, and through, his death, in the community of those who believed in him. But it is still a serious objection to this explanation, in either form, that if Jesus himself was the first to use the phrase from Daniel in this way, he would not have been understood by his hearers unless he explained just what he meant (all the more since '*the* Son of Man' is not mentioned in Daniel, but only one 'like a son of man'), and there is no record that he ever did explain what he meant, nor that anyone felt that an explanation was needed.

This difficulty is best met if Jesus' use of the phrase is understood in the light of the frequent use of it in Ezekiel, where the prophet is addressed by God as 'Son of Man'. There, too, the meaning of the term is not explained, but no explanation seems to be needed—it suggests at once the littleness of the prophet as a man, and the greatness to which God calls him in his service; through him, man though he is, God speaks to men, and carries out his high purposes. In this sense 'Son of Man' is not properly a title at all. But, as has been pointed out above, it is doubtful, for purely linguistic reasons, whether *bar-nasha* could have been used as a title meaning '*the* Son of Man'; to have used it in that way would almost certainly have led to misunderstanding, and it has been suggested that, e.g., in Mark 2.9, what Jesus really meant was, 'that ye may know that *man* hath power on earth to forgive sins'. No misunderstanding would have arisen, however, if in referring to himself Jesus said 'this son of man', or the like. The difficulty would still remain of explaining how such a phrase came to be mistranslated into Greek, and then misunderstood as a title. But, on the other hand, this suggestion does account for the strange fact that (except for Acts 7.56) Jesus is the only one who ever uses the phrase—he was the only one who could speak of himself as 'this son of man'. In any case, it seems probable that the old understanding of the phrase, as a reference to the real humanity of our Lord, contains an essential element of truth; it was a fitting self-designation for him who was made in all points like unto his brethren, the sons of men, that he might make them sons of God. (*V.* also FAMILY, II.)

J. Y. CAMPBELL

SONG *v.* WORSHIP

SONS OF AARON *v.* SACRIFICE III(*a*)

SOUL *v.* SPIRIT I(*c*) and MIND

SOUND *v.* SPEAK, WORD

SPEAK, VOICE, SOUND

Speaking is an *effective* activity according to Hebrew thought. Words are the expression of the will and purpose, and if the whole soul is put into the speaking then the words carry, as it were, the whole force of the personality. We may think of three categories of words, those directed towards good ends such as blessings, those directed towards evil ends such as curses, and those that are spoken emptily, with the lips only (cf. Isa. 29.13) and are vain words. Thought, word and deed are not three separate processes or acts but are organic elements of the same single process, an act of volition. The word and the thing are, to the Hebrew mind, one and the same thing, and the same word is used for both. If the spoken word is charged with the personal power of the speaker it is but natural to regard it as having objectivity, at least until such time as it has achieved its end and has, as it were, spent its power. Thus in Zech. 5.1–4 the roll containing the words of the curse is seen being borne to those against whom the curse was directed, and we may recall the familiar words of Isa. 55.11: 'my word . . . shall not return unto me void, but it shall accomplish that which I please . . .'. The uttered word cannot be revoked: the blessing that should have been given to Esau remained with Jacob. There are other means of giving effective expression to will and effort, facial expressions and gestures, the use of arms and hands, but speech remains at once the most arresting and significant, the most elastic and far-reaching. The subject of speech need not be either visible or tangible. For these reasons, doubtless, it came to be regarded as the normal medium for the effective communication of God's power and activity. This was all the more natural for the Hebrews because they soon came to regard vision of God as a mortally dangerous experience (Exod. 33.20), whereas to be able to *hear* God, though still a privilege of extreme value, was not fraught with such danger (Deut. 5.26).

The conceptions of the VOICE and of the word of God have become so integral a part of religious thought and vocabulary, and their metaphorical and symbolic use is so firmly established, that we normally give no thought to their origin. The Hebrews, however, were realists, and when they used the term voice of God or word of God we should expect to find an actual physical experience behind it. The reality is not far to seek. With their undeveloped scientific and philosophical mind they knew nothing of primary and secondary causes. Such sounds as could not readily be explained as the result of man's activity would naturally be ascribed to the presence and activity of God. But we can never satisfactorily separate what is heard from how it is heard and understood, that is to say, we must reckon not only with the fact of natural sounds beyond the immediate understanding of men, we must reckon too with the background of faith against which those sounds were heard and interpreted. What sounds are they, and what is that background of faith? Generally speaking, the SOUND may be that of light or strong winds, heavy rain, running water, volcanic eruptions or earthquakes and, not least frequently, thunderstorms. These all appear as elements in OT descriptions of theophanies or of other indications of God's presence on earth. Adam and Eve heard God walking in the garden in the cool evening breeze. They heard the *sound* as he walked: the Hebrew word *qol* means either 'sound' or 'voice' or 'thunder'. David was told to listen for the sound of marching in the tops of the mulberry trees 'for then is Yahweh gone out before thee' (II Sam. 5.24). Elijah heard the sound of a gentle murmuring as of a breeze (the word *demamah* may mean silence, but it may also mean a murmuring or moaning sound such as a breeze might make: the LXX translates by *aura*, breeze, I Kings 19.12). The Sinai theophany and subsequent allusions to it have details that belong both to volcanic phenomena and to thunderstorms. In Ezekiel (1.24) there is conscious development into simile: 'like the noise of great waters, like the voice of the Almighty, a noise of tumult like the noise of an host'. The second question may be answered by saying that the Hebrews believed in the presence of God on earth in human form, and that he exercised his creative power very largely through word of mouth. 'By the word of the Lord were the heavens made, and all the host of them by the breath of his mouth' (Ps. 33.6). 'The worlds have been framed by the word of God' (Heb. 11.3). The priestly writer ascribed every act of creation to a deliberate fiat of God (Gen. 1). The utterance of a name, or of a new name, by God is a creative activity (Isa. 40.26, 65.15). Indeed, God's whole activity towards man and the world is revealed either as creative or redemptive, and every sound and utterance coming from him will be involved in creating, maintaining or transforming, redemptively, what has been made. 'When he uttereth his voice, there is tumult of waters in the heavens' (Jer. 10.13). With the realism so characteristic of them the Hebrews would naturally *expect to hear* something of God's effective speaking, naming and calling into being. If their expectation was realized they found themselves sharing in God's creative and redemptive work either as agents or as witnesses. A suggestive explanation of the name Yahweh has been put forward to the effect that the root of which the name is an imperfect tense means *to speak*. Yahweh would therefore, if this etymology should prove correct, mean 'He speaks' or 'He declares'. Either of these meanings would fit OT experience of him. Did not Deutero-Isaiah love to dwell on the power of Yahweh both to predict and to perform?

It is often difficult to determine where realism merges into symbolism. Sometimes, indeed, the developed symbol is patent, as in Num. 7.89: 'he heard the Voice speaking unto him . . . from between the two cherubim'. Symbolism was bound to enter sooner or later because what man hears, whether literally or spiritually, is but a whisper of the ultimate fullness of God's reality (cf. Job 26.14). The actuality on earth is but a part of and a symbol of the greater thing in heaven. The transition from actual to metaphorical usage may perhaps underlie the fact that although Deutero-Isaiah uses the accepted formula, 'Thus saith Yahweh', yet when he wishes to make clear that there was an actual auditory experience, such as must originally have underlain that phrase, he uses the phrase 'a voice crying' (or, 'Hark! one crying') (40.3). For him, therefore, the old phrase must have come to stand for intuitive perception of God's word.

The phrase 'The word of Yahweh' came to be a technical term for what was revealed through the prophets. There was nothing exclusive in the fact that it was to prophets that the word was normally revealed. Prophethood might become universal: 'would that all Yahweh's people were prophets' (Num. 11.29). Indeed, it may be claimed that this is just what the Incarnation made possible that all men might be priests and prophets of God. Tradition and experience alone gave the prophets the monopoly. In the days of Samuel's youth 'the word of Yahweh was precious . . . there was no open vision' (I Sam. 3.1). In later times there were bitter heart-searchings over the truth and authenticity of the word of Yahweh as proclaimed by prophets. The false prophet arose who was more concerned with worldly matters than with the word of Yahweh. Jeremiah in particular was troubled by this problem. 'The prophet that hath a dream, let him tell a dream; and he that hath my word, let him speak my word faithfully. . . . Is not my word like as fire? saith the Lord; and like a hammer that breaketh the rock in pieces?' (Jer. 23.28f.). The ultimate proof that the prophet uttered God's word was its fulfilment, for as he uttered the word of God he was acting as God's agent on earth. It was the duty of the prophet to release God's creative word. Jeremiah clearly traces the ultimate origin of the prophet's 'word of God' to direct audition in the council of Yahweh (23.18).

It is only when we set the Johannine conception of Christ as *the* word of God against this background of Hebrew thought that we can truly understand all that this expression implies for NT Christology: the word of God which took flesh and became incarnate in Christ is none other than the effective instrument of God by which the world was created and is redeemed. (*V.* also WORD.)

L. H. BROCKINGTON

SPEAKING WITH TONGUES *v.* SPIRIT V, VIII(e)

SPIRIT, HOLY SPIRIT

I. INTRODUCTION

The word 'Spirit' almost defies analysis; but we may begin by noting briefly some of the less important meanings of its Heb. (*Ruach*) and Gk. (*Pneuma*) equivalents:

(*a*) WIND, the beneficent or destructive, invisible gust of air: frequently in the OT, e.g. I Kings 18.45, Ps. 103.16, Jer. 4.11; rare in the NT. Two examples in the latter (John 3.8, Heb. 1.7—quoting Ps. 104.4), and such passages as Gen. 8.1, Num. 11.31, Amos 4.13, Isa. 11.15 depict the wind as an instrument of the equally unseen God. It may be observed that the Stoics spoke of a warm air or Spirit as the source and goal of everything (see T. R. Glover, *The Conflict of Religions in the Roman Empire*, pp. 37f.). Probably the ancient world conceived even the wind as material; something like a reverse of this seems to be characteristic of our modern age.

(*b*) BREATH, the air that is vital 'stuff', Gen. 6.17, Job. 34.14f., II Thess. 2.8, Jas. 2.26, Rev. 11.11, 13.15. Throughout the Bible, of course, the real source of life is God; and as religious thought developed, 'Spirit' came to be associated particularly with the life created by God, Gen. 1.2; cf. II Macc. 7.22, Luke 8.55 (for OT ideas see N. H. Snaith in *The Doctrine of the Holy Spirit*, Headingley Lectures, p. 23). Hence to 'expire' or to 'give up one's spirit' is to die, Matt. 27.50 and pars., Acts 7.59f.; cf. II Macc. 14.46, Wisd. 2.3. Thus even as breath 'Spirit' carries with it the over-tone of God's dynamic, creative activity.

(*c*) SOUL. For the Hebrews man is of the earth; he is flesh, Isa. 31.3; yet as the creature of God he is a living soul marked out for a special relationship and destiny, Gen. 2.7, 1.26, 6.17, 7.15.

In the post-exilic period 'Spirit' became a virtual synonym for 'soul' and 'heart', the seat of intelligence and emotion in man (cf. Job 20.3, 32.18, Isa. 57.15, Dan. 5.20). Human characteristics are described in 'spiritual' terms; the quiet or humble (Isa. 66.2), the depressed (Isa. 54.6; cf. Wisd. 5.3), the energetic (Hag. 1.14—where G. Adam Smith paraphrases 'spirit' as 'their conscience and radical force of character', *The Book of the Twelve Prophets*, Vol. II, p. 241; with this compare the earlier use of spirit=energy, Judg. 15.19, I Kings 10.5). Once again the highest reaches of human life are set within the framework of a divine dimension (cf. Isa. 57.16); and God not only commands heaven and earth, he forms the inner life of man—his spirit, the 'real' personality (Zech. 12.1; cf. II Macc. 7.22). So he may be called 'the God of the spirits of all flesh' (Num. 16.22, 27.16; cf. II Macc. 3.22, Heb. 12.9).

When we turn to the NT, the situation is complicated by the fact that room must often be found for the distinctive conception of the Holy Spirit at work within Christians. But Spirit=soul or the inner self appears in Mark 2.8, 8.12, Luke 1.80, John 11.33, 13.21; cf. also Luke 1.47 (soul and spirit), Mark 14.38 (spirit and flesh—the intention of the will contrasted with physical disability). The same usage occurs in Acts 17.16 and possibly Heb. 4.12. In the Pauline literature we find examples in I Cor. 2.11, II Cor. 7.1,13; less certainly II Cor. 2.13; much less clearly I Cor. 5.4.

(*d*) SPIRITS (GOOD OR EVIL). Belief in supernatural beings, alive in the woods, in numinous stones, and so on, is a legacy from primitive religion. The early Heb. view gives its God control over these spirits (cf. Judg. 9.23, I Sam. 16.14, I Kings 22.21). It is God who tests and distracts mankind (Amos 3.6). Later a distinction is made between the Heavenly King and the ministers of his court—the winds are his messengers or angels (Ps. 104.4; cf. Heb. 1.7,14, Zech. 6.5). Ezekiel may have believed that an angel 'spirited' him about and communicated with him (1.20, 2.2, 11.1–6). Reference may be made to A. Lods's article in *Record and Revelation*, ed. H. W. Robinson, pp. 195f., and to *Hebrew Religion, Its Origin and Development*, by W. O. E. Oesterley and T. H. Robinson, pp. 111ff., 318f.

For similar ideas in the NT, see I Tim. 4.1 (demonic doctrines taught by Satan's emissaries; cf. I John 4.1), II Cor. 11.4, Rev. 16.13f. The general pattern of thought is that the whole world lies in the power of the Evil One (I John 5.19) and Christians must wage war against supernatural forces of wickedness (Eph. 6.12). Faith in the God of Christ is a safeguard, for he is the deliverer (Matt. 6.13). Men and women are unhealthy as sinners or as vexed by evil spirits; hence Jesus frequently exorcised the demons (Mark 1.23ff., 3.11, Luke 11.24–6) as a sign of divine power effective in the world ('the finger of God', Luke 11.20; 'the Spirit of God', Matt. 12.28). Cf. Acts 5.16, 19.15. Freedom from the evil influences at work in the human personality remains as an essential offer of the Gospel. (See P. S. Minear, *Eyes of Faith*, pp. 68ff.). 'Spirits' may also refer to the dead—insubstantial ghosts (Mark 6.49, Matt. 14.26, Luke 24.39, Heb. 12.23, I Pet. 3.19, where according to the legend the dead are still able to listen to Christ's preaching).

II. THE THEOLOGICAL MEANING OF SPIRIT

The Spirit of God has an essential place in the earliest proclamation of the Christian Message or *Kerygma* (C. H. Dodd, *The Apostolic Preaching and Its Developments*, pp. 42f., 51f.). At the heart of the message was a true story about Jesus, the Christ of Israel and Lord of all (Acts 2.36, Phil. 2.11); and he had been anointed for his office by the Spirit of God (Acts 4.26f., 10.38; cf. Luke 1.35, John 1.32f., Rom. 1.1–4).

This story had a *setting*:

(*a*) It concerned the one, living *God*, whose mighty acts in the past history of his People, Israel (Pss. 44, 66, 78, Neh. 4.6ff., Isa. 43.7ff.) were now excelled (Luke 10.23f.; cf. 11.31f.). His Kingdom had arrived within reach of all seekers (Mark 1.15, Luke 11.20=Matt. 12.28, Luke 17.21).

(*b*) Through the ministry and resurrection of Jesus the hopes of *Israel* were fulfilled (Luke 7.18–23). But this had happened because of unexpected suffering and a unique conquest of death (Matt. 26.24, Luke 18.31, Acts 2.24). Following Jesus' own insight (Mark 9.31), the suffering of Messiah=Son of Man was found to be anticipated in the OT (Acts 3.18ff., I Pet. 1.10–12). Then the Church naturally defined this 'Kingdom Come' in terms of Jesus himself, for it had to define God's reign in this way (Gal. 4.4, Phil. 2.11, Heb. 1.1f., John 1.1–18). Here again it was faithful to the mind of Jesus (Matt. 11.27). Confession of Jesus meant entrance into the Kingdom, involved obedience to the Father he revealed, and demanded the self-sacrifice of which love is capable. (See T. W. Manson, *The Teaching of Jesus*, pp. 129ff.)

This story had tremendous *consequences*:

(*1*) God's great act in Jesus ensured *the forgiveness of sins* and men were called to *repent*. Jesus as dying and alive again was the founder of the New Covenant (Heb. 7.22, etc.; cf. I Cor. 11.25, Jer. 31.31ff.). Israel as the People of the Old Covenant was offered this salvation (Acts 5.31, Rom. 10.8f.), and the world also (John 3.16, 16.8–11, I John 2.2, 4.14). To hear the Gospel is to face the issues of destiny, for man is accountable to the God revealed in Jesus (Matt. 16.27; cf. Ezek. 20.3f., Matt. 25.31–46—an early sermon?—G. D. Kilpatrick, *The Origins of the Gospel according to Saint Matthew*, p. 97, John 5.27, Acts 10.42, Rom. 2.16, II Cor. 5.10, I Thess. 1.10: in some of these passages Jesus is the judge; cf. W. A. Curtis, *Jesus Christ the Teacher*, p. 142).

(*2*) As a part of the blessings of 'Kingdom Come' *the Spirit of God was bestowed on those who did believe and repent* (Acts 2.38; cf. Gal. 3.2). This gift marked them off from Israel as such and from mankind in general (Acts 2.33, 5.32); yet the promise of it is first of all for Israel (Acts 2.39, 3.25f.; cf. Rom. 1.16, 3.1–4, 5.1,5, 8.2,9,11).

(*3*) In their invitation to others the spokesmen of the Message proclaimed themselves as *eyewitnesses, equipped for their task by the Spirit* (Acts 10.38–42, Luke 24.46–9; and note Acts 5.32, John 14.26, 15.26f.). Paul stood in the same tradition (Rom. 10.12–15, 15.18f.). Such testimony might lead to martyrdom (John 15.18ff.; see R. P. Casey, Addn. Note V, *The Beginnings of Christianity*, pt. I, Vol. V, ed. F. J. Foakes Jackson and K. Lake).

Thus the sweep of the original Christian Proclamation was from the beginning when the Word was with God to the unending climax when God will be all in all (I Cor. 15.28, Phil. 2.6–11, Rev. 21.22f., 22.3–5, John 1.1). In this whole process the Spirit of God was seen to be active in Israel, the Church, and the world.

III. THE OLD TESTAMENT

An adequate discussion of the place of the Spirit in the OT would require an historical as well as a theological examination of the evidence; but our purpose here is merely to indicate that convictions about the Spirit and its influence belong to the Christian inheritance from Israel. These were transformed by the events of the Christian revelation and subsequent religious experience.

Some of the principal ideas were as follows:

(*a*) The Spirit is sent forth by God in the act of creation and in maintaining human life (cf. above under *Breath* and *Soul*).

(*1*) Gen. 1.2, Ps. 18.15 (RV, 'the breath of thy nostrils'), 33.6 (RV, 'the breath of his mouth'), 104.30, Job 26.13, Isa. 34.16, Jdth. 16.14.

(*2*) Job 33.4, Isa. 42.5 ('breath and spirit to the people and them that walk therein').

'In Hebrew consciousness, man lives within the orbit of God's immediate action, from moment to moment under the direct control of the divine Hand. God is the Creator who acts in every situation, whether in nature or history' (P. S. Minear, *Eyes of Faith*, p. 149, with a ref. to A. Guillaume, *Prophecy and Divination*, p. 184).

(*b*) Extraordinary endowments of body or leadership for God's people are due to the 'invasion' of the Spirit: 'And the Spirit of the Lord came upon him, and he judged Israel; and he went out to war . . .', Judg. 3.10; cf. 6.34, 14.6, Gen. 41.38. (On the other hand, men might be troubled by an evil spirit from God: Judg. 9.23, I Sam. 16.14ff. The divine purpose seemed to be served by conflict or by loss of insight and initiative. We might prefer to explain such cases from the human point of view.)

(*c*) Wisdom and discernment are especially gifts of the Spirit; cf. Num. 11.25f. (a given 'amount' that can be shared by others in the task of governing the chosen people) and Deut. 34.9 (Joshua as the successor of Moses was full of the spirit of wisdom, 'for Moses had laid his hands upon him'—so Num. 27.18; but the transmission of the Spirit is not present in the latter passage). In Prov. 1.23 Wisdom cries, 'Turn you at my reproof: Behold, I will pour out my spirit unto you, I will make known my words unto you'; Exod. 31.3–6, one craftsman's skill is 'inspired'; Sus. 45—a (holy) spirit of sagacity in Daniel: cf. the notable passage in Ecclus. 39.6 on the man that meditates on the Law: 'If the great Lord will, he shall be filled with the spirit of understanding. . . .' In the later literature such wisdom is predicated of the promised Branch of Jesse, Isa. 11.2 (cf. *Pss. Sol.* 17.35–42, 18.7f.). And the close relationship between the divine Spirit and wisdom is beautifully told in the Wisdom of Solomon (e.g. 7.22ff., 'For there is in her a spirit quick of understanding, holy, . . . For she is a breath of the power of God, and a clear effluence of the glory of the Almighty; . . . she maketh men friends of God and prophets'; 9.17, 'And who ever gained knowledge of thy counsel, except thou gavest wisdom, and sentest thy holy spirit from on high?'; cf. 1.5ff., 7.7, 12.1). Dr. A. J. Macdonald thinks that we have here 'the connecting link, on the one hand, with the pneumatology of the earlier writings of the Hebrew OT, and, on the other, with the pneumatology of the NT' (*The Interpreter Spirit and Human Life*, p. 46; cf. also J. C. Rylaarsdam, *Revelation in Jewish Wisdom Literature*, pp. 99ff.).

(*d*) Prophecy is a characteristic mark of the Spirit's presence amongst men. At first this is a strange, ecstatic power induced suddenly in certain 'holy men': I Sam. 10.6, 19.23f. ('Is Saul also among the prophets?'), Ecclus. 48.12,24 (Elijah was wrapped in a tempest, and Elisha was filled with his spirit; Isaiah saw by an excellent spirit what should come to pass at the last). The interpretation of dreams may be included here: Dan. 4.8f.,18, 5.12,14. Everything depended on the conception of the supernatural and, as development in the understanding of God's true nature proceeded, there was a corresponding ability to distinguish true from false prophetic inspiration. Such understanding, of course, meant a fuller appropriation of God's revealing Word. We reach the heights with the 8th-cent. prophets and their successors: Mic. 3.8, 'But I truly am full of power by the spirit of the Lord . . .' (the whole chapter should be read), Isa. 42.1 ('I have put my spirit upon him'), 61.1 ('the spirit of the Lord God is upon me'). At this high level there is much less of the trance and clairvoyance elements, for the prophet retains his reasonable faculties; he has eyes to see (cf. Isa. 29.10), is sensitive to the activity of the living God in history and in his own experience (cf. Jer. 1.11ff.), and publishes his oracles in intelligible speech or writing, whether sober prose or lyric verse. Indeed, the great prophets themselves rarely speak of their own inspiration, because of the misconceptions about Spirit-possession. 'There is no invasion of the man's personality overwhelming and obliterating it, and there is always the certainty that it is Yahweh with whom he has to do. . . . Moreover, it is the content of the word which is important' (N. W. Porteous in *Record and Revelation*, ed. H. W. Robinson, p. 245; see also C. H. Dodd, *The Authority of the Bible*, pp. 48ff.).

The prophecies speak to Israel as the consecrated, though disobedient nation, and to its people as those who are bound in covenant to God, to do his will. Early Judaism preserved them and interpreted them for new generations. It is noteworthy from this point of view that the litany for the sin-offering includes the petition:

> 'Cast me not away from thy presence;
> And take not thy holy spirit from me.'
> (Ps. 51.11; cf. Ps. 143.10.)

Israel's greatest souls longed, like Moses in Num. 11.29, to dwell in a nation where all were prophets because the Lord had put his Spirit upon them. For them the apocalyptic message of Joel brought hope of a New Age: 'I will pour out my spirit upon all flesh; and your sons and your daughters shall prophesy' (2.28). Or they might turn to Ezekiel's promise of a resurrection for Israel: in the valley of dry bones the divine Creator shows the prophet earthquake and tempest of wind, the breathing of new life into the dead frames; and promises that this is a parable of his action in the nation; for he will put his spirit in them and they will live (37.1–14). With this we may compare the demand for repentance in 18.31, and the divine offer in 11.19f., 36.26f. (one heart, a new spirit, a heart of flesh). Lastly, we may notice Isa. 63.7ff. Whether it comes from a very late period or from Second Isaiah, this passage shows the religion of the Old Covenant at its best. It proclaims the fatherhood and saviourhood of God in his relationship to Israel. He is merciful and loyal, exceedingly kind; he has led them gloriously in bygone days. But the faithless nation has 'grieved his holy spirit' and God seems to have become their enemy. Now in a time of desolation the prophet passionately cries for a rending of the heavens, for terrible and mighty acts of the Lord, for cleansing and renewal. Let the spirit of the Lord once more cause them to rest (Isa. 63.14); let God put his holy spirit again on his holy people (Isa. 63.11,18, 64.9). The work of the Spirit is in fact the work of God himself.

(*e*) We may sum up by saying that the Spirit is the divine Power immanent in human history, but chiefly in Israel's. It is immanent only because it is essentially transcendent, coming forth out of the supernatural life of a God who deals directly with men. Passages like Ps. 139.7 ('Whither shall I go from thy spirit?'), and Isa. 34.16, 48.16 imply 'some sort of personalization', yet 'the most the Hebrews did was to approach that half-dreamed intangible representation which appears in Job 4.15 ["then a spirit passed before my face"]' (N. H. Snaith, *The Doctrine of the Holy Spirit*, Headingley Lectures, p. 31). The supernatural element in the working of the Spirit according to the OT needs to be stressed. Israel knew that in this realm God was active and awe-inspiring, that to him must be ascribed the peculiar character of the seer and the prophet, that when the Spirit came it did so revealingly and marvellously. And Israel was constituted God's holy nation no less by the presence of his Spirit than by the covenant of Sinai. Yet Judaism in the main could not point to the Spirit's power amongst its adherents in the century before John the Baptist. It was this vacuum which Christianity announced to be filled and filled to overflowing as a result of Jesus' ministry and death.

IV. THE SYNOPTIC GOSPELS

On this an important recent discussion by C. K. Barrett, *The Holy Spirit and the Gospel Tradition* (London, 1947), should be consulted.

In the Third Gospel more than the others we find several refs. to the presence of the divine Spirit in the ministry of Jesus:

(*a*) *The Birth and Boyhood Narratives:* Matt. 1.18,20, Luke 1.(15),35,(41),(67), 2.25ff. These passages reflect a developed belief (in Hellenistic-Christian circles, probably) that the Lord of the Church had a special origin in history; yet the traces of the miraculous do not loom large. The conception by the Spirit is an act of divine power which many will accept as an attempt to say that in the coming of the God-man the creative activity of the lifegiving Spirit was peculiarly present. Whether this further demands Virgin Birth (q.v.) is another matter. The relative unimportance of the latter in the main stream of NT thought is notable (cf. John 1.1–18). In the case of John the Forerunner, the Spirit is similarly active.

(*b*) *The Baptism and Temptation:* Mark 1.8,10,12, Matt. 3.11,16, 4.1, Luke 3.16,22, 4.1, and Luke 4.14. Once again supernatural power descends upon Jesus at the critical hour when his ministry begins, to instal and fit him for the unique vocation of being God's servant and Israel's King. This may be the interpretation of the Evangelists, but it is true to other strands in Jesus' teaching. The promise of John the Baptist (Mark 1.8) means that he foretold the coming of the new or Messianic Age when great gifts of the Spirit would be received by the faithful. Its fulfilment came after the resurrection (Acts 2.33, John 20.22; cf. John 1.26,33; contrast Acts 1.5, 11.16).

(*c*) *Luke 10.21, Matt. 11.25*: 'in holy Spirit' is a typical Lucan addition.

(*d*) *The Great Commission:* Matt. 28.19. The trinitarian formula here betrays a late date, probably near the close of the 1st cent.; contrast Acts 19.5 and Rom. 6.3ff.

(*e*) *The Teaching of Jesus:*

(*1*) *Mark 12.36* (cf. Ps. 110.1, Acts 2.34f.): if genuine it reflects the idea that the OT writers were moved by the Spirit. In the light of later doctrine (cf. I Pet. 1.11) this single example is significant, though it tells us little about Jesus' own views. When we relate it to such a saying as Luke 16.16, to Luke 11.29–32, and Jesus' knowledge of Joel's great prophecy, we may believe that Jesus thought that he in whom the Kingdom comes (the 'something greater') also brings the revelation and powers of the Spirit (cf., below, on Mark 3.29).

(*2*) *Luke 11.13:* the par. in Matt. 7.11 has 'good things' instead of Luke's 'the Holy Spirit' and is to be preferred.

(*3*) *Matt. 12.28:* here Luke's par. 'by the finger of God' (11.20; cf. Exod. 8.19) is a more striking phrase and almost certainly original. Luke's tendency is to multiply references to the Spirit. Yet Jesus might have used both forms at different times, and in any case the meaning (the power of God) is the same.

(*4*) *Mark 3.29;* Matt. 12.31f. par. to Luke 12.10: blasphemy against the Holy Spirit. The new Age of the Kingdom has come within men's reach and the work of the Spirit in Jesus is part of its reality; blindness to this means inevitable exclusion from the Kingdom's blessings. The Church may have interpreted this in the light of Isa. 63.10ff. and may even have applied it to Christian apostasy (Barrett, *op. cit.*, pp. 104ff.), but the double tradition of Q and Mark suggests that the saying is genuine. The realism and insight of the passage ring true to the mind of our Lord. If so, note that Jesus believes in the Spirit as God's, immanent in himself, and effective for the conquest of evil. Is the Spirit for him also 'personal'?

(*5*) *Mark 13.11;* cf. Matt. 10.19f. and Luke 12.11f., both perhaps placed too early in the ministry. The disciples will be inspired to make defence before persecutors. There is a variant, 'a mouth and wisdom', at Luke 21.15 which sounds authentic. If any weight could be given to the Johannine tradition (John 14.26f., 15.26f.), we might accept this saying in Mark, but the balance of the evidence is against it (cf. Barrett, *op. cit.*, pp. 131f.).

(*6*) *Luke 4.18*, quoting Isa. 61.1f., 'The Spirit of the Lord is upon me'. With this should be compared Matt. 11.5 and Luke 7.22. 'Luke has taken the narrative of Mark 6 . . . as foundation for a representative and symbolic scene to open the public ministry of Jesus, and . . . himself is mainly responsible for the section as it stands' (J. M. Creed, *The Gospel according to St. Luke*, p. 65). Nevertheless, we may hold that the prophecies of Isaiah regarding the Servant of God were before the mind of Jesus and that the early Church has elaborated an essential aspect of his interpretation of his Mission (see, for example, Mark 1.11, 7.6f., 11.17, 12.1–12, 14.24, Matt. 5.4, 8.17, 12.18–21). The Lucan programme in 4.18ff., therefore, is a stroke of genius! (Vincent Taylor, *Jesus and His Sacrifice*, pp. 46ff., should be consulted.)

The authentic sayings thus seem to be few—only two or three. More surprising, however, in the light of Acts and the Pauline Epistles is the restraint of the Evangelists' rewriting of the teaching. Each genuine strand is of first-class importance. Jesus believed in the Spirit. He called it the Spirit of God and related its work of power closely to his own activity in the eschatological crisis of 'Kingdom Come'. Hence he has been rightly described as a 'pneumatic' or spiritual man. We may legitimately go farther and hold that sayings about the Spirit are few in the recorded words of Jesus because of his humility (Phil. 2.6f.) and the necessity that his special status could not be a blinding wonder, but only an incognito which they alone could recognize who had eyes to see. He was the *Messias moriturus*, the Messiah who had to die in the sacrifice love offers in a sinful world (see my book, *The Doctrine of the Church in the New Testament*, pp. 54–6), and this was a secret which none divined before his resurrection. Similarly he knew himself to be endowed with the Spirit for this kind of filial, Servant Messiahship; consequently, he could no more speak openly of the Spirit than he could of the Father (T. W. Manson, *The Teaching of Jesus*, pp. 101f.). Such reserve was in the prophetic tradition (Barrett, *op. cit.*, p. 157). But John may be correct in his account of Jesus offering fuller teaching to the disciples privately; though Barrett makes a strong case against this view (*op. cit.*, pp. 153ff.).

One word may be added: the doctrine of the Holy Spirit in the rest of the NT depends not only on experiences verified by their fruit in Christian lives, but also on the fact of the Christ who died and is alive again (cf. I Pet. 3.18). The Spirit is known henceforward as God's gracious power and equally *as the presence of Christ himself* (cf. Rom. 8.9, Phil. 1.19). 'The general gift of the Spirit belongs to the time of the vindication and manifestation of the Messiah and of the Messianic Kingdom' (Barrett, *op. cit.*, p. 159).

V. PENTECOST

(Acts 2.1, 20.16, I Cor. 16.8.) We start with the second chapter of Acts, which is the continuation of Luke's Gospel. As in the first volume the author began with a programme in terms of the divine Spirit in Jesus, so here he prefaced the story of the expansion of the Church with an account of the outpouring of the Spirit on the eyewitnesses of the resurrection and their fellow-believers. The Lord's promise (Luke 24.49, Acts 1.8) was fulfilled at Pentecost. Moreover, the prophecy of Joel had at last come true—the disciples spoke with strange tongues in an ecstasy of divine speech or prophecy; there were signs of supernatural forces at work—the mighty wind, the fire, the 'intoxication' of the recipients. And all because the crucified Jesus is God's Messiah (2.36; cf. the use of Servant or Child in 3.13,26, 4.27,30); he is now at God's right hand (fulfilling Ps. 110.1; cf. the early poem, Phil. 2.6–11). On this day the Church was constituted as a reality in history and its growth began (2.37–41). Its life was marked by unity; common contributions (RV, fellowship) of wealth; adherence to the Apostolic teaching; the sacrament of the Bread Broken; and prayers (2.42). Worship at the Temple in Jerusalem was also maintained (2.46), and the outstanding mark of the new community was joy.

This picture is almost certainly idealized by the author on the basis of early traditions. He confuses the gift of tongues (*glossolalia*, cf. I Cor. 14.2–19) with the ability to speak foreign languages (2.6–11) and makes it symbolical of the universality of the Church. He emphasizes the favour with which the new movement was received (2.47) and exaggerates its success (2.41). We must note further that the Fourth Gospel dates the gift of the Spirit to the Day of Resurrection when the risen Jesus breathed on the disciples and said, 'Receive ye the Holy Ghost' (John 20.19–23). Can we reconcile the traditions? Acts 2.33 also ascribes the coming of the Spirit to the initiative of the risen Lord: 'he hath poured forth this, which ye see and hear'. John similarly alternates between 'I will send him unto you' (16.7) and 'whom the Father will send in my name' (14.26; cf. 14.17f., 15.26). There seems to be no reason for doubting the historical accuracy of the account in Acts: Pentecost was the occasion when the whole body of the disciples had this overwhelming experience. Theologically, John is right in his emphasis. The resurrection appearances (probably first in Galilee) made new men out of Peter and the rest of the Eleven; and it may well have been some weeks before the larger community was joined in one faith and heart, thus making possible the event recorded in Acts 2. Was Pentecost related to the appearance 'to above five hundred brethren at once' (I Cor. 15.6)?

The 'Gentile Pentecost' in the house of Cornelius (Acts 10.45f.) is likewise marked by speaking with tongues and the praise of God; a pattern doubtless often repeated when the Gospel message was received.

We may go on to notice that the beginnings of the Church, according to Acts, were characterized by the constant presence of the Spirit *as supernatural power*: in the original Apostles through whom it witnessed to God's work in Christ (4.8, 5.3,9,32), in the Seven (6.3,5,10, 7.55, 8.29,39), in Barnabas (11.24), Agabus the prophet (11.27f.); in the Church at Jerusalem (4.31); and at Antioch (limited perhaps to the prophets and teachers?—13.2,4). Throughout the Pauline missions the same thing was true, 13.9,52, 16.6f. (forbidden to preach in the province of Asia and, by '*the Spirit of Jesus*', to enter Bithynia), 19.21, 20.23, 21.4 (Tyre), 21.11 (Agabus at Caesarea). Many signs and wonders accompanied the gift of the Spirit: 3.6, 5.12,15f. (healing and exorcism), 8.6f.,13, 10.19 (Peter had a vision), 13.9–12 (Elymas the sorcerer was blinded), 16.18. Scripture (i.e. the OT) is the book of the Spirit: 1.16, 3.21, 4.25, 7.51f. (persecution of the prophets meant resisting the Holy Spirit), 28.25. The elders of Miletus were designated bishops, appointed by the Spirit to feed the Church (20.28). All that is true to the general thesis.

But another strain in the tradition is more confusing. The Spirit was not bestowed, apparently, except after the laying on of hands, 8.17, 9.17; cf. 6.6, 13.3, 19.6. It is not difficult to see that this may sometimes mean nothing more than a commissioning of certain men for special duty with prayer for an appropriate *gift* of the Spirit. But to reconcile an initial inspiration of Christian believers with such an act (cf. Gal. 3.2) is less easy. Probably we have in the case of Samaria and the baptists of Ephesus a reflection of later ecclesiastical practice.

A similar perplexity arises when the relation of Baptism to the reception of the Spirit is concerned; for the original community of Apostles and other disciples Pentecost was a 'baptism with the Holy Ghost' (cf. Acts 1.5), but new converts required Baptism in the name of Jesus (2.38), presumably a water-baptism; yet at 8.12–16 such Baptism failed to bring the desired inspiration. What is still more strange is that Peter, though recognizing that Cornelius and his house had experienced a Pentecost 'as well as we' (10.47, 11.15), asked, 'Can any man forbid the water . . .? And he commanded them to be baptized . . .' (10.47f., but not at 11.15–17). The connexion in Paul's case is obscure (9.17f.). Rom. 6.4 and 8.11, as well as I Cor. 12.13, show that the new life in the Spirit and therefore in Christ's Body, the Church, is very closely linked with the baptismal experience. Yet Paul seems to discount Baptism in I Cor. 1.13–17, perhaps leaving it to his assistants; and Gal. 3 strongly ties together the profession of faith and the gift of the Spirit. We are really in the dark on this subject, though several conjectures have been offered in explanation: for Leipoldt's see R. N. Flew, *Jesus and His Church*, p. 165; consult also Jackson and Lake, *Beginnings*, Pt. I, Vol. V, pp. 121ff. Probably we ought to allow room for an initial diversity before any regular practice became established as the eschatological expectation dimmed (*v.* also BAPTISM).

Dr. Newton Flew protests against unduly emphasizing the idea that for the first community the Spirit was 'regarded as the mysterious wonder-working power of God . . . not connected . . . with the normal religious acts of daily life, nor with the interpretation of the divine purpose in history' (*op. cit.*, p. 149). He properly draws attention to (*1*) the conviction that the living God was at work; (*2*) the Spirit was received by all Christians; (*3*) the Spirit was no private possession, but was shared by the whole group (*ibid.*). Thus the Church was established as a new fact, marked by a new quality of life, a society of love and joy and hope. This is the real meaning of Pentecost: there is no genuine Christianity 'on the wrong side of Pentecost' (W. R. Forrester, *Conversion*, p. 5).

VI. OTHER NT BOOKS

Several of the later New Testament books may be considered very briefly:

I Tim.: There is one reference to Christ's spiritual nature (so 3.16 probably; cf. I Pet. 3.18), and one to the Spirit in contrast with seducing spirits (false prophets or teachers) and devilish doctrines (4.1; cf. Acts 20.29—the Spirit had spoken through Paul or through some other prophet).

II Tim.: According to 1.14 the indwelling Spirit, received at ordination (1.6), enabled the bishop to maintain the tradition. This implies that in time of heresy the bishop was divinely inspired and should be obeyed. He possessed authority and the right to discipline because of his spiritual endowment; these he must use boldly and yet in love (1.7).

Titus 3.5 is important. As RV margin shows, the grammar is ambiguous. The renewal of the Spirit may be an effect of the washing (Baptism) or may be a second instance of the divine method in salvation. 3.6 may be a reference to Pentecost ('poured out'; cf. Acts 2.17f., 33, 10.45, Rom. 5.5), but if so it is a

Pentecost continually repeated and a close connexion with Baptism is implied—the sacrament of the Church involved the gift of new life in the Spirit. Hence it is perhaps better to consider renewal as an effect of Baptism (so Swete, *The Holy Spirit in the New Testament*, p. 247, and E. F. Scott, *Moffatt Com. in loc.*). Pauline parallels may be found in Rom. 6.3ff. and I Cor. 5.11; but the absence in Titus of any ref. to faith is significant. The tendency was toward an *ex opere operato* conception of the sacrament; yet the action of the Holy Spirit is too clearly evident to permit us to say that there was any magical idea in this.

James 4.5 cites an unknown 'scripture'. 'The spirit which he made to dwell in us' may be, as in 2.26, the breath of life in man as God's creature. (For a contrary view, Swete, *op. cit.*, pp. 257f.)

Jude 19f. is an attack on false teachers (cf. I Tim. 4.1), perhaps Gnostics whose claim to be 'spiritual' is disproved by their ethic. True Christians should hold the Apostolic faith, remain within the love of God, await Christ's coming to Judgment, and 'pray in the Holy Spirit'. They are the truly 'spiritual' and they are dependent on the power of the divine Spirit; for the thought of prayer in the Spirit, cf. Rom. 8.26, Phil. 3.3, John 4.24. 'Prayer is love in need appealing to Love in power, and the upbuilding of the church depends upon this living intercourse between God and His People' (James Moffatt, in the *Moffatt Com.*, *ad* Jude 20).

Revelation

(*a*) There are satanic spirits (16.13f., 18.2), but John the prophet or seer is a man inspired on the Lord's Day (Resurrection Day; perhaps in church?), 1.10, 4.2, 17.3, 21.10; and like his fellow-servant, the angel, he bears witness to Jesus, 19.10 (for testimony to Jesus [RV, 'of'] is the spirit of prophecy).

(*b*) Through the prophet the Spirit speaks to the churches in warning, rebuke or encouragement: 2, 3, *passim*; cf. 14.13, a message about those who die in the Lord.

(*c*) The seven spirits (1.4, 3.1, 4.5, 5.6) probably denote the perfect fullness in the divine Spirit.

(*d*) In 22.17 the Spirit is associated with the Bride—that is, the Church—in calling for the advent of Christ in glory. If this refers to an ecstatic response of the prophets in the Church (so M. Kiddle, *Moffatt Com. in loc.*), it should be observed that for the writer these prophets are indeed instruments of the supernatural Spirit who dwells within the Christian community.

Here we are in touch with notions very similar to those of the OT. The Spirit is the God who speaks in prophets; and prophets now testify to Jesus (Rev. 19.10) as the Apostles did and the first preachers (Acts, *passim*). In the Pastoral Epistles, however, and in Jude, we notice a tendency to link inspiration (i) to those who are orthodox (holding the Apostolic tradition in face of Gnostic heresies) and (ii) to ecclesiastical officials, duly ordained.

VII. HEBREWS AND I PETER

Hebrews. This document is an important witness to the common pattern of the early Christian preaching, but it concentrates on the symbolic nature of the OT preparation and on the high-priestly office of the Son. This did not mean that the OT was outmoded entirely, for the writer treats it consistently as Christian Scripture and ascribes certain passages to the utterance of the Holy Spirit (3. 7–11, 10.15; cf. 9.8).

9.14: Christ offered himself 'through the eternal Spirit' (RV), and this should be explained in terms of Christ's essential nature as the effulgence of the divine glory (1.3), as one who abides for ever (7.24), the perfect High-Priest (5.5–10, 7.24f., 8.2), who after death entered into the holiest of all in the realm of Spirit (cf. I Tim. 3.16, I Pet. 3.18). His sacrifice therefore 'had the whole power of His deathless personality in it' (H. A. A. Kennedy, *The Theology of the Epistles*, p. 214).

There are three other passages which must be given their fullest significance for the author's views:

2.4: signs, wonders, powers, and 'gifts of the Holy Ghost' accompanied the preaching of the Apostolic witnesses. This is an obvious reference to the supernatural events of the first Pentecost (or the earliest period of Christian history). God is the donor of the gifts: contrast I Cor. 12.4–11; but there is no real contradiction of the Pauline doctrine.

6.4: Christians are partners in the Spirit (cf. II Pet. 1.4, I Cor. 10.17, Phil. 2.1, Heb. 2.11). The author almost takes it for granted that this is the position of the ordinary believer. He is true to the tradition of Acts and the assumptions of Paul. Hence in 10.29 he can go on to define apostasy, which is unforgivable, as the mockery of the Spirit (cf. Mark 3.29). For 'Spirit of grace' cf. Zech. 12.10. Here too the Spirit is personified. He is the God who spoke by the prophets and enters the lives of Christian believers. The Church thus blessed should be loyal in time of danger and reliant on divine grace (4.16, 6.10–12, 10.23f.,32ff., 12.5,28); it is sanctified because of Jesus' death in self-sacrifice (2.9–11, 9.11–15, 10.1ff., 13.12); it belongs to the true Age, the Age of the new and better Covenant by which sins are forgiven; it is the People of God for whom the real Sabbath rest has been prepared. Note the promise of the Holy Spirit in 10.15 as our witness (cf. Acts 5.32, John 15.26f., I John 5.6–12). Hence the doctrine of the Spirit 'may have held a more prominent place in the author's thought than we are allowed to see' (Flew, *op. cit.*, p. 231).

I Pet.: As before, OT prophets were moved by the Spirit (1.11, 'Spirit of Messiah'; cf. II Pet. 1.21), and Christian preachers were similarly inspired (1.12, 'in holy Spirit'=with the power of the Spirit).

But the whole Church is the sphere of the Spirit's work (1.2; cf. 2.5). Christians are saints, dedicated to God, marked out by the presence of the Spirit, the Holy People of a Holy God (1.15, 2.10). In this conception the Church takes the place of Israel as the Bride of God (cf. Hos. 2.19–23), called by him to this dignity (1.1, 2.4,9, 5.13), the elect race, the royal priesthood, the holy nation, the house of the Spirit (2.5,9). With this compare Isa. 43.20f., Exod. 19.5f., Isa. 61.6, Deut. 7.6ff. True worship is possible in the Church (2.5, 'to offer up spiritual sacrifices'; 2.9, 'shew forth the excellencies' of the electing God; cf. Rom. 12.1, Phil. 3.3, John 4.24, Eph. 5.1f., Jude 20).

This replacement of Israel by the Church and the consequent fulfilment of prophecy, like the consecration of the Spirit, clearly depended on the life, death and resurrection of Jesus Christ (1.2, his death; 1.11, his sufferings; cf. 1.19, 2.21ff., 3.18f., 4.1,13, 5.1; and for resurrection see 1.3,21, 3.18,21f.). The Spirit came as part of the signs that the last day was at hand; Christ will come again and his people will share in his glorious triumph by entering on their heavenly inheritance (1.4–9,13, 2.12, 4.5–7,13f., 5.10; esp. 4.14 for the Spirit). Hence the faithful who have been regenerated (1.23) ought to be meek and quiet in spirit (3.4), loving to one another (1.22), growing up in the life of the redeemed (2.2), acting as good citizens (2.11ff.) and in their several spheres (2.18–3.7). Suffering is part of this vocation. But its reward is glorious life, life according to God in Spirit (4.6; cf. 3.18, of the victorious Christ). The Spirit present is the guarantee of life everlasting to those who remain loyal. He is 'the Spirit of God' (4.14).

But the author does not take us farther in understanding the relationship of the Spirit to God the Father and to Jesus Christ, nor in perceiving how the Spirit sanctifies Christians and enables them to display the glorious power of God (see James Moffatt in the *Moffatt Com. ad.* 4.14). We have advanced from the OT conception of the Spirit as the immanent Power of God so far as to relate this to the historic Jesus who is the risen Lord, the Son of God, and to the Church of God which is composed of all who confess that Jesus Christ is Lord. And probably one thing more: that the character of Spirit-led Christians is an imitation of Christ's and as such is acceptable to his Father.

The theologians of the Spirit are Paul and John, to whom we now turn.

VIII. THE PAULINE DOCTRINE

Paul had entered the Christian tradition of faith and life through a remarkable transformation. He had seen the light of God in the risen Christ (II Cor. 4.6); he had been moved out of 'the body of this death' (Rom. 7.24) into 'newness of life' (Rom. 6.4). And all was due to the gracious activity of the eternal God (cf. I Cor. 1.27–9, 2.6f., II Cor 5.18). What had happened and what continued in the believer he interprets in terms of God or Christ or the Spirit.

(*a*) Supernatural, divine power had been exercised in the Christ who was crucified and is alive again; the same power was effective in the Apostle (II Cor. 13.4) for all his ministry (I Thess. 1.5, Rom. 15.18f., I Cor. 2.4, 4.20f., II Cor. 6.6f.). He coveted this for his converts and found it being realized in a congregation (Rom. 15.13; cf. Eph. 3.16; and I Cor. 12.10,28f., 'powers'; RV, 'miracles' or 'workers of miracles'). In this Paul is at one with the first community established at Pentecost. He had seen demonstrations of the Spirit's power, signs and wonders on the mission field. God in Christ had been mightily at work to renew men and women (cf. I Cor. 1.24); thus fulfilling the OT scriptures and promising world-empire for God the King (I Cor. 4.20, Rom. 1.1–5, on which see A. M. Hunter, *Paul and His Predecessors*, pp. 25ff.).

(*b*) This gift of the Spirit came from heaven as an act of God's love (I Thess. 4.8, Gal. 3.5, 4.6, I Cor. 2.10,12, II Cor. 1.22, 5.5; cf. II Thess. 2.13). It was bestowed on all the faithful as the adopted sons of God (Rom. 8.9,14,16f. and Gal. as above) that they might know God's secret purpose of blessing (I Cor. 2.7,10ff.—though converts needed the instruction of an Apostle like Paul before they could fully understand).

More important, the sons of God received the Spirit as the divine pledge of *immortality* (II Cor. 1.22, 5.1–10; cf. Rom. 8.23, Eph. 1.14; and possibly II Thess. 2.13). Christians have 'resurrection-life' (Rom. 6.11), life in the Spirit (Rom. 8.2,10f.); and this will be perfected in the resurrection of the dead (Rom. 8.23, I Cor. 15.20–3,43f. [note, 'a spiritual body', a new organism]; cf. Phil. 1.21ff., 3.9–11, Col. 3.1–4). For Christ himself, as the last Adam, had become a life-giving Spirit (I Cor. 15.45).

(*c*) Accordingly, Paul holds that it is essential for Christian individuals to be holy in life, in character. God called them for 'sanctification' (I Thess. 4.3,7f.). Their new nature is quite different. Though they remain creatures of flesh and blood, intelligent beings, now they are 'spiritual' (*pneumatikoi*; Gal. 6.1, I Cor. 2.15, 3.1, 14.37). At several places this adjective almost certainly has the work of the Holy Spirit in view (Rom. 1.11, 7.14, 15.27, I Cor. 2.13, 9.11, Col. 1.9, 3.16; cf. Eph. 1.3, 5.19). So close is the believer's relationship of love to Christ that his bodily organs are 'members of Christ' and they become, as in a sacred marriage, 'one Spirit' (I Cor. 6.15–17). Or, the body of the Christian is a temple of the Holy Spirit who dwells within (I Cor. 6.19). The new personality is one intended to be wholly governed by the divine Life and its purposes —the Life known in Christ and sustained by the incoming Spirit (I Cor. 2.16, 7.40, Rom. 8.27, 12.2). By contrast, the unredeemed man lives 'according to flesh' (Rom. 8.4) and is ruled by a sinful tendency. The end of such a life can only be that 'death' which is the penalty of opposition to God (Rom. 8.6ff., Gal. 5.16–21)—that is, he cannot inherit God's Kingdom. (In I Cor. 7.34 and II Cor. 7.1, Paul seems to use 'spirit'=soul in a non-technical sense.)

The virtues of the sanctified Christian are the harvest of the Spirit co-operating with him as he obeys his Lord (cf. Phil. 2.12f.). Gal. 5.22 gives a famous list: see also Gal. 6.1 and I Cor. 4.21 (a spirit of meekness), Rom. 8.15,21 (freedom as children; cf. II Cor. 3.17), Rom. 15.30, Col. 1.8 (love). 'Love is the supreme and all-inclusive gift of the Spirit (I Cor. 12.31–13.1). Conformably with the teaching of the Gospels, the objects of such love are God (Rom. 8.28) and our neighbour (13.8–9); but it is upon the latter that the emphasis falls. . . .' (C. H. Dodd, *Moffatt Com.* on Rom., p. 197). 'The love of God hath been shed abroad in our hearts through the Holy Ghost which was given unto us' (Rom. 5.5). This is one of the central notes in the Pauline ethic and should be used to illuminate all other passages in the Epistles bearing on the life of the Christian. Note, too, the appeal for a sanctified enthusiasm buttressed by hope, patience, and unselfish devotion to others (Rom. 12.10ff.).

(*d*) The ethic of love leads inevitably to an ethic for the Churchman. Christians form a brotherhood in the Body of Christ; they constitute the Family of God. Similarly, they participate in the Spirit (Phil. 2.1). From the divine side the Holy Spirit fashions a community (II Cor. 13.14: here the 'participation' in the Spirit, which is the correct linguistic usage, almost certainly involves the idea of fellowship between the partners). It follows that Christian virtues are ecclesiastical too. Love means 'love of the brethren' (Rom. 12.10, I Thess. 4.9); and the converts or associates of Paul are his 'beloved'.

(*e*) THE GIFTS (*Charismata*). The marks of the Spirit's activity in the Church include the *mighty signs* wrought through the Apostle (Rom. 15.18f., II Cor. 12.12, Col. 1.29); but also the *ecstasies* of believers (II Cor. 12.1–7, I Cor. 12.10,28–31, 13.1f.,8, 14, *passim*), and *prophecy* (I Cor. 12.10, 13.2,8, 14.6,22, I Thess. 5.19f.). In I Cor. 12–14 Paul is wrestling with the dangers of the marvellous elements in Spirit-possession and pleading that the good of the Church is of primary importance. He insists, for example, that intelligent prophesying does edify the Church, because through it the influence of the Spirit is brought to bear on human lives. Yet the Apostle does not attempt to quench the *Glossolalia* (Speaking with Tongues—a kind of inspired gibberish); they were too unpredictable, and besides they did give evidence of divine power in the inspired Christian. Here is a fact which marks out the Church as the true People of God, the 'Israel' of the last days (Gal. 4.4,26,28ff., 6.15f.), the 'Seed of Abraham' (Gal. 3.14,16ff., Rom. 9.6ff.,29f.; cf. 4.13ff., 11.1, II Cor. 11.22, Heb. 2.16, John 8.31ff.), set free from the Law and reconciled to God through faith in him who raised Jesus from the dead (Rom. 10.9). True circumcision is 'in Spirit', not 'in letter'; it is inward, of the heart (Rom. 2.29; in fulfilment of Deut. 10.16, Jer. 4.4; cf. Mark 7.5ff.). This true People worships God 'in Spirit', united to the Christ who died and rose again (Phil. 3.3,8–11); consecrated in the New Covenant, which the Lord's Supper recalls (I Cor. 10.16ff., note 'Israel after the flesh', 11.25, II Cor. 3.6–18). A new spiritual order has arrived, putting out of court the Jewish legalism of scribe and Pharisee and providing the one clue to the meaning of the OT. For the Church reflects the glory of its Lord, who has taken the place of the *Shekinah* or Presence of God in the former dispensation (cf. John 1.14 and the Seven Signs of that Gospel; on II Cor. 3–4 consult R. H. Strachan's commentary in the Moffatt series). Hence a congregation, as an *ecclesiola in Ecclesia* may be called a Temple of God in which the Spirit dwells (I Cor. 3.16f.; cf. John 2.21, Eph. 2.11–22, I Pet. 2.5ff.).

Membership in the Church is dependent on the influence of the Spirit (I Cor. 12.3; perhaps referring to an ecstatic cry during service), among whose gifts faith is listed (I Cor. 12.9, 13.2—faith to do anything because it is faith in God, Mark 11.23; cf. Eph. 2.8). And the sacrament of Baptism, the natural result of a man's response to the Gospel, means being plunged into the new 'atmosphere' of the Spirit; the longing for real life in fellowship with God is satisfied because the Spirit quenches one's thirst (I Cor. 12.13, Rom. 6.3ff. with 8.2ff.; cf. John 7.37–9).

The constitution of the Church as a society of which the 'life-blood' is the Spirit of Christ leads to the ideal of unity, but a unity in diversity (I Cor. 12.4–13); and this unity may be called the Body of Christ; it is a single organism set in the world as a visible sign of its Lord's glory. God through the immanent Spirit appoints members to fulfil certain duties in the Church (I Cor. 12.14–30); but there is no legalistic hierarchy of officials (despite the unique place of the Apostles as the eye-witnesses of the resurrection and the inevitably strong moral authority of a founder of Churches like St. Paul; contrast the tone of the 'painful letter', II Cor. 10–13, with the one that follows, II Cor. 1–9).

Notice also that praise and prayer are 'inspired' (I Cor. 14.15, Col. 3.16, Eph. 5.19), but more valuable is intelligent utterance of the enthusiastic faith. Paul is realistic enough to see that Christians may not find this easy; for many of them are more carnal than spiritual. After all, it is only an 'instalment' they have received—the 'earnest of the Spirit' —and they must grow in wisdom. Even prayer may be difficult, but the Spirit comes to their aid as Intercessor (Rom. 8.26; cf. 34, Christ is the Intercessor). Christians are holy, but by no means perfect. They wait with patience for the glory that is to be. They must therefore pray without ceasing . . . and not quench the Spirit (I Thess. 5.17–19); for the Spirit is divine in love, in meekness, in patience. The character of the Spirit is the character of Christ. This explains both the idealism and realism of St. Paul; besides allowing us to find in offences against the Spirit of love a reason for low periods in the history of the Church (cf. Gal. 5.16–25, 6.7–9). Christians are washed, consecrated, justified 'in the name of the Lord Jesus Christ, and in the Spirit of our God' (I Cor. 6.11)—let them become what they are!

(*f*) From all that has gone before it is clear that Paul ascribed personal activity to the Holy Spirit, though he does speak otherwise from time to time. The Spirit reveals . . . indwells . . . helps . . . witnesses . . . works and divides (I Cor. 2.10ff., 3.16, Rom. 8.16,26, I Cor. 12.11). God searching the heart knows 'the mind of the Spirit' (Rom. 8.27); but the Spirit searches the deep things of God (I Cor. 2.10). Paul can speak indifferently of the Spirit of Jesus Christ, of Christ, of God's Son, of God, or of the living God (Phil. 1.19, Rom. 8.9,14, Gal. 4.6, II Cor. 3.3; cf. Rom. 8.11). This rich thought has been prompted by real events in religious experience: visions, speaking with tongues, heroic faith, a new, sacrificial love, graces of Christian life, chastity, absolute certainty of confidence in God the Father and a living communion with Jesus Christ. The Spirit as immanent deity and as equivalent to divine Wisdom, the Spirit that spoke in the prophets, is now for Paul to be equated with new powers that flowed from the resurrection of Christ and transformed believers. Only God can know God as the Spirit does according to the Pauline epistles. But the Spirit, like God himself, is revealed in Jesus Christ; so that Paul can write, 'the Lord is the Spirit' (II Cor. 3.17). Religiously they are one, for Lord (*Kyrios*) is in fact the all-excelling Name bestowed on the Risen Christ (Phil. 2.11)—and *Kyrios* is the OT Name for God. (Here we go a step farther than Bishop Rawlinson, whose exegesis seems to be correct: *The New Testament Doctrine of the Christ*, p. 155, n. 6.) Spirit is to the divine life what blood is to physical human life, essential for activity, thought, and personal relationships. It is 'a continuously vitalizing and energizing force, to which the Apostle assigns the attributes of personality because the effects of its presence correspond so widely and so closely to what was known of the self-consciousness and self-direction of Christ' (C. A. Anderson Scott, *Christianity according to St. Paul*, p. 173). Paul does not go beyond this to state explicitly what is involved for a Christian theism. He does not, for example, attempt a modalist doctrine: that at one stage man knows the deity as Father, at another as Son in Jesus Christ, at yet a third as Holy Spirit. A chapter like Rom. 8 shows that his apparently trinitarian conceptions of God are held simultaneously; but he has not worked out an articulated idea of the eternal Son and the eternal Spirit united in the Godhead equally with the eternal Father. Indeed, so far as the evidence goes, we cannot be sure that he would have spoken of 'equality' at all.

(*g*) *Ephesians*. A word should be added about this epistle, which the present writer considers non-Pauline. By contrast with Colossians, its companion, Ephesians has many references to the Spirit; actually inserting some in places where the parallel to Colossians is otherwise very close; e.g. Eph. 3.16 (power through his Spirit in the inward man), and 6.18 (praying at all seasons in the Spirit); similarly at 1.3, 2.18, 4.30, 5.18, 6.17, we have an original emphasis on the work of the Spirit or on the spiritual status of Christians.

Eph. 1–3 reads like a *Eucharistic meditation* in adoration of God who chose us in Christ and sealed us with the Holy Spirit for final salvation (1.3–14): thanksgiving and a prayer for spiritual enlightenment (1.15–23), followed by a note on the divine mercy in redemption (2.1–10) and a great passage describing the Church as the Commonwealth of God's Israel, the Body of Christ, and the Temple of the Spirit (2.11–22; it is also an Apostolic society). 3.1–13 speaks of the mystery of Universalism revealed by the Spirit, and the first half closes with a prayer for (*a*) the power of the Spirit and (*b*) the power of Christ dwelling within Christians in love (3.14–19); then comes a Doxology (3.20f.).

The second part might be headed: '*Be filled with the Spirit.*' 4.1–16 enlarges magnificently on the unity of the Spirit in the growing Church, the Body of Christ. 4.17–5.20 describes what it means to put off the 'old man' and be 'renewed in the spirit of [one's] mind', so as not to grieve the Holy Spirit. After a section on the positive duties of the Churchman and the Churchwoman (5.21–6.9, a section containing the idea of the Church as the Bride of Christ), we have a noble passage on the spiritual warfare of the Christian (6.10–20), and the rather lame ending (6.21–4).

Here is magnificence and grandeur in the language of the liturgy and in the hope of the Church's perfection as the 'fullness' of the Lord, his necessary completion, his Bride! Churchmanship, as ideally at Pentecost, is an 'intoxication' in the Spirit with power and love and faith—and the fullness of very God, to whom be glory.

IX. THE JOHANNINE DOCTRINE

(*a*) Jesus, the Word made flesh, is the one upon whom the Spirit rested and remained (John 1.32f.). He has received the Spirit not 'by measure' (John 3.34); that is, God has endowed him with completeness of spiritual insight and power as his Son and as the King of Israel. There is an implied contrast with the earlier prophetic revelation and with John the Baptist. Hence Jesus speaks 'the words of God' (John 3.34); his words are 'spirit and life' (John 6.63), for in him men face the Word of God incarnate, the life-giver (John 6.35,39f., 48–51), the one who baptizes with Holy Spirit (John 1.33, 20.22). This is a sign that God's New Age has come in Jesus (cf. Acts 2.17).

(*b*) Christians are those who have experienced rebirth, the birth of the Spirit (John 3.5–8); cf. John 1.12f., those who believe on the Name of Jesus Christ become children of God: they are born of God (cf. I John 3.1f.,14,23f., 4.13–15, and 3.9, 'his seed abideth in him'—the child of God has received a new life-principle). If the reference to water be correct in the text of John 3.5, there is probably an allusion to Baptism—but to Baptism less as an ecclesiastical rite, the conventional entrance to the Church. Rather the Evangelist is in the tradition of Paul (I Cor. 12.13) and Ezekiel (36.25–7: 'I will sprinkle clean water upon you . . . a new heart also will I give you, and a new spirit will I put within you . . . my spirit'; cf. John 13.1–11, 15.2f.). Something supernatural (John 3.3) must happen to them—and it cannot be automatically induced (John 3.7f., the wind is a symbol of the Spirit; indeed, in Greek the same word means both).

As such they have communion with God (I John 3.24, 4.13). Their fellowship is with the Father and his Son (I John 1.3) and they possess 'an anointing from the Holy One' (I John 2.20), probably the gift of the Spirit (but see C. H. Dodd in the *Moffatt Com. ad. loc.*). They worship 'in spirit and in truth' (John 4.23), not in one place (cf. H. H. Wendt, *The Teaching of Jesus*, I, p. 287). It is the offering made by those who here and now possess eternal life, which consists in the knowledge of the true God and his Son, Jesus Christ (John 17.3). 'In truth' therefore means 'with an awareness of the reality of the Father revealed in the grace and truth of Jesus Christ'. The final revelation has come, and worship is transformed as a result. External form is of less significance than spiritual devotion and likeness to God (as being his children). 'A formal act of worship, however sacred in itself, "profiteth nothing", and may even be a positive power for evil' (E. F. Scott, *The Fourth Gospel*, p. 127; cf. John 6.63, Isa. 58.5–7). Worship must be seen in the context of love for the brethren (John 15.13, I John 2.10, 3.11, 16–18, 4.21); but also of orthodoxy (John 17.3, I John 2.18,22f., 4.2–6, 5.5–12). If the former is to have weight, it must be œcumenical; if the latter is stressed aright, it must be centred in the historic faith in the Christ who was incarnate and who rose from the dead. But that puts the Gospels and the Apostolic testimony in the Epistles at the very centre of worship. (The OT has its place too, as the *Kerygma* proves.) All the more is John's emphasis on the Spirit required, lest the Book introduce legalism and credal forms without life (see John 14.26, 15.26f.). By the living testimony of the Spirit of truth the Gospel tradition comes alive in new generations. The Church at worship and in its work must bear witness to Christ. Probably it is through the Church that the Spirit brings the world (the organized system of evil and indifference) face to face with judgment, sin, and righteousness (John 16.8–11; cf. I Cor. 14.22–5); and it is through the Church because it appears in history as the fruit of God's mighty act in the resurrection of Jesus (John 16.10). The Church is the community of believers, whereas the world attacks both Jesus and his friends (John 16.9; cf. 16.33, 17.13–26);

the Church is submissive to its King, the world to its Prince who is condemned because of the victory Jesus wins by suffering and glorification (John 16.11, 13.11ff., 17.1f.; cf. 3.19–21, I John 2.8,15–17, 3.8–10,13f.).

(*c*) As in Paul, it is God the Eternal who 'gives' the Spirit (John 3.34, 14.16, 15.26). But John goes so far as to say that Spirit may be predicated of God's nature: John 4.24, 'God is Spirit'. This is the reason why in Christianity 'the particularism of *place*, the particularism of *race*, and the particularism of *book*' are transcended. (See C. J. Wright in *The Mission and Message of Jesus*, H. D. A. Major, T. W. Manson and C. J. Wright, p. 748.) Spirit is as good a term as John can find to express what God the Father is like essentially; and as such he is the Truth and he is Love. In all these aspects of his being he is revealed in Jesus Christ: 'grace and truth' dwell gloriously in Christ (John 1.14); and the love of God is declared in Christ's glorious death (John 3.13–16, I John 3.16, 4.7–10,14,16). To this revelation the Spirit, who comes after Jesus is glorified (John 7.39), bears witness (I John 5.7–10, John 15.26, 16.14). Accordingly he is the Spirit of truth (John 14.17, 15.26, 16.13; cf. I John 2.27, 5.7); and the love that Christians must manifest as those who live in communion with the Father and the Son is a fruit of the Spirit who abides in them (an inference from I John 3.24, 4.13, John 14.15f.; cf. John 17.26, the love of the Father for the Church means Christ's presence in them, and that presence is realized by the coming of the Spirit, John 14.18). It is also implied in this 'God is Spirit' that God is active in the world like the wind (cf. John 3.8), unseen, but not unknown. He 'is not a mere immanent principle in the world he has made, and . . . he is not aloof from the affairs of earth or the needs of men' (R. H. Strachan, *The Fourth Gospel* (1941), p. 156).

If all this defines God in spiritual terms, does it not also define the Spirit as divine? John proceeds to use the personal pronoun (John 14.16f., 'that he may be with you for ever . . . he abideth'; 26, 'he shall teach you'; 15.26, 'he shall bear witness'; 16.7, 'I will send him'; 16.8,13f., 'he will convict the world . . . He shall guide you . . . He shall glorify me'). And he uses a personal name for the Spirit; namely:

(*d*) *The Paraclete* (RV, COMFORTER, 14.16,26, 15.26, 16.7; cf. ADVOCATE, I John 2.1). The verb from which this noun is derived means in class. Gk. 'to call to one's aid', and the noun therefore may be translated as Advocate or Intercessor. In the LXX the verb is common in Second Isaiah to signify the encouragement or restoration to new life of Israel (cf. Isa. 40.1, 51.3,12); but it may also denote exhortation to a change of mind, sometimes to godly sorrow or repentance. In the NT the verb means to exhort or to summon. 'Paraclete' in I John obviously should be trans. 'Advocate'; but this scarcely fits the Gospel passages. As indicated earlier, John 14.26f. and 15.26f. may be compared with Mark 13.11 and pars.: the disciples in the world will have peace and will bear their witness despite tribulation (see also John 16.33, peace in Christ; and 14.18, to have the Spirit is to be in Christ). But the office of the Spirit is to 'bring to . . . remembrance' all that Jesus has said to his friends, the disciples (John 14.26, 16.14), and to 'guide . . . into all the truth' (John 16.13). Thus the Spirit is both Champion and Teacher of the Church, taking up the same office that the incarnate Lord had discharged. He vindicates the Christian community precisely because he brings the living presence of Christ himself. 'The fulfilment of the promise takes place after the Resurrection, and *is* the Resurrection in their experience' (R. H. Strachan, *op. cit.*, p. 286). In relation to the world outside the Church, the Paraclete is a Judge. Professor N. H. Snaith sums up an important discussion of the meaning of Paraclete by rendering it, for the Gospel, as ' "Convincer", i.e. He who convinces men of the things of God, and accomplishes in them a change of heart'. The idea of comfort is not involved in John 14.18, for the Gk. means 'orphans' (RV margin) (*Expository Times*, Vol. LVII, No. 2 (Nov., 1945), pp. 47ff.). In I John 2.1 the Advocate is Jesus Christ the righteous one; he is the Intercessor with the Father on behalf of Christians who commit acts of sin (see the valuable exposition by C. H. Dodd, the *Moffatt Com.* on the Johannine Epistles, pp. 24f.).

(*e*) One of the main themes of I John is that denial of the Incarnation is proof that Antichrist (the spirit of evil) is at work. Against this the author (whom one supposes to be also the writer of the Fourth Gospel) sets the Apostolic tradition and the witness of the Holy Spirit as the Spirit of Truth (2.22, 3.23f., 4.1–6, 5.7f.; cf. II John 7,9).

(*f*) It has been remarked that in John 14–16 we find five sayings about the Spirit as the Paraclete and that they form a unity. But they look like insertions into the Farewell Discourses and raise the question of what reliance can be placed on them as expressing Christ's own teaching. A most helpful examination of this question will be found in W. F. Howard, *Christianity according to St. John*, pp. 72ff., 122ff. We have seen that there is some important evidence in the Synoptic Gospels for Jesus' teaching on the Spirit, and that what is said there illuminates the Johannine doctrine.

Yet the latter is also the fruit of the Church's experience in the first two generations after the resurrection. Hence in John the Spirit proceeds from the Father, but is also the *alter ego* of Jesus Christ and in a sense takes Jesus' place. The five sayings therefore fit integrally into their context, 'for they form part of the eschatological hope. It is because of the sure and certain hope which is represented by the Parousia that a present union with Christ in the Spirit is possible. The work of the Spirit . . . is a continuation of the ministry of the incarnate Word' (Howard, *op. cit.*, p. 123). In this way the Johannine doctrine liberates and enriches the Apostolic tradition of God's 'Kingdome Come' whilst still proclaiming a 'last hour' and a 'last day' (I John 2.18, John 6.39f., 44,54). Such an hour is a time when the whole foundation of Christianity is at stake. John is not concerned with mere orthodoxy. 'For the Church . . . heresy is more deadly than hypocrisy, or even than conscious sin' (W. Temple, *Readings in St. John's Gospel*, p. 38). Such a last day is 'the *decisive* day, the *culminating* day, the day when the sifting is complete'. The Fourth Evangelist 'is thinking of the *resurrecting spiritual Ministry* of Jesus: this life of which Jesus was the incarnate vehicle is the means to the complete entrance to Eternal life' (C. J. Wright, *op. cit.*, p. 772). Christians have already passed from death into real life, have communion with the Father and the Son, are indwelt by the Spirit—nevertheless live in the not-yet. The end is not, till they are both 'not of the world' and 'not in the world'. Temporal language has to be used for the expression of timeless realities. Hence Howard rightly says: the Spirit 'was more than the pledge and foretaste of the future Kingdom. Though with St. John we are still in the predogmatic stage of the Trinitarian teaching, the sayings about the Paraclete carry us a degree farther than any other writing in the development of the New Testament doctrine of the Godhead' (*op. cit.*, p. 80).

(*g*) The doctrine that is implied about the Church as the society of those who are really alive may be summed up briefly as follows:

The eternal Spirit 'becomes' the other Paraclete when Christ departs from his disciples; and these disciples become the Apostolic Church when the glorified Christ imparts to them the gifts of the Spirit (John 20.19–23: as the Father has sent me as his Apostle, even so I send you as my Apostles to declare the Gospel of judgment on sin and of forgiveness for sin). Alternatively, the Father 'sends' the Spirit and the disciples become his Family. As the Word became flesh in the man Jesus, so the Spirit is incarnated in the Church that adores the Risen Lord, the Saviour of the world.

X. CONCLUSION

We noted earlier that the Primitive Preaching included the effusion of the Holy Spirit as one of the great consequences of the life, death and resurrection of Jesus. This note has been sounded throughout the NT teaching on the Spirit and his work. This means that for the NT as a whole the Church is a distinctive, indeed a unique society:

(*a*) *It shares a new and common life* (cf. II Cor. 3.6, Rom. 8, John 6.63).

(*b*) *It shares a new and common love* (Gal. 5.22, Col. 1.8, Rom. 13.8, Heb. 13.1, II Pet. 1.7). A similar thought pervades the chapter on the Vine in John 15 (cf. I John 4.7–13).

(*c*) *It must therefore be one*. This is an implication of theology, but is made a reality by the Spirit; so that Ephesians can sum it up as 'the unity of the Spirit . . . There is one body, and one Spirit' (4.3f.).

(*d*) *It is Apostolic, yet is served by a charismatic ministry* (Acts 1.8, 5.32, I Cor. 12.28ff., Eph. 4.11ff.). In II Tim. 1.14 and the Pastorals generally the charismatic element (the endowment of the Spirit of the living Christ for office) is giving way to a more formal appointment under an episcopal system in the first half of the 2nd cent.

And all this is possible because God has fulfilled his promises and Christ his: the life-energy of the Eternal has flowed into the lives of the believers. That is the meaning of the power of the Spirit. By this men and women become reconciled to God and are made new creatures (I Cor. 12.3, John 3.6, II Cor. 5.17). By it virtue grows in the redeemed personality (Gal. 5.22), the virtue of humanity as God longs for it to be (cf. Gal. 3.28; F. J. A. Hort, *The Christian Ecclesia*, pp. 228f.). The ethic of the Spirit follows inevitably from the faith in the Spirit. Another result of the Spirit's presence is the missionary movement of the Church as an essential activity of its life (Acts 1.8, 5.32, John 15.27). Power, life, glory, joy—these are the characteristic marks of the Holy Spirit's influence. But of course there is no magical endowment of Christians, for their God is the One known as Father, as Creator, as Righteous Saviour. They must make a personal response to the God Christ reveals and, as they do, they know that God grants them powers of his Spirit to accomplish with him his saving purpose for the world. In the possession of these powers, the *charismata* of grace, they acknowledge the Spirit as the Paraclete, the Spirit who is very God. (Also *v*. MIND.)

BIBLIOGRAPHY

F. W. Dillistone: *The Holy Spirit in the Life of To-day*, London (1946). R. Birch Hoyle: *The Holy Spirit in St. Paul*, London (1927).

A. L. Humphries: *The Holy Spirit in Faith and Experience*, London (1917). H. Wheeler Robinson: *The Christian Experience of the Holy Spirit*, London (1928). E. F. Scott: *The Spirit in the New Testament*, London (1923). N. H. Snaith: *The Doctrine of the Holy Spirit* (Heading Lectures), London (1937). H. B. Swete: *The Holy Spirit in the New Testament*, London (1909). L. S. Thornton: *The Common Life in the Body of Christ*, London (1942). C. Williams: *The Descent of the Dove*, London (1939). E. W. Winstanley: *Spirit in the New Testament*, Cambridge (1908).

GEORGE JOHNSTON

STATUTE, ORDINANCE

The principle governing the use of these words for translating the technical terms for positive legal enactments in Heb. and Gk. is by no means clear. The difficulty arises within the Bible itself, where the varying practice of the LXX translators has affected NT usage. It is not even clear that the term commandment (*q.v.*) should always be given a meaning decisively different from these other terms.

In the OT, the RV has tended to replace the use of ordinance in the AV by statute wherever possible. The constituent element in Heb. law which the terms indicate may perhaps be described as *permanently valid declarations of what is right*. This element is distinguishable, on the one hand from the positive Commandments, and on the other hand from the judgments which arise out of particular cases and which may or may not become an element in the law of the community. It is significant that the term statute (ordinance) is most often applied to the enactments which regulate the cult. Social conduct, it is suggested, should be regulated in a more flexible manner, by judgments. But as the Heb. for this (*mishpat*) is often rendered in the LXX by *dikaiōma*—one of the two equally common 'statute' words—this point should not be pressed very far. The use of the words does however seem to be bound up with the conviction that the form of man's religious duties has been prescribed once for all in clear-cut terms. Further, the Gk. usage suggests that the terms carried no conscious reference to an author of the statute, whereas the terms translated commandment did. Obedience to a statute or ordinance was not obedience to a person.

This may help to explain the NT use of *dogma*, a word properly translated as ordinance. It is used of imperial decrees, and of the ordinances decreed by the Apostles and Elders in Jerusalem (Acts 17.7 and 16.4). In Eph. 2.15 and Col. 2.14, Paul uses it in a careful definition of the law of Judaism, 'the law of commandments in ordinances', 'the bond which was against us by its ordinances'. Statutes and ordinances, by their very nature, give only an ambiguous testimony to the command of God. (*V.* also COMMAND, JUDGE, LAW.)

W. A. WHITEHOUSE

STONE *v.* CORNER-STONE, ROCK

STRAITEN *v.* SUFFER

STRENGTH *v.* MIGHT, ROCK

STRIFE *v.* STRIVE

STRIVE, STRIFE, VIOLENT, VIOLENCE

A. In the ordinary sense of conflict between individuals or peoples (Exod. 2.13, Judg. 12.2); of turmoil within a people (II Sam. 19.9). Violence as overpowering force (Gen. 21.25, Acts 21.35).

B. In relation to the biblical conception of peace (*q.v.*), which is 'the most comprehensive denomination of happiness as it designates healthy development in all forms, both of harmony within the covenant and of all progress in life' (Pedersen), strife is the greatest of evils, especially between brethren (Gen. 13.8), friends (Ps. 55.9ff.), those within the covenant (Amos 1.9). The 'enemies' of the Psalms are often men of strife whose weapon is the tongue (Ps. 31.20, 35.1, etc.); the man who causes strife, generally verbal, is a particular danger to the community (Prov. *passim*). It is especially grievous for the prophet to be compelled by his calling to be a man of strife (Jer. 15.10), and for the nation to be an object of contention (Ps. 80.6). The prophets condemn Jerusalem as full of strife (Isa. 1.21—also called 'breaches', Jer. 14.17); widespread strife is a reproach to Jehovah (Hab. 1.3).

Strife is the chief enemy of the community of Christ's disciples, and proceeds from the centrality of the self, and the worldliness which identifies greatness with power and superiority, in contrast to the self-giving and service of the life of the Son of Man (Luke 22.24–7, Mark 9.33–7, 10.35–45, 8.34). It is characteristic of the life of the world (Rom. 1.29), of the flesh (Rom. 13.13, I Cor. 3.3, Gal. 5.20), and it destroys the life of the Church (I Cor. 1–4, II Cor. 12.20, Phil. 2.3; cf. John 17.20ff.), having its root in the envy and jealousy which betray a divided self (Jas. 3.14–4.2). It will manifest itself in the latter days in verbal disputes of false teachers (I Tim. 6.4, II Tim. 2.23, Tit. 3.9).

Also of striving with God by doubting his power and putting it to the test (Isa. 45.9, Job 33.13) as at Meribah (Num. 27.14; cf. Deut.

33.8 for a variant tradition); of acting against his will (Jer. 50.24; cf. Acts 5.39).

Closely connected with strife is violence, a breach in the community and of the covenant, which is regarded with abhorrence as displaying the very nature of sin (Gen. 6.11, Ps. 73.6, Prov. 16.28f., Ezek. 18.7ff.); a synonym for wickedness and falsehood, for the deviation from what is straight and true (Ps. 11.5, 58.2, Prov. 4.17), which thrives on social discord (Isa. 59.6, Jer. 6.7, Ezek. 7.23), is manifested in the oppression of the poor by the rich and mighty (Amos. 3.10, Mic. 6.12, Jer. 22.17, Zeph. 1.9) and in the cruelty of extortion (Luke 3.14) and of the nation which executes the Lord's judgment (Hab. 1.9). Violent death is an evil (Jer. 34.4f.). Jehovah as saviour delivers from violence (II Sam. 22.3, Ps. 72.14); absence of violence will be characteristic of the new Jerusalem (Isa. 60.18, Ezek. 45.9). The Servant of the Lord is to perform his redeeming work without violence (Isa. 42.3, 53.9). Only in Matt. 11.12 (Luke 16.16) is violence used in a good sense of those who answer such demands as 'if thine eye offend thee pluck it out', and who stop at nothing in the way of self-sacrifice to gain the kingdom of God.

To strive is used metaphorically in the hellenistic books of the OT (Wisd. 4.2, 10.12) and in the NT of the effort needed to attain the spiritual goal (Luke 13.24), of prayer (Rom. 15.30), self-discipline and suffering (I Cor. 9.24ff., II Tim. 2.5, Phil. 1.30, Heb. 12.4, I Tim. 4.10), in which all are of one mind (Phil. 1.27) and the strength is supplied by Christ (Col. 1.29ff.). (*V.* also WAR, PEACE.)

C. F. EVANS

STUMBLING-BLOCK

This word occurs 8 times in the OT (twice in the plural) and 5 times in the NT. The Heb. word so translated is derived directly from a verb meaning 'to stumble', and so means 'what causes one to stumble'. It is used literally in Lev. 19.14, 'Thou shalt not . . . put a stumbling-block before the blind', figuratively in Jer. 6.21. In Ps. 119.165, where the literal translation is, 'There is not for them a stumbling-block', the AV has, 'Nothing shall offend them', and the RV, 'They have none occasion of stumbling'. In Ezekiel, in which the word occurs 8 times (twice oftener than in all the rest of the OT), idols are called 'the stumbling-block of their [his] iniquity', 14.3,4,7, as is 'their silver and their gold' in 7.19—doubtless partly because idols were made of the silver and the gold; in 44.12 the Levites who 'ministered unto them before their idols' are said to have become 'a stumbling-block of iniquity unto the house of Israel' (so RV; AV paraphrases). In 18.30 the word seems to mean the 'ruin' which results from stumbling; in 21.15 (AV, ruins; RV, stumblings) the Heb. text is probably corrupt.

A very difficult passage in Isaiah speaks of God himself as becoming a stumbling-block to his faithless people: 'He shall be . . . for a stone of stumbling and for a rock of offence to both the houses of Israel, for a gin and for a snare to the inhabitants of Jerusalem', Isa. 8.14. In this figurative use of the words there is no real difference of meaning between 'stone of stumbling', 'rock of offence', 'gin', and 'snare'. Even literally a 'stone of stumbling' and a 'rock of offence' are the same thing, and so are 'gin' and 'snare'. But there is a clear difference between the literal meaning of the first pair and the literal meaning of the second pair of synonyms. Twice in the NT the phrase 'a stone of stumbling and a rock of offence' is quoted and applied to Christ, Rom. 9.32f. and I Pet. 2.8. Here the Gk. for 'offence' (which has the now obsolete sense of 'stumbling') is *skandalon*. But properly *skandalon* means a 'trap' or 'snare'. The word occurs some 15 times altogether in the NT, and in the EVV it is always taken to mean 'stumbling-block', though the actual wording of the translation varies: 'stumbling-block' (3 times), 'occasion of stumbling' (once, I John 2.10), 'occasion to fall' (once, Rom. 14.13), 'offence' (9 times), and 'things that offend' (once, Matt. 13.14). Since it is always used figuratively, it probably makes little difference whether the literal meaning is supposed to be 'stumbling-block' or 'snare'—in the Christian life a hindrance is also a temptation. But it does add to the significance of some passages to remember that for a Gk.-speaking reader *skandalon* would suggest, not simply a hindrance to the doing of what is right, but an enticement to do what is wrong. Thus when Jesus told Peter that he was a *skandalon* to him, Matt. 16.23, he may have meant, 'You are a temptation to me'.

From *skandalon* the verb *skandalizein* is formed; in the NT this is always translated 'to offend', but the meaning is never 'to commit a wrong', and seldom 'to cause resentment to', but 'to cause [one] to commit wrong' (e.g. Matt. 5.29, Mark 9.42, etc.).

J. Y. CAMPBELL

SUFFER, SUFFERING, AFFLICTION, PERSECUTION, TRIBULATION, TROUBLE, WOE

The J narrative traces suffering back to the beginnings of the human race; sorrow is part of the lot of mankind (cf. Gen. 3.16f.). As God is conceived of as the cause of all phenomena, the OT did not shrink from attributing to him the cause of all evil (cf. Amos. 3.6, Isa. 45.7), although evil agents might be immediately responsible.

The simplest view was that suffering, whether apprehended individually, in the form of sickness or poverty, or nationally, in the form of subjection to surrounding peoples (the background to most of the prophetic writing), was of a punitive or retributive character. This view arose from the deep-seated conviction that the universe was ruled by God, and that he gave to men their deserts. The sense of corporate personality was strong throughout most of the pre-exilic period, so that the sinfulness of the nation was seen to be the cause of any national disaster. Ezekiel might protest against the view 'that the fathers have eaten sour grapes, and the children's teeth are set on edge' (Ezek. 18.2), but he none the less applied the principle that sin would bring with it suffering. The prophetic writers saw the judgments of God in history, but also looked beyond history to the full manifestation of the wrath of Jehovah in the day of woe even to those who had seemingly escaped their due retribution.

The problem of suffering presents itself with particular intensity in the Book of JOB. Most commentators suggest that the poem is an examination of the retributive view of suffering, especially as applied in its more individualist forms. Ezekiel had held that 'the soul that sinneth, it shall die' (Ezek. 18.4), and there were those who sought to give the obverse to the classic Deuteronomic statement of reward that the blessings of obedience are prosperity in every department of national life, and that disobedience would lead to defeat, fevers, barrenness and other national and social ills (*v.* Deut. 31, 32, *passim*). It has been pointed out that in a this-worldly ethic 'the idea that divine rewards in retribution are manifested in an outward manner passes rapidly and naturally into the idea that the outward circumstances of life are an index of character' (O. S. Rankin, *Israel's Wisdom Literature*, p. 79). Now, the Book of Job presents Job as the sufferer *par excellence*. Is his suffering, then, an index of his character? There is also another issue at stake. Can man rely on the moral consistency of God? If a man, like Job, is patently righteous, and yet suffers, is this a pointer to the absence of any true equity in the universe? Traditional teaching had asserted that all suffering and misfortune were the visible signs of the wrath of God upon human sin. The logical corollary of this would be that the wicked should be sufferers in some form or another, and the righteous should always enjoy health and prosperity. Experience, however, did not seem to corroborate the theory. As many a psalmist complained, the wicked seemed to prosper, and there was danger that God's servant would go down into Sheol before succour was brought. 'Is God just to let the wicked prosper and the righteous suffer? Can such conduct be reconciled with the righteousness and justice of God?' Such were the questions before the writer of the Book of Job.

In the face of contemporary theory Job protests his innocence. He suffers, but he claims to be no sinner, and so will not accept the arguments of the 'comforters' who uphold the traditional morality. Even Elihu (perhaps a later addition) holds that suffering is linked with transgression: 'And if they be bound in fetters, and be taken in the cords of affliction; then he sheweth them their work, and their transgressions that they have behaved themselves proudly' (Job 36.8,9); but he also suggests that it has a probationary, if not even a redemptive quality: 'He delivereth the afflicted by his affliction' (Job 36.15). (N.B. It is possible that the last verse should be translated as 'in his affliction'—i.e. the affliction is the context rather than the means of divine deliverance).

A different view is given by Professor Stevenson. 'The theme of the poem of Job is the revolt of a suffering, helpless man against a pitiless and all-powerful God. Job has been driven to question the justice and fair dealing of the Almighty. His own unmerited suffering has opened his eyes to the prevailing misgovernment of the world. God does not rule, as he ought, for the benefit of men, still less does he dispense to each the fortune he deserves. Job stands for the human race in his protest against the evils of human life' (W. B. Stevenson, *The Poem of Job*, p. 45). The latter writer holds that Job's suffering was not the result of disease, as is commonly accepted, but that he was enduring injustice at the hands of miscreants. He would argue that none of the comforters expressed the view that all suffering is God's punishment for sin, and 'that misfortunes are always proof of a man's wickedness' (*op. cit.*, p. 38). The standpoint of Eliphaz is that 'men are born to misery as surely as sparks fly high' (Job 5.7). This would suggest the belief that suffering is a part of God's ordering of human existence, and would imply that good and bad alike cannot escape misfortune. The good man, however, could be differentiated from the bad in that he could survive and surmount disaster. The tyrant, says Eliphaz, eventually meets his end, and, accordingly, God cannot be accused of ultimate misgovernment.

The *dénouement* of the poem suggests that the events of life are subject to the control of a divine intelligence which man, with his natural limitations, is not always able to perceive: 'Who is this that darkeneth counsel by words without knowledge? . . . Where wast thou when I laid the foundations of the earth? Declare, if thou hast understanding' (Job 38.2,4). Moreover, it is no mechanical force which is immanent in nature, but rather an interested, personal being, who can be trusted as the ultimate guarantor of reward and retribution. Such a God will be able to vindicate his servant. Although there is no kinsman to act as Job's avenger (Heb. *Go'el*), yet at the last assize God will be there to speak for Job, proclaiming his innocence: 'But I know that my redeemer [RV marg. reads 'vindicator'] liveth, and that he shall stand up at the last upon the earth' (Job 19.25). For many there could be no other attitude than a sincere agnosticism, coupled with the conviction that all would be clear, when Jehovah revealed his final judgments. As Professor Rankin puts it: 'A man's good and evil deeds might not be observed to bear appropriate fruit in his lifetime, but Jahve would bring them to light in his descendants with whom his personal life was bound up' (*Israel's Wisdom Literature*, p. 81).

The prose sections (i.e. prologue and epilogue) of the Book of Job seem to take the standpoint that suffering can be probationary. Job's integrity is being tested to see whether his obedience to God is self-interested or not. Once the test has been made, due restitution is made by God, thus corroborating in the end the traditional doctrine of rewards. (A probationary view of suffering appears in Judg. 2.22–3.6, where the Israelites are beset by the surrounding nations 'that by them I may prove Israel, whether they will keep the way of the Lord to walk therein, as their fathers did keep it, or not'; cf. Hab. 2.4: 'The just shall live in his faithfulness' (RV marg.), where the interpretation seems to be that the Chaldean menace cannot be immediately averted, but endurance in the face of tribulation will bring ultimate deliverance. In the case of the Suffering Servant, there is a sense in which his reward will be the greater because of his service in the midst of affliction (Isa. 53.10–12).)

The Psalter reflects a mixed attitude to the problem of suffering. Most of the writers would accept the traditional belief which linked sin and suffering directly, although experience made a strict adherence difficult; e.g. Ps. 1 depicts the blessedness attendant upon the man who meditates upon the law; the lot of the ungodly is contrasted with his: 'The wicked are not so; but are like the chaff which the wind driveth away' (vs. 4). The sum of conduct is that 'the Lord knoweth the way of the righteous: but the way of the wicked shall perish' (vs. 6); and cf. the certitude of the prosperity of the righteous in Ps. 15: 'He that doeth these things shall never be moved' (vs. 5). Some psalmists, however, have a more pessimistic view of life, which arises out of a realistic approach to suffering, e.g. Ps. 39, where the writer pleads with God to 'remove thy stroke away from me': 'I am consumed', he cries, 'by the blow of thine hand' (vs. 10). The wicked are prosperous and the godly are in adversity, but man is too insignificant a thing to worry about. One must either be resigned to one's lot or plead for a respite 'before I go hence, and be no more' (vs. 13). Another interpretation of the same type of experience is that the prosperity of the wicked is merely apparent or, at most, of short duration; it is the well-being of the righteous which continues and abides permanently: 'Mark the perfect man, and behold the upright: for the latter end of that man is peace. As for the transgressors, they shall be destroyed together: the latter end of the wicked shall be cut off. But the salvation of the righteous is of the Lord: he is their stronghold in the time of trouble' (Ps. 37.37–9); cf. Wisd. 3.1–6, where the ungodly, who had taunted the righteous so confidently, are troubled with terrible fear, and acknowledge their error. The righteous have been through the test and have been found worthy in the midst of trouble and persecution, and their souls are accordingly in the hand of God. In Ps. 49 the ungodly receive their just deserts in Sheol, but the righteous are received by God: 'God will redeem my soul from the power of Sheol: for he shall receive me' (vs. 15). There is a hint that in the world to come the incongruities of this world will be put right. Present existence is but an incomplete episode, and so seeming inequalities will not be fully resolved in this life.

It was the consciousness of affliction which evoked in Israel the yearning for deliverance, and also enabled the prophetic and priestly writers to perceive deliverances experienced as the saving acts of God. The affliction in Egypt leads to the deliverance of the Exodus. The 'bread of adversity and the waters of affliction' (Isa. 30.20) are the prelude to the joyfulness of deliverance (cf. the phrase used in the service for the Passover in the Jewish Prayer Book: 'Lo! this is the bread of affliction, which our ancestors ate in the land of Egypt.' The former lot of the people is contrasted with their present ease). Jehovah perceives the affliction of Israel, and comes as deliverer: 'I have surely visited you, and seen that which is done to you in Egypt: And I have said, I will bring you up out of the affliction of Egypt' (Exod. 3.16f.). There is general agreement in the OT of this readiness of Jehovah to vindicate his people in their trouble. Their backsliding from the demands of Jehovah has intensified their calamities, but he was ready to receive their 'turning' and deliver them. It was the trouble which made Israel mindful of Jehovah, and Israel discovered that Jehovah had been and was still mindful of them; e.g. 'But when in their distress they turned unto the Lord, the God of Israel, and sought him, he was found of them' (I Chron. 15.4); 'then they cried unto the Lord in their trouble, and he delivered them out of their distresses' (Ps. 107.6,13,19, 28). Similarly with the individual, it is out of his afflictions that Jehovah becomes known as 'the God of my salvation' (Ps. 88.1).

Whilst the commonest word for trouble or distress has the notion of 'straitness'—that thing which hems in the sufferer, the root meaning of another common word is 'poor' or 'humble'. The 'poor' becomes the title of the oppressed or afflicted classes. It is this group which ultimately has no vindicator (no *go'el* to carry on the blood-feud on its behalf), no saviour but God. Basically, the Heb. word used signifies the 'poor and needy', those lacking material goods. From here the transition is to the 'poor and weak', those oppressed by the rich and powerful (*v.* Amos and Micah, *passim*), and hence, in turn, afflicted Israel, hemmed in by heathen forces, or the pious remnant in Israel, which suffers at the hands of the irreligious in the nation. God does not forget them, and the demonstration of divine righteousness in the Day of Jehovah will mean their deliverance and salvation. God has compassion on them: 'Sing, O heavens, and be joyful, O earth; and break into singing, O mountains; for the Lord hath comforted his people, and will have compassion upon his afflicted' (Isa. 49.13); and God saves and delivers them: 'The angel of the Lord encampeth round about them that fear him, and delivereth them' (Ps. 34.7). It is for this cause that 'righteousness' adds to itself the notion of 'deliverance', and that the 'righteous God is also known as "Saviour" '—cf. 'Deliver me in thy righteousness' (Ps. 71.1).

Some of the OT writers suggest that suffering has a disciplinary and purificatory value: 'Blessed is the man whom thou chastenest, O Lord, and teachest out of thy law' (Ps. 94.12; cf. Ps. 119.67,71, where it was the affliction which turned the psalmist back to the path of the divine statute; Zech. 13.9: 'And I will bring the third part through the fire, and will refine them as silver is refined, and will try them as gold is tried'; Mal. 3.2f.: 'He is like a refiner's fire, and like fuller's soap: and he shall sit as a refiner and purifier of silver. . . .'). Later Judaism was to follow in this tradition. It was very conscious of the fact that 'obedience to the Torah did not secure immunity from the slings and arrows of outrageous fortune' (W. D. Davies, *Paul and Rabbinic Judaism*, p. 263). As the Jew found himself subject to foreign powers, there was the clash of loyalties, and at times the yoke of the Torah was incompatible with the demands of Greek or Roman powers (e.g. the crisis under Antiochus Epiphanes). The ensuing persecution was to be accepted in some sense as a purgation of sin—i.e. suffering had atoning efficacy. 'Beloved are chastisements, for just as sacrifices atone, so also chastisements atone', says Rabbi Nehemiah (quoted by W. D. Davies, *op. cit.*). W. D. Davies (*op. cit.*, p. 265) suggests that this recognition, that obedience to the Torah could bring suffering, influenced St. Paul to take the position that 'the death of the Messiah could only have one meaning . . . it would be the expression of obedience to the demands of God' (cf. II Cor. 10.5, Rom. 5.13–18, Phil. 2.8).

The final interpretation of suffering is to be found in the Servant Songs of Deutero-Isaiah, and particularly in the fourth (Isa. 52.13–53.12). The Servant is represented as 'despised and rejected of men; a man of sorrows and acquainted with grief' (53.3), but his suffering is neither the result of his own sin nor the chastisement that might lead to his own perfection. Whether the Servant be understood to be a corporate or an individual figure, the suffering still remains vicarious and redemptive: 'the Lord hath laid on him the iniquity of us all' (vs. 6). The suffering apparently gains for itself a merit which is transferable. Professor North draws out the likeness between the suffering of the Servant and that of Jesus: 'The essential likeness between the Servant and Jesus lies in this: that whereas prophets like Jeremiah suffered in the course of, or as a result of, their witness, for both the Servant and Jesus suffering is the means whereby they fulfil their mission and bring it to a triumphant conclusion. This conception is unique in the OT. Hosea's suffering may have taught him his message, but it can hardly be said that he suffered in order to save Gomer or Israel. Jeremiah did not suffer uncomplainingly. Nor is the case of Job really parallel: Job suffers to vindicate God's faith in him in the face of the cynical aspersions of Satan; he does not suffer for others, and even his friends get no further than the Gentiles did in their first confessedly wrong estimate of the Servant, that he was "smitten of God, and afflicted" ' (C. R. North, *The Suffering Servant in Deutero-Isaiah*, pp. 208–9).

In the so-called 'Messianic Woes' suffering is given an important place as the prelude to the advent of the new age, when it is to become a thing of the past. In the OT prophetic books predictions of the future golden age—whether for Israel or the world—occur alongside of denunciations which threaten direct calamities. It was this juxtaposition which gave ground for the belief that when evils of all kinds had reached their climax deliverance would be at hand. Out of the travail of affliction and persecution the new age would be born. The origin of the idea may be found in Mic. 4.9ff.: 'Be in pain, and labour to bring forth, O daughter of Zion, like a woman in travail' (vs. 10); 'Therefore will he give them up, until the time that she which travaileth hath brought forth: then the residue of his brethren shall return . . .' (Mic. 5.3). The travail is not that of the Messiah himself, but the throes of mother Zion which is in labour to bring forth the Messiah. The idea is in itself an obvious one—that the path to happiness should pass through pain and tribulation. In Dan. we read '. . . and there shall be a time of trouble, such as never was since there was a nation even to that same time' (Dan. 12.1)—a prelude to the vindication of the 'saints of the Most High'. The later Apocalyptic books elaborated the idea. *Baruch* (xxvii–xxix) depicts twelve woes: 'Into twelve parts is that time divided, and each of them is reserved for that which is appointed for it.' These woes are to be universal and usher in the Messianic Age. 'And it shall come to pass when all is accomplished that was to come to pass in those parts, that the Messiah shall then begin to be revealed' (*Apocalypse of Baruch*, xxix. 3). The *Book of Jubilees* points to like tribulation: 'Behold the earth shall be destroyed on account of all their works, and there shall be no seed of vine, and no oil, for their works are altogether faithless, and they shall all perish together, beasts and cattle and birds, and all the fish of the sea, on account of the children of men' (xxiii. 18). It is by reason of the destruction that comes to the old world in the 'day of destruction' (cf. *Enoch* xcix. 4) that the new age must involve also a re-creation; it is then that 'the former troubles are forgotten' and there arise 'new heavens and a new earth' (cf. Isa. 65.16–17, Rev. 21.1). The notion that the threatening troubles will be announced by omens of all kinds is carried into the NT in the apocalyptic passages in the Gospels (Matt. 24.3ff., Mark 13), where the whole of nature falls into commotion and confusion. It is after these preliminaries that the Messiah is revealed: 'And then shall they see the Son of Man coming in clouds with great power and glory' (Mark 13.26). In the Apocalypse the woes are the prelude to the final entrance of the Kingdom of God (Rev. 11.15).

The NT largely reflects the different views enunciated in the OT, although the place of vicarious and redemptive suffering looms large in the description of Christ's passion (*q.v.*). Suffering is of the essence of the mission of the Messiah (cf. Mark 8.31); the floods, which had been a symbol of trouble for OT writers, introduce the notion of the 'baptism' which he is to endure (Luke 12.50). It is antagonism to Jesus and his message which is the immediate cause of affliction, as antagonism gives way to persecution (cf. John 3.19f.). His followers are to become participants in this affliction: 'If they persecuted me, they will also persecute you' (John 15.20; cf. I Pet. 4.13). The Church is to live in the days of the Messianic Woes, and only at the *Parousia* will it find its final release (cf. Acts 14.22, John 16.33).

Jesus fulfils perfectly the mission of the Suffering Servant of Deutero-Isaiah, for, sinless himself, no connexion could be made between his character and his afflictions, so that they must be of a vicarious character (cf. I Pet. 2.19–23). His life is offered up as a sacrifice for others (cf. Heb. 13.12); he brings deliverance to the captives through his atoning death: 'For verily the Son of Man came not to be ministered unto, but to minister, and to give his life a ransom for many' (Mark 10.45). Not only does the Church encounter a like affliction by following in the way of the cross, but as the 'body of Christ' it becomes a participant in the vicarious suffering of Christ himself; cf. 'I . . . fill up on my part that which is lacking of the afflictions of Christ' (Col. 1.24).

The NT does not dispense with the law of retribution: 'Be not deceived; God is not mocked: for whatsoever a man soweth, that shall he also reap' (Gal. 6.7), but Jesus expressly repudiates the popular view which made suffering (e.g. a physical defect) the direct result of some sin (Luke 13.1–5, John 9.2ff.). God's providential care is shown to be world-wide; his gifts are not sharply apportioned with respect to deserts (cf. Matt. 5.45). A naïve interpretation would not explain why the followers of Jesus would suffer even more than unbelievers, which Jesus said would come to pass (*v.* Matt. 5.10ff., 10.16–25, John 15.18–20, 16.23).

There is place for a probationary interpretation: 'Knowing that the proof of your faith worketh patience', or, 'Blessed is the man that endureth temptation: for when he hath been approved, he shall receive the crown of life, which the Lord hath promised to them that love him' (Jas. 1.3.12; cf. I Pet. 1.7, 4.17). But, further, suffering may be a means of discipline —a view which is also applied to the sufferings of Christ: 'Though he were a son, yet learnt he obedience through the things he suffered' (Heb. 5.8). 'Let us also rejoice in our tribulation', writes St. Paul, 'knowing that tribulation worketh patience; and patience probation, and probation hope' (Rom. 5.3). St. Paul welcomes a 'thorn in the flesh' as the means of learning that strength is to be found in a consciousness of personal weakness (II Cor. 12.7–9): 'Wherefore I take pleasure in weaknesses, in injuries, in necessities, in persecutions, in distresses, for Christ's sake: for when I am weak, then am I strong' (II Cor. 12.10). The paradox of Christian living is to be found in the joy that is the concomitant of the tribulation (cf. II Cor. 4.9ff.: 'Pursued, yet not forsaken . . .'; II Cor. 6.10: 'Sorrowful, yet always rejoicing'). (*V.* also HEAL, PASSION, REWARD.)

R. J. HAMMER

SUPERSTITION, SUPERSTITIOUS

Only in NT at Acts 17.22 and 25.19. The Gk. word used (*deisidaimonia*, here only) means 'respect for or fear of the supernatural'. The context would suggest that Paul uses it in a complimentary sense in the former instance, and hence RV marg. (religious) is to be preferred; in the latter instance Festus is speaking with the cynical disdain of the Roman official for the 'queer' religious beliefs of subject races, and therefore probably RV marg. is to be preferred (superstition). Festus is doubtless treating Agrippa as a man of the world like himself, as doubtless Agrippa wished to be treated by the Romans; he is not gratuitously insulting Agrippa. The biblical attitude towards what we call 'superstition' cannot be discovered in these passages; we must turn rather to the prophetic denunciation of false gods and idols (e.g. Ps. 115, Isa. 44, Jer. 44.15ff.), although the word does not occur in these passages. That the early Church was alive to the dangers of superstition (in the modern sense) is indicated by such passages as Col. 2.8–23, I Tim. 1.3f., 4.1–7, etc. (*V.* also RELIGION.)

A. R.

SWEAR *v.* OATH

SWORD *v.* ARMOUR

SYNAGOGUE *v.* CHURCH, MINISTER, PRAYER I

* * *

TABERNACLE *v.* SACRIFICE II(*b*)

TABERNACLES, FEAST OF *v.* SACRIFICE IV(*a*) and esp. (*d*)

TAMMUZ *v.* GOD, GODS IV

TARRY *v.* TIME

TEACH, TEACHING *v.* PREACH

TEACHERS *v.* MINISTER

TEMPLE *v.* SACRIFICE II(*a*) and (*b*)

TEMPT, TEMPTATION

The English word 'tempt' has narrowed in meaning since the AV was made (1611), and now usually means only to 'entice'. But its biblical meaning is often 'prove' or 'test' (*v.* note VI of Appendix to NT in the RV). God often makes trial of a person and tests his fidelity (Gen. 22.1, Exod. 20.20, Deut. 8.2, etc.), but he does not entice to sin (Jas. 1.13). (For the notion of Satan as the 'angel of testing', *v.* ADVERSARY.) It is forbidden to men to test God (Deut. 6.16, quoted by Jesus in Matt. 4.7 =Luke 4.12). Jesus himself makes trial of persons (e.g. the Syrophoenician Woman, Mark 7.25–30), and he also is tempted by human agents (e.g. Mark 8.11, 12.13, etc.). But the supreme temptations which he endured were spiritual ones, a truth which he graphically illustrates in his colourful story of his temptation in the desert (Matt. 4.1ff., Luke 4.1ff.). As the Chosen People was tested for forty years in the Wilderness after its baptism in the Red Sea, so Jesus, the Messiah who recapitulates the history of his People, was tested for forty days in the desert after his baptism by John in the Jordan. The temptations to misuse his wonderful powers for selfish ends were endured and overcome: he would not employ them for his own comfort (turn stones into bread), or for the purposes of self-display (the pinnacle of the temple), or to achieve political power (the kingdoms of the world). These temptations, of course, recurred to Jesus throughout his ministry: they are temptations which recur to his Church in every century. Jesus was 'tempted in all points like as we are' (Heb. 4.15); it is because he was victorious in the struggle that he is our High Priest, able to succour us (Heb. 2.17f.).

There is no reason why in Jesus' picture-story of his Temptation we should take literally the hypostatization of temptation in the person of Satan: the whole story is obviously symbolical. On the other hand, it is clear that the NT writers themselves believed in the existence of a personal Satan or tempter (cf. I Thess. 3.5, I Pet. 5.8, etc.). The important matter is that we should not minimize the reality of evil or the seriousness of temptation, however we rationalize these things.

The clause in the Lord's Prayer, 'Lead us not into (the) temptation' (Gk. *peirasmos*), raises difficulties. Jesus can hardly be thought to be praising a 'cloistered virtue' or advocating a withdrawal from the world in which temptation is inevitable. Blessing comes from the struggle with and victory over temptation (cf. Jas. 1.12). It is possible that there is here an eschatological reference: 'keep us out of the *peirasmos* or trial at the end of the age'—the final convulsion in which this world will perish. This would turn the clause into a prayer for salvation. But in view of the general trend of Jesus' teaching (though there may well be such a secondary implication), we should probably look for a moral interpretation of the clause. The two clauses, 'Lead us not into t., but deliver us from evil [or the Evil One]', would then mean: 'Keep us away from situations fraught with moral peril, where our resistance might be broken down; but, if we are tempted, do not let us succumb to evil'. However much of the eschatological meaning we may read into the clause, it is clear that we must not on any account read this simple moral meaning out of it. As with many of the sayings of Jesus, it has doubtless both an eschatological and an ethical reference. (*V.* also ADVERSARY.)

ALAN RICHARDSON

TESTAMENT *v.* COVENANT

THANK, GIVE THANKS, THANKSGIVING (EUCHARIST), etc.

OT: According to Young's *Analytical Concordance to the Bible* (AV), t., etc., always represent Heb. root *yadah*, except in II Sam. 14.22, where Heb. is *barak*.

(*a*) Root *yadah*, according to Young, is trans. t., etc., 64 times, PRAISE 55, CONFESS 18. Where trans. t., etc., it always (where trans. 'praise' nearly always) refers to men thanking or praising God. *Yadah*='confess' is used of men confessing sin to God or confessing God's name. The noun *todah* (thanksgiving) sometimes means a sacrifice offered as a thank offering (in II Chron. 29.31, 33.16 it is trans. 'thank offering'). Sometimes the phrase *zebach-todah* (sacrifice of thanksgiving) occurs. The sense of indebtedness to God is to be found throughout the OT. In Pss. esp. prominent (e.g. 18.49, 30.4,12, 79.13, 92.1, 118.1,29, 136,1ff.,26).

(*b*) Root *barak*, trans. BLESS, etc., *c.* 370 times, other words (incl. once 'thank') *c.* 30 times. See BLESS, and also H. W. Beyer in *TWNT*, II, pp. 751-63. Used of men blessing men (though God always regarded as the ultimate source of blessing), of God blessing men, sabbath, sheep, corn, etc., of priests' repetition of God's blessing in liturgy, of men blessing (i.e. praising) God. This last use comes very near to that of *yadah* above. So in Ps. 103.1ff. it denotes thankful praise called forth by remembrance of all God's mercies. Deut. 8.10 is the OT warrant for the Jewish graces over food and wine. These were called 'blessings' (*berakoth*), as were any prayers beginning 'Blessed . . .'. The special tract about these in the Talmud (*Berākoth*) says: 'It is forbidden to taste of this world without saying a blessing; whoever tastes of this world without saying a blessing commits unfaithfulness' (*v.* Ber 35*a*, and (*c*) below.

NT: (*a*) Gk. words rep. by t., etc.: (*1*) compounds of *homologeo* (like Heb. *yadah*, also= confess), Matt. 11.25, Luke 10.21, 2.38. (*2*) *Charis, eucharisteo*, etc. *Charis* (usually 'grace') is trans. t., etc., Luke 6.32,33,34, 17.9, Rom. 6.17 (7.25 in some MSS), I Cor. 15.57, II Cor. 2.14, 8.16, 9.15, I Tim. 1.12, II Tim. 1.3, I Pet. 2.19 (AV). *Eucharist-eo* (verb) 39 times, *-ia* (noun) 15 times, *-os* (adj.) once, are always trans. t., etc.

(*b*) Thankfulness to God is often enjoined (e.g. Eph. 5.20, Phil. 4.6, Col. 2.7, 3.15,17, 4.2, I Thess. 5.18, I Tim. 2.1). Paul often begins his letters with thanks to God for those to whom he is writing, for their faith, etc. (Rom. 1.8, I Cor. 1.4, Eph. 1.16, Phil. 1.3, Col. 1.3, I Thess. 1.2, II Thess. 1.3, Philem. 4). The supreme ground for thanks is Christ (e.g. II Cor. 2.14), and, where no special ground is mentioned, we may safely assume that God's grace in Christ is chiefly intended. Thanksgiving is not meant to be merely words, but the very mainspring of Christian living, the right motive of all service. This is clearly indicated in passages where t., etc., do not occur. So the third main division of Rom. is introduced (12.1ff.) by a 'therefore' which refers back to the preceding main division on justification, and by an appeal to 'the mercies of God', i.e. God's grace in Christ of which Paul has been writing. We are to express our thanks by presenting our lives as a sacrifice, the manner of which is indicated by what follows in 12–15.13. Christian obedience is not a method of earning our salvation (Pharisaism), but simply the expression of gratitude to God. So it is to be free from the Pharisee's ulterior motive. Our obedience cannot be more than a token of thanks; we can never by our obedience equal our indebtedness to God (cf. Luke 17.10). Thankfulness, i.e. the glad and free recognition of our infinite indebtedness to God, is the one true motive of Christian living; cf. Matt. 10.8, 18.32f., I Cor. 6.20, Eph. 4.32. The same idea is behind Matt. 25.31ff.; for our gratitude to Christ is to be rendered to the neighbour who comes as his representative. The whole idea is well expressed in the General Thanksgiving, 'that our hearts . . . all our days'. Cf. Heidelberg Catechism, the third main division of which is entitled 'Of Thankfulness' ('*Von der Dankbarkeit*'); in Qu. 2 the last of the three things a Christian must know is 'how I may thank God for this redemption'.

(*c*) T., etc., frequently used in connexion with food and drink (Matt. 15.36=Mark 8.6, Matt. 26.27=Mark 14.23, Luke 22.17,19, John 6.11,23, Acts 27.35, Rom. 14.6, I Cor. 10.30,

11.24, I Tim. 4.3f.), and refer to the Jewish grace or *berakah* (*v.* OT(*b*), above). Elsewhere 'bless' (*eulogeo*) is used in this connexion (Matt. 14.19=Mark 6.41=Luke 9.16, Mark 8.7, Matt. 26.26=Mark 14.22, Luke 24.30, I Cor. 10.16). Comparison of the two lots of refs. will show that *eucharisteo* and *eulogeo* are used indifferently to rep. Heb. *barak*. (According to Jewish usage, it was the name of God, not the food, that was blessed; but in Mark 8.7 and Luke 9.16 most MSS represent Jesus as blessing the food. This change of ideas is significant; cf. the tendency in eucharistic thought to concentrate attention on the sacramental elements rather than on the action as a whole. Cf. H. W. Beyer in *TWNT*, II, p. 760.) At every Jewish meal, whether private, social or religious, the head of family or host took BREAD in his hands, said the *berakah* or thanksgiving ('Blessed art thou, O Lord our God, King of the world, who bringest forth bread from the earth' was the regular form); the others said, 'Amen'; then he broke the bread, ate a fragment of it himself, and then distributed it to the others. It seems that there was something unique about Jesus' way of doing this (Luke 24.35): perhaps during the bread-*berakah* he used to look upward (Mark 6.41), instead of downward, as was usual; or perhaps he varied the form of words. After the meal followed the final *berakah* said by head of house or chief guest. After the invitation 'Let us give thanks', he took the cup and, with his eyes upon it, said the long thanksgiving, then took a sip and handed the cup to the others. This cup after the meal had a special name—'the cup of blessing' (*kos shel berakah*, cf. I Cor. 10.16). There was the same procedure at the Passover meal, only with additional special usages, the cup of blessing being then the third cup of the meal.

(*d*) *The Eucharist*

(*1*) At the *Last Supper*, as at other meals with his disciples, Jesus followed the usual customs of Jewish piety. Hence the prominence of t., etc., and 'bless', etc. (*eucharisteo* and *eulogeo*) in this connexion. The word 'thanksgiving' (*eucharistia*) is used as a technical term for the sacrament in Ignatius (*c.* 115), though never in the NT. The earliest names appear to have been the BREAKING OF BREAD (Acts 20.7; in 2.42,46 not specifically religious) and 'the Lord's Supper' (I Cor. 11.20). 'Communion' in I Cor. 10.16 is a predicate, not a name. 'The Lord's Supper' in I Cor. seems to have included a real supper. Later (by *c.* 100, or perhaps, as Dix suggests, between the writing of I Cor. and Mark) the particular parts of the supper, to which Jesus had given new meaning, were separated from the rest; and these parts were called the *Eucharist*, while what was left of the supper, when the eucharistic parts were taken away, became the *agape* (in NT in this sense of a meal only Jude 12, and acc. to some MSS, II Pet. 2.13). So G. Dix, *The Shape of the Liturgy*, pp. 77f., 95ff.

(*2*) Our *primary sources* are I Cor. 11.23ff., Mark 14.22ff., Matt. 26.26ff., Luke 22.15ff., giving three types (Mark and Matt. belonging together). In addition we have I Cor. 10.16ff., 16.20*b*,22*b*, Acts 20.7,11, John 6; and, outside NT, passages in *Didache* ix, x, xiv, Ignatius and Justin. Of the 4 primary sources the Pauline is the oldest. The tradition common to Paul and Mark consists of 3 parts: a narrative framework (Jesus takes bread, prays, breaks it, says explanatory word about it, takes cup, prays, says explanatory word); formulas concerning bread and wine; an eschatological saying (Mark 14.25; cf. I Cor. 11.26). There are considerable differences between the sources in the bread-formulas and cup-formulas, so that we cannot be certain of the words Jesus actually used; but it seems likely that the bread-formula was simply 'This is my body', and that the cup-formula was 'This is the new covenant in my blood' (in Mark the cup-formula being assimilated to the bread-formula). The explicit command to repeat this in remembrance of him is only in I Cor. In the Lucan text at this point there is an instance of a 'Western non-interpolation' (*v.* RV margin), and the most probable text omits 1½ verses. In this text we have no ref. to the cup after supper, but a ref. to the first cup of the Passover meal before supper.

(*3*) The Synoptics seem to identify the Last Supper with the Passover meal, but John 18.28, 19.14 seem to contradict this. On this question *whether the Last Supper was, or was not, a Passover meal*, scholars are still divided, Wellhausen, Beer, Lietzmann, Huber, Hupfeld, F. Spitta, Drews, G. H. Box, F. C. Burkitt, W. O. E. Oesterley, G. Dix maintaining that it was not, while Merx, Chwolson, Dalman, Strack and Billerbeck, Jeremias, Behm maintain that it was. For convenient summaries *v.* A. E. J. Rawlinson, *The Gospel according to St. Mark*, pp. 262–7, W. O. E. Oesterley, *The Jewish Background of the Liturgy*, pp. 158–92, J. Behm in *TWNT*, III, pp. 731–4. Behm (1938) argues strongly for its having been a Passover meal, and it must be said that the tendency of some British scholars to assume that the question has been settled the other way is premature.

(*4*) *What was the meaning Jesus intended?* It is important to remember that the bread-saying and cup-saying were originally separated by a whole meal, and so were independent of each other. This being so, it is improbable that Jesus was thinking of body and blood as the two elements which make up a person.

Taking the bread-saying separately, it is natural to understand 'my body' as equivalent to 'me', a meaning the Aramaic word which was probably used (*guphi*) could certainly have. So the bread-saying probably meant originally 'This is me'. Jesus knew that it was the last time he would have this meal with his disciples—it was a farewell. At the same time his thought went forward to the heavenly feast when he would eat with them in glory. They were about to enter the time of separation, the time between the present supper and the final reunion. During that interval they would again and again eat together, but without him. So he gives them a token and pledge of his real personal presence with them during the days of separation. The bread broken and distributed in the familiar way was to have a new meaning: it was henceforth to be the pledge of his real personal presence in their midst, though unseen.

The cup-saying connects the cup of blessing after supper with the new covenant God is about to make with his people by the Cross. If the I Cor. form is original (assimilation to the bread-saying would account for its change into Marcan form), then no great stress is laid on the identification of the wine with the blood. This cup is henceforth to be for the disciples the visible, tangible pledge of their share in the new covenant. 'The promise of the bread-saying is that he will be there, the promise of the cup-saying that he will be there as the Saviour who initiates the new covenant by his death' (Behm). So Jesus put new meaning into old familiar usages: the bread and cup of the fellowship meal were henceforward to be the pledges of his real personal presence, till the disciples' fellowship with him should be perfected in the heavenly feast.

(*5*) *Developments*. Paul's eucharistic teaching is essentially as above, but we may note certain developments or working-out of implications. (i) The parts of the meal to which Jesus had given new meaning, though still outwardly connected with the meal, are seen to be essentially distinct, in themselves a solemn religious service; the beginning of the separation of Eucharist and *Agape* is discernible. (ii) This involves the bringing into direct contact with each other of the bread-saying and cup-saying, which were originally separate, thus emphasizing the identification of the two material elements of bread and wine with the body and blood as the two elements of the person (cf. I Cor. 10.16, 11.27). Concentration of attention on the elements rather than on the rite as a whole was a later development from this, which has had misleading effect. (iii) I Cor. 10.17 makes explicit something implicit in Jesus' own action—that the supper is the expression of fellowship between those who partake together. (iv) The command to repeat the action, already implicit in Jesus' words that are common to I Cor. and Mark, is made explicit by the addition of 'this do in remembrance of me', 'this do, as oft as ye drink it, in remembrance of me'. (v) This remembrance is not to be understood in the sense of the pagan memorial meals, but in the light of the Passover meal, in which the historical deliverance from Egypt, God's intervention in the past on behalf of his people, was celebrated and proclaimed as a present reality. (vi) I Cor. 11.27ff. makes explicit the moral implications of the real presence of the Lord.

For the Johannine eucharistic teaching, see John 6, esp. 41–59, J. Behm, *op. cit*., pp. 740–2, E. C. Hoskyns, *The Fourth Gospel*, I, pp. 309–47, W. F. Howard, *Christianity according to St. John*, pp. 143–50, etc.

(*6*) There are certain *negative points* that must be made here. (i) The fact that the Supper is firmly rooted in history marks it off decisively and absolutely from the sacramental meals of Hellenistic religion with which some have sought to connect it. (ii) Sacrificial ideas are absent from the NT references to the Supper. There is no trace in NT of idea of our offering the bread and wine (unless Matt. 5.23f.?) or Christ to God; the only thing offered to God is our thanks and praise. The attempts to find in the 'remembrance' (*anamnesis*) the idea of ritual memorial directed to God are unconvincing, as also are the attempts to show that 'communion' in I Cor. 10.16 implies a *sacrificial* meal or that 'do' in I Cor. 11.24f. means 'offer'. Even when the term 'sacrifice' is used in connexion with the Eucharist in *Didache*, xiv, it is with ref. to the thanksgiving prayer, not the elements. (iii) The NT gives no support to any mechanical or magical ideas in connexion with the elements or the rite as a whole (though such ideas can be discerned as early as Ignatius, e.g. 'the medicine of immortality', *Smyrn*., xxiv, 6, 'antidote against death', *Eph*. xx.2), nor on the other hand does it support any idea that the Supper is merely a symbol; in contrast with both these misunderstandings it declares the gift of the Supper to be a presence, that is personal not mechanical, real not symbolic.

(*7*) *Summary*. We must now try to sum up the NT teaching on the Eucharist. (i) The *gift* of the Eucharist is the real personal presence of the risen, glorified Lord. That this was the faith of the disciples in the earliest days of the Church in Palestine, the Aramaic *Marana tha* in I Cor. 16.22 (whether trans. 'Our Lord, come!' or 'Our Lord is here!') is witness, for it appears from *Didache*, x, 6 that it was a fragment from the liturgy. (Cf. Behm, *op. cit*.,

p. 736, K. G. Kuhn, *ibid.*, IV, pp. 470–5.) The Supper is the Lord's appointed tryst with his own. Those who keep tryst with him can know he will assuredly come to meet them. The connexion with Easter and the note of joy need to be stressed more than has often been the case (cf. K. Barth, *Dogmatik im Grundriss*, p. 132). (ii) The Eucharist proclaims the Cross of Christ, the institution of the new covenant in his blood, and is the pledge of our share in its benefits. (iii) At the same time it points forward to the final consummation and is a foretaste of the final reunion with Christ in glory. (iv) It is a pledge and expression of fellowship between Christians. (v) It is Eucharist—thanksgiving. This is implied by 'remembrance' in I Cor. As Jews at the Passover meal called to remembrance and gave thanks for the mighty intervention of God in delivering them from slavery in Egypt, so Christians, remembering and celebrating their redemption as a present reality, cannot help but give thanks to God. (*V.* MEMORY.)

See, further, H. W. Beyer in *TWNT*, II, pp. 751–63 (on 'bless'); J. Behm, *ibid.*, III, pp. 726–43 (on 'break'), which includes a fairly full bibliography on the Eucharist in NT up to 1937, I, pp. 351f. (on 'remembrance'); M. Barth, 'Das Abendmahl', *Theologische Studien*, 1945; E. Schweizer, 'Das Abendmahl eine Vergegenwärtigung des Todes Jesu oder ein Eschatologisches Freudenmahl?', *Theologische Zeitschrift*, 1946, pp. 81ff.; T. Preiss, 'Le Dernier Repas de Jésus fut-il un Repas Pascal?', *Theologische Zeitschrift*, 1948, pp. 81ff.; G. Dix, *The Shape of the Liturgy*, esp. pp. 48–102; E. C. Ratcliff in *The Holy Communion, a Symposium*, ed. H. Martin, pp. 12–32; and (esp. important) J. Jeremias' *Eucharistic Words of Jesus*. (Also *v.* MEMORY.)

C. E. B. CRANFIELD

THOUGHT

Heb. has a number of verbs expressing mental action, but the commonest of them (*chashab*, *damah*, *zamam*), with their cognate nouns, signify thought with a view to action; hence plan, device, purpose, rather than abstract thought. Disinterested, academic reflection is not a mark of the Heb. mind, but is characteristic of the Gk., and in the NT we find verses where the noun 'thought' represents Gk. words which have this less practical sense, e.g. Luke 24.38, Rom. 2.15 (Gk. *dialogismos*), Matt. 9.4 (Gk. *enthumēsis*).

For the noun derived from the Heb. *chashab* see Gen. 6.5 (every imagination of the *thoughts* of his heart: the same combination, I Chron. 28.9, 29.18) Ps. 94.11, Isa. 55.7–9, Jer. 29.11. The verb *chashab* is sometimes trans. 'imagine' in EVV, e.g Ps. 10.2, Zech. 7.10 (where note the sinister shade of meaning). (Also *v.* IMAGINATION.)

The Hebraic sense is sometimes preserved in the NT even in Gk. words which at first suggest something much nearer to philosophical reasoning, e.g. Mark 7.21 (*dialogismos*), Heb. 4.12 (*enthumēsis*), Acts 8.22 (*epinoia*).

The phrase 'take thought' in the AV of the Gospels (7 times in Matt., 4 times in Luke, once in Mark) is a rendering of the quite different verb *merimnao* which properly means 'worry', 'be anxious' (so RV). This is condemned by Jesus because it fundamentally implies forgetfulness of God's providence, i.e. lack of faith. (*v.* CARE.)

The Gk. verb *phroneo* sometimes appears as 'think' in our EVV. Its connotation is, however, considerably wider than is suggested by our 'think'. It implies the activity not of the reasoning faculty alone, but of all the mental powers, including feeling and willing. Thus it corresponds to the Heb. word *nephesh*, soul (*v.* MIND). For example, 'what thou thinkest' (Acts 28.22) means 'your whole attitude to religion', not simply ideas. In I Cor. 13.11, RV rightly alters the 'understood' of AV to 'felt'; it is the third of the verbs here used which more definitely means reasoning. Similarly in Phil. 1.7 RV changes 'think this' of AV to 'be thus minded'; an even better rendering would be '*feel* like this about you', particularly in view of the clause which follows immediately, viz. 'because I have you in my heart [*kardia*]'. In Phil. 4.10, AV is to be preferred to RV, with 'your care of me' rather than 'your thought of me'.

In other places the verb is rendered by some phrase containing the noun or verb 'mind' (*v.* MIND), e.g. Rom. 11.20, 'be not highminded', i.e. conceited, and in the phrase 'be of the same mind', i.e. agree, share a common outlook, Rom. 15.5, etc. For the interpretation of the famous passage Rom. 8.5ff., it must be remembered that 'mind', whether verb as in vs. 5, or the cognate noun as in vss. 6, 7 and also 27, signifies the whole outlook or attitude, which may be influenced either by what Paul calls 'the flesh', i.e. roughly speaking, the merely instinctive part of man, the lower nature, or by divine influences, 'the spirit'. The AV is almost unintelligibly literal here, and RV is no improvement, but the Moffatt translation has great merit, 'those who follow the flesh have their interest in the flesh, and those who follow the Spirit have their interests in the Spirit'.

In another classic passage, Phil. 2.5, AV and RV are both wrong, and we should prefer 'let this be your attitude', as also Phil. 3.15 and 19. In Col. 3.2 'set your mind on' (RV) is perhaps better than 'set your affection on'

(AV) and is not inadequate because it clearly implies more than thinking about heaven or forming mental images of it. (Also *v.* MIND.)

E. C. BLACKMAN

THRONE *v.* AUTHORITY, HEIGHT

TIDINGS *v.* GOSPEL

TIME, SEASON

Modern speech preserves a duality of thought and expression about time that appears also in the Biblical writers, though the emphasis within that duality is the opposite of that in the Bible. The two modes of thought and expression may be termed the 'chronological' and the 'realistic'. For modern Western man the emphasis is on the 'chronological': he thinks of time as something to be measured, measured by a clock. The Bible recognizes this character of time (the NT uses the word *chronos*, time), but has little to say about it and makes little or no contribution to our ability to measure time. But modern man has other ways of talking about time: he can talk about doing things 'at the right time', though with little capacity to become articulate as to what the phrase means. But here, where modern speech and thought are comparatively weak, the Bible is possessed of a rich vocabulary and penetrating insights.

The contrast between 'chronological' and 'realistic' is exhibited in the NT distinction between *chronos* (measured time, duration) and *kairos* (time of opportunity and fulfilment). *Chronos* may refer to a short time ('a moment of time', Luke 4.5) or a long ('time of forty years', Acts 13.18). The characteristic meaning of *kairos* can be seen in such phrases as 'time of temptation' (Luke 8.13) and 'time of harvest' (Matt. 13.30).

The OT has a word (*'eth*) which can translate *kairos*; indeed, it has a rather rich variety of words with this meaning; but it has no word which can properly translate *chronos*. The idea of measured, chronological time of course was there, in days and months, new moons, and years; though it is interesting to note that chronology (as we know it) was a late achievement of the Hebrew mind, and that, when it was developed, it was largely borrowed. The development of chronological reckoning following the use of realistic terms for time can be seen in a study of the names of the months in the OT. The final set of names [Nisan (Neh. 2.1), Iyyar, Sivan (Esther 8.9), Tammuz, Ab, Elul (Neh. 6.15), Tishri, Marcheshvan, Kislev (Zech. 7.1), Tebeth (Esther 2.16), Shebat (Zech. 1.17), Adar (Ezra 6.15)] was derived from Babylon, and some of these are not even used by the Biblical writers. These late, Babylonian names, part of a whole system of chronology, replaced the previous exilic habit of naming the months by their numbers (cf. Jer. 36.9, 39.2, Ezek. 8.1, 24.1, 32.1, I Kings 6.1, etc.); and this numerical reference itself replaced an earlier and probably Canaanitish system in which the months were named by what happened in them. Four only of these names survive: Abib (month of ripening ears), Exod. 13.4; Ziv (month of flowers), I Kings 6.1; Ethanim (month of perennial streams), I Kings 8.2; and Bul (month of rain), I Kings 6.38. This designation of a 'time' by its content is characteristic of the whole biblical tradition, and is connected with the understanding of time 'realistically' in terms of opportunity and fulfilment.

Throughout the Bible the word 'time' is used realistically. Thus we read of the time of natural events—evening (Gen. 8.11), harvest (Jer. 1.16, Matt. 13.30), rain (Ezra 10.13); of social events—marriage (I Sam. 18.19), mealtimes (Ruth 2.14), campaigning seasons (I Chron. 20.1); of human life—birth (Gen. 38.27), death (I Sam. 4.20), its duties (Gen. 24.11), and its religious observances (Dan. 9.21). Particularly interesting is the long catalogue of 'times', each distinguished by its content, in Eccles. 3.1–8. But while all these times are known in terms of their content, their fulfilment is a matter of man's seizing an opportunity. Eccles. makes this abundantly clear in its assertion that 'to everything there is a season, and a time to every purpose under the heaven' (Eccles. 3.1). To revert to another illustration, it is of no avail for a farmer to try to reap a harvest in sowing time, and while the harvest is ripe he must seize the right time for gathering it. Thus, events that happen in time derive their location from two factors—an opportunity (a time, *'eth* or *kairos*) that presents itself to man, and man's response to the opportunity in appropriate action.

At this point the Bible takes us a step further. It is not enough to recognize the fabric of events as being woven of the warp of opportunity and the web of human response; far more important is it to recognize that it is God the Creator who provides the opportunity. Natural events are of his ordaining. God gives to Israel 'the rain of her land in its season' (Deut. 11.14), controls the harvests (Hos. 2.11), feeds all living creatures 'in due season' (Ps. 104.27, 145.15) and maintains the constancy of day's following upon night (Jer. 33.20). Even in responding to the contents of times that seem most natural, man is thus really responding to God. What is true of the realm of nature is equally true of the realm of history. The great prophets speak of the time (Jer. 51.6) or the day (Isa. 34.8) of the Lord's vengeance, and refer to a future occasion when the Lord will produce certain historical events. Indeed, the whole mission of a prophet consisted in making plain to Israel that contemporary events were not a mere aggregation of happenings, but rather a series of times-with-contents sent by God for his own purposes, and demanding certain appropriate responses from the chosen people. The prophet was concerned, that is, to offer an interpretation, or rather *the* interpretation, of history; and for him history consisted of a continuum of times, each with its own specific character, but all of them at bottom of religious and theological significance. In interpreting his own contemporary situation a prophet may speak now of judgment and doom, now of promise and hope; that depends upon the course of events. But he will speak of these things, and demand appropriate response, in any and every historical situation, precisely because God ordains what is to happen. His word goes forth, and the 'time' is thereby filled with a certain content. God it is that 'performeth the counsel of his messengers, that saith of Jerusalem, She shall be inhabited; and of the cities of Judah, They shall be built, and I will raise up the waste places thereof: that saith to the deep, Be dry, and I will dry up thy rivers: that saith of Cyrus, he is my shepherd, and shall perform all my pleasure: even saying of Jerusalem, She shall be built, and to the temple, Thy foundation shall be laid' (Isa. 44.24–8). Thus at every point of history true prophecy can echo the Deuteronomist's word in its understanding of historical time: 'I call heaven and earth to witness against you this day, that I have set before thee life and death, the blessing and the curse: therefore choose life, that thou mayest live, thou and thy seed' (Deut. 30.19).

We have so far dealt with the 'concrete' or 'realistic' use of the word 'time', and noticed that times are known by their contents and that their content is always in nature and in history, endowed by God. But to enter into the full richness of the biblical understanding of time we need to retrace our steps somewhat, and return to the fundamentally theological interpretation of history characteristic of the Bible by another route. This is supplied in the use made by biblical writers of certain technical phrases of the historian.

The most revealing is the simple and unavoidable phrase, 'at that time'. At first sight this would seem to offer no problems, nor provide any room for investigation. But amongst its uses we may quickly and readily distinguish two. It may be used in an historical narrative to indicate that the event about to be recorded took place 'at the same time' as the one just reported, as when the historian tells of the dedication of Solomon's temple and continues: 'at that time Solomon held a feast, and all Israel with him' (I Kings 8.65). No one can mistake that for anything else than a clear attempt at precise chronological location. But the same phrase may be used when the event about to be recorded cannot be held to have this relation of temporal succession to that immediately preceding it in the narrative: it then becomes a formal phrase rather like 'once upon a time'. A good example is the story of Tamar (Gen. 38.1), about which Dr. Skinner has written: 'it is obvious that [it] belongs to a cycle of tradition quite independent of the story of Joseph'—told in the previous chapter (*v.* Skinner, *ICC*, *Genesis*, p. 450).

But it seems that these two uses do not necessarily exhaust the functions of this phrase, as we may see in considering its 15 occurrences in the first ten chapters of Deut. There the phrase is used to introduce a whole number of events, all of which took place between the crossing of the Red Sea and the entry into Canaan. Driver, in his *ICC*, *Deuteronomy* (p. 15), has noticed the difficulty of giving any satisfactory interpretation to the tense of 'I spake unto you at that time' (Deut. 1.9) if, as the narrative presupposes, the speaking was at the close of, or subsequent to, the Israelites' sojourn at Horeb. He goes on to suggest that either we are here reading a piece of narrative that originally depended on a text in which Exod. 18 was followed by Num. 10.29–36, or that this Deuteronomic retrospect 'was written at a time when the interval between Jethro's visit (Exod. 18) and the departure from Horeb (Num. 10.33) had so dwindled that both could be included in the expression "at that time" '. But it would seem possible to advance another explanation, for which some additional and independent reasons could be advanced, viz. that by the time this Deuteronomic retrospect was written, all the various times instanced in these first ten chapters of Deut. were already looked back upon as severally part of, and together constituting, 'that time', that classic time of God's activity in which, by the wonder at the Red Sea, by the giving of the Law, by the discipline of the wilderness, God had called, constituted and corrected his people.

There is no doubt at all but that the phrase 'at that time' may refer to the past. It can be used, suitably adapted, to refer to the present (cf. Esther 4.14). But it can also be used to refer to the future. Thus Isaiah uses it to indicate the certainty of Ethiopia's doom (Isa. 18.7), Jeremiah to speak of God's future favours (Jer. 3.17, 31.1) as well as of his judgments (Jer. 4.11, 8.1). Micah (3.4) and Zephaniah (1.12) both use it of God's coming judgment, and Zephaniah also to assure his people of their restoration (3.19,20). The writer of Daniel refers by it to the time of trouble and deliverance at the 'end' (Dan. 12.1). Lastly, the phrase is added to 'in those days' in both Jeremiah (33.15, 50.4) and Joel (3.1) to refer to the divine action by which God will gather, restore and establish his scattered people. The point of all this is not that the prophet should use an historian's phrase about the past to refer to the future—there is no other speech that can be used—but that without exception the words should indicate some future act of God. The formal phrase has been given new power and meaning by the profound prophetic conviction that the central and basic fact of all history and all historical incident is that God is Lord of it, and active in and through it.

If, then, by the time of Jeremiah it was possible to think of 'that time' as the coming event (or sequence of events) in which God would restore and re-establish his people, it would seem no less possible and no less likely that 'that time' in the past could be invested with the meaning of that past event (or sequence of events) in which God had first made and established his people. Just as all nations shall be gathered unto Jerusalem 'at that time' (Jer. 3.17), so were Sihon and Og conquered, judges appointed, the law given, and the Levites separated, we believe, 'at that time'. These were not discrete, unrelated events. They were distinct chronological occasions, but they were, fundamentally, one event, God's calling and making of a people for his possession.

Thus the whole of history, past, present and future, consists of times that are all, in the Psalmist's phrase, 'in God's hands' (Ps. 31.15). But in that history, two times especially can be discerned—the time of God's making of his people, and the time of his remaking of them. In the meantime all that happens, for weal or woe, is under divine control. God called Israel to serve him, and when Israel failed, it was God who punished. 'Ho, Assyrian, rod of mine anger', cries out Isaiah (10.5), though he can see beyond the immediacy of Israel's punishment: 'I will punish the fruit of the stout heart of the king of Assyria, and the glory of his high looks' (10.12). Jeremiah is even more emphatic on this last point: 'I will bring Israel again to his pasture. . . . In those days, and at that time, saith the Lord, the iniquity of Israel shall be sought for, and there shall be none; for I will pardon them whom I leave as a remnant' (Jer. 1.17–20). God's will and purpose, then, are the ultimate determinants of history. To disobey his will is to court disaster, though human disobedience will not therefore finally frustrate God's plans. Forgiveness, as well as judgment, enters into history, has its 'time'. Indeed, forgiveness is a profounder element in events, for while judgment constitutes incidents in history, forgiveness will mark its consummation. The 'time' of restoration is God's in a way that the 'time' of judgment is not, for forgiveness is solely an act of divine love and mercy.

Because God's activity so determines the events of human life, piety is inescapably necessary. 'Let everyone that is godly pray unto thee in a time when thou mayest be found' (Ps. 32.6). Prayer should be offered in an 'acceptable time', i.e. a time of acceptance (Ps. 69.13; cf. Isa. 49.8). This does not mean that there are times when God cannot be trusted. He is the stronghold of the righteous in time of trouble (Ps. 37.39), and can be trusted at all times (Ps. 62.9; cf. Pss. 31.14–16, 34.2). The God whose activity and will condition all the 'times' of nature and of history is the one God with whom living personal communion can be had. Hebrew piety derives its characteristics from its concern with a God who is Lord of all time.

Before we turn back once more to see how the two 'classic times' of God's activity regulate the whole biblical story, we may pause to consider some particular words and expressions which, in one way and another, throw light on the Hebrew understanding of time. One has already been quoted in an expression where it is used as a parallel to 'time', the word 'DAY.' In many of its 2,000 occurrences in the Old Testament it is used to distinguish the period of light from that of darkness, or to mark off one period of twenty-four hours from another. But also, both in the singular and in the plural, it acquires meanings which are unambiguously supra-temporal in their reference. Thus the phrase 'in that day', like the parallel 'at that time', can refer to past (Gen. 15.18), present (I Sam. 3.12—a future tense with a present meaning—'*futurum instans*') or future (Isa. 17.4) activity of God. And 'that day', as 'that time', became an eschatological term referring to the final activity of God in judgment and mercy (cf., e.g., Joel 3.18, Zeph. 3.16), and was used in the same way as 'that time' to indicate the time when God delivered his people from Egypt (Ezek. 20.5.6).

Days, like times, are known by their contents (e.g. Gen. 35.3, Hos. 2.5, Ps. 95.8, Amos 1.14), though one content—God's—is emphasized as fundamental. The OT refers to the day of God's anger (Lam. 2.1), of his vengeance (Isa. 61.2) or power (Ps. 110.3), but the most interesting expression of all is 'THE DAY OF THE LORD'. Amos, on whose lips the expression is first found (Amos 5.18ff.), is attacking a popular misconception of what the term means. His contemporaries apparently used it of a coming time when God would intervene in history to deliver his people from every oppression and give them lordship in the earth. This irreligious optimism of popular religion, Amos and the other great prophets attacked. 'Wherefore would ye have the day of the Lord? . . . Shall not the day of the Lord be darkness, not light? even very dark and no brightness in it?' (Amos 5.18–20). The Lord's Day will indeed be the day of his coming and his action, but he will come in righteousness and therefore in judgment: in that day sin and unrighteousness must perish, and holiness and peace triumph. This double character of God's decisive intervention in history is familiar to all the prophets: in Isaiah's great words it appears: 'The spirit of the Lord God is upon me . . . to proclaim the year of the Lord's good pleasure, and the day of vengeance of our God.' This last 'day' is no ordinary day, for 'the sun and moon are darkened, and the stars withdraw their shining. And the Lord shall roar from Zion . . . and the heavens and the earth shall shake . . . then shall Jerusalem be holy' (Joel 3.15–17). These patently supernatural events are a clear indication that the final arbiter in history is the Lord God, and the Lord God alone. That day would be the end of the present historical order: 'In that day Egypt shall be a desolation, and Edom shall be a desolate wilderness' (Joel 3.19), but it would also inaugurate a new trans-historical order: 'But Judah shall abide for ever, and Jerusalem from generation to generation.' Prophecy has merged into eschatology, and the categories of time are strained with the tensions of eternity.

What has been said about 'day' can be said, in varying degree, of other words for time, which beget a special significance as they are used of God's activity in history. The word 'YEAR' may be predominantly chronological ('the eleventh year of Zedekiah', Jer. 1.3), but it can also be defined by its content ('year of recompense', Isa. 34.8), especially by the content of God's decisive action in history ('the acceptable year of the Lord', Isa. 61.2). The word 'SEASON' shares in the characteristic of the words it translates, words often rendered elsewhere as 'time' or 'day'. But there is one use of the Hebrew word *mo'ed*, sometimes rendered 'season', that calls for special remark. It is used in the phrase 'tent of meeting', where the word that can refer plainly enough to a human tryst (cf. I Sam. 20.35) is applied to the tent where, at certain times, indicated by the descent of a pillar of cloud (Exod. 33.7–11), God meets with Moses. The same word is used for the 'set feasts' of the Hebrew year ('solemn assemblies' in the AV), for these too are of God's appointment. It is also used to indicate the natural seasons which were marked in Israel by religious observances, viz. each NEW MOON (cf. Gen. 1.14). The MOON is a natural object, but it has been put in the heavens by God in order to remind men of the 'times' when he will tryst with them. So the succession of days and MONTHS and years was more than a mere temporal sequence; it was a divinely ordered and a divinely penetrated succession in which, at appointed times, the eternal kept tryst with the mortal.

The various words used for time in the OT are thus seen to express a view of history as made up of various times which are in God's appointment. Their content may be varied, but ultimately all times belong to him, and serve his purposes. Man experiences times of God's anger and judgment and times of his mercy and favour. But there is an important qualification to be added, which finds expression in the OT in the use of the word 'moment'. 'MOMENT' is used to emphasize the transcendent power of God which can accomplish great things in little time (cf. Exod. 33.5), but its characteristic meaning is in the prophets and singers of Israel, who contrast the 'moment' of God's anger with the 'everlasting' nature of his kindness (cf. esp. Isa. 54.7,8). The same thought appears when Isaiah contrasts the 'day' of God's vengeance with the acceptable 'year' of God. In this temporal contrast a qualitative distinction is being drawn. Anger is but a reaction, albeit a divine reaction: kindness is God's very nature and is his constant attitude to men. It is even the condition of his anger, for he would not be angry with men if he had no care for them. Anger is thus an 'accident' and kindness a 'property' of the divine nature; and mercy is more fundamental than judgment in history, if the prophetic doctrine is right that God's anger lasts but a moment, while his kindness endures for ever.

This contrast is not to be discovered in the light of contemporary history alone. We must refer to the two classic 'times' of God's activity in history if we are to see its validity. There was a time when God was active in Israel's history to call and establish his people. There will be a time in the future—such is the prophet's conviction—when God will again recognizably intervene in history to create a new Israel, bound to him in an indissoluble covenant. These two times were essential ingredients of the Hebrew judgment upon contemporary history: without them the prophetic understanding of history would have been impossible, for the present cannot be interpreted save in the light of some ultimate direction, any more than one can describe a journey unless it begins in some place and ends in another.

The most noteworthy thing about the NT terms for time is not that they contain a word for temporal duration (*chronos*), but that throughout the whole book there runs the conviction that the 'time' looked forward to by the prophets has in fact arrived in history with the advent of Jesus Christ. The NT equivalent for the OT 'time' or 'season' is *kairos*—time: and the affirmation that the expected time has arrived appears first on the lips of Jesus himself. 'The time is fulfilled'—this, Mark tells us (Mark 1.15), summarizes his first preaching when he came into Galilee. But what 'time' was this? And what is meant by its fulfilment? The latter question needs answering first, and we can see the meaning of 'fulfilled' in another context—Luke 4.21. Jesus was in the synagogue at Nazareth, and had read Isa. 61.1,2. He closed the book, returned it to the attendant, sat down and said, 'To-day hath this scripture been fulfilled in your ears.' In the earlier days of prophecy in Israel the word spoken by the true prophet, being God's word, was expected to come true, to be fulfilled, immediately. God's word was itself creative, and if the prophet spoke it, then it would create the conditions of its fulfilment. But as Jeremiah knew, in the agony of his own heart-searching, sometimes the word of the Lord seemed to tarry. Jeremiah, after much inner wrestling, could not conclude that the word given to him had not come from God, and so drew the only other possible inference—that fulfilment must wait. Messianic prophecy could indeed be explained in no other way, and in the synagogue Jesus asserted that the time spoken of by Isaiah and defined by its content had now in historical fact arrived. Fulfilment is thus the arrival of the time foretold—and the 'time' of Mark 1.15 can only be the Messianic 'time' of Hebrew religion. Now had come the time when God would create his new Israel in an indissoluble covenant.

The time of Jesus is *kairos*—and so is a time of opportunity. To embrace the opportunity means salvation, to neglect it disaster. There is no third course. In rejecting Christ, in failing to seize their opportunity, the Jews court disaster. By contrast Christians, discerning the times aright, are the heirs of salvation. They 'know the season' (Rom. 13.11), 'redeem the time' (Eph. 5.16, Col. 4.5); and 'now is the acceptable time; behold, now is the day of salvation' (II Cor. 6.2, quoting Isa. 49.8). God's activity in history by which he constitutes his people in an indestructible fellowship are events contemporary with the men of the NT. Yet though the people of God is constituted in history, in a time which is properly called a *kairos*, its proper existence is not in time, but in what the NT calls 'THE AGE TO COME' (*aion*, age, not *kairos*, time)—an age beyond history whose life is said to be 'eternal'. The life of God's people, then, participates in two WORLDS or AGES, this world of historical time comprising various *kairoi*, or opportunities, of which that offered in Jesus Christ is the most fundamental, decisive and significant; and the world to come, which is beyond history and yet not wholly 'outside' it or unrelated to it, since it can be entered from within history, where its special life can in some measure be enjoyed. 'He that heareth my word, and believeth him that sent me, hath eternal life, and cometh not into judgment, but hath passed out of death into life' (John 5.24). Jesus knows this contrast (cf. Mark 10.30, etc.), as do Paul and other writers of the NT (cf. Rom. 8.18, I Pet. 1.4,11, Heb. 12.28, etc).

The 'time' of Jesus was thus fraught with great issues. But how should men know and discern the opportunity of that time? The answer is that the contents of that time were so plainly related to those by which God established his old Israel that men, and especially the covenant people themselves, were without excuse if they could not discern what was going on. The grave charge Jesus brought against his contemporaries was that though they could read the signs of the weather, they could not 'discern the signs of the times' (Matt. 16.3; cf. Luke 12.56). He wept because Jerusalem did not know the 'time of [her] visitation' (Luke 19.44). Jerusalem and the Jews should have recognized the signs of the times, because, as the NT writers are so zealous to show, the events of Jesus' time were so patently fulfilment of prophecy. In order to share their judgment it is not necessary to follow them in each and every application of prophecy to the life of Christ. It will suffice if we recognize the principle on which they worked and accept their intention. This can be done by exhibiting the significant parallels between the divine action in the history of the Exodus by which God once constituted the Old Israel and those actions in the life, death and resurrection of Jesus Christ by which he constituted the New Israel of God.

Paul states explicitly that 'our passover also hath been sacrificed, even Christ' (I Cor. 5.7), and with that clue so plainly given it is impossible not to be struck by the way in which the whole series of events connected with the

Exodus is focused in the death and resurrection of our Lord. Jesus spoke of his own death as his 'baptism' (Mark 10.38, Luke 12.50); but baptism was that ceremony in which a man, by a symbolic action, shared in the historical action of the people of God when they went out of Egypt through the waters of the Red Sea and were thereby made a people for God's possession. In the 'baptism' of the cross and the issuing from the 'perils of the waters' in the resurrection, God now constituted his people indissolubly anew. At the Last Supper Jesus speaks of the outpoured wine as his blood of the new covenant (Mark 14.24, with parallels in Matt. 26.28, Luke 22.20), thereby linking the passover blood of the old covenant with Jeremiah's prophecy of the new, and interpreting them together in his sacrificial death. Nothing could be clearer than that what is taking place in the life, death and resurrection of Jesus is precisely what was meant to take place at the Exodus—the establishment of a people for God. Thus, perhaps even more forcibly than the application of particular prophecies in the manner of Matthew can the parallels between 'Exodus time' and 'Messianic time' persuade us of the meaning and mission of the life of Jesus Christ. As he approaches his death he has become 'the people of God' who are all represented in him. He is the lamb slain, by whose blood men are sprinkled for the passing over of God's judgment. As he dies upon the cross and descends into the tomb he passes from the 'captivity' of his flesh into the waters of the Red Sea (his baptism). When he rises from the tomb he has issued from the waters to new life and possession of the land of God's promise. After this it is interesting and significant to note that if we translate literally, as we surely may, the Greek of Luke 9.31, we are told that at the Transfiguration Moses and Elijah talked with Jesus of the 'Exodus which he was about to fulfil at Jerusalem'. It would seem, therefore, that the time of Jesus Christ was not only a fulfilment of prophetic Messianic time (i.e. the time when that was accomplished which the prophetic word was intended to accomplish), but also a fulfilment of Exodus time (i.e. the time when that was accomplished which the historical events of the Exodus were meant to accomplish, viz. the creation of a people, an Israel, of God). Once more we see that the biblical conception of time is not that of evolution or progress, or even of chronological succession: it is at bottom one of promise (prophetic and historical) and fulfilment, in which history consists of times bringing opportunities, the basic time and the decisive opportunity being that of the coming of Jesus Christ, in whom all the promises of God, prophetic and historical, are yea, Amen.

These considerations serve to emphasize the immense significance of the word *kairos* (time) and its cognates in the NT. It would be almost true to say that wherever *kairos* is used some of these overtones can be heard. Luke may say, in an apparently chronological fashion, that 'at that time Herod the king put forth his hands to afflict certain of the church', but such action by Herod was itself conditioned by what had happened at *the kairos*, *the* time of Jesus Christ. There are also a number of words and expressions which in the OT and NT alike are found to have theological as well as temporal meaning because of their relation to the activity of God in the historical order.

There is a group of words such as 'HENCEFORTH', 'HENCEFORWARD', 'HITHERTO', 'heretofore' and 'no longer' which already in the OT have some theological meaning (cf. Num. 18.22, II Chron. 16.9, Gen. 4.12, Isa. 41.23) indicating the qualitative difference of two times in consequence of God's action, or the dependence of the future upon it. But in the NT these same words are used to refer to the absolute differentiation between times that God has made in Jesus Christ (cf. Matt. 23.39, 26.64, Mark 11.14, Luke 1.48, 5.10, John 13.7, 15.15, 16.24, Rom. 6.6, II Cor. 5.15, Eph. 4.17). There is something quite incommensurable between the world as it was (and is) without Christ and the world as it has been redeemed in Christ. 'Hitherto' and 'henceforth' are the temporal words that mark the slopes of the watershed. The watershed itself is represented by the word 'NOW'. The decisive significance of this term is foreshadowed here and there in the OT when some act of God has made a quite new situation for men (cf. Jer. 34.15, Gen. 26.22,29). But in the NT 'now' carries a full and profound meaning embracing all that God has established in his Son. This is true of all the Gk. words that lie behind 'now', but of none so much as *nun*. The fullness of its meaning is manifest in such a phrase as 'now is the day of salvation' (II Cor. 6.2), the 'now' being not merely chronological but realistic, referring to the contents of God's acts of redemption in Christ, which are effective over a long period of history. If psychologists speak of a 'specious present', theologians might well say that 'now' refers to a divine, redemptive present. This fullness of meaning should be read in many places, e.g. when Paul refers to 'things whereof ye are now ashamed' (Rom. 6.21), and it colours many more, particularly the usages of the fourth Gospel, e.g. 'draw out now, and carry to the master of the feast' (John 2.8). 'Now' is also used in an almost opposite sense, though in the light of the same divine acts of redemption, e.g. 'Blessed are ye that hunger now; for ye shall be filled' (Luke 6.21; cf. Matt. 26.65, 27.42, etc.).

Johannine terminology has other characteristics of its own, of special interest being his preference for 'HOUR' to 'time' (*kairos*), the word time being used but three times in the fourth Gospel (twice in 7.6 and once in 7.8) in a phrase in which Jesus speaks of the time of his death as 'my time' (see below: 'my hour'). The word 'hour' occurs in the OT in Daniel only (3.6,15, 4.19,33, 5.5) in characteristically eschatological settings. It is known to the Synoptic writers in the NT, who with John find both chronological (e.g. Matt. 27.46) and theological (Matt. 8.13) uses for it. But John charges the word with ultimate meanings, using it to refer to what we have called the 'divine redemptive present' ('the hour cometh and now is', 4.23, 5.25), and to that hour in which the divine redemptive present was decisively inaugurated ('my hour', 'Father, the hour is come', cf. 7.30, 8.20, 12.23,27, 13.1, 17.1, 19.27). The word is thus eschatological in its essence, and it is therefore not surprising to find it in Revelation, as in Daniel (Rev. 3.3,10, 9.15, 11.13, 14.7, 17.12, 18.10,17,19).

We must now turn to a set of words which refer to the durational aspects of temporal experience, which likewise acquire theological significance in association with the divine activity, and lead us to other expressions related to the last things and to eternity. Verbs that express the action of WAITING are frequently used, as is natural, of men waiting for one another (I Sam. 10.8), but are also associated with men waiting for or upon God, or even with God 'waiting' so as to be able to show mercy (Isa. 30.18). To wait for God is a frequent phrase upon the lips of psalmists and prophets (Ps. 33.20, 37.9, 62.5, Isa. 8.17, 64.4, Jer. 14.22, Micah 7.7, Hos. 12.6, Zeph. 3.8), and refers to the faithful in Israel who were really expecting and awaiting the promised activity of God in Israel's history. In the NT, although that activity is regarded as having taken place in Jesus Christ, there is still reference to a waiting by his disciples. Jesus tells the Apostles to 'wait for the promise of the Father' (Acts 1.4), but Paul goes beyond this to think of all disciples, indeed the whole creation, waiting for the consummation of what God had done in Christ (Rom. 8.19,23,25), a process which can also be referred to as 'waiting for the revelation of our Lord Jesus Christ' (I Cor. 1.7).

The word 'TARRY', used less frequently in a theological context, introduces a new meaning in the OT, God being asked to 'make no tarrying' (Ps. 40.17, 70.5), or asserting through his prophet that his salvation 'shall not tarry' (Isa. 46.13). Temporal imminence thus becomes an expression of religious certainty: 'The vision will surely come, it will not delay' and 'though it tarry, wait for it' (Hab. 2.3). The NT uses the word of human activity (e.g. Acts 21.4), but also in the OT sense of waiting for God's action (Luke 24.49, 'for the power from on high'; John 21.22,23, for the 'coming' of the Lord).

Another word, used only in the NT, and there very little (4 times in all), has found much currency in more recent times—DISPENSATION. Only in Eph. 1.10, 3.2 has the word any temporal significance. It does not supply any basis for the division of history into 'dispensations', Christian and Mosaic, or any other. The word translates the Gk. word 'economy', and is plainly a metaphor, expressing the belief that the *kairoi* that constitute history are part of 'God's economy' or 'stewarding' of the world, by which the divine purpose is effected.

These words of duration remind us in various ways that *the kairos*, initiated by the birth of Jesus Christ, is not yet closed. The day of opportunity is still here; and we in the twentieth century can use the 'now' of the divine redemptive present with the NT writers. The *chronos*, the duration, of *the kairos*, is not yet run out. In this statement we may see how *kairos* and *chronos* are related, and so understand the phrase 'times (*chronoi*) and seasons (*kairoi*)' in Acts 1.7 and I Thess. 5.1. God provides the opportunities (*kairoi*) for men in history and determines how long (*chronoi*) they shall last. But as surely as the opportunities of history come, so surely will they go. Even *the* opportunity given to men in Christ is for a limited duration. There will be a crisis when 'there shall be time no longer' (Rev. 10.6), i.e. when the termination of this opportunity will no longer be delayed (see RV margin). Thus both NT words for time belong to the realm of the historical: we must look elsewhere for expressions of what lies beyond history, though before we do, it behoves us to consider the words used for the end itself.

These fall into two groups, those that talk about LAST (*eschatos*) or latter things or events, and those that speak of the END. The word 'last' can be used in both testaments in a non-theological meaning (e.g. last words, II Sam. 23.1; last farthing, Matt. 5.28), but in conjunction with the word 'day' or 'time(s)' it develops an increasingly rich theological significance. In the OT it begins (as 'latter' or 'last' days) by indicating the farthest remove in time conceivable to a certain individual (e.g. Abraham, Gen. 49.1), and while this usage persists a long time, it becomes clear when the phrase is used in a Messianic prophecy that a new eschatological meaning has been attained (e.g. Isa. 2.2 = Micah 4.1). There is another theological usage in the phrase 'first and last', which is used secularly by the Chronicler to express all the acts of a king (e.g. II Chron. 9.29), but theologically by Deutero-Isaiah to indicate the sole sovereignty of God (e.g. Isa. 44.6). In the NT these uses are reflected, though, as our investigation leads us to expect, the last days are there identified both with the time contemporary with the events reported (e.g. Acts 2.17; cf. also Jesus' identification of the resurrection at the last day with his own presence in history in John 11.24,25), and with a time of preparation for the final consummation (II Tim. 3.1, etc.) as well as with the final manifestation of Christ (John 6.40, I Pet. 1.5). The term 'first and last' is taken up in the Book of Revelation and applied as a title to him who had risen from the dead, i.e. Jesus Christ (Rev. 1.17, 2.8, 22.13). Another use of the word is in the distinction between the first and the last Adam (I Cor. 15.45), by which the parallels and the differences between Adam and Christ are drawn. Clearly this variety of NT usage shows that the 'last' time of God's decisive action began in Jesus Christ (*the kairos* whose duration is not yet exhausted) and will end in its own 'last times' or 'days' which will herald the approach of the 'last day' in which Christ shall be finally revealed.

The word 'END', like the word 'last', has secular uses, both spatial (e.g. Exod. 28.23) and temporal (e.g. Deut. 11.12). It is in the idea of the end of an action or event that its theological significance can be seen and traced. 'End' may partake of three sources of meaning—as cessation, as a final period, as outcome. In all these the theological emphasis is on the fact that God bestows the end. The cessation may be of an individual life (Ps. 39.4), of a people (Amos 8.2), or of the world (Gen. 6.13); but it is seen to be God's action. The 'end' of a vision or revelation may be limited to the fulfilment of a particular vision (Hab. 2.3), or it may refer to the time of the end of the world (Dan. 8.17, etc.); but it is God who is the surety of fulfilment. Various ways of life may lead to varying consequences, but God adjusts the end to the condition (Ps. 73.17). This transcendent lordship of God over history also finds expression when God is said to be he who declares 'the end (latter part) from the beginning' (Isa. 46.10), and when the kingdom of the (Messianic) prince is proclaimed as having 'no end' (Isa. 9.7). The limits of temporality do not apply to the divine.

The NT echoes and amplifies these theological usages. The 'end' or fulfilment of prophecy is in Christ's life and death (Luke 22.37). The 'end of all things is at hand' (I Pet. 4.7). There is to be no end to Christ's kingdom (Luke 1.33), though there will be an end to this world order (Matt. 24.6,14, Mark 13.7, Luke 21.9, I Cor. 15.24). Thus in the NT use of 'end' we have confirmation of the view that the Messianic age has come within this present world order, and this thought receives striking expression in a phrase of Paul's, that upon Christians 'the ends of the ages are come' (I Cor. 10.11). Paul's teaching about ages is that there are two—the present and that which is to come. The ends of both are come upon us: in other words, Christians live both in this age and in that which is to come, which is another way of saying that the new Messianic age has been inaugurated in Christ, though it still awaits consummation at the end of this present age. That consummation is depicted not only in the expression already noticed, but in another which occurs three times in Matt. 13 (vss. 39,40,49), and which means 'full end'. It is this word, filled with eschatological meaning, which Jesus uses in his promise to be with his disciples 'to the end of the world' (Matt. 28.20). That the 'end' is not simply a fact of temporal sequence, but an act of God's gracious nature, is again indicated by the phrase in which Peter writes of Christians receiving 'the end' of their faith, viz. their souls' salvation (I Pet. 1.9). The end, then, is God's gift and action; and it is the end which in fact shapes the process. But the promises that are made to those who endure 'to the end' are not made simply for those who are alive just before the end comes in history (if that be permissible language at all); they are all who endure to the point where the loyalties between this world and the one to come clash in decisive conflict, and who do not succumb to this present world, but endure as seeing him who is invisible.

We must now turn to the words used for ETERNAL. In the OT the word *'olam* predominates, and it originally implied a period of time, one at least of whose boundaries was not fixed. Its significance changes with the object to which it is applied. Thus, in reference to a man's life it can mean simply 'lifelong', as it does when Hannah promises to take her son to Shiloh to stay there 'for ever' (I Sam. 1.22). Its quantitative character is passing into a qualitative one when the OT speaks of the 'everlasting hills' (Gen. 49.26), and that process is evidently complete when the word is applied to God, whose existence cannot be thought of as circumscribed by our human temporal limitations. Nowhere is this more apparent than when the Psalmist tries to write of God's eternity: 'Before the mountains were brought forth, or ever thou hadst formed the earth and the world, even from everlasting to everlasting, thou art God' (Ps. 90.2). Hills are said to be 'everlasting' themselves—their origins are undiscoverable by man: but compared with God they are as beasts that perish. Indeed, the whole world that seems so constant and so sure is but an evanescence in comparison with God. We are here at the point where the OT itself realizes the inadequacy of temporal terms to depict the being and existence of God.

The word *'olam* has thus undergone an immense change in meaning. From being a secular, temporal word, it becomes a profound theological term applicable in its richest sense to God alone. This change has been effected by the prophets of Israel. Hosea uses it to assert that God will betroth Israel to himself 'for ever' if she returns to her wifely loyalties and duties (Hos. 2.21), and already here the term is sufficiently enriched to embrace the destiny of Israel. The Messianic prophecy of Isa. 9 emphasizes this, for the period of peace and prosperity that the new king will inaugurate shall know no temporal bounds (Isa. 9.6, where 'even for ever' parallels 'there shall be no end'). But it is Jeremiah among the pre-exilic prophets who most develops this concept, and he prophesies from the conviction that God has controlled history 'from of old' and will do so 'even for evermore' (Jer. 7.7). God's activity in Israel's history flows from his 'everlasting love' (Jer. 31.2), and will result in a new and 'everlasting covenant' being established (Jer. 32.40). We may say that Jeremiah, by the use of this word, was able to penetrate behind the manifold diversity of historical events to the enduring ground and reason of them all.

Thus it is that all the marks of God's care for Israel are called 'eternal'. God's righteousness (Isa. 51.6), his salvation (45.17) and his word (Isa. 40.8) are all 'EVERLASTING'. So are David's throne (Ps. 89.37,38), the possession of Palestine (Gen. 17.8), the divine statutes (Lev. 6.18, etc.), etc. The history of Israel is thus not to be understood, even in terms of her political institutions, without reference to the supra-temporal being of God. So deeply was this conviction held by the prophets that they saw it as a sin of blasphemy for any man or institution of men to lay claim to 'everlastingness' (Isa. 47.7). Mortality is the mark of man, and 'everlastingness' that of God (cf. Zech. 1.5; *v.* DEATH).

The 'everlastingness' of God in the OT never quite breaks clear of its temporal origins. The familiar parallelisms which help to interpret its meaning are 'throughout all generations' or 'from generation to generation'. It is sometimes opposed to a 'moment' of time (Isa. 54.8). But, as Ps. 90 suggested, there is the beginning of a qualitative differentiation between 'everlastingness' and time, which also finds expression in the late use of the plural of *'olam*. In any late passage, when the word had come to mean an *indefinite* period both in the past and in the future as applied to God, the plural cannot mean the literal addition of a number of indefinite, unbounded temporal durations: it can only be read as a poetic emphasis by which a quantitative plural is a symbol for a qualitative difference.

But God does not cease to be effective in history, though he is not of it. This distinguishes him from the 'fathers' of Israel, and makes him *the* Father of the nation. 'Thou art our father, though Abraham knoweth us not, and Israel doth not acknowledge us: thou, O Lord, art our father; our redeemer from everlasting is thy name' (Isa. 63.16). Thus the OT uses a temporal term to show that throughout the course of time there is active a supra-temporal being whose beginning and end baffle our comprehension, but whose effective reality we may know in his control of events, as of the world in which they occur.

The NT has as its characteristic words for eternity *aiōn* and *aiōnios*. The words are familiar in Greek literature though there is little evidence that such usages affected the NT. What is fairly certain is that, since the words were used to translate *'olam* from the OT, the NT usages have the OT world of thought behind them. In this connexion it is important to observe that neither there, nor in any Jewish literature current at the time, was the word *aiōn* used to express the view that the history of the world is made up of a number of *aiōns* or 'ages', nor even the notion of two *aiōns* or ages—the present and the one to come.

The word *aiōn* can be used of a man's lifetime, as when Paul contemplates eating 'no flesh for evermore' (I Cor. 8.13). The OT meaning of an indefinite past time influences some passages (e.g. Luke 1.70, Acts 3.21, 15.18, where *aiōn* is translated 'world'); and at other times the indefinite future is intended, quite in the manner of the OT (e.g. Mark 11.14, Luke 1.33,55, Heb. 13.8, etc.). But the distinctive fact about the NT is that not only the OT, but also, and more particularly, the events of Christ's life and death and resurrection, help to impart a new meaning to eternity. Thus St. John says that those who eat his flesh and drink his blood shall not die, but live for ever (John 6.50–8). This does not mean that such persons will continue in this mortal, temporal existence for ever; it means that by a new relationship to God set up through Jesus Christ, a new dimension of life is opened to man, eternal life. This is not life without temporal limits, but life-in-Christ and Christ-in-life. The transition to this eternal life can be made in time; but the temporal boundaries of human life do not affect it (cf. John 4.14, 8.51,52, 10.28, 11.26). The same thought of a new quality of life deriving from the priesthood constituted by the life and death of Jesus Christ is expressed in Heb. 5.6, 6.20, 7.17,21, etc.

One important feature of the NT use of *aiōn* is the distinction between the present *aiōn* or age or world, and that which is to come, a distinction which has temporal aspects (Matt. 13.39,40,49), but is more characteristically 'ethical' or 'concrete' (e.g. Luke 16.8, 20.35). This world is characteristically an evil world, in which the minds of the unbelieving are blinded by its god (II Cor. 4.4). But the world to come is a world of eternal (Mark 10.30), of resurrection life (Luke 20.35,36). Yet it must be clearly understood that these two worlds do not stand in an order of temporal succession. The peculiarity of man's situation *now* is that, the *kairos* being upon him, he may at any point of this world's time step into the world to come, and, in the phrase of the Fourth Gospel, have eternal life as a present possession. This is exemplified in Paul's phrase about the ends of the ages having come upon Christians, in his conception of the 'earnest' of our inheritance which we have here and now, in his conviction that God 'raised us up with Christ and made us to sit with him in the heavenly places' (Eph. 2.6); and it is established in Christ's teaching about the new kingdom which had appeared among men with his coming.

So the eternal in the NT is not an uncharacterized duration: it is a 'filled' magnitude—Christ-filled. The more metaphysical implications of that basic conviction begin to show themselves in phrases which the NT writers felt bound to use if they were to do justice to their data. Paul writes of God's wisdom, revealed in Jesus Christ, which had been 'foreordained before the worlds unto our glory' (I Cor. 2.7), i.e. before time began. He also writes of the mystery 'which from all ages hath been hid in God' (Eph. 3.9, Col. 1.26), i.e. from the beginning of time until now. Revelation speaks of a 'lamb that hath been slain from the foundation of the world' (Rev. 13.8), and in John 17.24 Jesus himself is given words referring to God's loving him 'before the foundation of the world'. Beyond history, then, the NT writers discerned the living ground of a purpose that had been latent and yet active all through history; active because the time of Christ's coming was the fulfilment of 'the time', and latent because only in that coming was the purpose fully revealed. But in that revelation man had been able to see at once both the real nature of time and history and the true character of the eternal.

BIBLIOGRAPHY

O. Cullmann: *Christ et le Temps*, Delachaux et Niestlé, Neuchâtel (1947). C. Orelli: *Die Hebräische Synonyme der Zeit und Ewigkeit* (1871). F. H. Brabant: *Time and Eternity in Christian Thought*, Bampton Lectures, London (1937); *Eternity, a Concordance of Biblical Words*, London (1882).

JOHN MARSH

TONGUES, SPEAKING WITH *v.* SPIRIT V, VIII(*e*)

TRANSFIGURE, TRANSFIGURATION

The story of the t. occurs in Mark 9.2–8, Matt. 17.1–8 and Luke 9.28–36. There is a close agreement between Mark and Matthew (although the latter expands instead of shortening Mark as is his usual practice). Mark is the earlier and more primitive, e.g. his description of the whiteness of Jesus' garments; Matthew contrives to stress the parallel with Moses on Mount Sinai. Luke's account is more varied, but it is unlikely he is using any other source; he is probably following his custom of rather free editorial re-writing, partly to correct misconceptions (he omits the actual word 'transfigured' lest it should suggest the metamorphosis of some pagan God) or to add explanations (he connects the t. with Jesus' prayer, and says that Moses and Elijah talked of the 'exodus (decease) which he was about to accomplish at Jerusalem'). The Fourth Gospel omits the t., for the writer has no need of a *particular* example of Jesus' glory; to him the whole life and death of Jesus is one visible continuous demonstration of God's glory dwelling with men. The only other reference to the t. in the NT is II Peter 1.16–18; this is part of a second-century pseudonymous letter which, following a literary convention of the time, tries to correct errors in current Church life by associating itself with the august name of an Apostle. It is particularly concerned with the time of the *parousia* (or appearance of Christ at the end of the world) and with the problem of the interpretation of Scripture. It takes the t. as a foretaste and assurance of the *parousia*, and as a witness to the sureness of the prophetic tradition. In both points there is a slight shift of emphasis from the view of the Synoptists half a century or more earlier, which we are about to examine. Lastly, the use of the verb by St. Paul (II Cor. 3.18) should be noted, where he refers to the 'transformation' of the Christian believer.

In the Gospel narratives the t. follows directly upon Peter's confession of faith at Caesarea Philippi (after six days, Mark and Matthew; about eight days after, Luke). Jesus had made up his mind that Messiahship involved suffering and death, a conception so at variance with any current ideas of the role of the Messiah as to make it inconceivable even to his closest followers. At this moment he goes up into a mountain with Peter and James and John. Tradition has it that it was Mount Tabor, but it is not very high, and in any case had a fortress on top; it is much more likely to have been Mount Hermon, fourteen miles north of Caesarea Philippi, which reaches 9,000 ft. On the mountain he is transformed by a heavenly radiance, and a heavenly voice attests his mission, both of them counteracting what would be the natural conclusion to draw from Jesus' outward failure and death. Moreover, two OT heroes, who together sum up the significant features of the OT, are present and are subordinated to him (Mark 9.7 and parallels). As at his Baptism his Sonship was proclaimed by a voice from heaven, so that voice is heard at the decisive halfway stage of his ministry. If the t. came at a crisis in Jesus' own life, and was not only designed to fortify and enlighten the alarmed and bewildered disciples, then the three who were most closely associated with Jesus were with him at this moment as they were to be later at Gethsemane.

The t. is thus a turning point in our present Gospel narratives. The story is clearly full of symbolism, but before we turn to that we must face the historical question, 'What did happen?' It is impossible to be quite sure. Bishop K. E. Kirk has well said 'before the earliest Gospel assumed its present shape, the Church had fixed upon the t. as the central moment of the Lord's earthly life. It had surrounded that moment with a glamour of illusion and allegory so complex that it cannot now with any certainty be analysed into its constituent elements' (*Vision of God*, p. 101). It has been thought by some that the t. is a reading back by the Synoptists of the post-Resurrection glory into the life of Jesus, and that the story is misplaced in its present setting. Others have regarded it as purely symbolical or mythical. But we have learned a good deal more about psychical experiences in recent years, even if we had forgotten well-authenticated phenomena in Christian history. One of the best known examples is the *stigmata* of St. Francis of Assisi, which were the result of prolonged meditation on the passion of Christ and which remained with him until his death. To-day various kinds of visionary and auditory experiences have been investigated, e.g. *photisms* or sensations of bright light, and it has been pointed out that the *form* of such experiences is likely to be influenced by the conscious and unconscious minds of those involved. From this point of view the appearance of Moses and Elijah to Messianically-minded Jews is what we should expect: and in a far deeper sense they would appropriately be present in the mind of Jesus. It is, of course, precarious to build too much on psychological studies or to claim too great a certainty about our Lord's inner life, but it does seem likely that, after the spiritual crisis of Caesarea Philippi, Jesus as he was praying underwent a profound spiritual experience in which the disciples shared. This has been best expressed by W. K. Lowther Clarke: 'Whatever took place was primarily in our Lord's consciousness . . . for a brief space the disciples were able to enter into the Lord's consciousness and see with his eyes. Then their faith failed, and the vision passed; or, perhaps, he thought of other things, and the link which connected them with the unseen world was forthwith snapped. The cloud was not so much a material as a psychic cloud, if the expression may be allowed; though the great mystics would have felt no need to apologize for such a conception' (*New Testament Problems*, p. 35). If this is the nearest we can get in answering the historical question, a puzzle still remains: why did the disciples so clearly fail immediately after the Crucifixion to expect either a resurrection or a *parousia*? No satisfactory answer has been given to this question. Mark 9.10 looks like an attempt to supply one.

The symbolism of the t. story is so pervasive that it has been the despair of commentators and at the same time a stimulus to their ingenuity. Moses and Elijah represent the Law and the Prophets. Furthermore Moses was traditionally also a prophet, as well as the mediator of the old covenant. Both were thought to have been translated into heaven, Elijah according to II Kings 2, Moses according to popular tradition in *The Assumption of Moses*, an apocalyptic work of the 1st cent. AD (this had grown out of Deut. 34.6). Elijah was expected to reappear as a forerunner of the Messiah, see Mal. 4.5–6 and II Esdras 6.26 (which refers also to Enoch), and there is a possibility that the same was expected of Moses, though the rabbinic evidence is late and slight. Both had conversed with God (Moses, Exod. 20; Elijah, I Kings 19). Moreover, Moses' face had been transfigured (Exod. 34.32–5, quoted by Paul in II Cor. 3.7). And both appear again in NT times in connexion with the 'last things' in Rev. 11.3. In the t. story these two figures, summing up all this wealth of OT suggestion, are present when the divine voice says of Jesus, 'hear ye him', and the prophecy of Deut. 18.18 is fulfilled. The law and the prophets are at the same time fulfilled and superseded, and their representative forebears agree that it is so, and witness that it is in Jesus, the Messiah, the divine Son, that God's revelation is now to be seen. The Messianic era has dawned.

For the cloud as the symbol of the divine glory and presence, see under GLORY. Peter's desire to build three tabernacles, as at the Feast of Tabernacles, to perpetuate this dwelling of God with men is unnecessary and premature. God is already dwelling with men in Christ, and yet before Christ's glory can be permanently realized there must be the way of suffering and crucifixion.

In this wider setting the t. can be seen to link the beginning of the 'last days' in the earthly ministry of Christ both with his Resurrection triumph and with the *parousia*, when the end of the time process will see all things subjected to him. There has been discussion as to which of these last two emphases is primary, but it is a minor question compared with the fact that both are there. Thus the t. is one more instance of the close linking of the two Testaments, and of the age-long purposes of God in creation and redemption. It is a vivid illustration of the 'taking our manhood into God' which is the way in which the *Quicunque Vult* describes Christ's work. The Eastern Orthodox Church makes much of the t. as the supreme symbol of the t. of the whole of creation. In the English-speaking world we pay tribute to this, as A. M. Ramsey has pointed out (see Bibliography) in the place the word 'transfigure' has in our vocabulary. He also draws attention to a suggestive definition of transfiguration by C. H. Dodd in summarizing part of the argument of A. J. Toynbee's *Study of History*. Dodd says that to transfigure a situation is to 'bring the total situation as we ourselves participate in it, into a larger context, which gives it a new meaning' (*The Bible To-day*, p. 129). That is what the t. story does to the life of Jesus in the narrative of the Synoptic Gospels. (*V.* also PRESENCE, esp. sect. 'Glory'.)

BIBLIOGRAPHY

Standard Commentaries, *ad loc.* E. Underhill: *The Mystic Way* (1913), pp. 114–23. A. M. Ramsey: *The Glory of God and the Transfiguration of Christ* (1949), Part II.

RONALD H. PRESTON

TRANSGRESS *v.* SIN

TREE *v.* CROSS

TRESPASS *v.* SIN

TRIBULATION *v.* SUFFER

TRIUMPH *v.* VICTORY

TROUBLE *v.* SUFFER

TRUTH

'Jesting Pilate's' question (John 18.38), if historical at all, implies in the questioner no more than the intellectualist view of truth made familiar to that age by the Gk. philosophical tradition, and presupposed still in our modern usage. The biblical usage is different, and is fundamental, esp. in its thought about God.

In the OT truth is a quality which properly belongs to God. God is a God of truth (Ps. 31.5, Jer. 10.10), who 'keepeth truth for ever' (Ps. 146.6; cf. 100.5). Truth means essentially reliability, dependableness, ability to perform what is required. The Heb. words trans. 'truth' (*emeth, emunah*) are sometimes rendered 'faithfulness' (Hos. 2.20, Deut. 32.4; RV changes to 'faithfulness' where AV has 'truth'; cf. also Isa. 25.1). The verb *aman* is more common than the nouns, and it means 'confirm', 'stand firm', 'trust'. From the same root we have the adj. *amen* (*q.v.*) meaning 'true' in the sense of 'sure', 'reliable', 'valid'. In itself truth is a fact or state which is unalterable and has to be accepted; as applied to persons it means that there is something which regularly characterizes their behaviour; they are consistent.

Three passages in particular illustrate the fundamental meaning. Gen. 32.10 uses the word with reference to the continuing kindness of God made real in Jacob's experience by outward prosperity. I Kings 17.24 similarly implies that God's truth is related to his goodwill and may be expected to manifest itself in tangible blessings. The prayer of the Psalmist (Ps. 54.5) that God will cut off his enemies 'in thy truth' is perplexing. There is no need, however, to follow those commentators who would emend the Heb. text here, for the use of 'truth' is consistent with other passages. It refers to the abiding characteristic of God; he is of such a nature as to react hostilely to human sin, and the pious man may call upon God to act as it were 'in character'. In view of this, it is clear how different the Heb. conception of God was from the pagan view of the caprice and unaccountability of the gods. Not so had Israel learned Jehovah in the school of her great prophets.

From the primary conception of a quality inherent in God, truth develops into a quality of his activity, e.g. his 'judging' (Ps. 96.13); God 'sends it forth' (Ps. 57.3). Notice, further, the collocation of 'truth' with 'mercy' (Gen. 32.10, Ps. 25.10, 108.4, etc.).

Truth is also regarded as what God demands of man. He desires it in the inward parts (Ps. 51.6); man must speak it (Ps. 15.2); and seek it (Jer. 5.1); and walk in it (II Kings 20.3). Here it means unwavering conformity with God's will as made known in the Law: 'all thy commandments are truth' (Ps. 119.151); also, more generally, faithfulness, trustworthiness.

Passing on to the NT, we find 'truth' representing the Gk. *alētheia*, and therewith picking up Gk. connotations, which are much nearer our modern ones. But the possibility of a Heb. meaning must always be considered. *Alētheia* in Gk. means the actual state of affairs as contrasted with rumour or false report or mythology; to the philosophers it means that which really exists as opposed to what only appears to exist or comes into existence only to pass away. Thinking—the philosopher's business—does lead to truth, and when this goal is attained right action should follow; wrongdoing may be put down to ignorance. This at any rate was the Platonic belief. Not all Gk. thinkers however agreed with Plato that *alētheia* could be found by disciplined thinking, and in the Hellenistic Age we find it regarded as accessible only by revelation. This is the line of development in Gnosticism and Neo-Platonism.

The fusion of these two senses—the Heb. and the Gk.—in varying degrees in the NT yields some interesting developments of meaning. The meaning 'that which has validity or stability', when carried over into the NT, makes it possible to speak of truth as something to be done (cf. John 3.21, I John 1.6) rather than simply believed or thought of, and to set truth in contrast with unrighteousness (cf. the immediate contexts of the two passages just mentioned). For truth as that on which one can rely see Rom. 3.3–7, where God's faithfulness and truth are together set over against human falseness.

A meaning practically identical with our modern one, esp. in the phrases 'truly', 'in truth', is found in the NT. This is sufficient to explain the few occurrences in the Synoptic Gospels and Acts, and also Rom. 2.2, 9.1, II Cor. 12.6, 13.8, Eph. 4.25, Phil. 1.18, I Tim. 2.7. Similarly, moreover, in the Johannine writings this meaning is adequate for John 8.40,44–6, 16.7,13, I John 3.18. In these writings, however, a deeper sense is generally implied; cf. John 17.17,19. For such an inward, deeper sense we may compare Rom. 1.25, 3.7, 15.8, where the phrase 'truth *of God*' occurs; II Cor. 11.10, 'truth *of Christ*'; and Gal. 2.5,14, Col. 1.5, where there is an alternative, 'truth *of the gospel*'. In these passages the word is moving towards the meaning: the Christian revelation, or the truth as revealed by Christ and as taking precedence over all other human apprehensions of truth. Such a meaning is required in II Cor. 4.2, Gal. 5.7, Eph. 1.13, 4.21, II Thess. 2.10–12, Jas. 1.18, 5.19, I Tim. 3.15, and the five occurrences (I Tim. 2.4, 4.3, II Tim. 2.25, 3.7, Tit. 1.1) in the Pastoral Epistles of the phrase 'knowledge of the truth' as the hallmark of a Christian, as also in Heb. 10.26. In II Pet. 1.12 the rather strange phrase 'the present truth' practically means 'Christianity'.

This paves the way for the distinctive Johannine usage, which is the most developed and suggestive in the Bible and demands a closer investigation. The dominant meaning is here divine truth, revelation, without the unparticularized connotation of truth in ordinary English speech. For example, John 8.32 is not a motto for the metaphysician or scientist; truth here is that which God has made known of himself in Jesus, and similarly freedom is not a general freedom of thought or conscience but freedom in the strictly moral and religious sense of freedom from sin. Truth in the intellectual sense is far from being all that man needs; the primary thing is not to understand and make sense of the universe, but to know God and live a good life, and Christ's work is directed to this end (John 17.3); it is truth of this kind that he offers. In fact he brings it into the world (John 1.17; cf. 1.9) and may even be identified with it (John 14.6). After the resurrection it will be the function of the Holy Spirit to lead men into 'truth in its entirety' (John 16.13). Truth so understood is a stimulant of conduct rather than matter for contemplation; something which we do, to be obeyed or disobeyed (John 3.21, I John 1.6; cf. also Gal. 5.7, I Pet. 1.22). It makes men fit not only for good living in fellowship with one another, but fit also for divine life in fellowship with God: 'I am the way, the truth and the life; no man cometh unto the Father, but by me' (John 14.6). It is a means of sanctification for those who receive it (John 17.17,19), a thought which is easier to understand if the embodiment of truth in Jesus the Revealer is kept in mind; in this connexion he is conceived as performing a priestly function, mediating between God and worshipper. In the light of this we can interpret the famous statement about true worship (John 4.23f.); worship such as God requires is 'in spirit and in truth', i.e. conformable to the divine nature which is spirit, and determined by the truth which God has made available concerning himself. Here again the thought of Jesus as the personal embodiment of truth is not far away, and it is right to interpret vss. 23f. in the light of vss. 25f.: in so far as men see the truth in Jesus they will both worship and live acceptably to God, but such worship and conduct are not possible apart from Jesus. In certain Johannine passages the OT background shows through unmistakeably, viz. John 17.17 ('Thy word is truth'), III John 3–4.

E. C. BLACKMAN

TURN, TURN AGAIN *v.* REPENT

TWELVE, THE

The 'disciples' of Jesus have already been mentioned several times in the Gospel of Mark when we hear that Jesus 'appointed twelve, to be with him and to be sent out to preach and to have authority to cast out demons' (Mark 3.14). It is not clearly stated when this happened, but it must have been some little time after Jesus had begun his public ministry. Though Mark alone says explicitly why Jesus chose twelve out of the larger number of his disciples, Luke says that he called them 'apostles', which indicates that his purpose was to send them out (Luke 6.13; *v.* APOSTLE). Neither Mark nor Luke here indicates why *twelve* were thus chosen, but a saying of Jesus reported by Luke alone much later in his Gospel suggests that the number had some connexion with 'the twelve tribes of Israel' (Luke 22.30). The chosen twelve were not at once sent out by Jesus; Mark does not report their dispatch on their mission till 6.7, while Luke does so at 9.1, and says that it was then that Jesus gave them authority to cast out demons and to cure diseases—Mark repeats his previous statement that Jesus gave them authority over the unclean spirits. Matthew omits any mention of the choice or appointment of the twelve, but introduces them as an already existing group ('he called his twelve disciples', 10.1) when he comes to tell of their mission. But he seems to put the mission earlier in the ministry of Jesus than Mark and Luke do. In Mark the only indication of the real purpose of the mission (which can hardly have been simply to drive out demons and to heal the sick) is in the words, 'And they went out and preached that they should repent' (Mark 6.12). Luke says they were sent forth 'to preach the Kingdom of God and to heal the sick' (9.2); Matthew tells us that what they were to preach was, 'The Kingdom of heaven is at hand' (10.7). Matthew also reports the injunction that they were not to go to Gentiles or to Samaritans, but only to the lost sheep of the house of Israel (10.5), and the assurance that they would not have gone through the cities of Israel before the Son of Man came (10.23). Of the outcome of the mission we hear nothing, only that when the twelve returned they reported to Jesus what they had done (Mark 6.30, Luke 9.10; Matt. does not report their return at all). It would seem that the tradition embodied in the Gospels had failed to preserve any clear recollection either of the purpose or the result of this mission; was this perhaps because it had failed to achieve what Jesus intended and expected? The explicit limitation of its scope to Israe and the assurance that there would not be time to complete it even so, are very hard to explain. But they may perhaps be held to give some confirmation of the suggestion that the choice of *twelve* disciples was determined by the fact that their work was to be for Israel only. (Similarly the number 70 in Luke's account of another mission is commonly supposed to have a symbolic significance; it corresponds to the number of the nations of the world in Gen. 10.)

The first three Gospels all give lists of the names of the twelve, and there is a fourth list in Acts, Matt. 10.2ff., Mark 3.6ff., Luke 6.14ff., Acts 1.13ff.; John refers to 'the twelve' at 6.67ff. and mentions Thomas as one of them, 20.24, but has no more to say of them. The lists in Matthew and Mark agree except in order, as do those in Luke and Acts. But the latter two differ from the former two in having 'Judas (son) of James' instead of Thaddaeus. Since we know nothing more either of Thaddaeus or of Judas (except that 'Judas, not Iscariot' is mentioned in John 14.22), it is useless to try to account for this divergence.

After their return from their mission, the twelve appear in the Gospels only as the constant companions of Jesus, to whom some of his teaching was specially addressed (Mark 9.35, 10.32) and along with whom he partook of the Last Supper. Matthew and Luke, but not Mark, sometimes call them 'the twelve disciples' (Matt. 10.1, etc., but only once, 9.1, in Luke) or 'the twelve apostles' (Matt. 10.2 and Luke 22.14, where, however, many good authorities omit 'twelve'). Sometimes it is fairly clear that 'his disciples' means only the twelve. But nowhere is there any suggestion that in choosing the twelve Jesus intended that they should be the leaders, after his own death, of the community of his followers.

Yet it was only natural that those who had been Jesus' closest companions during his life should after his death and resurrection take the leading place among those who believed in him. According to the Acts this is what happened. The story of the election of Matthias to fill Judas' place shows the importance attached to the number twelve. But it is doubtful whether it was really so quickly felt that there must be *twelve* apostles, for there are indications that for a time 'the eleven' was an accepted designation for the apostolic group (cf. Matt.28. 16; Luke 24.9, 33; Acts 1.26, and probably even 2.14, since by usual Greek idiom, 'Peter with the eleven' means 'with the eleven of whom he was one' rather than 'with the eleven others'). Only once in Acts are the apostles referred to as 'the twelve' (6.2). And soon the leadership of the church in Jerusalem passed from the original apostles to another group in which James, the Lord's brother, who had not been one of the twelve, took the leading place. (See also APOSTLE, MINISTER.)

J. Y. CAMPBELL

* * *

UNBLAMEABLE *v.* INNOCENT

UNCLEAN, DEFILE, PROFANE, CLEAN, PURIFY, WASH

'Ye shall put difference between the holy and the common, and between unclean and the clean' (Lev. 10.10). The primitive sense of numinous awe includes both reverence and fear, i.e. holiness and uncleanness (*tm'*); in both senses contact with certain persons and objects is dangerous and forbidden. Holiness is the condition of approach to God, cleanness of intercourse with all society. The opposite of holiness is common or PROFANE—that which does not pertain to God—and it may be clean and so permitted to man; or unclean and so prohibited (contrast the same root *hll* in Gen. 49.4, where a taboo is broken; and in Deut. 20.6, where the vineyard is profaned, i.e. brought into common use, after the holy firstfruits have been given to God).

The following are unclean in themselves, and association with them conveys uncleanness: sexual intercourse (Gen. 34.5), especially adultery or within the prohibited degrees, Lev. 18; childbirth (Lev. 12; the period is twice as long for a girl as for a boy); sexual or other issues from the body (Lev. 15); certain animals (Lev. 11, Deut. 14); leprosy (Lev. 13f.); dead bodies (Num. 19). Uncleanness is more contagious than holiness (Hag. 2.11f.), and no one can escape it. It is closely allied to sin, except that uncleanness comes from outside; and even unwitting defilement makes a man guilty (Lev. 5.1ff.). In Hebrew psychology the CLEAN is what supports the total psychic activity of person or group, the unclean what counteracts it; a pure heart is one which preserves the integrity of the soul unbroken by contaminating elements (cf. Matt. 5.8). When an animal is eaten part of a strange soul is absorbed, and therefore the Israelite may only eat what can be assimilated into the soul, i.e. familiar animals, and not those sacred to other nations. Every warrior must be absolutely pure or the psychic activity of the army is destroyed (Deut. 23.9ff.) and drastic purifications must be undertaken by the victors if they are to gain ascendency over the spoil without injuring their souls (Num. 31.19ff.). Any alien element may DEFILE, and therefore contact with all things foreign is dangerous, especially idolatry (Ezek. 23.17) In the context of the prophetic message, this religious defilement took on a strongly ethical meaning (Isa. 6.5). In NT times Pharisaism stressed strict ritual purity in obedience to God's revealed will; but Jesus gave overriding authority to the moral claims of the Law (Mark 7.1–23; see Branscomb, *Jesus and the Law of Moses*, pp. 156–82). This teaching was rediscovered in the early Church (Acts 10f., Rom. 14.14), and, against a gentile background, defilement took on a thoroughly ethical sense (e.g. Heb. 12.15, II Pet. 2.20); though the tender conscience might still be defiled by contact with pagan ritual, affecting both flesh and spirit (I Cor. 8.7, II Cor. 7.1).

Cleanness is indispensable for being sanctified: no one may enter the sanctuary or touch sacred objects when they are unclean (so in Deut. 12.15 clean/unclean mean ready/unready for religious duties; cf. Lev. 22). This is especially true of the priest (Exod. 30.19), who may also be disqualified if he is branded as abnormal by a physical defect (Lev. 21.17ff.; so also the sacrificial animal, Lev. 22.20ff.). In the NT, Jesus is both the 'lamb without blemish and without spot' and also the sanctified priest (I Pet. 1.19, Heb. 9.14); so that Christians share his sanctity, and it is God's purpose for the Church to be ethically spotless (Eph. 1.4, 5.27, Col. 1.22, Phil. 2.15, Jas. 1.27, Jude 24).

Many forms of uncleanness may be removed by WASHING (e.g. Lev. 22.6f.), but an offering is necessary: for a woman after childbirth (Lev. 12.7f.); after contact with the dead (Num. 19; it is to be noted that David's conduct over his son, II Sam. 12.15ff., strikes at the root of the old idea of the uncleanness of death); and for a healed leper (Lev. 14; cf. Mark 1.40ff.). In the Gospels 'cleansing' usually means miraculous healing, and in John 9.7 a man receives his sight on washing. The priest effects 'atonement' for the Israelite, and obliteration of his sin, so making him clean. So as to be the great source of purification, the temple itself must be purified—in post-exilic times, once a year on the Day of Atonement (Lev. 16). (*V.* also WATER.)

In Heb. (esp. 9.1–10.25) the significance of this ritual is completely transformed. Sacrifice means cleansing from sin, but, since it is only the shadow of an eternal reality, cannot effect it. In the willing death of Christ in perfect obedience to the Father's will the eternal reality was perfectly revealed; so that Christians themselves can boldly enter the holy place having their hearts sprinkled from an evil conscience, and their body washed with pure water. This reference to baptism, taken up again in 'the washing of regeneration and renewing of the Holy Spirit' (Titus 3.5) is set within God's purpose to 'purify unto himself a people for his own possession' (Titus 2.14). Christ presented the Church to himself, holy and without blemish, 'having cleansed it by the washing of water with the word' (Eph. 5.26f.), i.e. not simply with the baptismal confession of Jesus as Lord, but with the word Jesus had spoken abiding in his disciples (John 5.3). This whole new meaning of cleansing is brought to a focus in the washing of the disciples' feet (John 13.3ff.). Throughout the NT ethical purity becomes the mark both of the individual and the church (II Cor. 6.6, 11.2,3), for 'we know that when he appears we shall be like him, for we shall see him as he is; and everyone who thus hopes on him purifies himself as he is pure' (I John 3.2f.). (*V.* also WATER.)

KENNETH GRAYSTON

UNDERSTAND

The Heb. word (*bin*) means discern, consider; and the cognate nouns (*binah*, *tebunah*) can mean both the act and faculty of understanding and also the object understood. The relevant Gk. verbs are similar in meaning (*noeo*, as Mark 13.14; *suniemi*, as Mark 4.12). 'They that seek the Lord understand all things', says Prov. 28.5. Contact with God, faith, is the spring of understanding as of wisdom (cf. WISE). Alternatively, God is the most important object of understanding: Isa. 43.10, Jer. 9.24; though in the more intellectual sense God is beyond man's understanding: Isa. 40.28, Rom. 11.33ff.

The verbs 'understand' and 'know' are in frequent juxtaposition, esp. in OT, and their meaning often is synonymous (*v.* KNOW).

E. C. B.

UNLEARNED

The passage chiefly requiring explanation is Acts 4.13, where the Apostles are described as unlearned and ignorant. Unlearned (lit. unlettered) means unable to read (cf. Isa. 29.11f., John 7.15), i.e. unable to understand the Law. Ability to understand and expound (cf. Isa. 50.4) the Law was for a Jew the chief reason for learning letters. As referring to Peter and John, the word therefore indicates that from the point of view of the Jerusalem authorities they were not recognized religious teachers. The word rendered 'ignorant' signifies a private person as contrasted with one holding public office, or a professional or expert; hence, with ref. to the Apostles, 'amateurs', local preachers rather than ordained ministers. In I Cor. 14.16, 23f. the same word (trans. unlearned) perhaps means catechumens as contrasted with church members.

E. C. B.

UNLEAVENED BREAD, FEAST OF *v.* SACRIFICE IV(*a*) and esp. (*b*) and BREAD

UNREPROVEABLE *v.* INNOCENT

UNRIGHTEOUS, UNRIGHTEOUSNESS

In the OT the word stands for that wickedness which results in sorrow and trouble (Isa. 10.1, 55.7), for violence (Exod. 23.1), sheer perverseness and injustice (Lev. 19.15 and 5 times elsewhere), and the exact opposite of righteousness (*q.v.*; Jer. 20.13). This last is the usual meaning in the NT, except for II Cor. 6.14 where the reference is to general lawlessness.

N. H. S.

UPRIGHT, UPRIGHTNESS

These are OT words, the only time the adj. is used in the NT being Acts 14.10, where it means 'stand erect'. It is commonly thought that the word 'upright' is primarily an ethical word, but this is not so. The original meaning of the root, as is clear from the Arabic, is 'be gentle, easy, tractable', whence Samson can say that a woman is *yashar* in his eyes (Judg. 14.3,7). Here the EVV have rightly translated 'she pleaseth me well', but the Hebrew word is that which is normally translated 'upright'. The word can be used of making a path straight and easy to travel (Isa. 40.3), or of gold being smoothly overlaid on graven work (I Kings 6.35). The next stage is the use common in Deuteronomic writers whereby certain actions are said to be 'good and right' in the eyes of the Lord (Deut. 6.18 and frequently), the meaning being 'agreeable to and pleasing to'. From this we get an ethical content to the meaning of the word, but it is important to understand that the meaning of the word is conditioned by the character of the one to whom the action is pleasing. This is shown, for instance, in Prov. 14.12, where the EVV have 'there is a way which *seemeth right* unto a man, but the end thereof are the ways of death', where 'seemeth' is interpolated by the translators.

N. H. SNAITH

* * *

VAIN, VANITY

These words refer to what is impermanent and unsubstantial, like breath (Heb. *hebel*), e.g. Ps. 62.9, 'men . . . lighter than vanity'; as contrasted with God, who alone is dependable (cf. vs. 7, 'the rock of my strength and my refuge is in God'). All men, rich or poor, high and low alike, are unreliable. This usage of the word is frequent in Eccles. The ref. to idolatry is also frequent, e.g. Jer. 8.19; and in the NT, Acts 14.15, Rom. 8.20 (Gk. *mataios*, *mataiotes*). Another Heb. word to which 'vain', 'vanity' often corresponds is *shaw'*, emptiness (Gk. *kenos*, Phil. 2.16); cf. Ezek. 13.8f., 22.28, where note the connexion with lying, and Hos. 12.11, Ps. 24.4, where note the connexion with idolatry. A similar word meaning 'emptiness' (*riq*) is rendered 'vain' in a few places, e.g. Ps. 2.1, Isa. 49.4. In Ps. 33.17, 'a horse is a vain thing for safety', the Heb. is *sheqer*, 'lie', the meaning being the unreliability of the horse. The phrase 'in vain' in the third commandment (Exod. 20.7, Deut. 5.11), literally 'for emptiness' (*shaw'*), means lightly, without due reverence for God; similarly in Ps. 139.20.

E. C. B.

VEIL *v.* SACRIFICE II(*d*)

VENGEANCE *v.* REWARD

VERILY *v.* AMEN

VESTMENTS *v.* SACRIFICE III(*d*)

VICTORY, CONQUER, OVERCOME, TRIUMPH

The Biblical faith in divine retribution involved the conviction that the oppressed, whether conceived of individually or nationally, would eventually gain the victory through the power of God. According to OT teaching, for Israel *victory* would mean 'ease' or 'security' (cf. II Sam. 23.10.12); when ascribed to God himself it was a picture of his pre-eminence (cf. I Chron. 29.11) or of the ultimate vindication of his purpose (cf. Isa. 25.8). It was the consciousness that victory belonged to God and could be granted by God that evoked Israelite confidence (cf. Num. 13.30). It also called forth the spirit of *triumph* or exultation —the pæan attendant upon the victory. At times this cry of rejoicing might be on the lips of the oppressor (cf. II Sam. 1.20, Ps. 25.2, 94.3), but in the end it would be proper only to those who trusted in God: 'Save us, O Lord our God, and gather us from among the nations, to give thanks unto thy holy name, and to *triumph* in thy praise' (Ps. 106.47). Both creation (cf. Ps. 92.4) and redemption (cf. Exod. 15.1,21) alike called forth the shout of triumph. In both cases it marked the recognition of an act of God.

The NT points to the achievement of this divine victory through Jesus Christ. Bishop Lightfoot (commenting upon Col. 2.15 in *The Epistles to Colossians and Philemon*) points out the significance of the conflict in the life of Christ, which was the prelude to the *victory*. 'Christ took upon himself our human nature with all its temptations (Heb. 4.15). The powers of evil gathered about him. Again and again they assailed him; but each fresh assault ended in a new defeat. . . . Then the last hour came. This was the great crisis of all, when "the power of darkness" made itself felt (Luke 22.53), when the prince of this world asserted his tyranny (John 12.30). The final act in the conflict began with the agony of Gethsemane; it ended with the Cross of Calvary. The victory was complete. The enemy of man was defeated. The powers of evil . . . were cast aside for ever. And the victory of mankind is involved in the victory of Christ' (pp. 256ff.). It is because of the victory of the Cross that Christ is represented as the triumphant general, leading the subjugated powers of evil in his train. The triumph lies in the cross itself, the symbol of shame and defeat becoming the emblem of victory and glory. 'The convict's gibbet is the victor's car' (Lightfoot, *op. cit.*). (In II Cor. 2.14—the other instance of the word *triumph* in the NT—the picture is different. There it is those liberated by the Cross, who are now the enchained participants in Christ's triumph. Man, redeemed from sin and death, becomes the booty of the divine conqueror.)

In John the *victory* is proclaimed proleptically—in anticipation of the glory that was to come from the Cross. 'Be of good cheer; I *have overcome* the world' (John 16.33). Archbishop Temple wrote: 'That these words should be spoken then is a fact that almost paralyses feeling, even the feelings of awe and adoration. He knew what was before him; yet he can say *I have overcome the world*. For what the world thought his shame was his glory, and what the world thought his defeat was his victory (Col. 2.15). . . . Not in gloom or depression, but in solemn triumph, "for the joy that was set before him" (Heb. 12.2) he moves forward to his death; soon the crown of glory and thorns will be upon his brow; soon upon his gallows-throne he will be *lifted up*; already he is the conqueror' (*Readings in St. John's Gospel*, p. 302).

For St. Paul the resurrection of Jesus was the sign that the victory had been won. Death —to him 'the wages of sin' (Rom. 6.23)—has been 'swallowed up in *victory*' (I Cor. 15.54). The truth of man's justification had been made manifest through the Resurrection (cf. Rom. 4.25). Through sharing in Christ's Resurrection (cf. I Cor. 15.22—'For as in Adam all die, so also in Christ shall all be made alive'), man becomes likewise a sharer in the divine victory wrought by Christ (cf. I Cor. 15.57, 'But thanks be to God which giveth us the victory through our Lord Jesus Christ'). Karl Barth points out that this victory is one that man can realize in the present—'Note the present tense: "which *giveth* the victory"! As God's gift, the victory, the "reality of the resurrection", is present; is a valid word spoken to us, not to be forgotten, not to be dragged down into the dialectic of *our* existence, not to be restricted, not to be weakened, not to be doubted' (*The Resurrection of the Dead*, p. 221).

The consciousness of this victory affects the Christian's attitude to present afflictions. 'If God is for us, who is against us?' (Rom. 8.31). The victory of Christ is pictured as super-abundant, and in this super-abundance St. Paul pictures the Christian as sharing—'Nay, in all these things we are more than conquerors [Gk. *hypernikomen*] through him that loved us' (Rom. 8.37). The same outlook appears in I John 5.4—'Whatever is born of God conquers the world' (Moffatt's Translation). Through faith an entrance is made into the sphere of victory, for a man is born into the family of the God to whom victory belongs. For the writer faith in Jesus Christ as the Son of God means that the enticements of a pagan world are overcome. C. H. Dodd comments: 'Here, then, is the way to victory over paganism, the paganism of the human heart, manifesting itself both in a godless world-order and in the power of evil inclinations, false standards and bad dispositions which we have to overcome in ourselves in obeying God's commands. The way to victory is not a confident assertion of our own better selves, but faith. . . . We have a faith against which all the forces of evil in the world and in ourselves are powerless to prevail' (*The Johannine Epistles*, pp. 126–7). Victory, then, whilst being fundamentally eschatological in its import—as signifying the final triumph of God—is at the same time something into which man may enter here and now. He becomes a member of the victorious community.

R. J. HAMMER

VINDICATOR *v.* REDEEM, REWARD, SUFFER

VINE, VINEYARD

Often in literal sense. As it does not bear fruit for several years after planting and needs much care, to sit under one's own v. (I Kings 4.25, Mic. 4.4, Zech. 3.10) or to eat of one's own v. (II Kings 18.31, Isa. 36.16) is a sign of security.

Israel frequently likened to a v. and sometimes to a vineyard: Ps. 80.8–19, Isa. 5.1–7, 27.2ff., Jer. 2.21, 12.10, Ezek. 15, 17.5ff., 19.10ff., Hos. 10.1; cf. II Esd. 5.23. So too in Rabbinic literature (for refs. *v.* J. Behm in *TWNT*, I, p. 346). J. H. Bernard, *St. John*, II, p. 478, says: 'The v. was the national emblem, and on the coins of the Maccabees Israel is represented by a v.' In the Syriac Apocalypse of Baruch the v. is a figure of the Messiah. In Ecclus. 24.17ff. the divine Wisdom is likened to a v. The figure of the v. for heavenly beings was widespread in the oriental religions, esp. in the Mandaean literature. (See Behm, *ibid.*)

For the vineyard in Mark 12.1ff. and pars., cf. Isa. 5.1ff. The most important passage is John 15.1–8. The background of this is on the one hand the institution of the Eucharist and on the other the use of v. as a figure of Israel. Three main points are made: (*1*) Jesus is the true vine; for he is the true meaning and life of Israel, the people of God. The true Israelites of the OT had lived by faith in him. This claim is in implied opposition to all other claims to be the true v.—so to the claims of unbelieving Israel, and possibly those of oriental religions. (*2*) There is an inward fellowship between Jesus and his disciples, which is a relationship of their complete dependence upon him. As the branches of the v. can only bear fruit if they enjoy the sap of the v., so the disciples can do nothing unless they abide in him. Cf. Pauline figure of body and limbs. (*3*) God the Father exercises a disciplinary care over the Church. He is the Husbandman, who takes away the worthless, and prunes the fruitful branches.

C. E. B. CRANFIELD

VIOLENCE, VIOLENT *v.* STRIVE

VIRGIN *v.* MARRIAGE

VIRGIN (BIRTH)

(*1*) *Factual.* The references to the Virgin Birth of Christ in Holy Scripture are few. Outside the familiar Christmas story of Matt. 1 and Luke 1f., there are none in the NT. Neither the Pauline 'born of a woman' (Gal. 4.4), nor the Johannine 'and the Word became flesh' (John 1.19) contain even a covert allusion. On the other hand, neither here nor elsewhere (esp. II Cor. 8.9, Phil. 2.6–8, John 3.13, 6.51, 8.58) is the Advent of our Lord or his pre-existence so presented as to be incongruous with the Matthean or Lukan accounts.

(*2*) *Critical.* Textual criticism brought to bear on these infrequent references fails to discover any real ground for regarding the allusions to the VB as interpolations. Internal evidence (atmosphere, linguistic style, and so on) goes to show that Luke may have found the source of his narrative among Palestinian Christians, familiar with Judaic life and religion, and acquainted with information supplied by the Mother of Jesus herself. Similar evidence indicates that Matthew may have acquired his information from Christians outside Palestine, possibly in Antioch, where the influence of Joseph may have reached and the memory of the part played by the Eastern magi might be expected to persist. The absence of all mention of VB by Mark may show that some early accounts of Jesus knew nothing of it. It may therefore be that the story of the VB was current in only limited circles at the early period when the material was being assembled and compiled, out of which the Gospels eventually emerged. At the later date, when the rest of the NT books were written, it is impossible to suppose that this knowledge had still such limited currency; and infrequency of mention in these later documents must be attributed either to the fact that so little credence was given to it that it was not worthy of mention, or to the fact that it was so universally accepted as to demand no special reference. The question which conclusion is to be drawn can be decided only by reference to other and wider considerations.

(*3*) *Historical.* It is possible and indeed necessary to press the question of the nature of the origin of the story of the VB still further back, to its place in history. Let it be allowed that Matthew and Luke find the story in existence and use it each in his own way. What historical foundation has the story? Apparently either (*i*) it rests on facts; or (*ii*) it is told in order to 'square' certain OT prophecies; or (*iii*) it is an inference from the total impression which Christ made on his disciples.

It is not really possible to maintain that the VB makes its appearance in the Gospel narratives as a face-saving device for OT prophecies. Isa. 7.14 is adduced at Matt. 1.22, and its meaning is strained to yield 'virgin', with the evident purpose of producing OT sanction for something accepted on other grounds. Again, it is certainly true that the total impression made by Christ on the disciples is prior in importance to their belief in the VB. But it is more than difficult to understand why this and no other inference was drawn from the supernatural character of Christ, unless there were factual evidence to commend it.

The other alternative remains: that the story of the VB is founded on historical fact. Neither of the Gospel accounts gives the impression of attempting by this means either to sanction or to prove a divinity that is in doubt, or to explain the method of Christ's Advent or indeed anything else. The VB is affirmed as plain fact. At this point the Roman doctrine of Immaculate Conception represents misunderstanding of the intention of the Gospel writers. Erecting this, as it were, second tier on the VB, Romans convert the whole into an explanation, instead of allowing it to stand as an affirmation of fact.

The Gospel accounts do indeed manifest wide divergences. But that both are fictions is not the only or indeed the most reasonable explanation of this fact. Discrepancy is likely to occur when, as in the case of the Birth of Jesus, the facts of the case first become the object of interest or scrutiny some thirty years after their occurrence. For only at this late date, after Christ's death and resurrection, could the facts concerning the birth of an obscure Jewish infant be in any sense noteworthy.

Nor is it plausible to suppose that the VB represents a Christian variant of the no doubt frequent and familiar allusions to divine generation through a human parent in pagan mythology. Against such an alleged origin, the pure ethical tone of the whole narrative (cf. esp. Luke 1.38) may be counted sufficient defence. On the positive side, there must be reckoned the evident care and balance with which Luke approaches the task of setting down in writing the story of our Lord (1.1–4); and the not unplausible suggestion that, to achieve that 'perfect understanding' of which he boasts to Theophilus, he may well have himself made contact with the Blessed Virgin Mary, and from her own lips heard such things as she had hitherto 'kept and pondered in her heart' (Luke 2.19; cf. 51). It is not unfair on the whole to pass the judgment that 'for history the really strong argument in favour of the VB is the difficulty of accounting for the story otherwise than on the assumption of its truth' (H. R. Mackintosh).

(*4*) *Doctrinal.* The Scriptural account does not accord such emphasis to the VB as to thrust it into a central and essential place in the Christian faith, such as is occupied by certain other elements (e.g. the Resurrection of Christ). To 'believe on the Lord Jesus Christ' is enough for salvation, and Scripture does not further exact confession of the VB. Yet the Church was not misled when it affirmed in the Creed its belief in the VB. The propriety of this action is a theological and not a philosophical one. To the question of the 'possibility of VB in general', Holy Scripture returns no answer; it is simply unconcerned with any such enquiry. What Scripture in the Matthean and Lukan accounts affirms is the VB *of Jesus Christ*; and the profession of the Creeds is similarly not in VB as such, but in 'Jesus Christ, born of the Virgin Mary'.

Just as little is the Scriptural VB 'scientific', in the sense that it is the attempted explanation of some aspect of Christ. For example, to read 'parthenogenesis' into the Gospel accounts is sheer perverse misconstruction. Nor does the VB wear the aspect of a rationalization of Christ's sinlessness; for it is clear that an account that would plausibly break the entail of sin would have to be much more clever than to leave him connected on even one side of his parentage with the human race and thus so far involved in corrupt human nature.

It is impossible to separate the factual account of the VB in the Gospel narratives from its manifestly theological significance. VB is not an explanation; it is the affirmation of mystery and miracle. It affirms that here God is at work. The enquirer is led by St. Luke through the stages of his own research, back to the Palestinian circle in which the story was current, back perhaps to the Blessed Virgin Mary herself, back to that perfect obedience in which she declared herself the 'handmaid of the Lord' (1.38), back to that divine intimation of a part she must play in the saving strategy of God. And then, like a vow of silence sealing careless lips, the enquirer lights upon a miracle. It is the Gospel's 'thus far and no further: here God is at work'. The VB is unequivocally supernatural.

There is therefore in the case of the VB a union of factual probability and theological propriety, a conjunction of excellent tradition and spiritual fittingness, which commends it to the credence of the Christian. At this point it becomes important to emphasize the Scriptural order of things. It is not the VB that guarantees the stature of Jesus; on the contrary, it is the stature of Jesus that makes the VB credible. The really improbable thing is not that the Son of God in taking flesh should be born of a virgin. It is rather that the Son of God should take flesh at all. The warrant of Scripture, factual and spiritual, offers the VB as outward sign of the divinity of the grace and truth that came by Jesus Christ (John 1.17). (*V.* also EMMANUEL.)

BIBLIOGRAPHY

Charles Gore: essay in *A New Commentary on Holy Scripture*, S.P.C.K., NT, pp. 315–20. Douglas Edwards: *The VB in History and Faith*, London (1943). V. Taylor: *The VB*, London (1920).

J. K. S. REID

VISION

Generally, vision means an ecstatic experience in which new knowledge is revealed through something seen. This is very common in the book of Daniel (*c.* 30 times). Such visions are attributed particularly to prophets. Among the prophets Ezekiel would seem to have developed most a capacity for visionary experiences, but the implication is that for most of the prophets vision was a normal medium for the reception of divine oracles (cf. Isa. 1.1, 21.2, Obad. 1, Nahum 1.1, Amos 1.1, 'words of Amos . . . which he *saw*'); cf. also for the non-writing prophets, II Sam. 7.4,17 and I Chron. 17.15 (Nathan), II Chron. 9.29 (Iddo), Gen. 15.1 (Abraham), Num. 24.4,16 (Balaam), I Kings 22.17,19 (Micaiah), and more generally Num. 12.6: 'If there be a prophet among you I the Lord will make myself known unto him in a vision, I will speak with him in a dream.' The well-known passage I Sam. 3.1, 'The word of the Lord was precious in those days; there was no open vision', is to be interpreted in line with Prov. 29.18, 'Where there is no vision, the people perish' (better, instead of 'perish', 'get out of hand'; cf. RV). Vision means that declaration of God's will without which community—one might almost say civilization—is impossible.

In the NT this sense is practically confined to the Lucan writings: cf. Luke 1.23 (Zacharias), 24.23 (the disciples), Acts 2.17 (Peter, quoting Joel 2.28), 9.10 (Ananias), 10.3 (Cornelius), 10.10ff., 12.9 (Peter), 16.9, 18.9, 26.19 (Paul). It is implied that these were men capable of direct awareness of God such as was the hallmark of the prophet. Paul himself, though undoubtedly to be regarded as a prophet, did not set much store by visionary experiences (cf. I Cor. 13.2, II Cor. 12.1ff.).

E. C. BLACKMAN

VOCATION (AV only) *v.* CALL, WORK

VOICE *v.* WORD

* * *

WAIT *v.* TIME

WAR, FIGHT

A. In ordinary sense of combat, single or between armies (I Sam. 17.9, Josh. 9.2, etc.); military operations (Luke 14.31).

B. In particular sense, that human life and the universe are the scene of the struggle between life and death, good and evil; that there is a divine kingdom to be established on earth; and that God reveals himself as God in victorious conflict with his enemies and in the destruction of evil and death. With this conflict the struggles of Israel and the Church are closely related. This view appears to have come less by way of mythological stories of primeval warfare between the gods, of which there are relatively few traces in the OT, than through the experiences of history interpreted by prophetic minds.

(i) In early Israel war was a natural condition by which the community was established and maintained. Jehovah is depicted as a warrior (the Lord of hosts), who made Israel his people by the overthrow of the Egyptians (Exod. 15.1–18, Deut. 4.34, Ps., *passim*), and who maintains her as such by fighting for her and by teaching her to fight (II Sam. 22.35, Ps. 144.1). The army of Israel is the hosts of Jehovah (Exod. 12.41), the victories of Israel are all ascribed to Jehovah, and no distinction is made between the enemies of Israel and the enemies of Jehovah (Judg. 5; cf. 'The Book of the Wars of the Lord', Num. 21.14). The existence of Israel as an elect people is held to require the extermination of all nations which threaten her and that which is peculiar to her (Deut. 7). War is holy, and great importance is attached to all that belongs to the successful conduct of war, leaders, prophets, kings, and the observance of ritual laws affecting the integrity of the army (*v.* Johs. Pedersen, *Israel,* esp. Vol. II, pp. 1–32). This view continues in some measure throughout the OT. Jehovah is always a God of action whose work, and therefore his nature, is discerned in the conflict with whatever opposes him, and the history of Israel from the Maccabean revolt onwards encouraged the identification of his enemies with the enemies of Israel (*v. I and II Macc., Psalms of Solomon*).

(ii) The prophets make a distinction between the enemies of Jehovah and the enemies of Israel. When Israel is apostate Jehovah becomes her enemy and fights against her (Jer. 21.5, Isa. 63.10), by means of the prophet (Jer. 1.10–19) and by means of the military power of foreign nations which he employs as instruments of judgment (Isa. 10.5f., Jer. 25.1–9,27, Ezek. 21.8–23). Sin rather than wars is the opposite of peace. War thus becomes a punishment for disobedience and unrighteousness, and those who prophesy security or victory for Israel are false prophets, concealing her sin (Jer. 28, Ezek. 13.8–16). (In the prophets, and in the accounts of the capture of Jerusalem, can be discerned a horror of war (Jer. 4.19f.) and the abolition of war is looked for in the coming age of God's reign (Isa. 2.2–4, Micah 4.1–4, Zech. 9.9f.)). War becomes a symbol, and the way is open for the belief that it is all evil and unrighteousness, of which Jehovah is the enemy. In the frequent references to 'enemies' in the Psalms it is not always possible to decide whether the psalmist is speaking of national or private enemies. From Jeremiah onwards there is a continual struggle within Israel between the faithful remnant and the ungodly, and sometimes this is described in general terms as the struggle between Jehovah and evil.

Yet the purpose of Jehovah remains the establishment of a redeemed and purified people, and when the heathen nations have served their purpose as instruments of judgment they will be brought low by war (Isa. 10.12–15, Jer. 51, Ezek. 38–9). Jehovah will fight on behalf of Israel to deliver her from her captors (Isa. 49.22–6—for descriptions of the divine warrior who comes to save, *v.* Isa. 59.17f., 11.4f., Wisd. 5.17–23), and to deliver the faithful Israelite from his persecutors in Israel (Ps. 35 and *passim*). The final salvation is depicted as the victory of Jehovah, or of his Messiah, over the nations and as the establishment of the reign of God in an ideal Israel (Dan. 7–12, Zech. 14, Isa. 9.1–7, 11.1–9, Ps. 110), when universal security will spread from Zion through the subservience of all peoples to Israel and her God (Isa. 49, Zech. 8). Under the influence of apocalyptic the temporal and spiritual struggles of the nation and of the individual are seen upon the background of, and in relation to, a final, cosmic and super-earthly conflict between personal, spiritual beings—God, or his representative (Messiah or Michael)—and the rival forces of the kingdom of evil under its leaders (Satan, Beliar or Mastema). Wars on earth, involving bitter suffering for the elect, are the prelude to this conflict. Ancient mythological ideas of primeval warfare, borrowed perhaps from foreign sources, are adapted in Judaism to serve this prophetic message. The cosmic conflict is between Jehovah and Chaos (Gen. 1, Ps. 104.6ff.), the dragon of the deep (Job 9.13), which is also a conflict between light and darkness (Job 26.10–13), and which will come to a final issue in the last days (Isa. 27.1). The fall of man results in a perpetual enmity between the serpent and the human race (Gen. 3) and the final salvation restores the harmony of nature (Isa. 11.6–9, 65.25).

In the NT the equation of the enemies of God with the enemies of Israel, and of the purpose of God with the domination of the Gentiles disappears. War is not a means of establishing the kingdom of God (Matt. 26.52, John 18.36). Wars will mark the tribulation which precedes the end, and the destruction of Jerusalem is a judgment upon an Israel which shows itself apostate in rejecting the Messiah (Mark 13.3–13, Luke 21.10–24, 13.34f., 19.41–4, 23.28–31). The warfare of the kingdom of God is with the power of evil embodied in 'the world' (Jas. 4.4) and 'the flesh' (Rom. 8.7).

Important is the fact that the ministry of Jesus for the most part is a scene of conflict (cf. Luke 2.34). This is indicated not only by the framework to the narratives provided by the Evangelists, but also by the contents of the narratives themselves. In his works he is in conflict with various manifestations of disorder in human life and the universe, disease, demon-possession, death and storm. In his words he is in conflict with sin, especially with the hypocrisy or practical godlessness of the religious leaders, which is exposed by his assertion of the absolute demands of God and of the law of love. He stands in the line of the prophets conducting the Lord's controversy, and he describes himself as a man of war because his word divides men in their allegiance (Matt. 10.34f.). The inner significance of this ministry is declared by the narratives of the Temptation to be the decisive battle between Jesus as the bearer of the Holy Spirit and the chief of the kingdom of unholy spirits. Whereas Israel had fought against God by 'tempting' him (Deut. 6.16) in the wilderness, Jesus, as the representative of Israel, succeeds where Israel had failed in obedience (Matt. 4.1–11); he restores the harmony of Eden (Mark 1.12f.). The conflict continues throughout his life (Luke 4.13, 22.28,31). Jesus interprets his own exorcisms, and those of his representatives, as signs of the victorious warfare which is being waged by the kingdom of God against the rival kingdom of evil, in which Satan has been bound and is being made to yield up his ill-gotten prey (Mark 3.20ff., Matt. 12.22ff., Luke 11.14ff.; cf. Isa. 49.24–5, Luke 10.18, 13.16). The final issue of this conflict is not reached until he has met the full force of sin and death in the Cross; therefore temptation to avoid the Cross is Satanic (Mark 8.33). His hostility to sin and his identification of himself with men lead inevitably to the Cross, where his obedience and sacrifice transform the passive suffering of opposition into the active overthrow of evil. Hence the Cross is spoken of in terms of triumph (*v.* G. Aulen, *Christus Victor*) which brings to an end the usurpation of the world by the evil one (I John 5.19, Eph. 2.2, Luke 22.53, John 12.31, 16.33, Col. 1.13, 2.15, Acts 26.18). Satan is expelled from heaven by the triumph of the Messiah, to make war for a limited time on the Messiah's disciples (Rev. 12.7–12).

Hence the Christian life is a warfare (I Tim. 1.18, 6.12, II Tim. 2.3ff., 4.7), and the enemy is not earthly, but the invisible and spiritual forces of evil and the Satanic rulers of the world (Eph. 6.12; cf. I Cor. 2.6ff.). Christians need to be exhorted to struggle (Heb. 12.4), but the dominant note of the NT is not that of struggle towards a future hope, but that of present possession and confident victory, in virtue of the fact that the Christian shares Christ's victory and wears God's own armour (I John 2.13f., 5.4f., I Cor. 15.57, Rom. 8.37, Eph. 6.10–20, I Pet. 4.1, II Cor. 10.3–5). Behind the struggles of the Church stands the heavenly warrior Christ (Rev. 19.11–16). There is one war and one victory, which the followers of the Messiah have to repeat in their own lives. By his weapons, which are his own blood of sacrifice and the sword of the word of God (cf. Ps. 45.3ff.), he continues to wage war until he secures both the overcoming of the world empires (Rev. 17.14) and the ultimate destruction of evil (Rev. 20.7–10, II Thess. 2.8f.). (*V.* also STRIVE, PEACE.)

C. F. EVANS

WASH *v.* WATER, UNCLEAN

WATER, DRINK, FOUNTAIN, SEA, WASH

The use of water as a theological image was governed and qualified by sacred history, and the theological adaptation of legendary material in the early books of the Bible. An examination of this symbol may conveniently be divided into the following headings:

(i) *Waters of Destruction.* The Bible uses the Flood legend (*v.* NOAH, FLOOD) to set forth two themes: God's judgment on sinners and the salvation of the Remnant (Gen. 6–8). The Waters of the Flood not only overwhelm and destroy the ungodly, but also are waters 'whereby eight souls were saved' (I Pet. 3.20). From this point onwards judgment and salvation are complementary aspects of each stage of revelation.

The same combination of waters of destruction and salvation is found in the history of the Exodus: where 'Pharaoh's chariots and host are cast in the sea . . .' but Israel is saved by water (Exod. 15.5f.). It is the theme of the Psalmist that God has led his people through the depths . . . 'and the waters covered their adversaries' (Ps. 106.11, 78.13). This primary act of God's revelation to Israel at the Red Sea is constantly being appealed to by leaders and prophets as a sign of God's covenant choice of his people (cf. Josh. 24.6f.). Overflowing waters of destruction and judgment will be the lot of the enemies of God's people. The Philistines will be overwhelmed by waters which 'will rise up . . . and become an overflowing stream' (Jer. 47.2–7). These waters of destruction and judgment will not come only upon Israel's enemies. They can come up against Israel herself if she refuses her place as God's people. Instead of the 'gentle waters of Shiloh' which she has refused, God will bring upon them 'the River strong and mighty even the King of Assyria and all his glory . . ., and he shall come up over his channels . . . he shall reach even to the neck' (Isa. 8.5–8). Perhaps the words of Amos refer to God's terrible judgment about to fall on the nation: 'Let judgment roll down as water and righteousness as a perennial stream' (Amos 5.24). Yet in such judgment God will remember the Flood and the promises to Noah. 'For this is as the waters of Noah to me, for as I have sworn that they shall not go over the earth, so have I sworn that I would not be wroth with them' (Isa. 54.9). The symbolism of overwhelming waters of trouble is used often in the Psalms, where the poor man and the innocent sufferer complains that he 'is come into deep waters where the floods overflow me' (Ps. 69.1). He receives the deliverance of God who sends 'down from on high to take him out of many waters' (Ps. 18.6). In the NT both the Flood and the Exodus are looked upon as types of Christian baptism (I Pet. 3.20 and I Cor. 10.2). The Passion is called a Baptism in the sense of Ps. 69.1, in Mark 10.35–42 and Luke 12.50. The disciples James and John are promised a share in it, and our Lord looks forward to its accomplishment (*v.* BAPTIZE).

(ii) *Waters of Cleansing*. In common with almost all other religions, the Hebrews found a place for water in ritual symbolism, which reaches its developed form in the Levitical ceremonial code (Lev. 14ff.). Within Solomon's temple the holy lavers stood as a reminder to the people of such cleansing (Exod. 30.8 and I Kings 7.23ff.). Yet more necessary was the warning of the prophets that the real cleansing needed was the inward removal of spiritual defilement. Israel, who had been taken by God as a foundling and washed as a new-born child, and adopted as his son (Ezek. 16), needed another cleansing which must come from God. The prophet Isaiah stresses this need: 'wash you, make you clean' (Isa. 1.16; cf. also Ps. 51.7). In the Exile it was given to Ezekiel to proclaim the promise of a new cleansing when on a restored People of God the Lord would sprinkle clean water . . . waters which the prophet sees proceeding from the restored Temple in such abundance that they are 'waters to swim in' (Ezek. 36.25, 47.1ff.). From this point onward the prophets look forward to the fountain of divine cleansing which will 'come forth out of the house of the Lord on that day' (Joel 3.18), and Zechariah takes up the theme in his promise that in that day living waters shall go out of Jerusalem (Zech. 14.8), and in that day shall be opened a fountain to the house of David for sin and for uncleanness (Zech. 13.1; cf. Ps. 46.4).

The NT takes up this theme of living cleansing waters proceeding from the presence of Jehovah and finds fulfilment of the prophecies in the outpouring of the Spirit first on Messiah himself and then upon the New Israel. The Spirit Baptism takes the place of the preparatory baptism of St. John Baptist, who used the waters of Jordan to seal and symbolize the repentance of those who await God's kingdom (Mark 1.4–8), and he promises the superior baptism of Holy Spirit which Messiah himself will bestow (vss. 8,9,10). Out of the individual Christian will the living waters flow (John 7.37); 'this he said of the Spirit' (*v.* Hoskyns, *Fourth Gospel*, pp. 321–7). But water remains the symbol and sign of Christian Spirit Baptism. To it Philip takes the Ethiopian eunuch (Acts 8.26), and the discourse with Nicodemus (John 3) links 'water and the Spirit', the earthly symbol and the heavenly reality, in the sacramental knot. Baptism for the Apostolic Church means having our bodies washed with pure water as the sign that our hearts are sprinkled from an evil conscience (Heb. 10.22). The Church herself has been cleansed as Israel is thought of as being washed (Ezek. 16), for Christ has cleansed it 'by washing of water and the Word' (Eph. 5.26). God has saved his people by a washing of regeneration and renewing of the Holy Spirit which he poured out upon us richly through Jesus Christ our Lord (Tit. 3.5).

(iii) *Waters to Drink*. Here again the sacred history of Israel provided the outward symbol for later theology. God provides water for his people in the desert—water from a rock (Exod. 17, Ps. 78.13,20). Israel is asked again to remember this as a sign of the Covenant (Deut. 8.15f.). But God is a Shepherd of Israel all through their history and provides waters for the godly Israelite all the days of his life (Ps. 23.2). Not only does God provide for the spiritual thirst of Israel but he himself is the fountain of living waters (Jer. 2.13), and with God is the fountain of life (Ps. 36.8f.). But Israel has committed two evils. She has forsaken the fountain of living waters and hewn for herself cisterns, broken cisterns, that can hold no water (Jer. 2.13, 17.13). Therefore God's judgment is to give her the waters of affliction (Isa. 30.20) and water and gall to drink (Jer. 8.15) or to send a famine and thirst, 'not a thirst for water but of hearing the words of the Lord' (Amos 8.11). Beyond judgment again lies salvation and the promise of water to quench the thirst of men. In that day Israel will say, 'God is my salvation; therefore with joy thou shalt draw water out of the wells of salvation', i.e. he will become once again the Fountain of Israel (Isa. 12.3). Deutero-Isaiah looks forward to the time when God will pour water upon him that is thirsty (Isa. 44.3), and when the Shepherd of Israel will lead them by springs of water (Isa. 49.10), and the prophet invites everyone that thirsts to come to the waters (Isa. 55.1ff.). Once more the NT takes up the theme and declares it fulfilled. The Samaritan woman in John 4.11,14 is told by Christ that he can provide the never-failing water, and the author of the Apocalypse speaks of the final quenching of Israel's thirst when the Lamb shall be a Shepherd to his people and shall guide them unto fountains of the waters of life (Rev. 7.17) and 'give to him that is athirst of the water of life freely' (Rev. 21.5). To Paul the rock of the wilderness is a type of

Christ, or rather, already Christ was their true spiritual drink—Christ the Rock whence Christians now receive the waters in the desert of this world (I Cor. 10.1ff.).

(iv) *Waters of Fruitfulness and Refreshment.* Water is used once more as a sign of God's good pleasure to his people, first of all in the actual restoration to them of the Holy Land after Exile when showers of rain and dew will make the land fruitful and when the 'glowing sand shall become a pool and in the wilderness water shall break out' (Isa. 35). From Exile Deutero-Isaiah promises that God will make the wilderness a pool of water for the fruitfulness of the desert where God will set the fir tree, pine and box (Isa. 41.17ff.). In fact the restoration is thought of as a new creation, a new fruitfulness (Isa. 43.19ff.). Water thus becomes part of the imagery of spiritual fruitfulness. In the day of Israel's restoration the Lord will keep his vineyard and water it every moment (Isa. 27.2), and Israel will be like a watered garden, like a spring of water (Isa. 58.9–14). When the Lord gathers Israel and makes his New Covenant with them 'they shall be as a watered garden' (Jer. 31.10–14). In the NT this day of Israel's fruitfulness has arrived: the Church is God's husbandry, and God is now watering his garden through the agency of his ministers (I Cor. 3.6–8); the river of life waters the City of God and the tree of life flourishes on its banks (Rev. 22.5).

Thus has the image of water in Holy Scripture been refined so that it may be used to convey pre-eminently the thought of God's activity in the world through the Holy Spirit, who as a living fountain cleanses, quenches thirst and refreshes the People of God. So we pray to that Holy Spirit: 'Heal our wounds, our strength renew, On our dryness, pour Thy dew, Wash the stains of guilt away.'

R. C. WALLS

WAVE-OFFERING *v.* SACRIFICE I(*h*)

WEALTH *v.* POOR

WEEKS, FEAST OF *v.* SACRIFICE IV(*a*) and esp. (*c*)

WHOLE *v.* RESTORE

WHORE *v.* ADULTERY

WICKED *v.* SIN

WIDOW

In I Tim. 5.3–16 directions are given about certain widows who evidently form a recognized class in the Christian community. Widows who have children or grandchildren to support them (vs. 4) or who are under sixty years of age cannot be 'enrolled', and only those who have been active in good works (vs. 10) are qualified. Some scholars interpret the passage as meaning that this official order or class of widows had special charitable duties in return for maintenance by the church; others hold that apart from the obligation of intensive prayer (vs. 5) these widows had no official duties and 'correspond not to our sisters of charity but to the occupants of our almshouses' (C. H. Turner, *Catholic and Apostolic*, Ch. XI; *q.v.* for further information). (*V.* also MARRIAGE.)

H. J. C.

WIFE *v.* MARRIAGE

WIND *v.* SPIRIT I(*a*)

WINE

OT: Often mentioned (in original under wealth of synonyms). Regarded as a good gift of the Lord, Gen. 27.28, Ps. 104.15, Isa. 55.1, Hos. 2.8f.,22, Joel 2.19,24, Amos 9.13. Bread and w. often together as main food and drink, Gen. 14.18, Judg. 19.19, Neh. 5.15; cf. corn and w. together. W. used for drink-offering to the Lord, Exod. 29.40, Lev. 23.13, Num. 15.5, 28.14. But dangers of abuse recognized, Gen. 9.21, Prov. 20.1, 23.30f., 31.4f., Isa. 5.11, 28.7f., Hos. 4.11. Priests forbidden to drink w. during their period of service, Lev. 10.9, Ezek. 44.21. Daniel avoids the king's meat and w. as defiling, Dan. 1.8,16. A Nazirite was forbidden to drink w. during period of his vow, Num. 6.3f., Judg. 13, Amos 2.12. (For Nazirites *v.* A. Lods, *Israel from Its Beginnings to the Middle of the Eighth Century*, Eng. trans., London (1932), pp. 305ff.) The Rechabites also abstained from w. along with other amenities of agricultural life, Jer. 35. In the wilderness Israel had had neither bread nor w., Deut. 29.6 (For Rechabites, *v.* T. H. Robinson, *Prophecy and the Prophets in Ancient Israel*, 1923, pp. 26f., 67f.)

It is clear from the above that there were two conflicting tendencies in OT with regard to w. While prophets like Hosea, accepting the change from nomadic to agricultural life and seeking to maintain the old loyalty to the Lord in the new circumstances, recognized w. as a gift from the Lord to be used gratefully but not abused (N.B. how anxious Hosea is to show w. is gift of the Lord, and not of a baal), the Rechabites, feeling that the Lord was a wilderness God, tried to avoid as foreign to him all that had not been known in the desert, e.g. permanent houses, sowing crops, etc. Their avoidance of w. not due to its being intoxicating, but to its belonging to agricultural as opposed to nomadic life. It is interesting that Ezekiel apparently tried to exclude w. from sacrifices (contrast Ezek.

45.24f. and 45.11,14f. with Exod. 29.40, etc.); Lods, *op. cit.*, p. 476. This was probably because of its use in heathen cults and the abuse to which it was liable.

The word w. also used metaphorically in OT. Of what is desirable—of reconciliation with God, Isa. 55.1; with eschatological reference, Isa. 25.6; with bread, of the benefits which divine Wisdom offers, Prov. 9.5. Cf. Ps. 16.5, 23.5, 116.13, where *cup* is used metaphorically in good sense. As metaphor for what is undesirable—three distinct though connected metaphors: (*a*) w. as metaphor for the Lord's anger and punishment of sin, Ps. 60.3, 75.8, Jer. 25.15 (cf. cup metaphor, Isa. 51.17,22, Jer. 49.12, etc.), perhaps suggested by similarity between drunkenness and the stunned bewilderment caused by God's punishments; (*b*) metaphor of winepress, in which the objects of God's anger are like grapes trampled in press, Isa. 63.2ff. (in vs. 6 metaphor (*a*) also appears), Lam. 1.15; (*c*) w. as metaphor for the seductive luxuries and vices of Babylon, Jer. 51.7.

NT: Regarded as a good gift, John 2.1ff., I Tim. 5.23. In contrast with John the Baptist, who was a Nazirite (Luke 1.15), Jesus drinks w., Luke 7.33f., Matt. 11.18f. W. used as a remedy by the Samaritan, Luke 10.34; offered to our Lord, mingled with myrrh, to deaden pain, Mark 15.23. Dangers of abuse recognized, Eph. 5.18, I Tim. 3.3 (cf. AV), 3.8, Tit. 1.7 (cf. AV), 2.3, I Pet. 4.3. Paul would avoid both meat and w., if it would save a brother being scandalized, Rom. 14.21.

The point of the saying recorded Mark 2.22, Matt. 9.17, Luke 5.37f. is probably that the Gospel cannot be contained within Judaism indefinitely. Jesus elsewhere emphasizes the continuity of the New Covenant with the Old (e.g. Matt. 5.17ff.), but here reference is not to the OT, but to the brittle and fossilized forms of Judaism. Luke adds a corollary (vs. 39), the point of which is probably that the Pharisees in their adherence to their legalism were unwilling to examine the claims of the Gospel: without tasting the new w., they are content to say, 'The old is good enough for us!' (*v.* J. M. Creed's commentary).

In the accounts of the institution of the Lord's Supper the word 'wine' does not occur, though in the Synoptics the phrase 'fruit of the vine' does. This phrase occurs because it was used in the Jewish blessing or grace over the w. For a discussion of the Lord's Supper, *v.* article on THANK. In the Synoptic accounts Jesus refers to drinking w. 'in the kingdom of God'. Cf. the Messianic feast, Matt. 22.1ff., Rev. 19.9.

The Lord's Supper is the clue to the significance of the miracle at Cana, John 2.1ff. John does not record the institution of the Supper; but it is clear that in Ch. 6 he refers to it (the bread). Probably here he means us to see a connexion with the wine of the Eucharist. The 'six waterpots of stone set there after the Jews' manner of purifying' are a witness to the need for purifying from sin. But the water could not itself wash away sin, it was only a sign pointing to the blood of Christ which alone could really cleanse. As the water is replaced by wine, so the signs and promises of the Old Dispensation are replaced by the reality of the New. In the Eucharist the Christian recognizes in the w. the blood of Christ.

The three distinct but connected metaphors in a bad sense which we found in the OT reoccur in the NT: (*a*) Rev. 14.10, 16.19. Perhaps in Mark 14.36 and pars. (*v.* article, 'The Cup Metaphor in Mark xiv.36 and Parallels', *Expository Times*, Feb., 1948, pp. 137f., and April, 1948, p. 195); (*b*) Rev. 19.15; (*c*) Rev. 14.8, 18.3.

C. E. B. CRANFIELD

WISDOM *v.* WISE

WISE, WISDOM

A number of Heb. words here call for consideration, but the most important are two: *chokmah* and *binah*. The latter is usually translated 'understanding' and is considered under that heading. The meaning of *chokmah* (and its adjective *chakam*) is wisdom, esp. in the sense of sagacity, skill in making thought issue in the appropriate action (*v.* THOUGHT), ability; it has a practical rather than a theoretical reference and is thus different from the wisdom of the Greek philosopher. For the meaning 'technical proficiency' see Exod. 35.30ff. (Bezaleel the craftsman), Isa. 10.13 (the soldier), Ps. 107.27 (the sailor: read 'their wisdom is swallowed up' rather than 'they are at their wits' end'; cf. also Ezek. 27.8).

There are a number of instances where 'the wise' are a professional class. This is clearly so in the book of Daniel (cf. the Wise Men of Matt. 2), but is also implied elsewhere, e.g. Gen. 41.8 and Exod. 7.11 refer to wise men of Egypt (? magicians), Esth. 1.13, Prov. 1.6, Eccles. 12.9, Matt. 23.34, I Cor. 1.19f.; to say nothing of the description of Solomon as *the* wise man pre-eminent not only among the Hebrews, but also among the wise of all nations (I Kings 4.30ff.). In early times an adept at proverbs or aphorisms (Prov. 1.6), fable (cf. Judg. 9.8–15) or allegory (cf. II Sam. 12.1–4) was doubtless called a wise man. Isaiah and Jeremiah have no great opinion of the wise of their day (Isa. 19.12, 29.14, Jer. 8.8f., 18.18). From these two references in Jeremiah we may infer that in his day (*c.* 600 BC) the prophet was to be distinguished as a religious leader not only from the priest, but also from the wise; and the 'counsel' which is attributed to the wise is possibly to be understood as instruction about the Law in cases where the Law itself as taught by the priest was not explicit. After the Exile there arose the class of scribes, professional exponents of the new codification of Law promulgated by Ezra. What place remained then for the wise, when Law has scribe to interpret it and priest to execute it, at least as far as it concerned the Temple system? To the wise men in this later period we owe the Wisdom Literature, of which the best example is the Book of Proverbs. The Book of Job is the work of an outstandingly gifted member of the class; while Ecclesiastes comes from the pen of a sceptical and very unorthodox wise man, such orthodoxy as the work in its present form possesses being due to later editors. Outside the OT we have Ecclesiasticus and Wisdom in the Apocrypha as representatives of Jewish Wisdom literature.

For the word in a general sense, cf. Deut. 4.6 (where note the connexion between wisdom and observance of the Law), Ps. 107.43, Hos. 14.9, Matt. 10.16, 11.25, 25.2, Rom. 1.14, Jas. 3.13. There are a number of cases where the meaning is between the general and specialized sense, e.g. Eccles. 7.23, Prov. 13.20 (here it almost means those who receive the instruction of the professional wise men).

Full consideration of the meaning of wisdom would take account of what the Bible means by folly; cf. Matt. 25.2, Rom. 1.22, Eph. 5.15.

The Platonic Socrates says: 'Whithersoever reason [*logos*] leads, thither we must go.' That would have seemed incomprehensible to the Hebrew mind, which was incapable of thinking without clear theological presuppositions; even Philo, the most Hellenized of the Jews, set forth his wisdom in the form of commentaries on the Mosaic Law. For the Hebrew true wisdom was rooted in a right attitude to God (Prov. 9.10, 15.33, Ps. 111.10, Job. 28.28). Moreover, it is God's gift (I Kings 3.11ff., Eccles. 2.26, Isa. 11.2, Dan. 1.17, Wisdom 7.7, Eph. 1.17, Acts 7.10, Jas. 1.5, 3.17).

These insights into the meaning of wisdom and its relation to God receive their most important development in two passages where St. Paul is endeavouring to bring out the significance of Christ: I Cor. 1.24,30 and Col. 1.15–18 (cf. also Col. 2.3). The wisdom of God is most manifestly operative in what Christ did and was (cf. Mark 6.2). The partial personification of wisdom in Prov. 8 made it easier to conceive wisdom as incarnate in Christ. Prov. 8.22–31 was also of service in its suggestion that wisdom was pre-existent before Creation, active in creation, and since then specially interested in mankind (vs. 31). It is a fair assumption that St. Paul's thought was also influenced by two other passages which move on similar lines: Wisdom 7.22–7 and Ecclus. 24.24–7; and by Rabbinic speculation which identified Wisdom and Law.

In attempting to do justice to the uniqueness of Christ, St. Paul affirms the closest possible relation between Christ and the Father, involving pre-existence and participation in the creation of the universe; cosmology as well as soteriology was Christ's proper work. The late Hebrew conception of wisdom seemed to offer an exact parallel, and the exegesis of Col. 1 is impossible without reference to Prov. 8.

This Pauline thought is parallel to the Johannine thought of Christ and the Logos or Word of God, and Col. 1 should be studied in the light of John 1.1–18. These two passages are the highest peaks of Christological speculation in the NT. Their witness is that physics as well as theology needs Christ as its interpretative principle. The Redeemer is none other than the Creator of the universe. (*V.* also FOLLY, UNDERSTANDING.)

E. C. BLACKMAN

WOES (MESSIANIC WOES) *v.* SUFFER

WONDER *v.* MIRACLE

WORD

Word in the OT is usually the translation of Heb. *dabar*, which means a spoken utterance of any kind, a saying, speech, narrative, message, command, request, promise, etc.—the precise significance can be determined only from the context. Some OT books, which are collections of written 'sayings' of different kinds, begin with what is in effect a title: 'The words of ——' (cf. Amos, Jeremiah, Nehemiah, Ecclesiastes; also Prov. 30.1, 31.1). But *dabar* also means a matter, affair, event, act, etc.; in this sense it is usually translated 'thing' in the EVV, and sometimes 'any thing', e.g. Gen. 18.14, 19.22. Naturally, it is sometimes difficult to decide whether 'word' or 'thing' is the meaning intended; cf., e.g. the AV and RV, Ps. 35.20. In the OT, 'the word of the Lord', a phrase which occurs nearly 400 times, means simply any communication made by God to men, especially through a prophet; *v.* Jeremiah *passim* (in this book the phrase occurs more than 50 times). In the frequent statement, 'The word of the Lord came to ——', 'came' represents the simple copula, 'was', in Hebrew (e.g. Gen. 15.1), and sometimes even this is not actually expressed (e.g. Gen. 15.4). It is seldom that there is any indication of the manner in which the communication was made, and it must not be supposed that it was always, or even usually, by 'words' spoken and heard. It was the common belief in ancient times that words, once uttered, had a strange inherent power of their own, especially words of blessing or cursing, cf. Isaac's blessing of Jacob, which once given could not be recalled (Gen. 27). The words of the Lord always had the power appropriate to their particular character, and were effective for their particular purpose; cf. Isa. 55.11, 'so shall my word be that goeth forth out of my mouth: it shall not return unto me void, but it shall accomplish that which I please, and it shall prosper in the thing whereto I sent it'. This, however, does not mean that the word of God was really 'personified'; when, e.g. it is said that the Lord 'sent his word, and healed them, and delivered them from their destructions' (Ps. 107.20), or that 'he sendeth forth his commandment upon earth: his word runneth very swiftly' (Ps. 147.15), this is no more than a literary and poetical 'personification'. Evidence for a real personification of the 'word of God' in later Jewish thought has sometimes been found in the way in which the phrase 'the *memra* (=word) of the Lord' is used in the Targums, the vernacular paraphrases of the OT used in the synagogue worship. But this is a mistake: *memra* is not used as a translation of *dabar*; 'the *memra* of the Lord' is simply a reverential periphrasis for 'the Lord', a translation device confined to the Targums.

In the NT *word* is almost always the translation of one or other of two Gk. nouns, *logos* and *rhēma*, which are derived from different verb roots meaning 'to say'. *Logos* occurs in the Gk. NT more than 300 times, and *rhēma* some 70 times. In the AV *logos* is translated 'saying' some 50 times (35 of which are in the Gospels) and *rhēma* 9 times (8 of which are in Luke); there seldom seems to be any special reason for this variation in rendering. In a few passages, all in Luke and Acts, *rhēma* is used, like Heb. *dabar*, in the sense of 'thing', and is so translated in the AV 3 times—Luke 2.15,19, Acts 5.32; it should be so translated also in Luke 1.65, 2.51 and Acts 13.42. Luke 1.37 is ambiguous; it may mean either 'For with God nothing shall be impossible' (AV), or, 'For no word from God shall be void of power' (RV). (The Gk. version of Gen. 18.14 is similarly ambiguous.) *Logos* too is used in this sense, Acts 8.21, 15.6 (EVV, 'matter'), but the use of 'matter' in Mark 1.45 (EVV), 'things' in Luke 1.4 (EVV), and 'things' again in Acts 5.24 (AV) is due to a slight freedom in translation—in each case *logos* by itself means 'account' or 'report' (of the matter or things). The use of the words in this sense is a Hebraism which seems to be found only in the writings of Luke in the NT. The contrast between 'word' and 'deed' (which is familiar in Gk. literature) is found in I John 3.18, and a similar contrast between 'word' and 'power' in I Cor. 4.19f. and I Thess. 1.5; cf. also 'word and deed' (with mention of 'power' in the context), Luke 24.19, Rom. 15.18. For the rest it is enough to say that *word* in the NT has all the various more precise meanings noted in the OT.

In the NT 'the word of God' is usually 'the *logos* of God', but there are 6 passages (one, Luke 4.4, an inexact quotation from the OT) in which *rhēma* is used, without any discernible difference of meaning. The plural ('the words of God') is used only 3 times, John 3.34 and 8.47 (both times the plural of *rhēma*) and Rev. 17.17. In essential meaning this phrase is the exact equivalent of the OT 'the word of the Lord', but its application is now, naturally, wider, and it often denotes, specifically, the Christian message, the gospel (cf., e.g. Acts 13.44, 'almost the whole city was gathered together to hear the word of God', i.e. the Christian message proclaimed by Paul and Barnabas). In Luke 5.1 the same phrase is used of our Lord's own preaching. In Acts 'the word of the Lord' is used with the same meaning (cf. also I Thess. 1.8, II Thess. 3.1), but 'the Lord' is now not God, as in the OT, but Christ. Sometimes, as in Acts 13.44 just cited, some manuscripts have 'God' and others 'the Lord'. In one passage, I Pet. 1.23, the abiding word of God spoken of in Isa. 40.6ff. becomes, in the quotation of the Isaiah passage, 'the word (here *rhēma*) of the Lord', and is explicitly declared to be the word of the Christian gospel. Some 8 times in the Gospel of John, Jesus himself speaks of 'my word' in the same sense; cf. also Rev. 3.8. Frequently, and esp. in Acts, 'the word' alone has the same meaning; cf., e.g. Mark 2.2, Acts 8.4, I Thess. 1.6, Jas. 1.21. Often, too, the *word* in this sense is further described, as 'the word of the gospel', 'of the kingdom', 'of the cross', 'of salvation', 'of life', 'of truth', etc. When 'the word of God' has other meanings, these are usually sufficiently plain in the context, though they range from the divine fiat in creation, Heb. 11.3, to grace before eating (doubtless in scriptural words), I Tim. 4.5.

In the Prologue of the Gospel of John (1.1,14) 'Word' is an inadequate and possibly misleading translation of *logos*, though it is difficult to find a better. Here the Logos is an eternal divine Person, through whom in the beginning everything was made, and he is identified with the eternal Son of God who became incarnate as Jesus Christ. The evangelist seems to assume that his readers are familiar with this conception of the personal, divine Logos, a conception which is of Greek origin. The word *logos* meant both 'word' and the thought or reason which is expressed in words. Greek philosophers, believing that the universe is essentially rational, used the term *logos* to denote the rational principle by which it is sustained. Jewish thinkers (probably influenced by Greek philosophy) reached a very similar conception of the divine 'Wisdom', cf. Prov. 8, esp. vss. 22–31, where the personification of Wisdom is more than merely a literary device. Later, Jewish thinkers writing in Greek combined the two conceptions, using by preference the term *logos*. Paul calls Christ 'the wisdom of God' (I Cor. 1.24; cf. 1.30, Col. 2.2f.), and 'the first-born of all creation', in whom 'all things were created' (Col. 1.15ff.); it was therefore easy for the fourth evangelist to take the further step of identifying him with the Logos of contemporary Greek and Jewish thought. How far the evangelist's own conception of Christ was really determined by this identification is a much discussed question, to which there is no generally accepted answer. But it is certain that this special use of the term *Logos* is confined to the Prologue; in the rest of the Gospel the word is used in the ordinary senses, and in 10.35 'the word of God' means specifically the divine utterance in Ps. 82.6 which Jesus has just quoted. And there are good grounds for thinking that in the Prologue itself the evangelist has made use of an existing 'hymn' of the *Logos*, which may not have originally been Christian at all. The probability, therefore, would seem to be that it was his *Logos*-conception which was determined by his previous thought of Christ, and not his conception of Christ which was determined by the *Logos*-conception.

In I John 1.1, 'the word of life' is commonly taken to mean the incarnate Word or *Logos* (so RV text, where 'Word' is printed with an initial capital), but it is equally possible that it means 'the gospel', as in Phil. 2.16 (so, apparently, RV marg.). The statement in Rev. 19.13, that the name of the rider on the white horse 'is called the Word of God', is no doubt a reference to the teaching of the Prologue of the Gospel. But the introduction of the *Logos*-conception here is very surprising, and the clause may be a later addition to the original text. (*V.* also SPEAK.)

J. Y. CAMPBELL

WORK, LABOUR

The contrast between the Gk. and the Heb. attitudes towards work has often been noted. To the Greeks w. was something to be left to slaves or mechanics; Aristotle's 'perfect man' will not soil his hands with it. It has even been suggested that this attitude towards manual labour is one of the reasons why the Greeks made little progress in natural science as contrasted with their achievement in philosophy or mathematics. The Hebrews, on the other hand, regarded w. as a divine command from which no man was exempted. Thus, it is written in the Decalogue, 'Six days shalt thou labour, and do all thy w.' (Exod. 20.9). It is noteworthy that the later editors of the sacred books did not deem it necessary to expunge the account of Saul's ploughing (I Sam. 11.5) in order to enhance his royal dignity. The only idle rich of whom we read in the Bible are those who form the objects of the most bitter denunciations of the prophets. All through the scriptures w. is regarded as a divine ordinance for human life. Amongst the Jews of NT times no rabbi was allowed to receive payment for his teaching or other professional activities, but each rabbi must learn a trade and support himself and his family by honest toil—St. Paul, for example, was a tent-maker like Aquila (Acts 18.3). Paul continued to follow the rabbis' practice of self-support, even though he held that in principle it was right for the missionary of the Gospel to be supported by the church, and that there was dominical sanction for such practice (I Cor. 9.4–15; II Thess. 3.7–10). He also found it necessary to teach that Christians are not yet exempted from the ordinance of w.: 'If any will not w., neither let him eat' (II Thess. 3.10); doubtless some of his converts had misunderstood his eschatological teaching, and had assumed that, since they were now living in the New Age, the ordinances of the former dispensation had been abrogated. In this, as in other matters, Paul discourages any attempt to anticipate the Lord's Return; in the period of waiting the ordinances must still be fulfilled, but they will be fulfilled not as out of obedience to law but as from a new power of love. This teaching must remain the Christian doctrine of w. until world-history comes to an end.

Sometimes we hear it said that the Bible teaches that w. is a curse which is laid upon humanity as a punishment for sin. Such statements are distortions of the meaning of the myths of Gen. 1–3. W. is a divine ordinance for mankind even apart from sin; before the 'Fall' man (*v.* ADAM) is created to 'replenish the earth and subdue it and have dominion' over all living things (Gen. 1.28), and he is placed in the Garden of Eden 'to dress it and to keep it' (2.15). This teaching is in line with the general standpoint of the Bible that w. is the normal, natural and healthy routine of human living; it is as obvious and regular an activity as that the sun should rise or that lions should hunt: 'man goeth forth unto his w. and to his labour until the evening' (Ps. 104.19–23).

Honest toil is blessed by God in the abundance of a good harvest or in the prosperity of a family (Ps. 65), but labour which is not blessed by God is fruitless (Ps. 127). Skill of craftsmanship is a gift of wisdom and understanding from Jehovah (Exod. 35.30–36.2). The prudential morality of the Wisdom literature is full of exhortations to industry and of warnings against idleness (e.g. Prov. 6.6); and even though Ben Sira deprecates the deadening effects of manual labour (Ecclus. 38.25–30) and recognizes that wisdom 'comes by opportunity of leisure' (38.24), he is well aware that without the labour and skill of artisans 'a city shall not be inhabited' (38.32), and his general attitude is thoroughly biblical: 'Hate not laborious w., neither husbandry which the Most High hath ordained' (7.15).

Thus, the biblical point of view is that w. as such is neither a curse nor a punishment but is an integral part of God's original intention in the creation of the world. Nevertheless, like every other aspect of human existence, it has fallen under the curse (*q.v.*) which is the consequence of human sin. There is a wide-awake realism about biblical thinking which does not allow us to escape into the sentimentalism of much modern speaking about a 'gospel of work', which is apparently designed to persuade working-men that they like doing something which they know to be burdensome. The myth of Gen. 3 goes much deeper than this. The whole field of man's w., which ought to be the sphere of his glad co-operation for the common good, has become the scene of bitter rivalry and fratricidal quarrelling (cf. the story of Cain and Abel, Gen. 4); the ground is full of 'thorns and thistles' (3.18). The world of labour, so far from becoming the happy workshop of the commonwealth of mankind, is disarranged as a consequence of human sin; and God's good purpose in the creation is frustrated. The biblical myth implies that all the drudgery, bitterness and wretchedness of man's workaday life is the consequence of his rebellion against God. It discourages the suggestion that Utopia can be reached by any social or political techniques. 'Cursed be the ground for thy sake; in sorrow shalt thou eat of it all the days of thy life; thorns and thistles shall it bring forth unto thee . . . in the sweat of thy face shalt thou eat bread, till thou return unto the ground, for out of it wast thou taken: for dust thou art and unto dust shalt thou return' (Gen. 3.17–19).

The result of man's sin is that w., which should have been a congenial and enjoyable activity, now becomes a discipline and a task to be endured in obedience to the law of God. Man is unfit to live in paradise, and the Cherubim with 'the flame of a sword' bar his return thither (Gen. 3.24). Man's perennial illusion that he can by his science or technology find his own way back into a workless paradise —if there are no slaves to do the drudgery in a modern democracy, at least there are machines!—is the self-deception that arises from his refusal to recognize the law of God. But that law stands: 'Six days shalt thou labour.' This commandment need not, of course, be taken in a literalist way as a condemnation of the five-day week, but it does surely mean that an honest week's work is every man's duty. The eternal law of God cannot be replaced by any modern substitutes. Man rebels against God's law, and through his disobedience his workaday life becomes a burden and sorrow to him, and the law which he disobeys accuses and condemns him.

But the Bible tells us not only of law but also of grace. The NT shows how through love God's law may be fulfilled—how in fact it was perfectly fulfilled by Jesus Christ. It is of the deepest significance that Jesus of Nazareth was a carpenter (though perhaps it should be noted that the word *tektōn* in Mark 6.3 is not quite so precise as this and strictly means 'artisan', 'craftsman'). In his life the intention of God in the creation is utterly fulfilled. Christian piety has (quite rightly) loved to dwell upon the picture of Christ the master-workman of whom it was said, 'He hath done all things well' (Mark 7.37; note the implicit ref. to Gen. 1.31, LXX). The Lord who spoke of his 'yoke' as easy was the good carpenter who knew the difference between a well-made and a badly made yoke which the poor oxen at the plough would have to wear. It is of the deepest significance for our Christian doctrine of work that God, when for the sake of our salvation he most wonderfully and humbly chose to be made man, was incarnate in a village carpenter and not in a king or statesman or general or philosopher. This was the only fitting image for the God whom the biblical tradition had all along represented as himself a worker: 'In six days the Lord God made heaven and earth . . . and on the seventh day rested from his work' (Exod. 20.11). In the biblical doctrine of God as himself the great Architect and Master-Workman of the universe we have the utter antithesis of the view that w. is degrading and fit only for slaves, and the theological justification of the view that w. is an honourable and necessary activity of the good life. It was wholly appropriate that the God of biblical faith, when he became man, should have been born into a working-class family (cf. John 5.17). The 'almighty Maker of heaven and earth' could have been adequately revealed only by 'taking the form of a servant' (*doulos*, properly a born slave, Phil. 2.6). The tragedy of our age is that the working classes of the world should have turned their eyes away from the workman of Nazareth and opened their minds to the false gospel of the bourgeois 'scribbler in the British Museum'.

To the world outside the Church, then, it is necessary to proclaim w. as a law of God for human life, a law from which there can be no immunity; but for those who are 'in Christ', or who are within the redeemed community, w. ceases to belong to the sphere of law and becomes what God intended it to be in the creation. When in Christ we are re-made in his new creation, we are enabled to fulfil the divine intention, which in our own strength we could never do. Then our daily w. ceases to be under the curse and becomes our glad and free service. The likeness of God in man then becomes clearly visible as men become truly creative—when through skill of brain and hand they share in the creative activity of God and find joy in their daily w. and see that it is good (cf. Gen. 1.31). In creative workmanship men most truly share God's lordship over the creation; they too become craftsmen, artists, scientists—creators; but now they work not for selfish ends but for the greater glory of God. In this way it may be said that the view of Luther and Calvin is a true conclusion from the biblical teaching, namely, that in his daily work the Christian man may find the proper sphere for his sincere and acceptable praise and worship of God. (It should perhaps, however, be added that the words 'calling' and 'vocation' in the NT mean God's call to repentance and faith, not one's profession or 'avocation': cf. I Cor. 7.20, Eph. 4.1,4, etc. *V.* art. CALL.) In the Church's Eucharist the biblical doctrine of w. is most strikingly set forth: bread and wine, symbols of the w. of our hands, are offered to God, and are given back to us as food for our souls and bodies, the very life of God himself, the body and blood of Christ. Man's offering, including all the labours of his hands, is joined with the perfect offering of Christ and is thus rendered acceptable to God. We do not earn our salvation by our work or 'works' (*v.* FAITH), but now our 'works' arise spontaneously, as it were, from the faith in Christ by which we are justified.

Finally, it should be noted that, though w. is a necessary and wholesome part of human life, it is nevertheless not the whole of it, nor is it man's most important activity. Under the law the seventh day was reserved for the sabbath-rest, the worship and enjoyment of God. As man is made to share in the joy of the Creator in his work, so man is also made to share in the Creator's rest; and man's rest from all his work on the seventh day is the token of that heavenly rest which remains for the people of God (Gen. 2.1–3; Exod. 20.11; Heb. 4.9–11). *V.* REST, SABBATH.

ALAN RICHARDSON

WORLD *v.* TIME

WORSHIP

Etymology

OT: The general word is *'abodah*, from *'abad*, to labour, to serve, and usually translated 'the service of God'. To describe the specific act of worship, the word commonly used is *hishtahawah*, from *shaha*, to bow, to prostrate oneself.

NT: Corresponding to *'abodah* is *latreia*, meaning originally servitude—the state of a hired labourer or slave, and thence the service of God—divine worship. Corresponding to *hishtahawah* we have *proskuneo*—to prostrate oneself, to adore, to worship.

As the conception of worship underwent development and change in the course of biblical times, historical treatment of the subject will be essential.

I. WORSHIP IN OT

The 'worship of God' and the 'service of God' are practically synonymous terms in the OT. The connexion between these ideas goes back to primitive times when the deity was conceived anthropomorphically as a being with human wants and appetites (Gen. 8.21, etc.). The true worship of God was therefore regarded as dutiful ministration to these wants by sacrifice and obedience to his behests. An amusing account of the 'service' of Babylonian deities is easily accessible in *The Dawn of History*, by Myres, p. 100, and illuminates the connexion between worship and service.

The conception of worship exhibits a twofold growth in the OT. On the external side it develops into the complicated ritual of the Levitical Code. But there is also the growing realization that service not rendered heartily is not true service. The inward spiritual attitude of the worshipper thus begins to come to the front as an important factor in worship (Deut. 11.13). This conception of worship as spiritual service of God is further developed by the prophets (esp. Jeremiah), and is even brought into opposition to the ritual service of sacrifice (Ps. 40.6, 50.12ff., Micah 6.6ff.). Nevertheless, the sacrificial and ceremonial aspect of the service of God maintained its place right down to the final destruction of the Temple in AD 70. Sacrifice (*q.v.*) was continued long after the primitive idea that God could be pleased by offerings of meat and drink had been left behind. The vitality of the ceremonial aspect of worship may be traced to the fact that it had come to be regarded as a matter of divine revelation.

This was the way by which God had commanded men to approach him; and the Jew took delight in the precise performance of the appointed ritual of approach (see Wheeler Robinson, *Religious Ideas of Old Testament*, ch. 6).

Thus the rival conceptions of worship which to-day divide the Protestant from the Catholic Churches were already present in the OT. The clash between the despiser and the lover of ritual approach to God is neatly illustrated in Ps. 51, the last two verses being probably a priestly addition designed to mitigate the contempt for ceremonial expressed in the original psalm. It is, however, unlikely that the average Israelite was seriously conscious of the tension between the ceremonial and the spiritual aspects of the service of God. With unconscious tact he blended both in his worship. But a race so dominated by the love of tradition as the Jews was inevitably tempted to an increasing concentration on the traditional ritual of worship at the expense of its spirituality. The NT shows how far this process had gone in the Pharisaism of Christ's day.

Place of Worship. The primitive rule that God was to be worshipped wherever he was known to have appeared (Gen. 28.16ff., Exod. 20.24) led to the growth of a multiplicity of local sanctuaries through which local communities maintained contact with God (I Sam. 9.12ff.). Worship at these sanctuaries became corrupt owing to inevitable contact with indigenous heathen worship, and an effort was made to suppress them in the time of Josiah. Worship was henceforth to be national, not an affair of clan or family, and was to be offered only in Jerusalem (II Kings 23.8ff.). The reform was not fully effective until after the Exile; but thereafter Jerusalem was unchallenged as the sole sanctuary where alone God's people might legitimately offer worship and sacrifice. (For this conception of centralized national worship, see Ezek. *passim.*)

Synagogue worship gradually developed to satisfy the religious longings of those who were prevented from attending Temple worship, prayers being offered as a substitute for sacrifice. Authority for the substitution may be found in Hos. 14.2. But the synagogue was primarily a place of instruction rather than of worship, and the passionate Jewish belief that the Temple was God's sole earthly habitation kept the synagogue in a subordinate position, especially in Palestine, so long as the Temple stood.

Times of Worship. Worship was offered daily in the Temple. Strict observance of the Sabbath did much to keep worship a vital factor in the life of the people. National worship culminated in the annual festivals of Unleavened Bread, Weeks and Ingathering. Primarily connected with the barley, wheat and grape harvests, they became linked also with the great events of Israel's history (Exod. 23.14–17), for God was no nature divinity or baal, but a God who manifested himself through historical events. With the deepening of the sense of sin, the Day of Atonement rose to special prominence as a time of special penitential worship. (For fuller discussion of festivals, etc., see SACRIFICE IV.)

Music and Song in Worship. It is not known when music began to be used in worship. The account of the elaborate musical arrangements of the first Temple (I Chron. 25) is probably post-Exilic idealization; but after the Exile there were certainly Levitical choirs (Korah, Asaph, etc.) attached to the Temple. The parallelism of the Psalms suggests antiphonal chanting; but it is not certain what part was taken by the congregation. Probably much originally sung by them was later taken over by the choirs—one choir answering the other, and leaving only minor responses to the people. It is reasonable to suppose, however, that when the Psalms were chanted in the synagogue, the congregation perforce took a larger part in the responsive singing. It is probable that music and song, with their immediate appeal to emotions and heart, did much to guard the vitality of Jewish worship against the deadening effects of external ceremonialism.

II. WORSHIP IN NT

We saw that in the OT a tension developed between the spiritual and ritualistic aspects of worship, the prophets being the exponents of the former, and the Temple priests of the latter. Jesus adopts the prophetic conception of worship, and gives the inward spiritual element absolute primacy. He does not so much attack ceremonial worship as simply ignore it. The true service (worship) of God is adoring and obedient love to him, together with loving service of one's neighbour as God's child. '*This* do, and thou shalt live' (Luke 10.25ff.). Implicit in this assertion is the denial that ritual, ceremony or sacrifice have any determinative effect on man's relationship to God. See also Matt. 5.23f., and John 4.20–4, where the same teaching is further enforced. This is not to say that external forms and rules of worship are valueless. Man being an embodied soul, his worship must be clothed in some form of external ritual, however simple. But the principle laid down by Jesus is that of the complete relativity of the external form of worship. *Any* form or rule is good which is proved by experience to be an aid to that worship which is in spirit and in truth. A further consequence of Jesus' teaching is that the barrier between sacred and secular, worship and daily living, crumbles away. Since worship means the service of God, and this in turn implies loving one's neighbour, it follows that every kindly act performed in this spirit and intention is an act of worship (Matt. 25.34–40; Jas. 1.27).

These principles of Jesus regulate the teaching of the Apostles. Thus as regards the observance of certain days as sacred, St. Paul refuses either to approve or condemn the practice. No absolute rule can be laid down. External observances are to be expressions of inward faith, not matters of outward regulation (Rom. 14.5,6). Let each man act according to conscience in this, subject only to regard for the conscience of his brother.

As with times of worship, so also with *places of worship*. It was a matter of indifference to the Christians of the NT where they met. Christ was with them always and everywhere, and wherever two or three gathered in his name he was in the midst. No building was sacred, because none was secular. Corporate worship was offered in the house of any believer who had a room conveniently large. Expectation of the Parousia discouraged the building of special places of worship.

Forms of Worship. Apart from the Eucharist, there appears to have been little uniformity of worship in NT times. Christian worship was based on the usages of the synagogue, with which most of the early converts were familiar; but these were progressively modified to give fuller expression to the spirit of Christian worship, each congregation apparently making such changes as it thought most fitting. It must be admitted that the principle of spiritual liberty led to some degree of unseemly disorder in worship (I Cor. 14.23ff.). It took time for the new faith to clothe itself in a new ritual.

Music and Song in NT Worship. As joy was the keynote of Christianity it is natural that singing should have played a leading part in worship (Col. 3.16, Eph. 5.19). The Psalms, set to Jewish melodies, were widely used after the pattern of the synagogue; but there is ample evidence that distinctively Christian hymns came early into existence. A fragment of one of them is quoted in Eph. 5.14. On the whole subject, see *The Music of the Bible*, by J. Stainer (London, 1914). (*V.* also THANK.)

BIBLIOGRAPHY

H. W. Robinson: *The Religious Ideas of the Old Testament*, Ch. VI, London (1913). A. C. Welch: *The Religion of Israel under the Kingdom*, London (1912). W. R. Smith: *The Religion of the Semites*, London (1894). J. Skinner: *Prophecy and Religion*, Ch. IX, Cambridge (1936). Oesterley and Box, *The Religion and Worship of the Synagogue*, London (1911). J. H. Srawley: *Early History of the Liturgy*, Ch. I, Cambridge (1947). Harnack: *History of Dogma*, Vol. I. T. M. Lindsay: *The Church and the Ministry in the Early Centuries*, London (1910). J. B. Lightfoot: *The Christian Ministry*, London (1901). F. E. Warren: *The Liturgy and Ritual of the Ante-Nicene Church*, London (1912). E. R. Micklem (ed.): *Christian Worship*, Oxford (1936). See also articles on Worship and related subjects in *HDB* and *ERE*.

J. S. McEWEN

WRATH, ANGER, INDIGNATION

God's attitude to sin is described in both OT and NT in terms borrowed from the human passion of anger, indignation, and wrath. It is not to be thought of as an irrational, irresponsible action on the part of God, but rather as the manifestation, sometimes suddenly and immediately experienced, of that aversion to sin which is part of his character. It is especially called forth for presumptuous sin, and it shows itself in the severe punishment and even utter destruction of the offender.

It has been the custom to distinguish between the OT as emphasizing the divine wrath and the NT as emphasizing the divine mercy and love, but such a sharp distinction is unwarranted. The OT is the story of God's steady anger against sin in every form, whether within Israel or outside, coupled with his forbearance to execute the fierceness of his anger (Hos. 11.9), that is, to wipe out Israel entirely by allowing her to pay the proper penalty for her sin. The extreme example of both God's wrath and his forbearance is to be seen in Exod. 32.7–14, the story of the golden calf, especially since it was a saying of the Rabbis that in every sin there is something of the golden calf. God's wrath waxed hot against the people because of this crowning apostasy, but, at the pleading by Moses, he 'repented of the evil which he said he would do' to them. In his wrath he remembered mercy (Hab. 3.2).

The NT shows everywhere the same twin attitude on the part of God, an intense anger against sin, and great forbearance towards the sinner. It is by his grace that he is full of forbearance, for though he is strong and firm in his judgment against sin, it is not his will that any should perish, but rather that they should turn to him and live. Nevertheless, there does come at length the Day of Wrath, which is the day of God's final and irrevocable judgment (*q.v.*) against sin and all unrepentant sinners. This Day of Wrath is spoken of in the Gospels, in the Epistles, and in the Apocalypse; and the NT nowhere says that mercy has the last word. God's last word is of condemnation and destruction of sin and stubborn sinners on the one hand, and of full pardon and restoration to the divine favour to all who truly repent and have faith in him. (*V.* also JUDGE, REWARD.)

N. H. SNAITH

WRONG *v.* **SIN**

* * *

YEAR *v.* **TIME**

* * *

ZADOK *v.* **SACRIFICE III(*b*)**

ZEAL, ZEALOUS *v.* **DESIRE JEALOUS**